TOKYO
Revengers

CONTENTS

CHAPTER 34: DARKEST HOUR

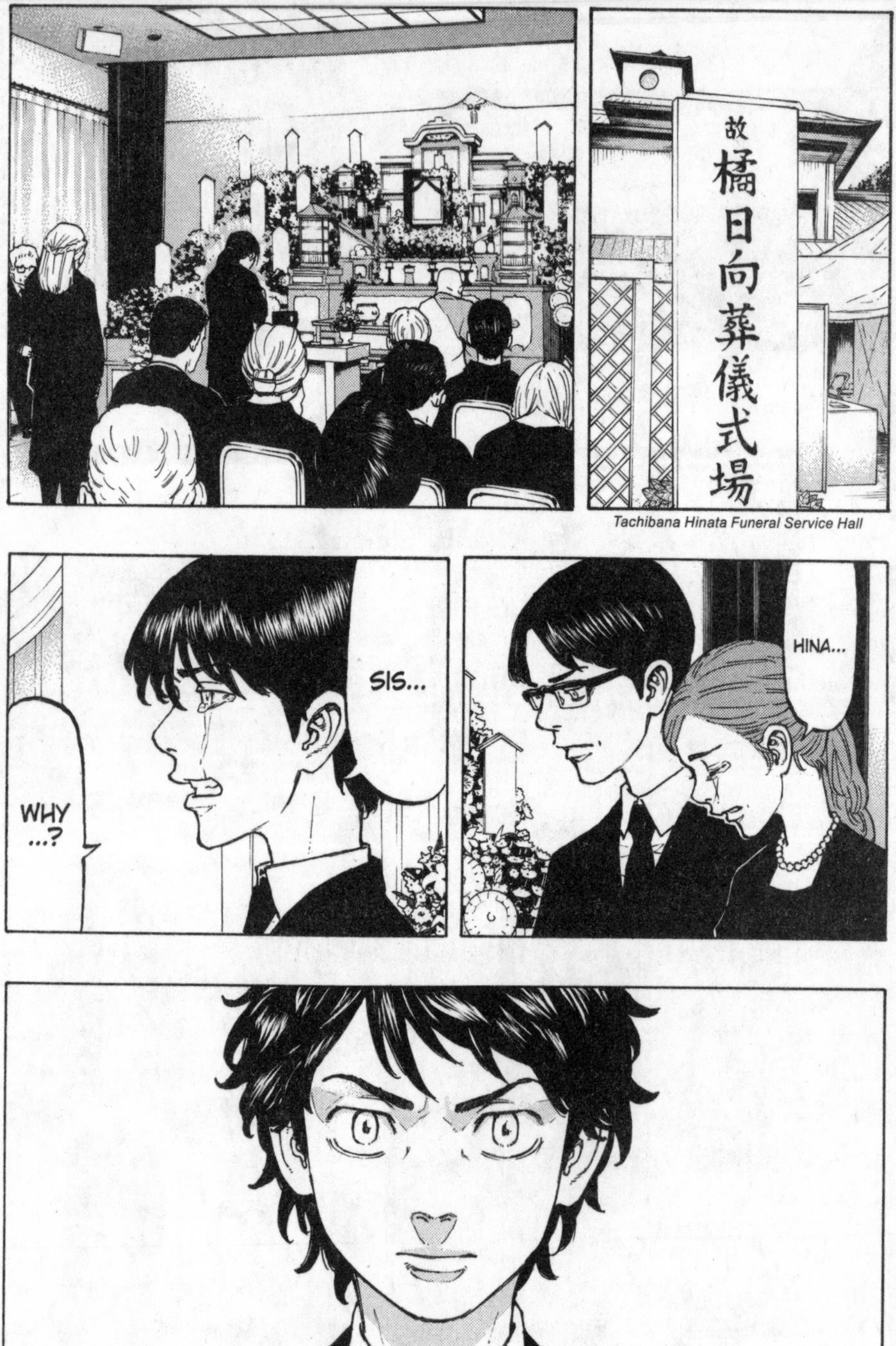
故
橘日向葬儀式場
HINA...
SIS...
WHY ...?

Tachibana Hinata Funeral Service Hall

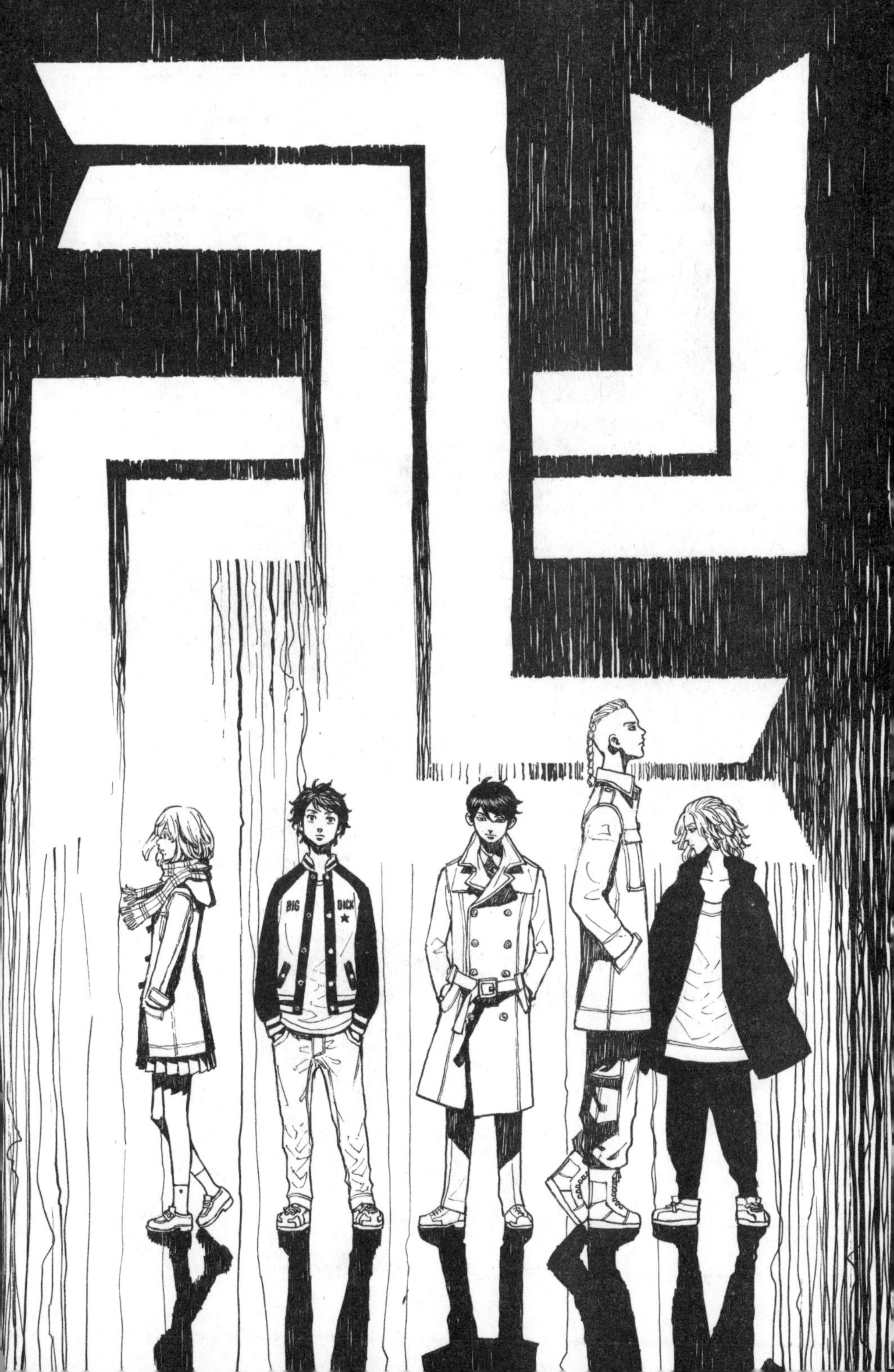
BIG
DICK

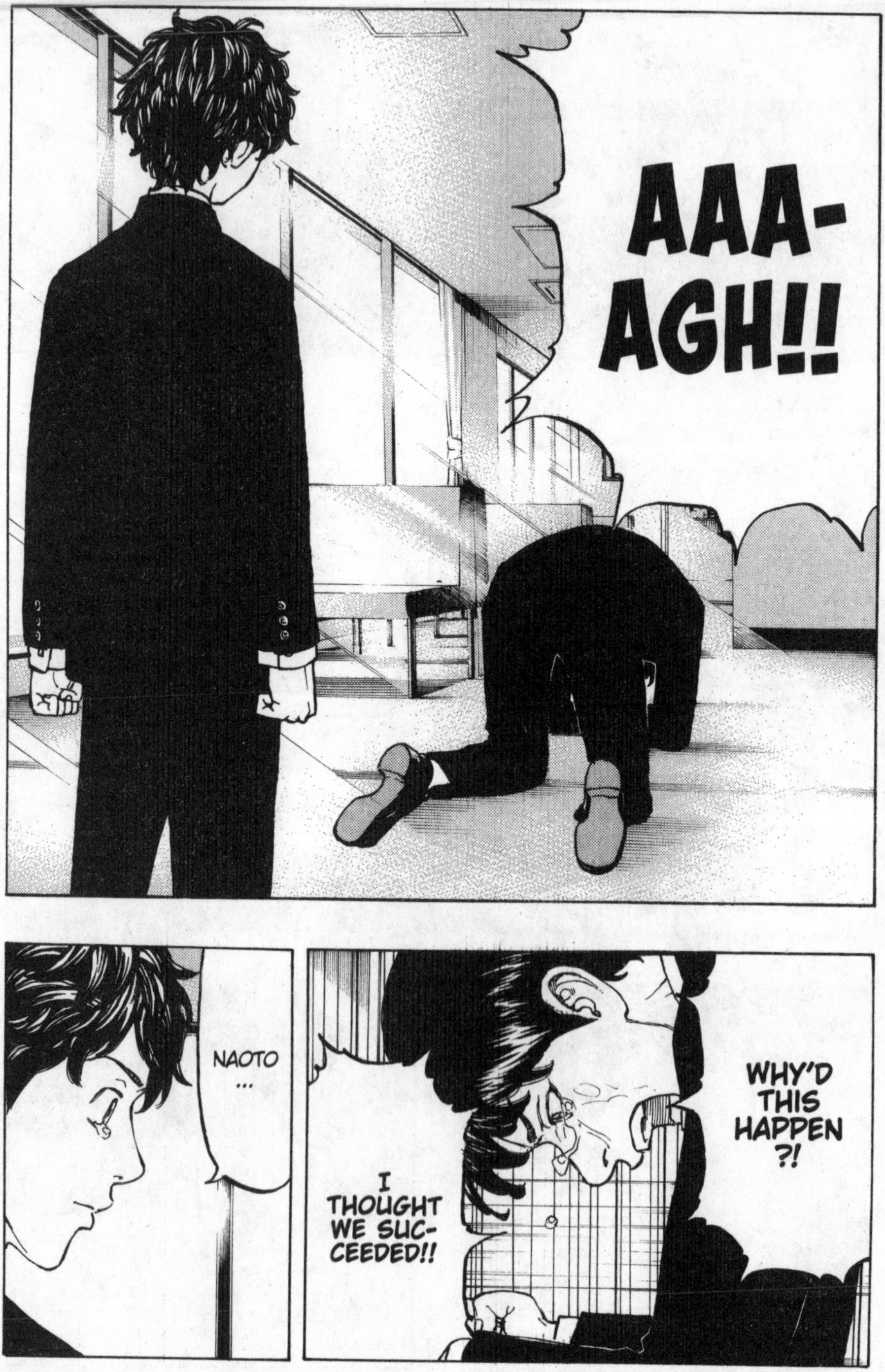
AAA-AGH!!
WHY'D THIS HAPPEN ?!
I THOUGHT WE SUC-CEEDED!!
NAOTO ...

OH.

HANAGAKI TAKE-MICHI-KUN?

BOW

I'M HINATA'S MOTHER.

YOU'VE CERTAINLY GROWN UP.

SHF

HERE...

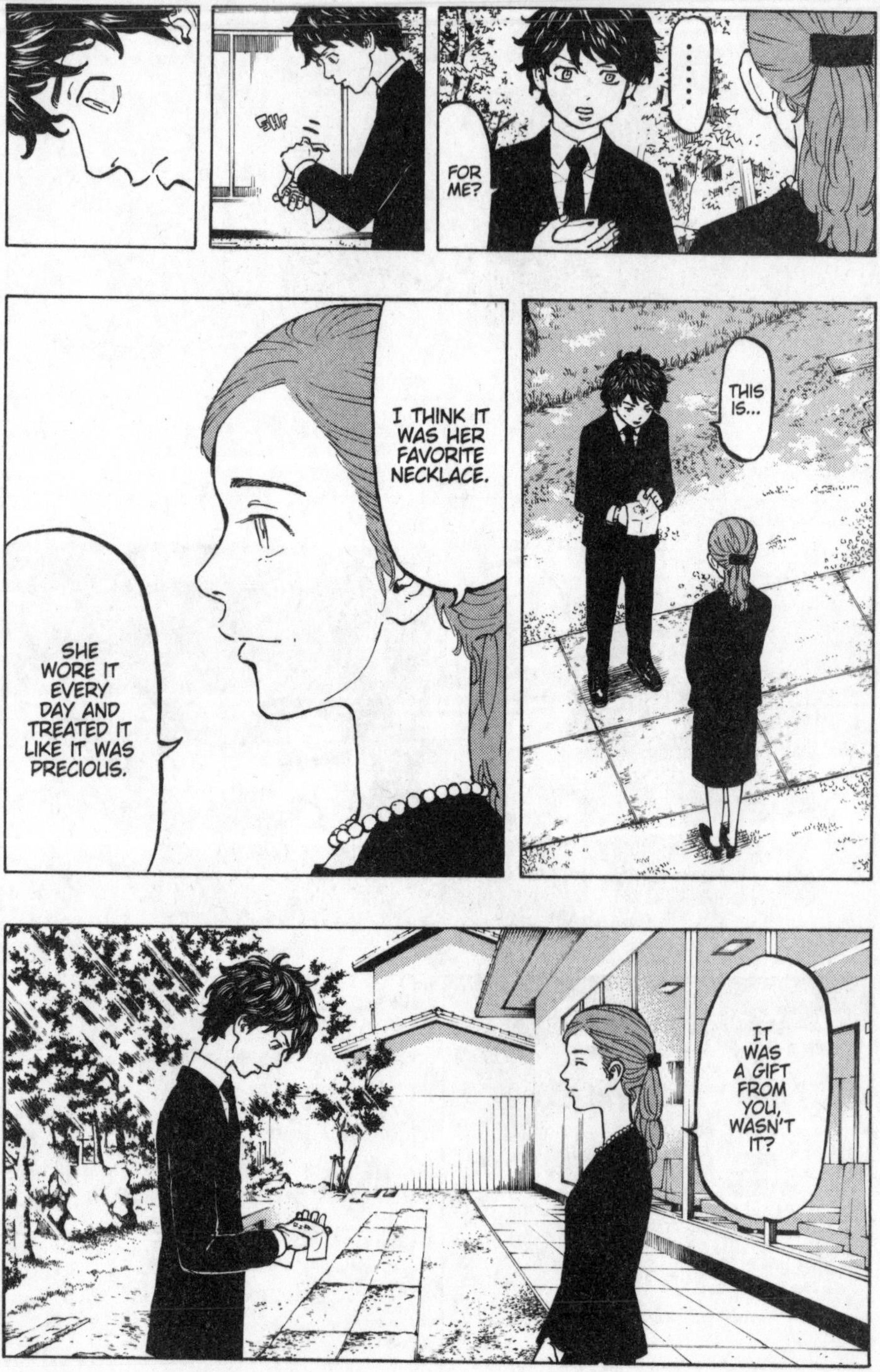
......
FOR ME?
SHF
THIS IS...
I THINK IT WAS HER FAVORITE NECKLACE.
SHE WORE IT EVERY DAY AND TREATED IT LIKE IT WAS PRECIOUS.
IT WAS A GIFT FROM YOU, WASN'T IT?

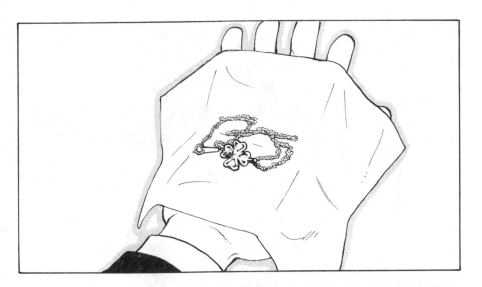

LOVED YOU VERY MUCH...

SHE MUST HAVE...

HINA ...

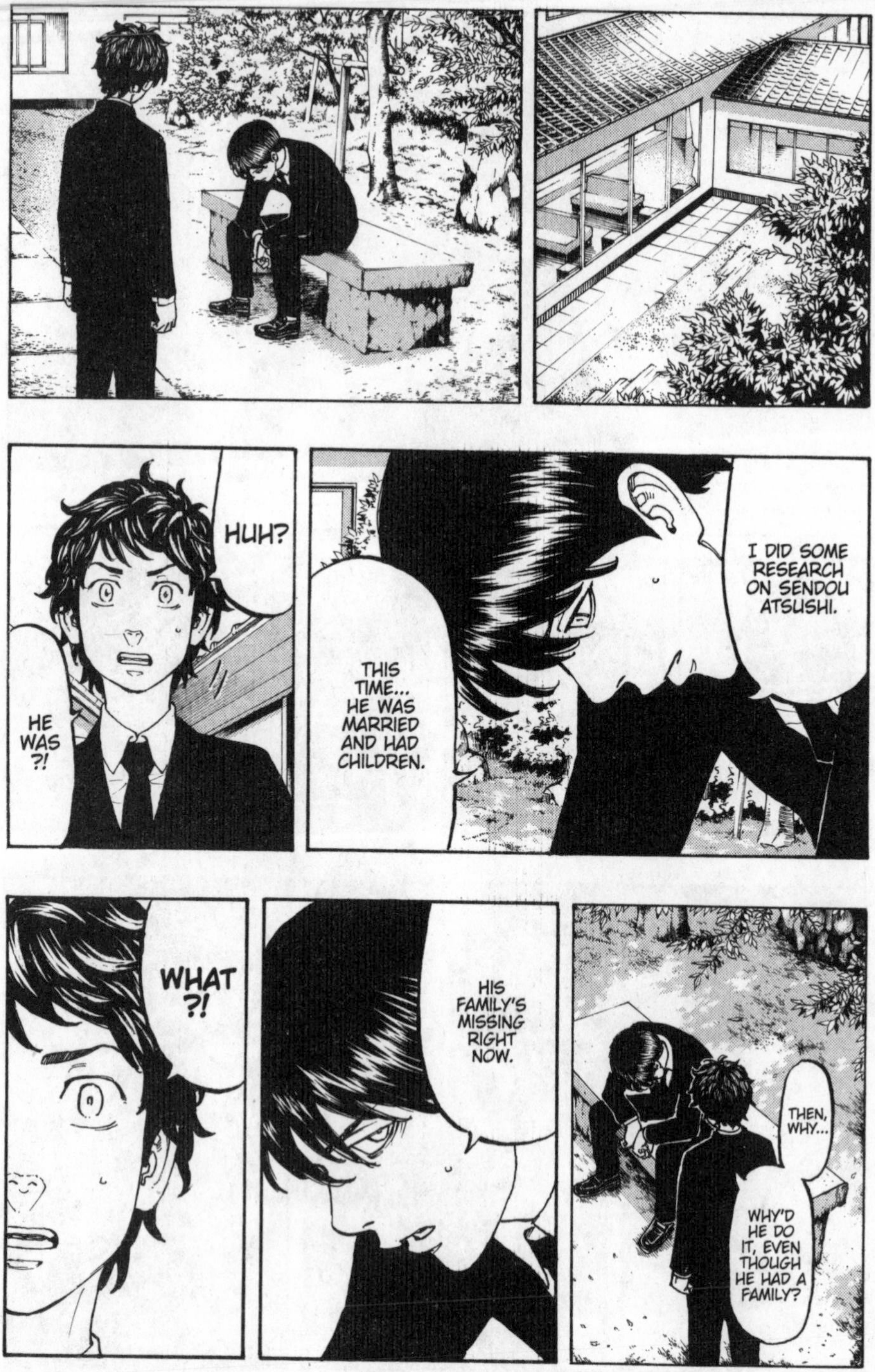
I DID SOME RESEARCH ON SENDOU ATSUSHI.
THIS TIME... HE WAS MARRIED AND HAD CHILDREN.
HUH?
HE WAS ?!
THEN, WHY...
WHY'D HE DO IT, EVEN THOUGH HE HAD A FAMILY?
HIS FAMILY'S MISSING RIGHT NOW.
WHAT ?!

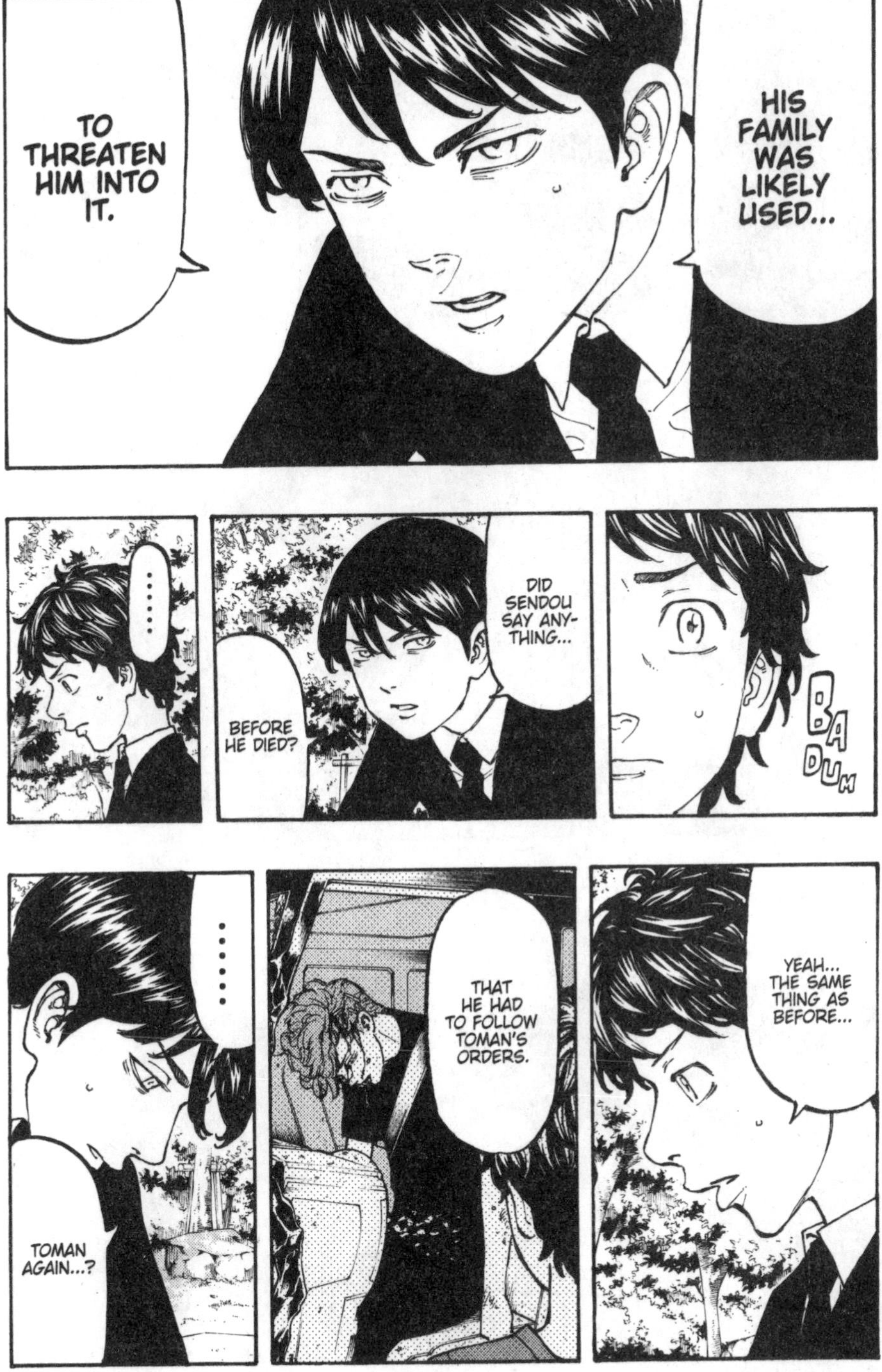
HIS FAMILY WAS LIKELY USED...
TO THREATEN HIM INTO IT.
BADUM
DID SENDOU SAY ANYTHING...
BEFORE HE DIED?
......
YEAH... THE SAME THING AS BEFORE...
THAT HE HAD TO FOLLOW TOMAN'S ORDERS.
......
TOMAN AGAIN...?

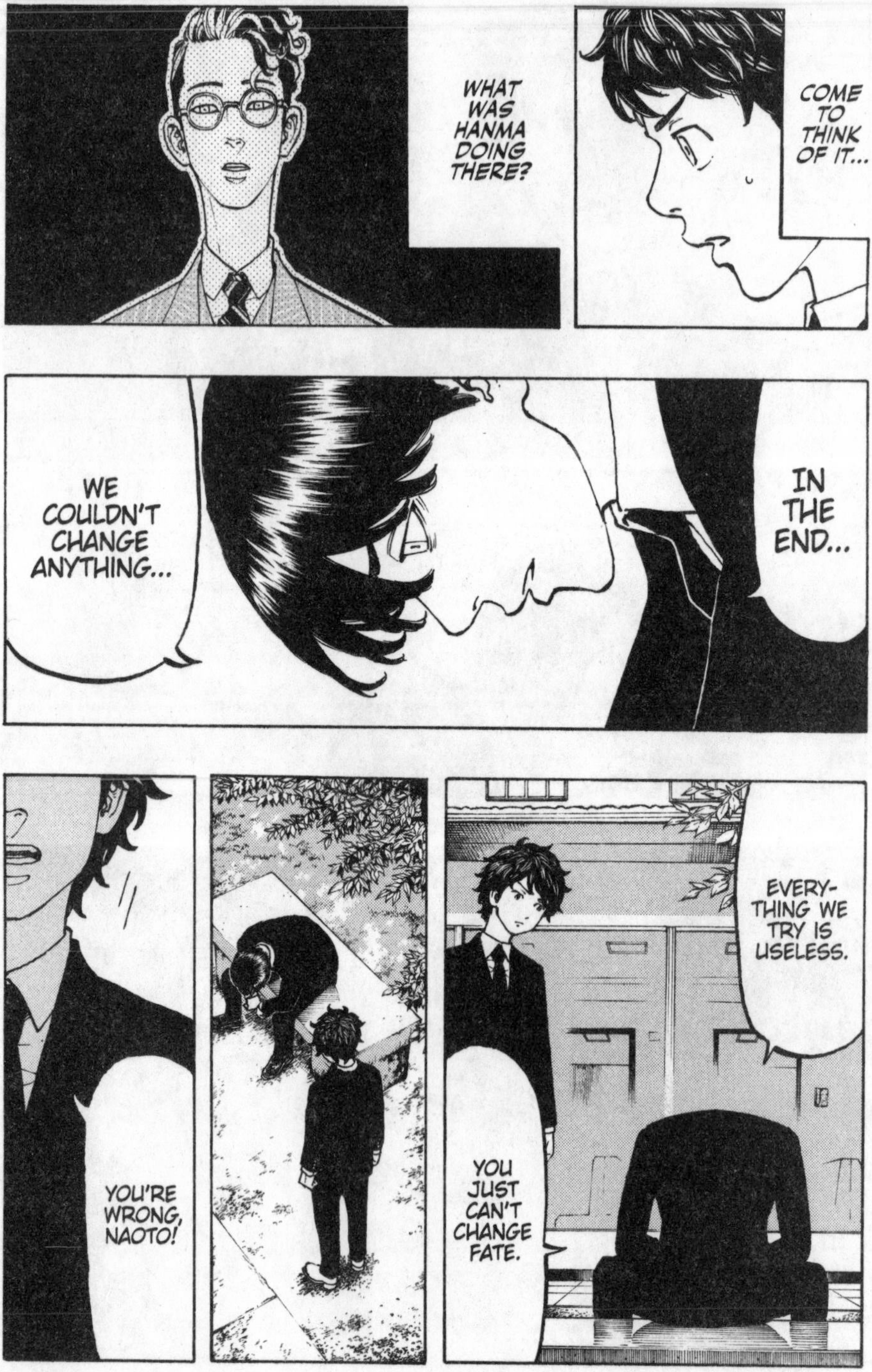
COME TO THINK OF IT...
WHAT WAS HANMA DOING THERE?
IN THE END...
WE COULDN'T CHANGE ANYTHING...
EVERY-THING WE TRY IS USELESS.
YOU JUST CAN'T CHANGE FATE.
YOU'RE WRONG, NAOTO!

SAVING DRAKEN-KUN DIDN'T CHANGE ANYTHING...
BECAUSE THAT WASN'T THE REASON TOMAN TURNED EVIL IN THE FIRST PLACE.
WHEN HINA DIED RIGHT IN FRONT OF ME...
AS I WATCHED THE FLAMES RISE UP...
I UNDER-STOOD SOMETHING.
WE'VE GOT TO GET TO THE ROOT. IT'S THE ONLY WAY!
......
THE ROOT?

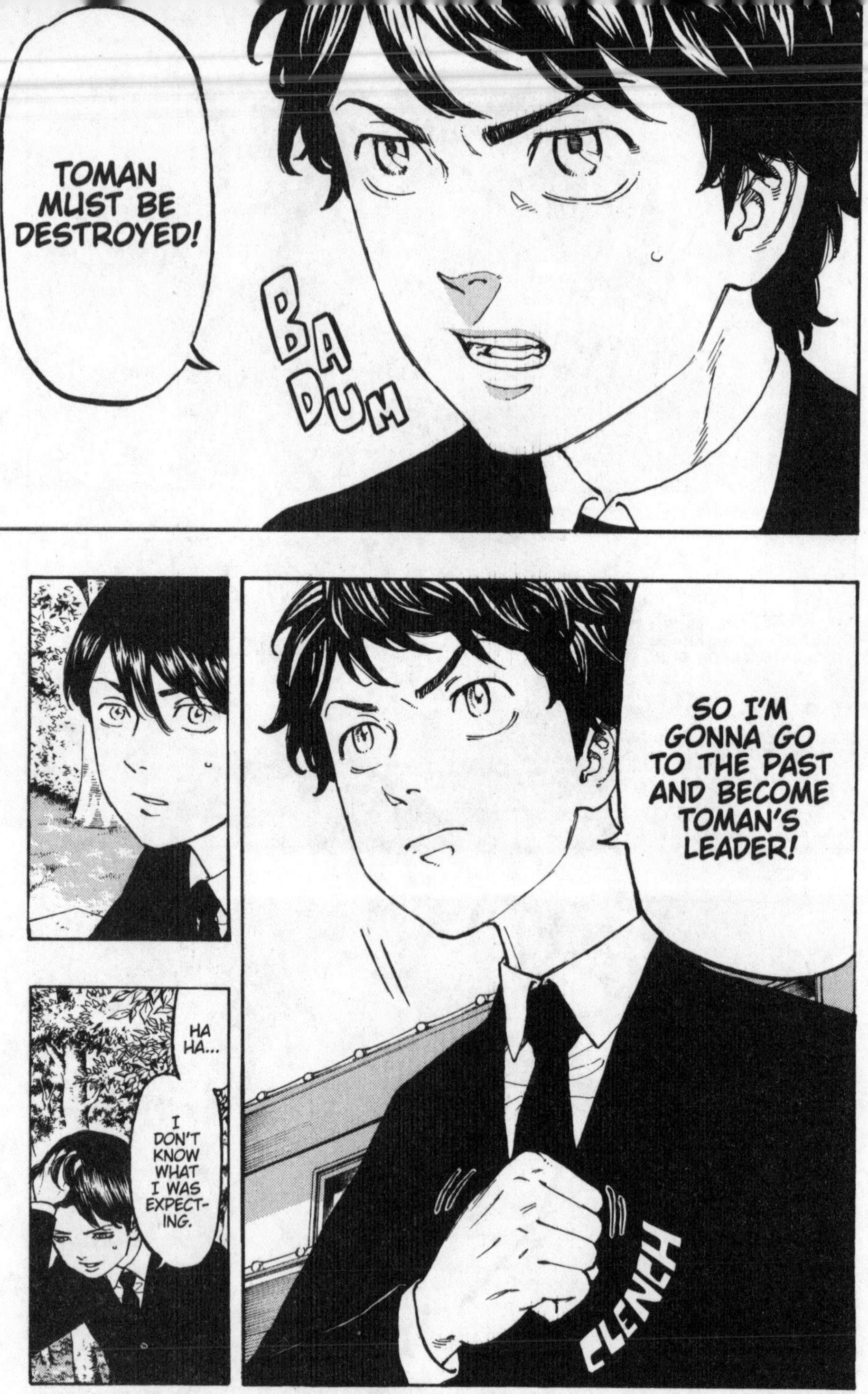
TOMAN MUST BE DESTROYED!
BADUM
SO I'M GONNA GO TO THE PAST AND BECOME TOMAN'S LEADER!
CLENCH
HA HA...
I DON'T KNOW WHAT I WAS EXPECTING.

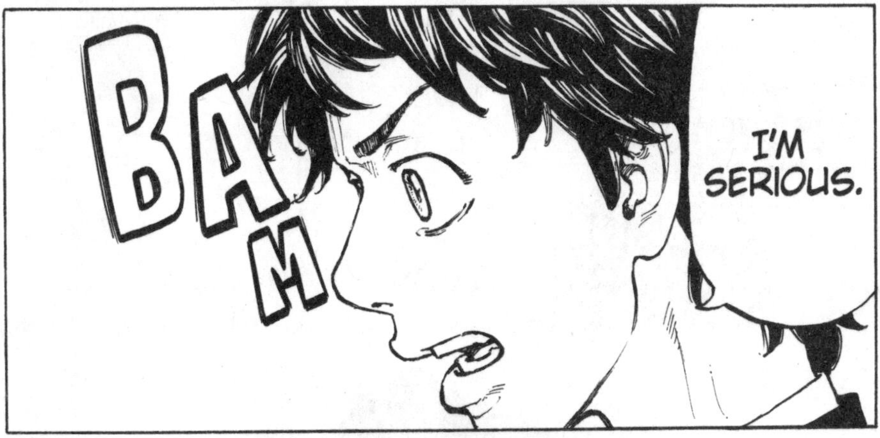
I'M SERIOUS.
BAM

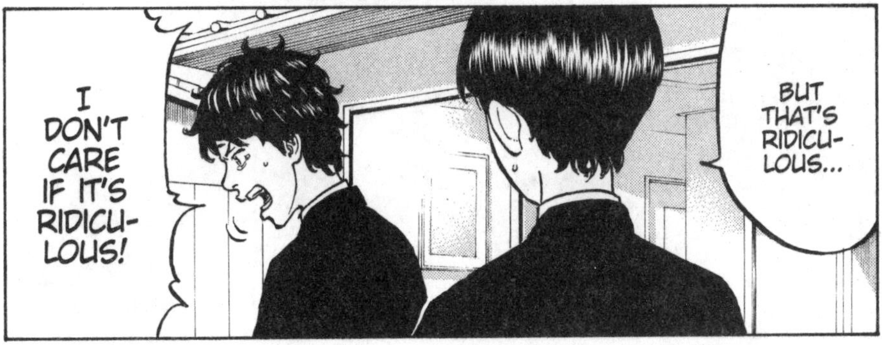
BUT THAT'S RIDICULOUS...
I DON'T CARE IF IT'S RIDICULOUS!

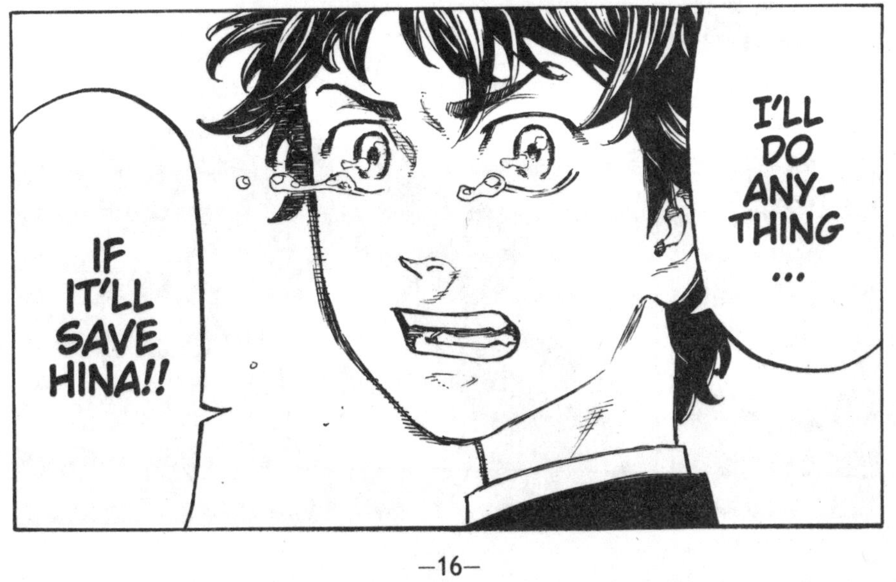
I'LL DO ANYTHING...
IF IT'LL SAVE HINA!!

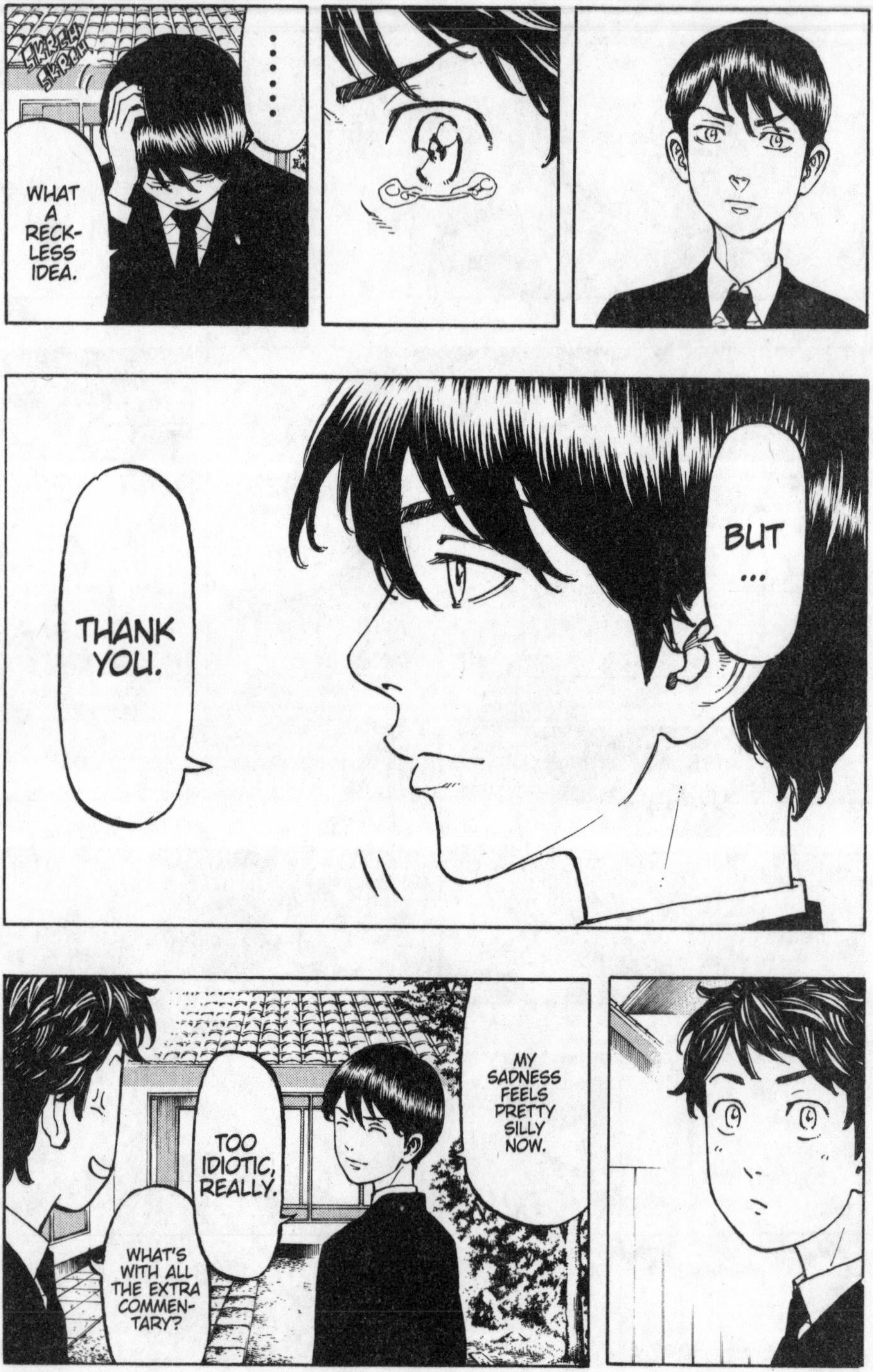
......
SKRCH SKRCH
WHAT A RECKLESS IDEA.
BUT ...
THANK YOU.
MY SADNESS FEELS PRETTY SILLY NOW.
TOO IDIOTIC, REALLY.
WHAT'S WITH ALL THE EXTRA COMMENTARY?

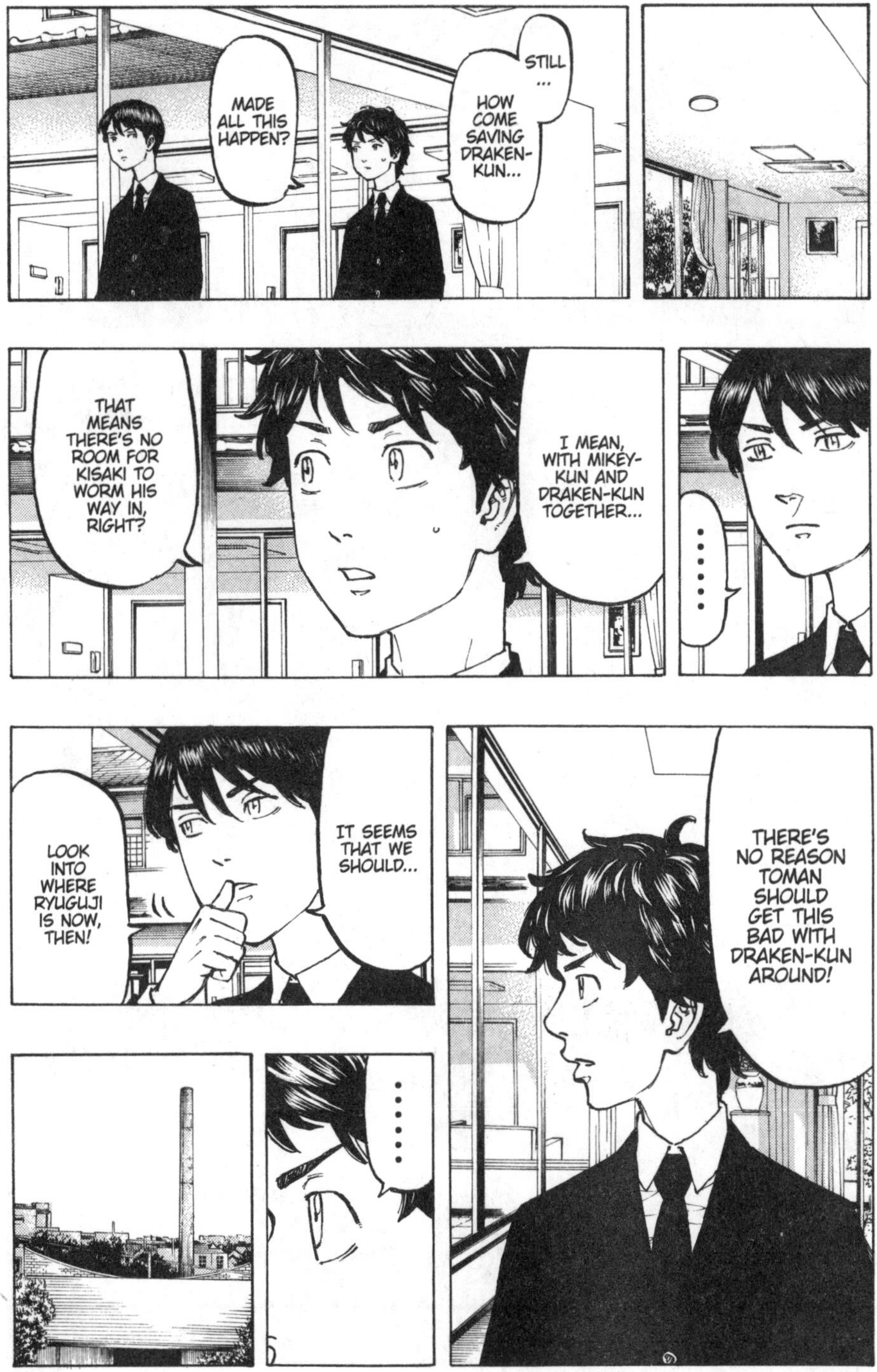
STILL... HOW COME SAVING DRAKEN-KUN...
MADE ALL THIS HAPPEN?
......
I MEAN, WITH MIKEY-KUN AND DRAKEN-KUN TOGETHER...
THAT MEANS THERE'S NO ROOM FOR KISAKI TO WORM HIS WAY IN, RIGHT?
THERE'S NO REASON TOMAN SHOULD GET THIS BAD WITH DRAKEN-KUN AROUND!
IT SEEMS THAT WE SHOULD...
LOOK INTO WHERE RYUGUJI IS NOW, THEN!
......

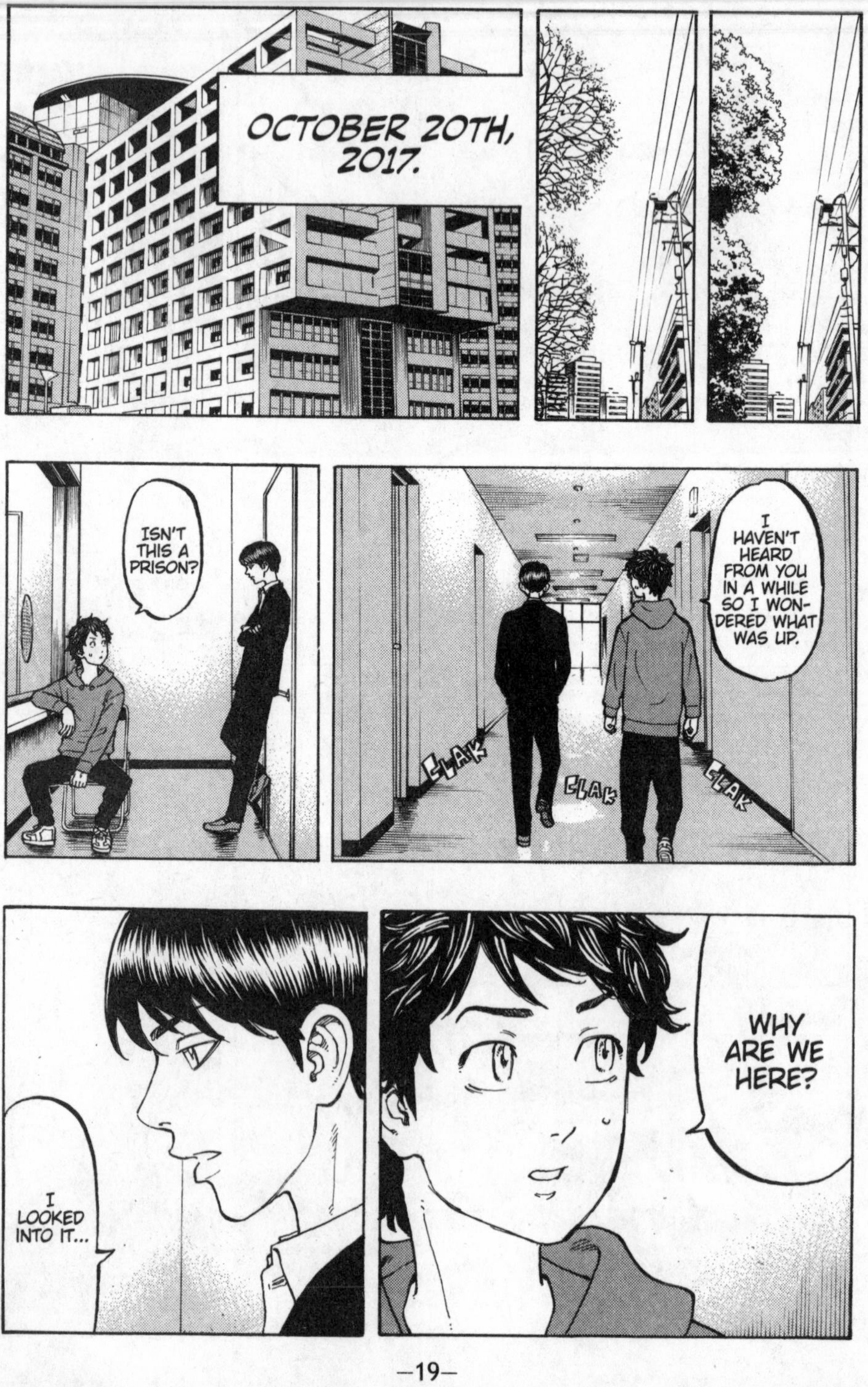

OCTOBER 20TH, 2017.
I HAVEN'T HEARD FROM YOU IN A WHILE SO I WONDERED WHAT WAS UP.
CLAK
CLAK
CLAK
ISN'T THIS A PRISON?
WHY ARE WE HERE?
I LOOKED INTO IT...

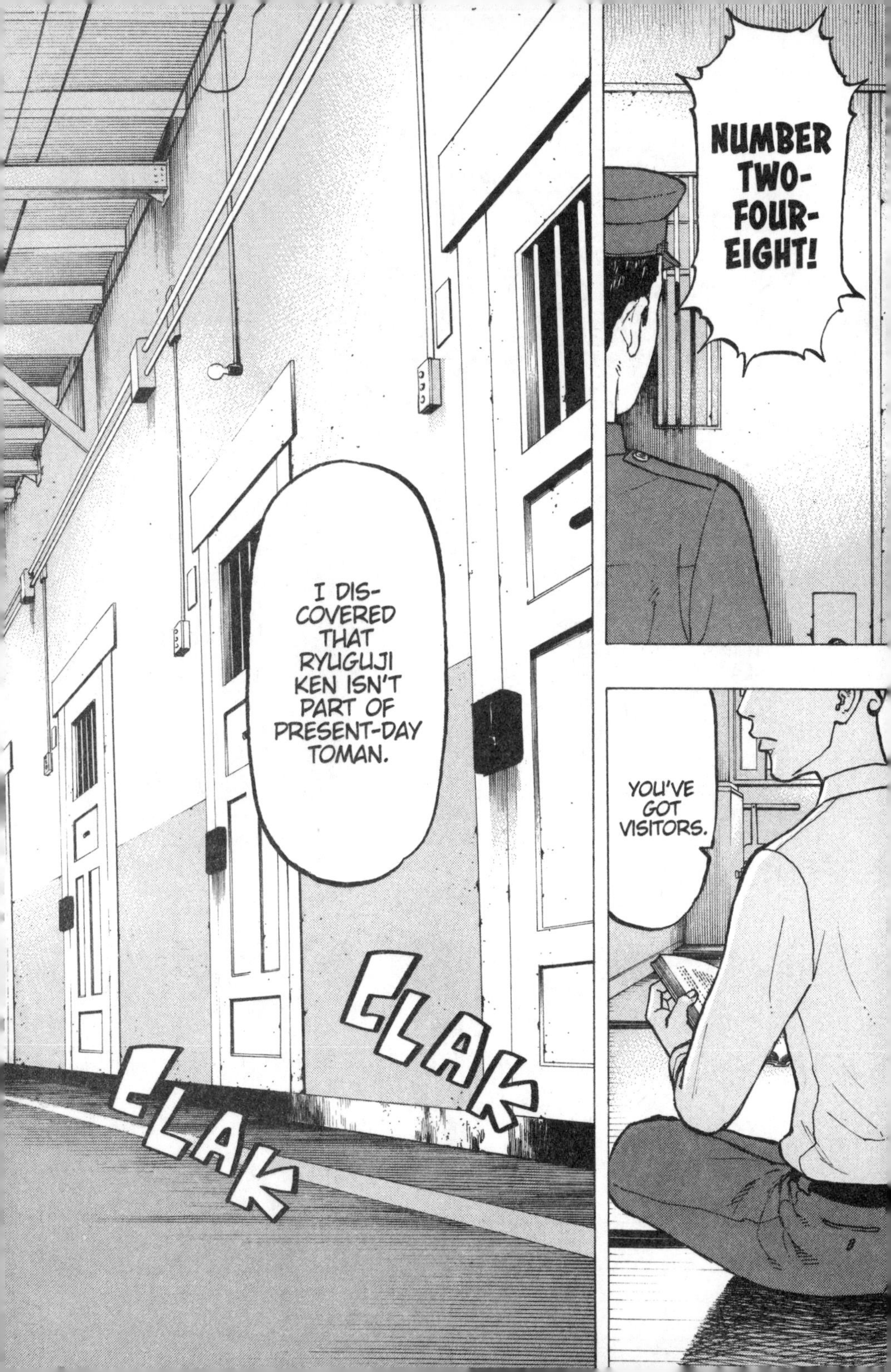
NUMBER TWO-FOUR-EIGHT!
YOU'VE GOT VISITORS.
I DIS-COVERED THAT RYUGUJI KEN ISN'T PART OF PRESENT-DAY TOMAN.
CLAK
CLAK

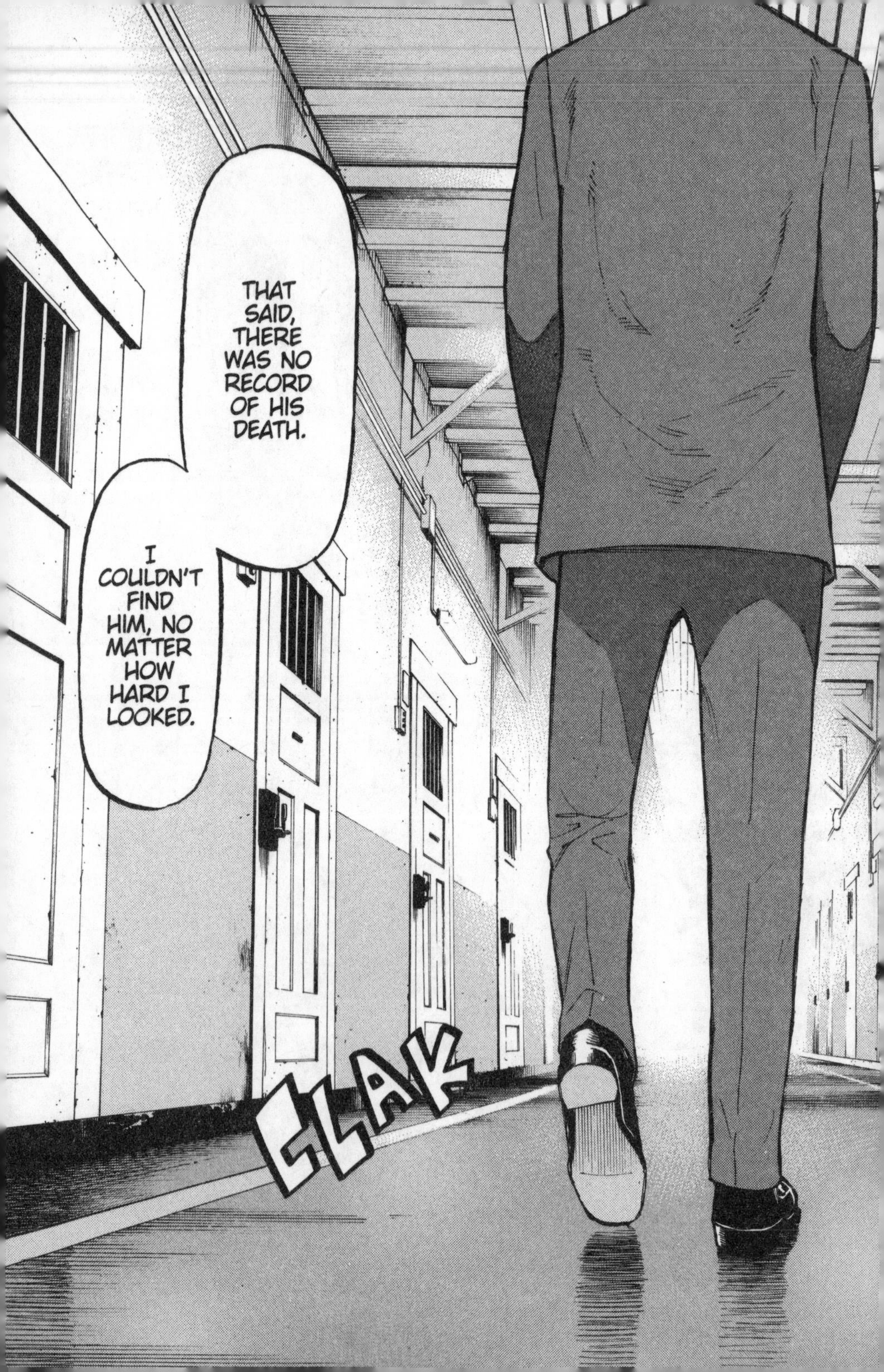
THAT SAID, THERE WAS NO RECORD OF HIS DEATH.
I COULDN'T FIND HIM, NO MATTER HOW HARD I LOOKED.
CLAK

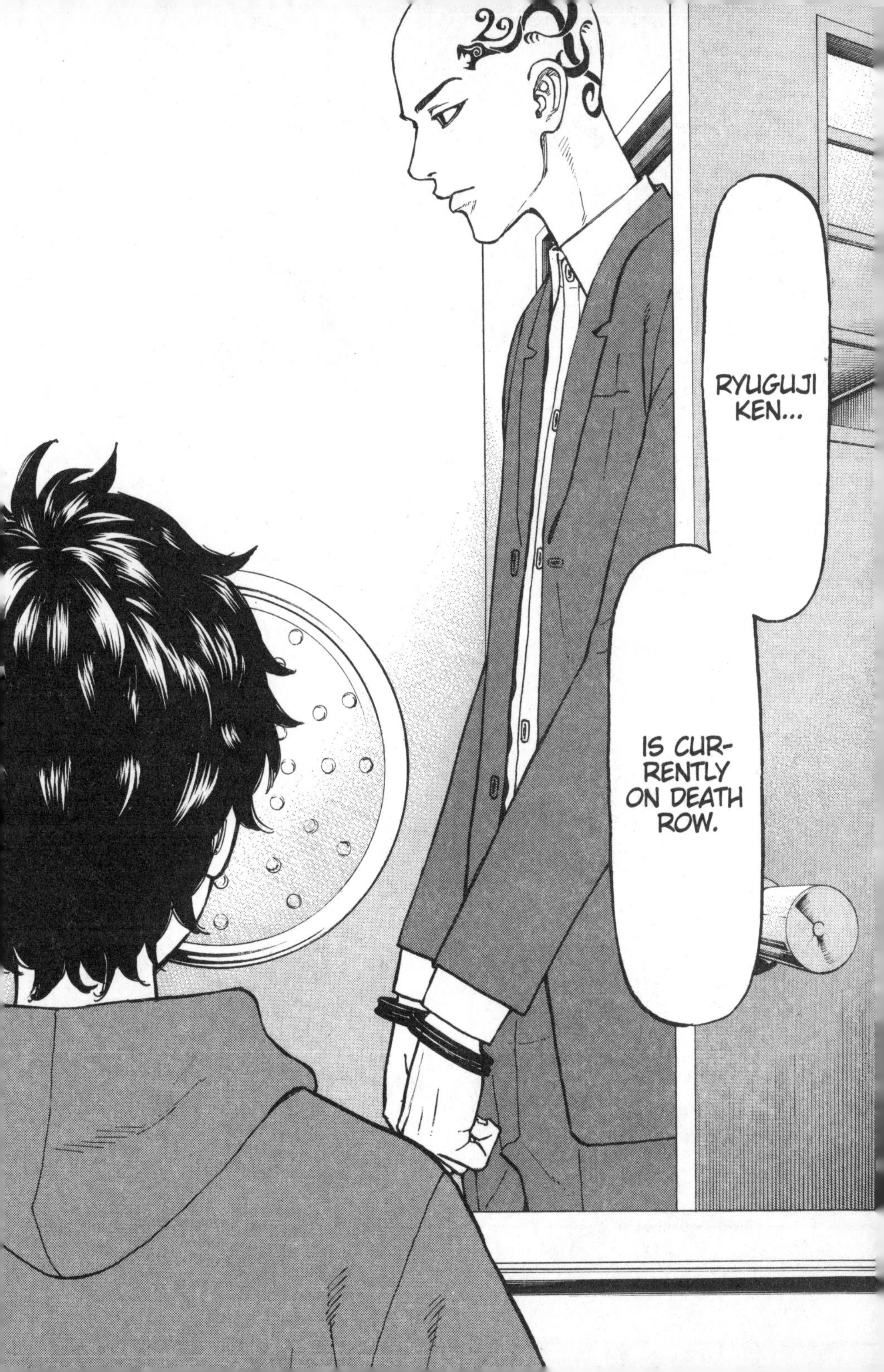
RYUGUJI KEN...
IS CUR-RENTLY ON DEATH ROW.

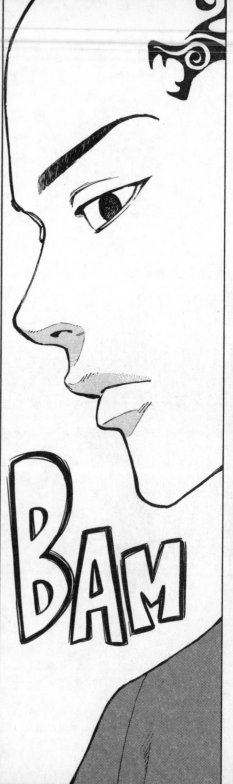

LONG TIME NO SEE, TAKEMITCHY.

THMMP

BAM

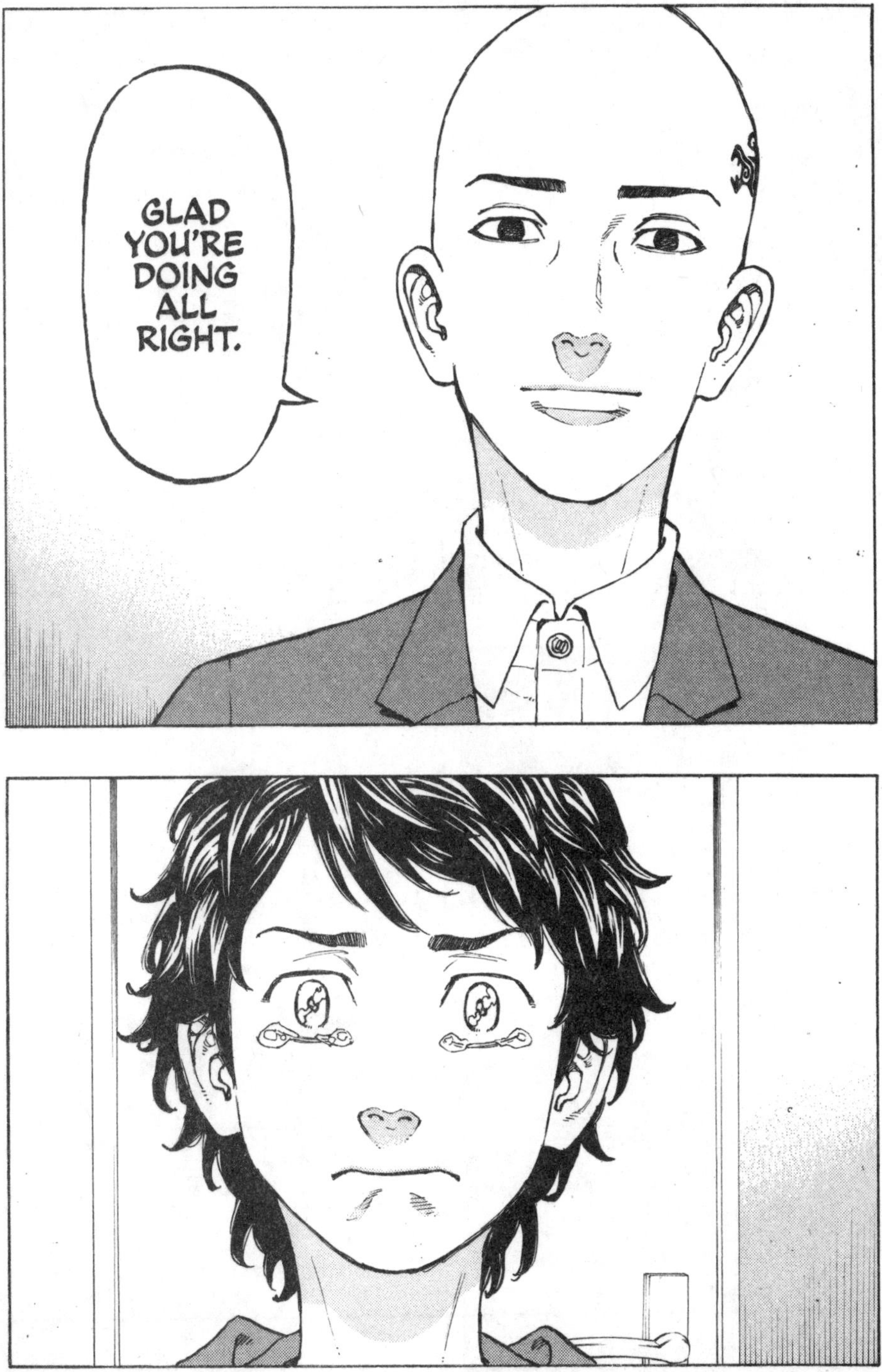
GLAD YOU'RE DOING ALL RIGHT.

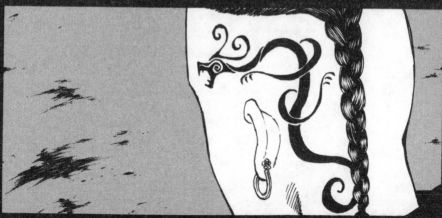

CHAPTER 35: ODDS AND ENDS

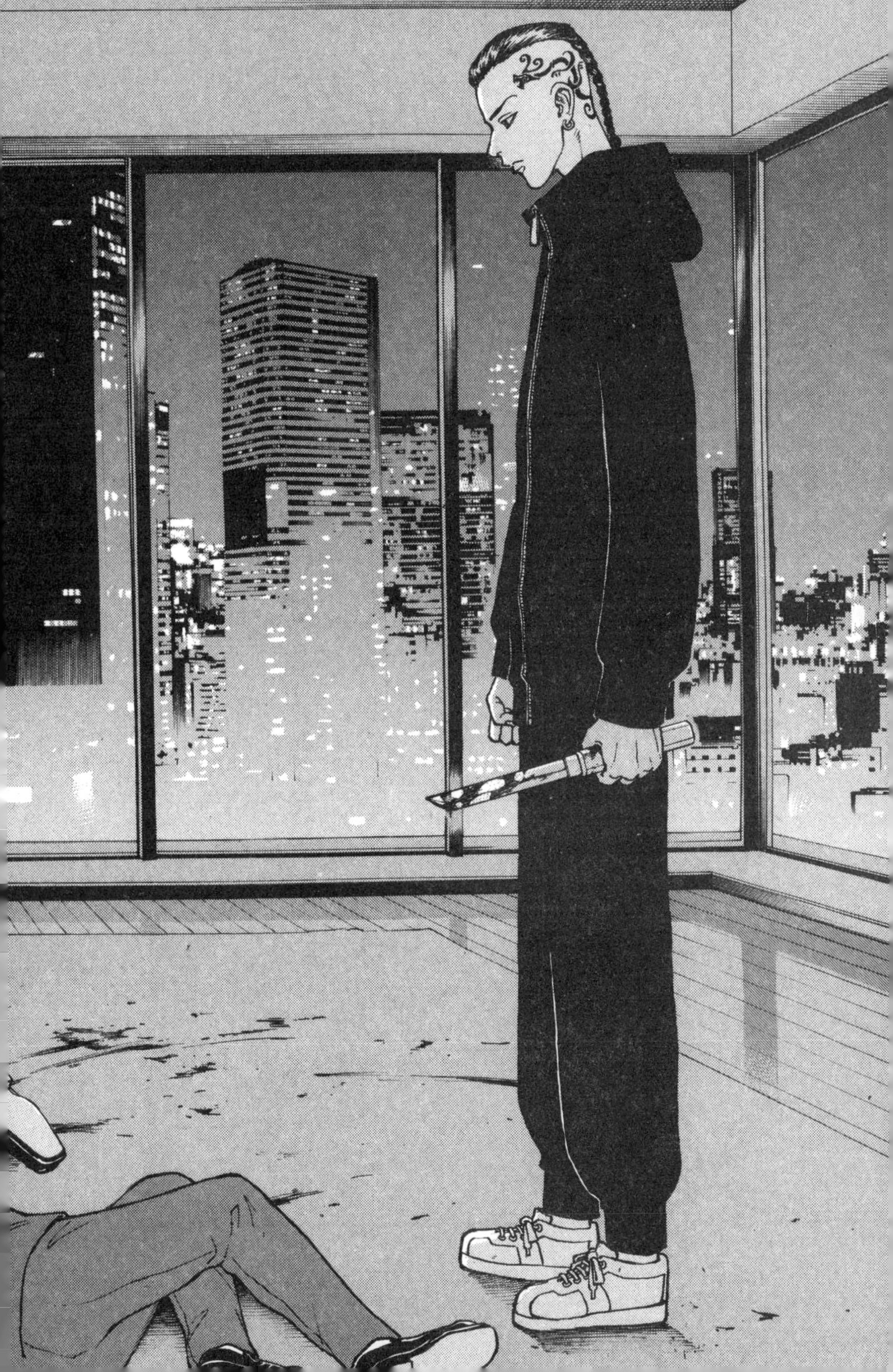

NUMBER TWO-FOUR-EIGHT, RYUGUJI!

......

YOU'VE GOT VISITORS.

KA CHK

NUMBER TWO-FOUR-EIGHT'S COMING NOW.

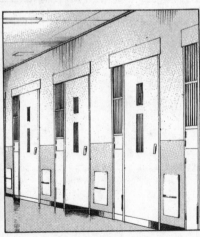

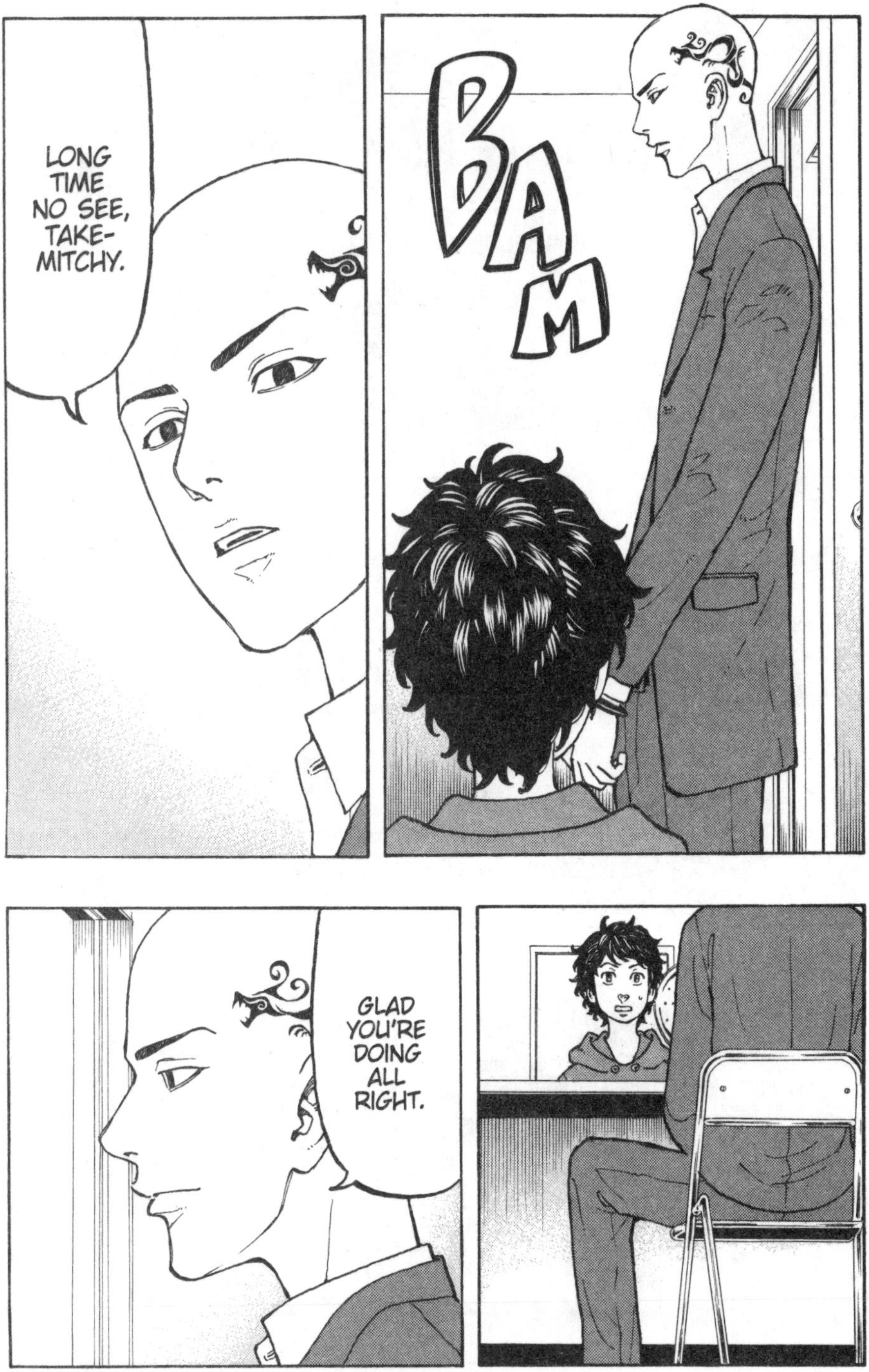
BAM
LONG TIME NO SEE, TAKE-MITCHY.
GLAD YOU'RE DOING ALL RIGHT.

HELLO. I'M TACHIBANA NAOTO.

GULP

......

DRA-KEN-KUN!

......

I SEE.

HE'S THE GUY WHO SET UP THIS VISIT FOR US.

THAT YOU'D COMMITTED MURDER AND BEEN SENTENCED TO DEATH...

I... I DIDN'T KNOW...

SO, WHAT IS IT?

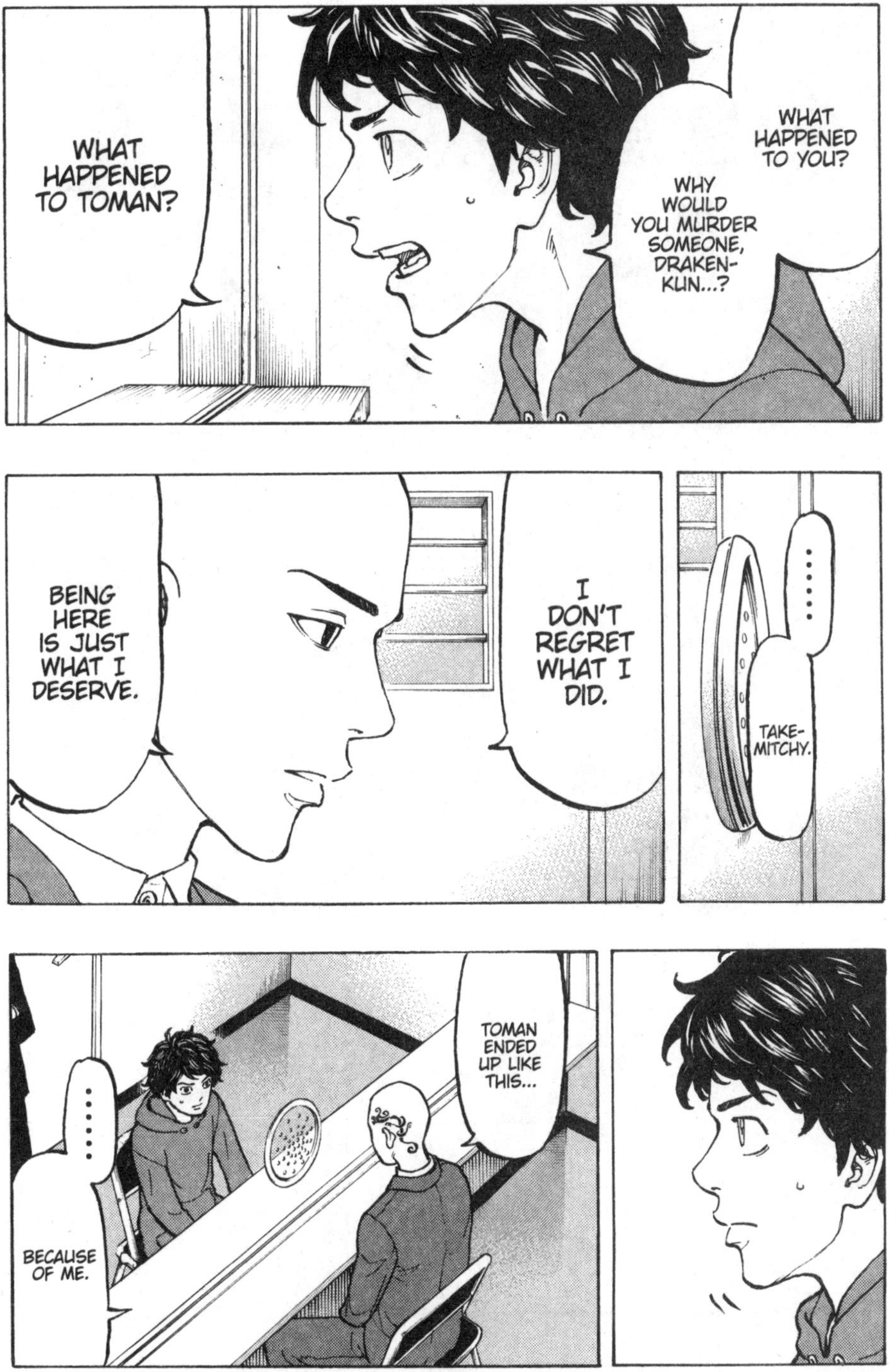
WHAT HAPPENED TO YOU?
WHY WOULD YOU MURDER SOMEONE, DRAKEN-KUN...?
WHAT HAPPENED TO TOMAN?
......
TAKE-MITCHY.
I DON'T REGRET WHAT I DID.
BEING HERE IS JUST WHAT I DESERVE.
TOMAN ENDED UP LIKE THIS...
......
BECAUSE OF ME.

BECAUSE I DIDN'T STOP HIM.

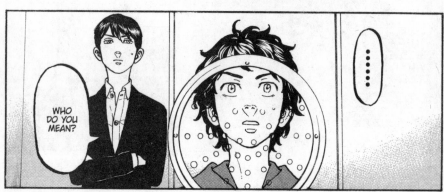

WHO DO YOU MEAN?

• • • • • •

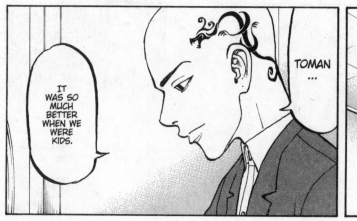

IT WAS SO MUCH BETTER WHEN WE WERE KIDS.

TOMAN...

• • • • •

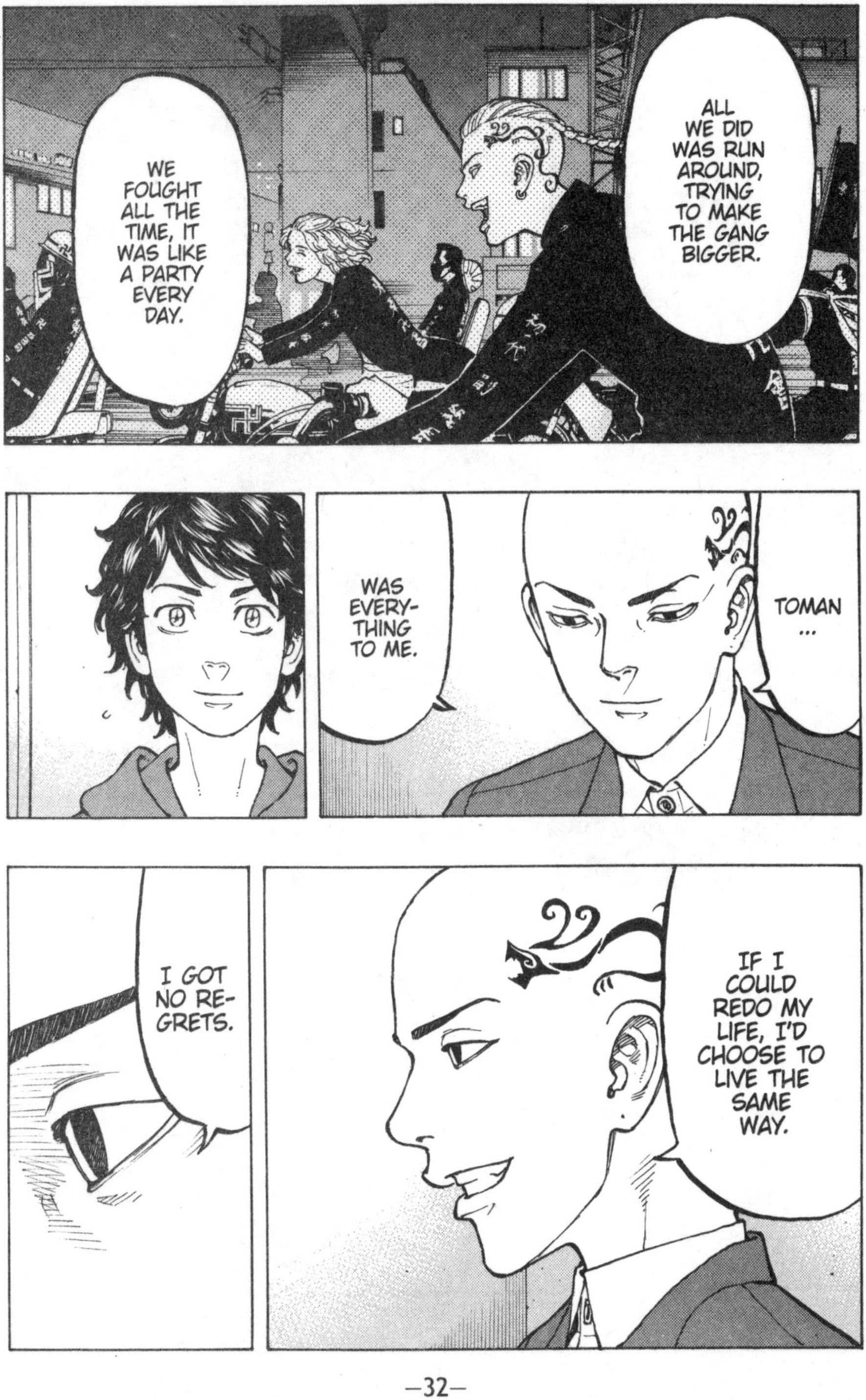
ALL WE DID WAS RUN AROUND, TRYING TO MAKE THE GANG BIGGER.
WE FOUGHT ALL THE TIME, IT WAS LIKE A PARTY EVERY DAY.
TOMAN ...
WAS EVERY-THING TO ME.
IF I COULD REDO MY LIFE, I'D CHOOSE TO LIVE THE SAME WAY.
I GOT NO RE-GRETS.

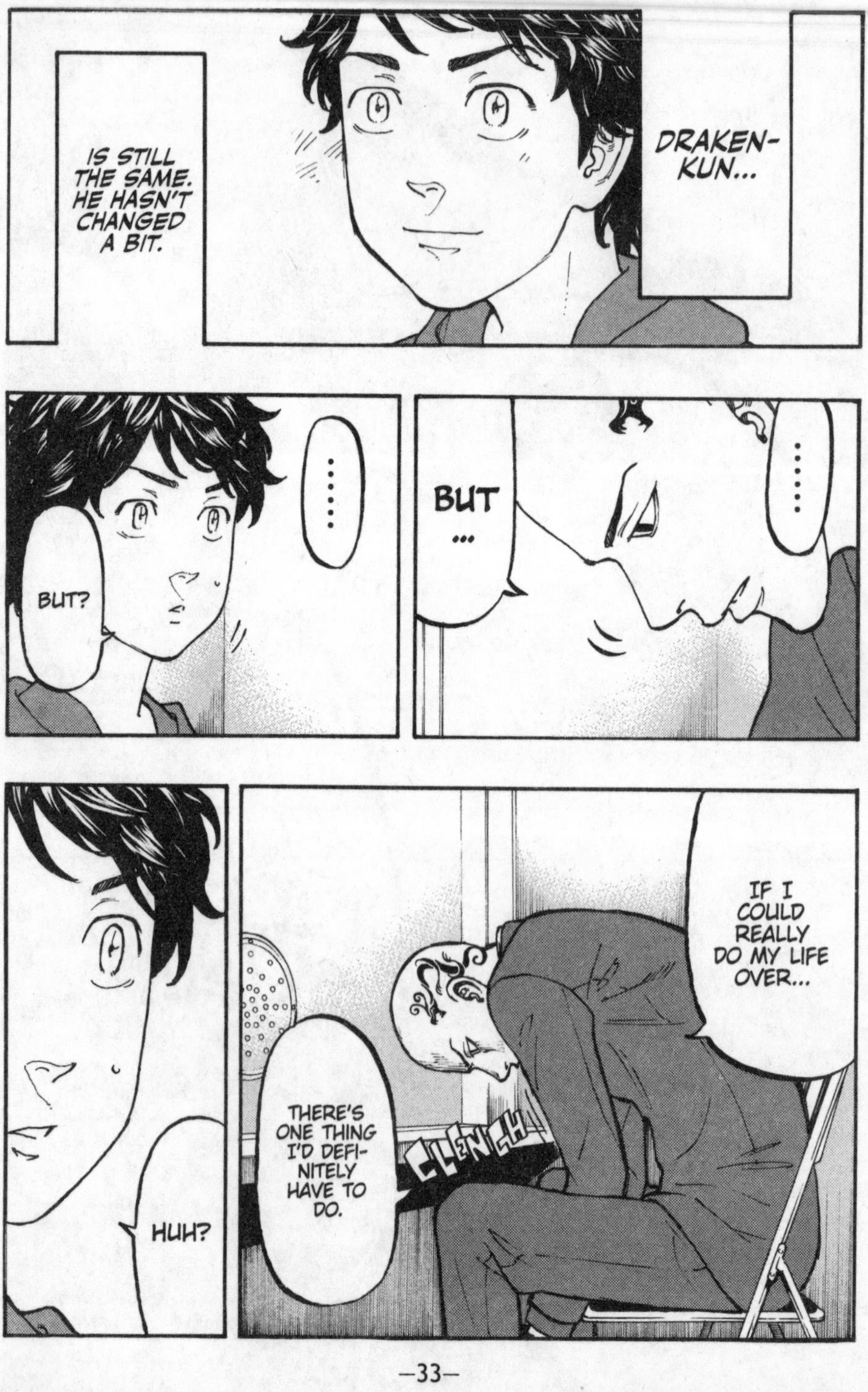
DRAKEN-KUN...
IS STILL THE SAME. HE HASN'T CHANGED A BIT.
......
BUT...
......
BUT?
IF I COULD REALLY DO MY LIFE OVER...
CLENCH
THERE'S ONE THING I'D DEFI-NITELY HAVE TO DO.
HUH?

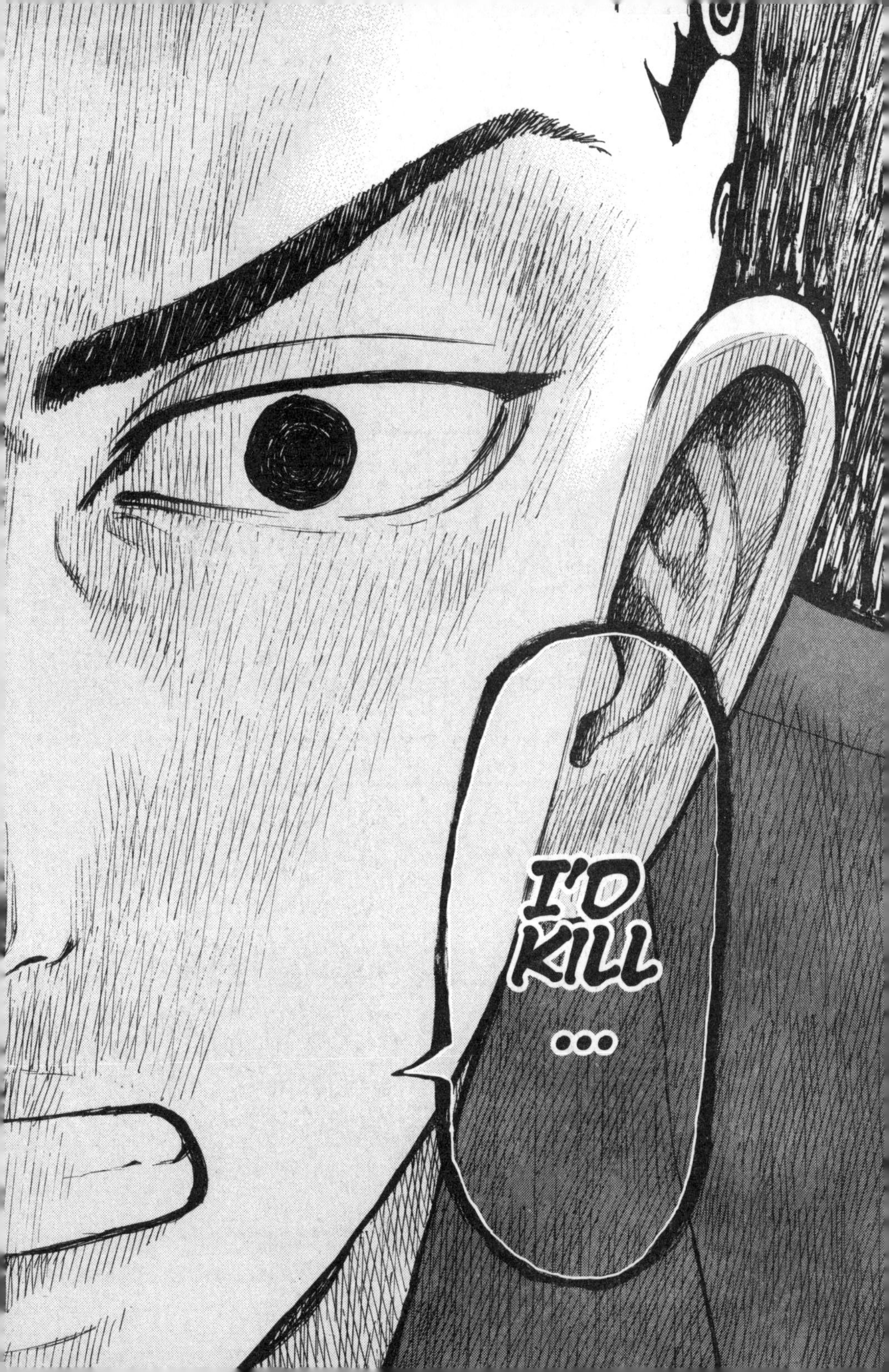
I'D KILL ...

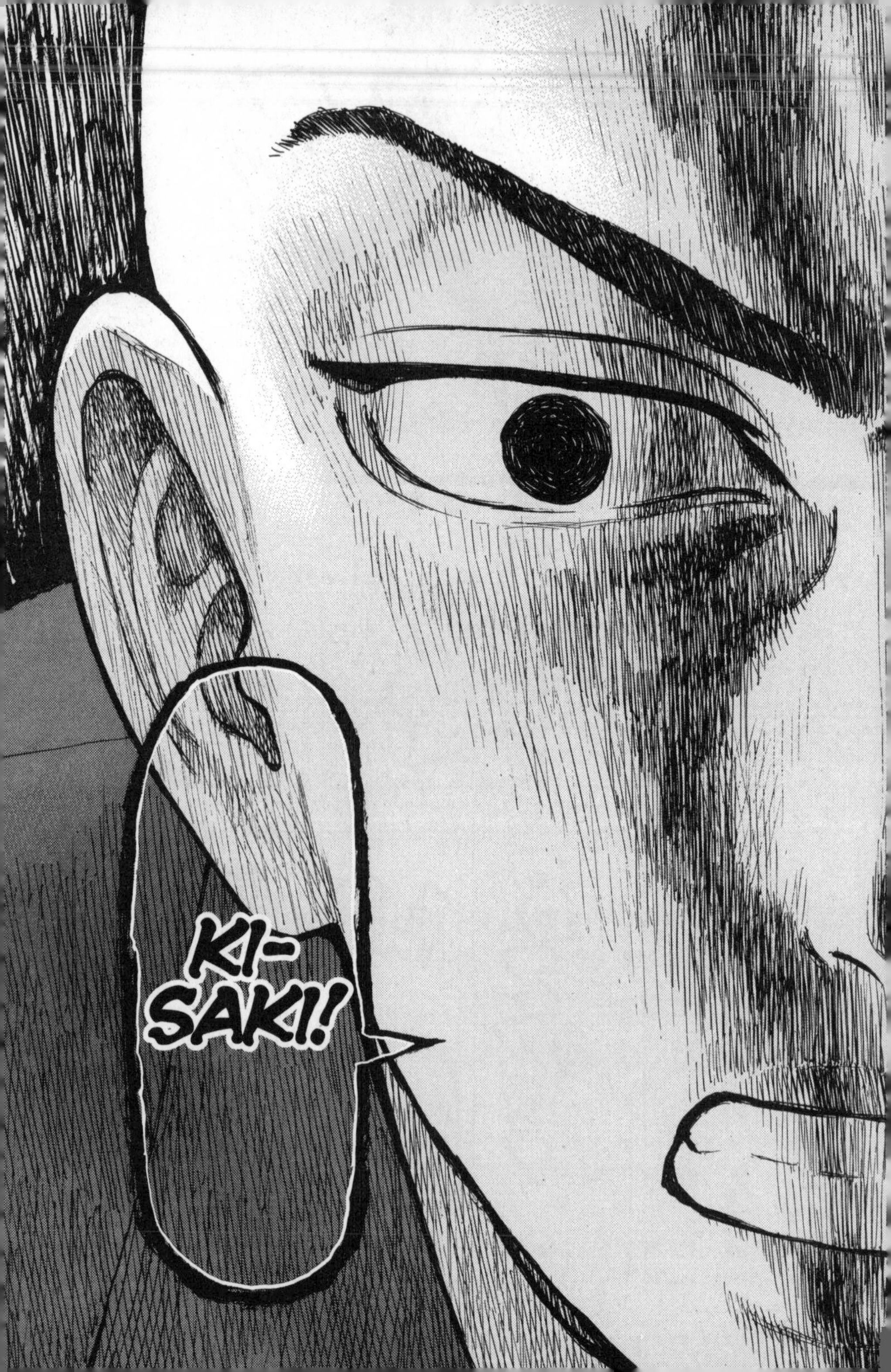
KI-SAKI!

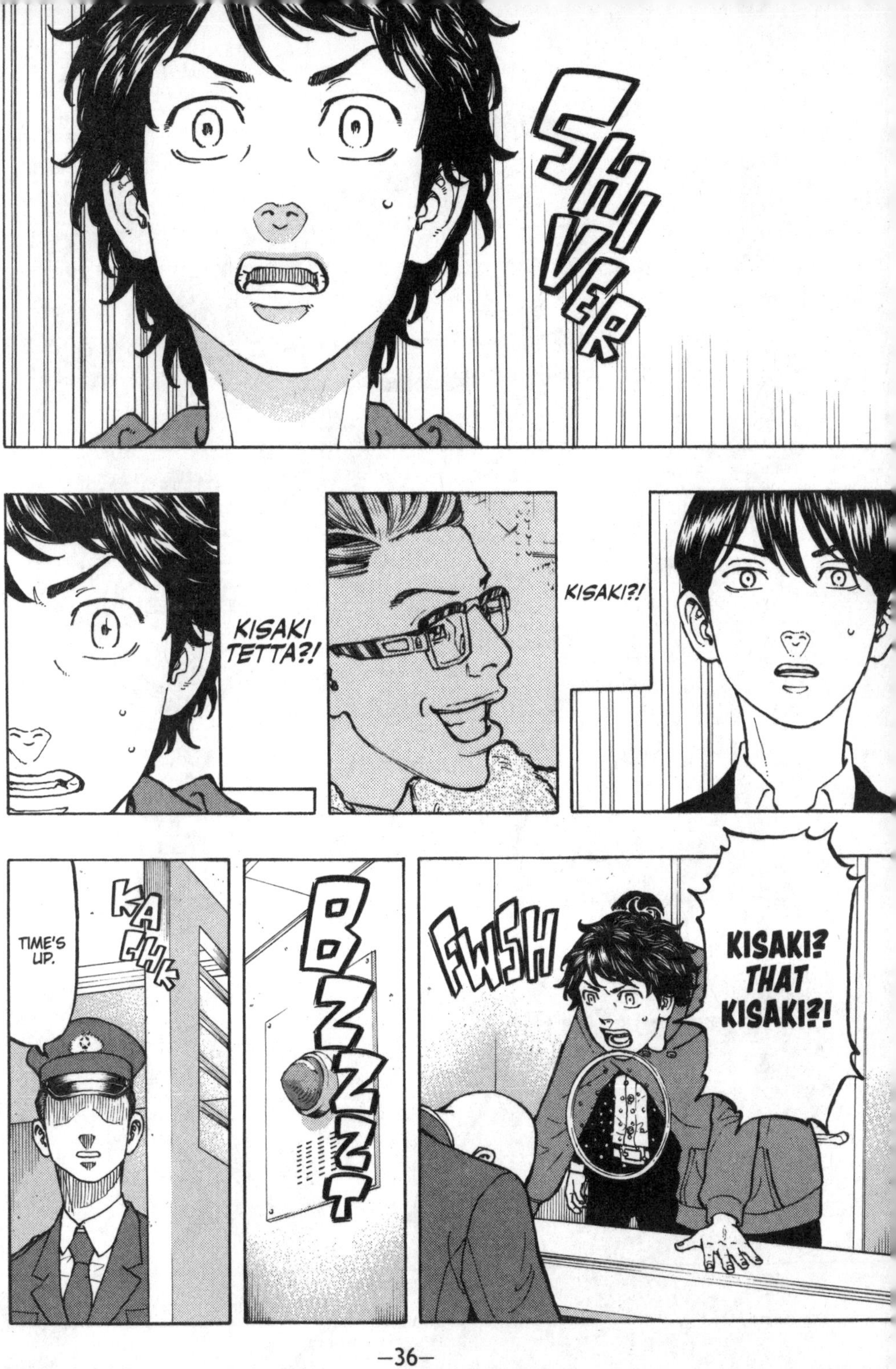
SHIVER
KISAKI?!
KISAKI TETTA?!
FWSH
KISAKI? THAT KISAKI?!
BZZZT
KACHK
TIME'S UP.

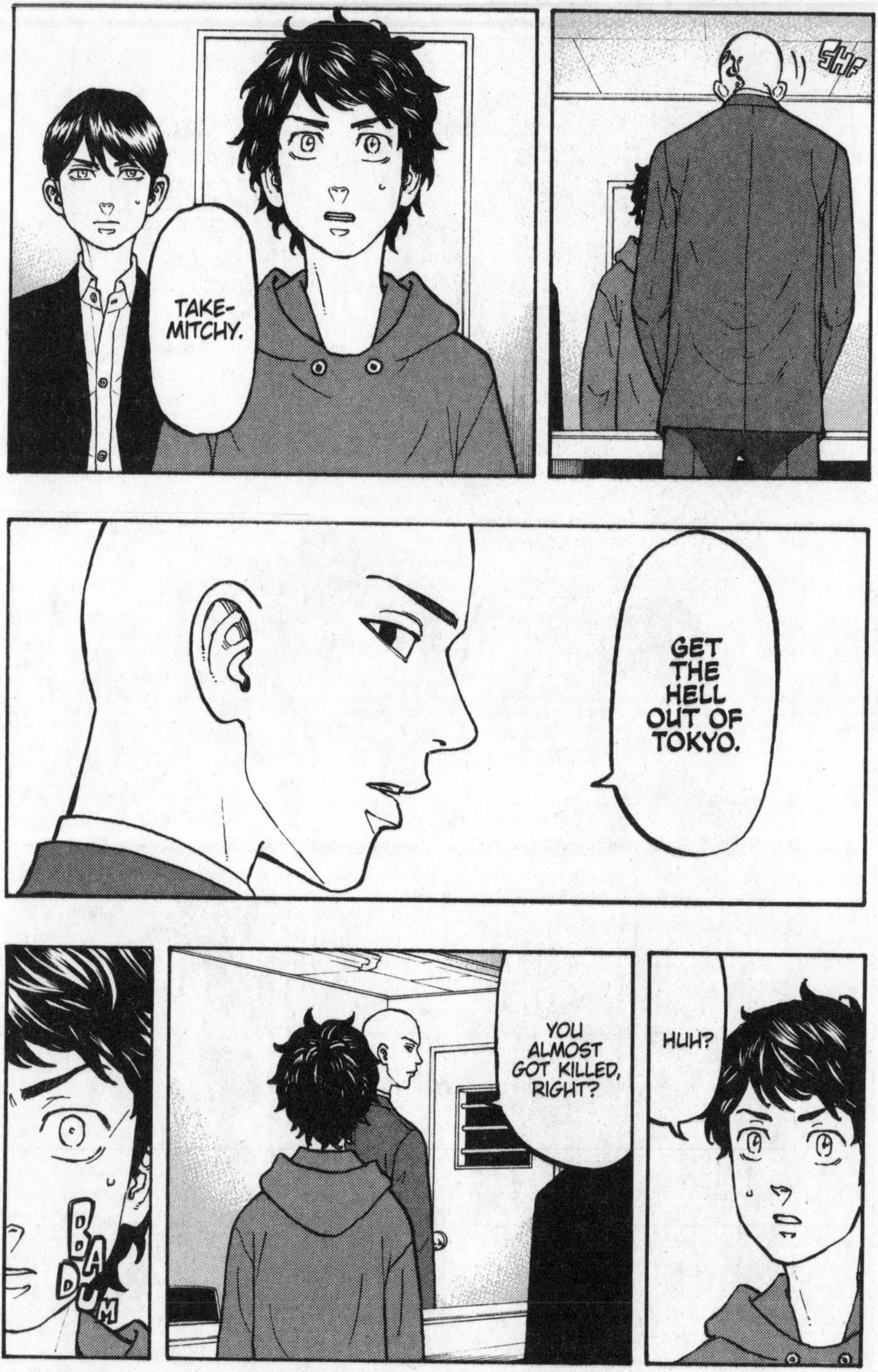
SHF
TAKE-MITCHY.
GET THE HELL OUT OF TOKYO.
HUH?
YOU ALMOST GOT KILLED, RIGHT?
BADADUM

THAT'S WHY YOU CAME TO SEE ME.

FOR KISAKI, KILLING PEOPLE...

IS JUST LIKE SQUASHING BUGS.

WAIT A MINUTE!!

GULP

WHY WOULD HE WANT TO KILL ME?!

WHY?!

Gulp

KISAKI ADORED MIKEY.

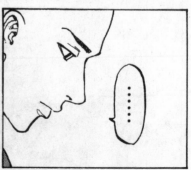

......

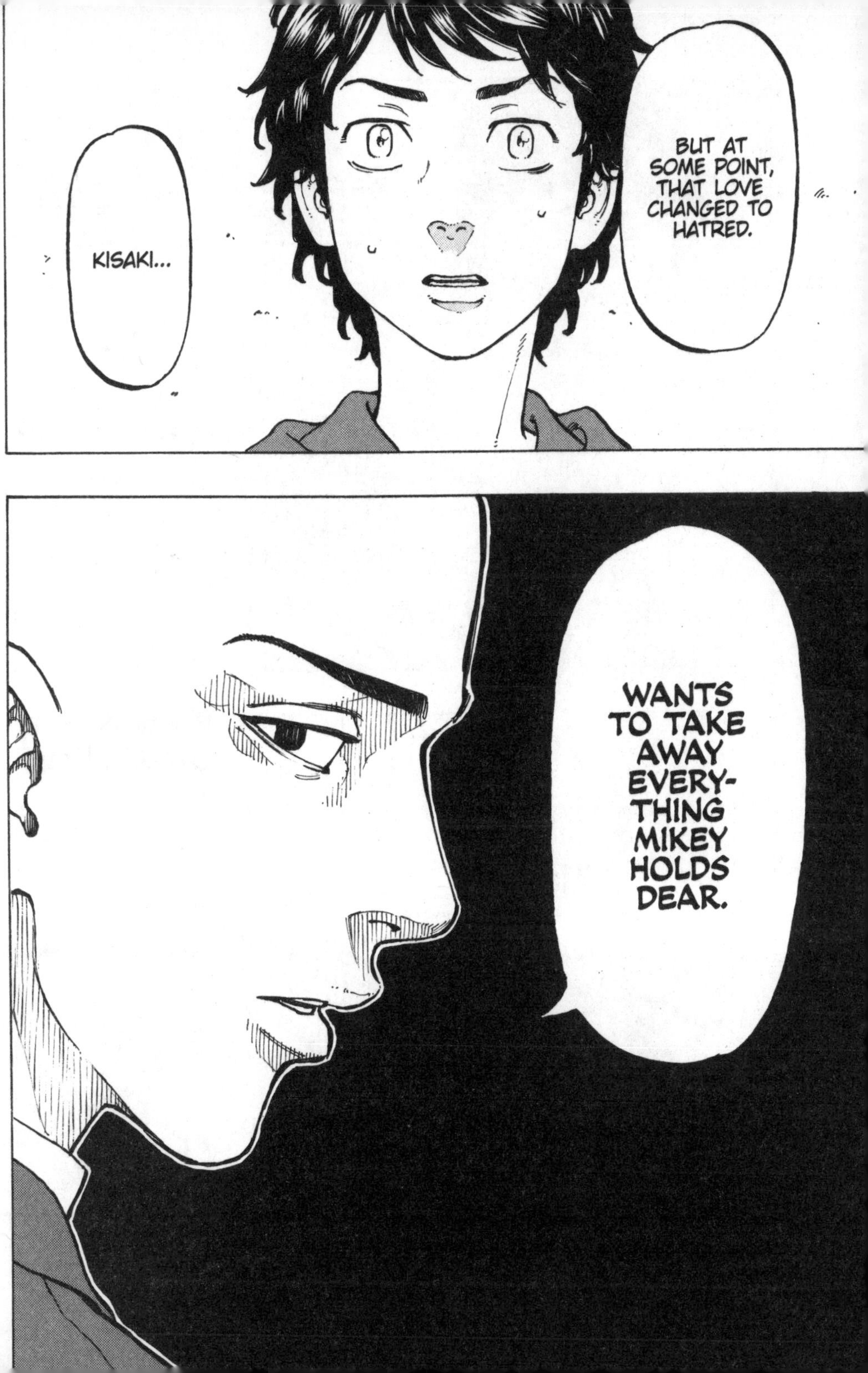
BUT AT SOME POINT, THAT LOVE CHANGED TO HATRED.
KISAKI...
WANTS TO TAKE AWAY EVERY-THING MIKEY HOLDS DEAR.

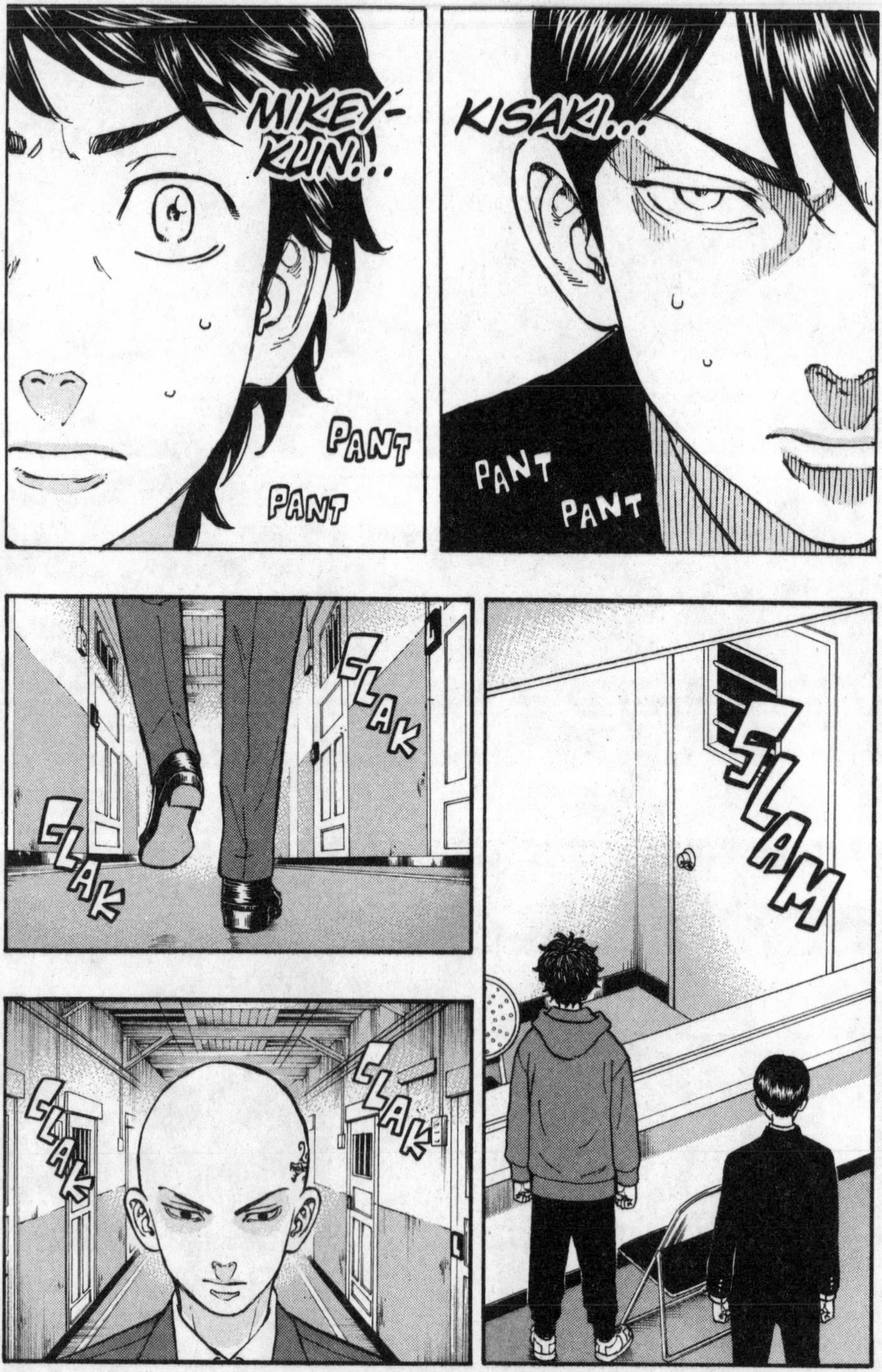
KISAKI...
PANT
PANT
MIKEY-KUN...
PANT
PANT
SLAM
CLAK
CLAK
CLAK
CLAK

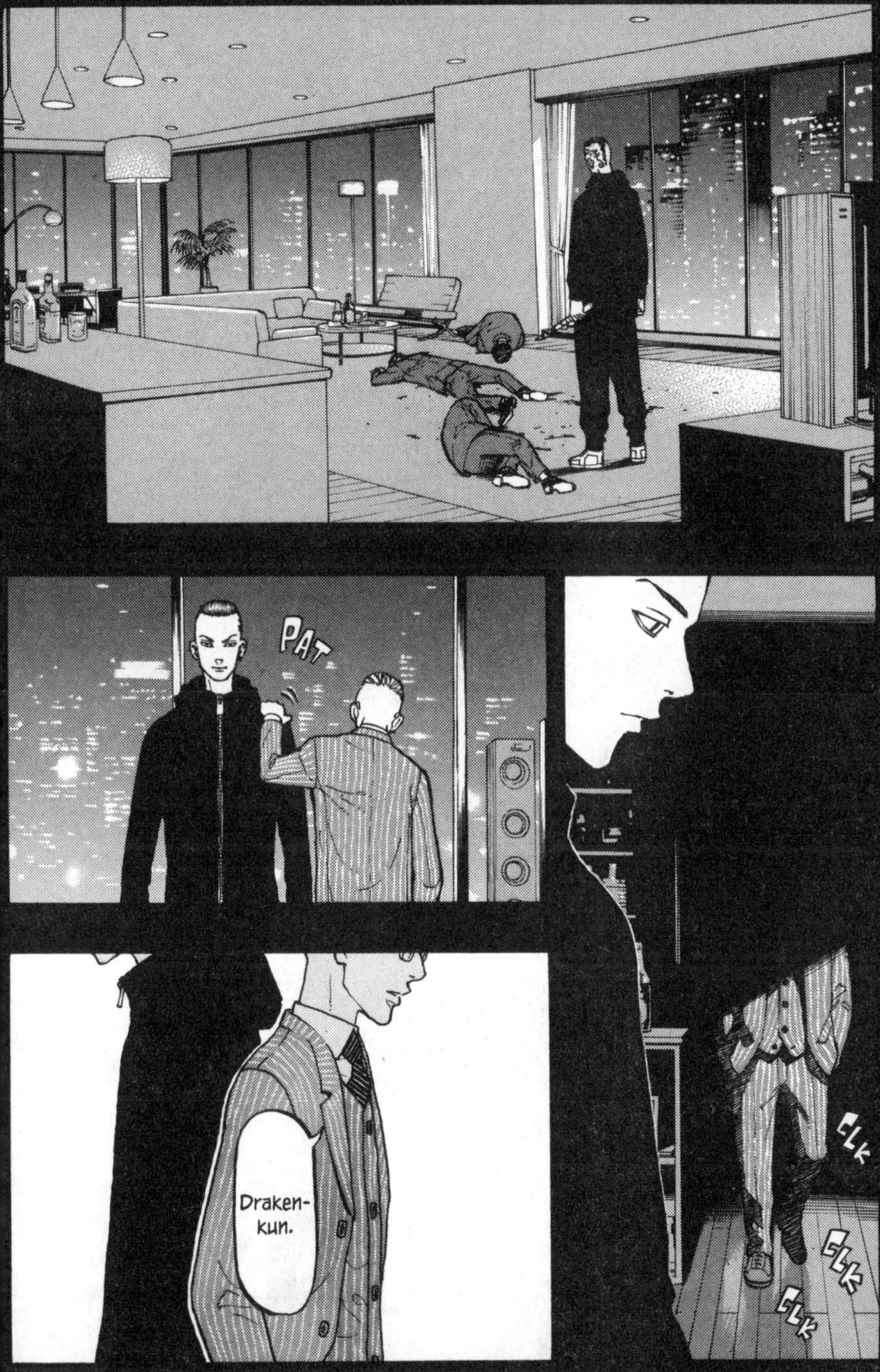
CLK
CLK
CLK
PAT
Draken-kun.

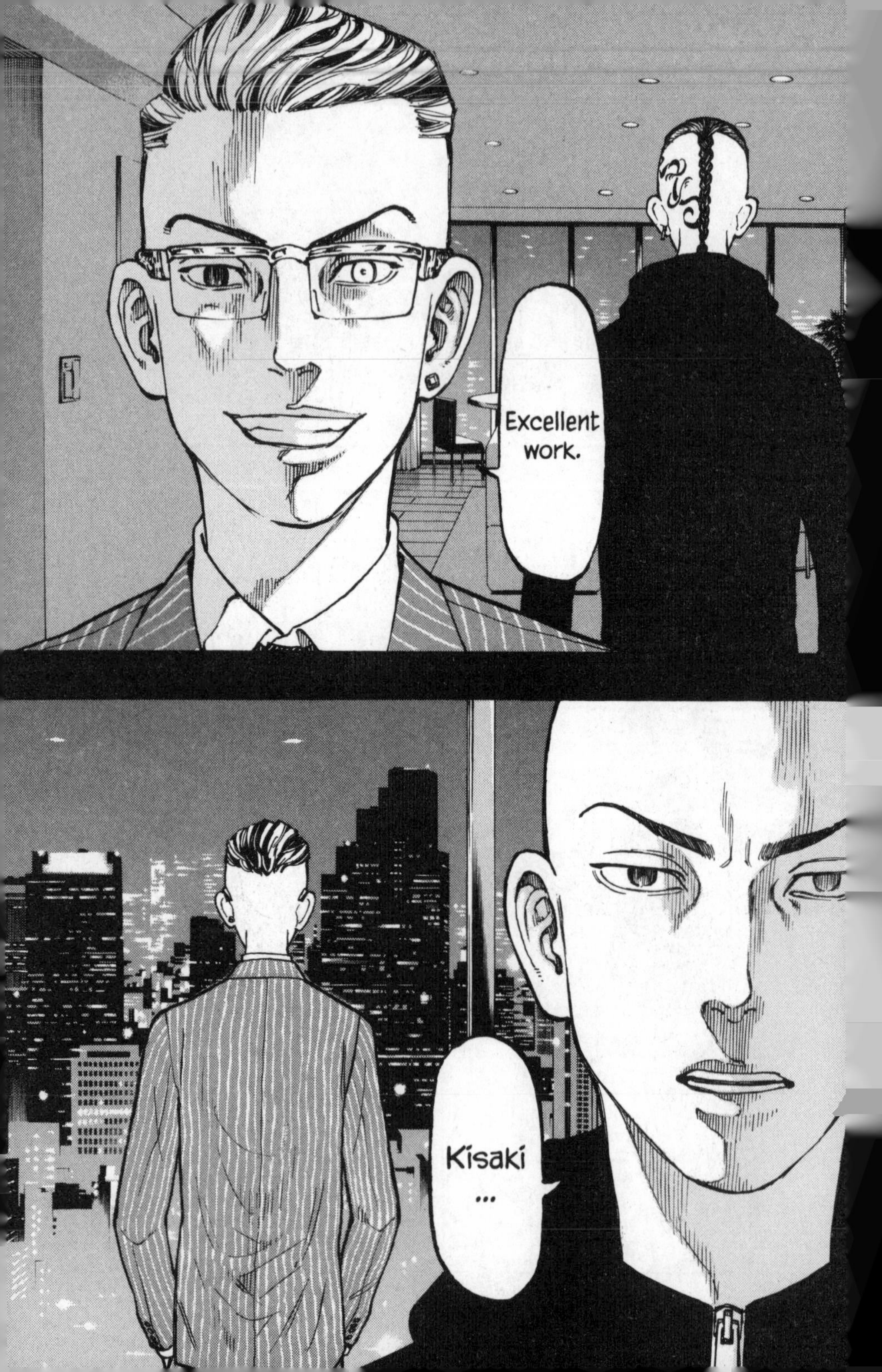
Excellent work.
Kisaki ...

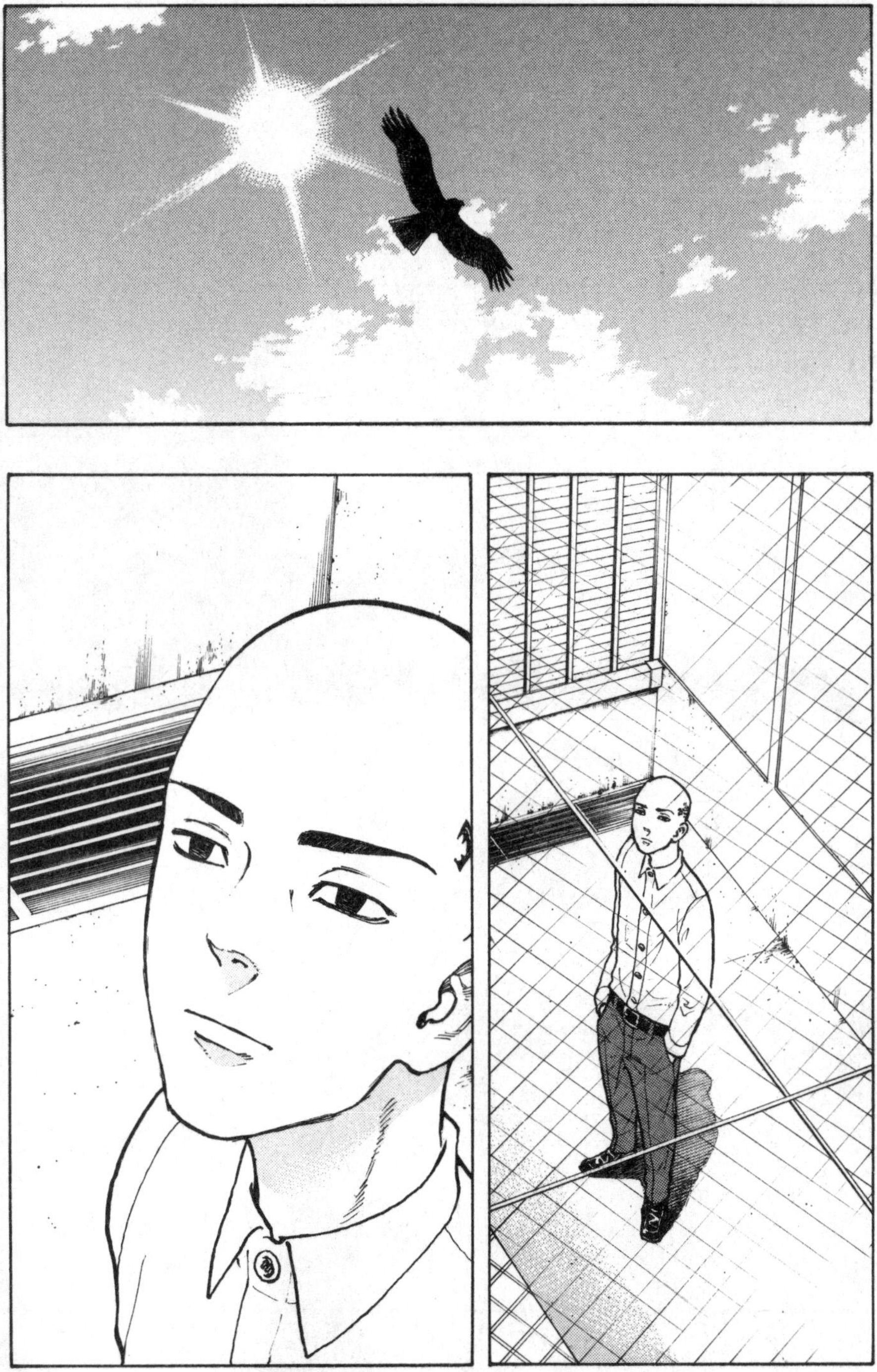

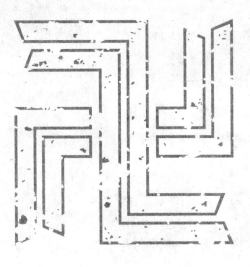

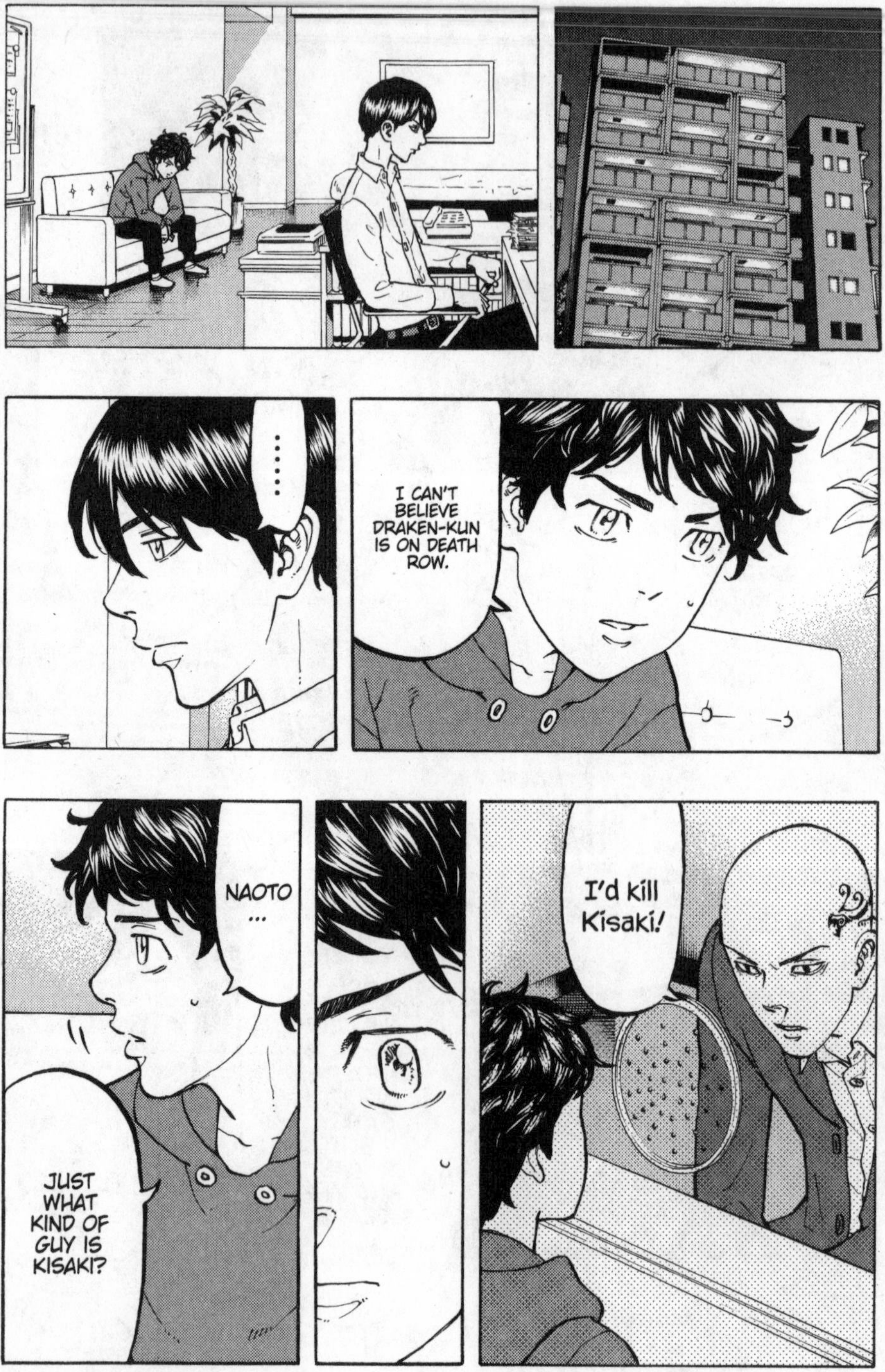
I CAN'T BELIEVE DRAKEN-KUN IS ON DEATH ROW.
......
I'd kill Kisaki!
NAOTO ...
JUST WHAT KIND OF GUY IS KISAKI?

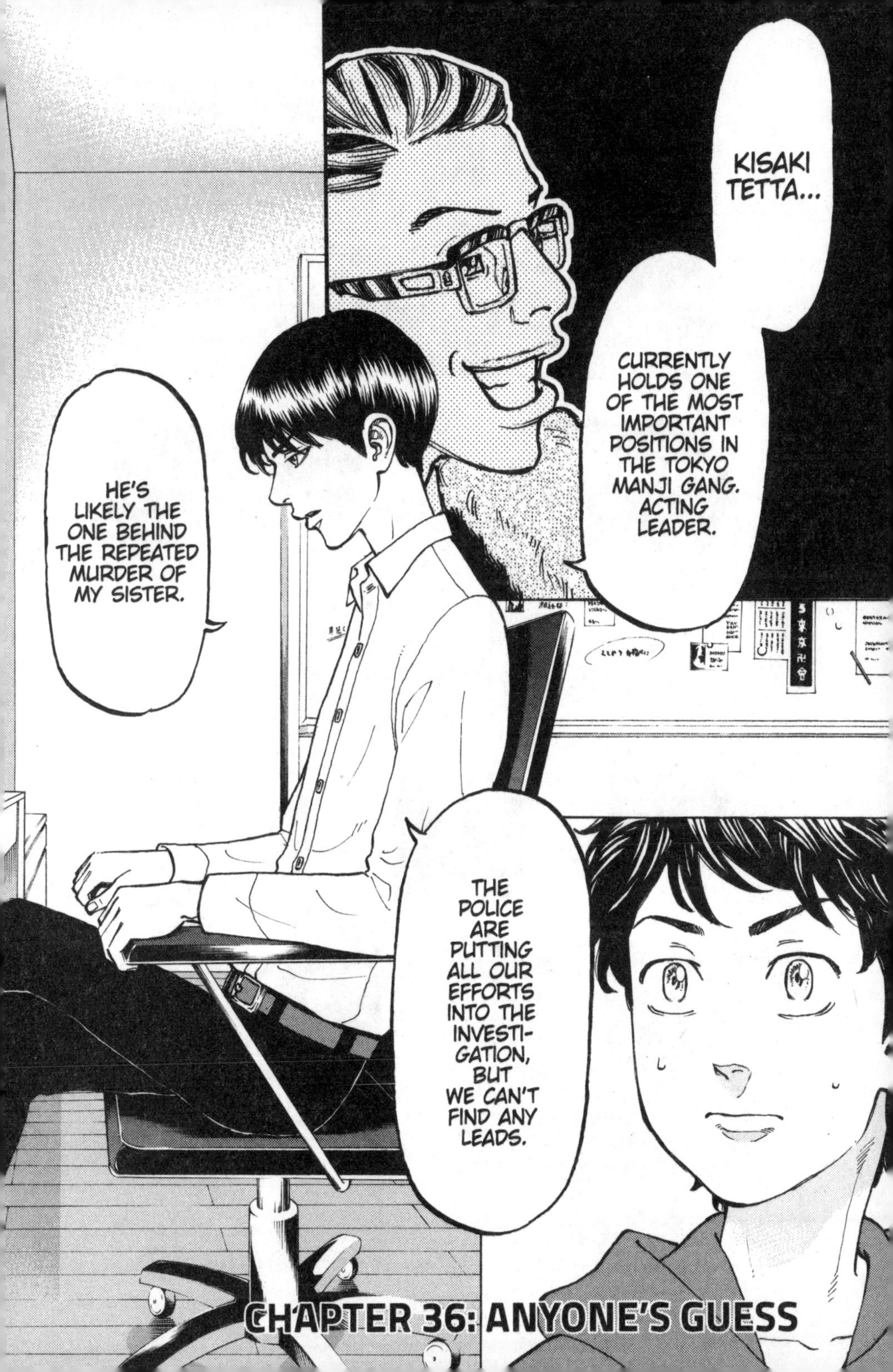
KISAKI TETTA...
CURRENTLY HOLDS ONE OF THE MOST IMPORTANT POSITIONS IN THE TOKYO MANJI GANG. ACTING LEADER.
HE'S LIKELY THE ONE BEHIND THE REPEATED MURDER OF MY SISTER.
THE POLICE ARE PUTTING ALL OUR EFFORTS INTO THE INVESTI-GATION, BUT WE CAN'T FIND ANY LEADS.

CHAPTER 36: ANYONE'S GUESS

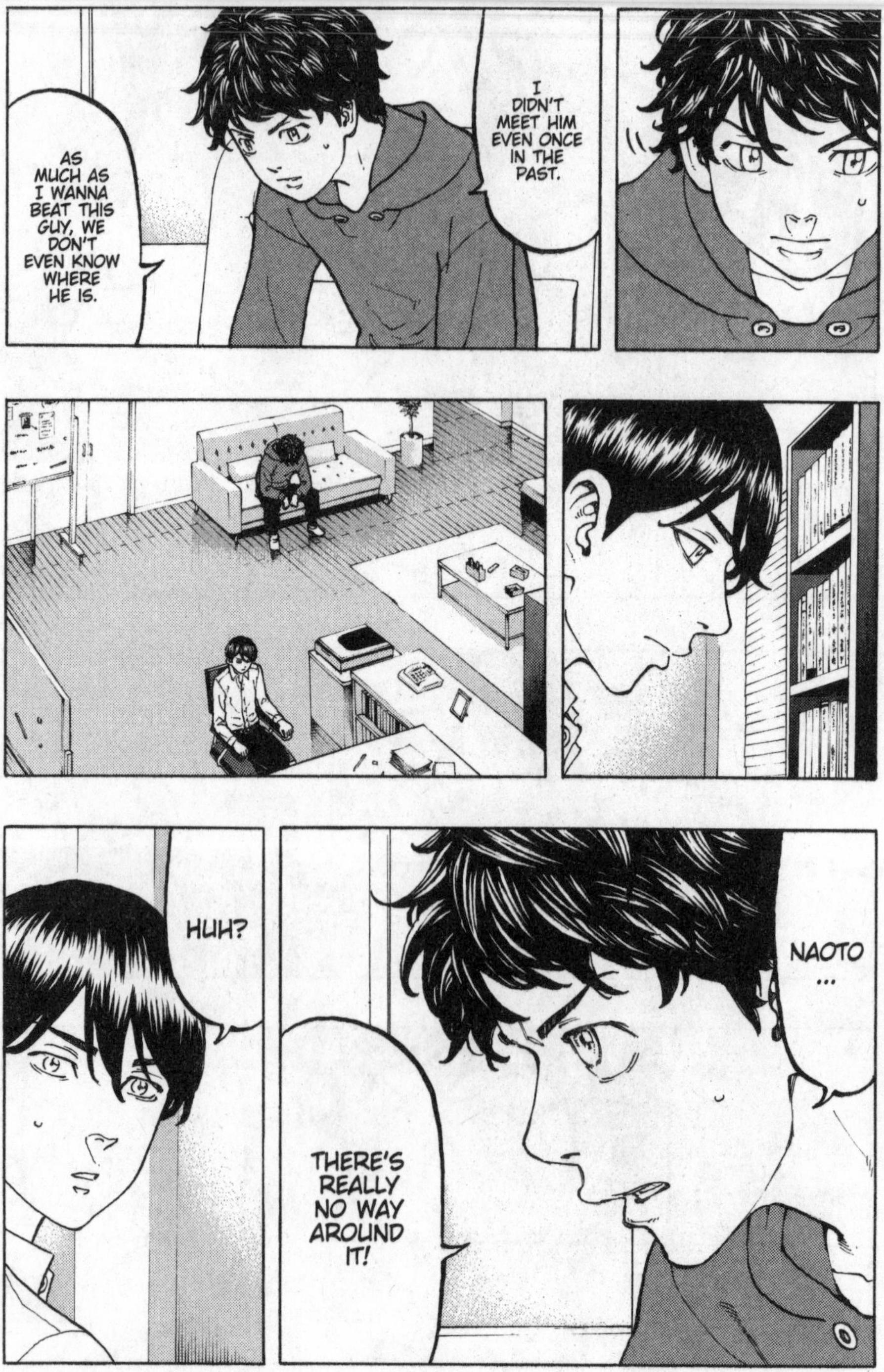
I DIDN'T MEET HIM EVEN ONCE IN THE PAST.
AS MUCH AS I WANNA BEAT THIS GUY, WE DON'T EVEN KNOW WHERE HE IS.
NAOTO ...
THERE'S REALLY NO WAY AROUND IT!
HUH?

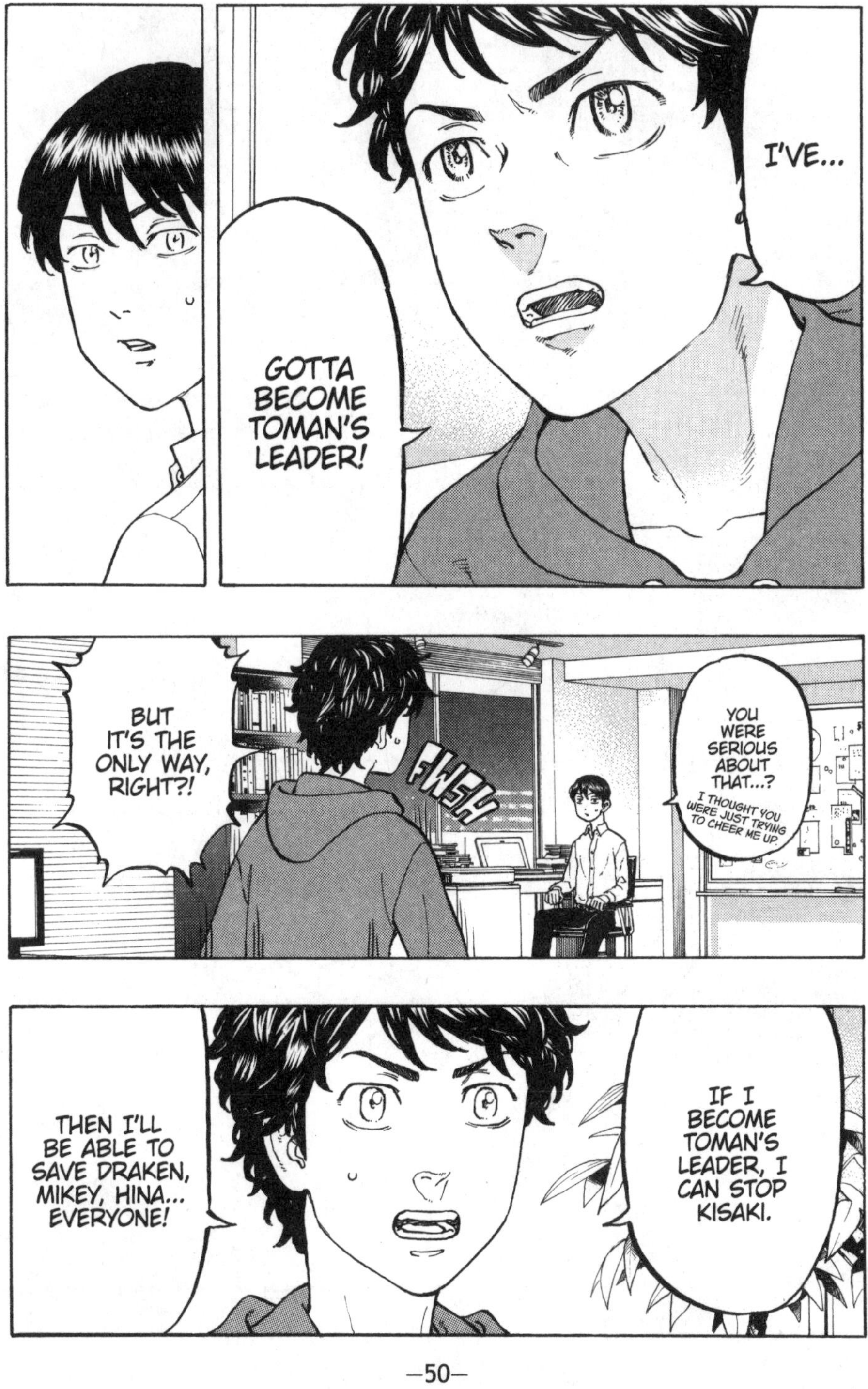
I'VE...
GOTTA BECOME TOMAN'S LEADER!
YOU WERE SERIOUS ABOUT THAT...?
I THOUGHT YOU WERE JUST TRYING TO CHEER ME UP.
FWSH
BUT IT'S THE ONLY WAY, RIGHT?!
IF I BECOME TOMAN'S LEADER, I CAN STOP KISAKI.
THEN I'LL BE ABLE TO SAVE DRAKEN, MIKEY, HINA... EVERYONE!

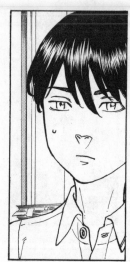

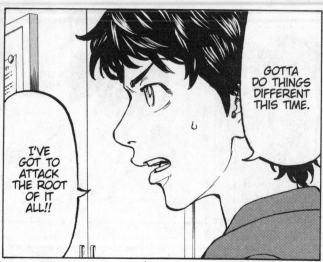

GOTTA DO THINGS DIFFERENT THIS TIME.
I'VE GOT TO ATTACK THE ROOT OF IT ALL!!
I'VE THOUGHT IT OVER.
FIRST, I'LL BECOME A CAPTAIN.
WITH PAH-CHIN GONE...
THE THIRD DIVISION DOESN'T HAVE A CAPTAIN RIGHT NOW.
I'LL AIM FOR THAT!

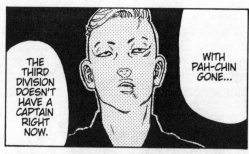

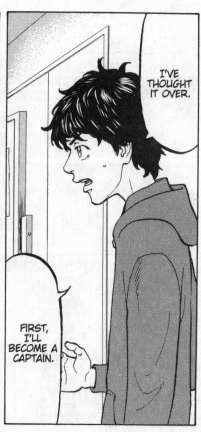

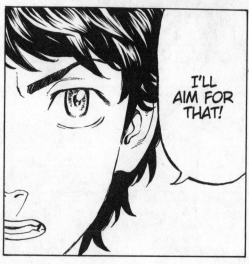

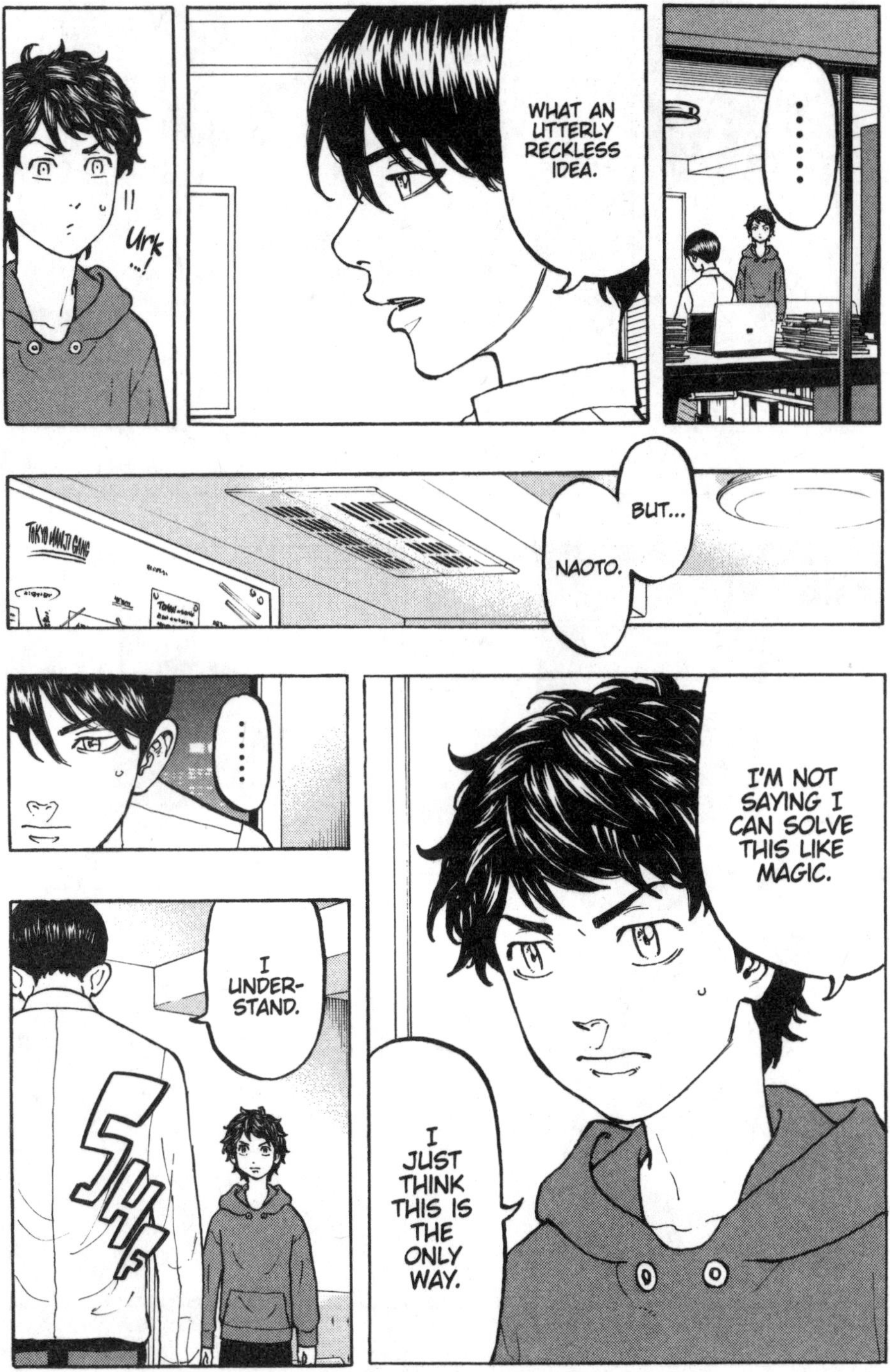
……
WHAT AN UTTERLY RECKLESS IDEA.
Urk …!
BUT…
NAOTO.
TOKYO MANJI GANG
I'M NOT SAYING I CAN SOLVE THIS LIKE MAGIC.
I JUST THINK THIS IS THE ONLY WAY.
……
I UNDER-STAND.
SHF

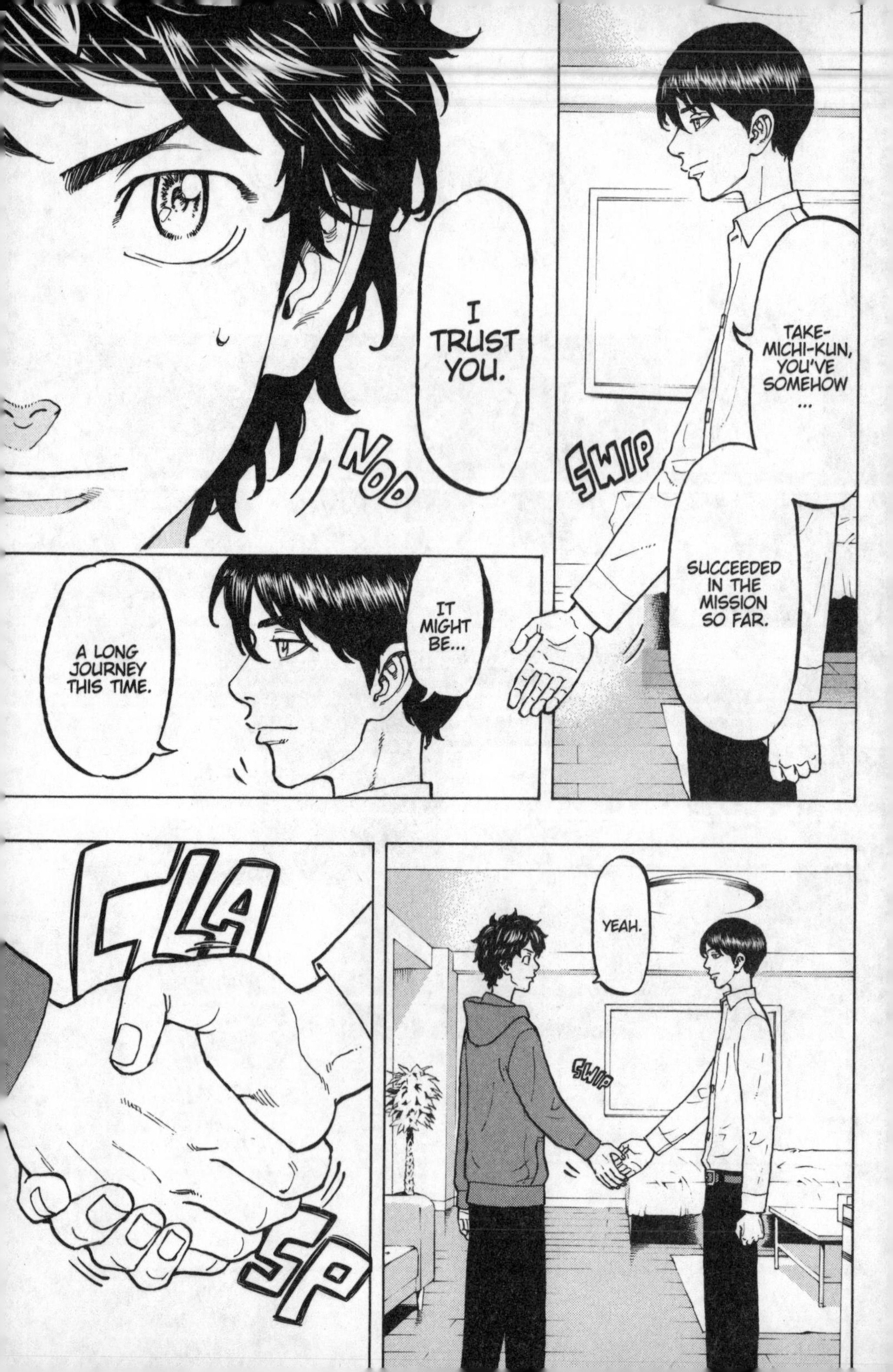
TAKE-MICHI-KUN, YOU'VE SOMEHOW ...
SUCCEEDED IN THE MISSION SO FAR.
SWIP
I TRUST YOU.
NOD
IT MIGHT BE...
A LONG JOURNEY THIS TIME.
YEAH.
SWIP
CLASP

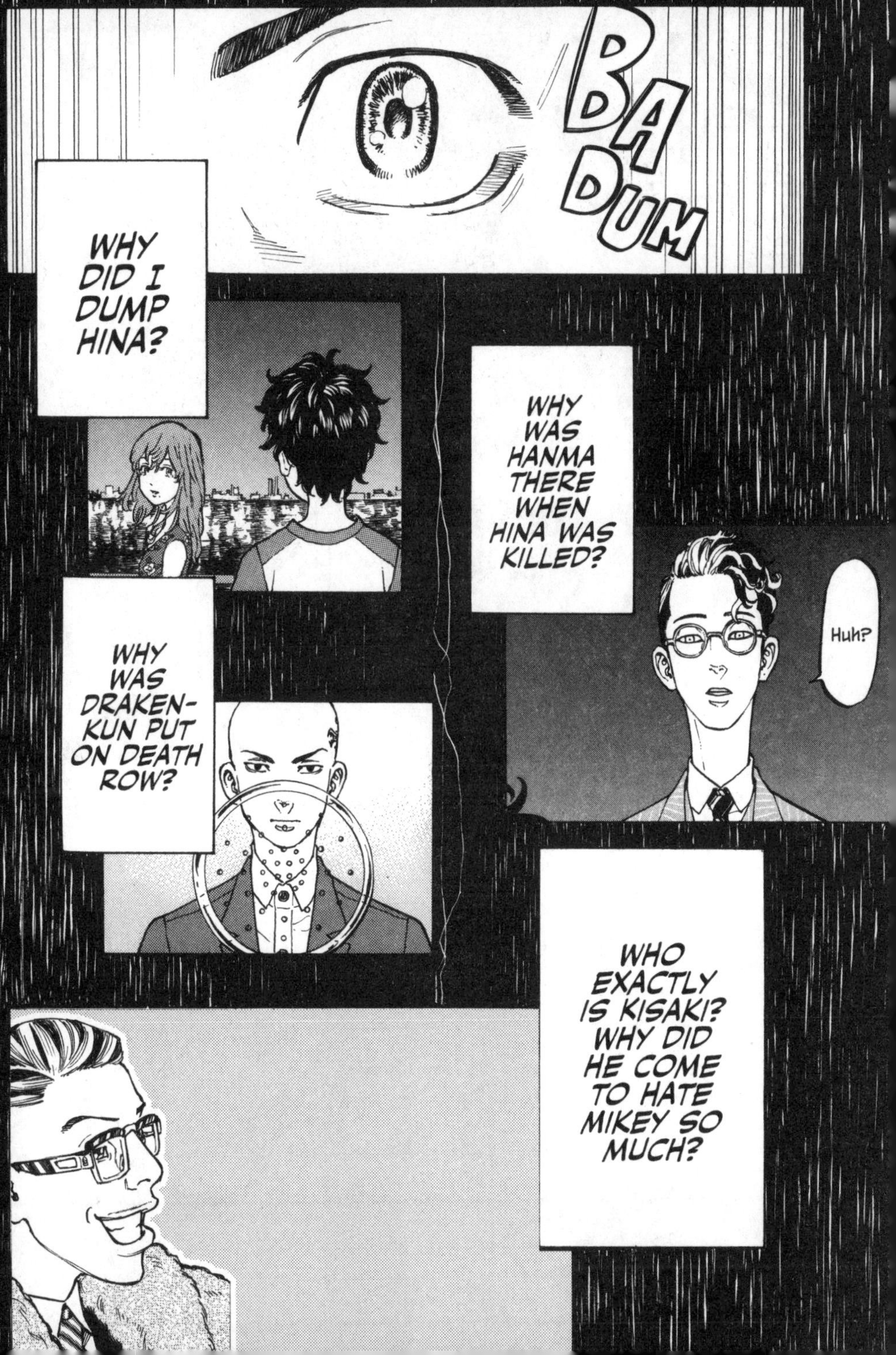
BA DUM
WHY WAS HANMA THERE WHEN HINA WAS KILLED?
Huh?
WHY DID I DUMP HINA?
WHY WAS DRAKEN-KUN PUT ON DEATH ROW?
WHO EXACTLY IS KISAKI? WHY DID HE COME TO HATE MIKEY SO MUCH?

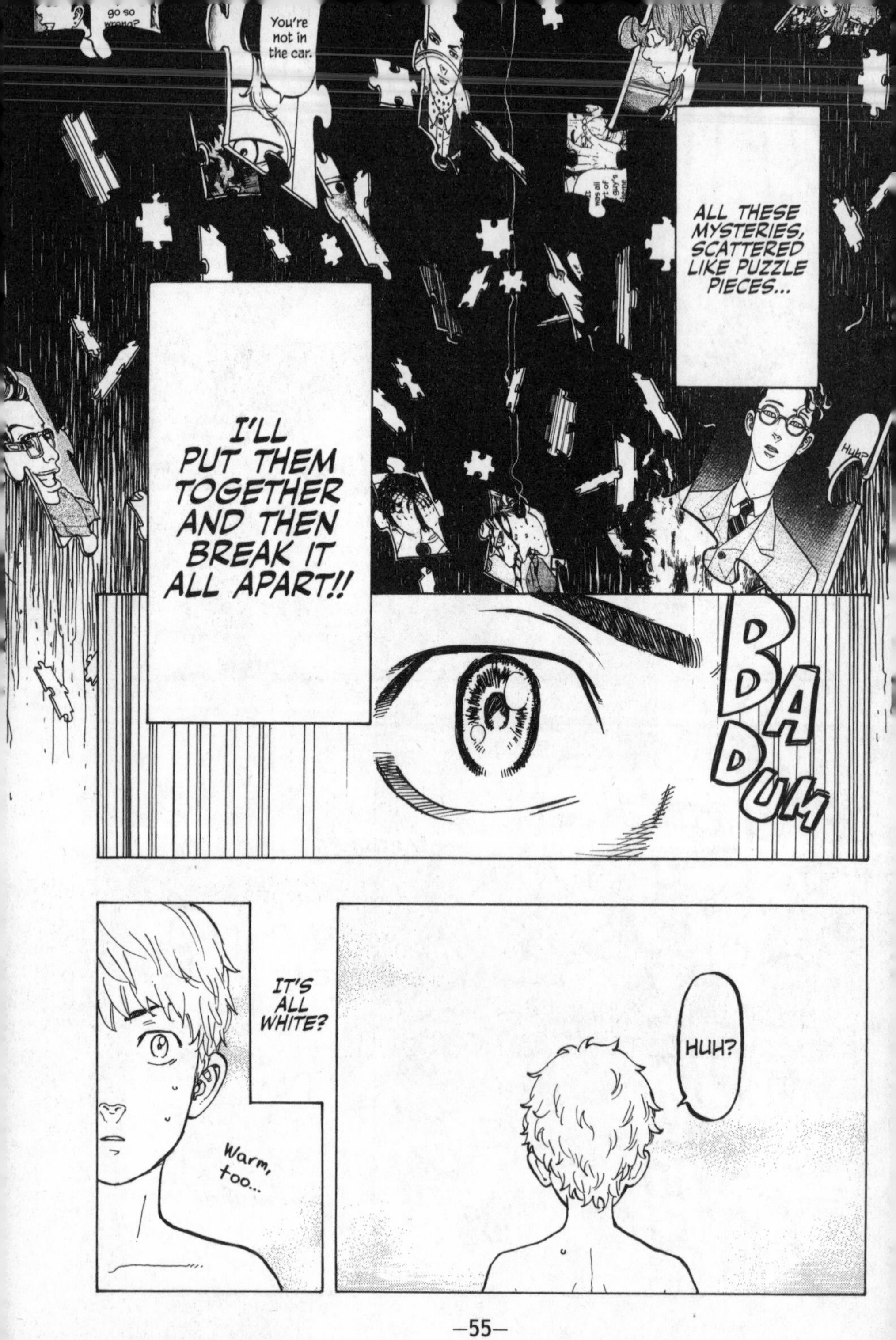
Huh?
ALL THESE MYSTERIES, SCATTERED LIKE PUZZLE PIECES...
You're not in the car.
go so wrong?
I'LL PUT THEM TOGETHER AND THEN BREAK IT ALL APART!!
BA DUM
HUH?
IT'S ALL WHITE?
Warm, too...

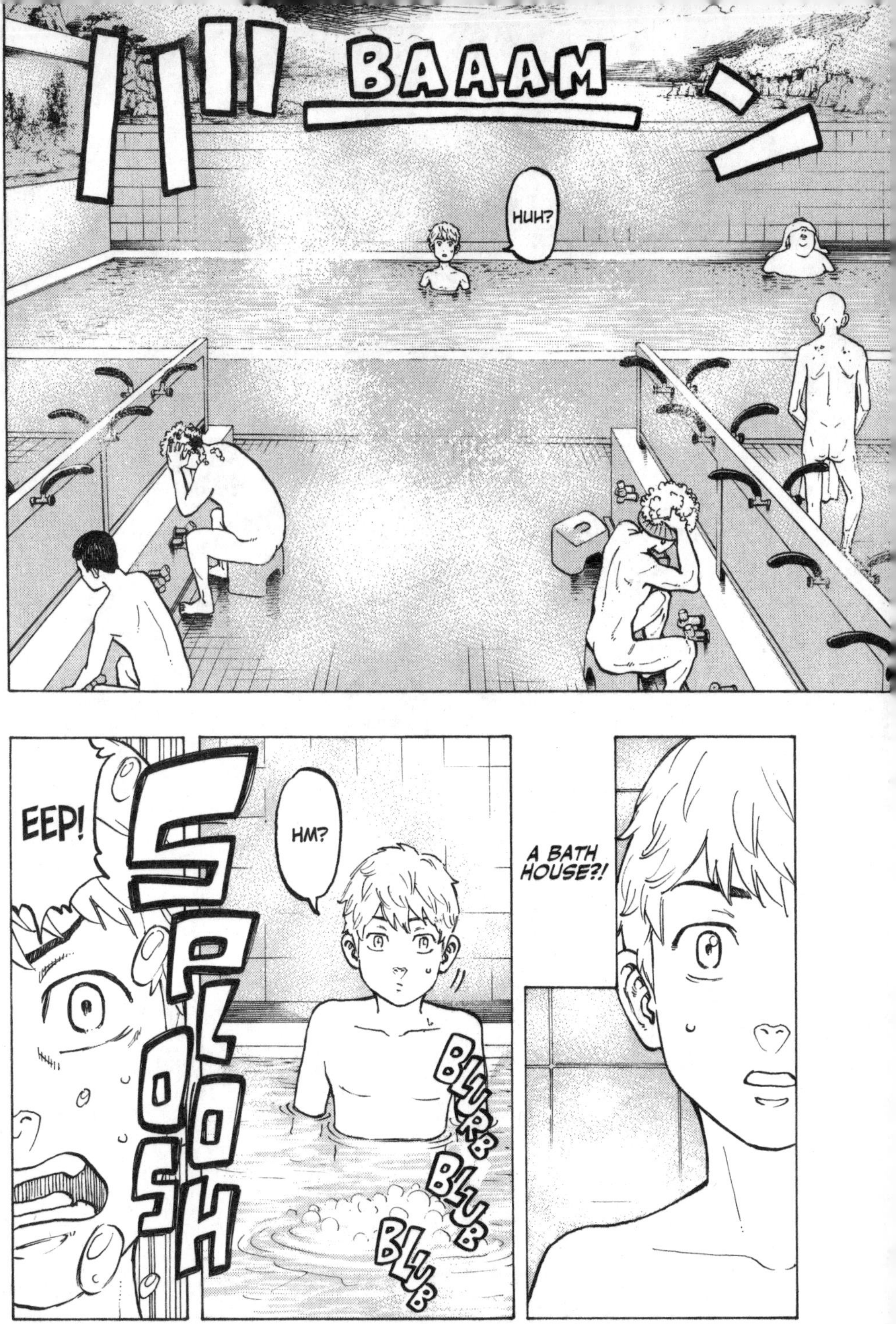
BAAAM
HUH?
A BATH HOUSE?!
HM?
BLURB
BLUB
BLUB
SPLOSH
EEP!

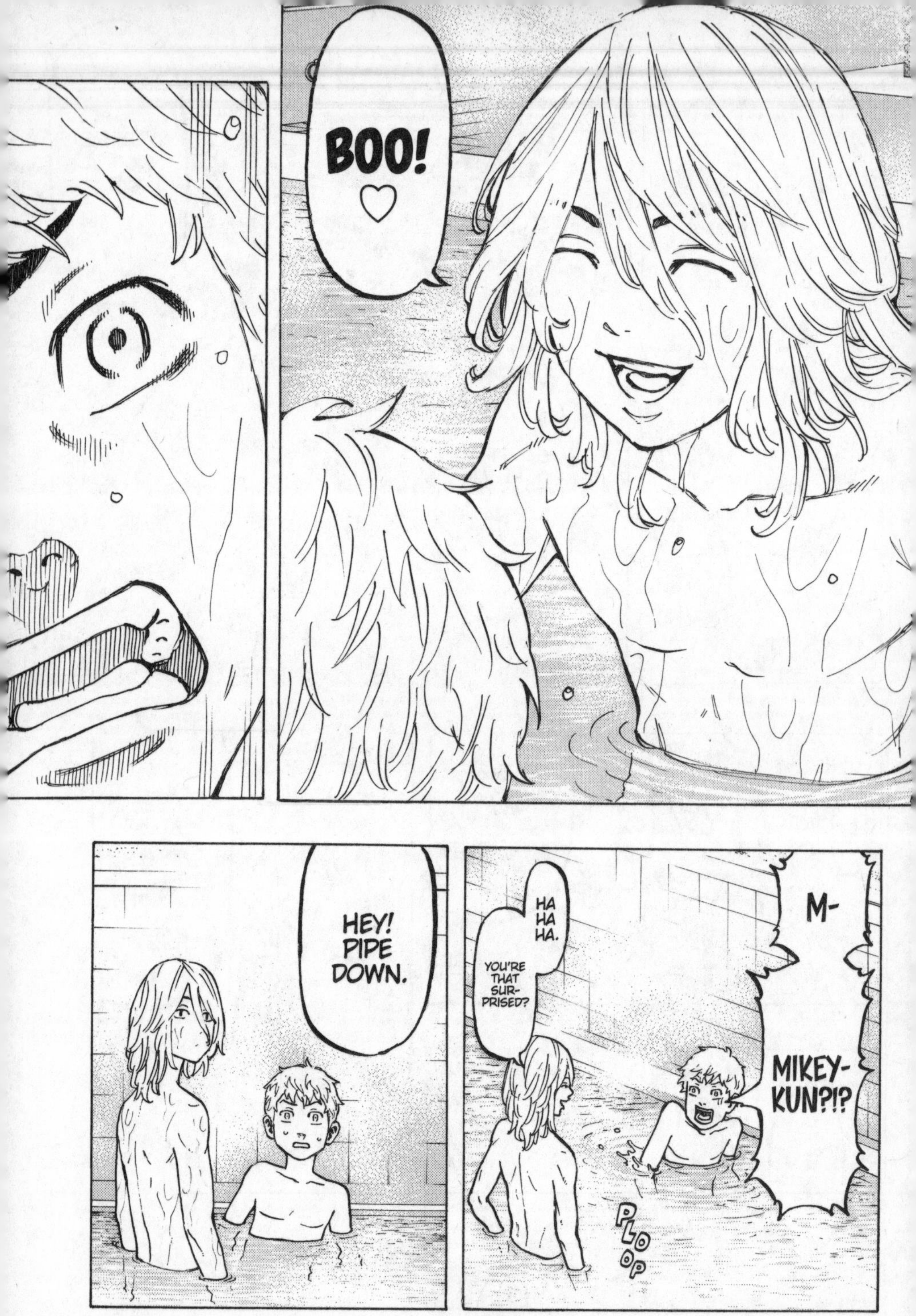
BOO! ♡
M- MIKEY-KUN?!?
HA HA HA.
YOU'RE THAT SURPRISED?
PLOP
HEY! PIPE DOWN.

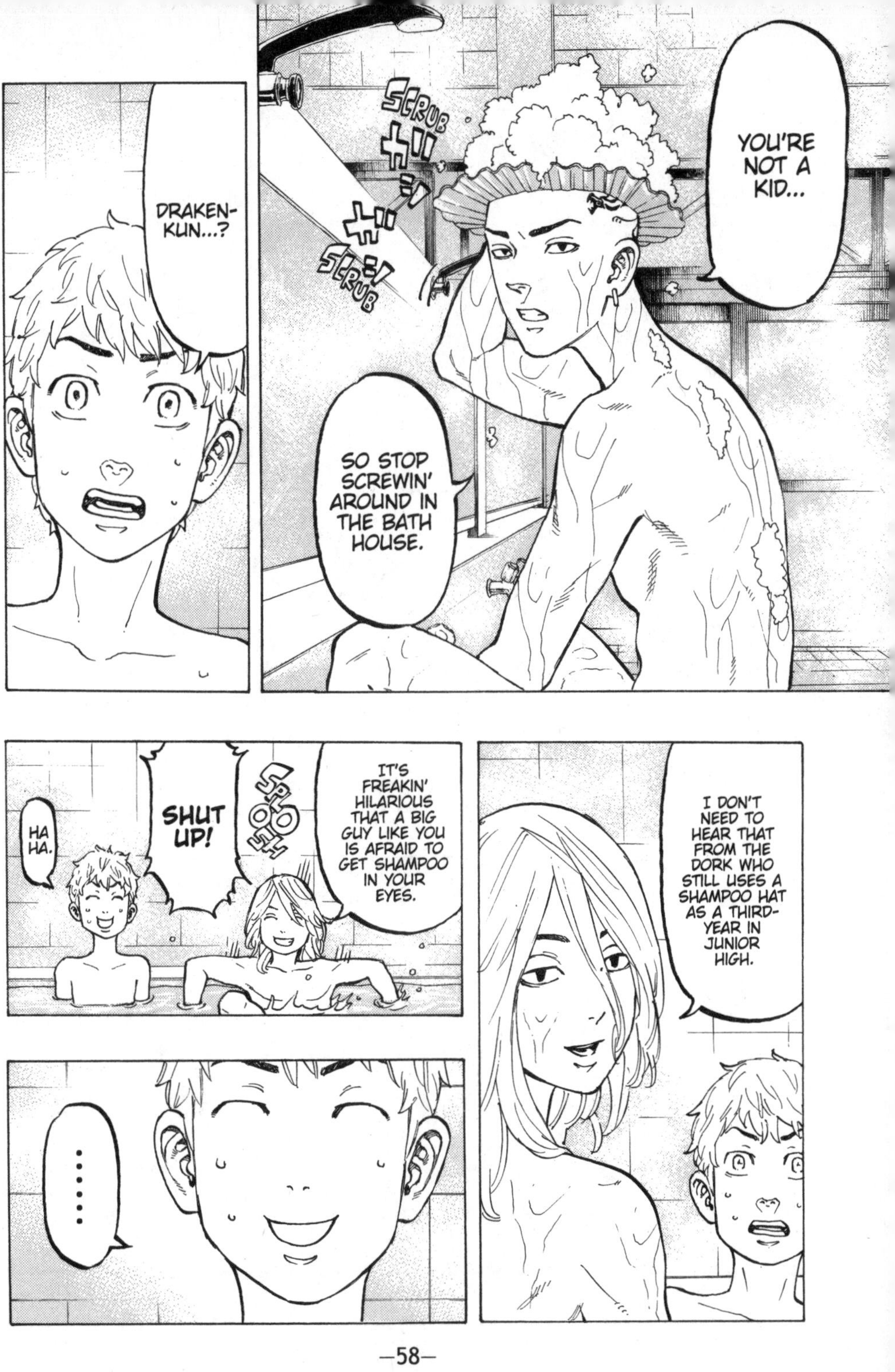
SCRUB
SCRUB
YOU'RE NOT A KID...
SO STOP SCREWIN' AROUND IN THE BATH HOUSE.
DRAKEN-KUN...?
I DON'T NEED TO HEAR THAT FROM THE DORK WHO STILL USES A SHAMPOO HAT AS A THIRD-YEAR IN JUNIOR HIGH.
IT'S FREAKIN' HILARIOUS THAT A BIG GUY LIKE YOU IS AFRAID TO GET SHAMPOO IN YOUR EYES.
SPLOOSH
SHUT UP!
HA HA.
......

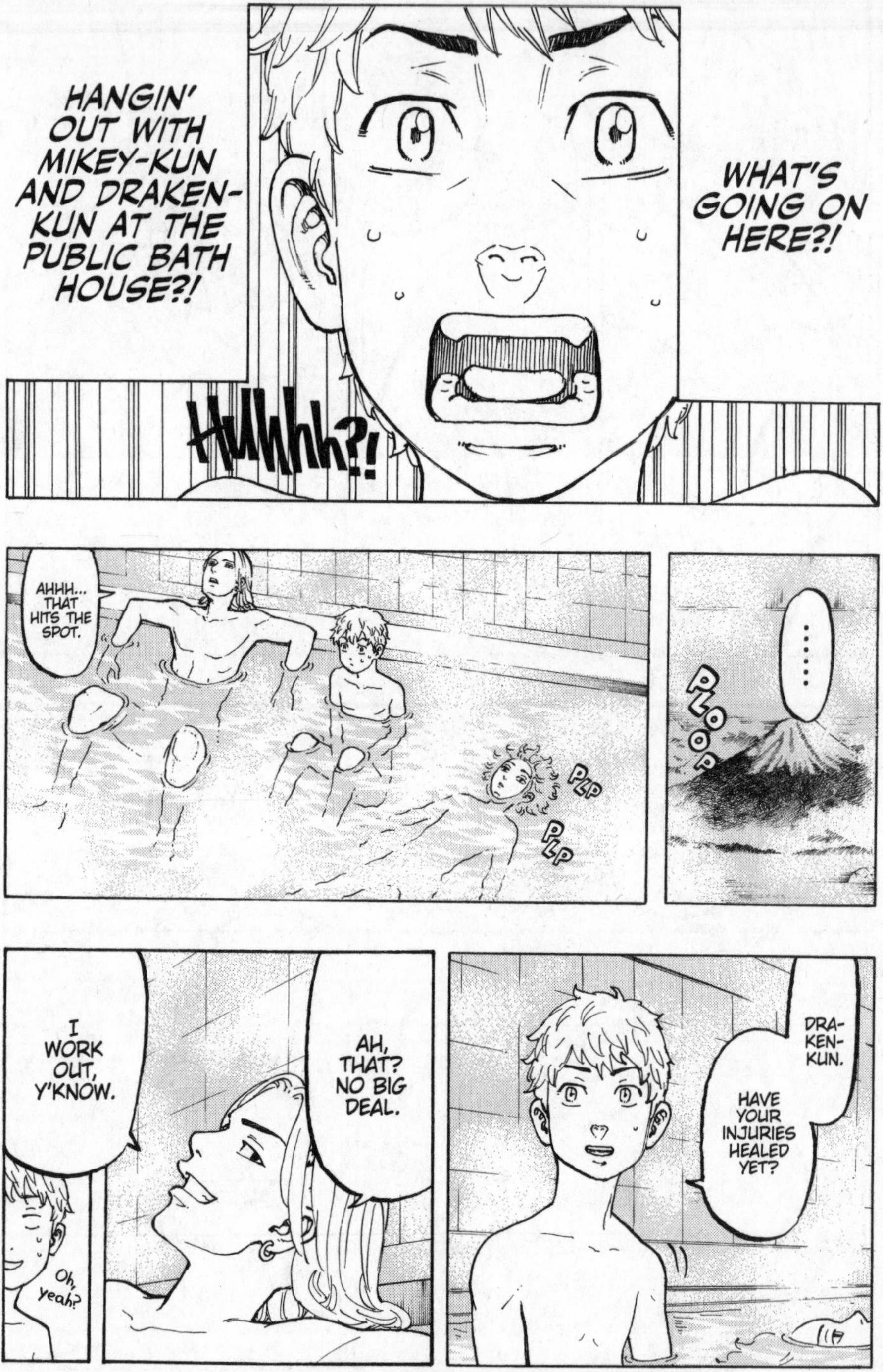
WHAT'S GOING ON HERE?!
HANGIN' OUT WITH MIKEY-KUN AND DRAKEN-KUN AT THE PUBLIC BATH HOUSE?!
Huhhh?!
......
PLOOP
AHHH... THAT HITS THE SPOT.
PLP
PLP
DRAKEN-KUN.
HAVE YOUR INJURIES HEALED YET?
AH, THAT? NO BIG DEAL.
I WORK OUT, Y'KNOW.
Oh, yeah?

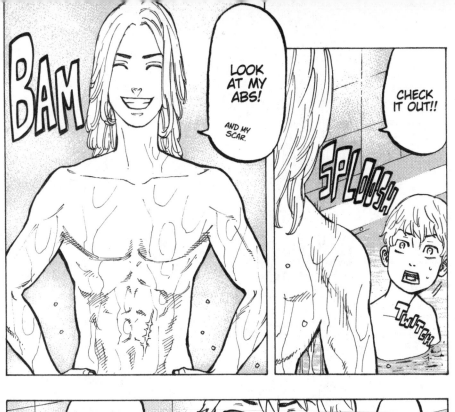

BAM

LOOK AT MY ABS!

AND MY SCAR.

CHECK IT OUT!!

SPLOOSH

TWITCH

YOU SERIOUSLY DON'T LOOK LIKE A JUNIOR HIGH KID.

NEITHER DOES THE SCAR.

HA HA.

GULP

HUH?

OHO.

SWSWH

I KNOW, RIGHT?!

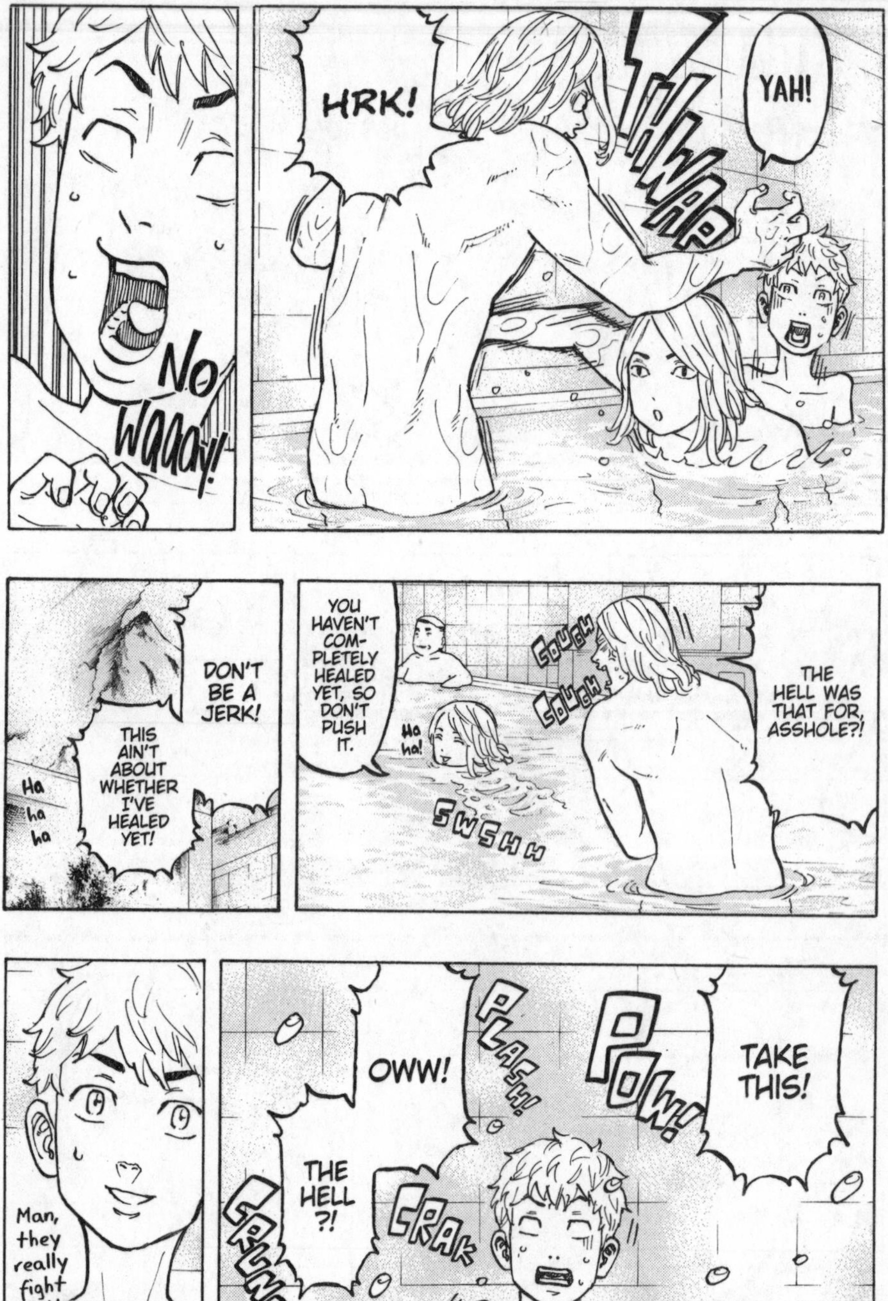
YAH!
THWAP
HRK!
NO WAAAY!
THE HELL WAS THAT FOR, ASSHOLE?!
COUGH COUGH
YOU HAVEN'T COMPLETELY HEALED YET, SO DON'T PUSH IT.
Ha ha!
SWSHH
DON'T BE A JERK!
THIS AIN'T ABOUT WHETHER I'VE HEALED YET!
Ha ha ha
TAKE THIS!
POW!
PLASH!
OWW!
CRAK
THE HELL?!
CRUNCH
Man, they really fight all the time.

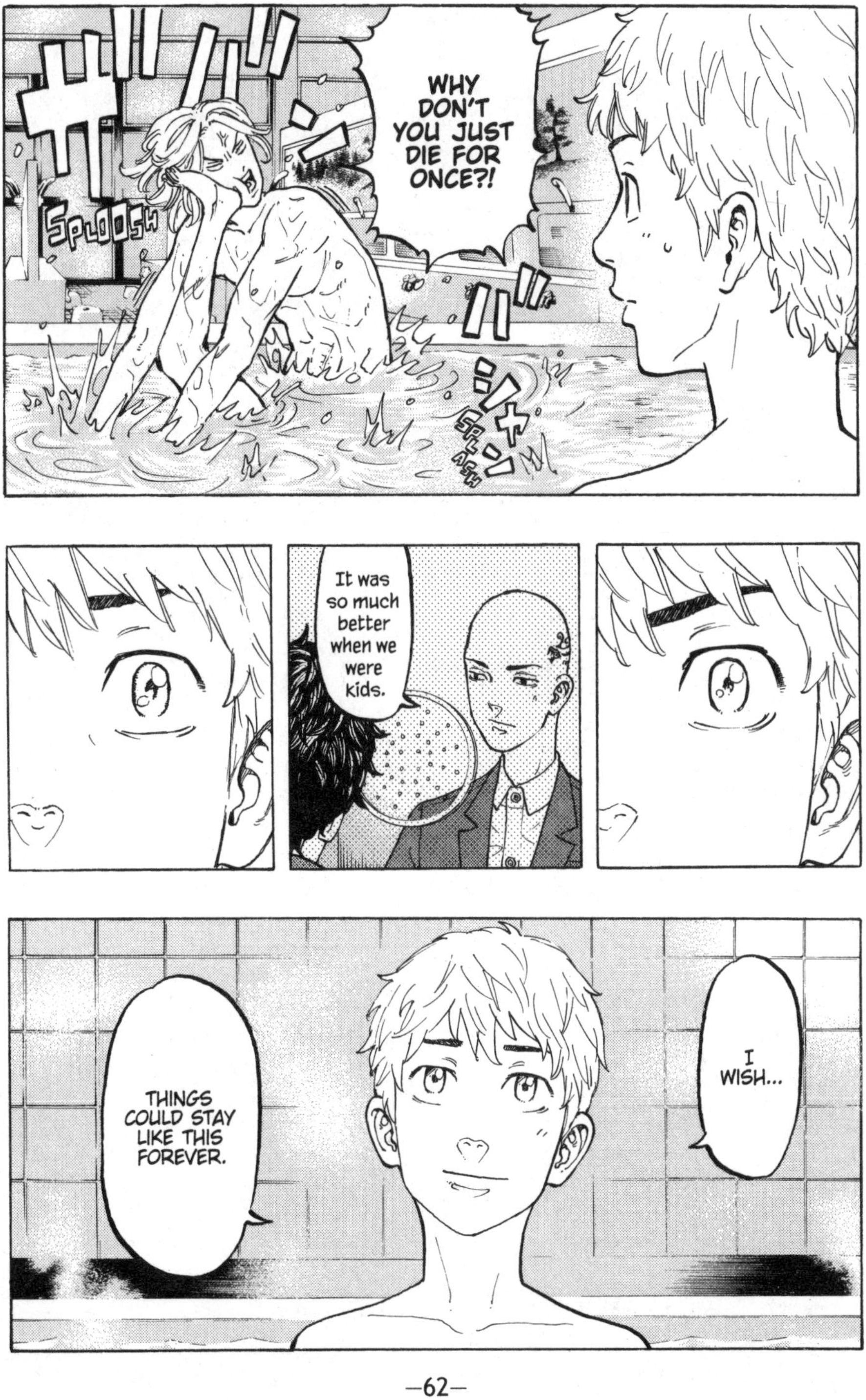
WHY DON'T YOU JUST DIE FOR ONCE?!
SPLOOSH
SPLASH
It was so much better when we were kids.
I WISH...
THINGS COULD STAY LIKE THIS FOREVER.

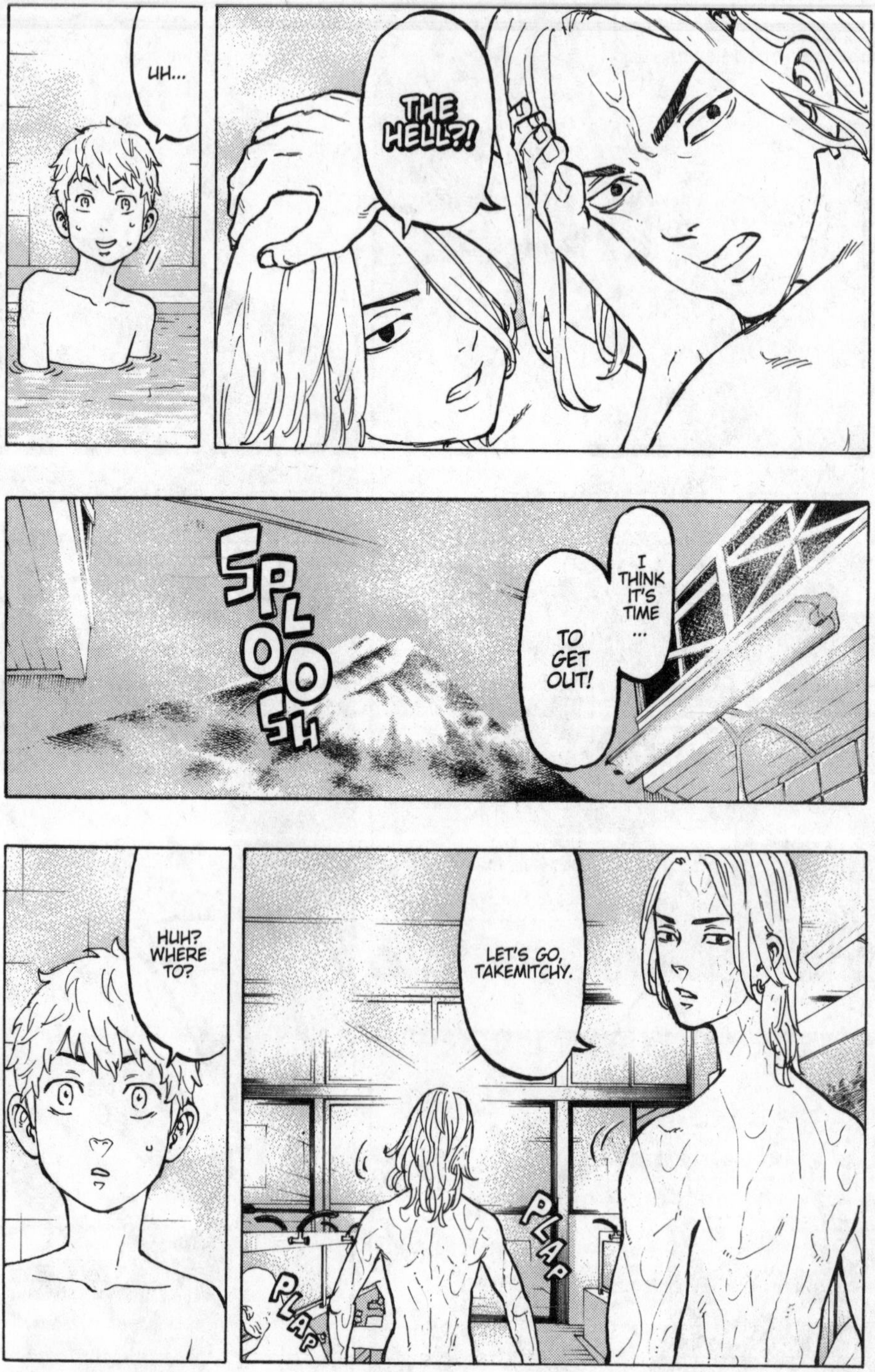
THE HELL?!
UH...
I THINK IT'S TIME ...
TO GET OUT!
SPLOOSH
LET'S GO, TAKEMITCHY.
PLAP
PLAP
HUH? WHERE TO?

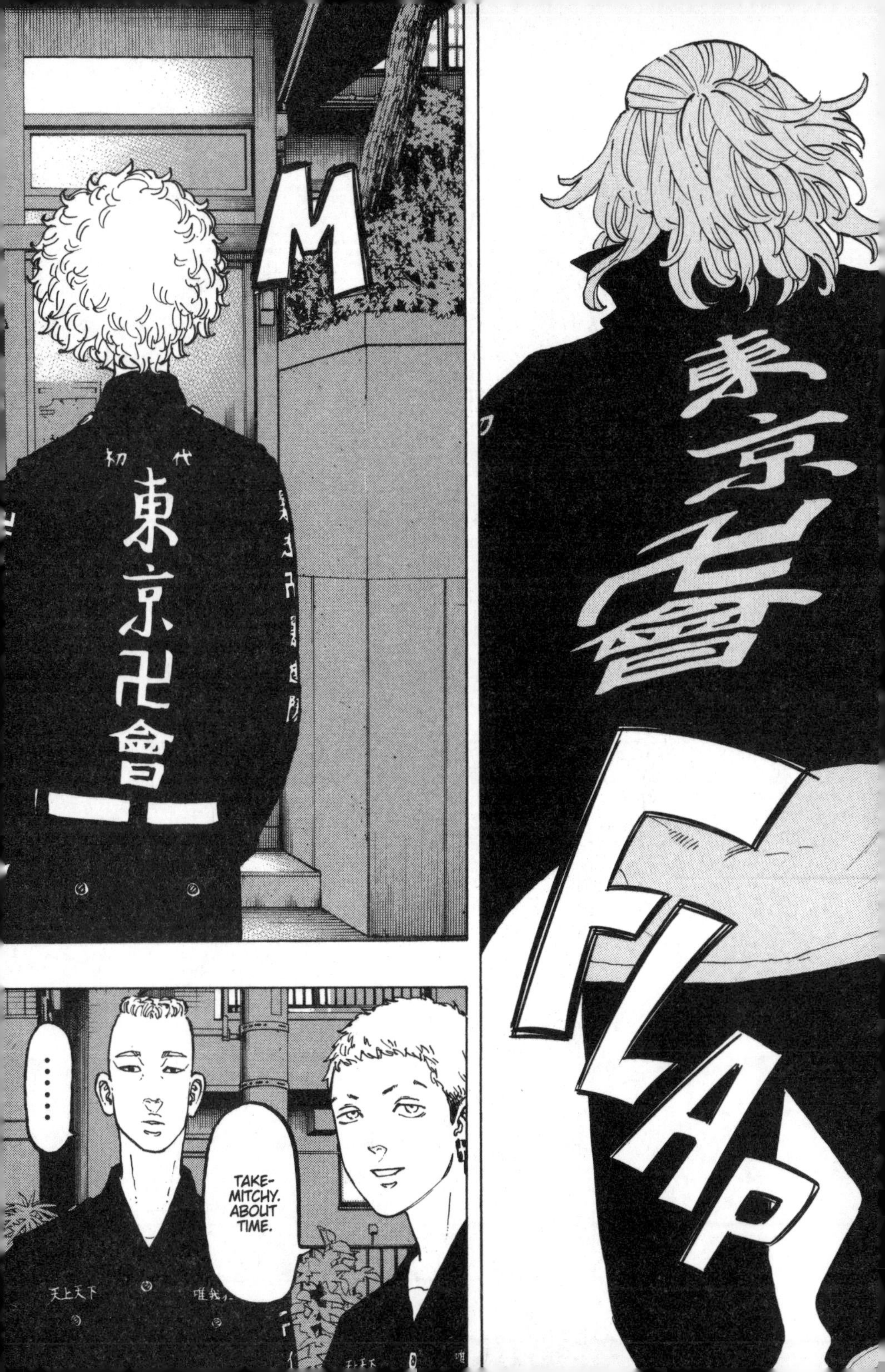
FLAP
M
……
TAKE-MITCHY. ABOUT TIME.

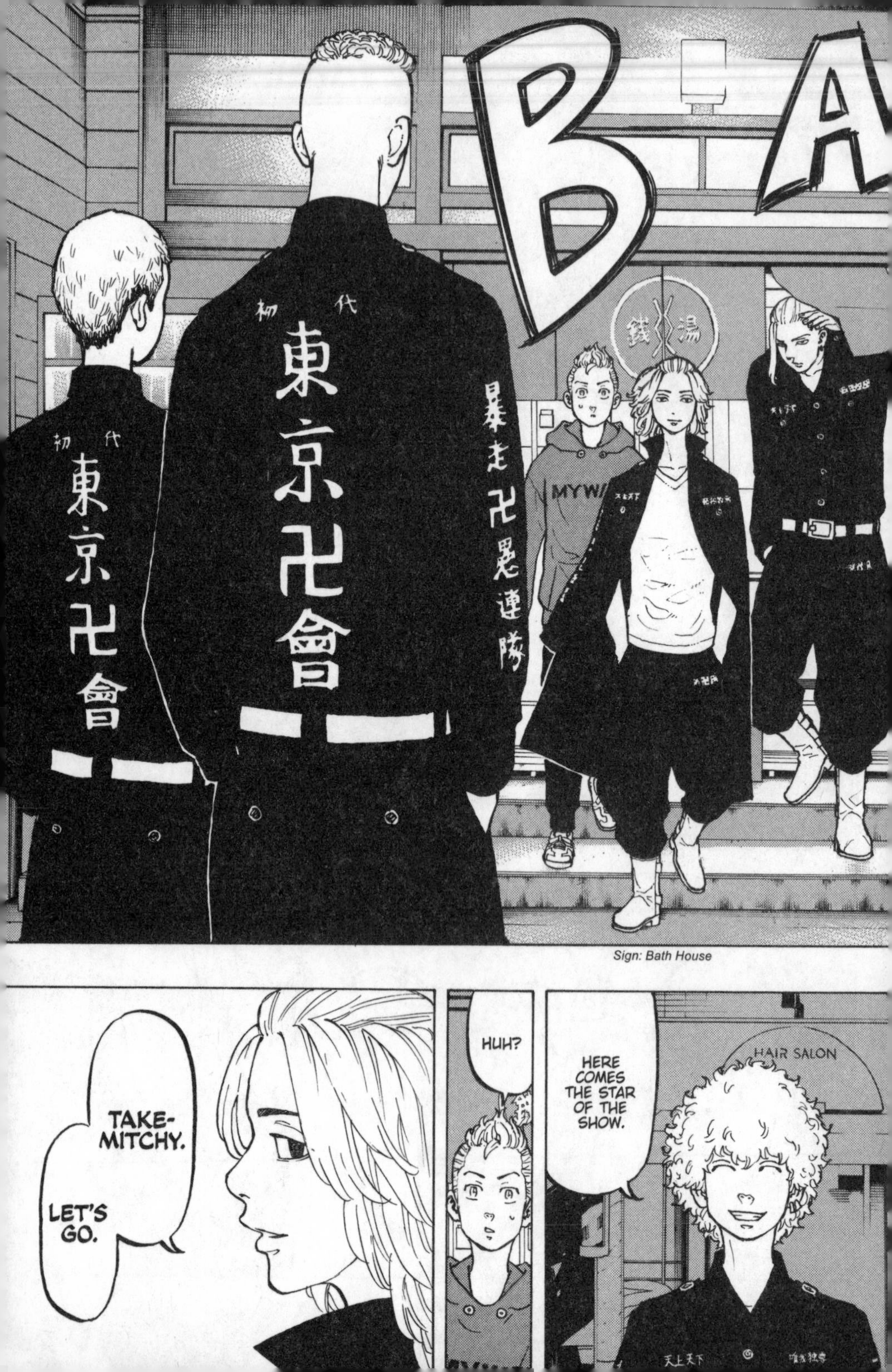

BA
初代
東京卍會
暴走卍愚連隊
銭湯
Sign: Bath House
HAIR SALON
HERE COMES THE STAR OF THE SHOW.
HUH?
TAKE-MITCHY.
LET'S GO.

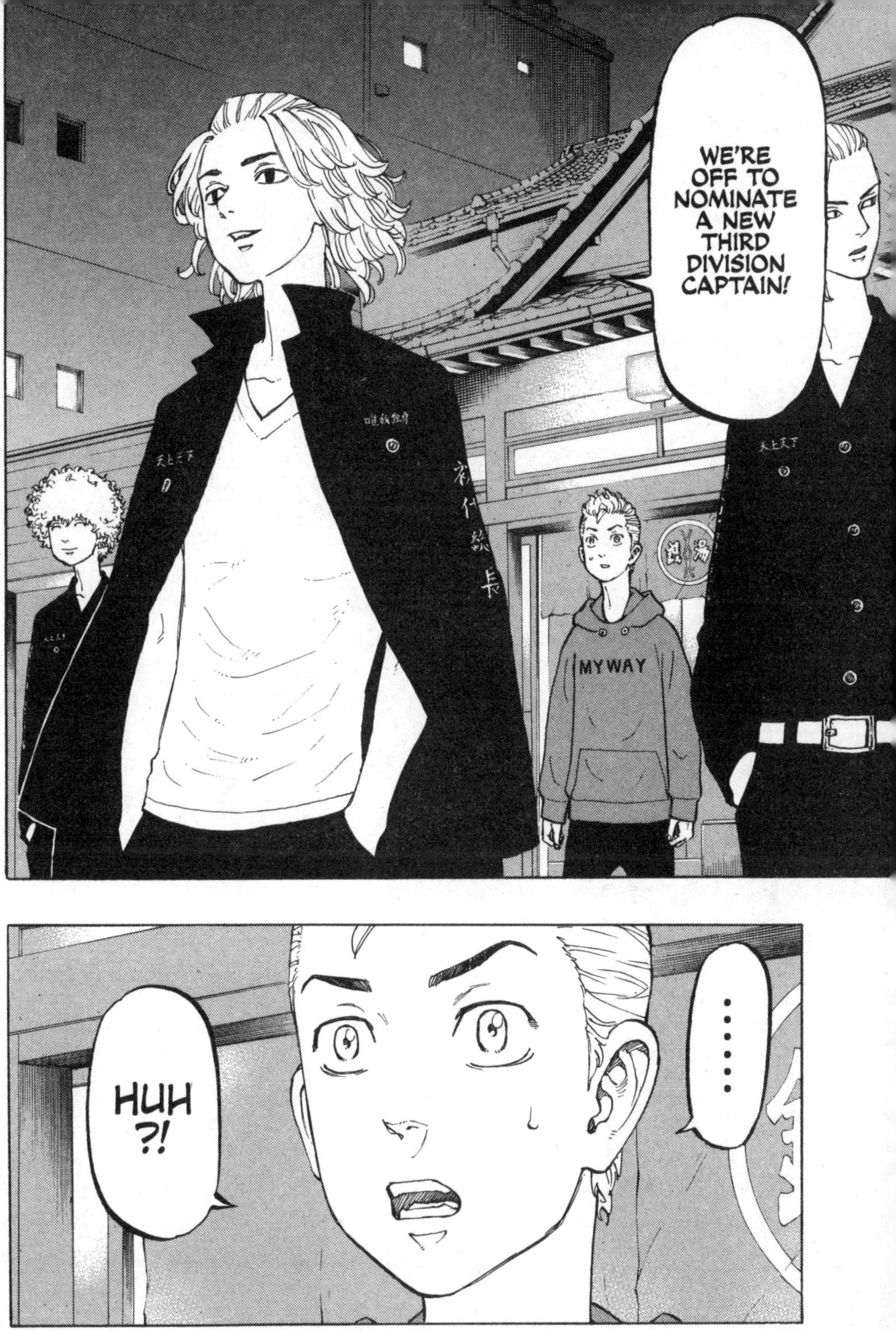
WE'RE OFF TO NOMINATE A NEW THIRD DIVISION CAPTAIN!
MYWAY
......
HUH ?!

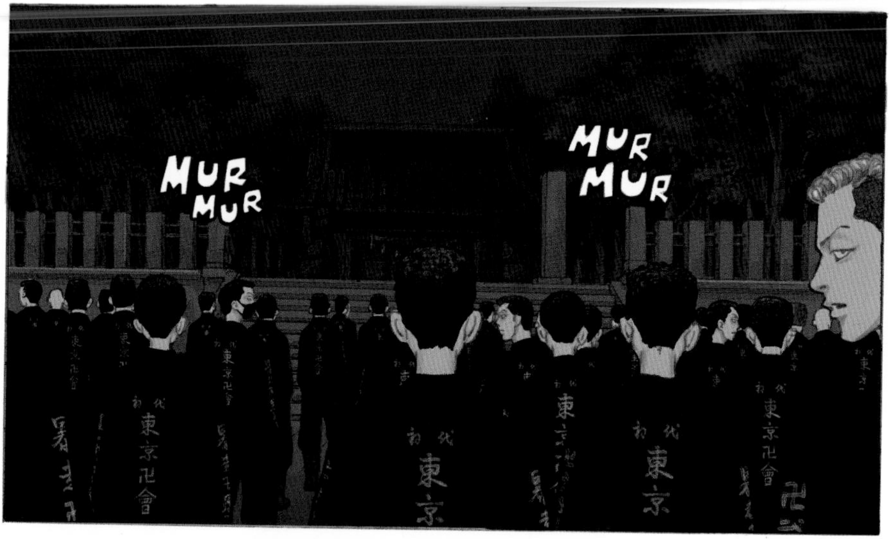
MUR MUR
MUR MUR

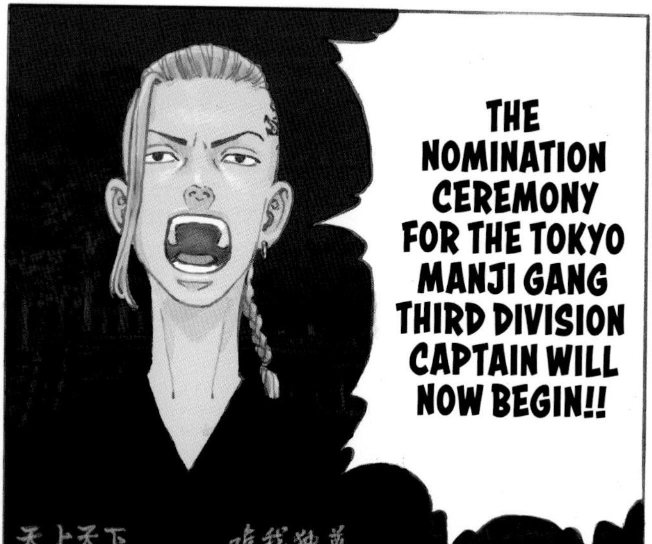
THE NOMINATION CEREMONY FOR THE TOKYO MANJI GANG THIRD DIVISION CAPTAIN WILL NOW BEGIN!!
天上天下 唯我独尊

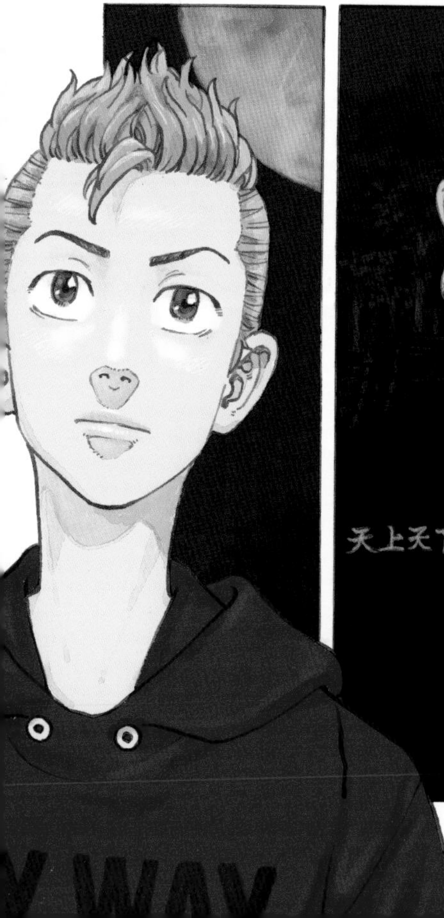

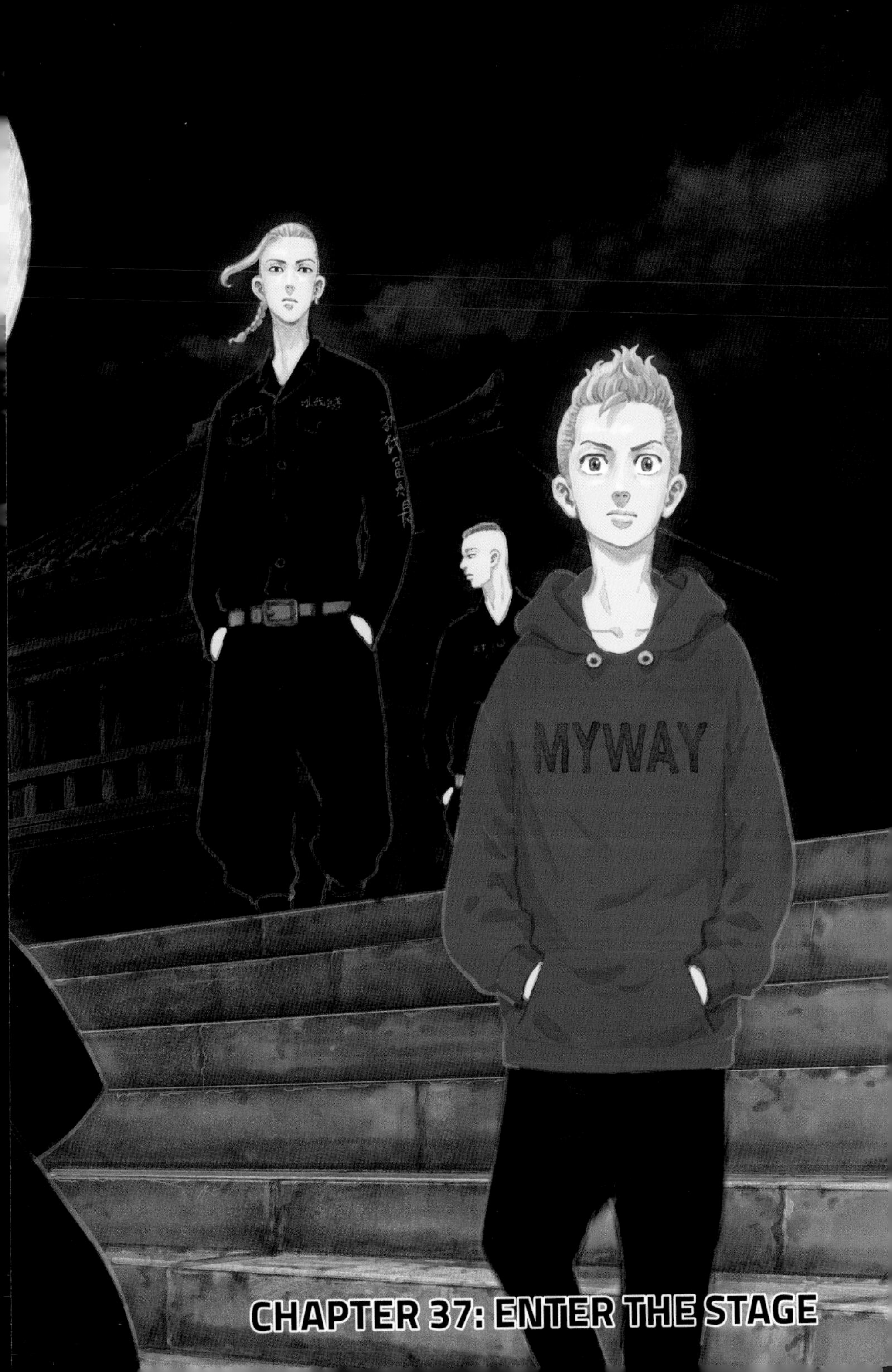
MYWAY

CHAPTER 37: ENTER THE STAGE

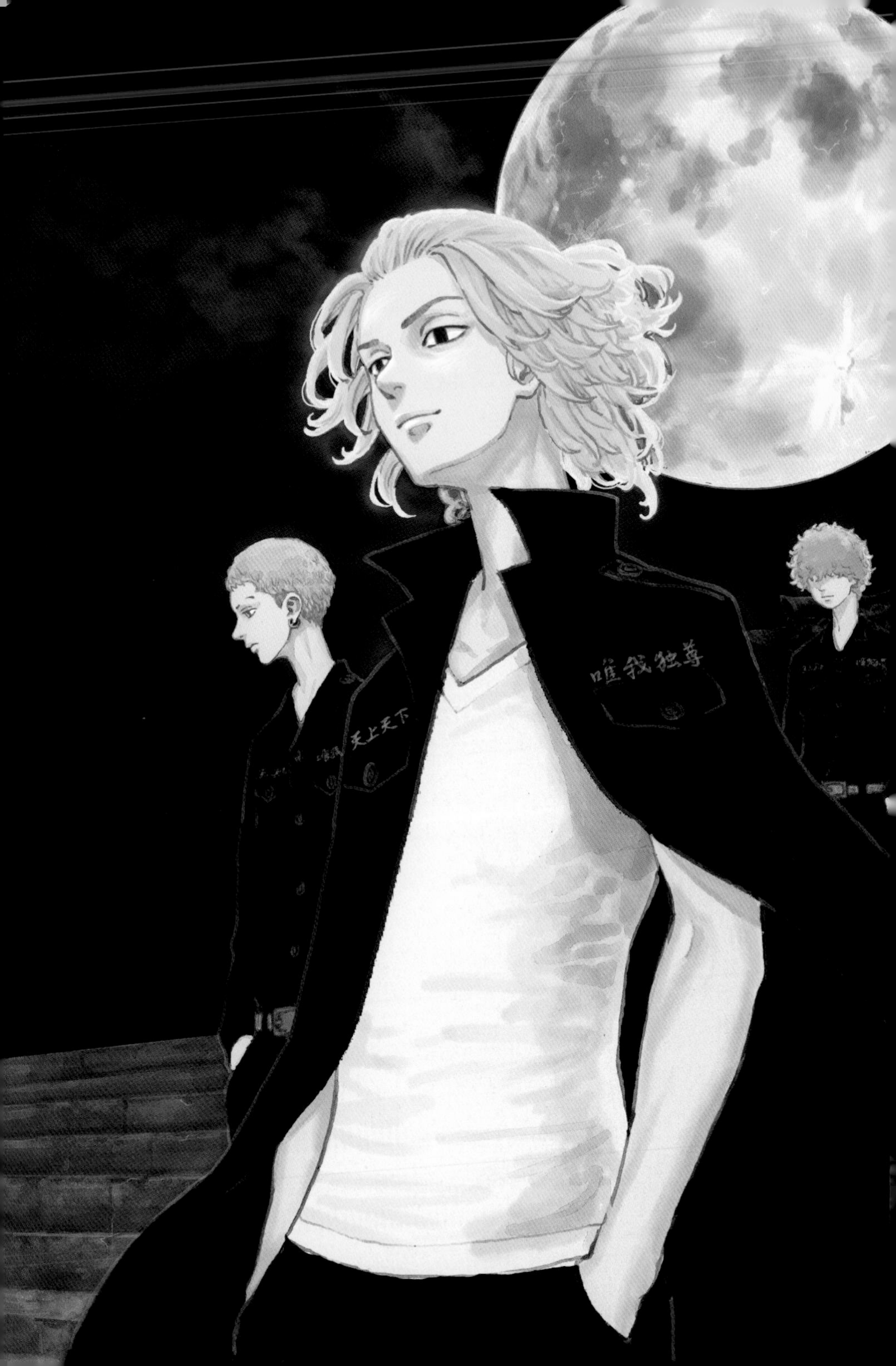
唯我独尊
天上天下

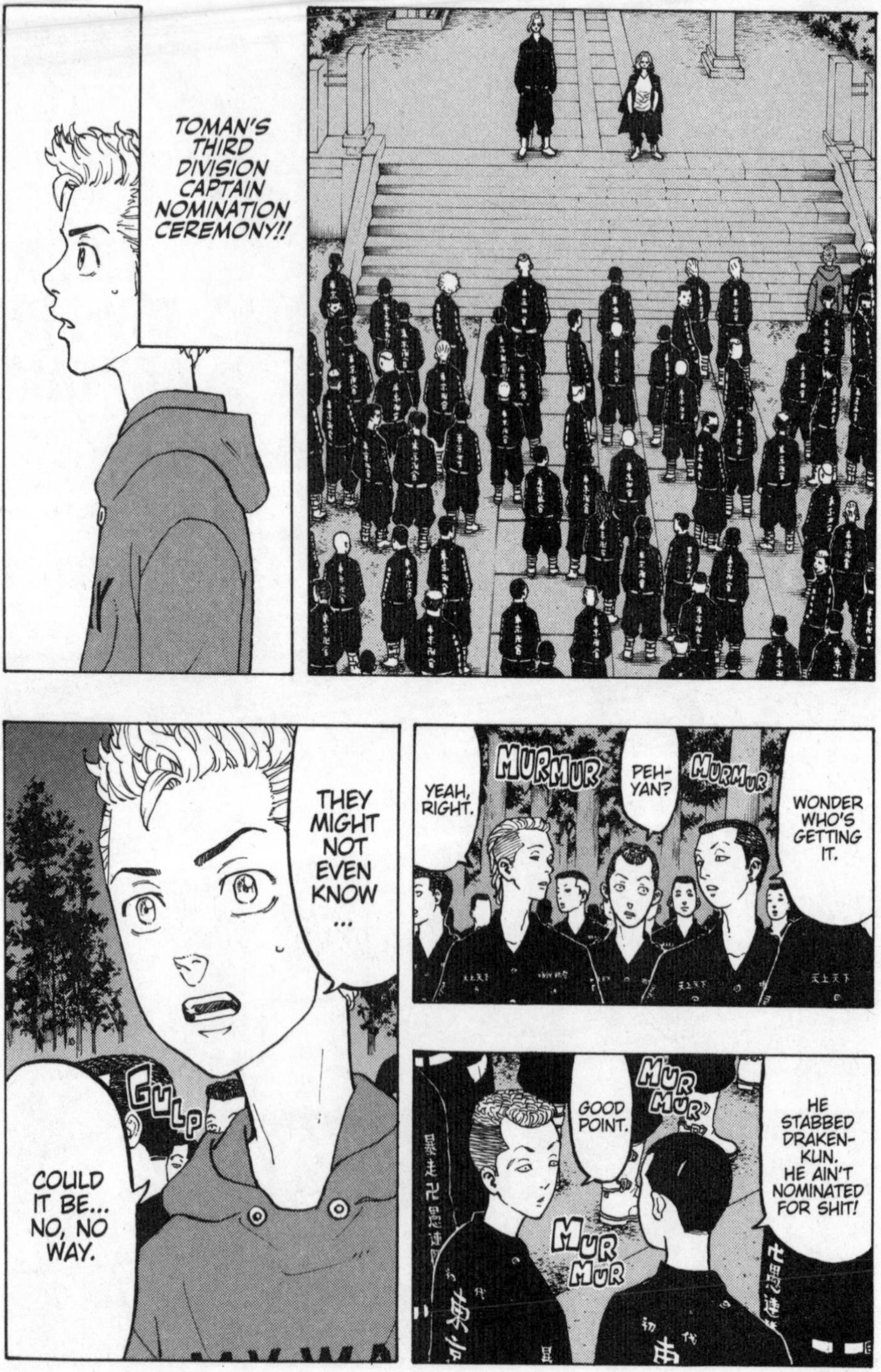
TOMAN'S THIRD DIVISION CAPTAIN NOMINATION CEREMONY!!
WONDER WHO'S GETTING IT.
MURMUR
PEH-YAN?
MURMUR
YEAH, RIGHT.
HE STABBED DRAKEN-KUN. HE AIN'T NOMINATED FOR SHIT!
MUR MUR
GOOD POINT.
MUR MUR
THEY MIGHT NOT EVEN KNOW ...
GULP
COULD IT BE... NO, NO WAY.

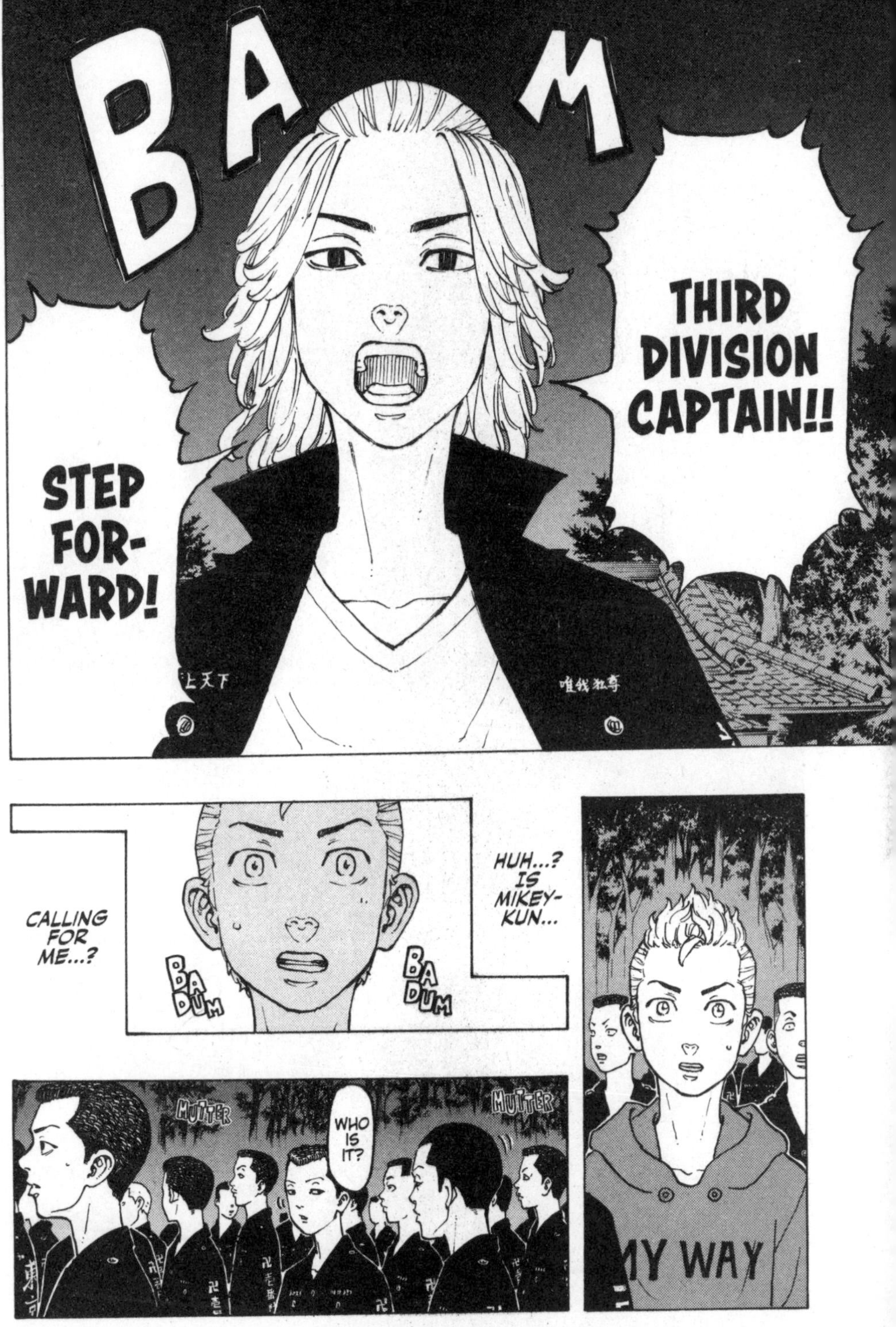
BAM
THIRD DIVISION CAPTAIN!!
STEP FOR-WARD!
HUH...? IS MIKEY-KUN...
MY WAY
BA DUM
BA DUM
CALLING FOR ME...?
MUTTER
WHO IS IT?
MUTTER

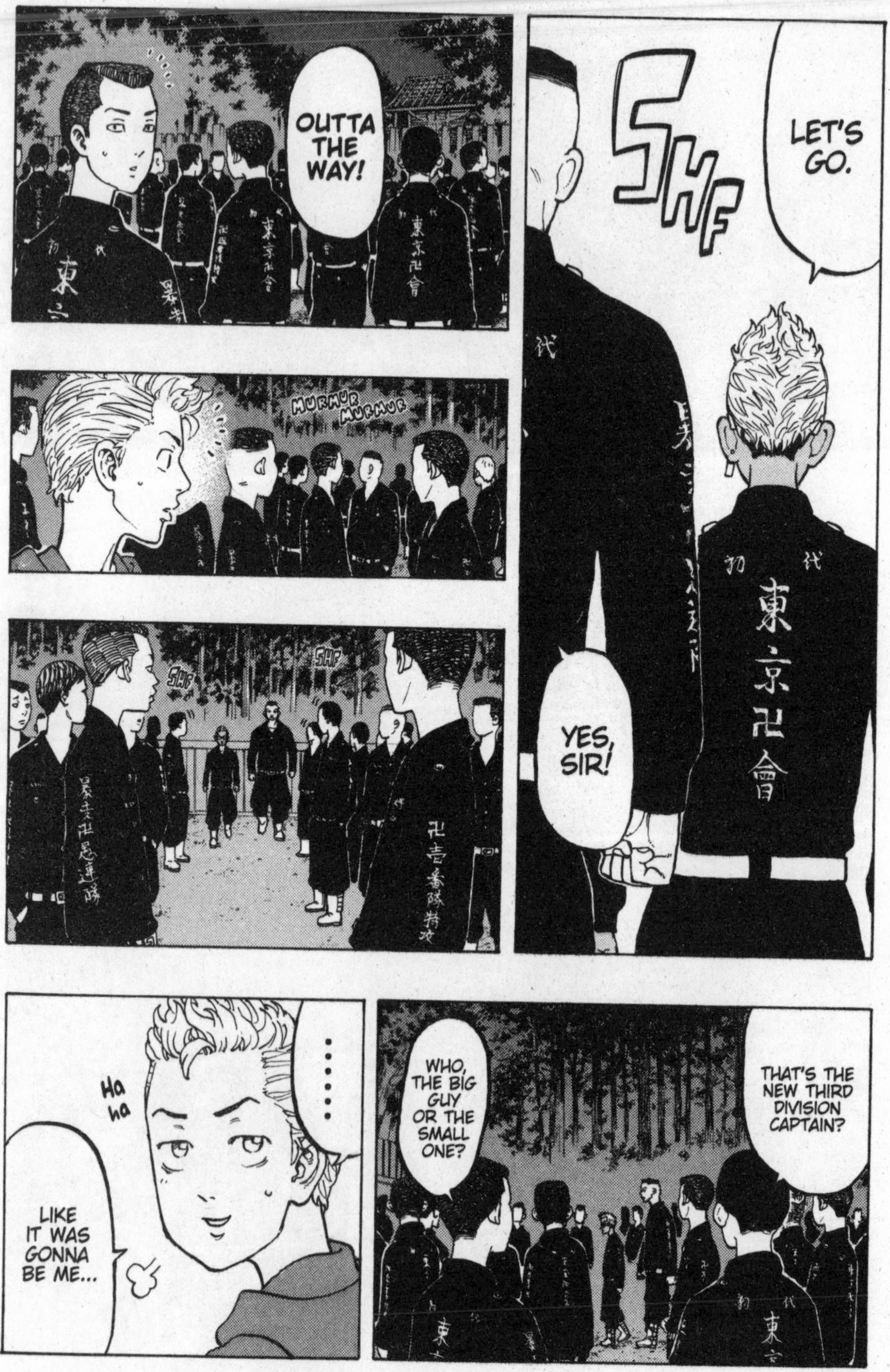
LET'S GO.
SHF
YES, SIR!
OUTTA THE WAY!
MURMUR MURMUR
SHF
SHF
THAT'S THE NEW THIRD DIVISION CAPTAIN?
WHO, THE BIG GUY OR THE SMALL ONE?
......
Ha ha
LIKE IT WAS GONNA BE ME...

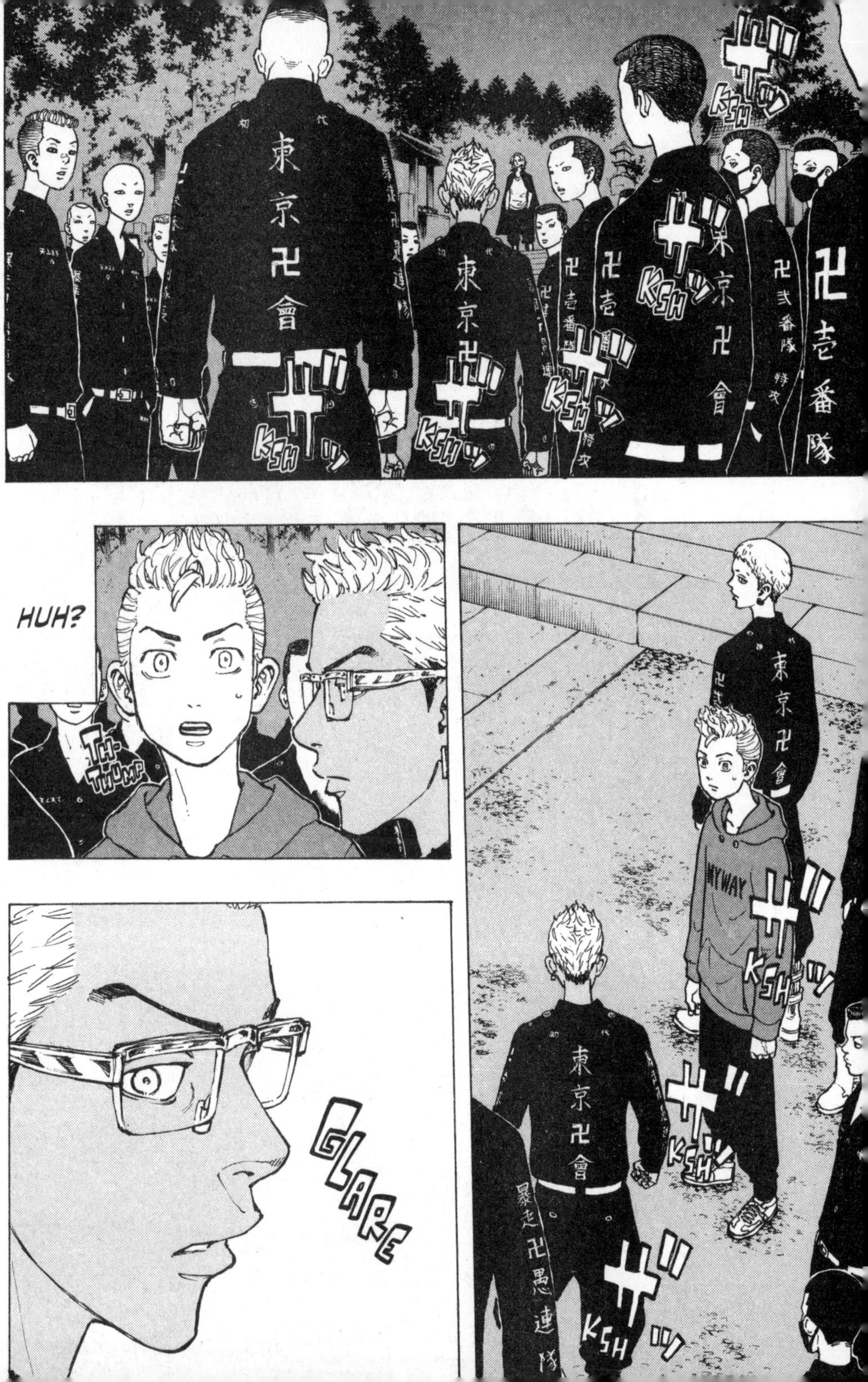
KSH
KSH
KSH
KSH
KSH
KSH
KSH
KSH
HUH?
TH-THUMP
GLARE

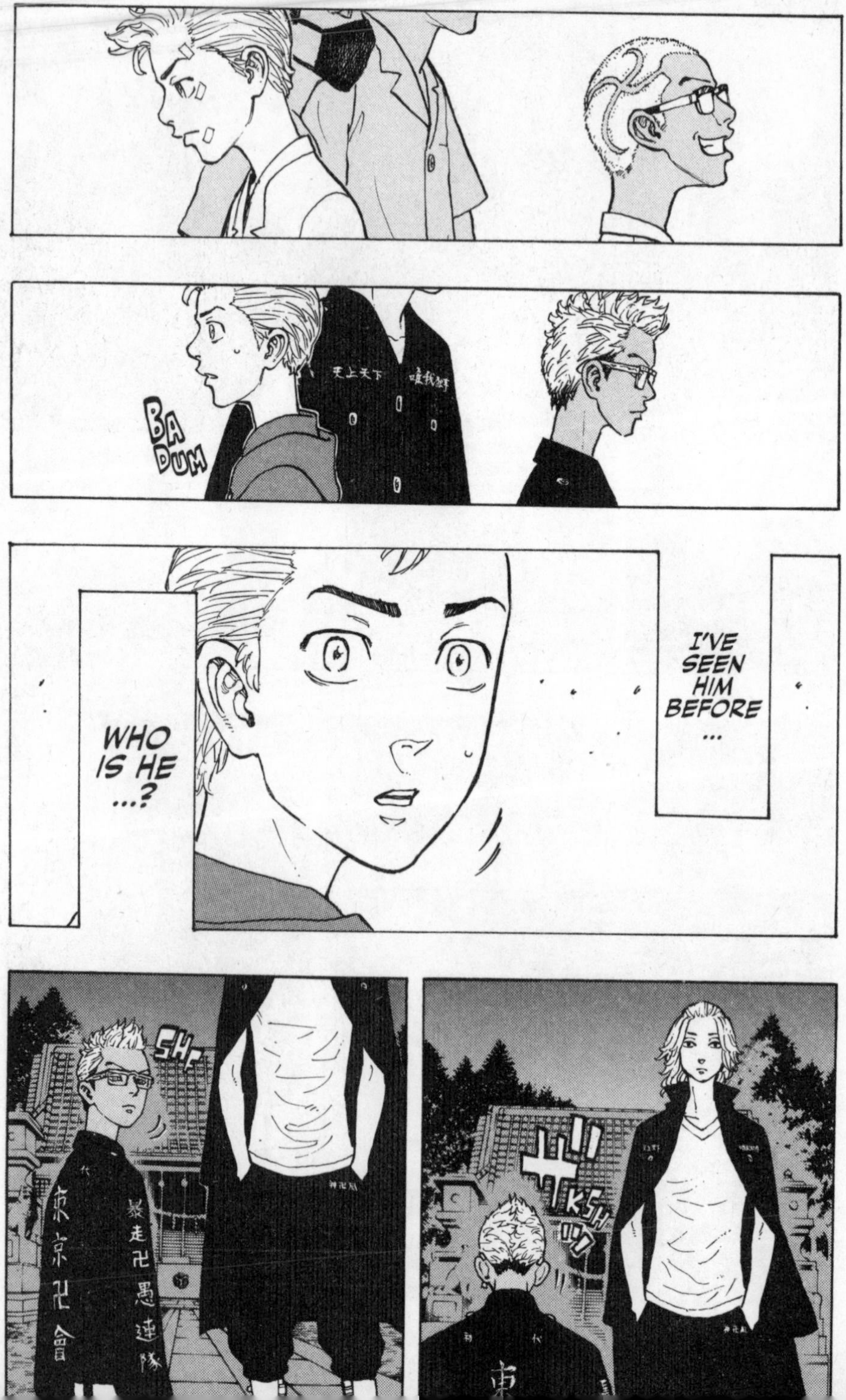
BA
DUM
I'VE SEEN HIM BEFORE ...
WHO IS HE ...?
!!
KSH
SHF
東京卍會
暴走卍愚連隊

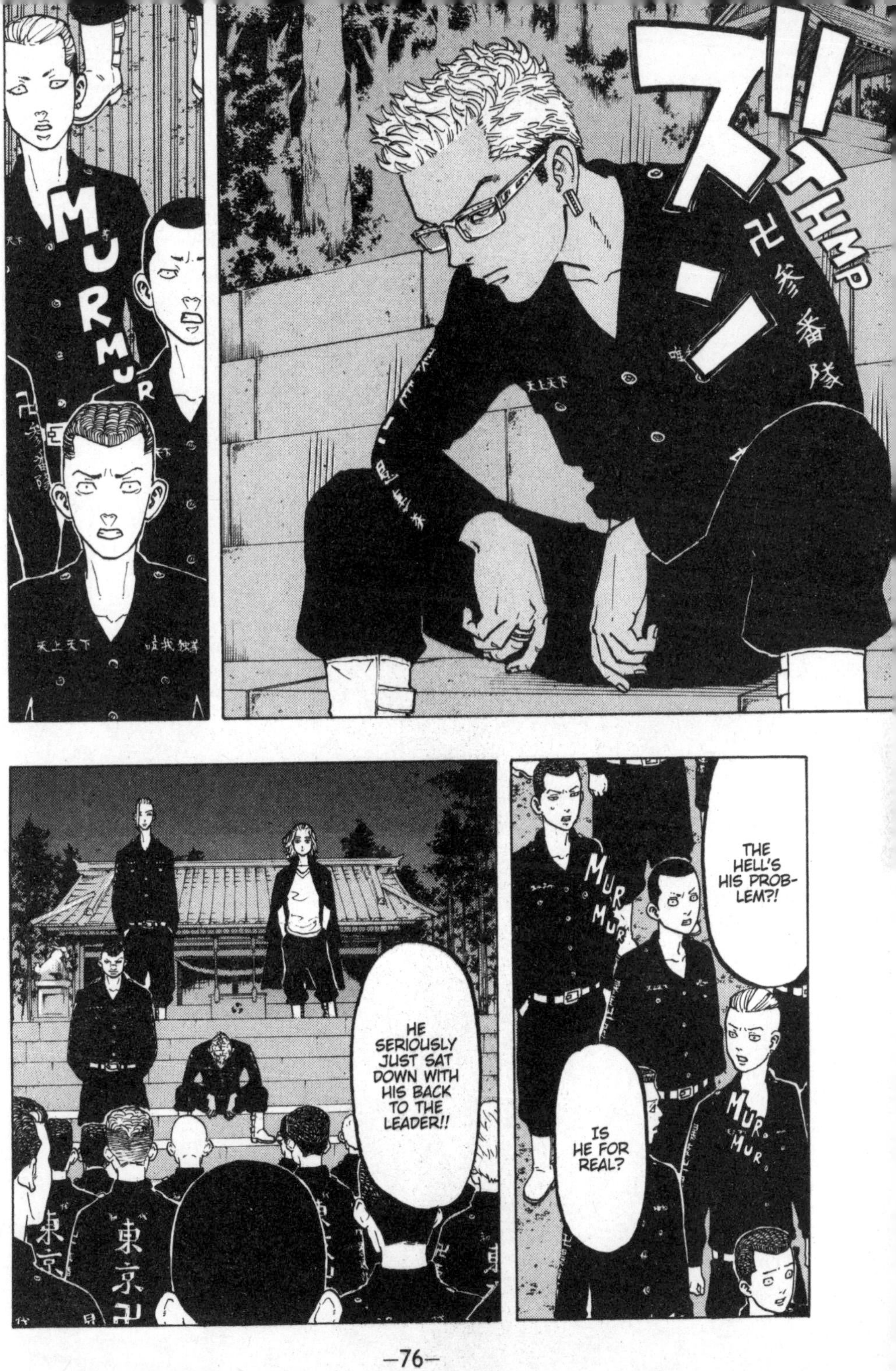
THMP
MURMUR
THE HELL'S HIS PROBLEM?!
MUR MUR
IS HE FOR REAL?
MUR MUR
HE SERIOUSLY JUST SAT DOWN WITH HIS BACK TO THE LEADER!!

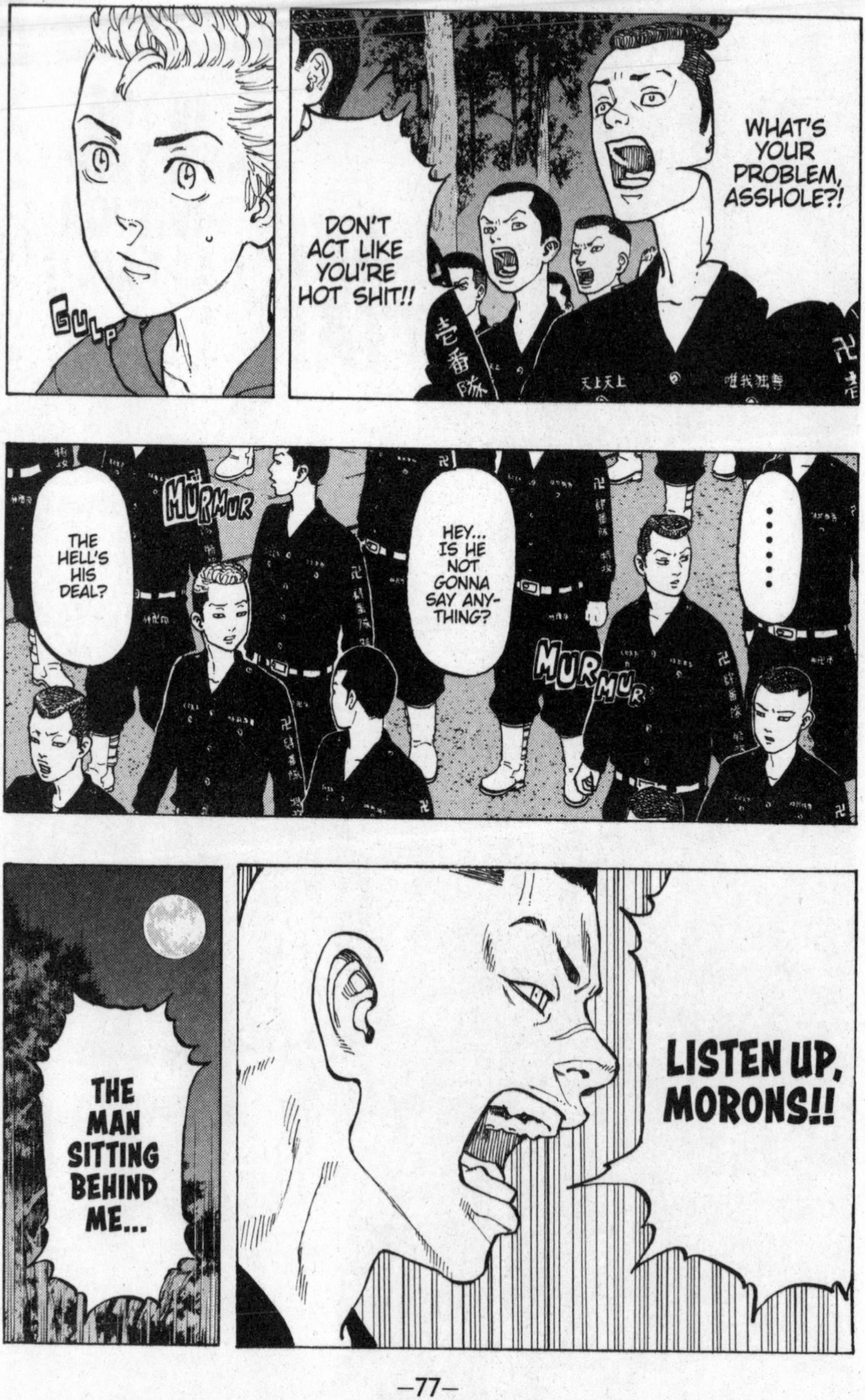
WHAT'S YOUR PROBLEM, ASSHOLE?!
DON'T ACT LIKE YOU'RE HOT SHIT!!
壱番隊
GULP
......
HEY... IS HE NOT GONNA SAY ANY-THING?
MURMUR
MURMUR
THE HELL'S HIS DEAL?
LISTEN UP, MORONS!!
THE MAN SITTING BEHIND ME...

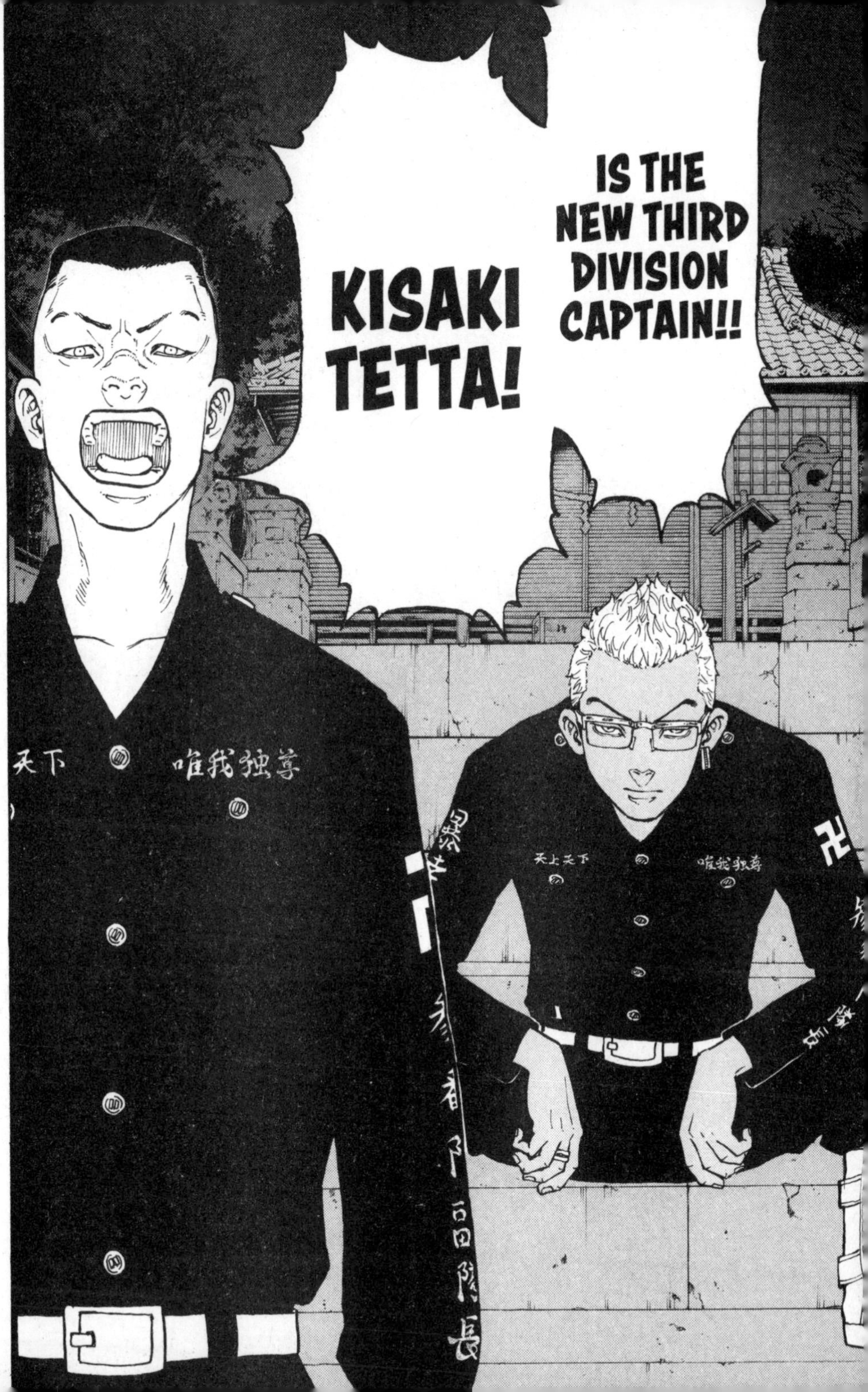
KISAKI TETTA!
IS THE NEW THIRD DIVISION CAPTAIN!!

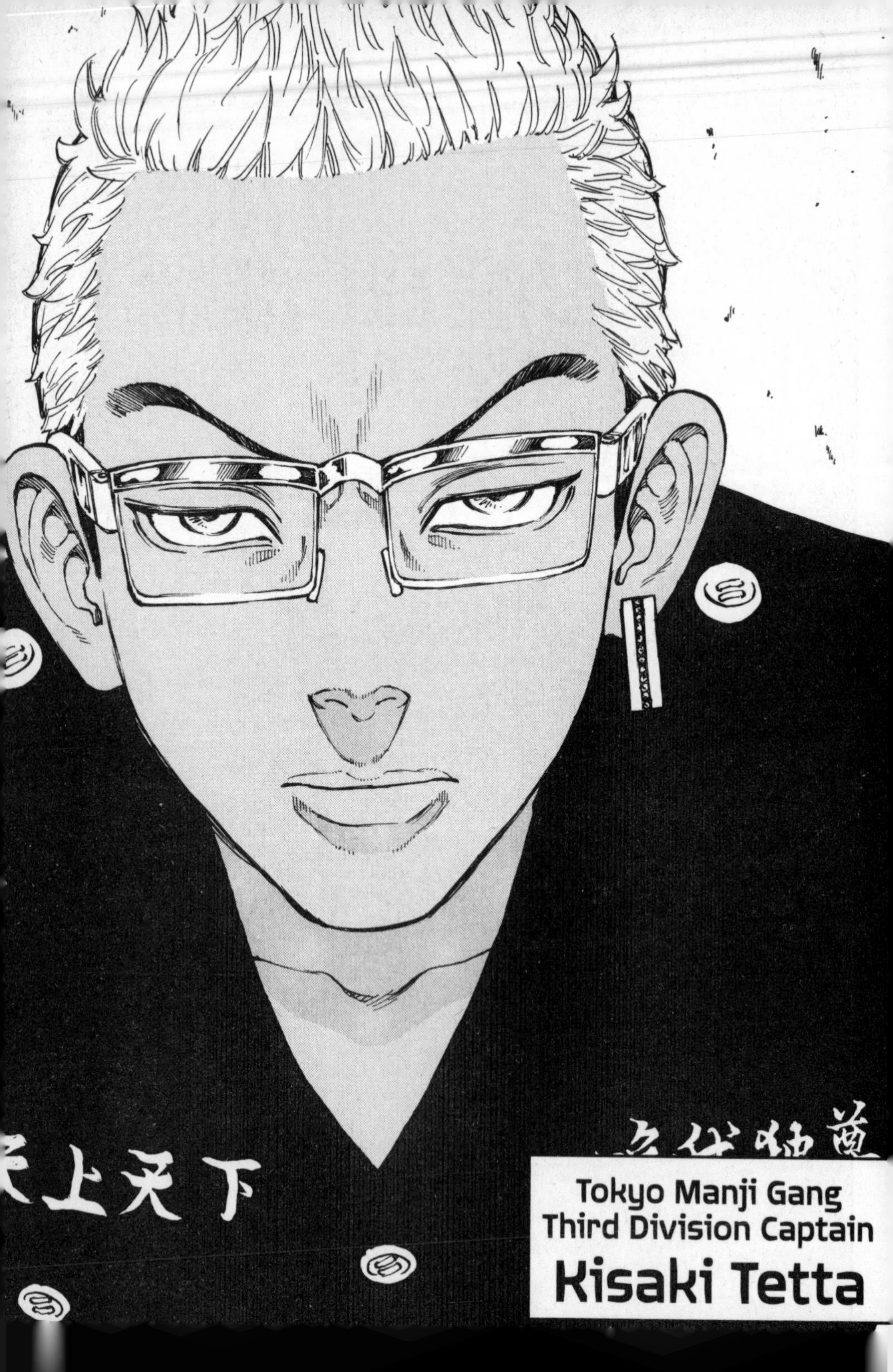
Tokyo Manji Gang
Third Division Captain
Kisaki Tetta

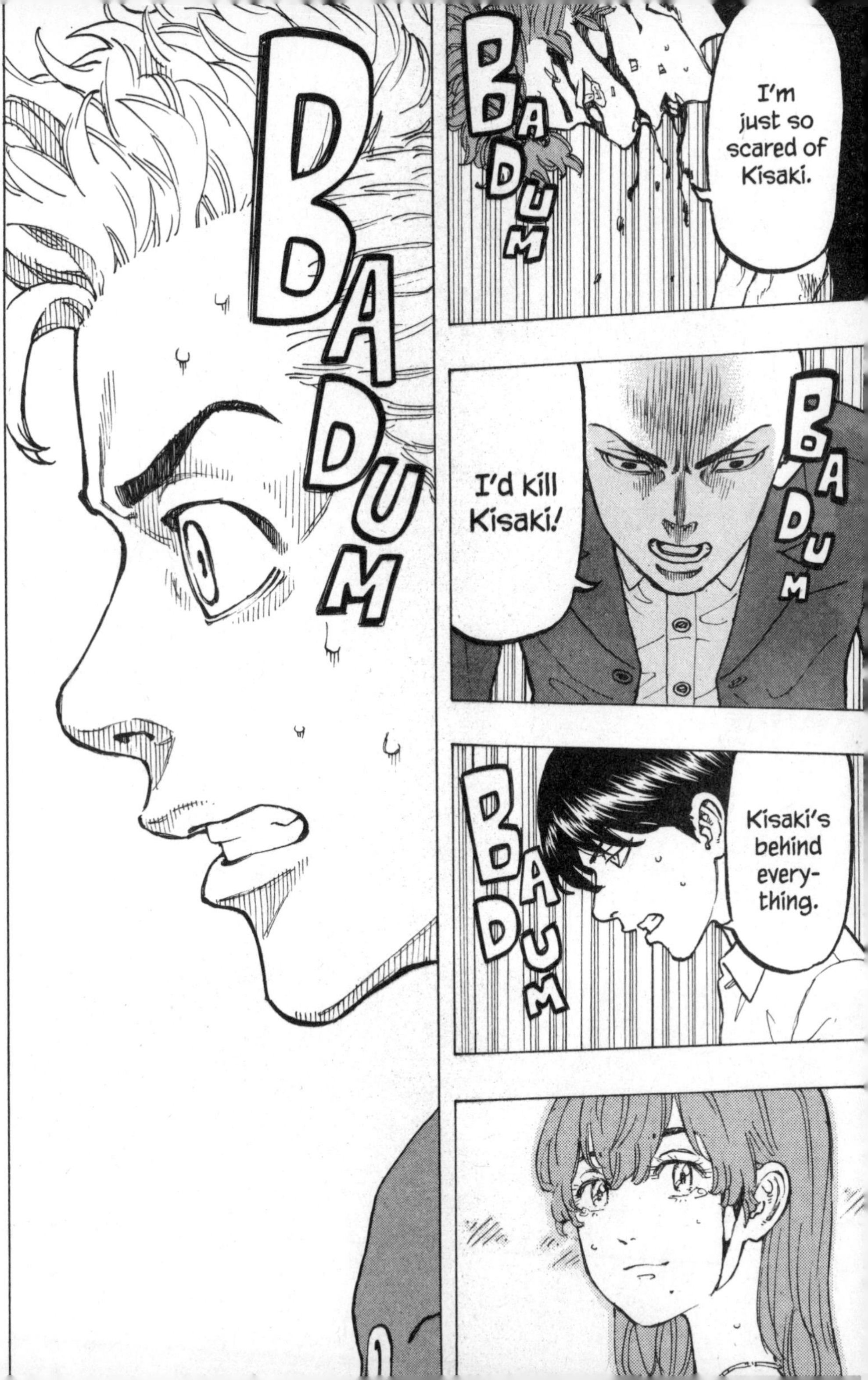
I'm just so scared of Kisaki.
BADUM
BADUM
I'd kill Kisaki!
Kisaki's behind everything.
BADUM
BADUM

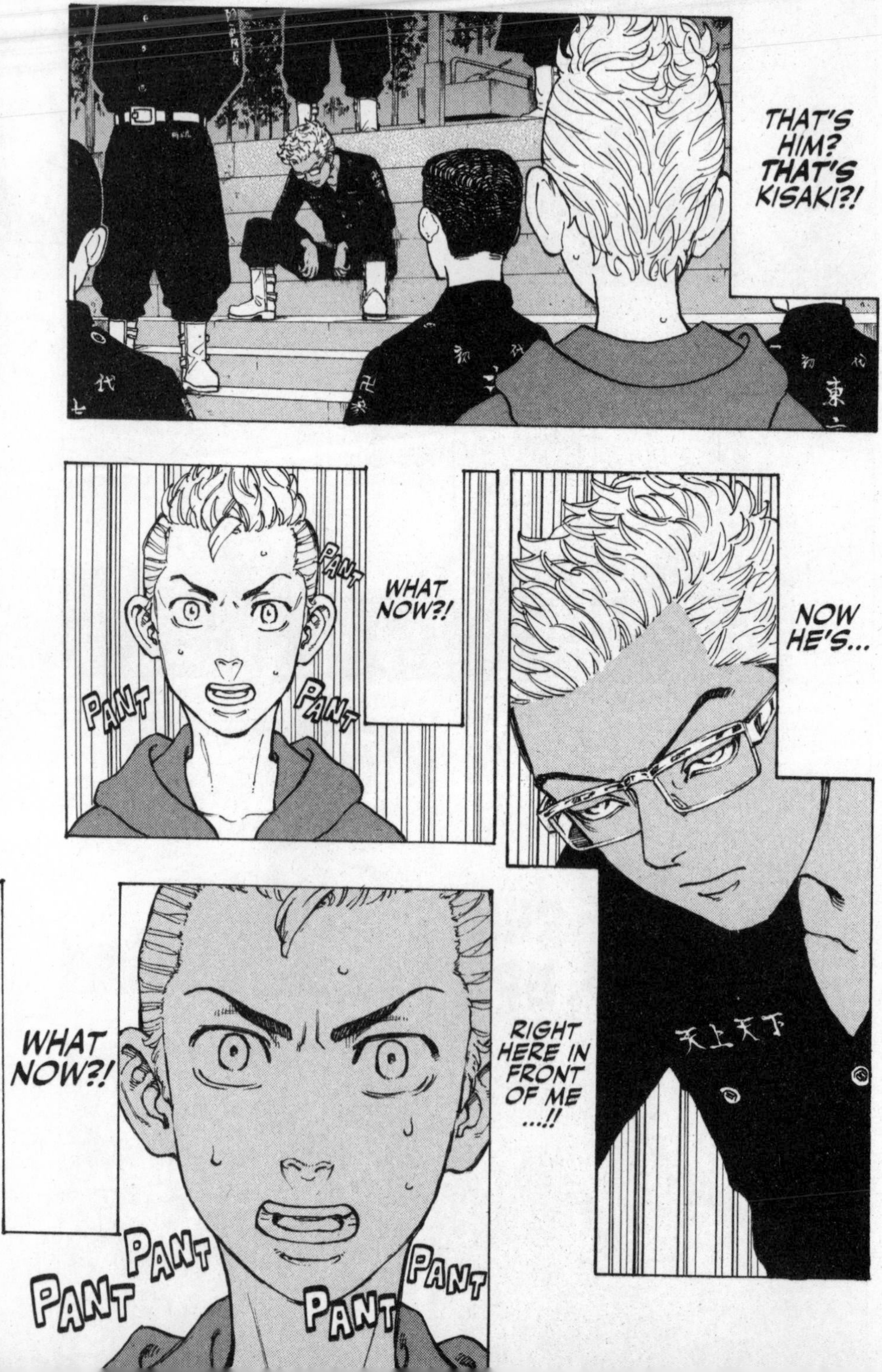
THAT'S HIM? THAT'S KISAKI?!
NOW HE'S...
RIGHT HERE IN FRONT OF ME ...!!
WHAT NOW?!
PANT
PANT
PANT
WHAT NOW?!
PANT
PANT
PANT
PANT

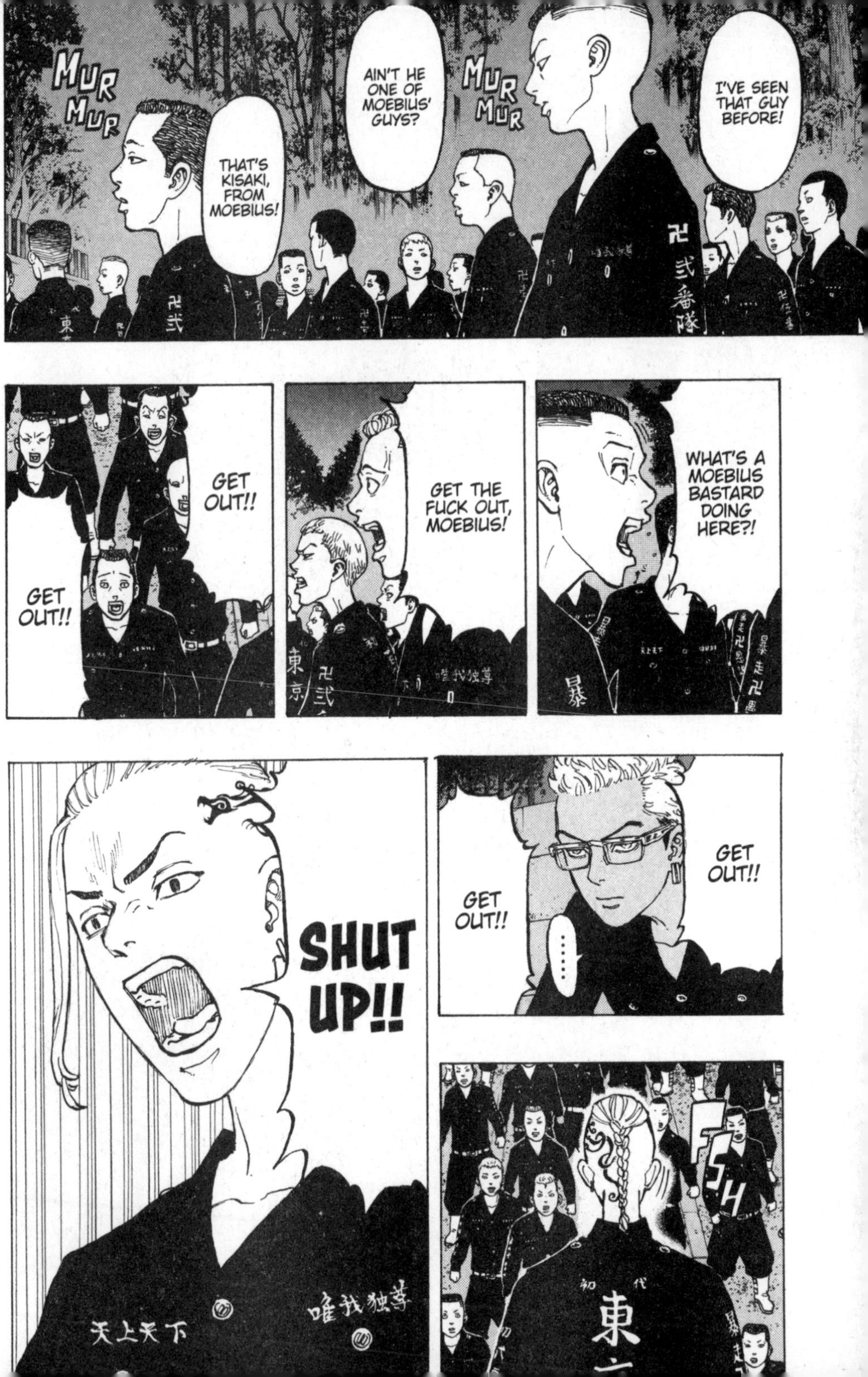
I'VE SEEN THAT GUY BEFORE!
MUR MUR
AIN'T HE ONE OF MOEBIUS' GUYS?
THAT'S KISAKI, FROM MOEBIUS!
MUR MUR
WHAT'S A MOEBIUS BASTARD DOING HERE?!
GET THE FUCK OUT, MOEBIUS!
GET OUT!!
GET OUT!!
GET OUT!!
GET OUT!!
......
SHUT UP!!

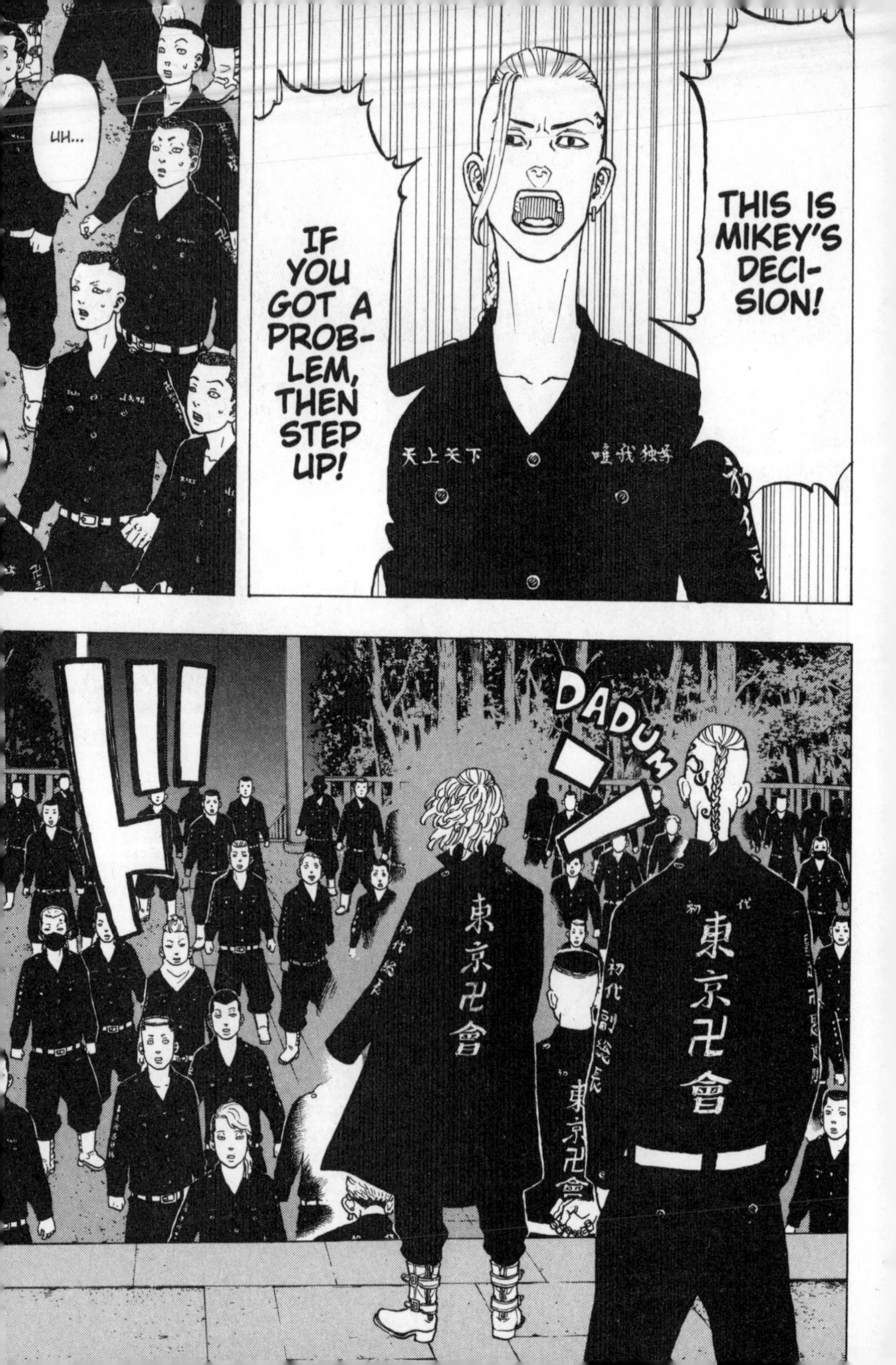
THIS IS MIKEY'S DECI-SION!
IF YOU GOT A PROB-LEM, THEN STEP UP!
UH...
DADUM

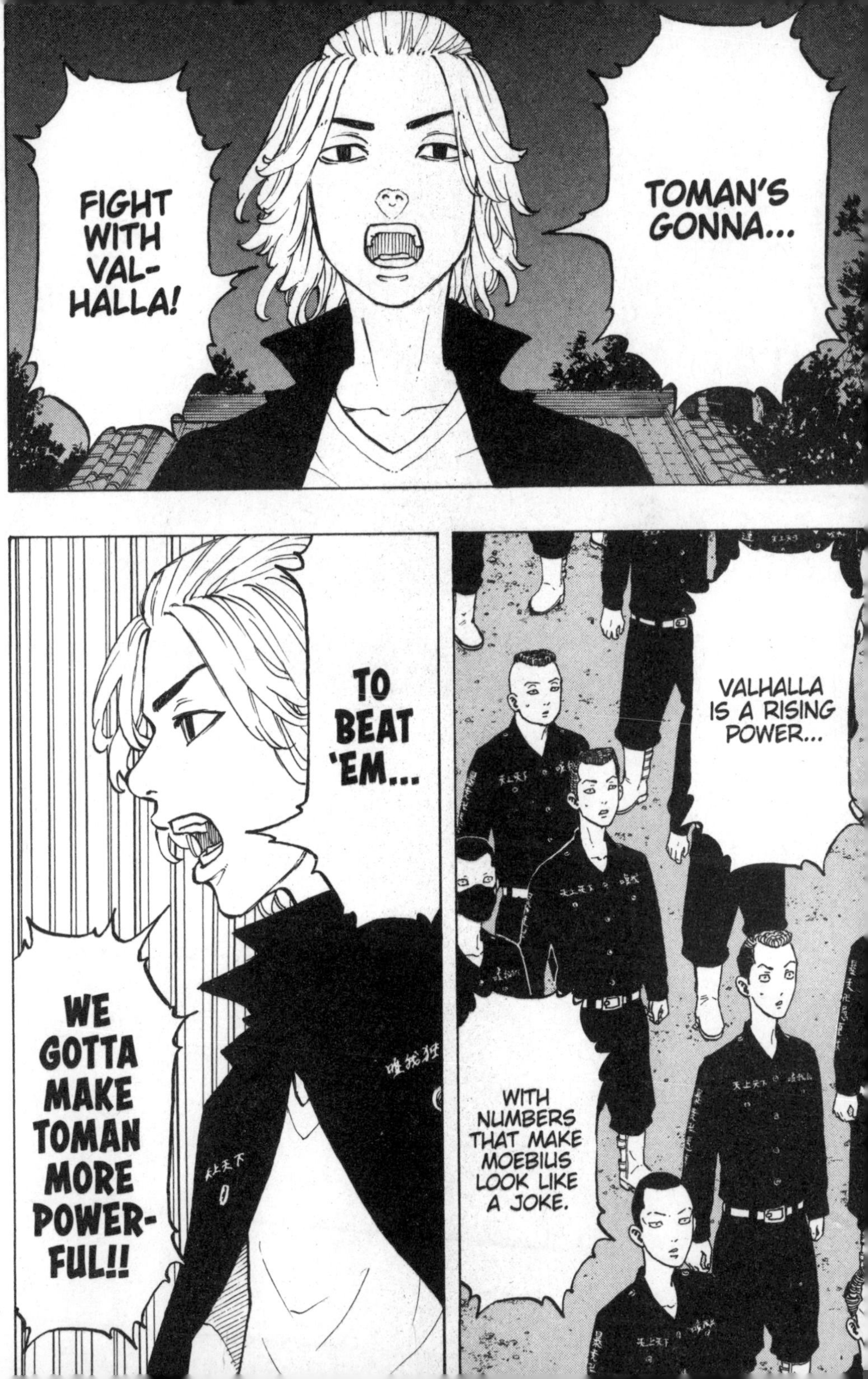
TOMAN'S GONNA...
FIGHT WITH VAL-HALLA!
VALHALLA IS A RISING POWER...
WITH NUMBERS THAT MAKE MOEBIUS LOOK LIKE A JOKE.
TO BEAT 'EM...
WE GOTTA MAKE TOMAN MORE POWER-FUL!!

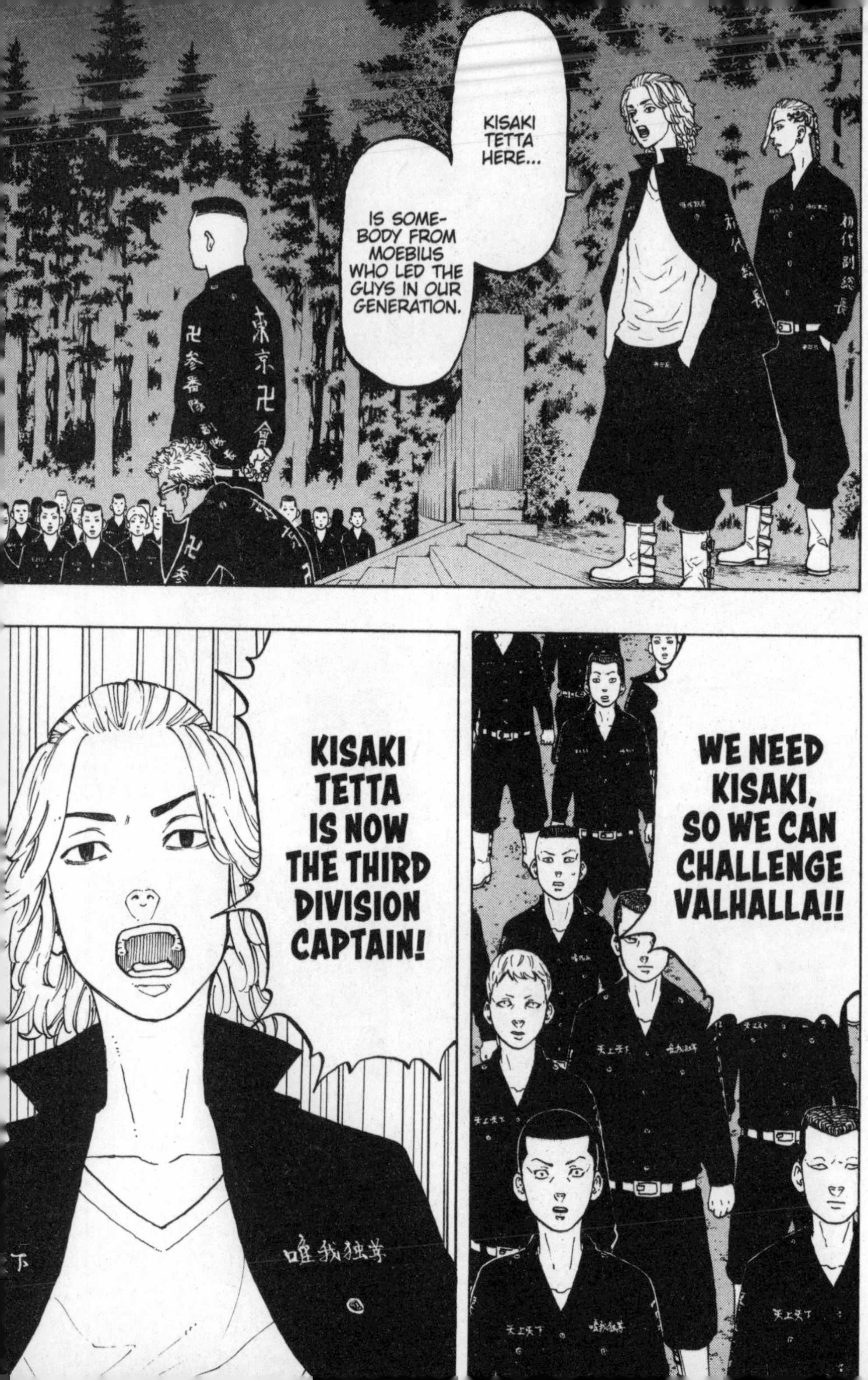
KISAKI TETTA HERE...
IS SOME-BODY FROM MOEBIUS WHO LED THE GUYS IN OUR GENERATION.
WE NEED KISAKI, SO WE CAN CHALLENGE VALHALLA!!
KISAKI TETTA IS NOW THE THIRD DIVISION CAPTAIN!

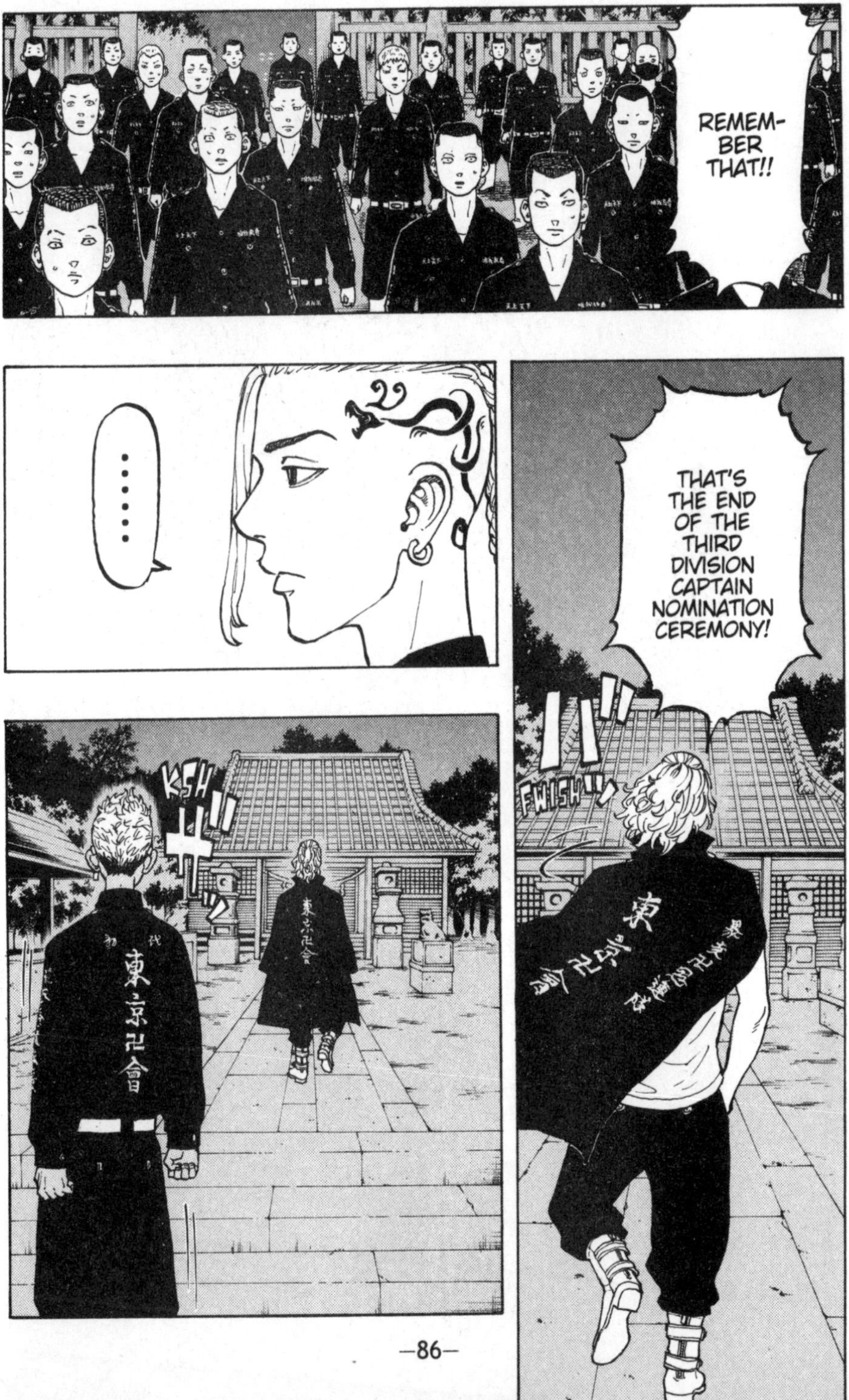

REMEMBER THAT!!
THAT'S THE END OF THE THIRD DIVISION CAPTAIN NOMINATION CEREMONY!
FWISH
......
KSH

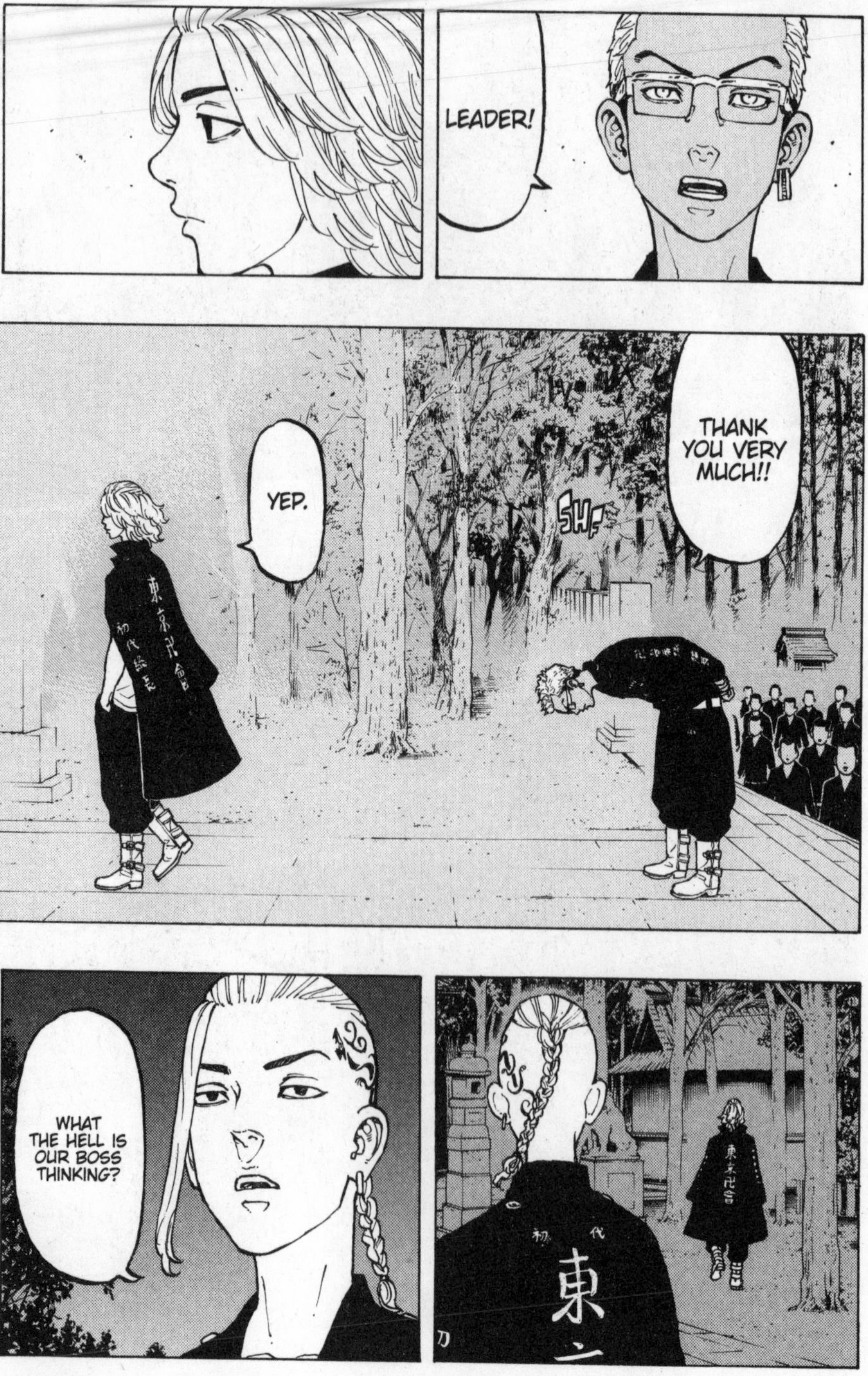
LEADER!
THANK YOU VERY MUCH!!
SHF
YEP.
WHAT THE HELL IS OUR BOSS THINKING?

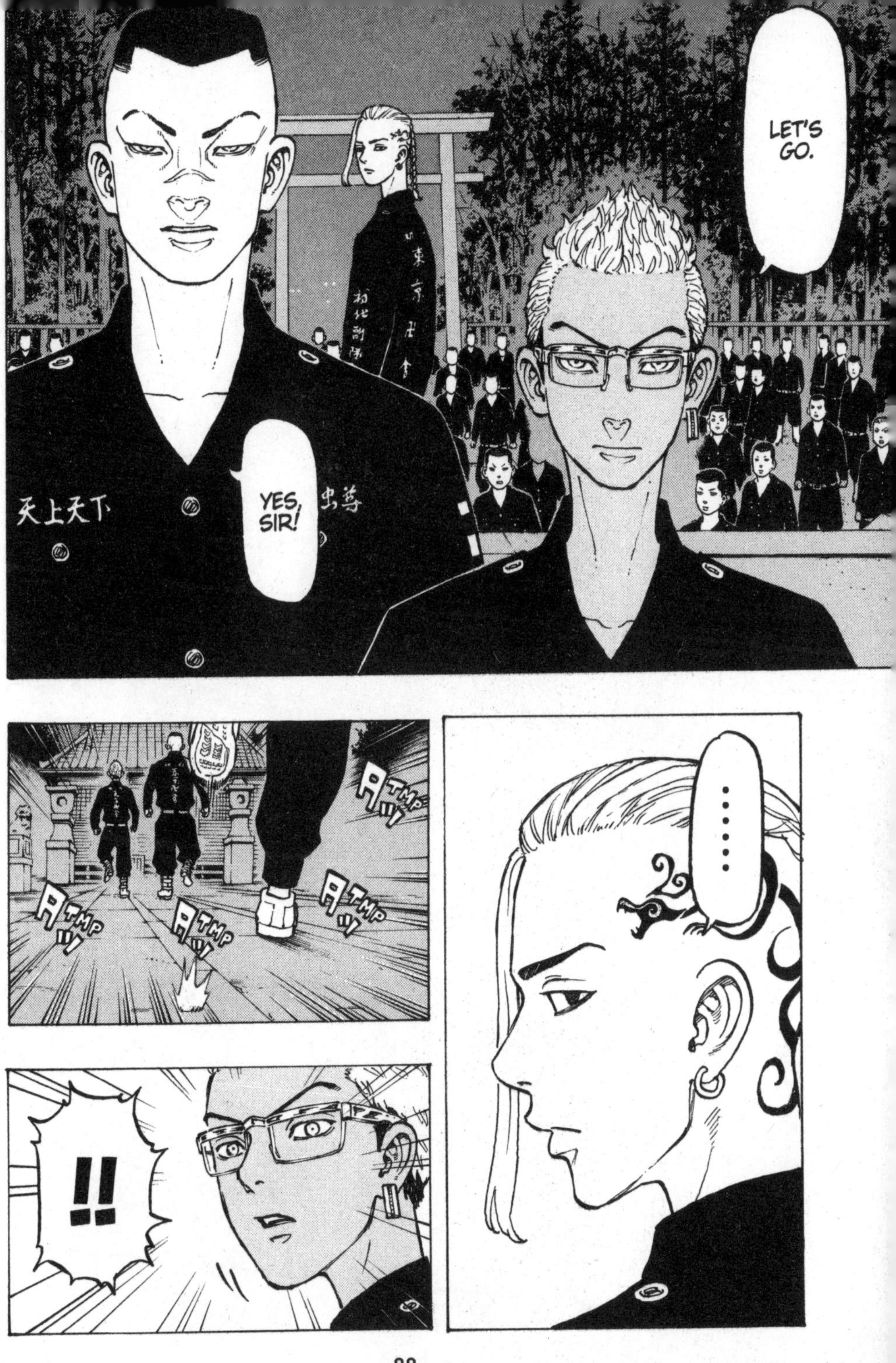
LET'S GO.
YES, SIR!
天上天下
......
TMP
TMP
TMP
TMP
!!

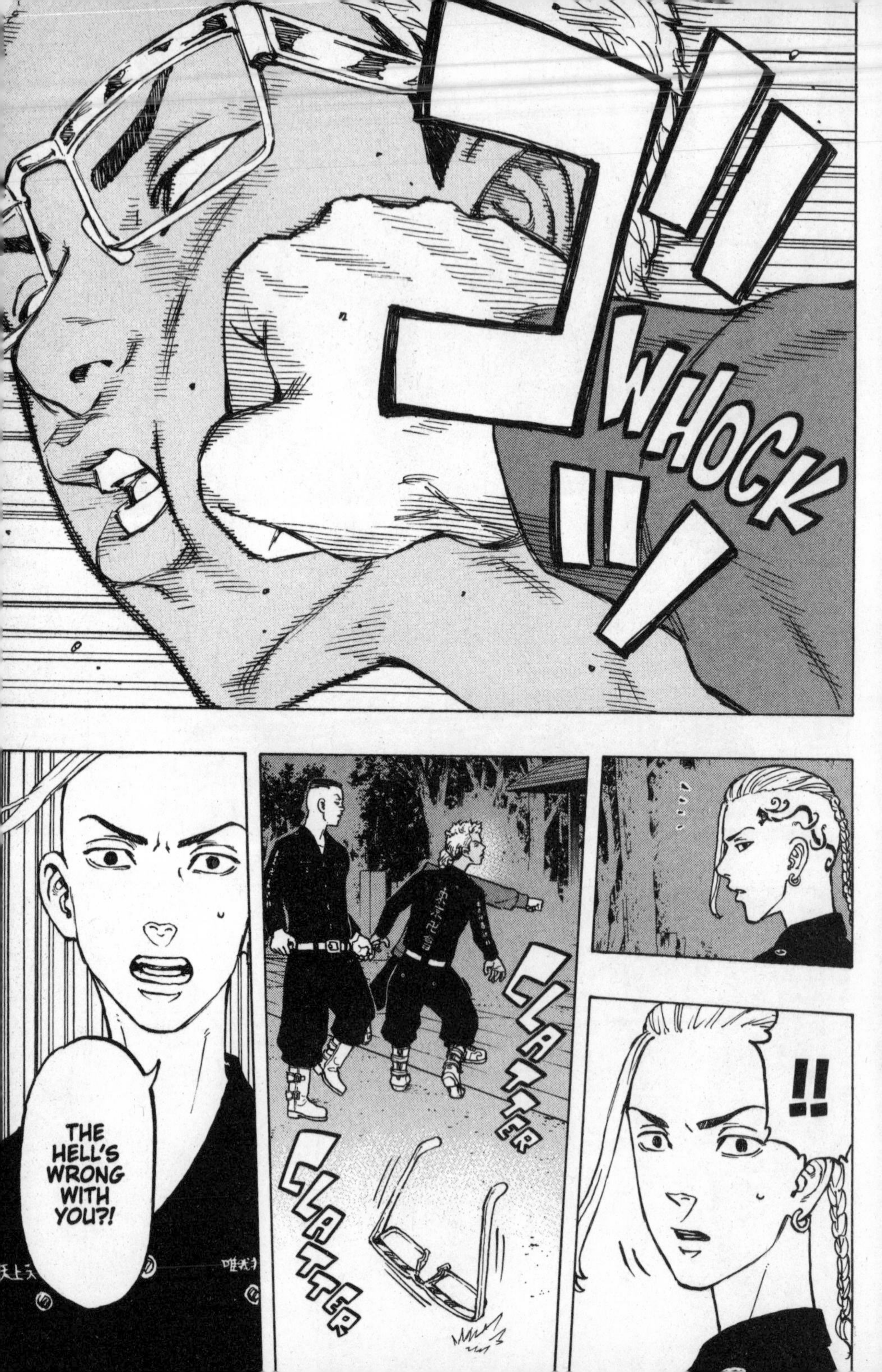
WHOCK!!
...
!!
CLATTER
CLATTER
THE HELL'S WRONG WITH YOU?!

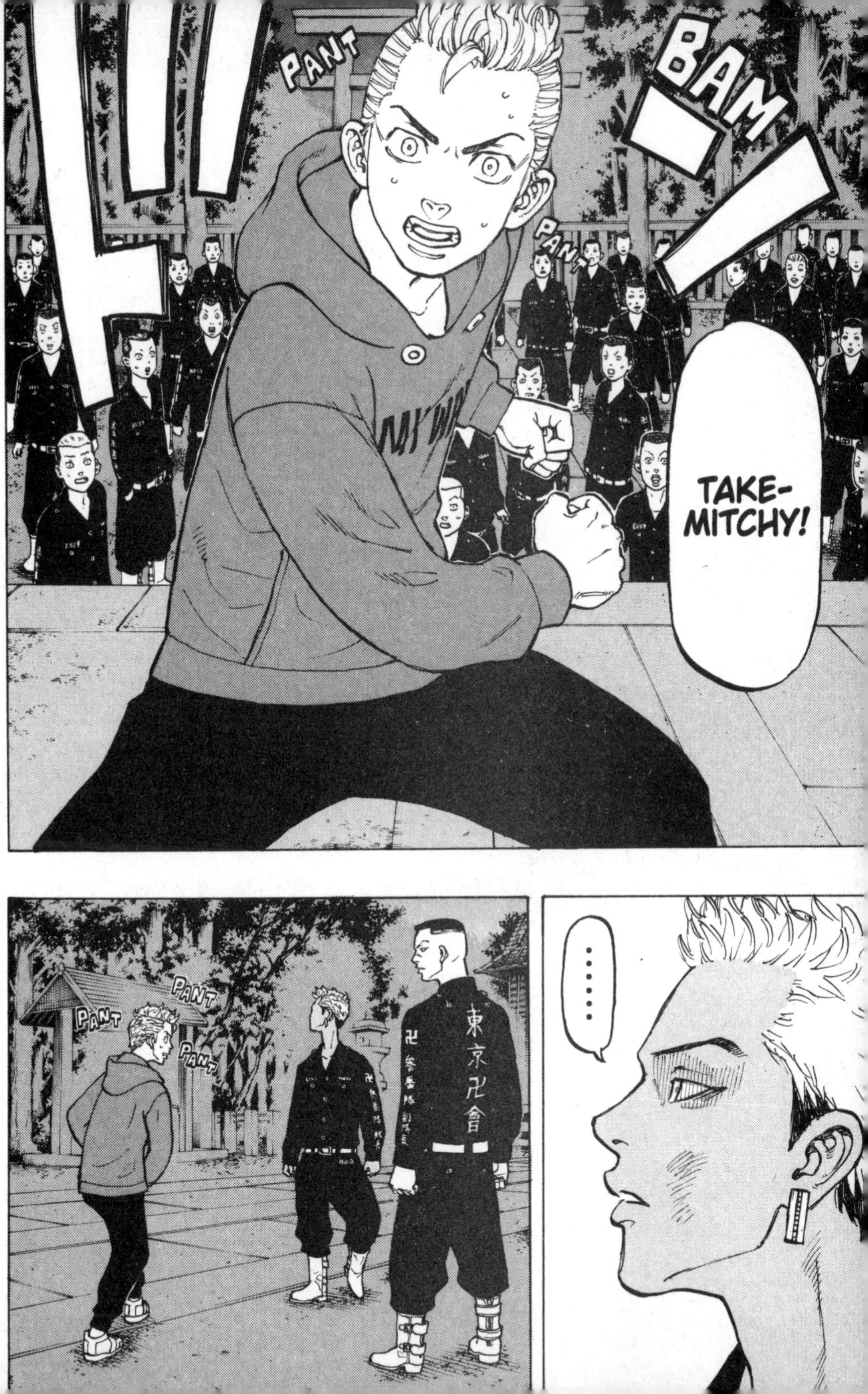
BAM
PANT
PANT
TAKE-MITCHY!
......
東京卍會
PANT
PANT
PANT

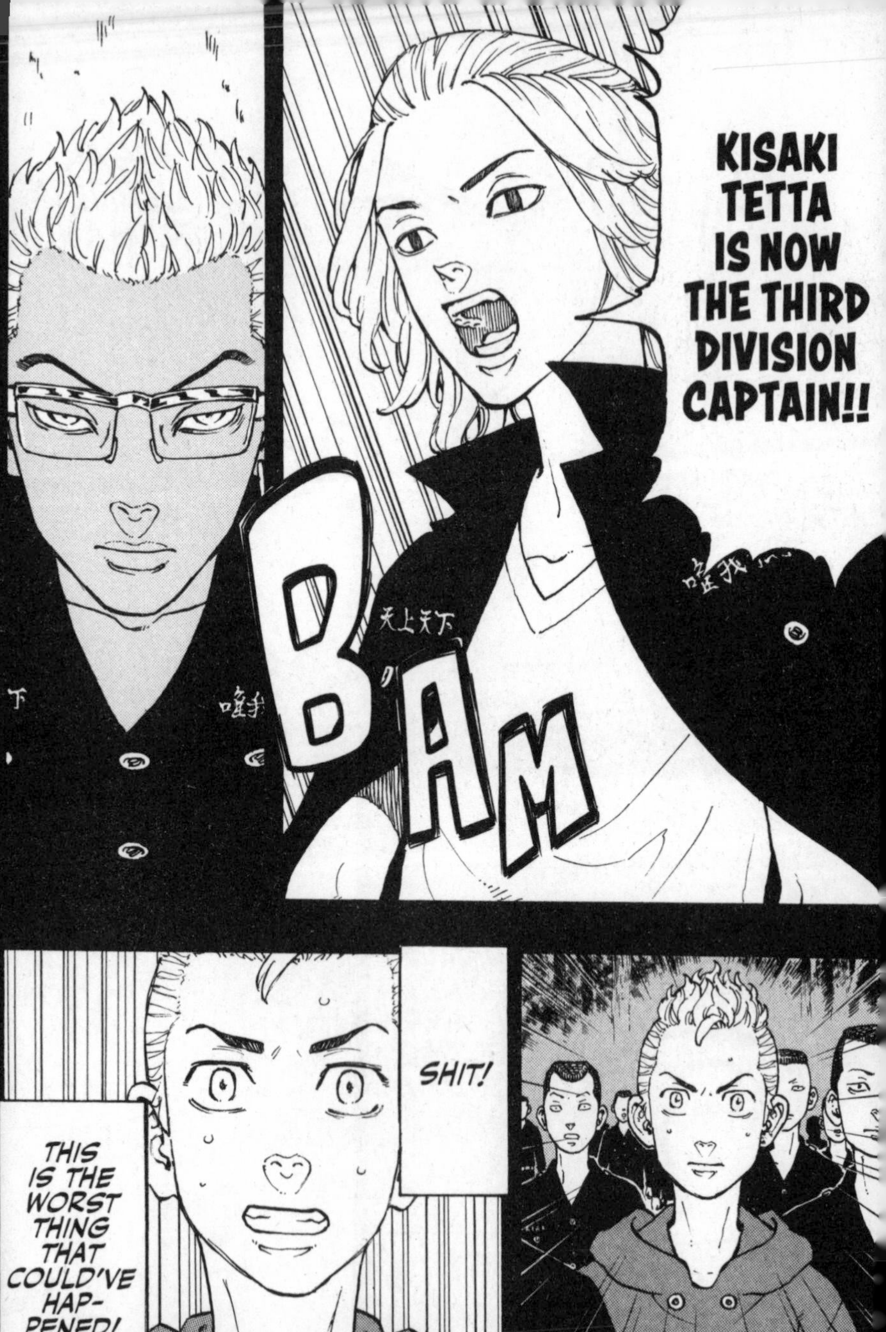
KISAKI TETTA IS NOW THE THIRD DIVISION CAPTAIN!!
BAM
SHIT!
THIS IS THE WORST THING THAT COULD'VE HAPPENED!

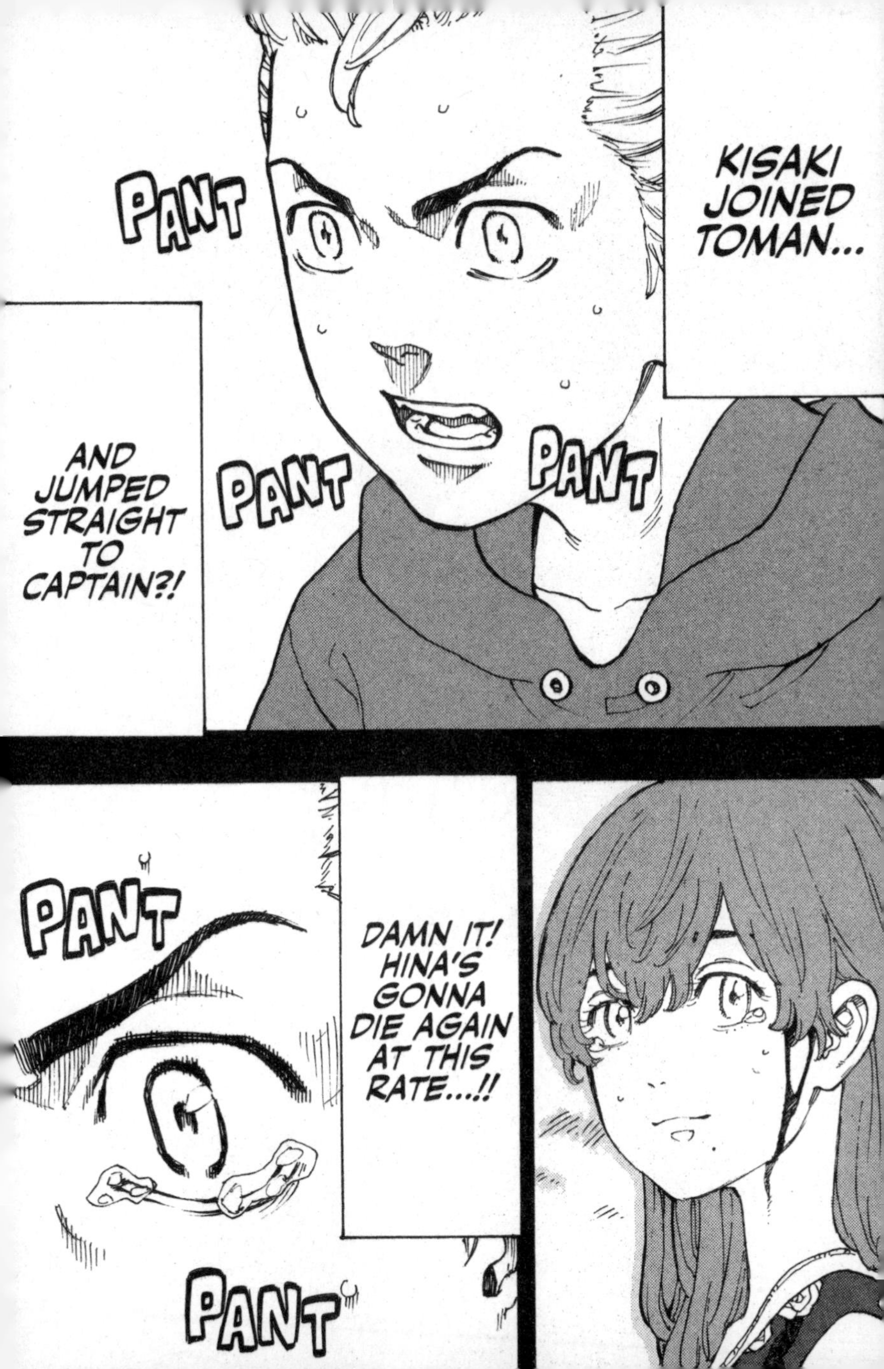
KISAKI JOINED TOMAN...
PANT
PANT
PANT
AND JUMPED STRAIGHT TO CAPTAIN?!
DAMN IT! HINA'S GONNA DIE AGAIN AT THIS RATE...!!
PANT
PANT

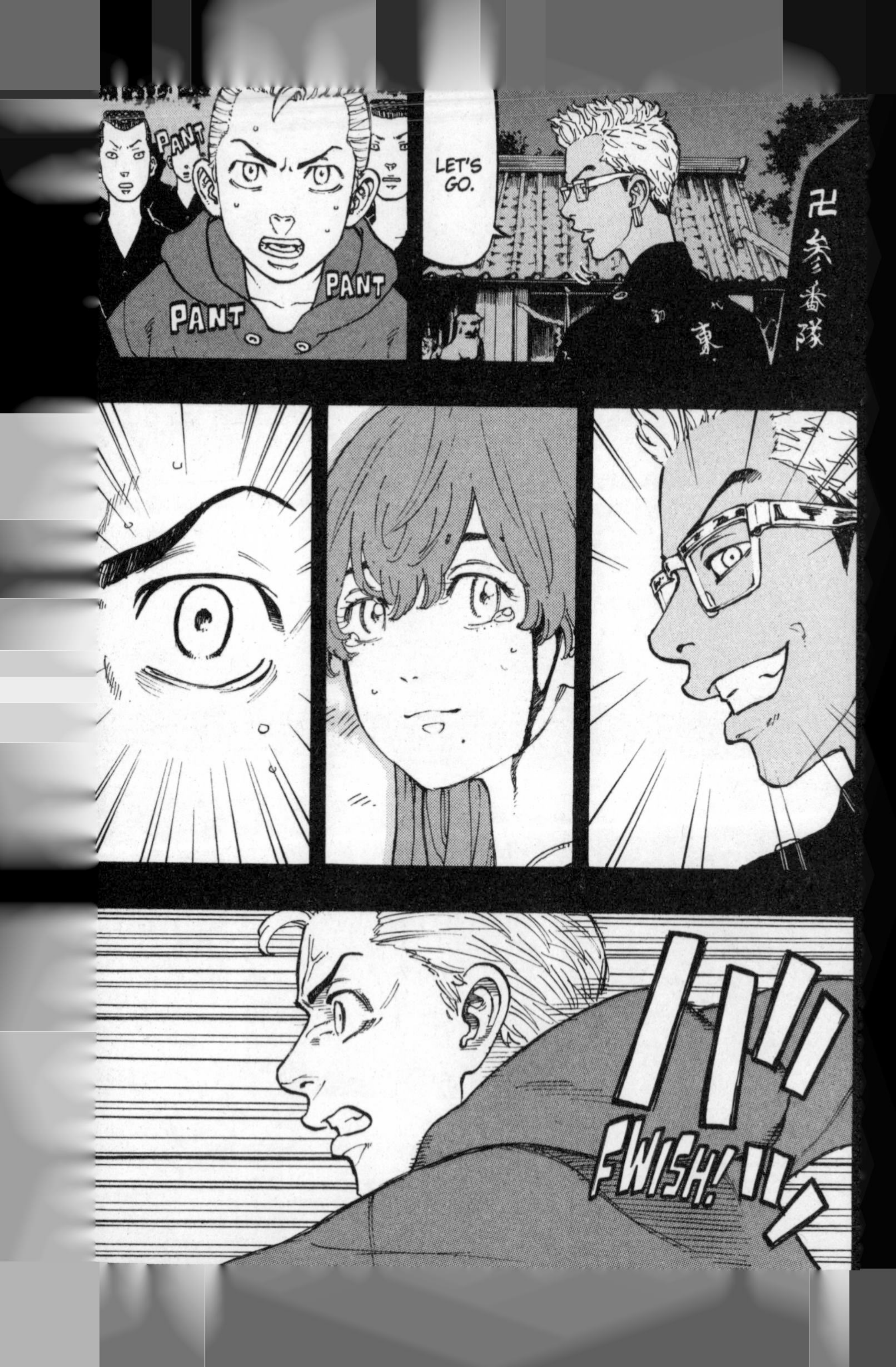
LET'S GO.
卍参番隊
PANT
PANT
PANT
FWISH!

CHAPTER 38: BREAK UP

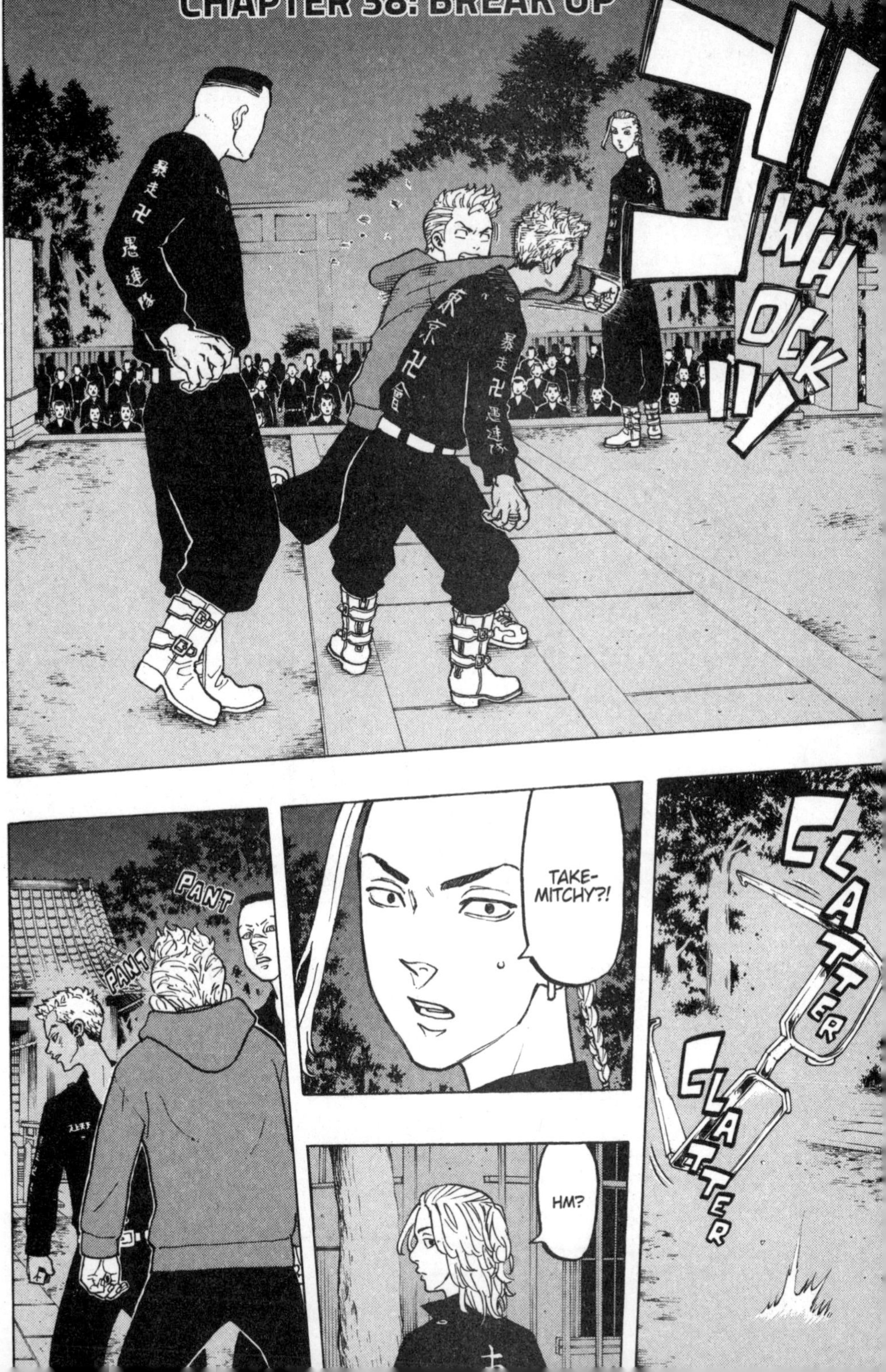
WHOCK
CLATTER
CLATTER
TAKE-MITCHY?!
HM?
PANT
PANT

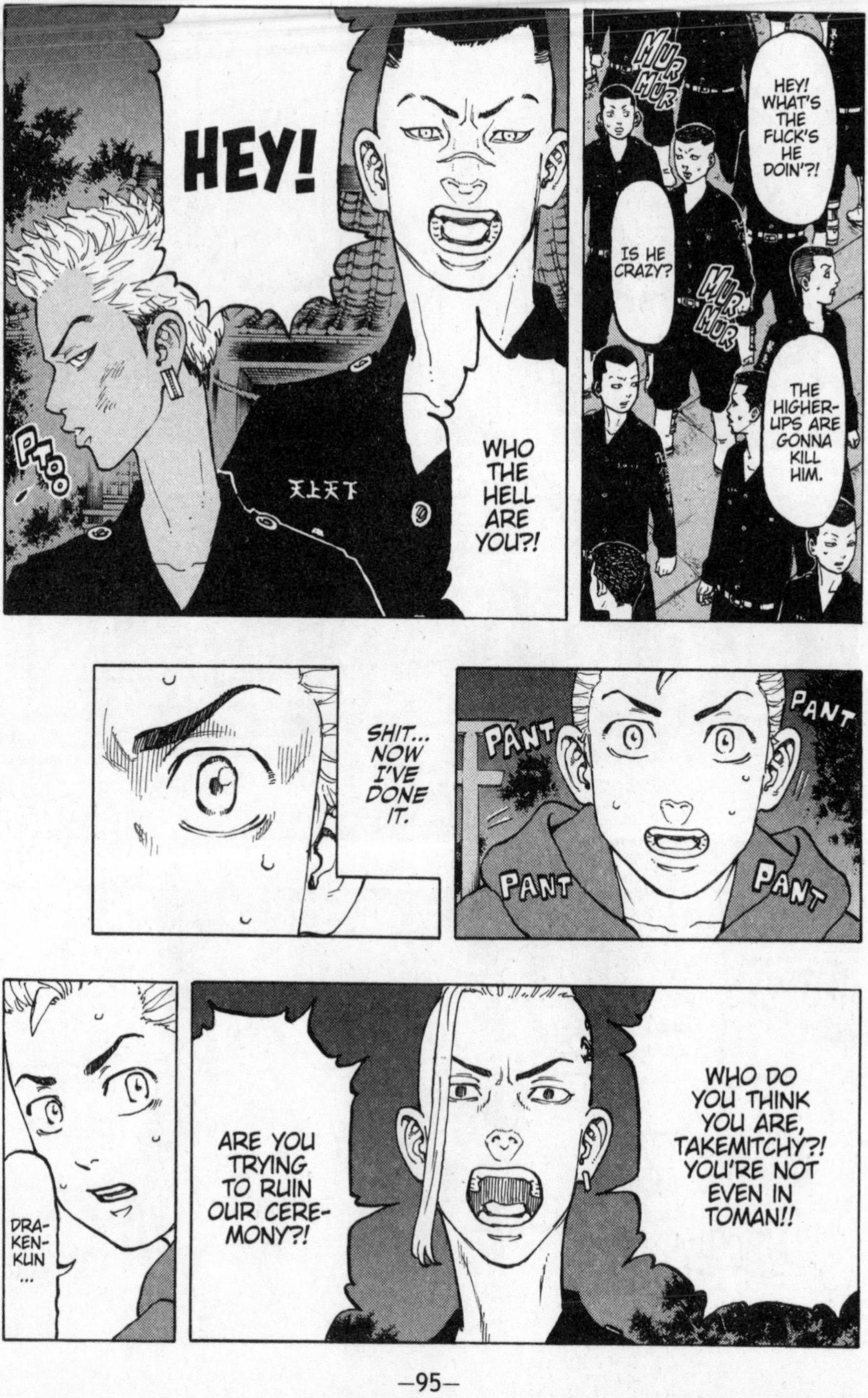
HEY! WHAT'S THE FUCK'S HE DOIN'?!
MUR MUR
IS HE CRAZY?
MUR MUR
THE HIGHER-UPS ARE GONNA KILL HIM.
HEY!
WHO THE HELL ARE YOU?!
PTOO
PANT
PANT
PANT
PANT
SHIT... NOW I'VE DONE IT.
WHO DO YOU THINK YOU ARE, TAKEMITCHY?! YOU'RE NOT EVEN IN TOMAN!!
ARE YOU TRYING TO RUIN OUR CEREMONY?!
DRAKEN-KUN...

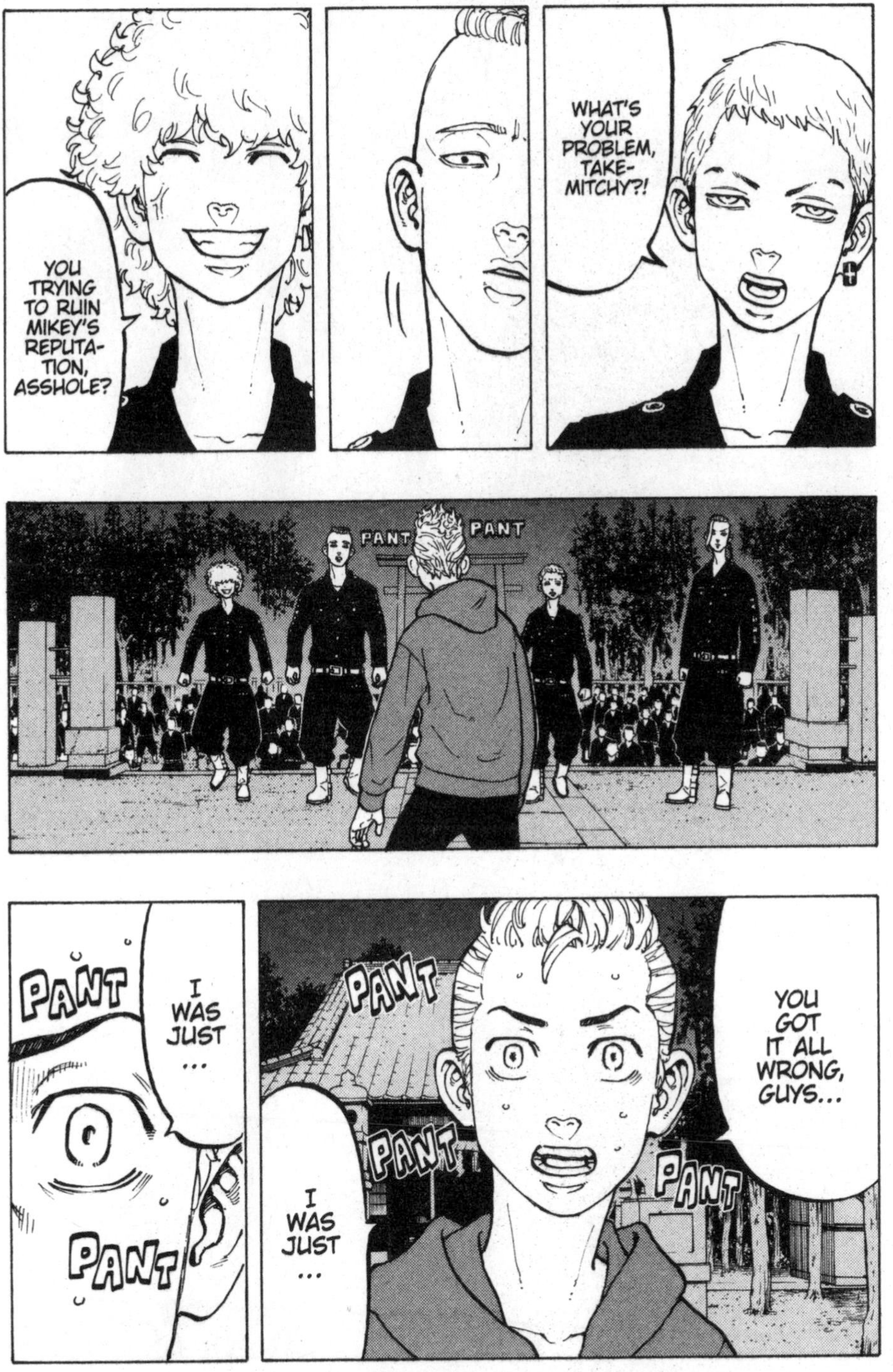
WHAT'S YOUR PROBLEM, TAKE-MITCHY?!
YOU TRYING TO RUIN MIKEY'S REPUTATION, ASSHOLE?
PANT PANT
YOU GOT IT ALL WRONG, GUYS...
PANT
PANT
PANT
I WAS JUST ...
I WAS JUST ...
PANT
PANT

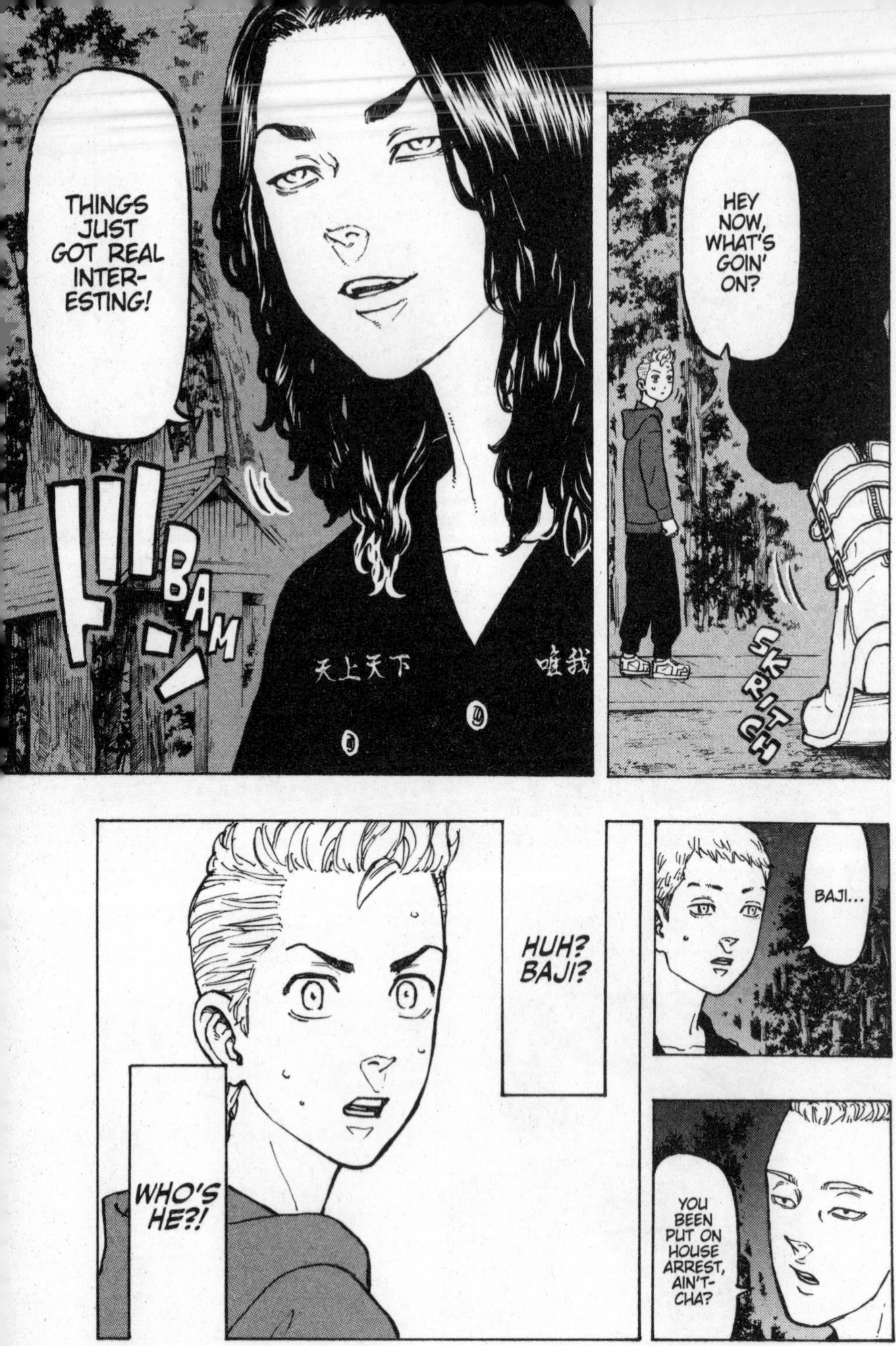
HEY NOW, WHAT'S GOIN' ON?
SKRITCH
THINGS JUST GOT REAL INTER-ESTING!
BAM
天上天下
唯我
BAJI...
YOU BEEN PUT ON HOUSE ARREST, AIN'T-CHA?
HUH? BAJI?
WHO'S HE?!

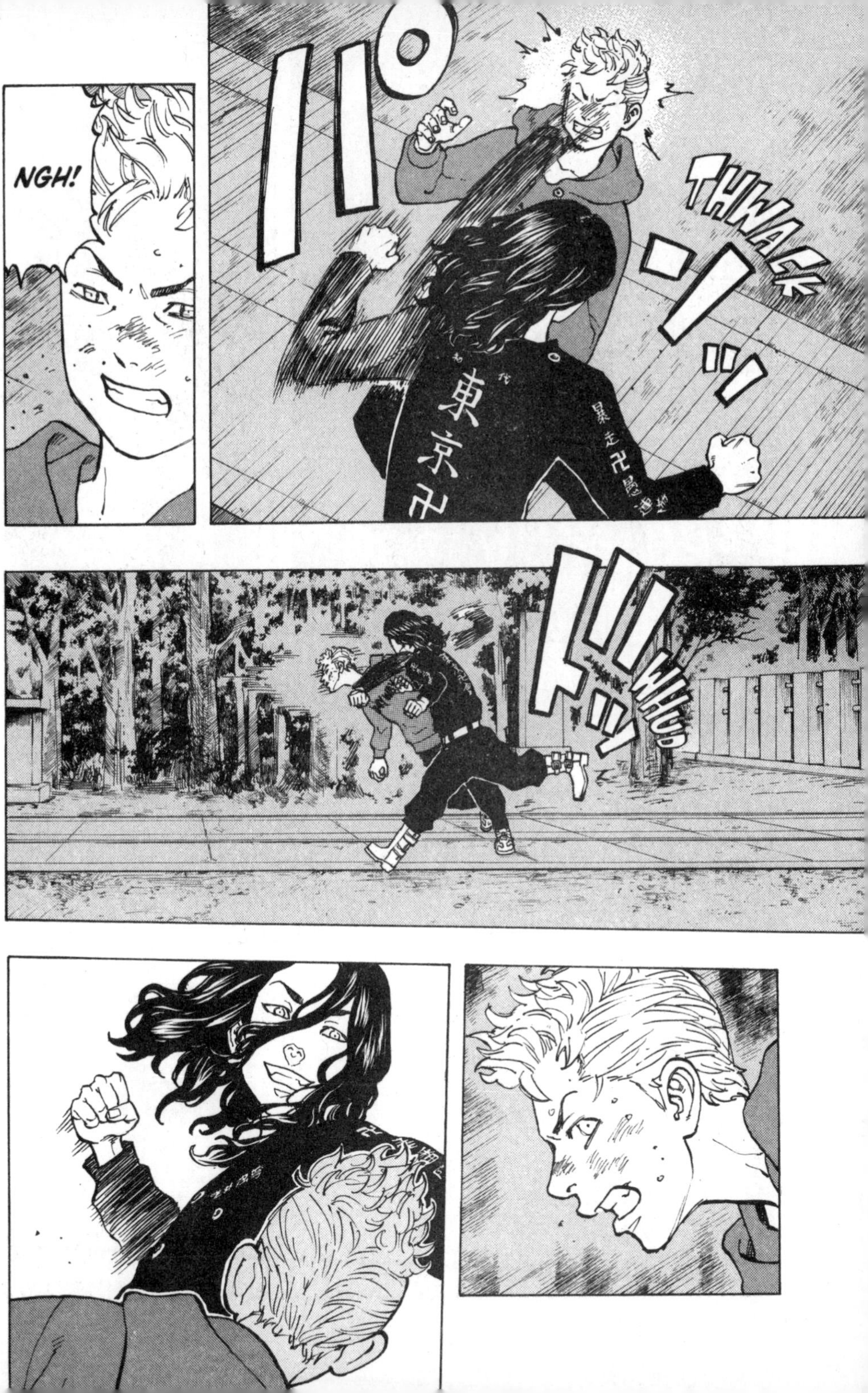
THWACK
NGH!
WHUD

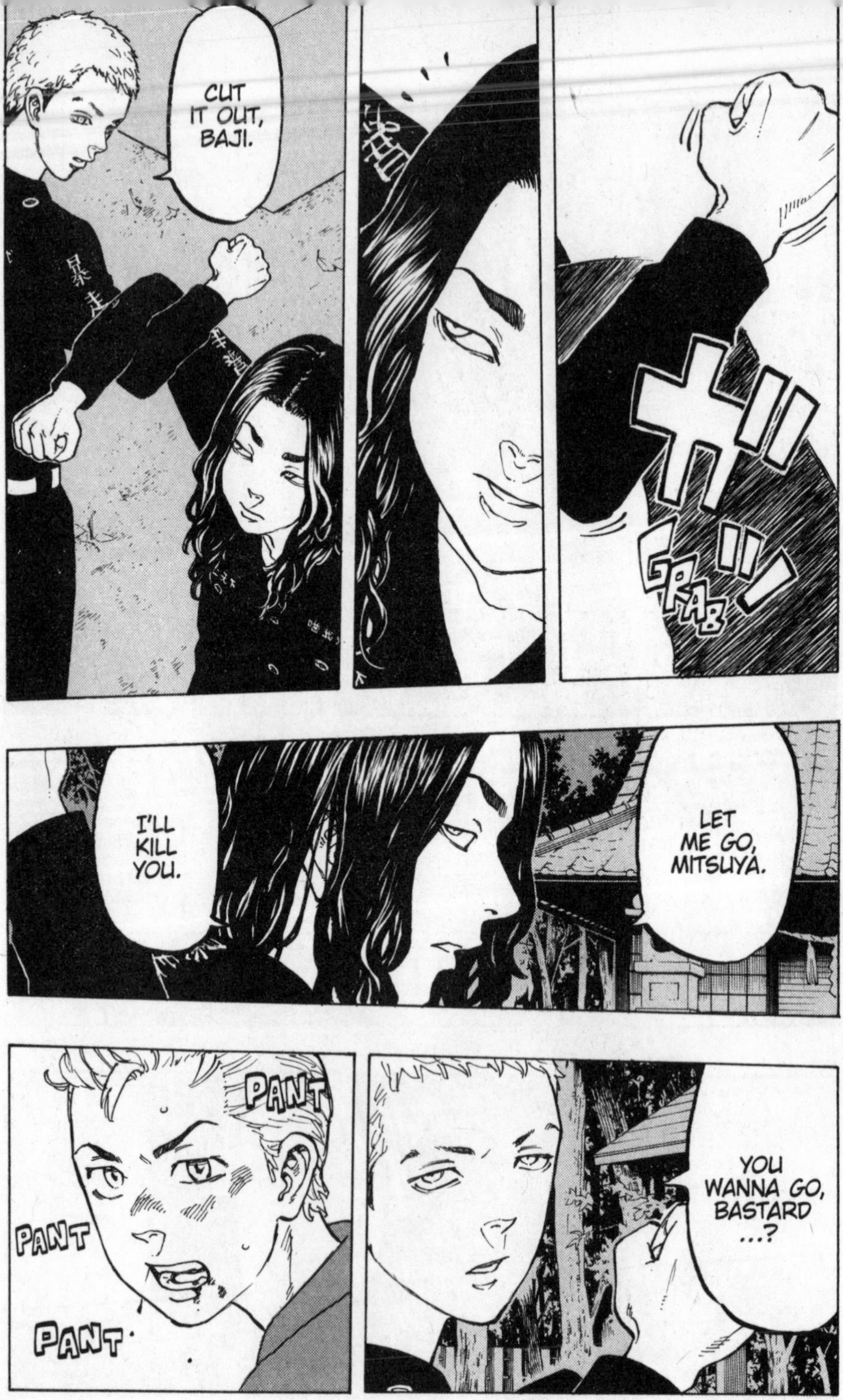
GRAB
CUT IT OUT, BAJI.
LET ME GO, MITSUYA.
I'LL KILL YOU.
YOU WANNA GO, BASTARD ...?
PANT
PANT
PANT

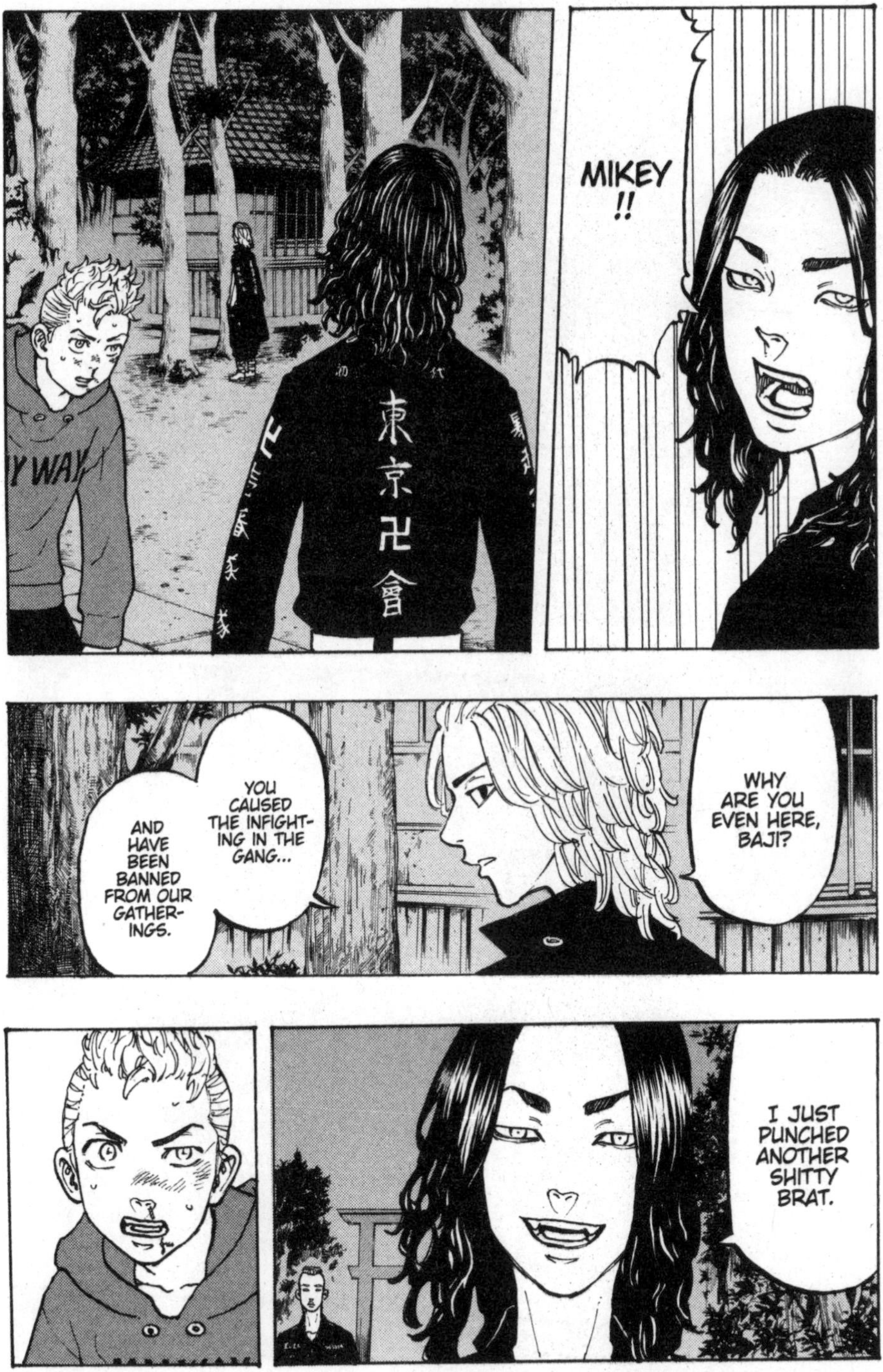
MIKEY !!
東京卍會
WHY ARE YOU EVEN HERE, BAJI?
YOU CAUSED THE INFIGHTING IN THE GANG...
AND HAVE BEEN BANNED FROM OUR GATHERINGS.
I JUST PUNCHED ANOTHER SHITTY BRAT.

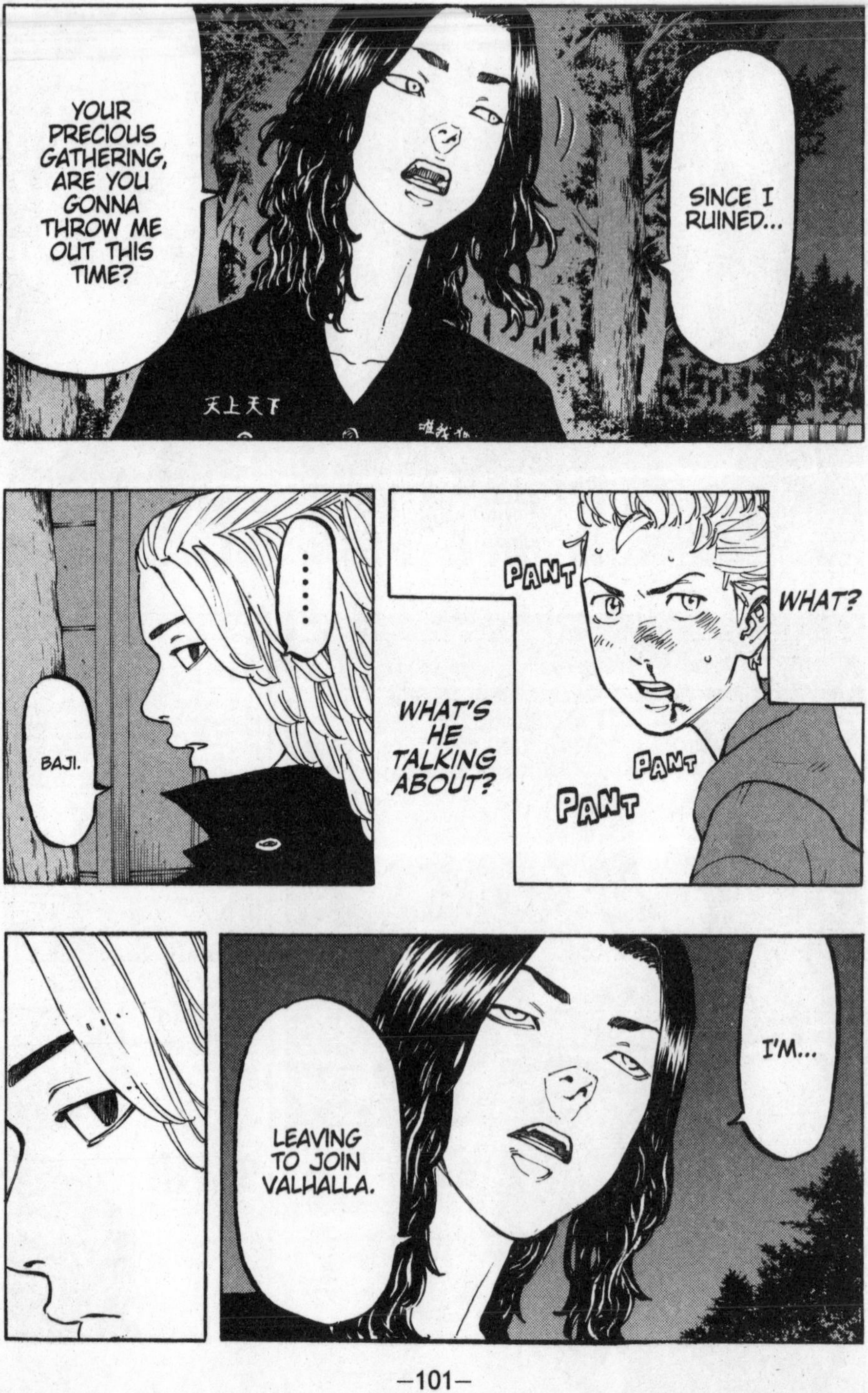
SINCE I RUINED...
YOUR PRECIOUS GATHERING, ARE YOU GONNA THROW ME OUT THIS TIME?
天上天下
WHAT?
PANT
WHAT'S HE TALKING ABOUT?
PANT
PANT
......
BAJI.
I'M...
LEAVING TO JOIN VALHALLA.

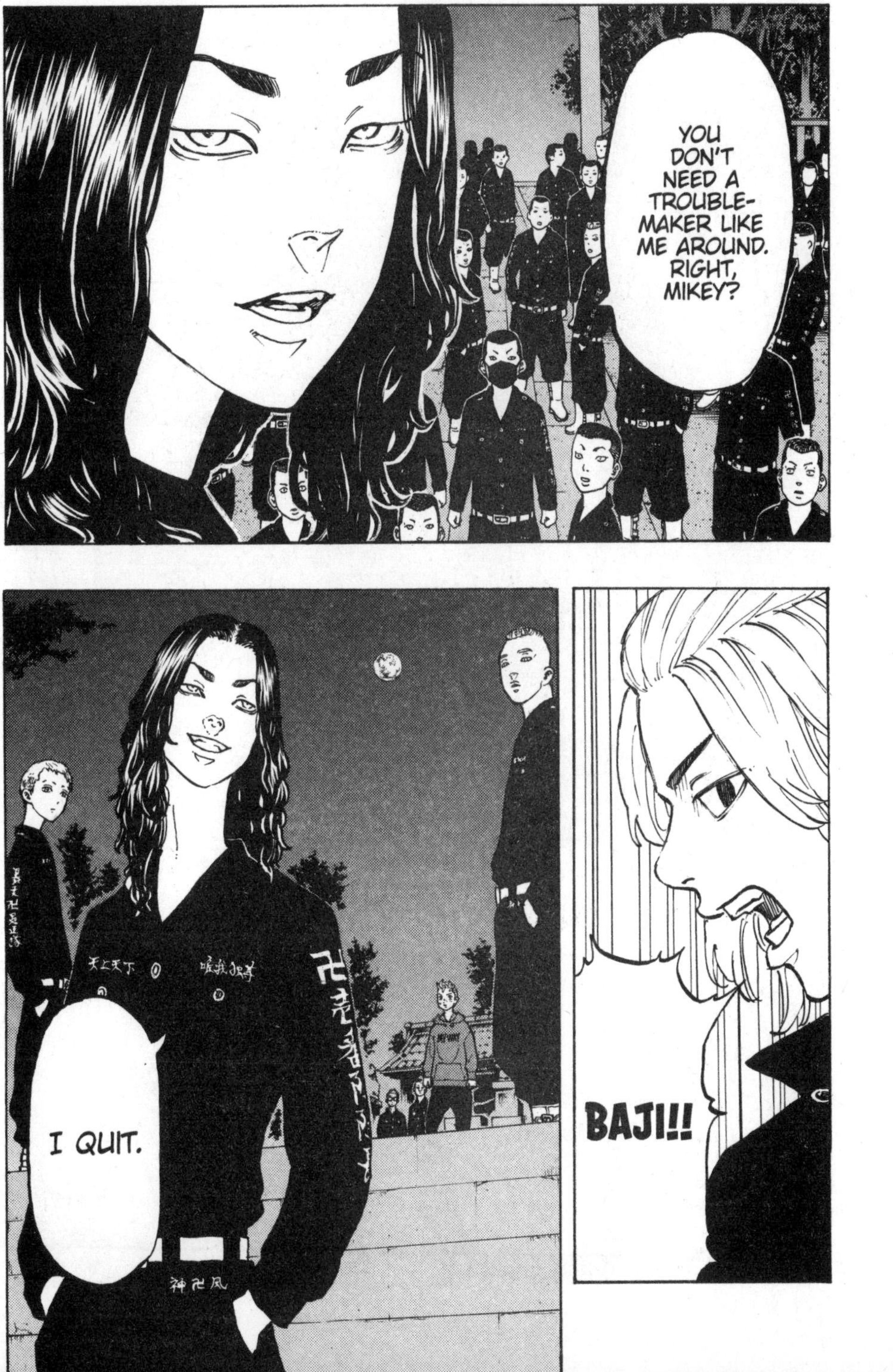
YOU DON'T NEED A TROUBLE-MAKER LIKE ME AROUND. RIGHT, MIKEY?
BAJI!!
I QUIT.

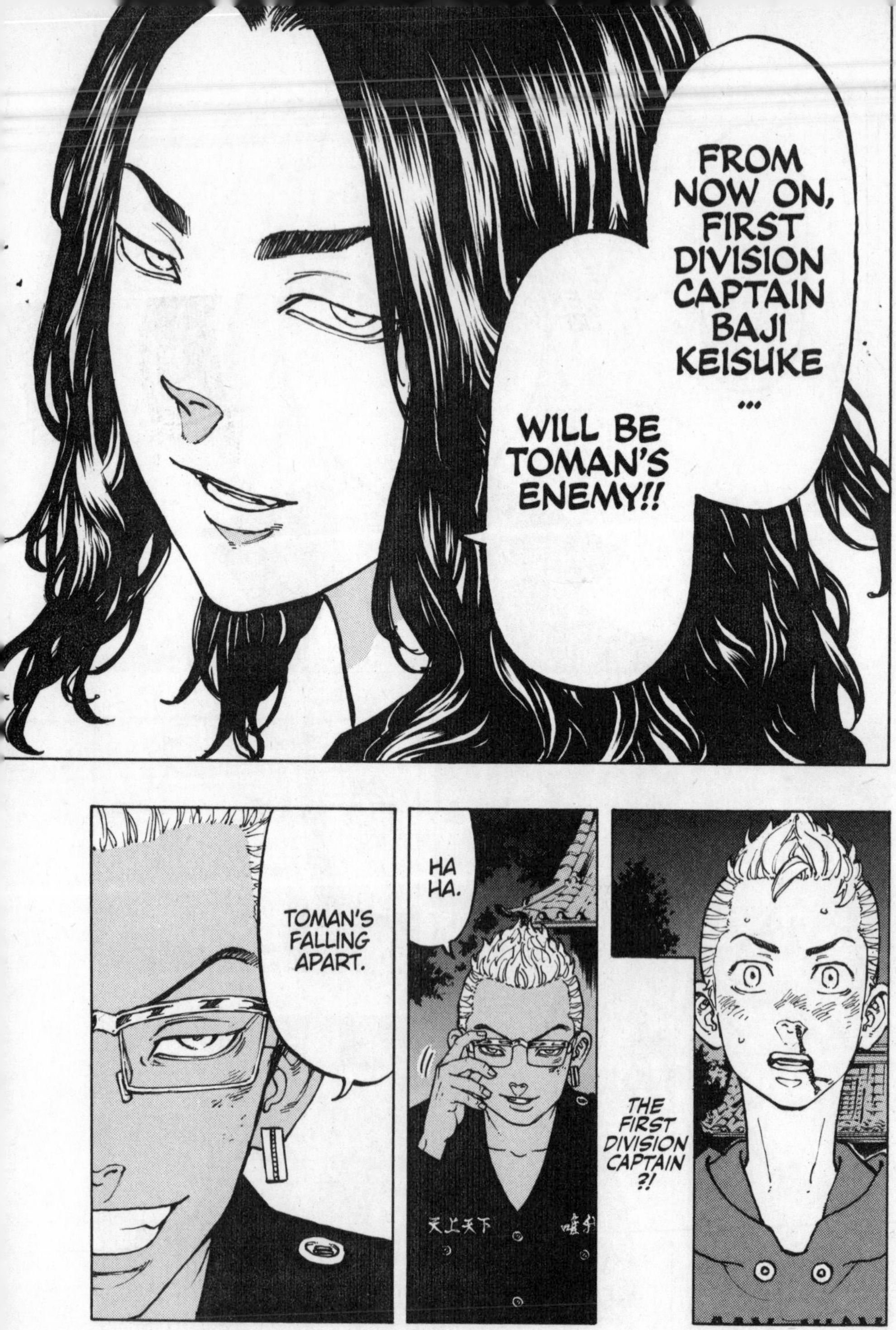
FROM NOW ON, FIRST DIVISION CAPTAIN BAJI KEISUKE ...
WILL BE TOMAN'S ENEMY!!
THE FIRST DIVISION CAPTAIN ?!
HA HA.
TOMAN'S FALLING APART.

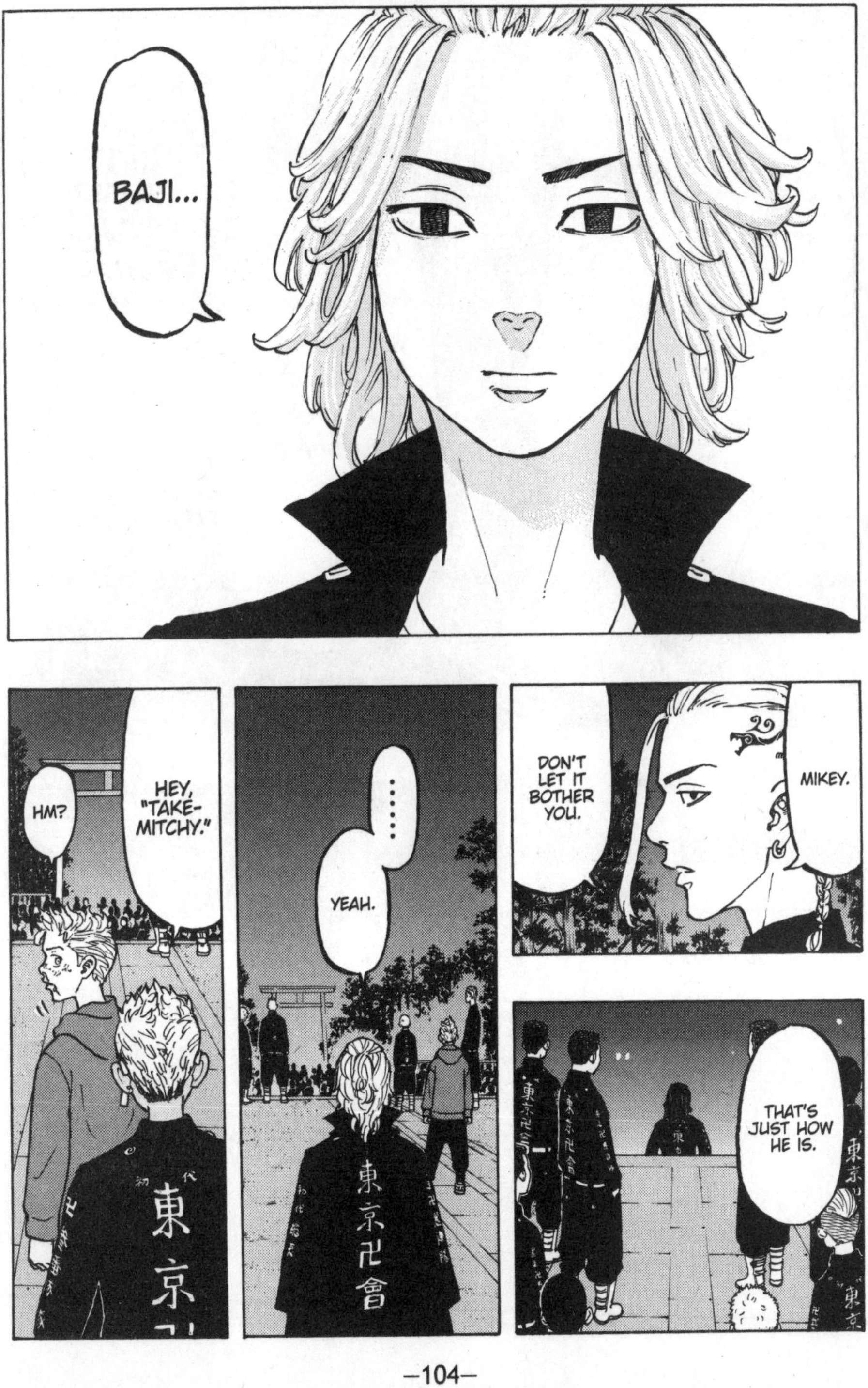
BAJI...
MIKEY.
DON'T LET IT BOTHER YOU.
THAT'S JUST HOW HE IS.
......
YEAH.
HEY, "TAKE-MITCHY."
HM?

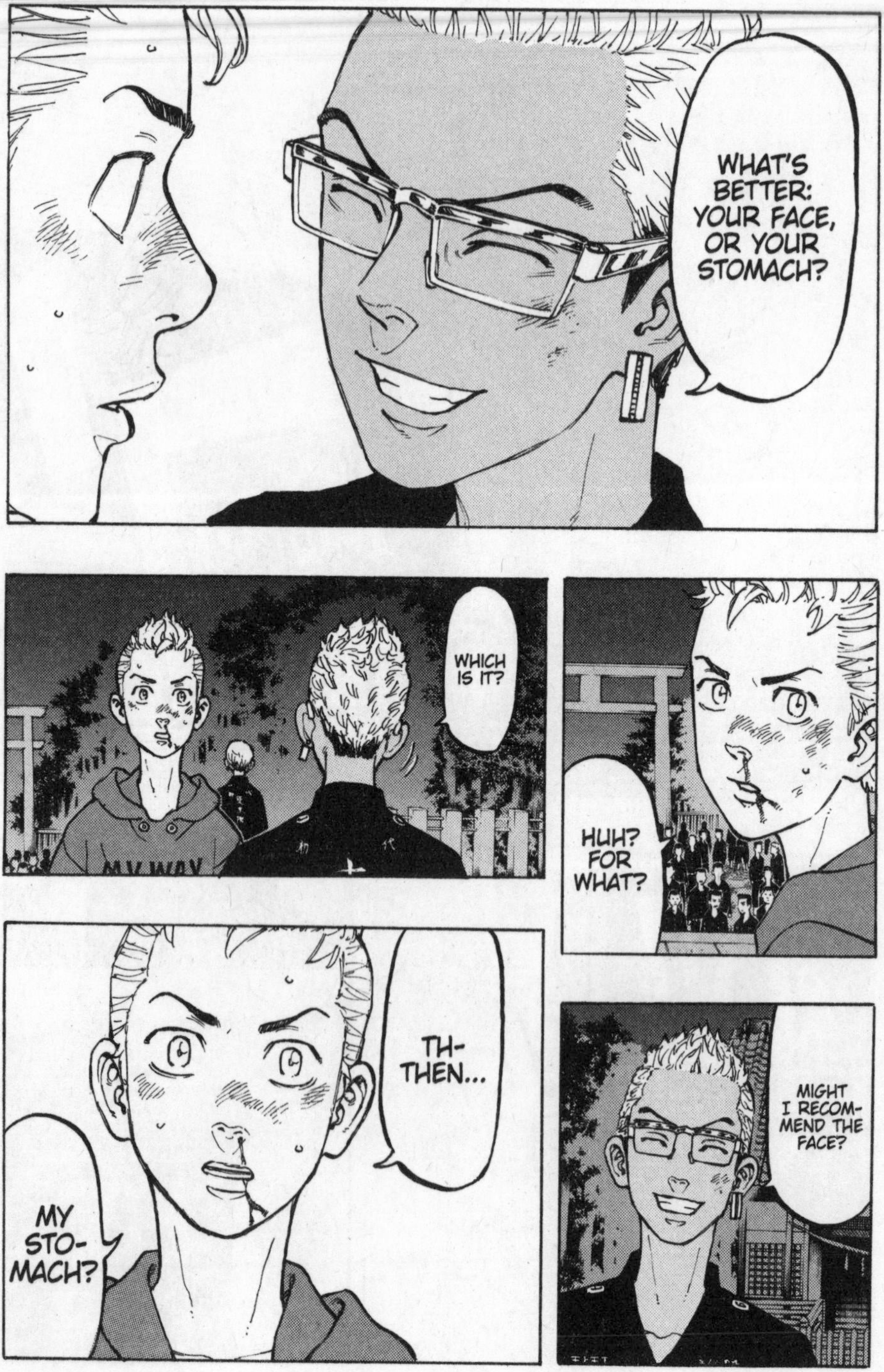
WHAT'S BETTER: YOUR FACE, OR YOUR STOMACH?
HUH? FOR WHAT?
WHICH IS IT?
TH- THEN...
MY STO- MACH?
MIGHT I RECOMMEND THE FACE?

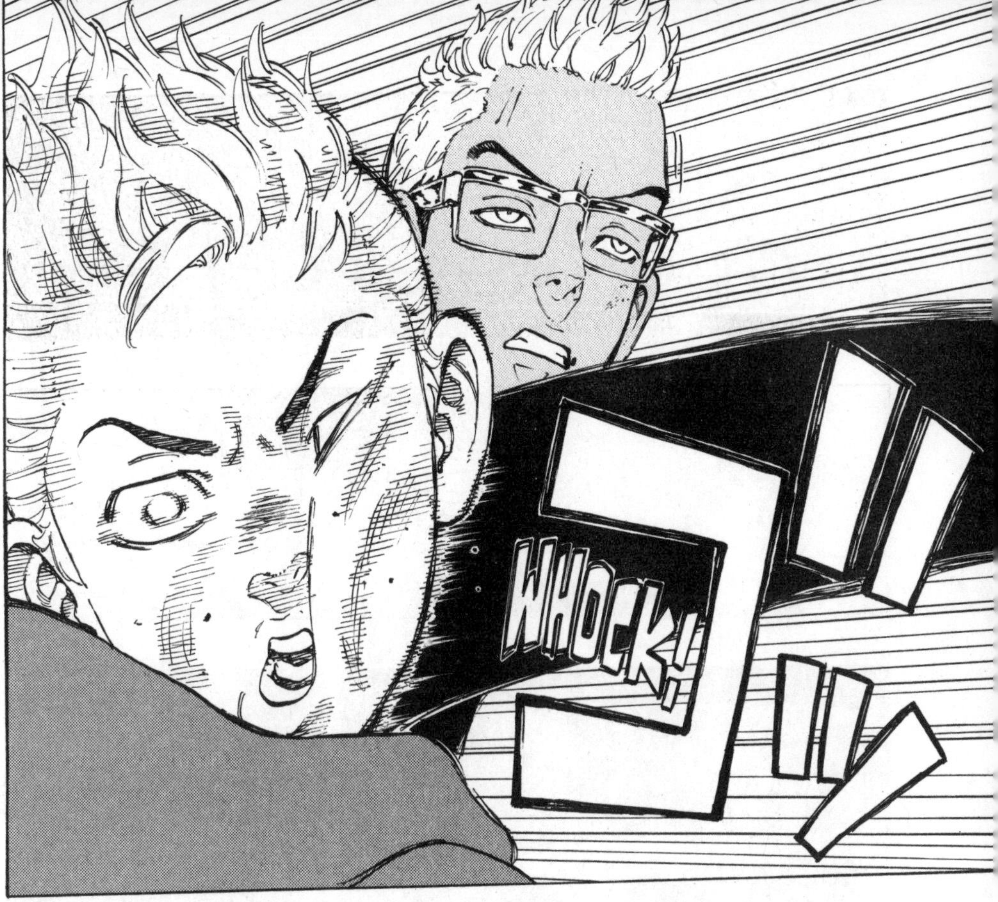
WHOCK!!
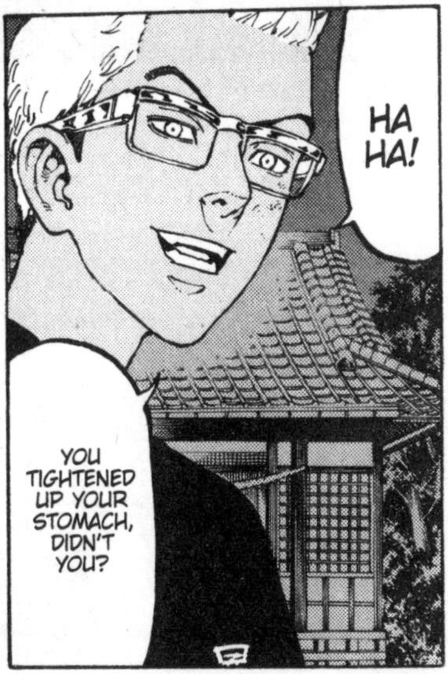
HA HA!
YOU TIGHTENED UP YOUR STOMACH, DIDN'T YOU?
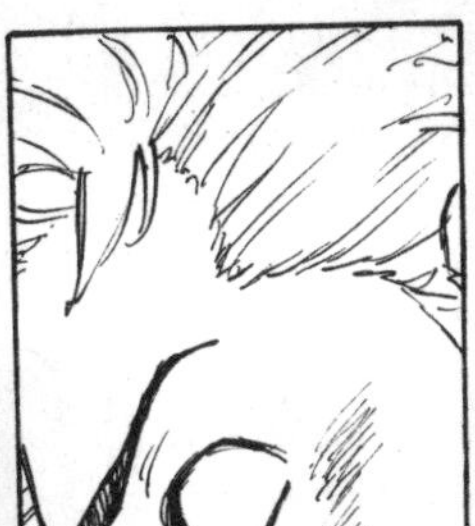
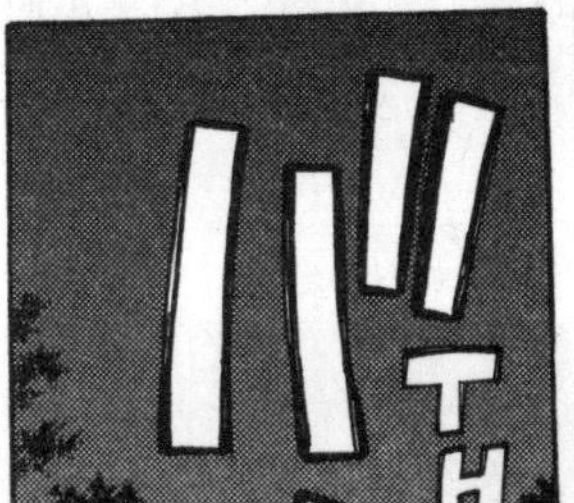
THUD

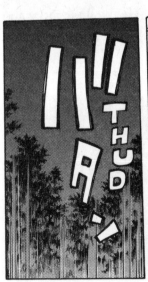

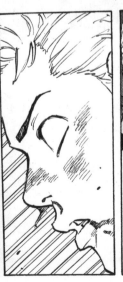

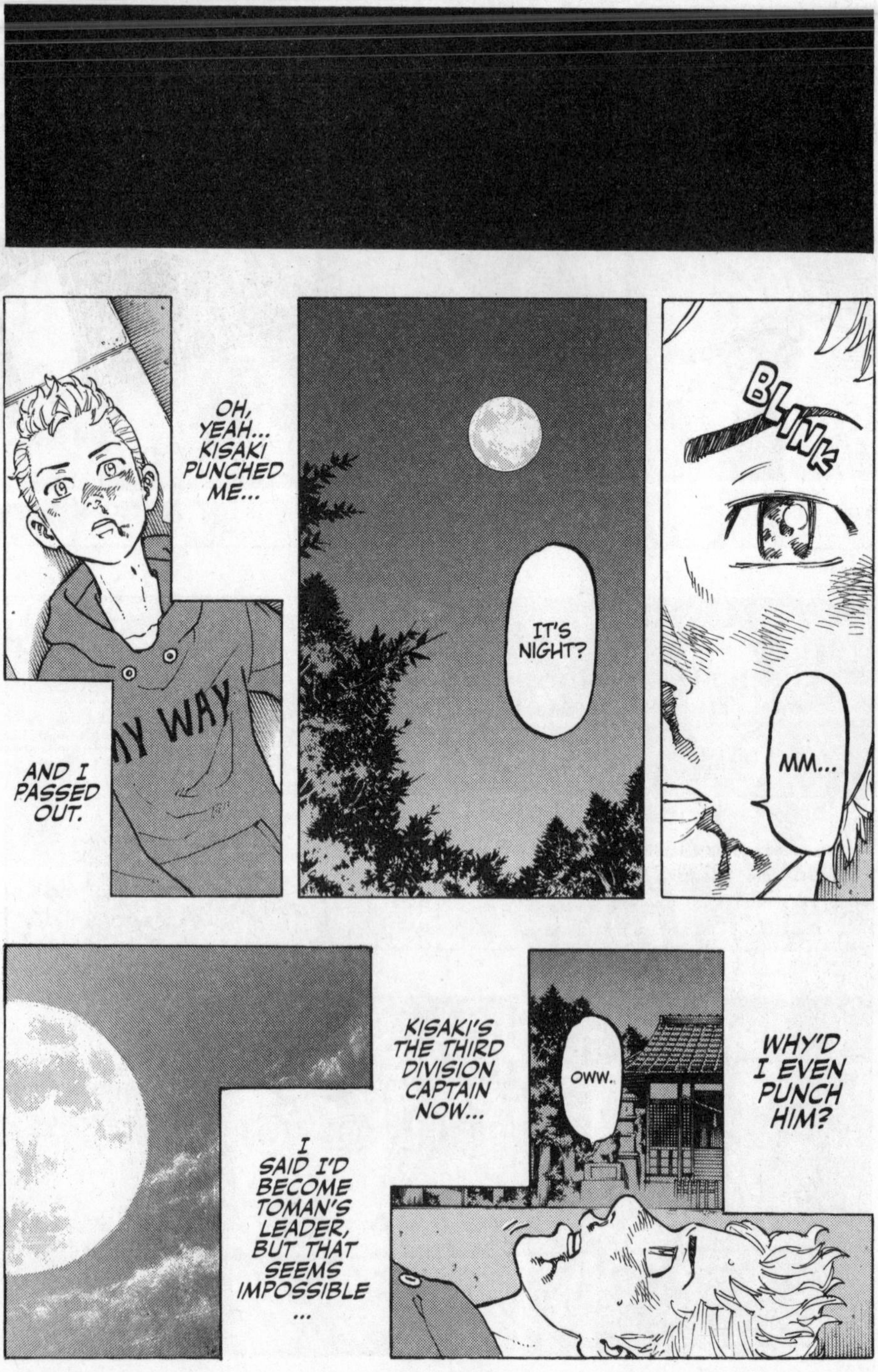
BLINK
MM...
IT'S NIGHT?
OH, YEAH... KISAKI PUNCHED ME...
AND I PASSED OUT.
MY WAY
WHY'D I EVEN PUNCH HIM?
OWW..
KISAKI'S THE THIRD DIVISION CAPTAIN NOW...
I SAID I'D BECOME TOMAN'S LEADER, BUT THAT SEEMS IMPOSSIBLE ...

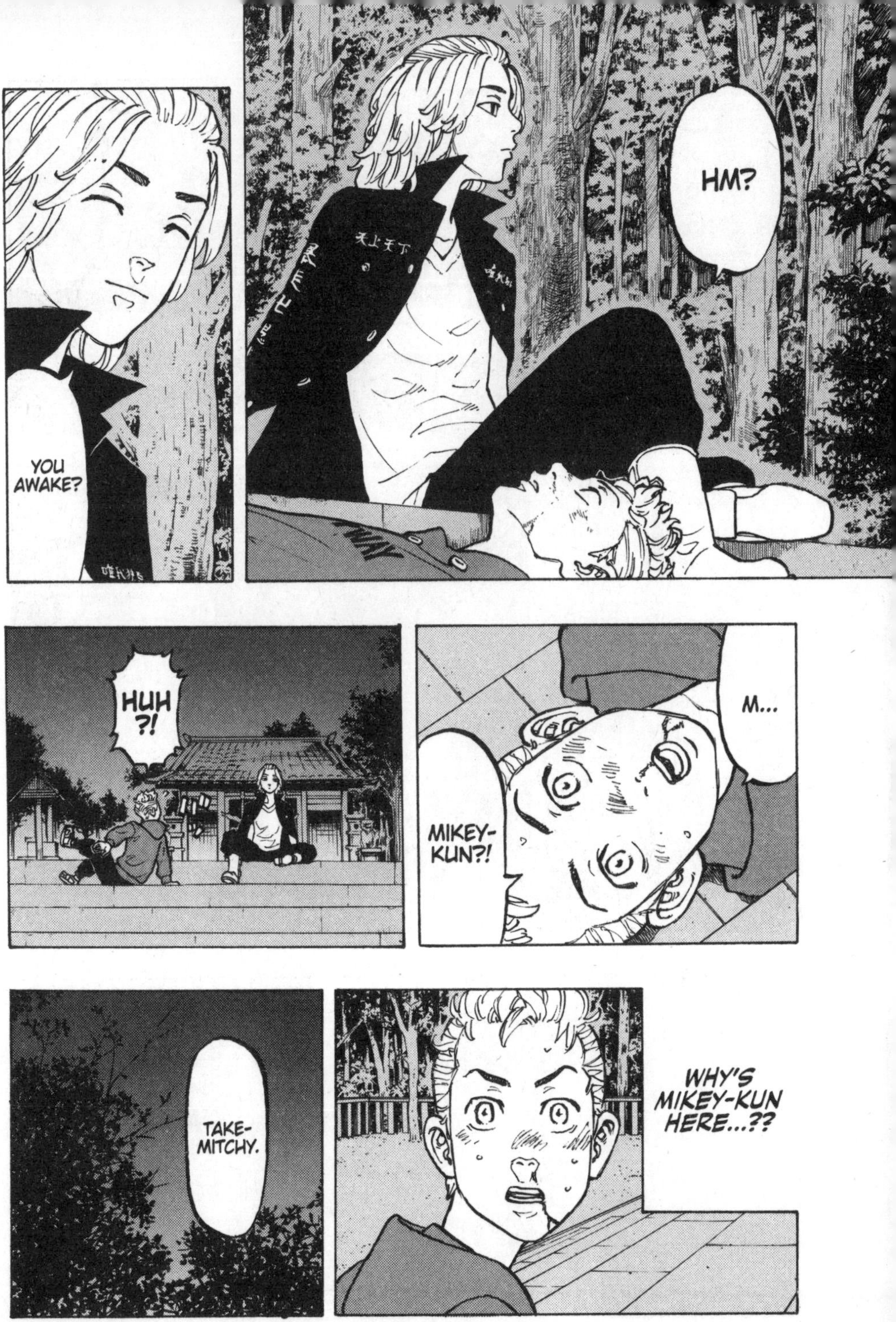
HM?
YOU AWAKE?
M...
MIKEY-KUN?!
HUH ?!
WHY'S MIKEY-KUN HERE...??
TAKE-MITCHY.

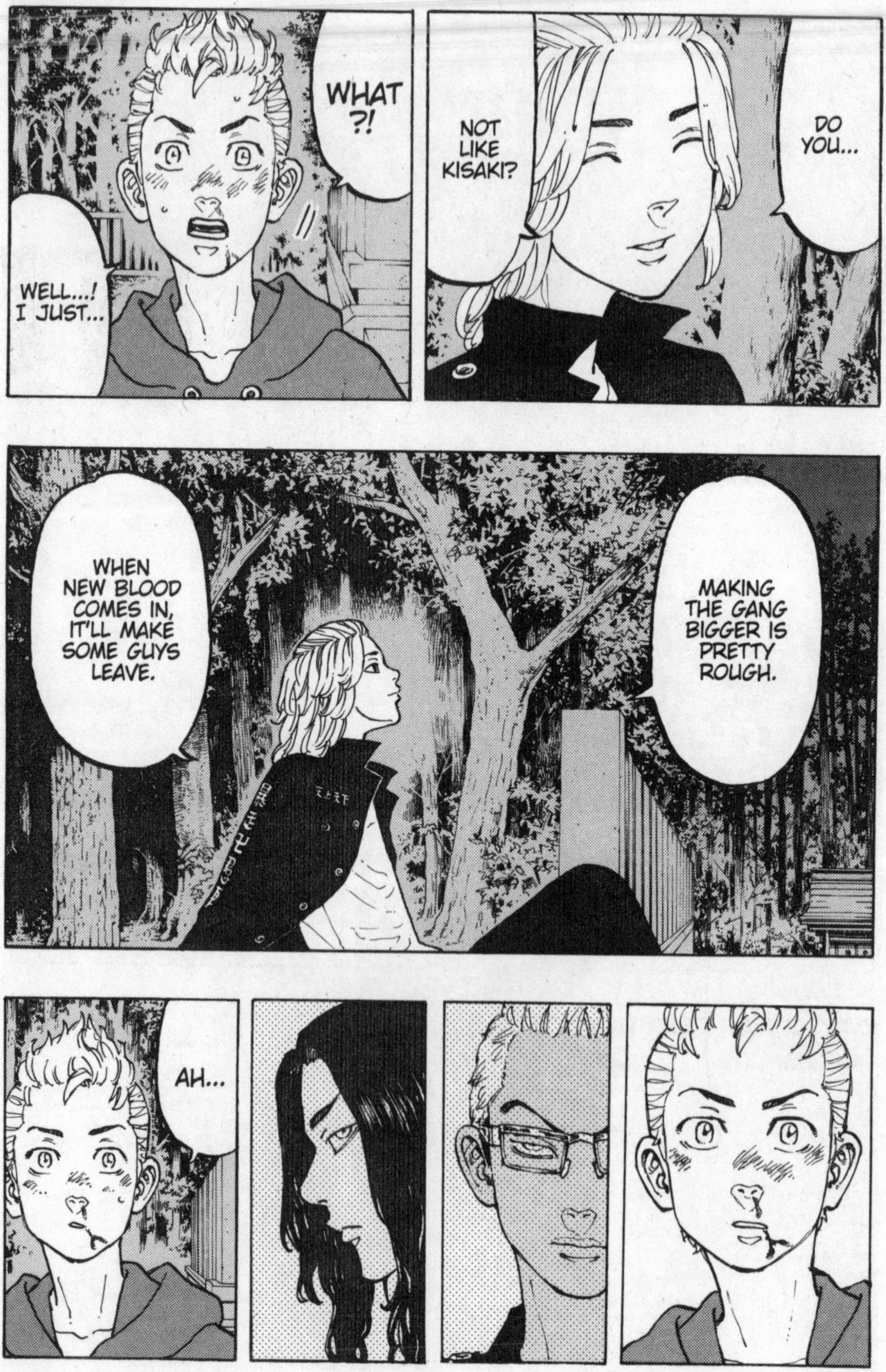
DO YOU...
NOT LIKE KISAKI?
WHAT ?!
WELL...! I JUST...
MAKING THE GANG BIGGER IS PRETTY ROUGH.
WHEN NEW BLOOD COMES IN, IT'LL MAKE SOME GUYS LEAVE.
AH...

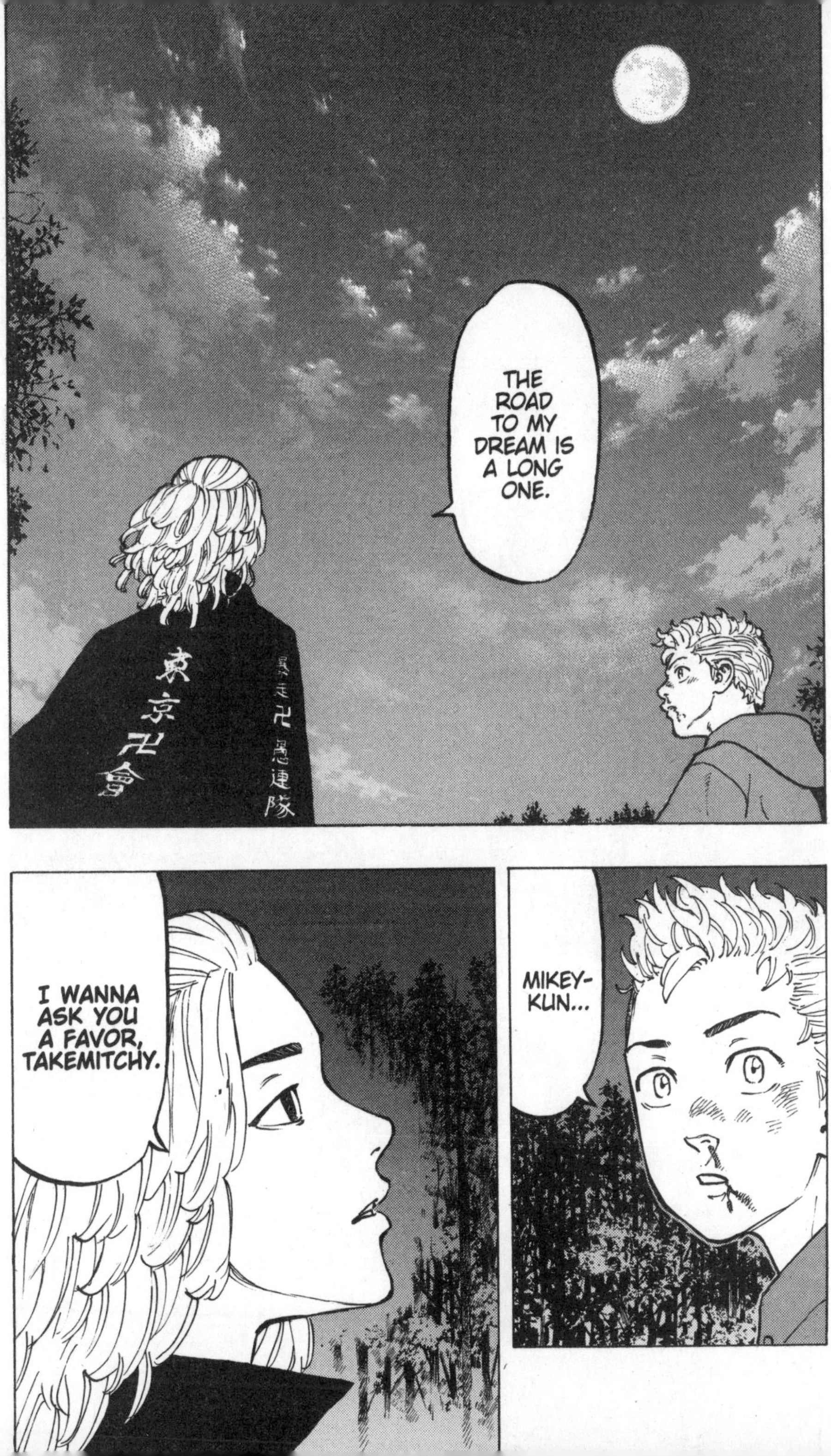
THE ROAD TO MY DREAM IS A LONG ONE.
東京卍會
暴走卍愚連隊
MIKEY-KUN...
I WANNA ASK YOU A FAVOR, TAKEMITCHY.

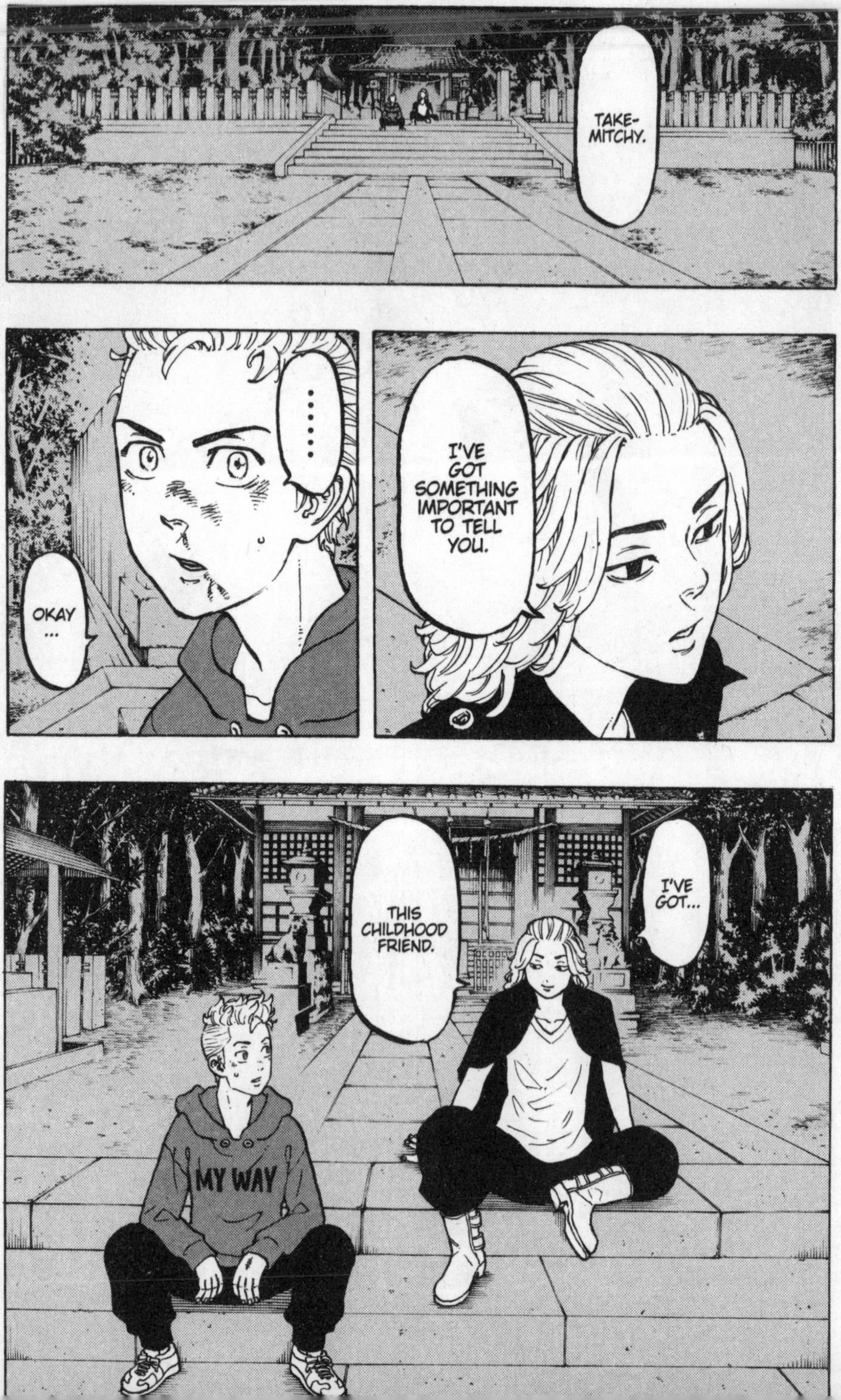
TAKE-MITCHY.
I'VE GOT SOMETHING IMPORTANT TO TELL YOU.
......
OKAY ...
I'VE GOT...
THIS CHILDHOOD FRIEND.

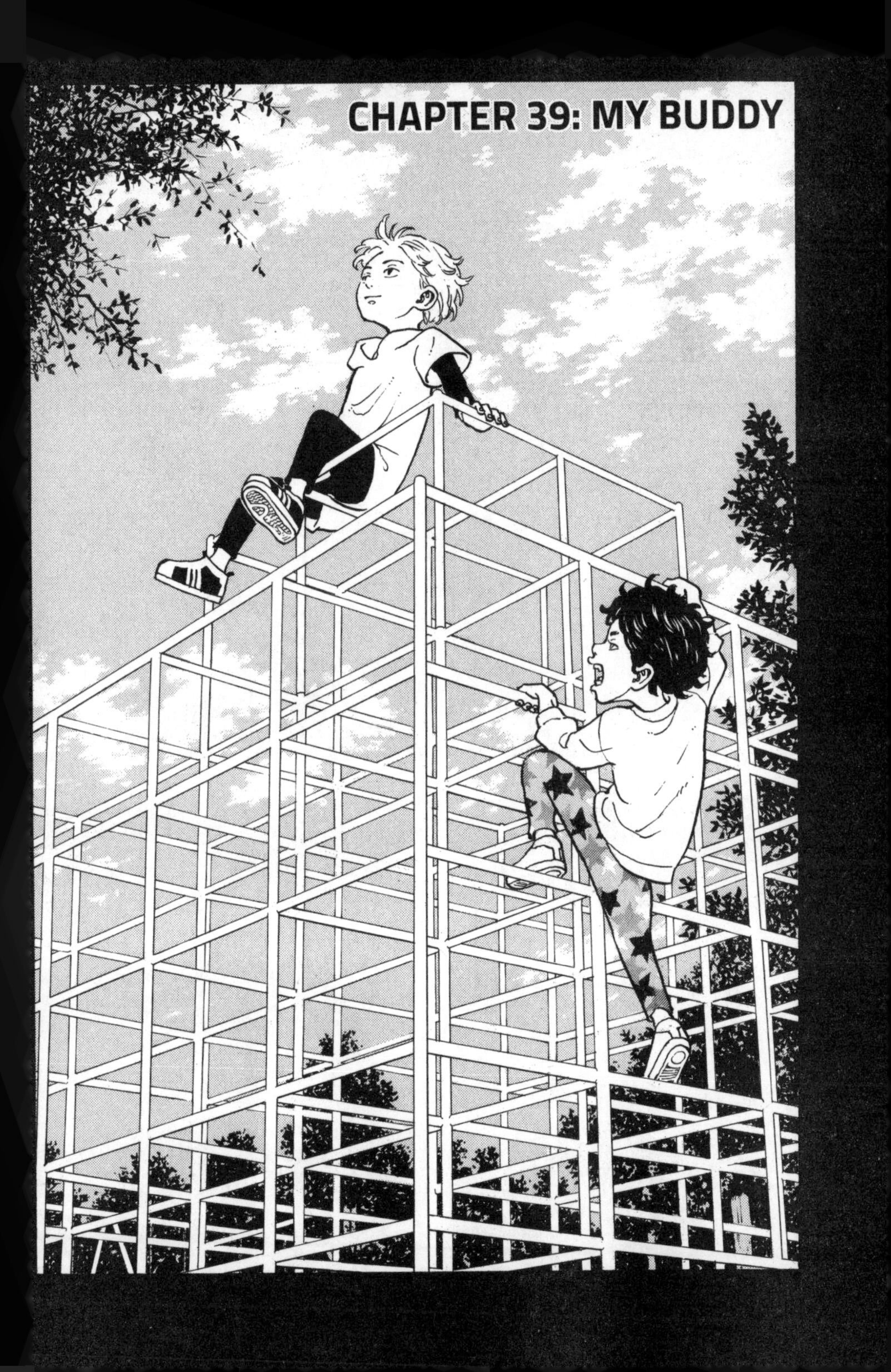
CHAPTER 39: MY BUDDY

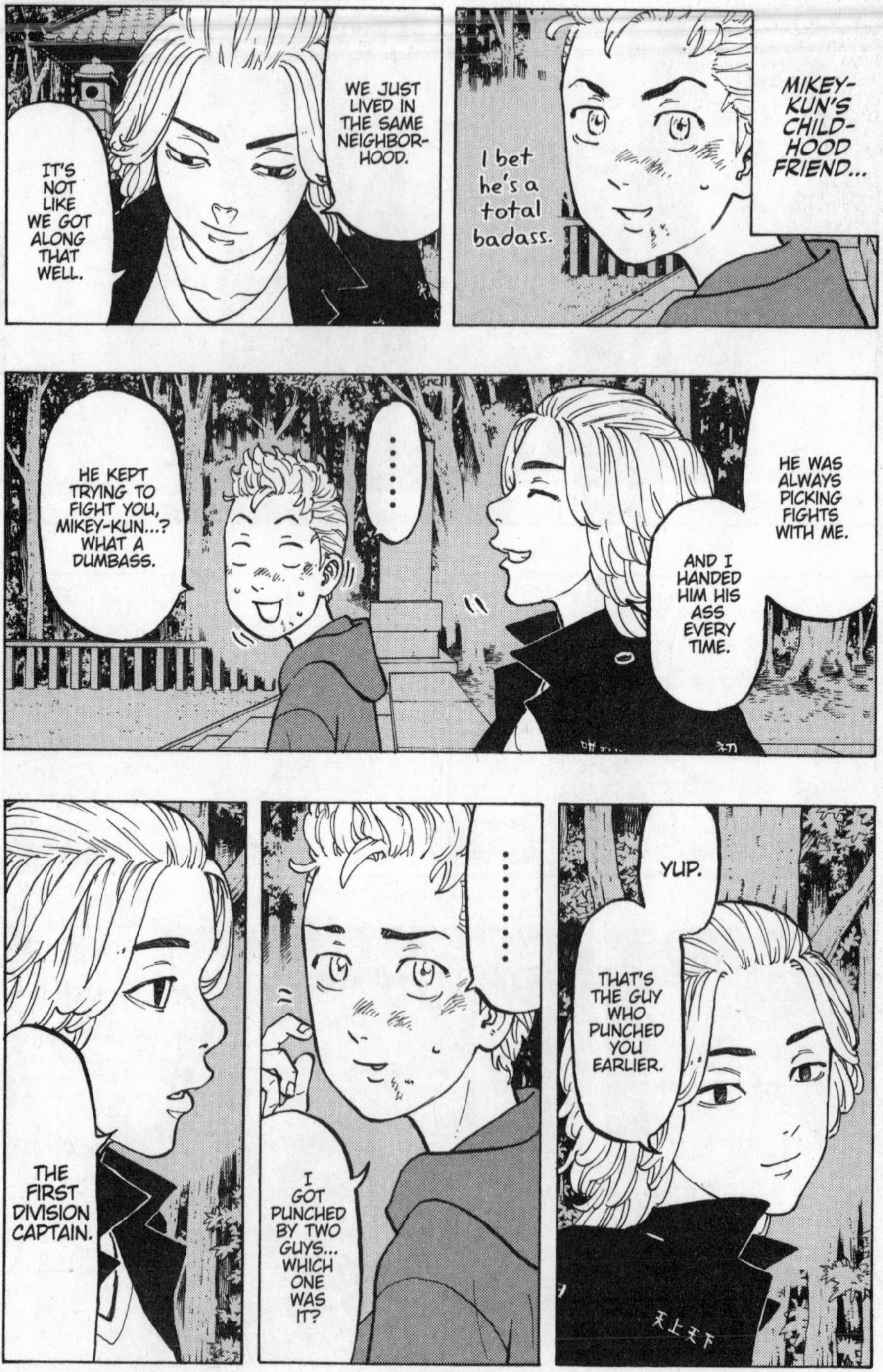
MIKEY-KUN'S CHILDHOOD FRIEND...
I bet he's a total badass.
WE JUST LIVED IN THE SAME NEIGHBORHOOD.
IT'S NOT LIKE WE GOT ALONG THAT WELL.
HE WAS ALWAYS PICKING FIGHTS WITH ME.
AND I HANDED HIM HIS ASS EVERY TIME.
......
HE KEPT TRYING TO FIGHT YOU, MIKEY-KUN...? WHAT A DUMBASS.
YUP.
THAT'S THE GUY WHO PUNCHED YOU EARLIER.
天上天下
......
I GOT PUNCHED BY TWO GUYS... WHICH ONE WAS IT?
THE FIRST DIVISION CAPTAIN.

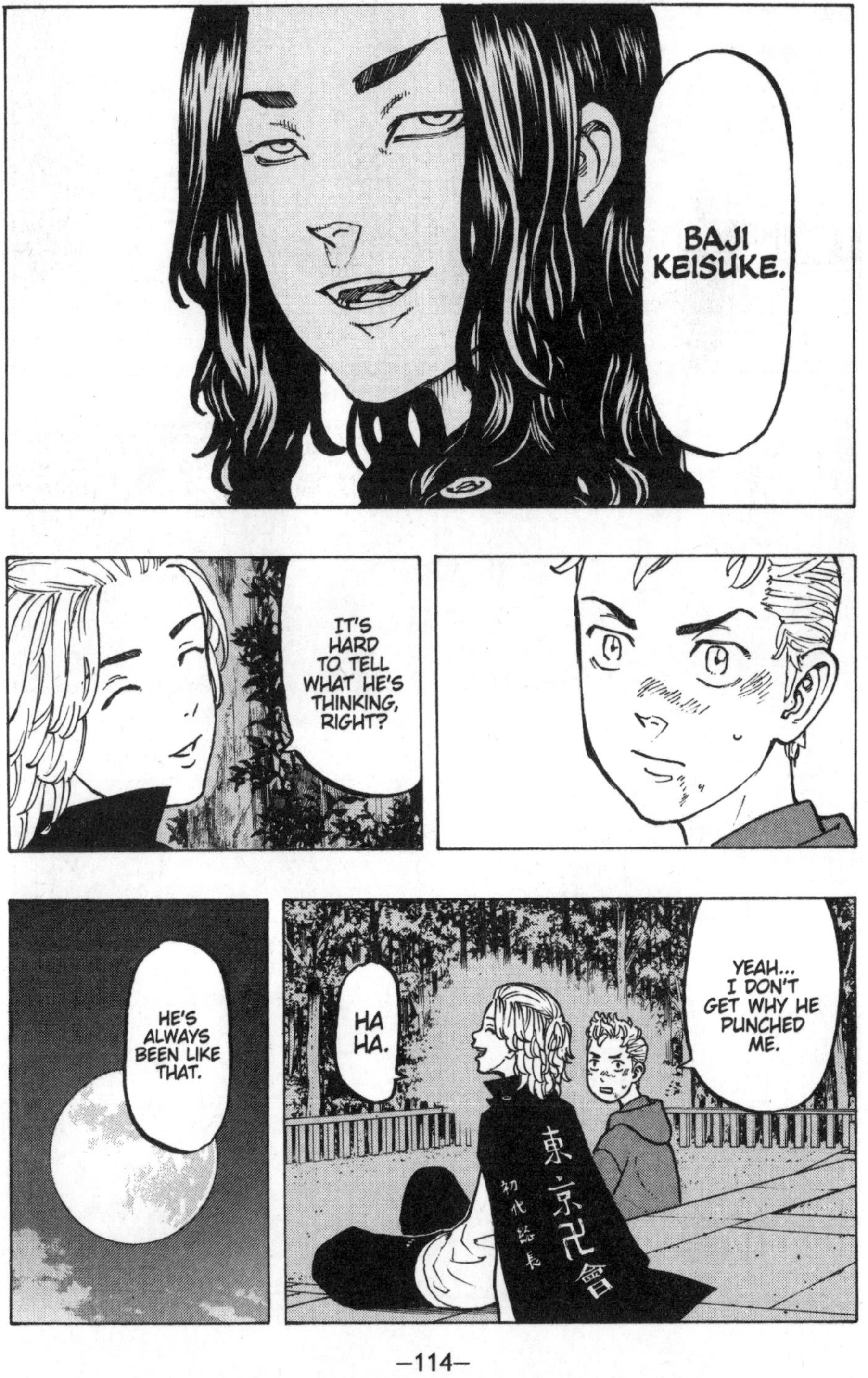
BAJI KEISUKE.
IT'S HARD TO TELL WHAT HE'S THINKING, RIGHT?
YEAH... I DON'T GET WHY HE PUNCHED ME.
HA HA.
東京卍會
初代総長
HE'S ALWAYS BEEN LIKE THAT.

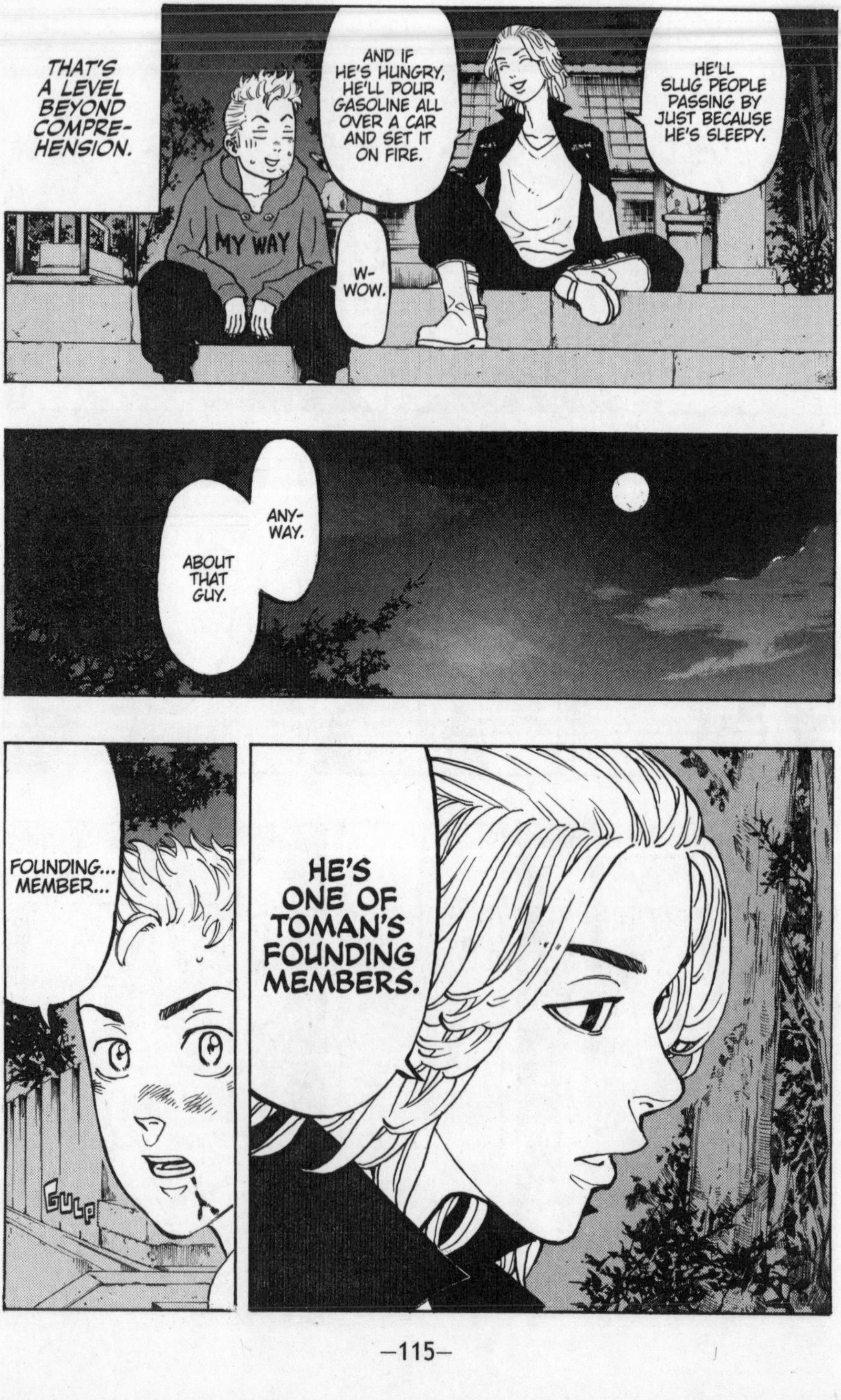
HE'LL SLUG PEOPLE PASSING BY JUST BECAUSE HE'S SLEEPY.
AND IF HE'S HUNGRY, HE'LL POUR GASOLINE ALL OVER A CAR AND SET IT ON FIRE.
W-WOW.
THAT'S A LEVEL BEYOND COMPRE-HENSION.
MY WAY
ANY-WAY.
ABOUT THAT GUY.
HE'S ONE OF TOMAN'S FOUNDING MEMBERS.
FOUNDING... MEMBER...
GULP

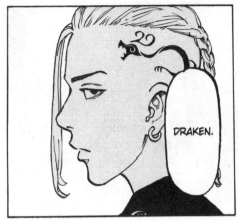

DRAKEN.

I STARTED TOMAN IN MY FIRST YEAR OF JUNIOR HIGH. ALONG WITH...

BAJI.

PAH-CHIN.

MITSUYA.

......

YEAH.

WITH THOSE FIVE...?

......

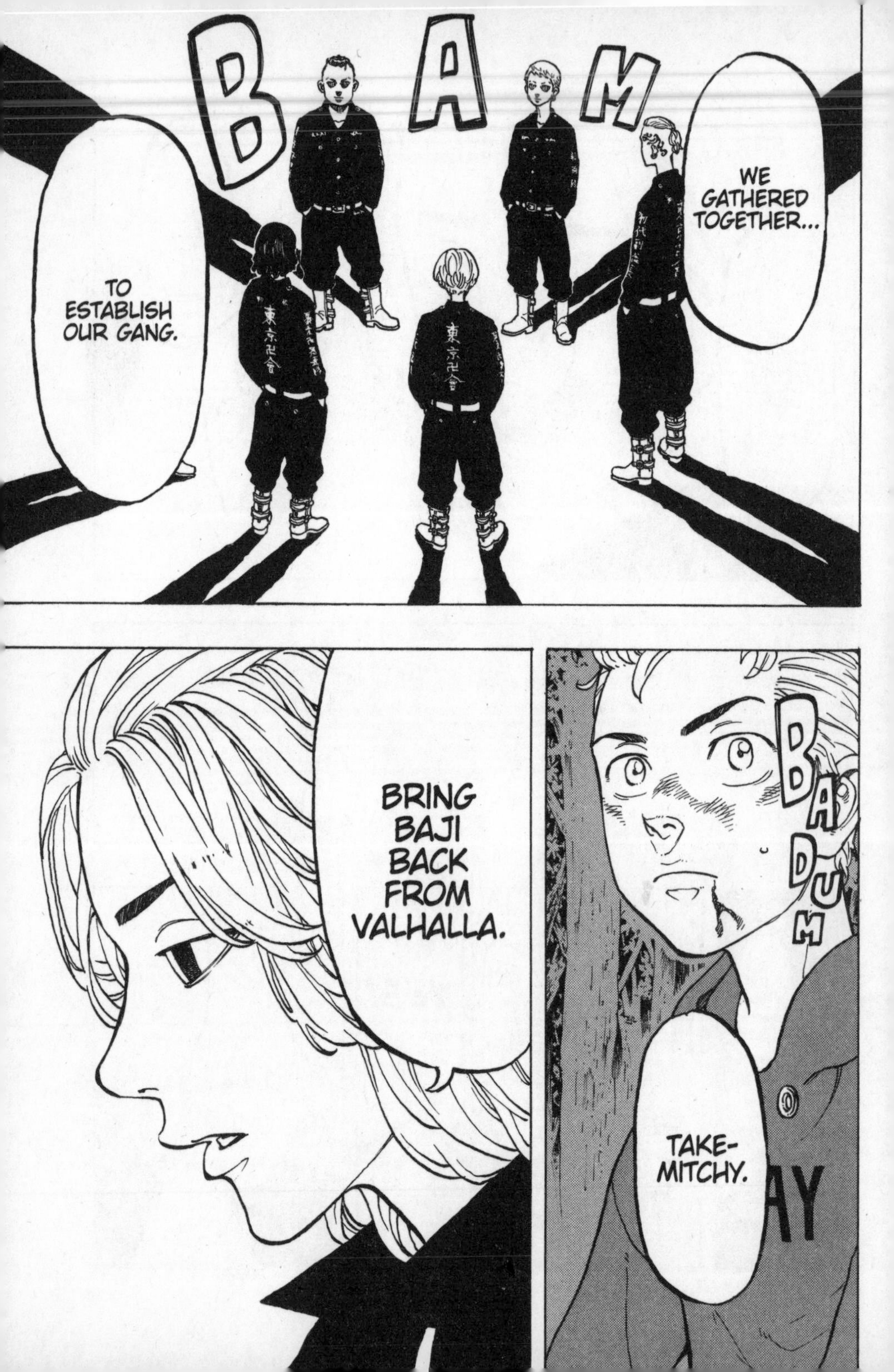

WE GATHERED TOGETHER...
BAM
TO ESTABLISH OUR GANG.
BADUMM
TAKE-MITCHY.
BRING BAJI BACK FROM VALHALLA.

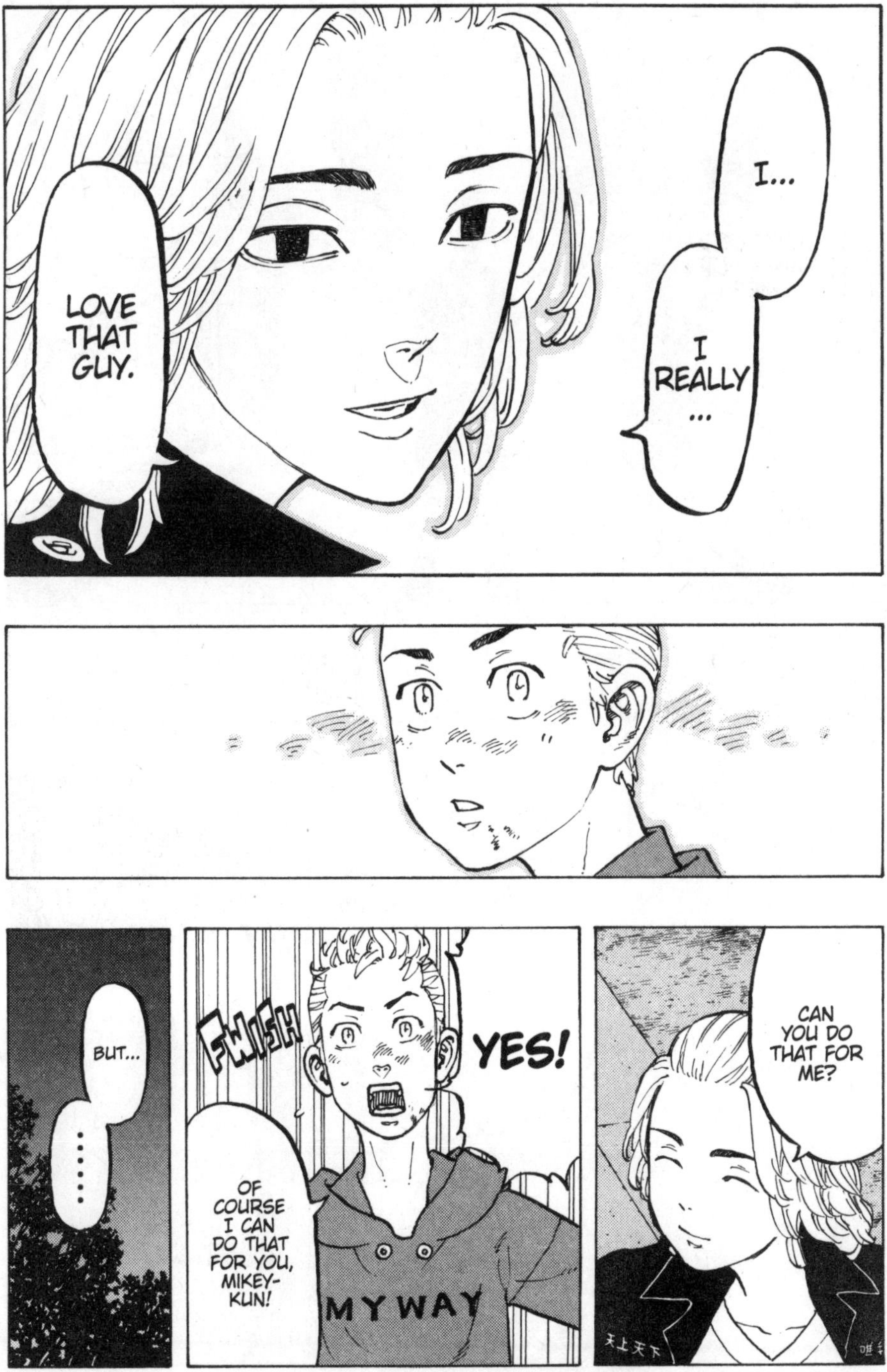
I...
I REALLY ...
LOVE THAT GUY.
CAN YOU DO THAT FOR ME?
YES!
FWISH
OF COURSE I CAN DO THAT FOR YOU, MIKEY-KUN!
MY WAY
BUT...
......

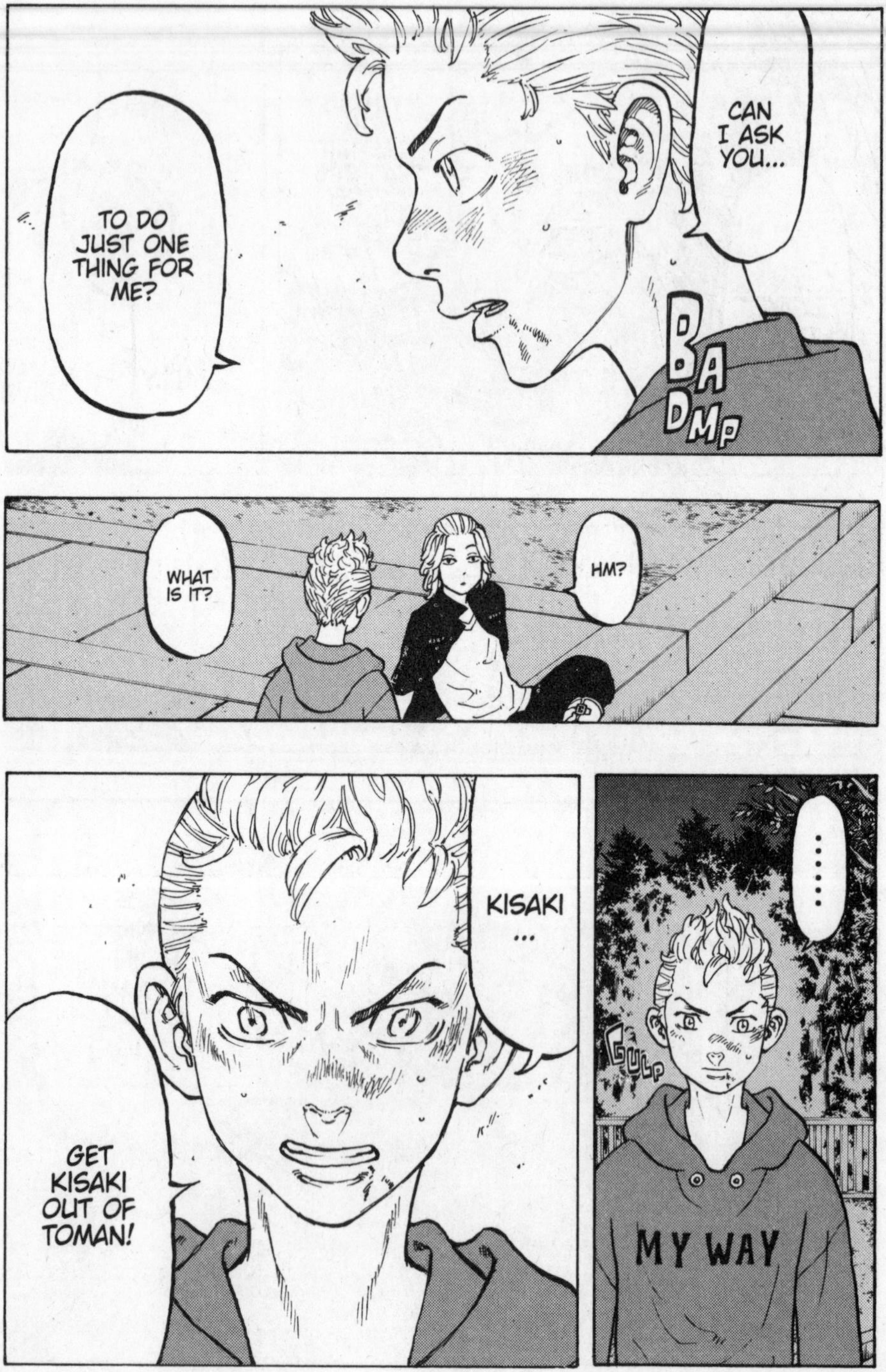
CAN I ASK YOU...
TO DO JUST ONE THING FOR ME?
BADMP
HM?
WHAT IS IT?
......
GULP
MY WAY
KISAKI ...
GET KISAKI OUT OF TOMAN!

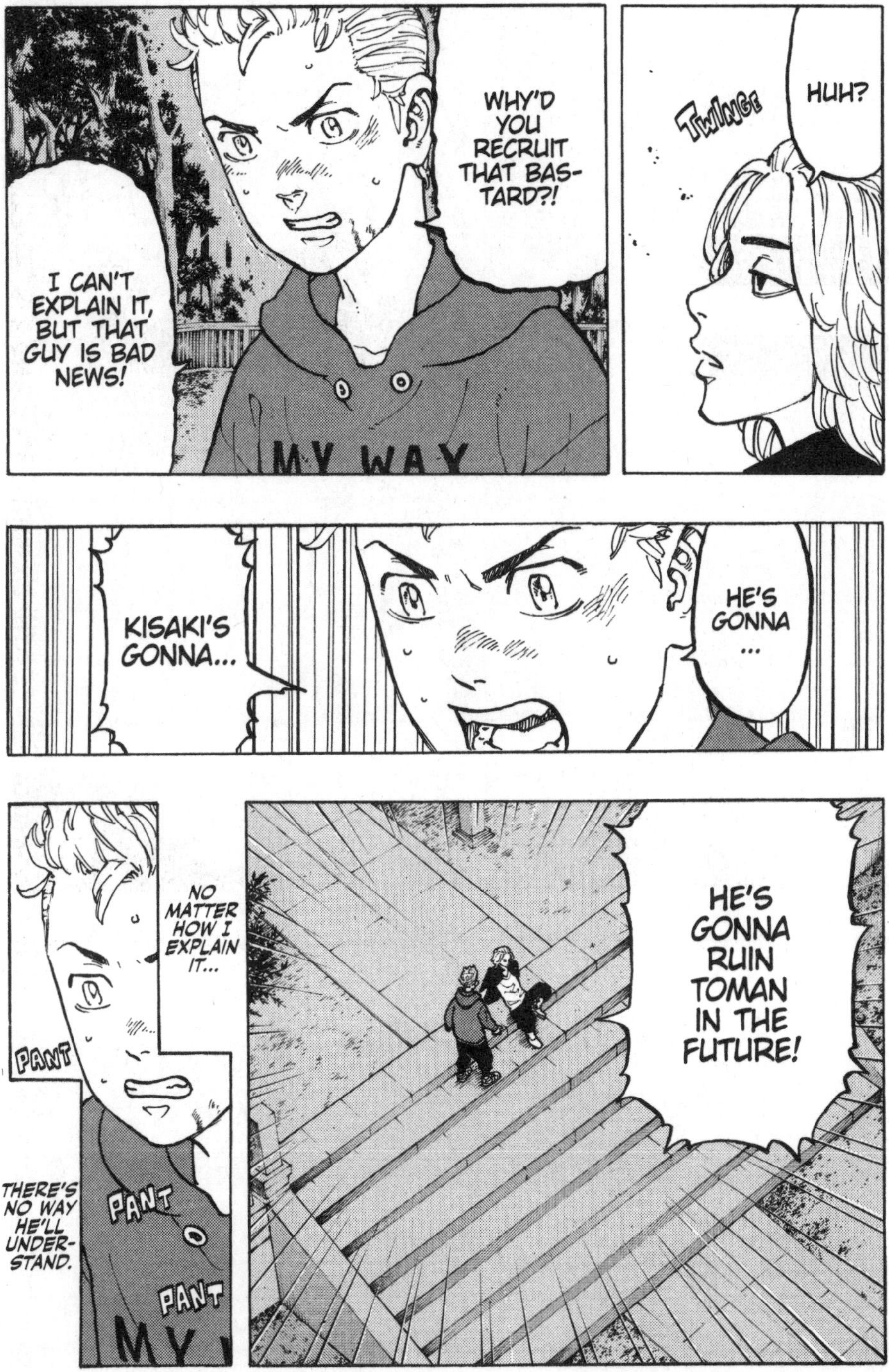
HUH?
TWINGE
WHY'D YOU RECRUIT THAT BAS-TARD?!
I CAN'T EXPLAIN IT, BUT THAT GUY IS BAD NEWS!
MY WAY
HE'S GONNA ...
KISAKI'S GONNA...
HE'S GONNA RUIN TOMAN IN THE FUTURE!
NO MATTER HOW I EXPLAIN IT...
PANT
THERE'S NO WAY HE'LL UNDER-STAND.
PANT
PANT
MY

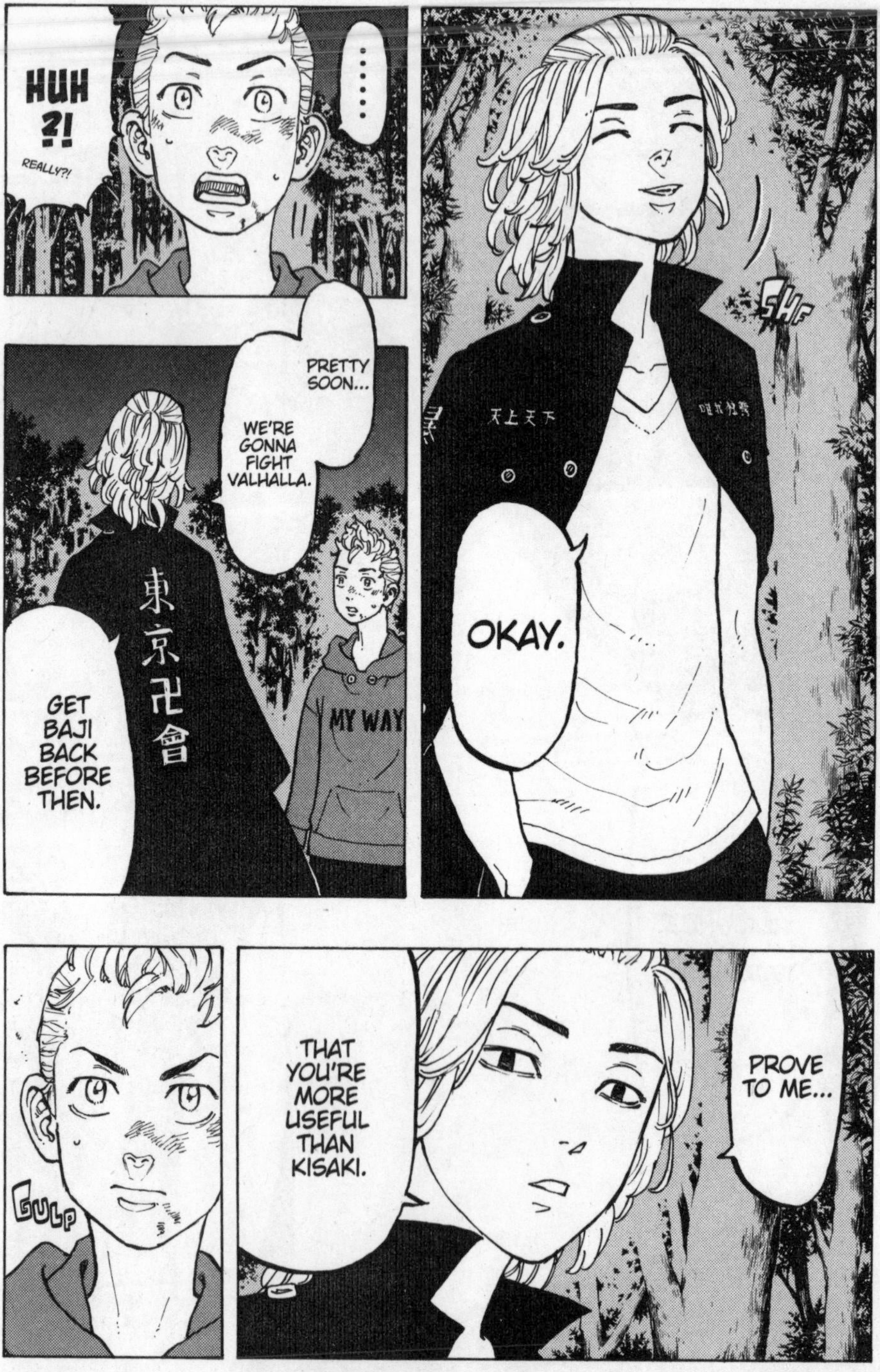
SHF
天上天下
OKAY.
......
HUH ?!
REALLY?!
PRETTY SOON...
WE'RE GONNA FIGHT VALHALLA.
GET BAJI BACK BEFORE THEN.
東京卍會
MY WAY
PROVE TO ME...
THAT YOU'RE MORE USEFUL THAN KISAKI.
GULP

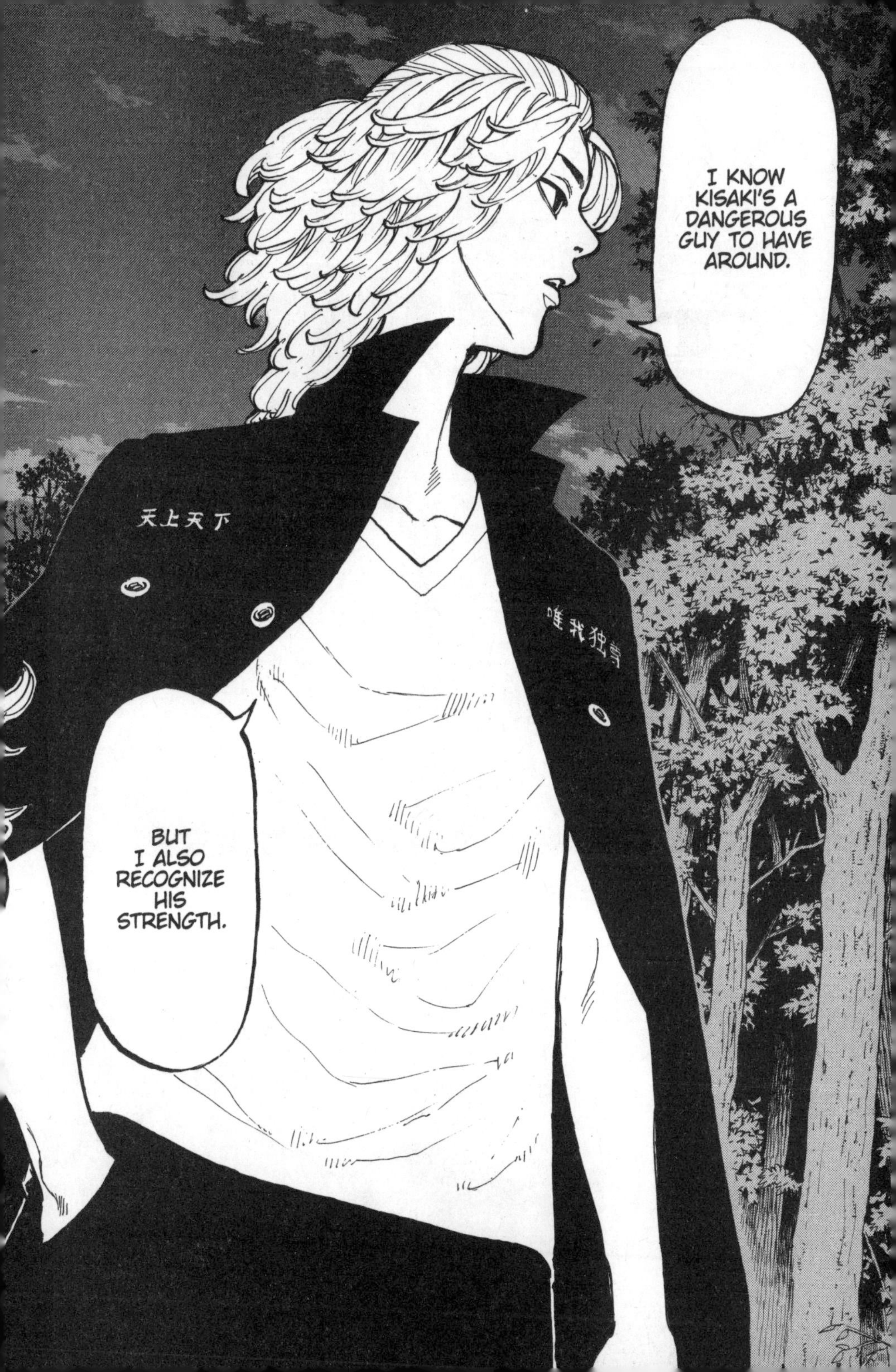
I KNOW KISAKI'S A DANGEROUS GUY TO HAVE AROUND.
唯我独尊
天上天下
BUT I ALSO RECOGNIZE HIS STRENGTH.

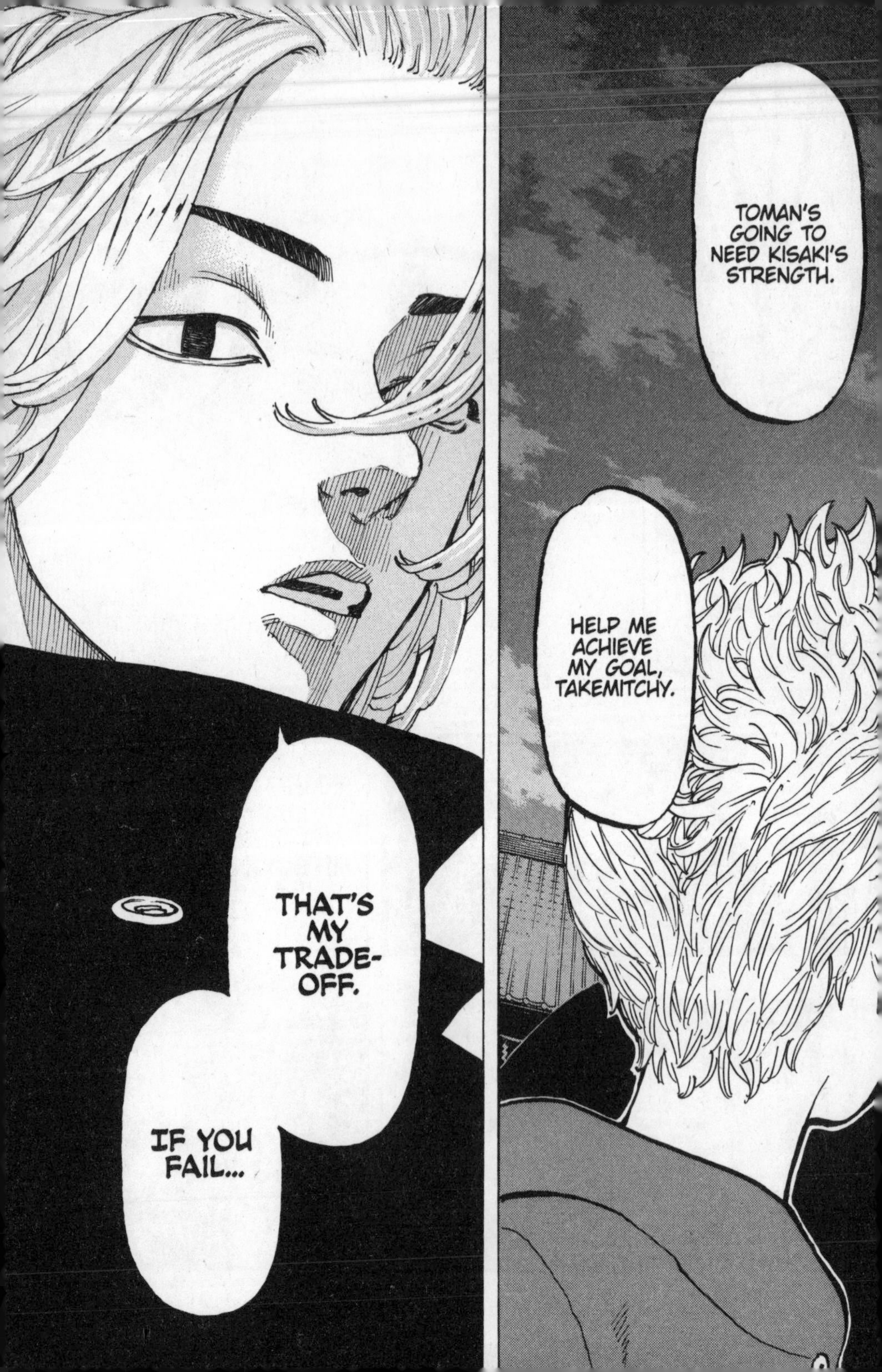
TOMAN'S GOING TO NEED KISAKI'S STRENGTH.
HELP ME ACHIEVE MY GOAL, TAKEMITCHY.
THAT'S MY TRADE-OFF.
IF YOU FAIL...

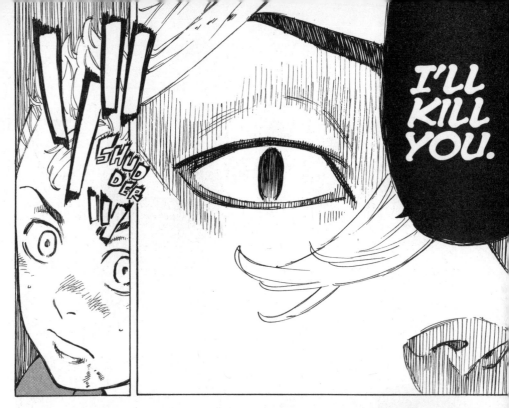

I'LL KILL YOU.

SHUDDER

YOU BEEN EAVES-DROPPING A WHILE, RIGHT?

FLINCH

MITSUYA!!

......

I CAN SEE YOUR SILVER HAIR PEEKING OUT FROM BEHIND THAT TREE!

C'MON OUT.

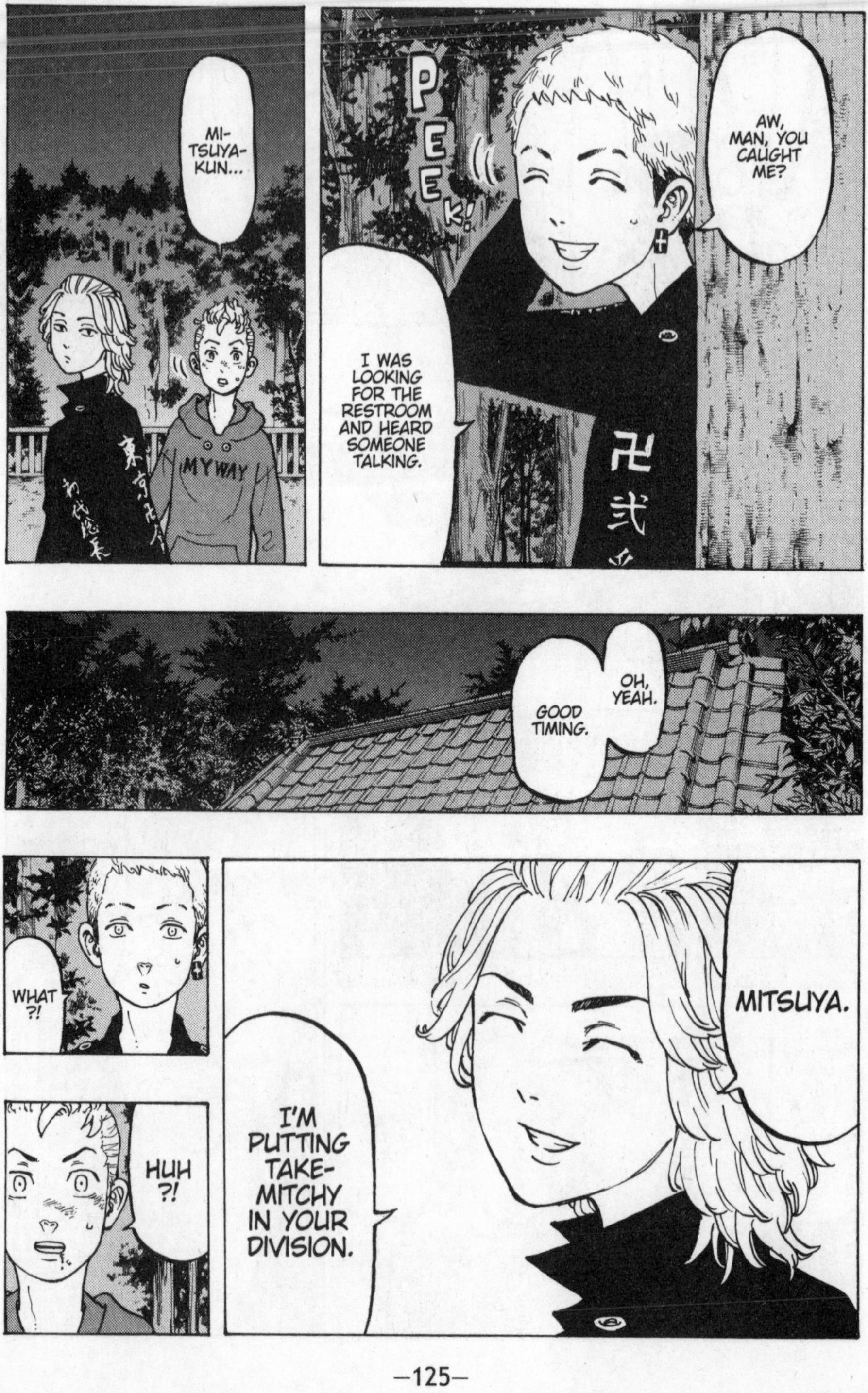
PEEK!
AW, MAN, YOU CAUGHT ME?
I WAS LOOKING FOR THE RESTROOM AND HEARD SOMEONE TALKING.
MI-TSUYA-KUN...
MYWAY
OH, YEAH.
GOOD TIMING.
MITSUYA.
I'M PUTTING TAKE-MITCHY IN YOUR DIVISION.
WHAT ?!
HUH ?!

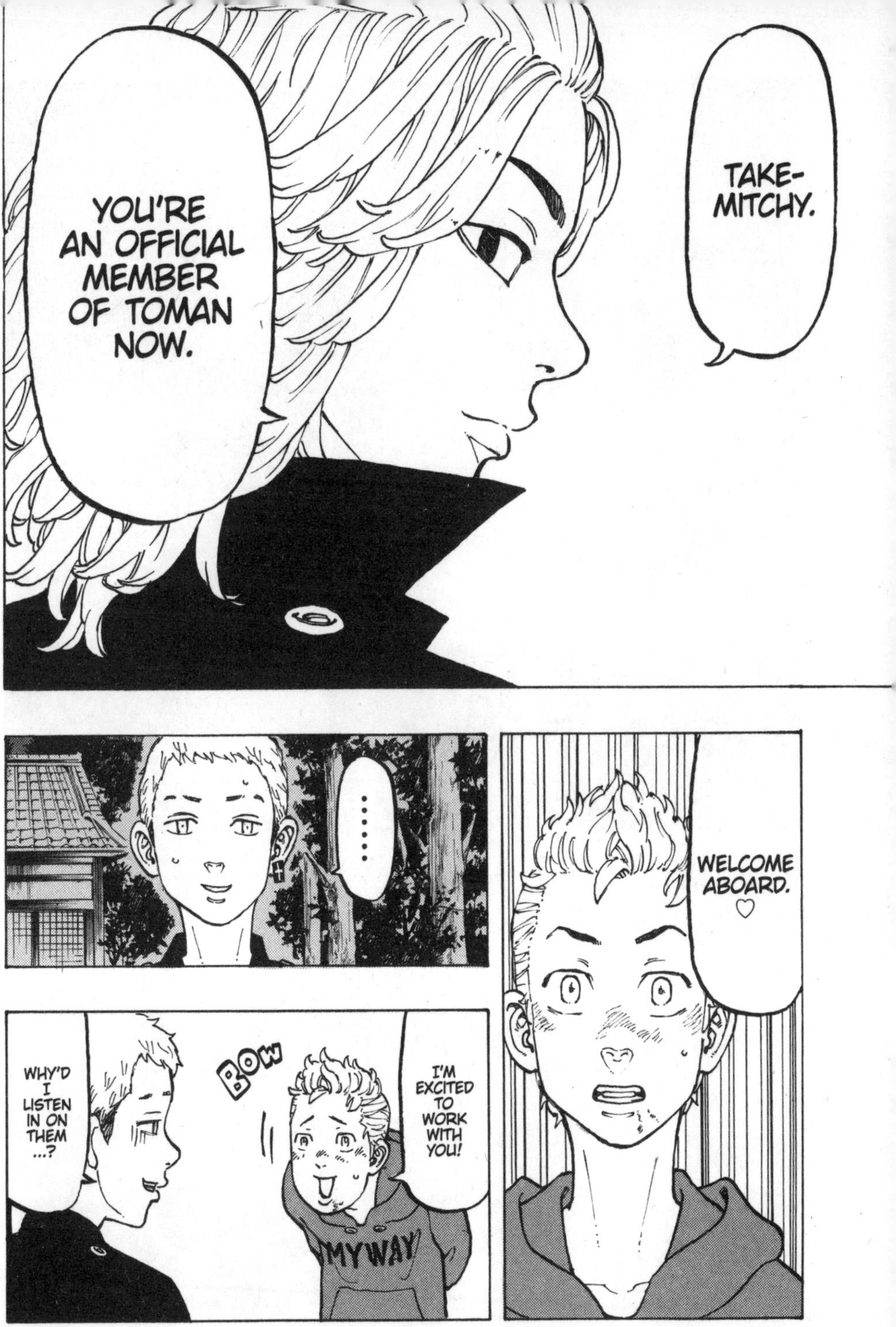
TAKE-MITCHY.
YOU'RE AN OFFICIAL MEMBER OF TOMAN NOW.
WELCOME ABOARD. ♡
......
I'M EXCITED TO WORK WITH YOU!
BOW
MYWAY
WHY'D I LISTEN IN ON THEM ...?

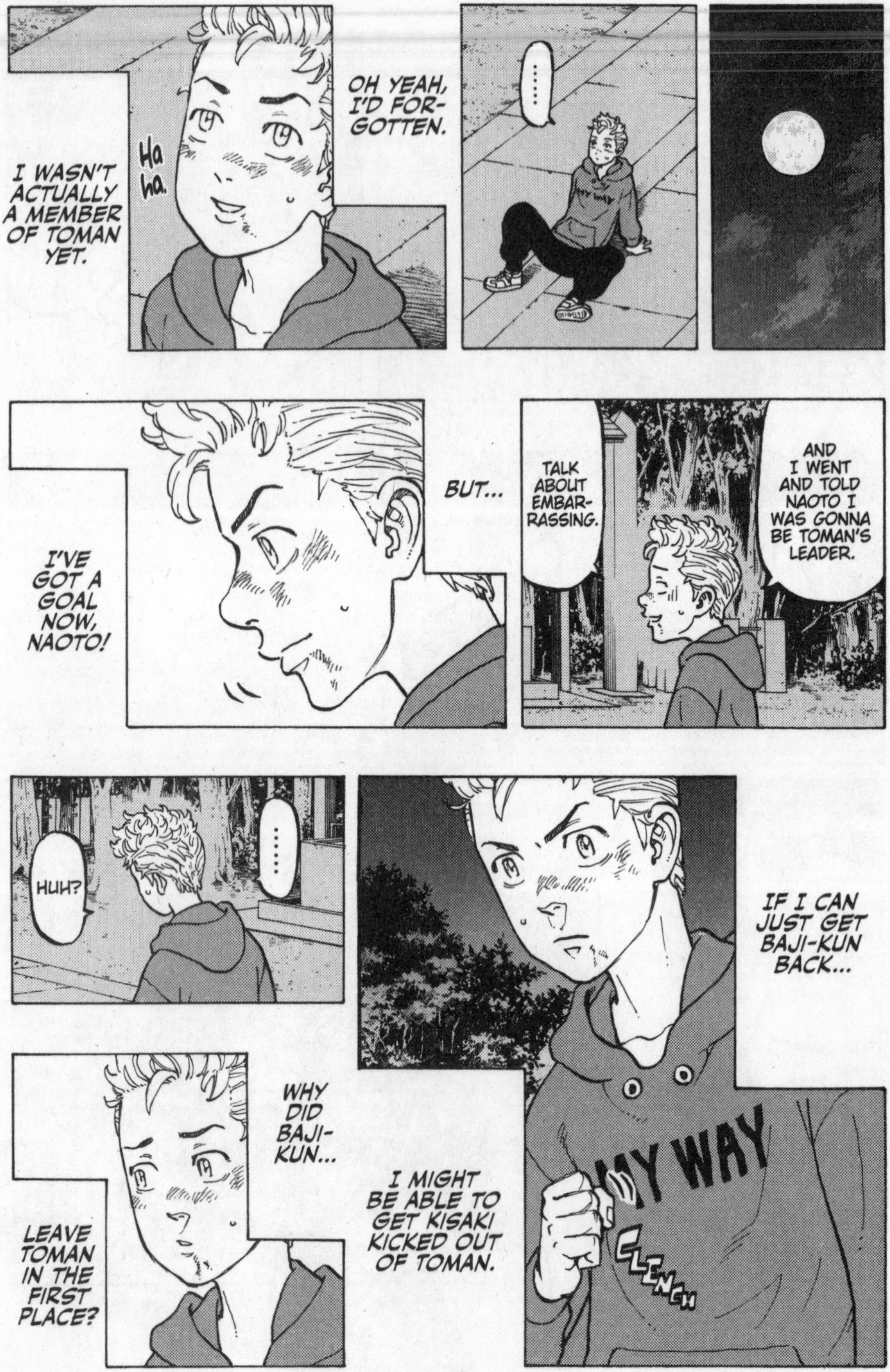
......
OH YEAH, I'D FOR-GOTTEN.
Ha ha.
I WASN'T ACTUALLY A MEMBER OF TOMAN YET.
AND I WENT AND TOLD NAOTO I WAS GONNA BE TOMAN'S LEADER.
TALK ABOUT EMBAR-RASSING.
BUT...
I'VE GOT A GOAL NOW, NAOTO!
IF I CAN JUST GET BAJI-KUN BACK...
I MIGHT BE ABLE TO GET KISAKI KICKED OUT OF TOMAN.
MY WAY
CLENCH
......
HUH?
WHY DID BAJI-KUN...
LEAVE TOMAN IN THE FIRST PLACE?

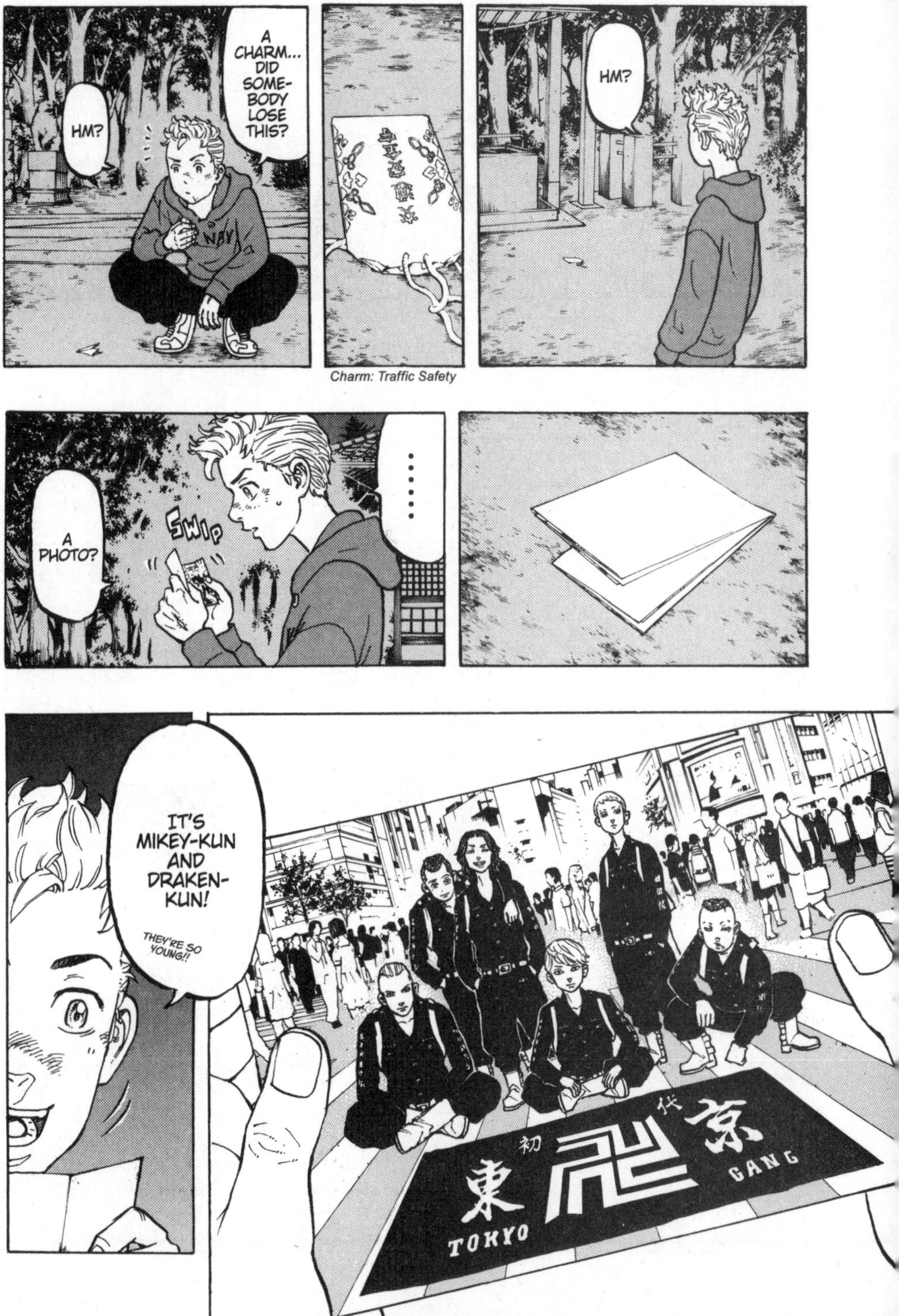
HM?
A CHARM... DID SOMEBODY LOSE THIS?
HM?
......
SWIP
A PHOTO?
初代
東京卍
TOKYO
GANG
IT'S MIKEY-KUN AND DRAKEN-KUN!
THEY'RE SO YOUNG!!

Charm: Traffic Safety

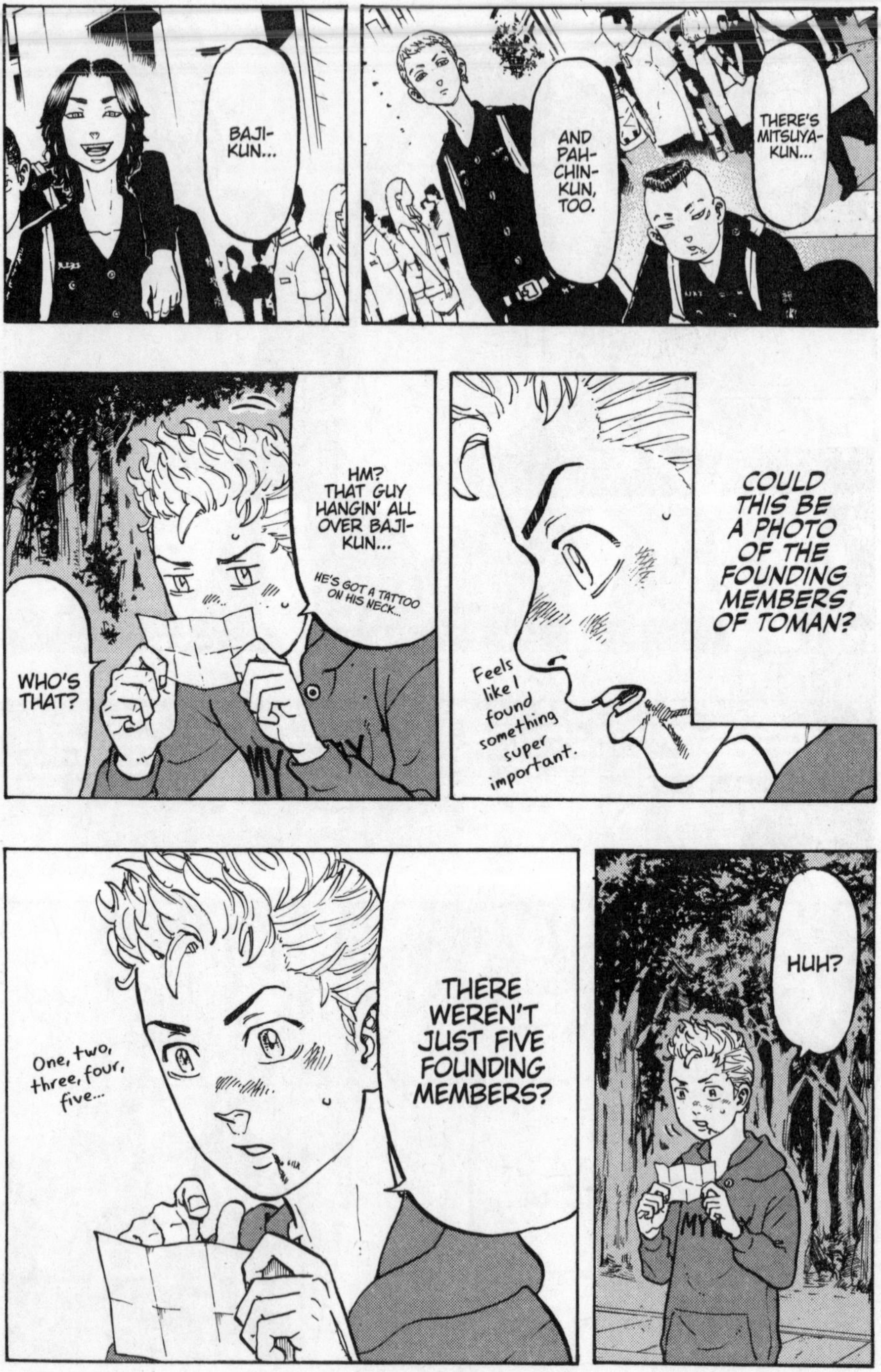
THERE'S MITSUYA-KUN...
AND PAH-CHIN-KUN, TOO.
BAJI-KUN...
COULD THIS BE A PHOTO OF THE FOUNDING MEMBERS OF TOMAN?
Feels like I found something super important.
HM? THAT GUY HANGIN' ALL OVER BAJI-KUN...
HE'S GOT A TATTOO ON HIS NECK...
WHO'S THAT?
HUH?
THERE WEREN'T JUST FIVE FOUNDING MEMBERS?
One, two, three, four, five...

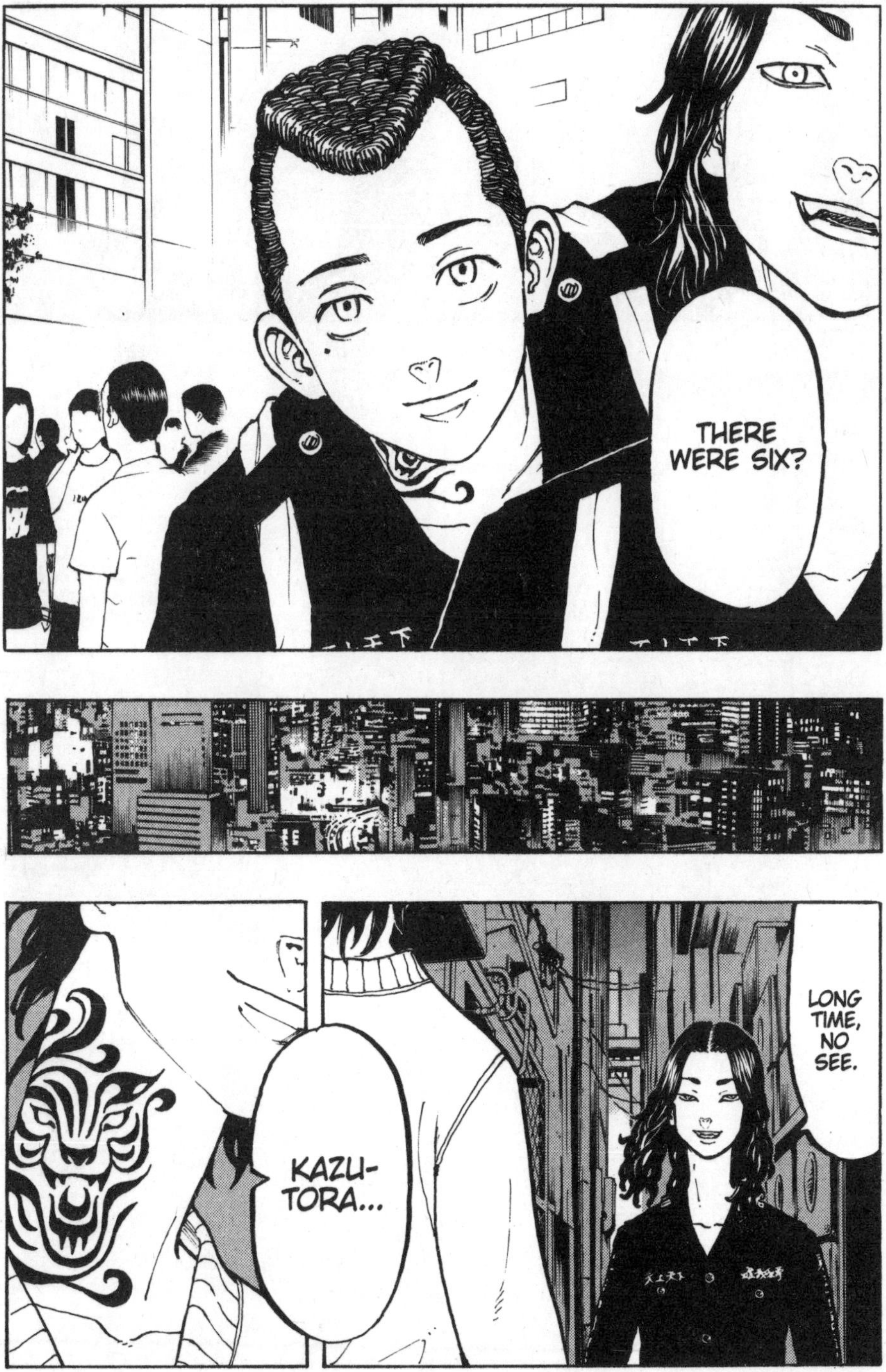
THERE WERE SIX?
LONG TIME, NO SEE.
KAZU-TORA...

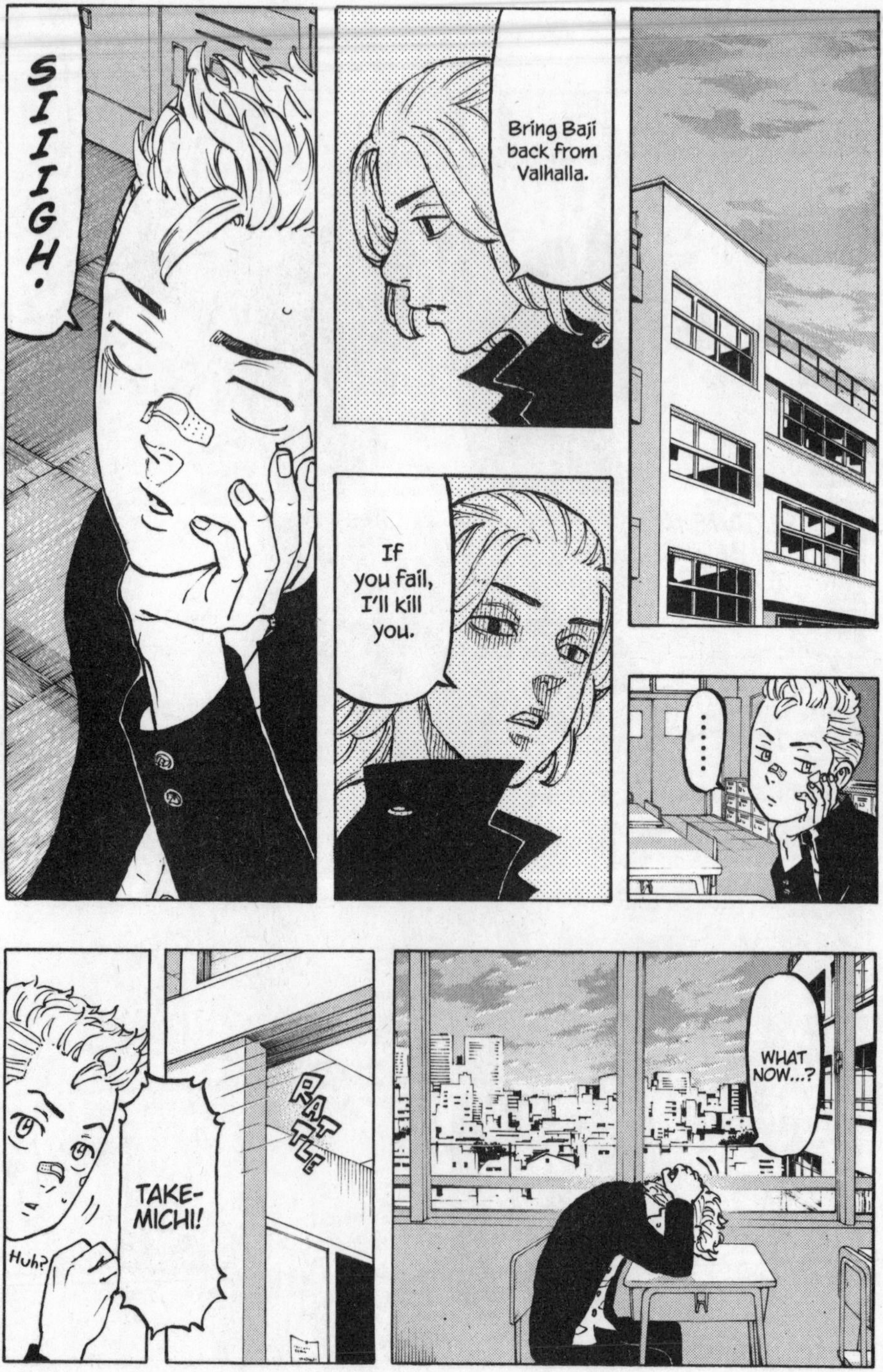

......
Bring Baji back from Valhalla.
If you fail, I'll kill you.
SIIIGH!
WHAT NOW...?
RATTLE
TAKE-MICHI!
Huh?

CHAPTER 40: NO PAIN, NO GAIN

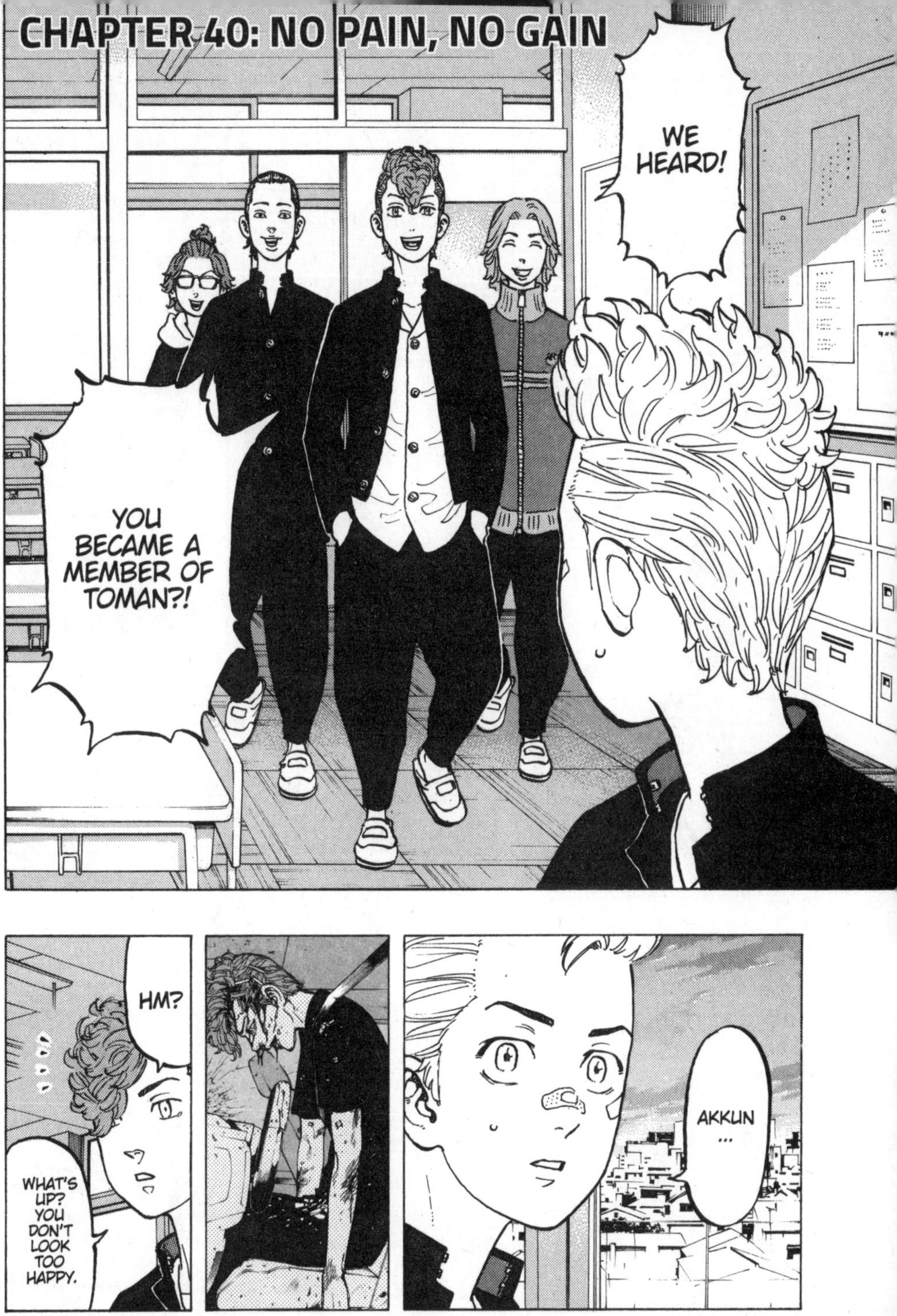

WE HEARD!
YOU BECAME A MEMBER OF TOMAN?!
AKKUN ...
HM?
WHAT'S UP? YOU DON'T LOOK TOO HAPPY.

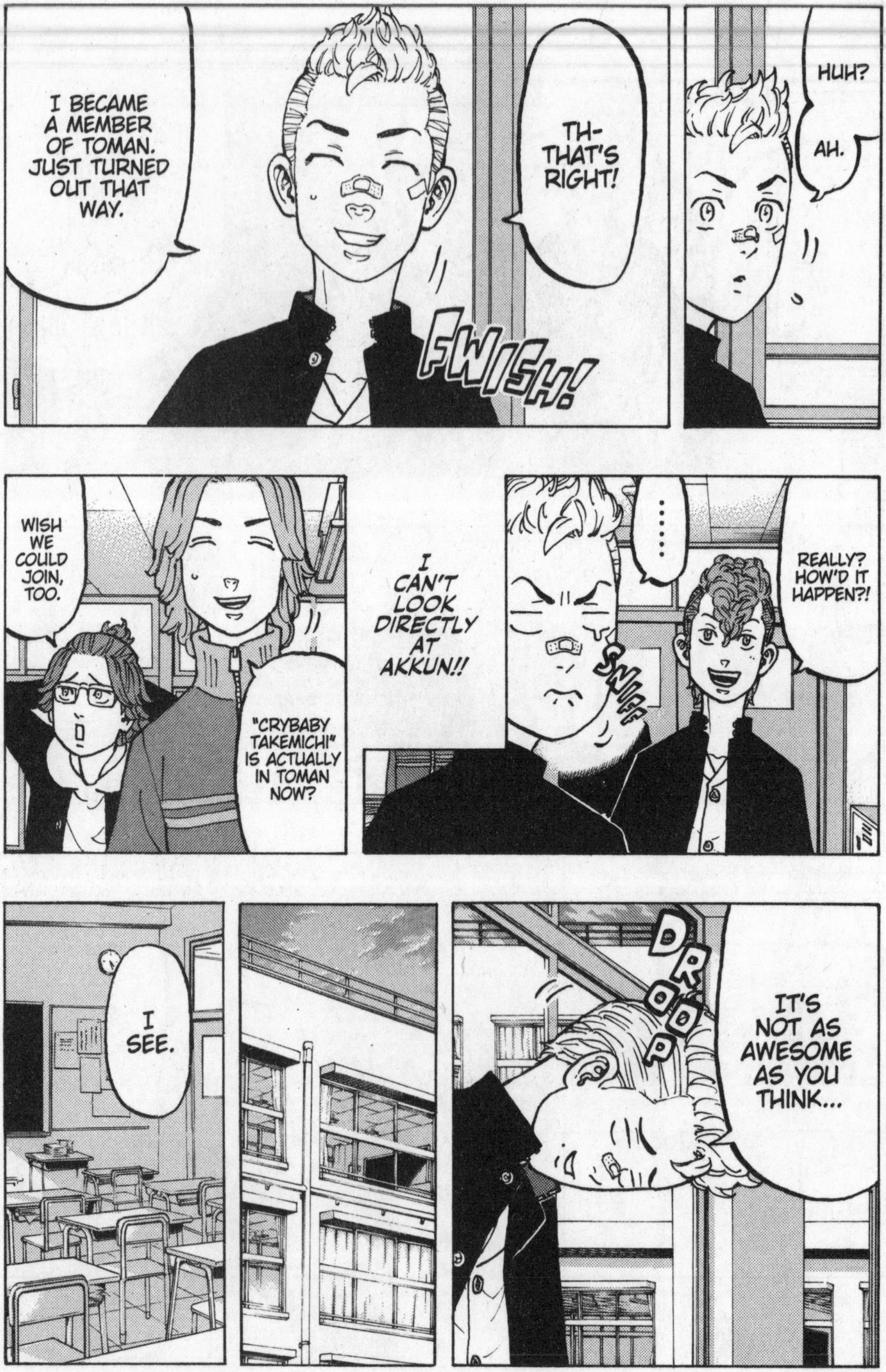
HUH?
AH.
TH-THAT'S RIGHT!
I BECAME A MEMBER OF TOMAN. JUST TURNED OUT THAT WAY.
FWISH!
......
REALLY? HOW'D IT HAPPEN?!
I CAN'T LOOK DIRECTLY AT AKKUN!!
SNIFF
"CRYBABY TAKEMICHI" IS ACTUALLY IN TOMAN NOW?
WISH WE COULD JOIN, TOO.
DROOP
IT'S NOT AS AWESOME AS YOU THINK...
I SEE.

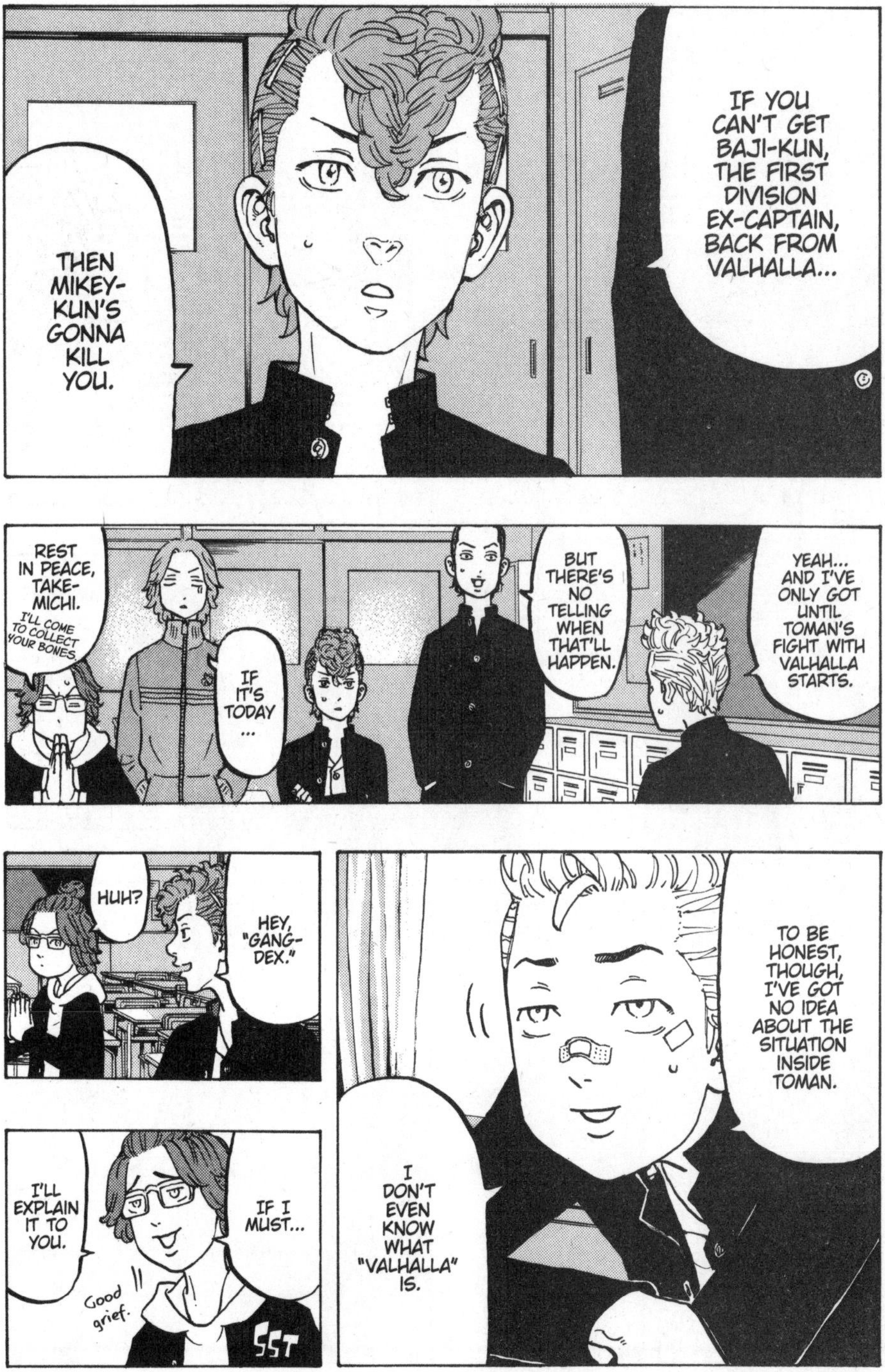

IF YOU CAN'T GET BAJI-KUN, THE FIRST DIVISION EX-CAPTAIN, BACK FROM VALHALLA...
THEN MIKEY-KUN'S GONNA KILL YOU.
YEAH... AND I'VE ONLY GOT UNTIL TOMAN'S FIGHT WITH VALHALLA STARTS.
BUT THERE'S NO TELLING WHEN THAT'LL HAPPEN.
IF IT'S TODAY ...
REST IN PEACE, TAKE-MICHI.
I'LL COME TO COLLECT YOUR BONES.
TO BE HONEST, THOUGH, I'VE GOT NO IDEA ABOUT THE SITUATION INSIDE TOMAN.
I DON'T EVEN KNOW WHAT "VALHALLA" IS.
HEY, "GANG-DEX."
HUH?
IF I MUST...
I'LL EXPLAIN IT TO YOU.
Good grief.
SST

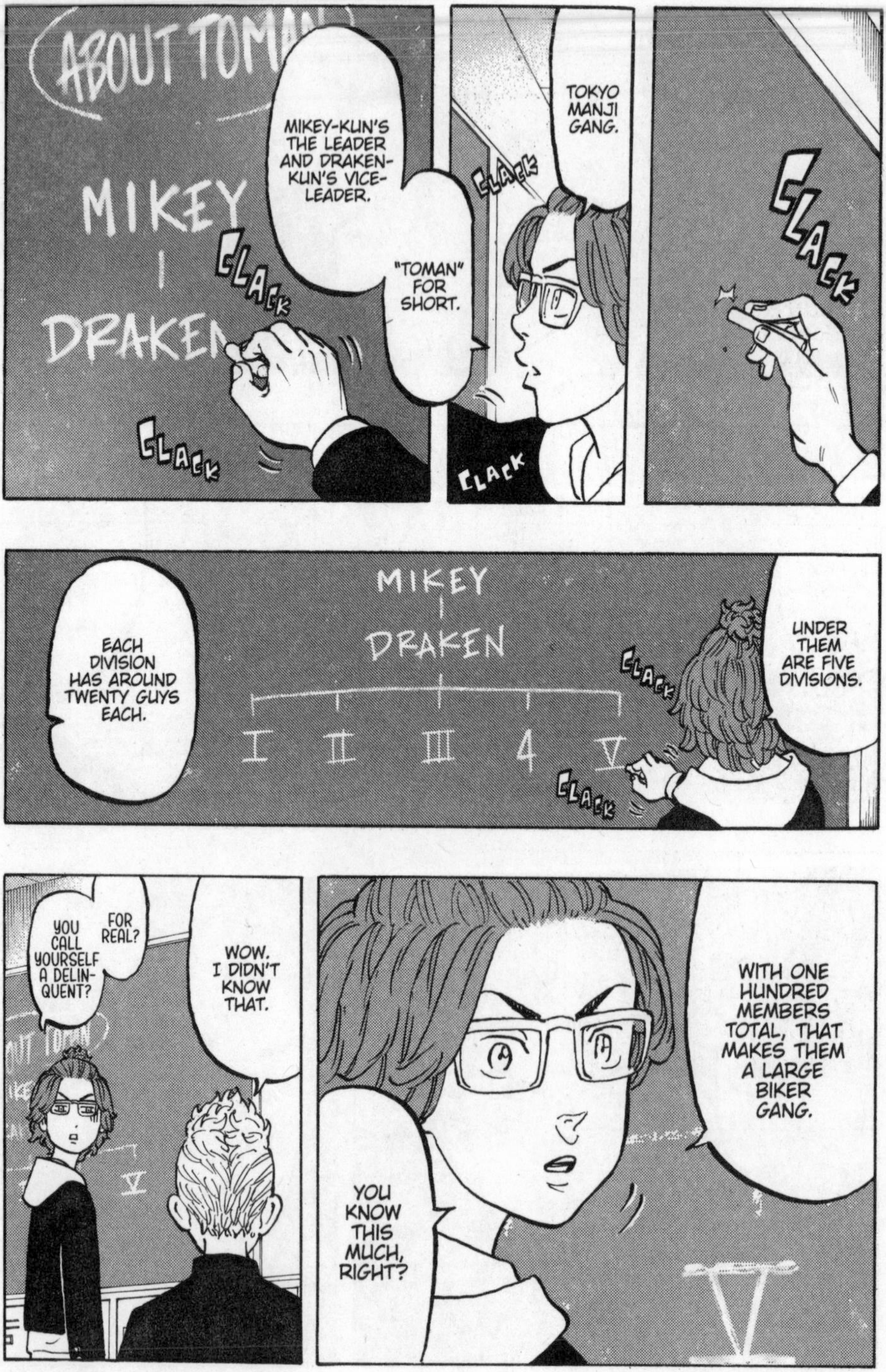
CLACK
TOKYO MANJI GANG.
CLACK
CLACK
"TOMAN" FOR SHORT.
ABOUT TOMA
MIKEY-KUN'S THE LEADER AND DRAKEN-KUN'S VICE-LEADER.
MIKEY
DRAKEN
CLACK
CLACK
UNDER THEM ARE FIVE DIVISIONS.
CLACK
CLACK
MIKEY
DRAKEN
I II III 4 V
EACH DIVISION HAS AROUND TWENTY GUYS EACH.
WITH ONE HUNDRED MEMBERS TOTAL, THAT MAKES THEM A LARGE BIKER GANG.
YOU KNOW THIS MUCH, RIGHT?
WOW. I DIDN'T KNOW THAT.
FOR REAL?
YOU CALL YOURSELF A DELINQUENT?

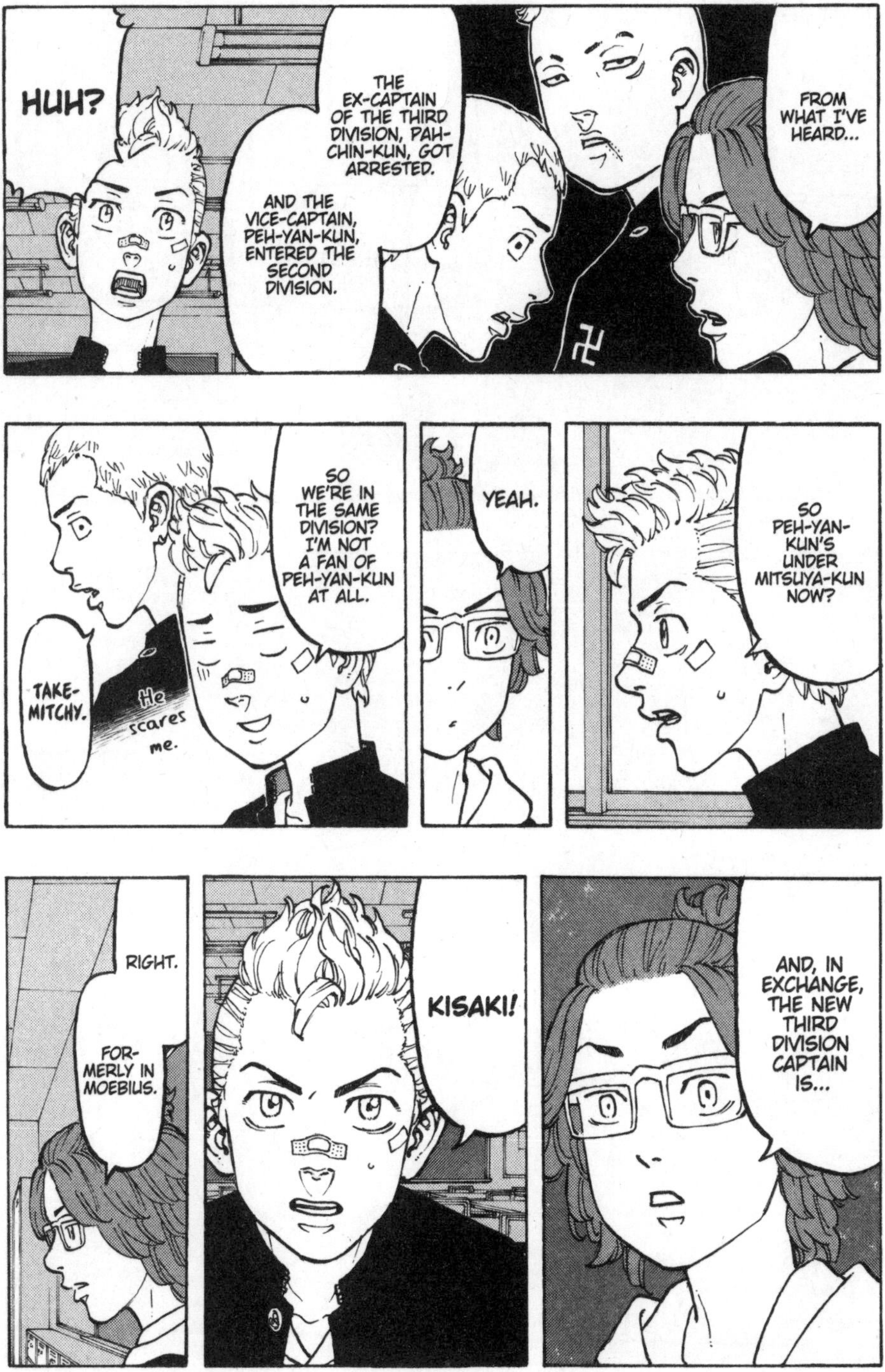
FROM WHAT I'VE HEARD...
THE EX-CAPTAIN OF THE THIRD DIVISION, PAH-CHIN-KUN, GOT ARRESTED.
AND THE VICE-CAPTAIN, PEH-YAN-KUN, ENTERED THE SECOND DIVISION.
HUH?
SO PEH-YAN-KUN'S UNDER MITSUYA-KUN NOW?
YEAH.
SO WE'RE IN THE SAME DIVISION? I'M NOT A FAN OF PEH-YAN-KUN AT ALL.
TAKE-MITCHY.
He scares me.
AND, IN EXCHANGE, THE NEW THIRD DIVISION CAPTAIN IS...
KISAKI!
RIGHT.
FOR-MERLY IN MOEBIUS.

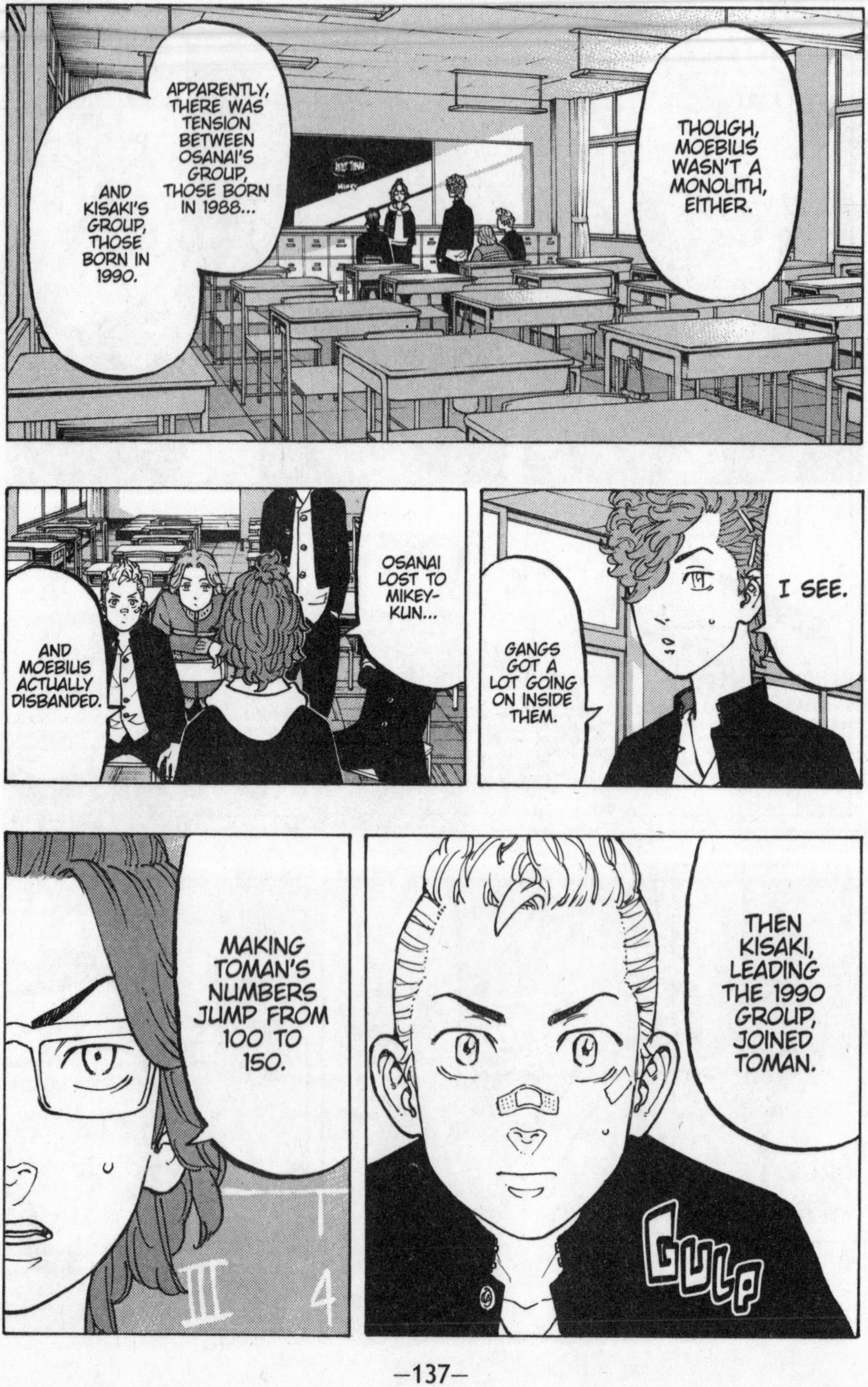
THOUGH, MOEBIUS WASN'T A MONOLITH, EITHER.
APPARENTLY, THERE WAS TENSION BETWEEN OSANAI'S GROUP, THOSE BORN IN 1988...
AND KISAKI'S GROUP, THOSE BORN IN 1990.
I SEE.
GANGS GOT A LOT GOING ON INSIDE THEM.
OSANAI LOST TO MIKEY-KUN...
AND MOEBIUS ACTUALLY DISBANDED.
THEN KISAKI, LEADING THE 1990 GROUP, JOINED TOMAN.
GULP
MAKING TOMAN'S NUMBERS JUMP FROM 100 TO 150.

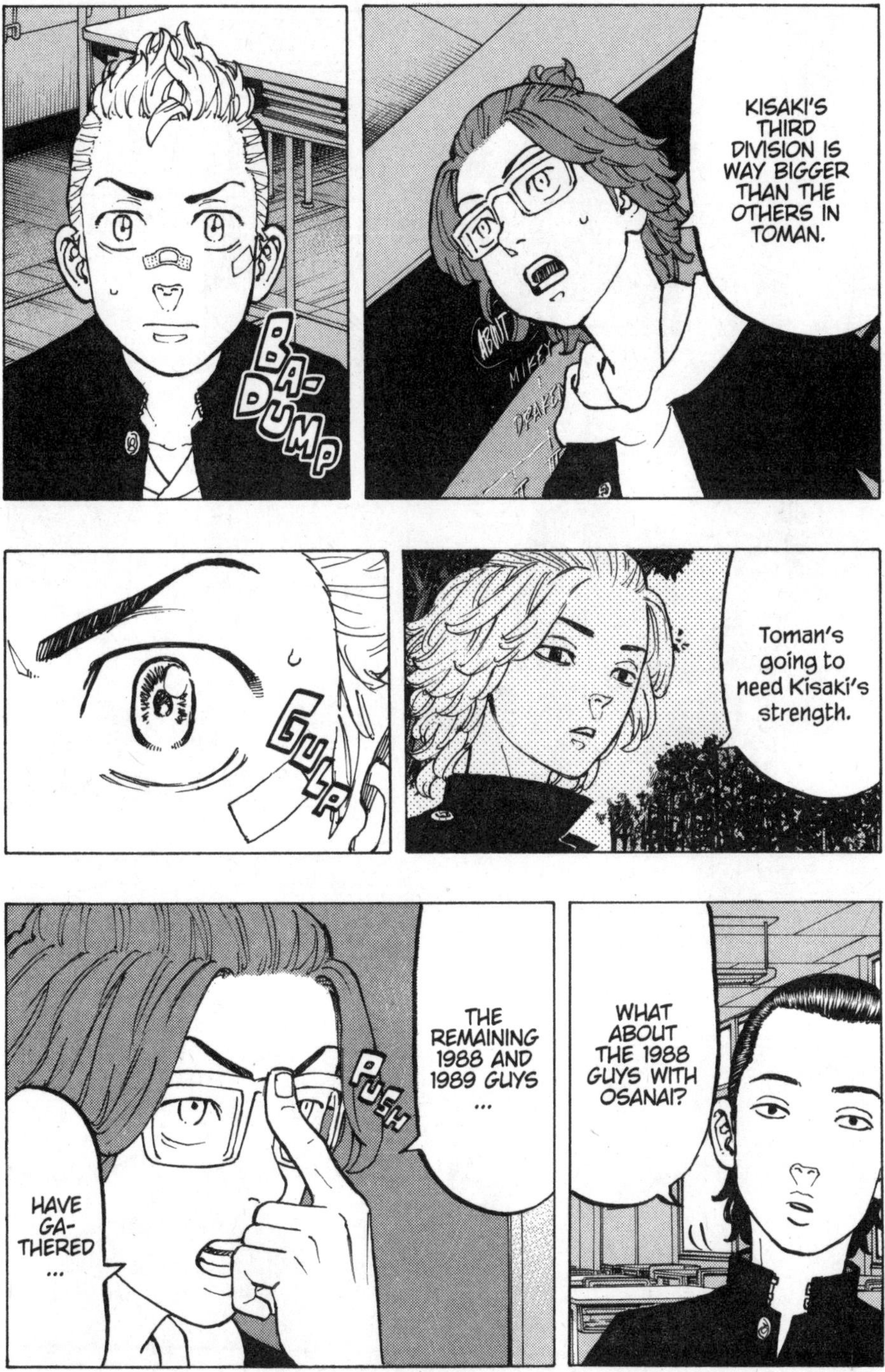
KISAKI'S THIRD DIVISION IS WAY BIGGER THAN THE OTHERS IN TOMAN.
BA-DUMP
Toman's going to need Kisaki's strength.
GULP
WHAT ABOUT THE 1988 GUYS WITH OSANAI?
THE REMAINING 1988 AND 1989 GUYS ...
PUSH
HAVE GA-THERED ...

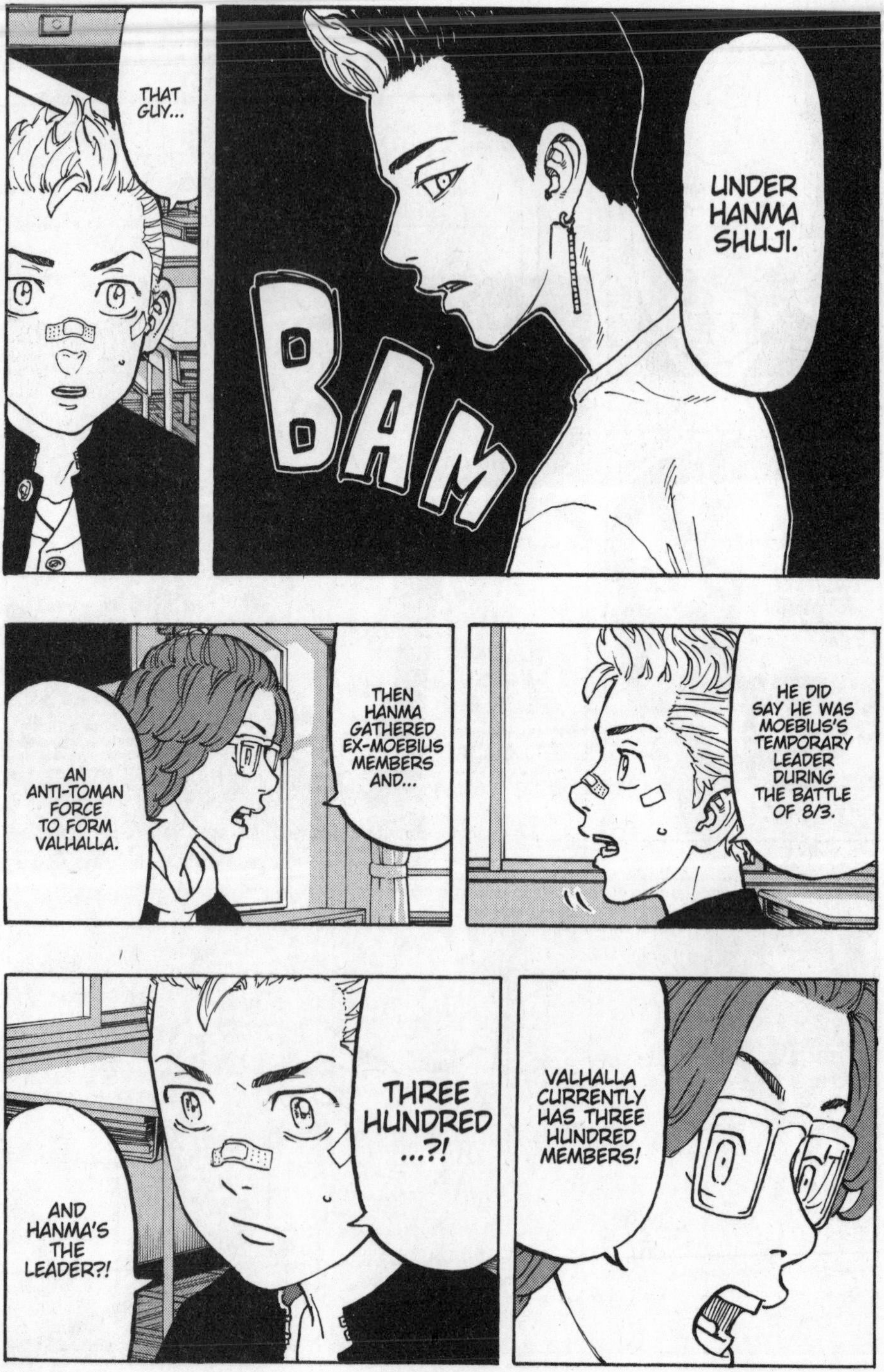
UNDER HANMA SHUJI.
BAM
THAT GUY...
HE DID SAY HE WAS MOEBIUS'S TEMPORARY LEADER DURING THE BATTLE OF 8/3.
THEN HANMA GATHERED EX-MOEBIUS MEMBERS AND...
AN ANTI-TOMAN FORCE TO FORM VALHALLA.
VALHALLA CURRENTLY HAS THREE HUNDRED MEMBERS!
THREE HUNDRED ...?!
AND HANMA'S THE LEADER?!

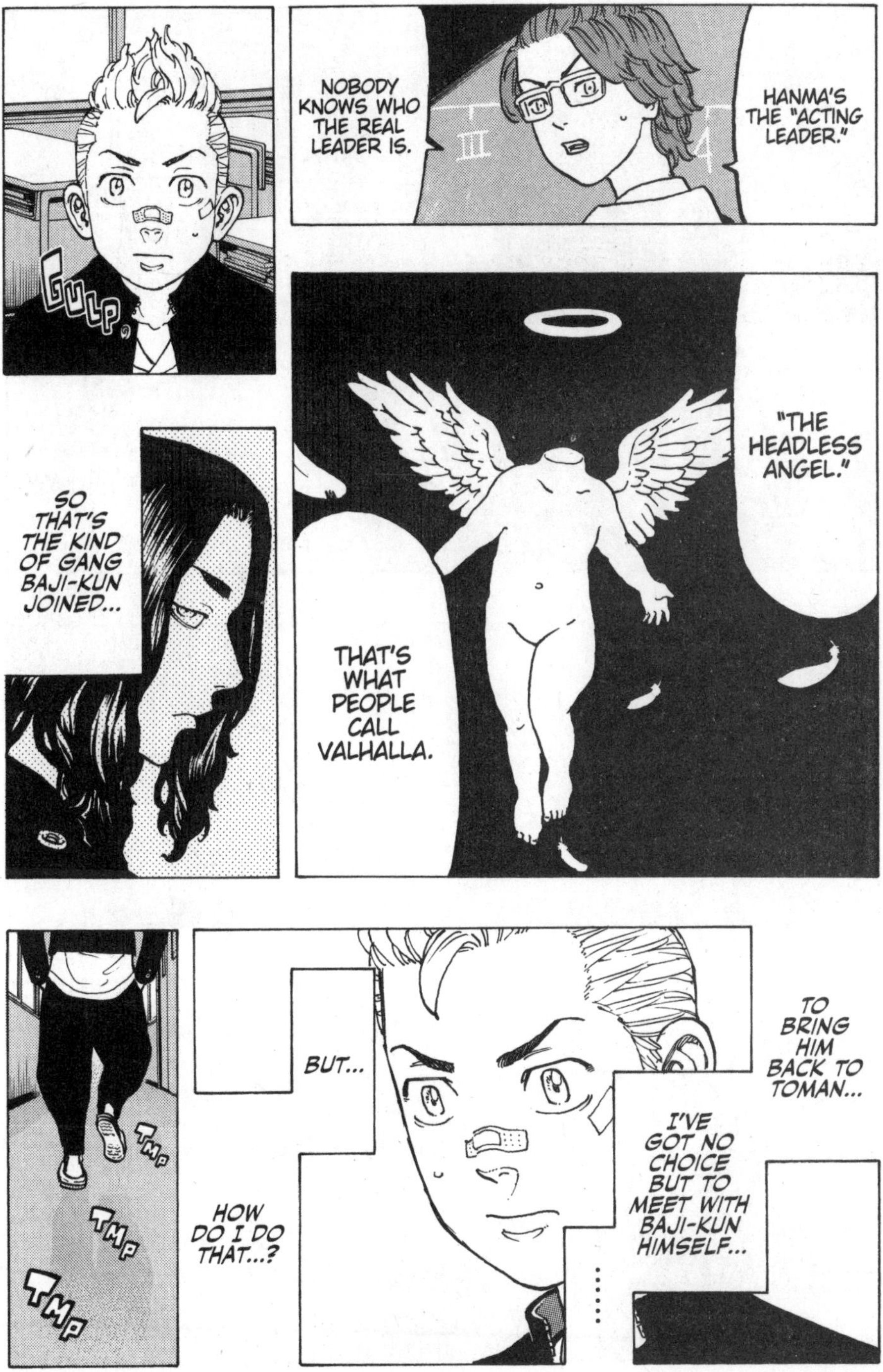
HANMA'S THE "ACTING LEADER."
NOBODY KNOWS WHO THE REAL LEADER IS.
GULP
"THE HEADLESS ANGEL."
THAT'S WHAT PEOPLE CALL VALHALLA.
SO THAT'S THE KIND OF GANG BAJI-KUN JOINED...
TO BRING HIM BACK TO TOMAN...
I'VE GOT NO CHOICE BUT TO MEET WITH BAJI-KUN HIMSELF...
BUT...
HOW DO I DO THAT...?
......
TMP
TMP
TMP

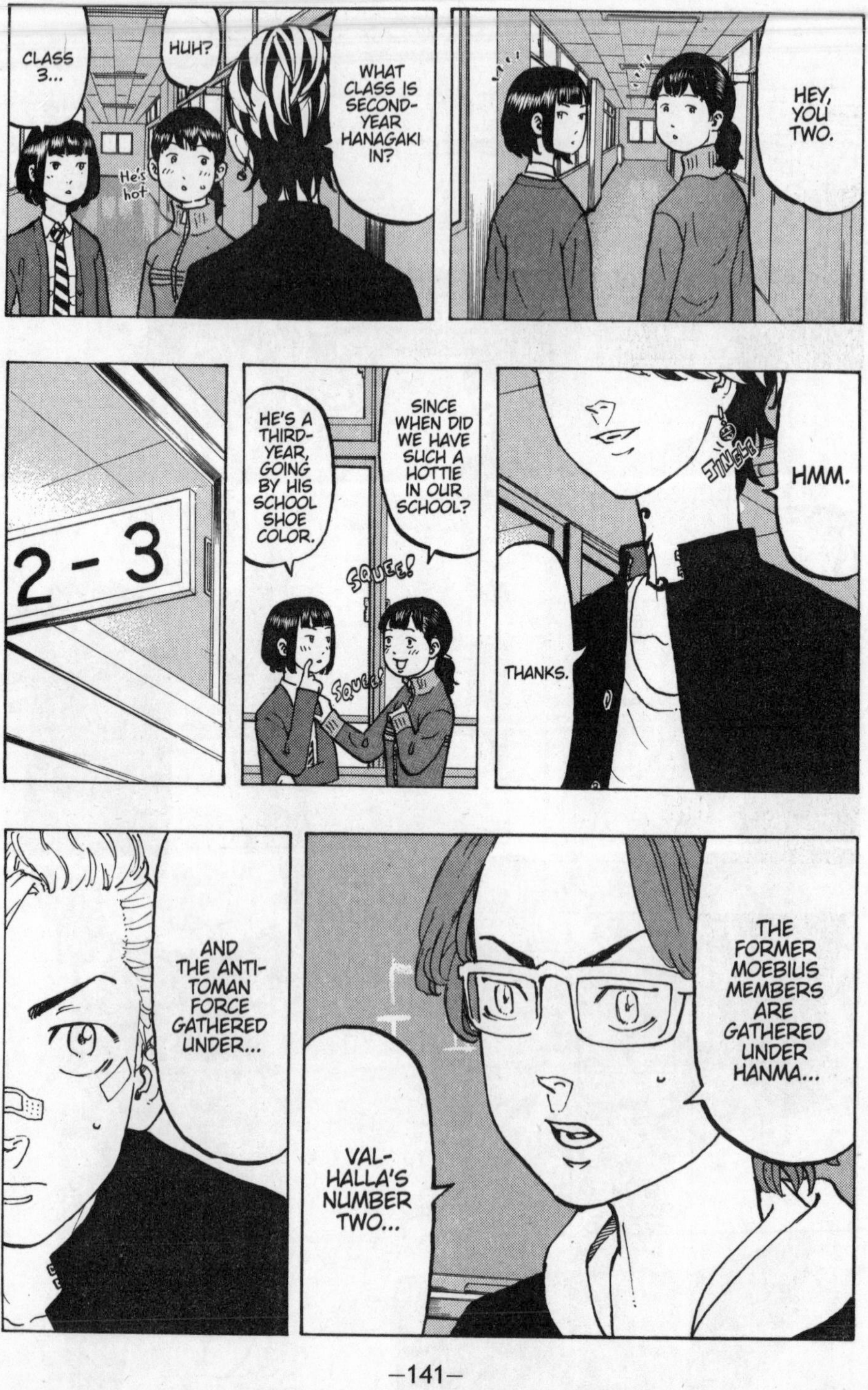
HEY, YOU TWO.
WHAT CLASS IS SECOND-YEAR HANAGAKI IN?
HUH?
CLASS 3...
He's hot
HMM.
JINGLE
THANKS.
SINCE WHEN DID WE HAVE SUCH A HOTTIE IN OUR SCHOOL?
HE'S A THIRD-YEAR, GOING BY HIS SCHOOL SHOE COLOR.
SQUEE!
SQUEE!
2 - 3
THE FORMER MOEBIUS MEMBERS ARE GATHERED UNDER HANMA...
VAL-HALLA'S NUMBER TWO...
AND THE ANTI-TOMAN FORCE GATHERED UNDER...

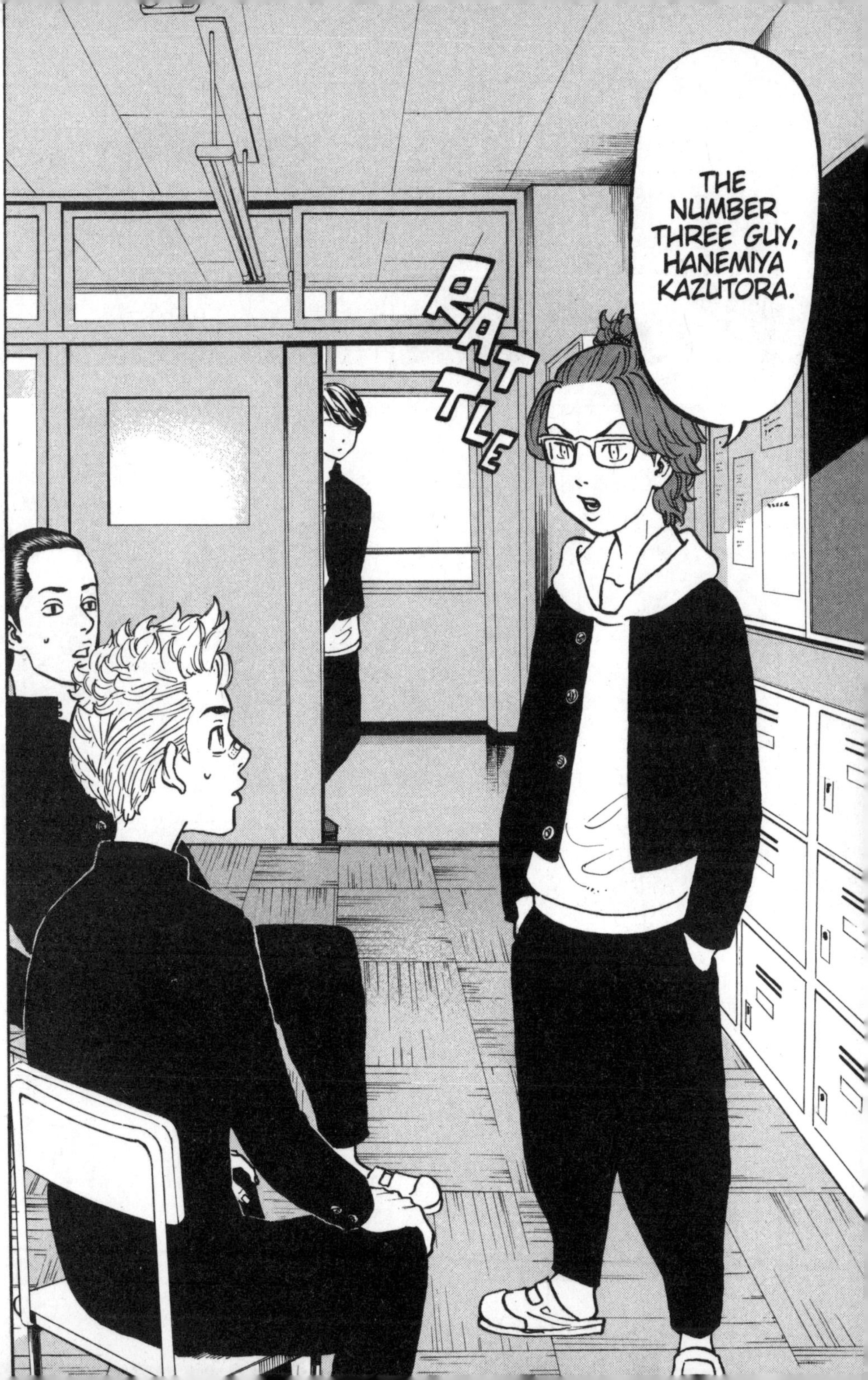
THE NUMBER THREE GUY, HANEMIYA KAZUTORA.
RATTLE

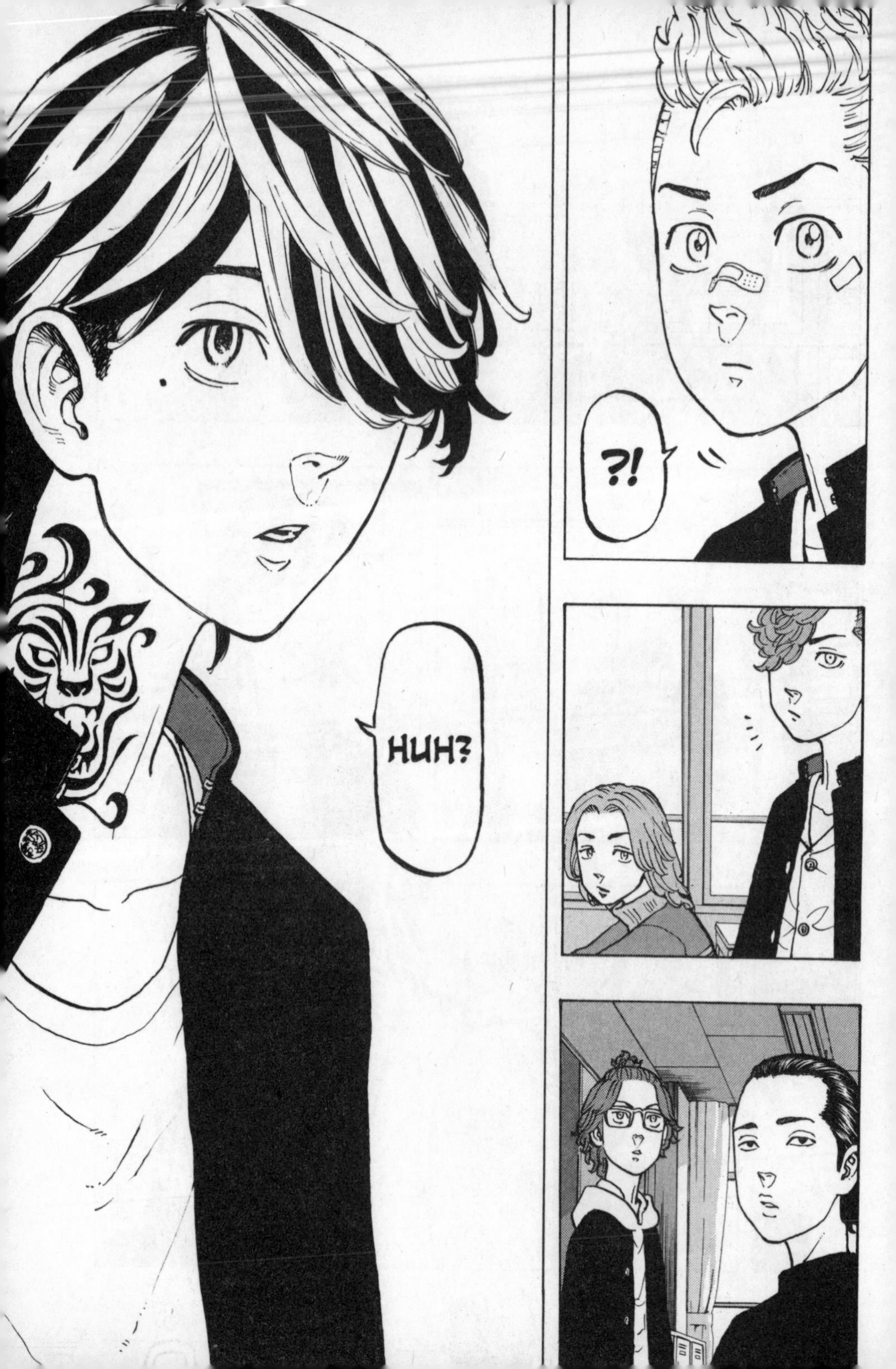
?!
HUH?

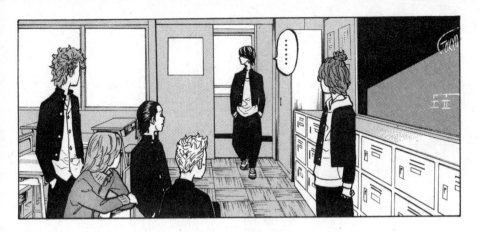

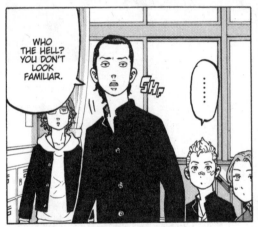

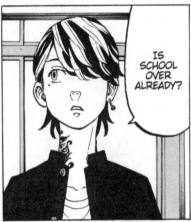

......
IS SCHOOL OVER ALREADY?
......
SHF
WHO THE HELL? YOU DON'T LOOK FAMILIAR.
THAT'S NOT VERY POLITE!
I *AM* YOUR JUNIOR HIGH SENPAI, AFTER ALL.
HUH?
WHO ARE YOU? NEVER SEEN YOU HERE BEFORE.
......

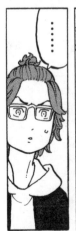

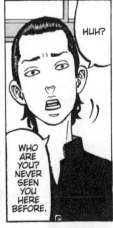

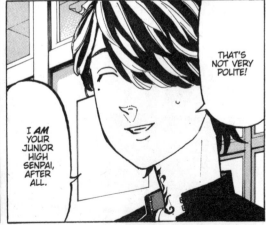

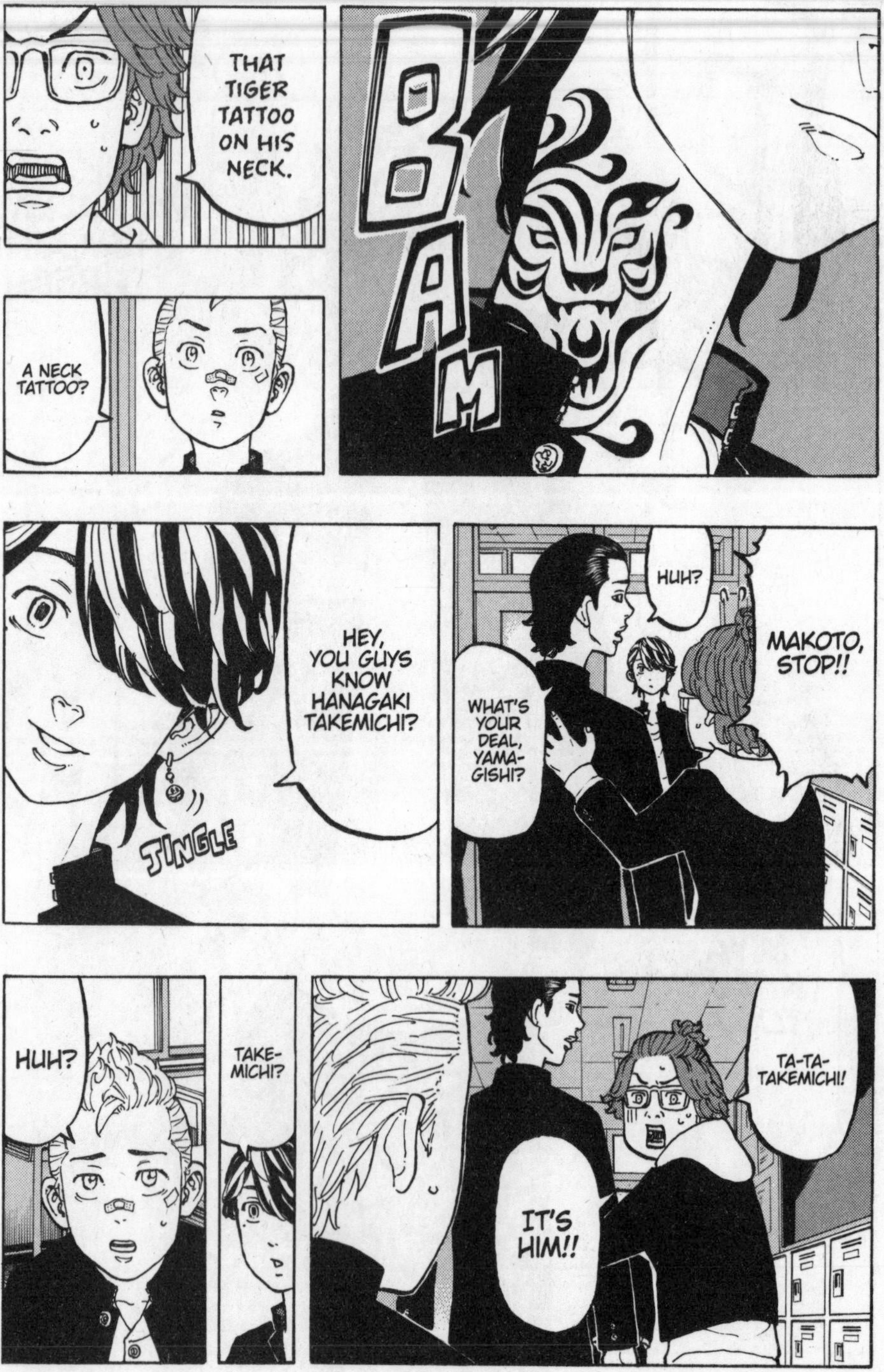
BAM
THAT TIGER TATTOO ON HIS NECK.
A NECK TATTOO?
MAKOTO, STOP!!
HUH?
WHAT'S YOUR DEAL, YAMAGISHI?
HEY, YOU GUYS KNOW HANAGAKI TAKEMICHI?
TINGLE
TA-TA-TAKEMICHI!
IT'S HIM!!
TAKE-MICHI?
HUH?

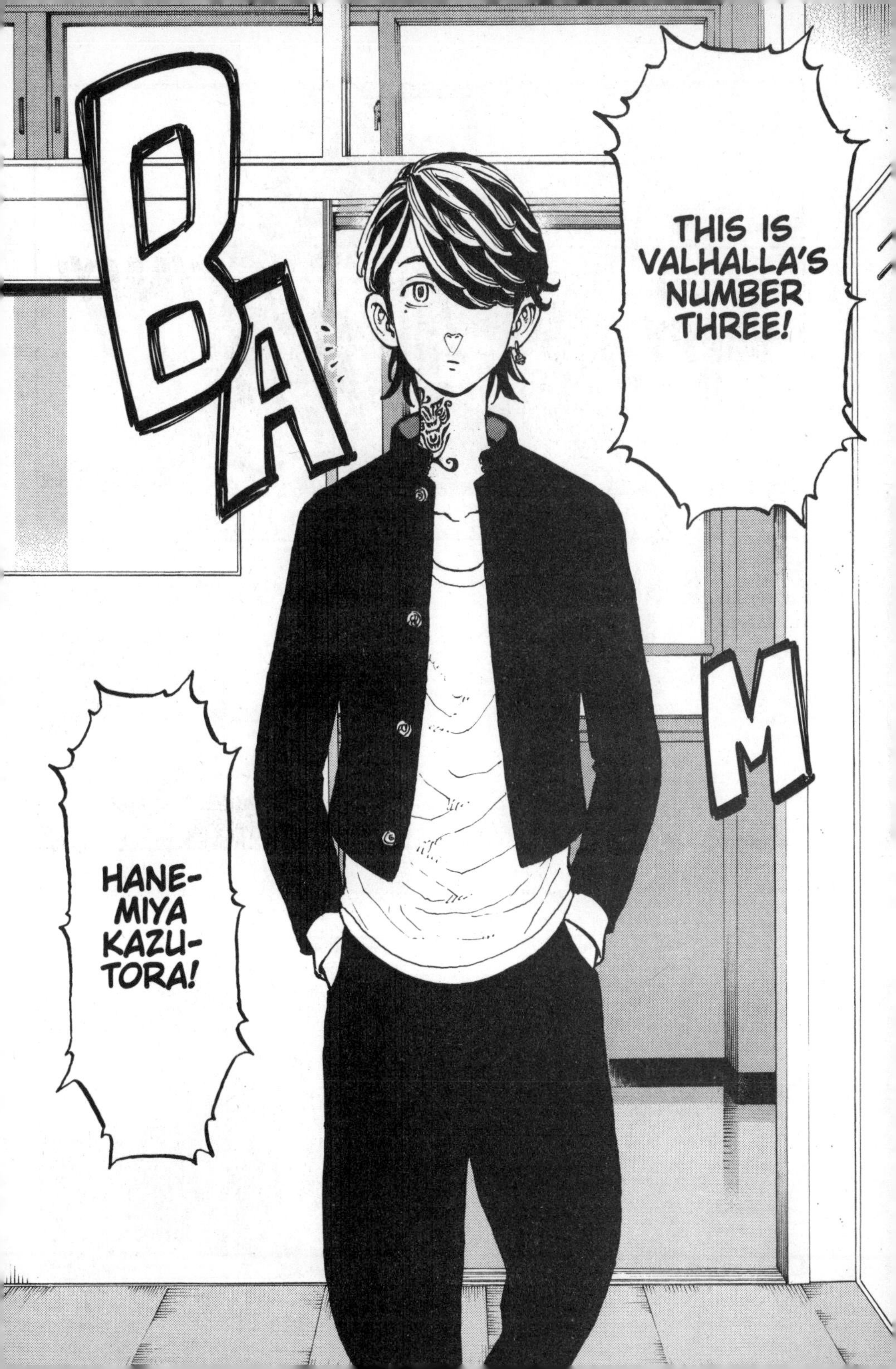
THIS IS VALHALLA'S NUMBER THREE!
BAM
HANE-MIYA KAZU-TORA!

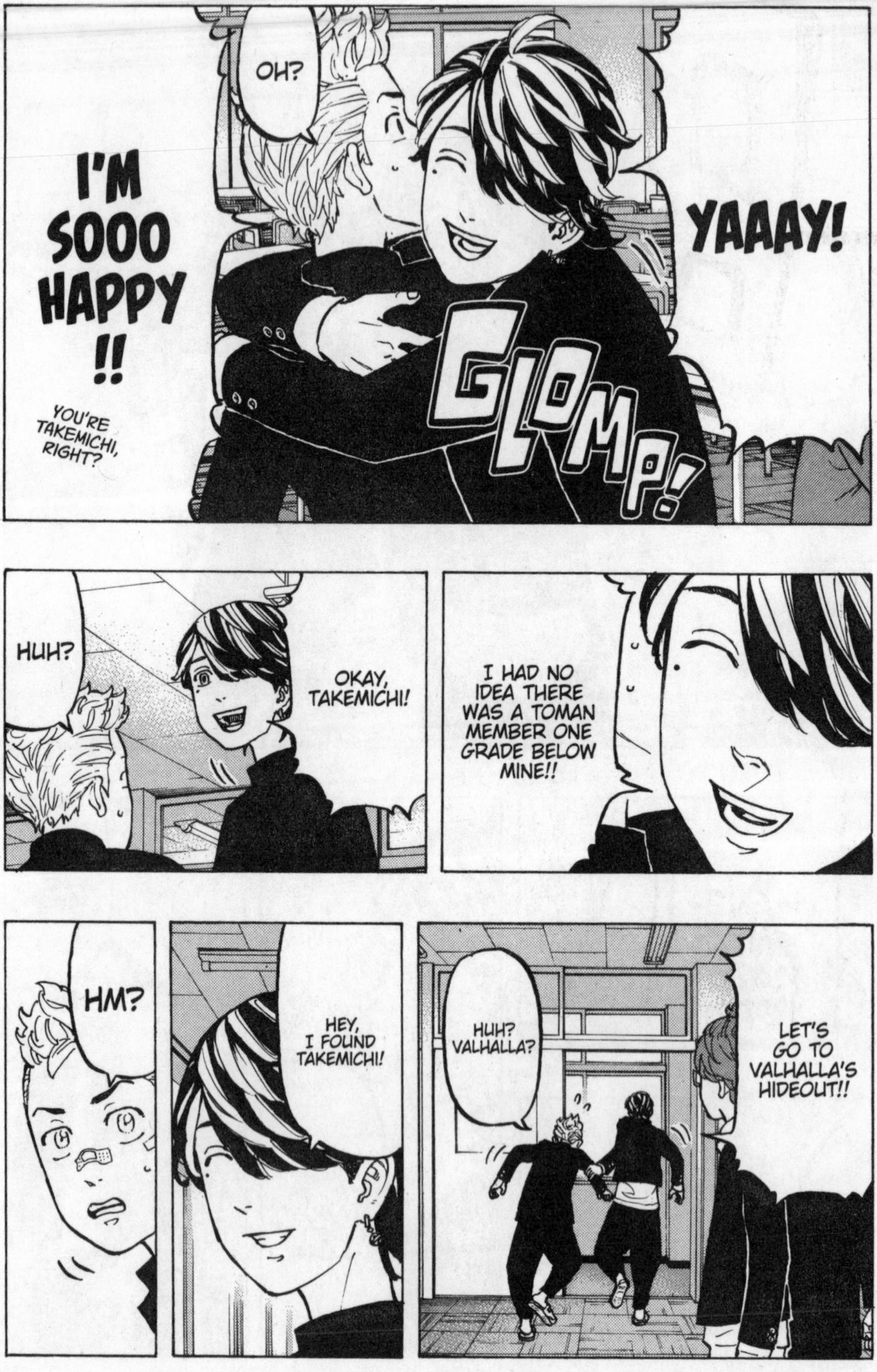

OH?
YAAAY!
I'M SOOO HAPPY!!
GLOMP!
YOU'RE TAKEMICHI, RIGHT?
I HAD NO IDEA THERE WAS A TOMAN MEMBER ONE GRADE BELOW MINE!!
OKAY, TAKEMICHI!
HUH?
LET'S GO TO VALHALLA'S HIDEOUT!!
HUH? VALHALLA?
HEY, I FOUND TAKEMICHI!
HM?

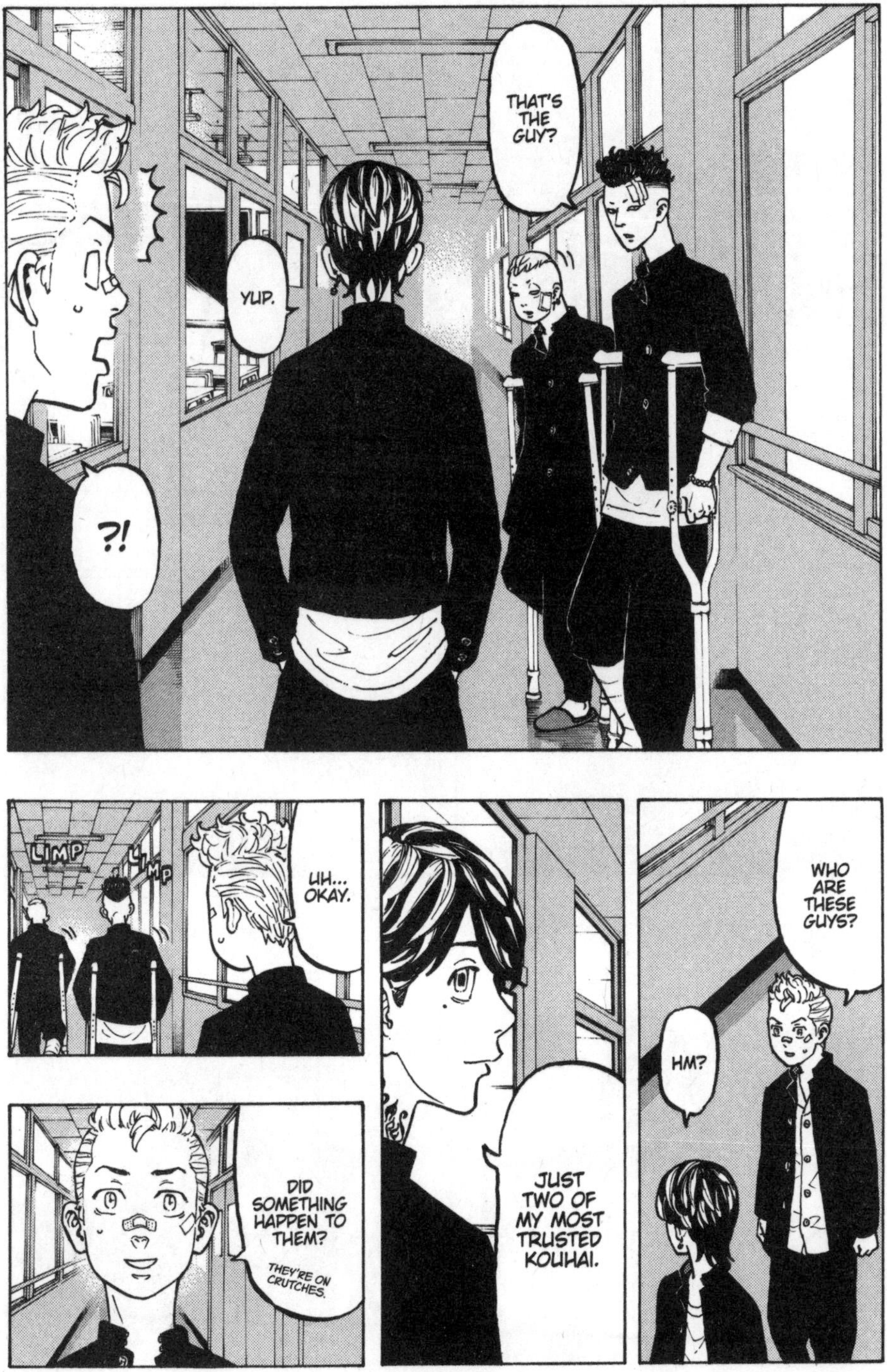
THAT'S THE GUY?
YUP.
?!
WHO ARE THESE GUYS?
HM?
JUST TWO OF MY MOST TRUSTED KOUHAI.
UH... OKAY.
LIMP
LIMP
DID SOMETHING HAPPEN TO THEM?
THEY'RE ON CRUTCHES.

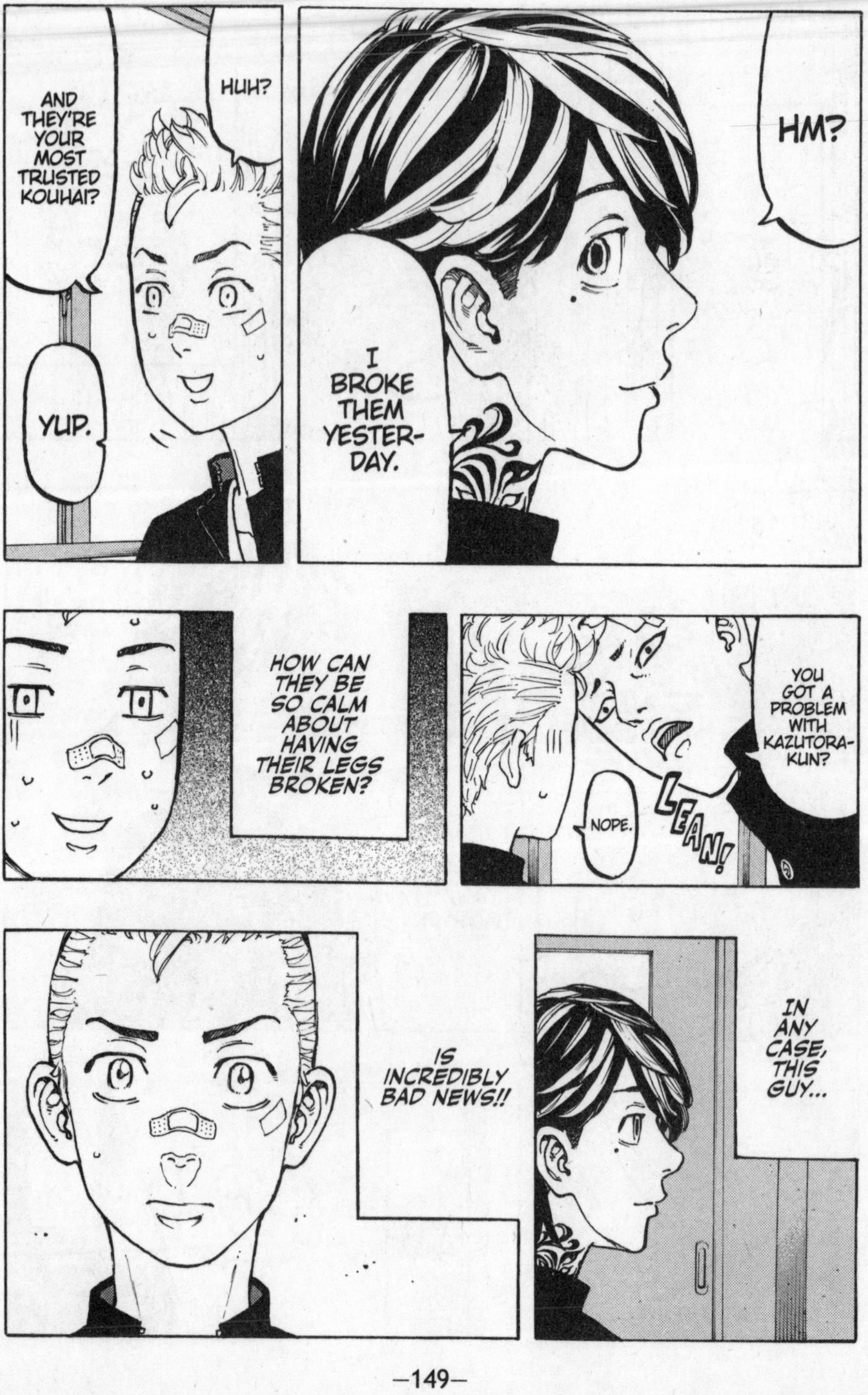
HM?
I BROKE THEM YESTER-DAY.
HUH?
AND THEY'RE YOUR MOST TRUSTED KOUHAI?
YUP.
YOU GOT A PROBLEM WITH KAZUTORA-KUN?
LEAN!
NOPE.
HOW CAN THEY BE SO CALM ABOUT HAVING THEIR LEGS BROKEN?
IN ANY CASE, THIS GUY...
IS INCREDIBLY BAD NEWS!!

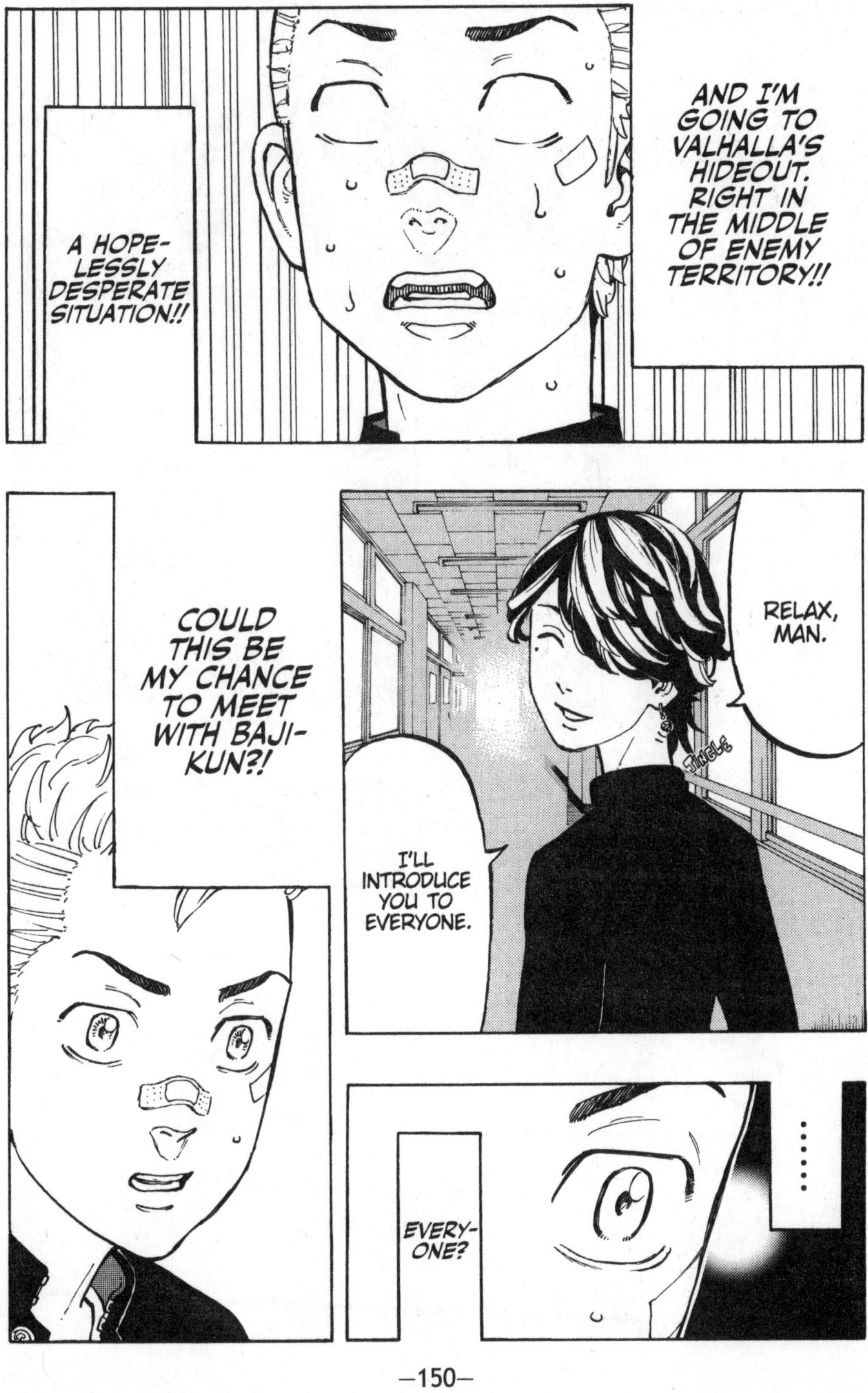
AND I'M GOING TO VALHALLA'S HIDEOUT. RIGHT IN THE MIDDLE OF ENEMY TERRITORY!!
A HOPE-LESSLY DESPERATE SITUATION!!
RELAX, MAN.
JINGLE
I'LL INTRODUCE YOU TO EVERYONE.
......
EVERY-ONE?
COULD THIS BE MY CHANCE TO MEET WITH BAJI-KUN?!

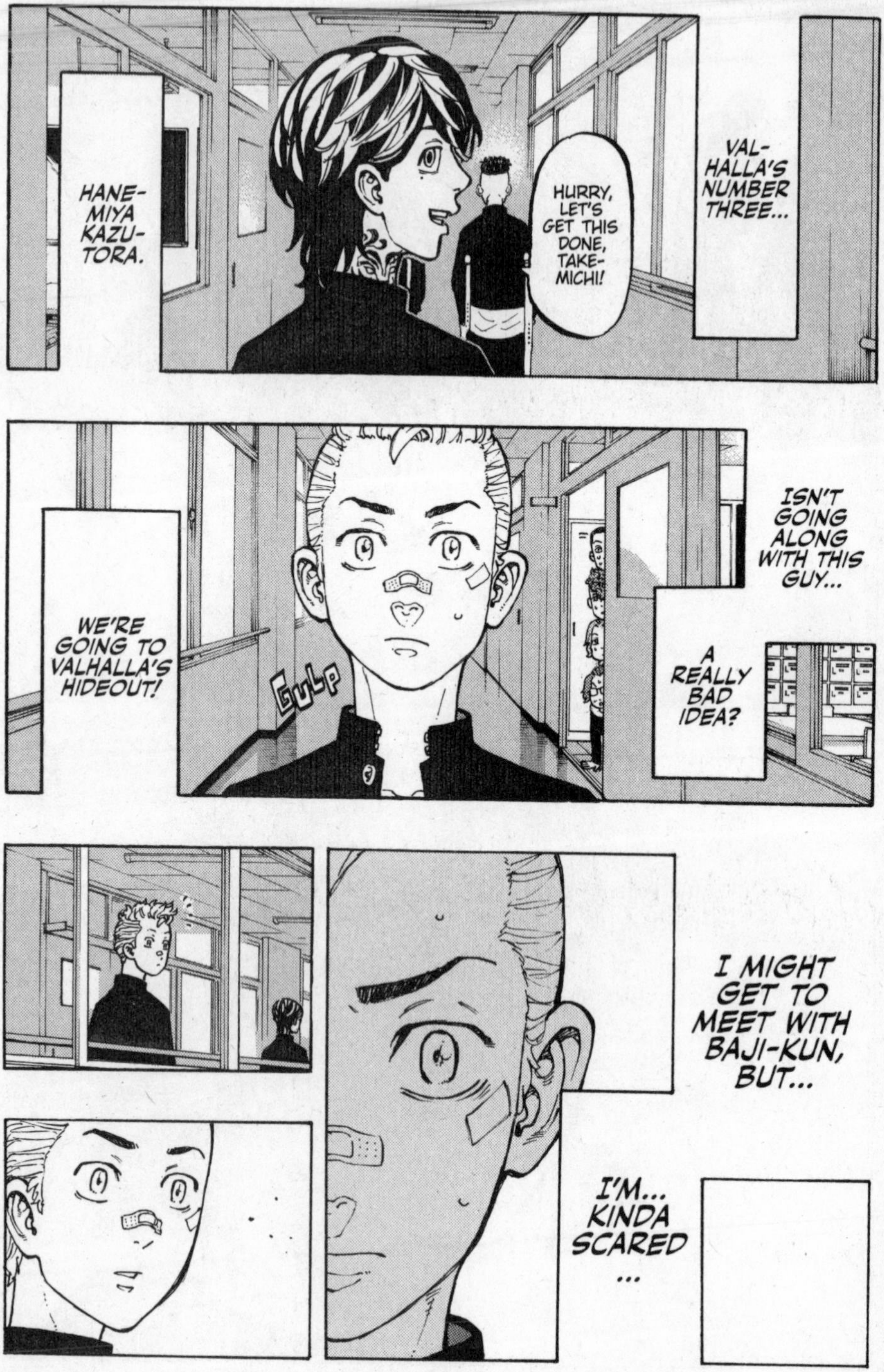
VAL-HALLA'S NUMBER THREE...
HURRY, LET'S GET THIS DONE, TAKE-MICHI!
HANE-MIYA KAZU-TORA.
ISN'T GOING ALONG WITH THIS GUY...
A REALLY BAD IDEA?
WE'RE GOING TO VALHALLA'S HIDEOUT!
GULP
I MIGHT GET TO MEET WITH BAJI-KUN, BUT...
I'M... KINDA SCARED ...

CHAPTER 41: DOUBLE CROSS

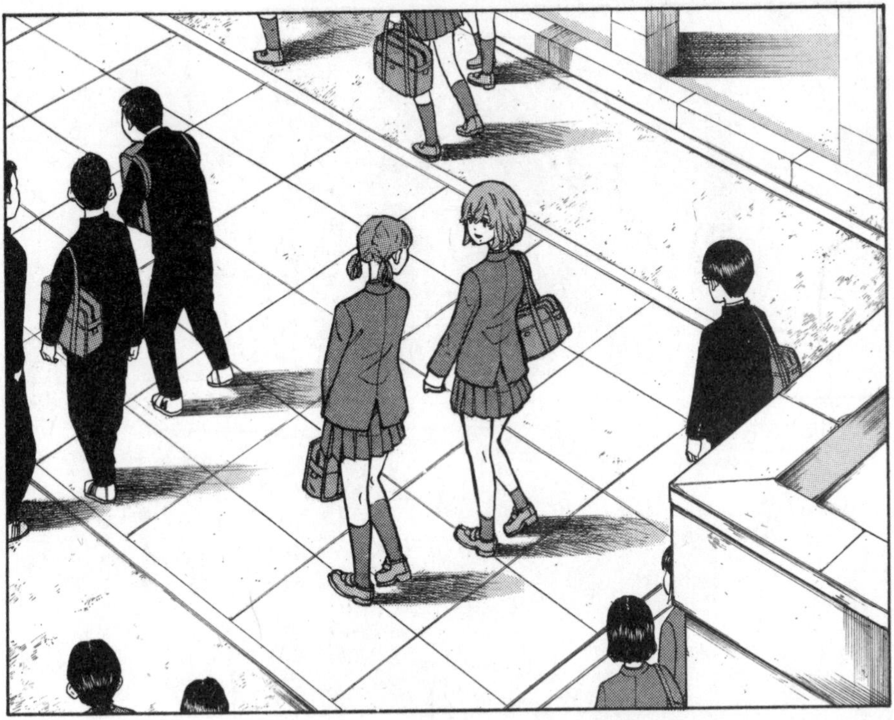

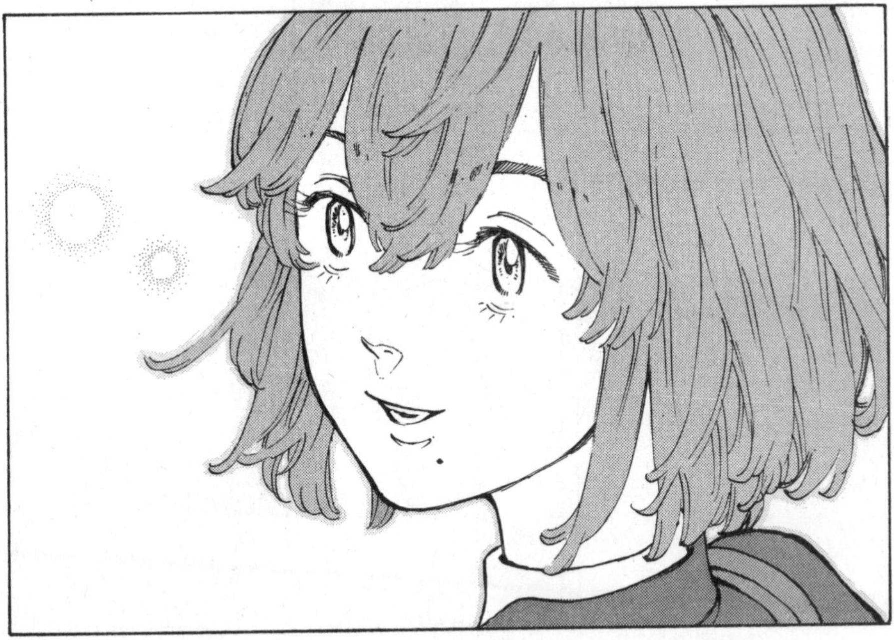

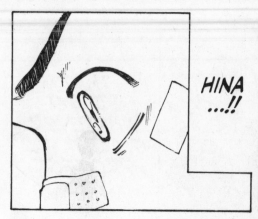

HINA ....!!

BA
DUM

I
SWORE
...

FWOOOOM

THAT
TIME...

BA
DUM

—153—

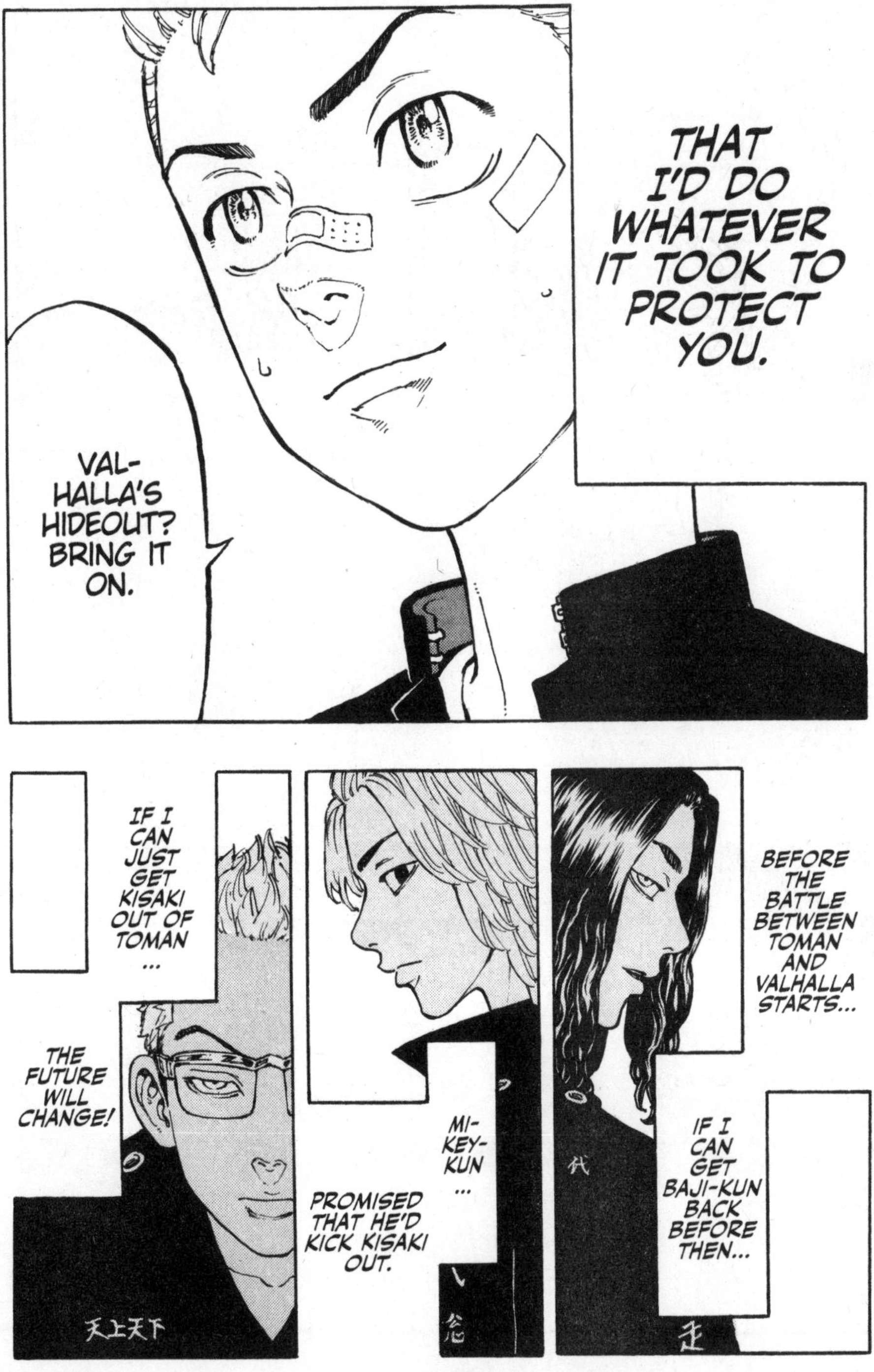
THAT I'D DO WHATEVER IT TOOK TO PROTECT YOU.
VAL-HALLA'S HIDEOUT? BRING IT ON.
BEFORE THE BATTLE BETWEEN TOMAN AND VALHALLA STARTS...
IF I CAN GET BAJI-KUN BACK BEFORE THEN...
MI-KEY-KUN ...
PROMISED THAT HE'D KICK KISAKI OUT.
IF I CAN JUST GET KISAKI OUT OF TOMAN ...
THE FUTURE WILL CHANGE!
天上天下

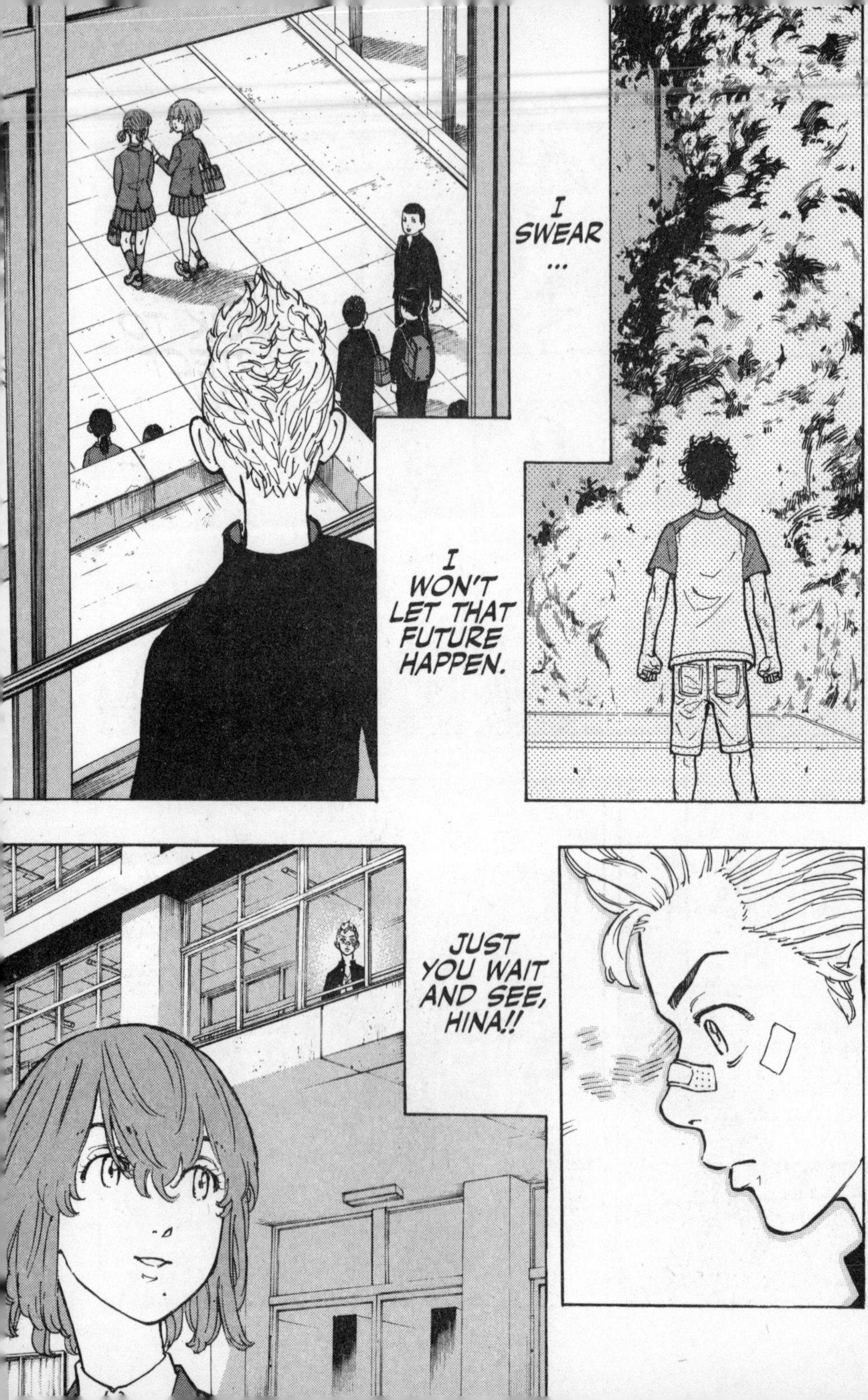
I SWEAR ...
I WON'T LET THAT FUTURE HAPPEN.
JUST YOU WAIT AND SEE, HINA!!

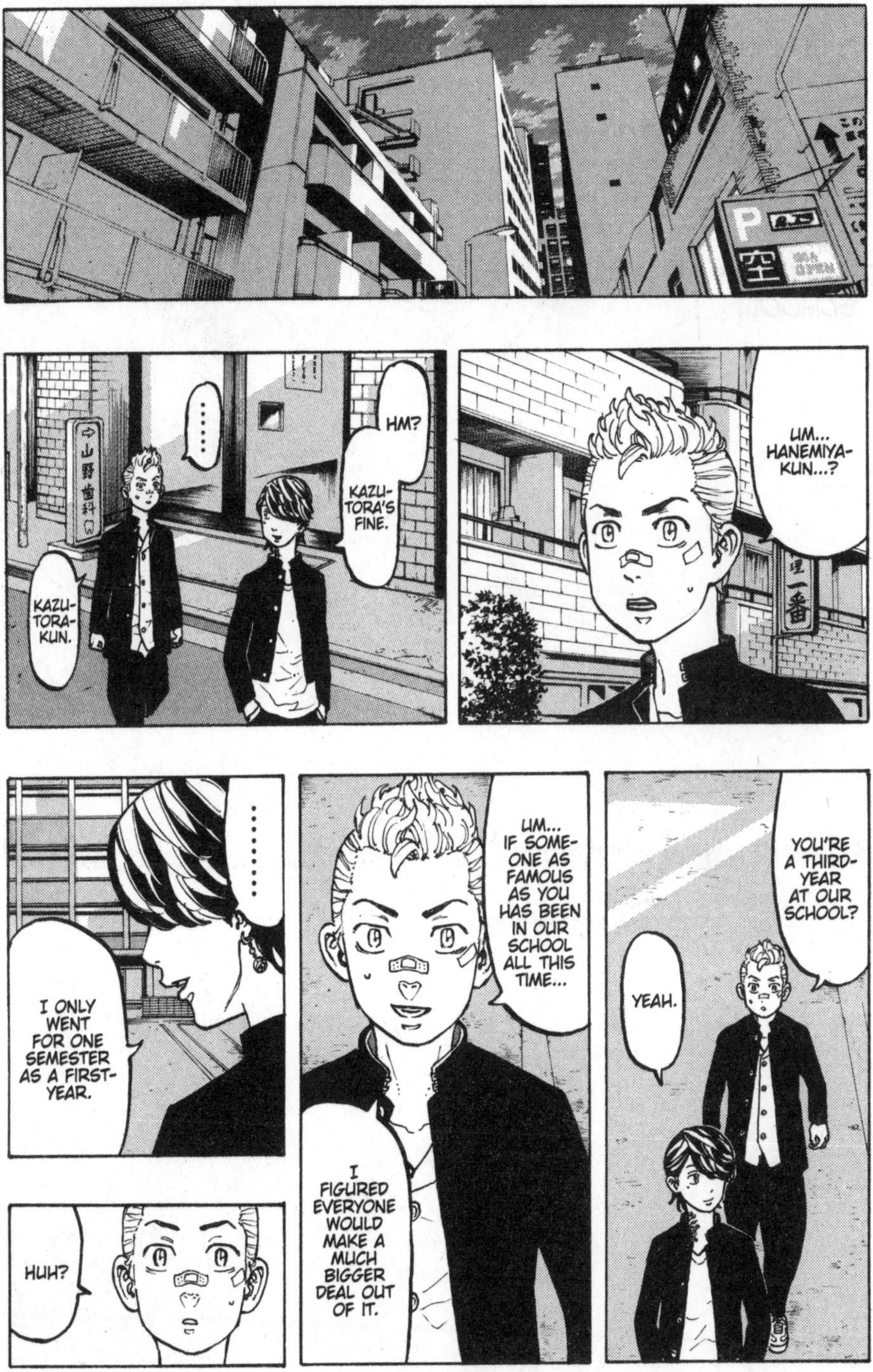
UM... HANEMIYA-KUN...?
HM?
......
KAZUTORA'S FINE.
山野歯科
KAZUTORA-KUN.
YOU'RE A THIRD-YEAR AT OUR SCHOOL?
YEAH.
UM... IF SOME-ONE AS FAMOUS AS YOU HAS BEEN IN OUR SCHOOL ALL THIS TIME...
I FIGURED EVERYONE WOULD MAKE A MUCH BIGGER DEAL OUT OF IT.
....
I ONLY WENT FOR ONE SEMESTER AS A FIRST-YEAR.
HUH?

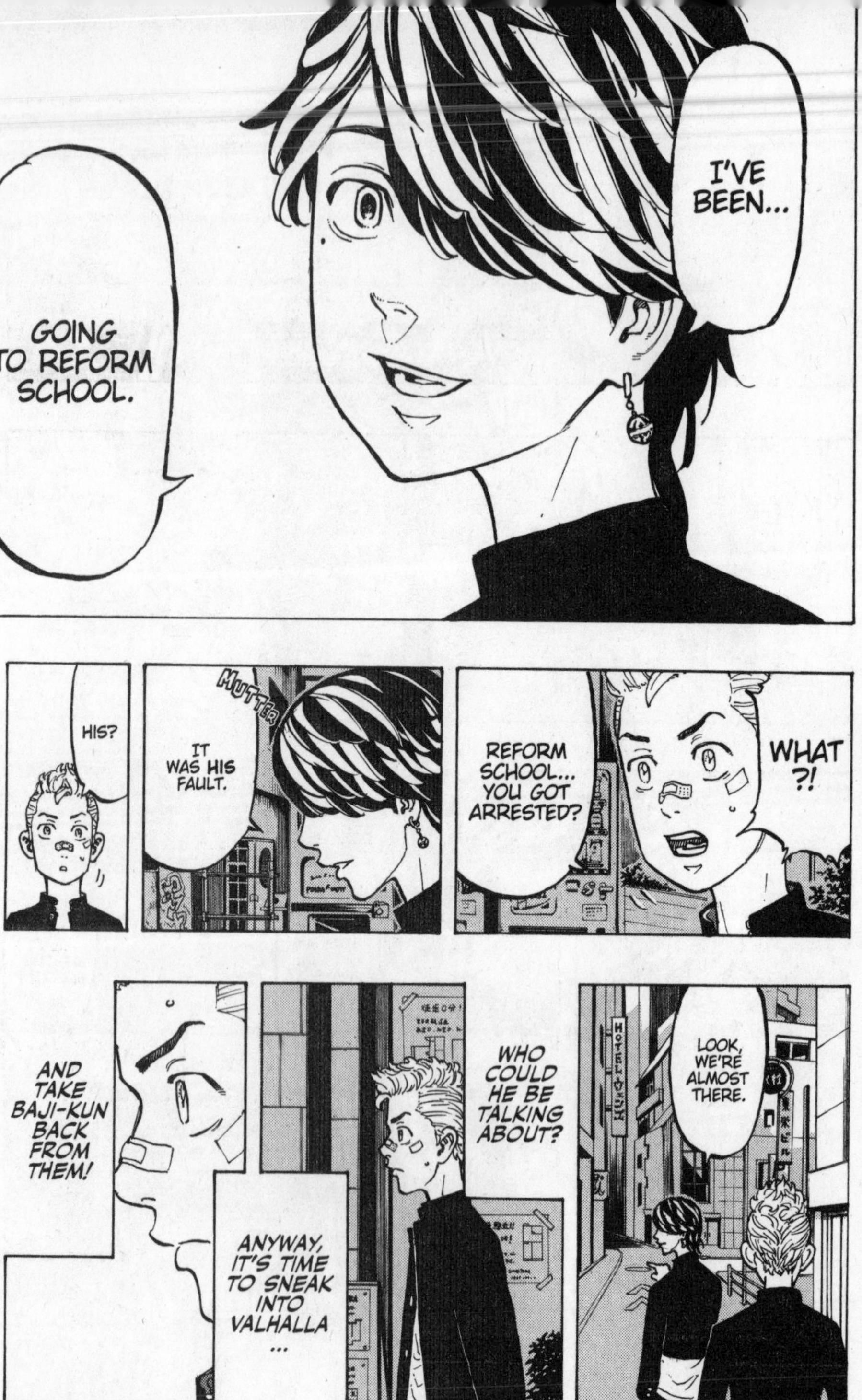
I'VE BEEN...
GOING TO REFORM SCHOOL.
WHAT ?!
REFORM SCHOOL... YOU GOT ARRESTED?
MUTTER
IT WAS HIS FAULT.
HIS?
LOOK, WE'RE ALMOST THERE.
WHO COULD HE BE TALKING ABOUT?
ANYWAY, IT'S TIME TO SNEAK INTO VALHALLA ...
AND TAKE BAJI-KUN BACK FROM THEM!

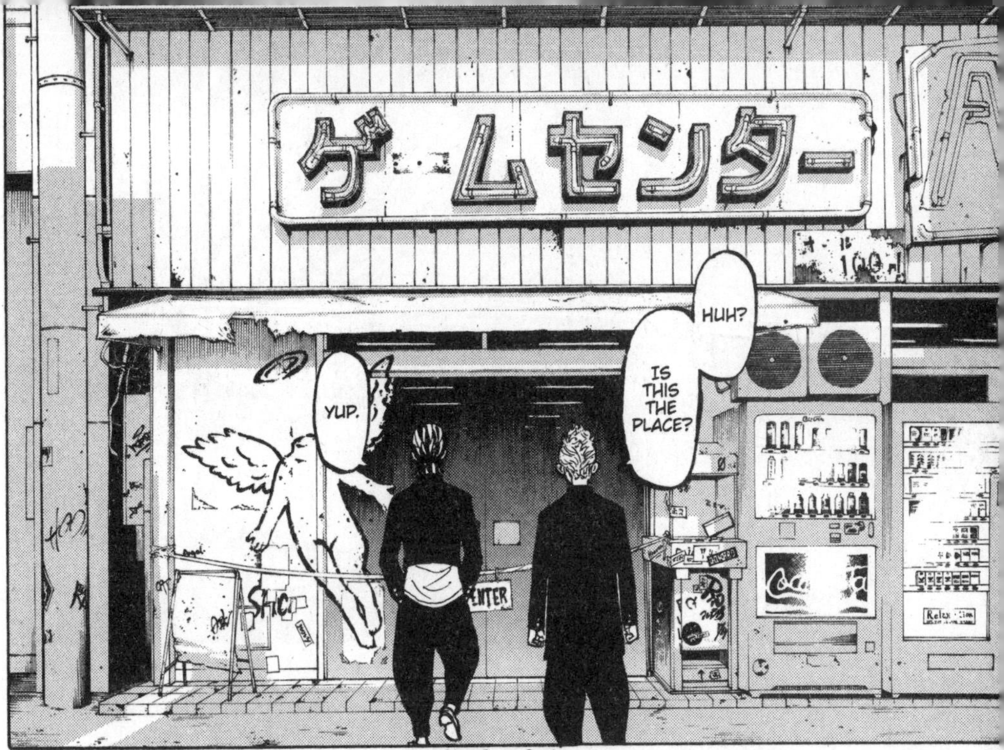
ゲームセンター
HUH?
IS THIS THE PLACE?
YUP.
Sign: Game Center

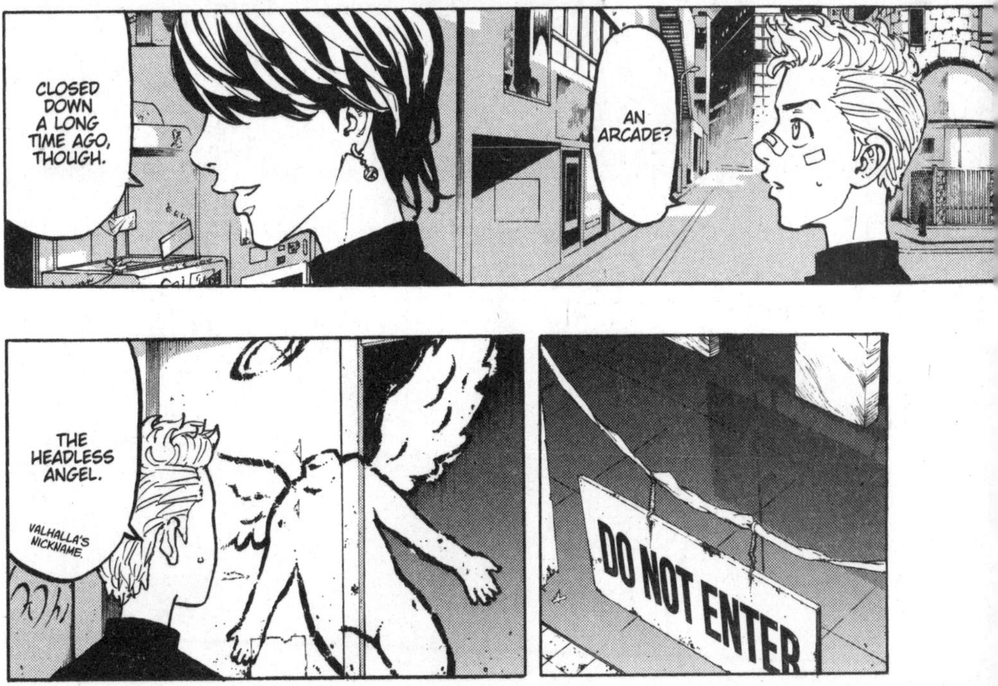
AN ARCADE?
CLOSED DOWN A LONG TIME AGO, THOUGH.
DO NOT ENTER
THE HEADLESS ANGEL.
VALHALLA'S NICKNAME.

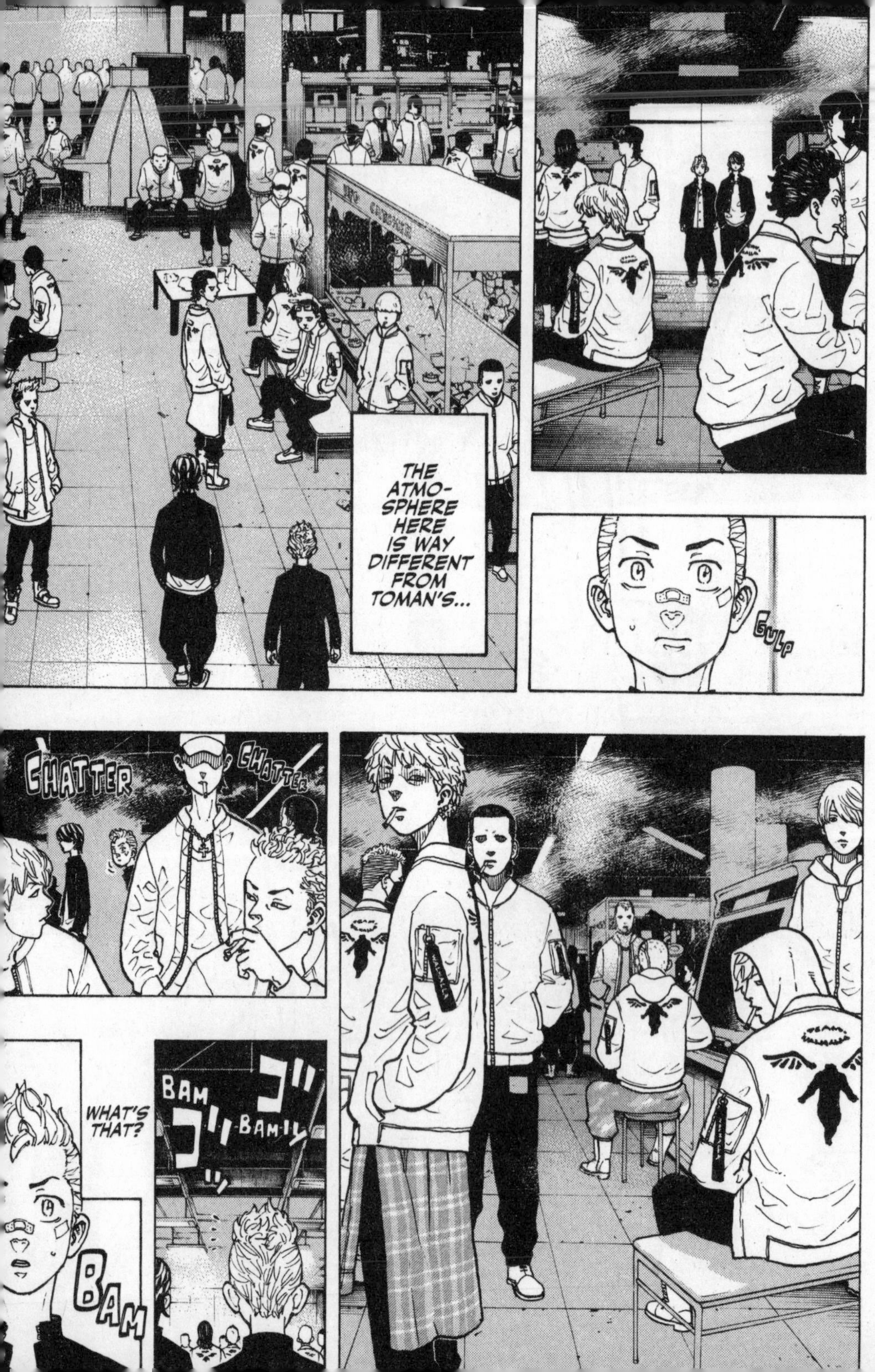
GULP
THE ATMOSPHERE HERE IS WAY DIFFERENT FROM TOMAN'S...
CHATTER
CHATTER
BAM
BAM
WHAT'S THAT?
BAM

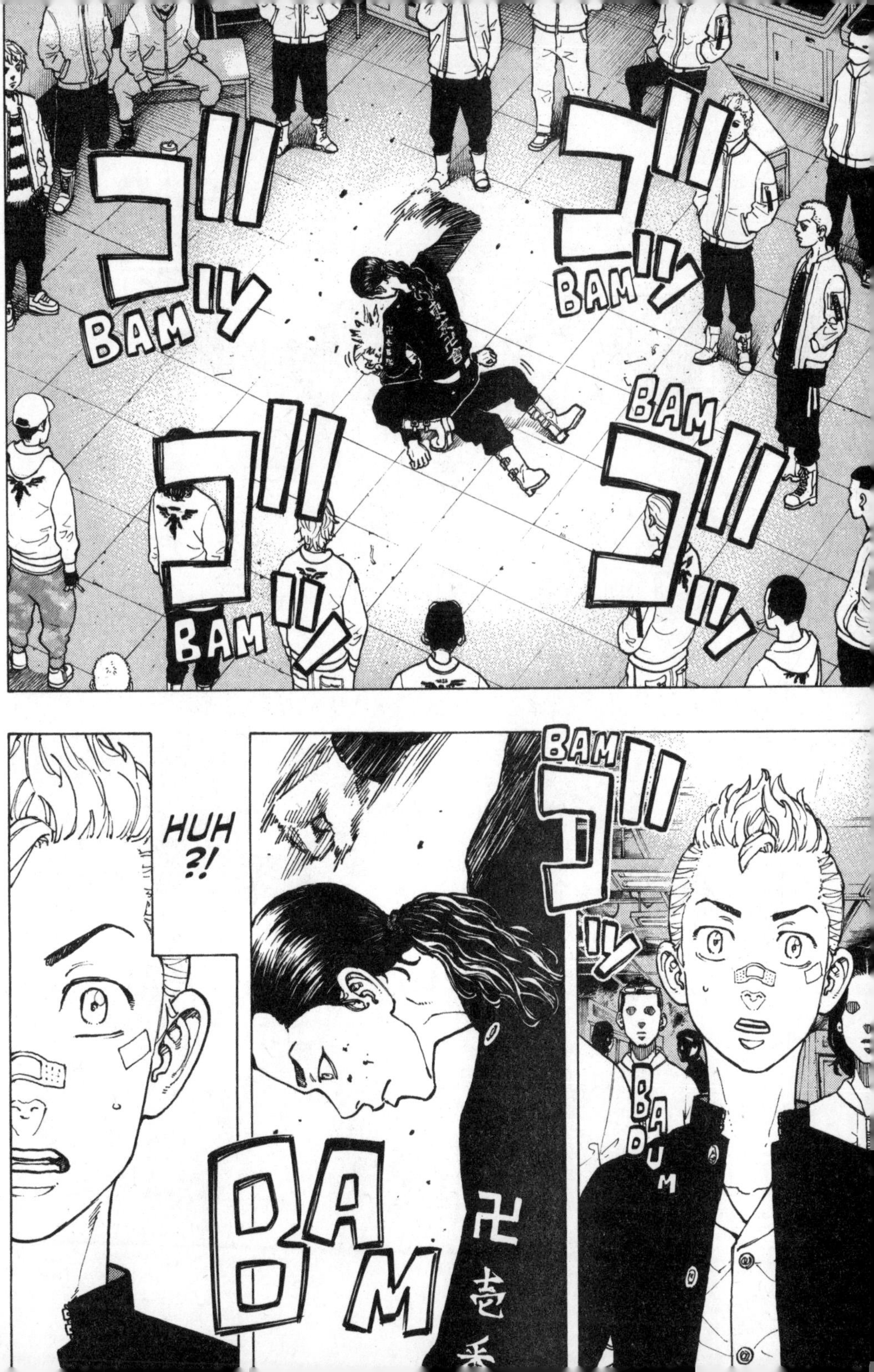
BAM
BAM
BAM
BAM
BAM
BA DUM
DA DUM
HUH ?!

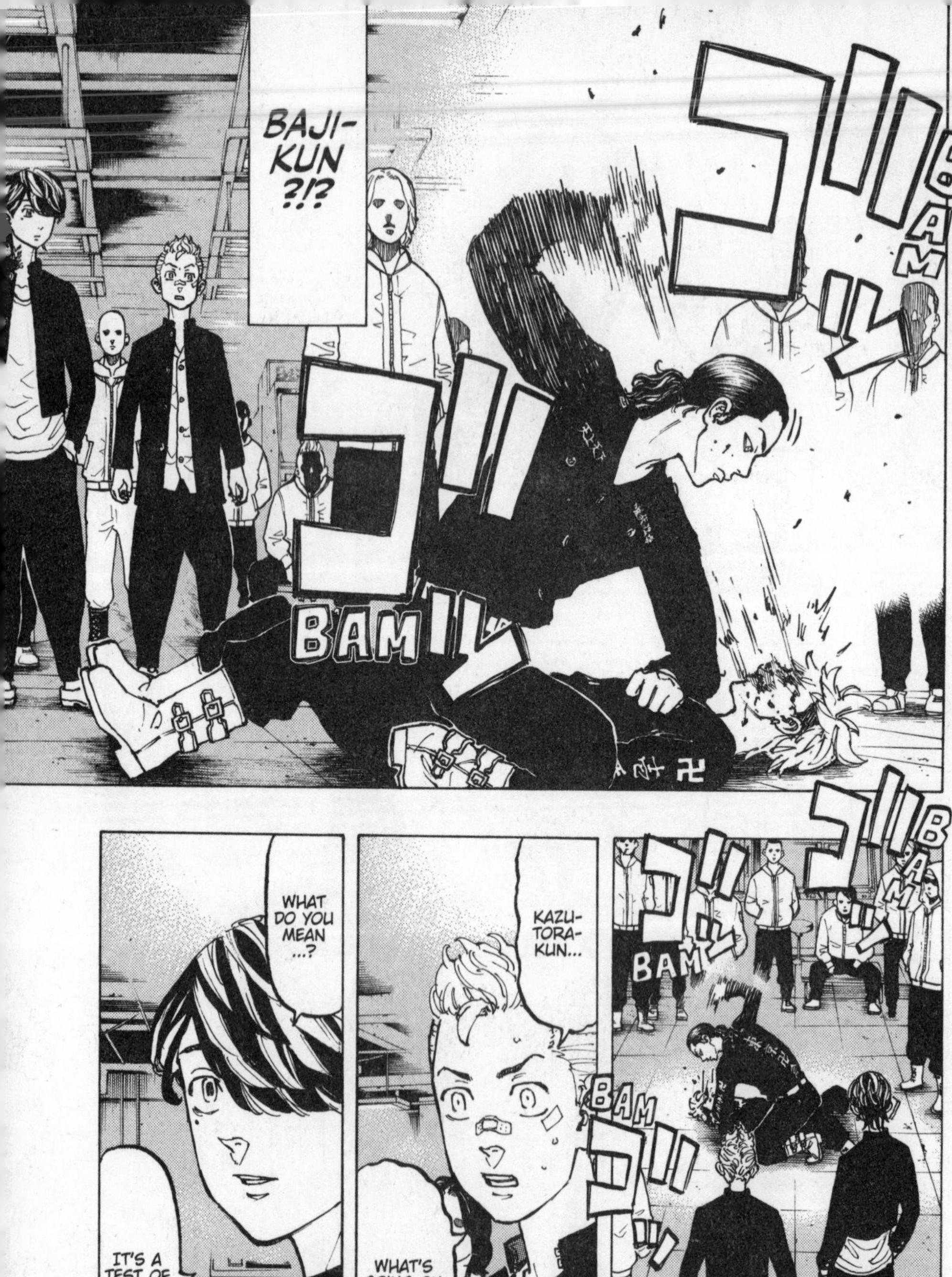
BAM
BAJI-KUN ?!?
BAM
BAM
BAM
BAM
KAZUTORA-KUN...
WHAT'S GOING ON HERE?
WHAT DO YOU MEAN ...?
IT'S A TEST OF FAITH.

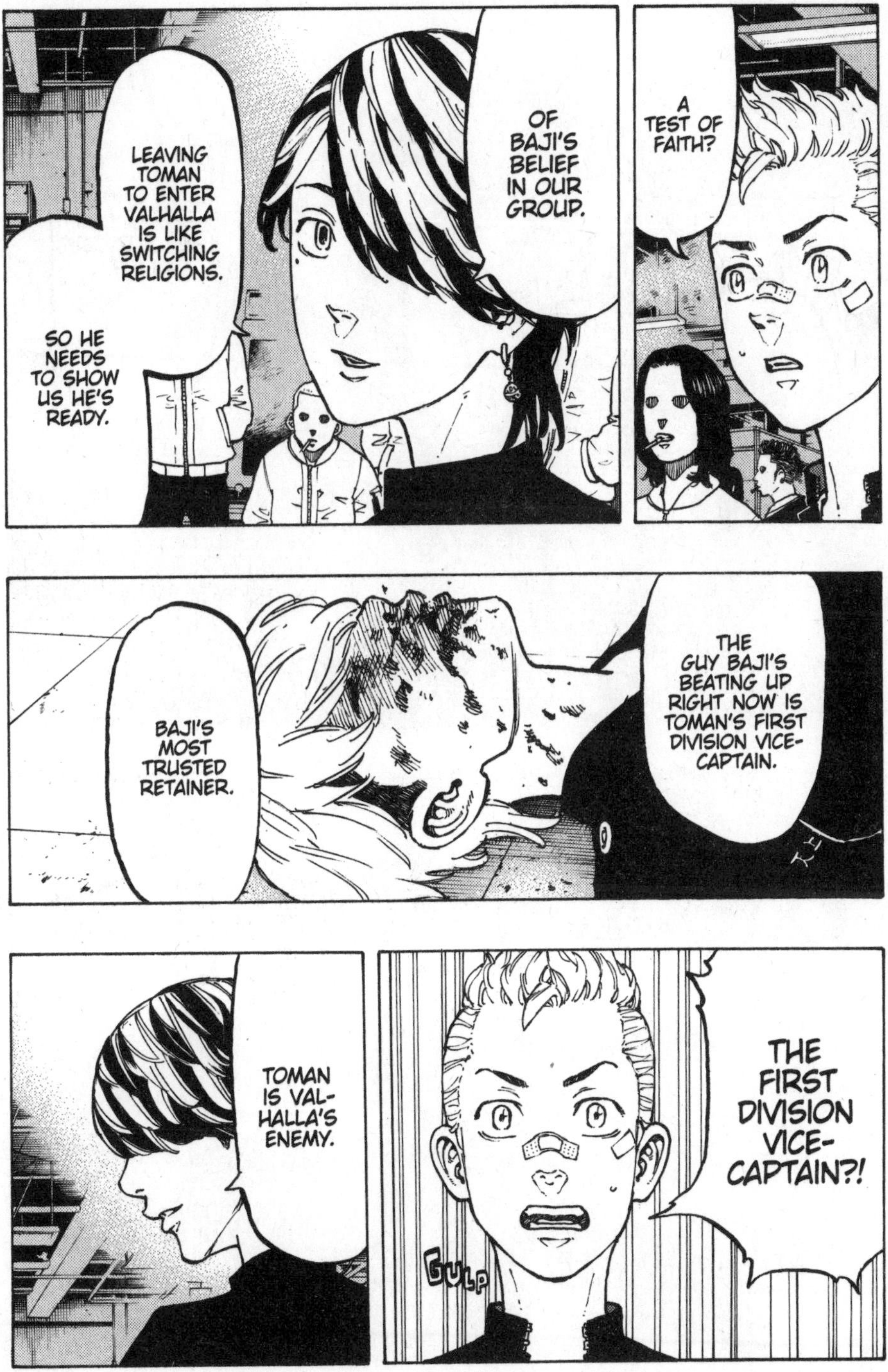
A TEST OF FAITH?
OF BAJI'S BELIEF IN OUR GROUP.
LEAVING TOMAN TO ENTER VALHALLA IS LIKE SWITCHING RELIGIONS.
SO HE NEEDS TO SHOW US HE'S READY.
THE GUY BAJI'S BEATING UP RIGHT NOW IS TOMAN'S FIRST DIVISION VICE-CAPTAIN.
BAJI'S MOST TRUSTED RETAINER.
THE FIRST DIVISION VICE-CAPTAIN?!
GULP
TOMAN IS VAL-HALLA'S ENEMY.

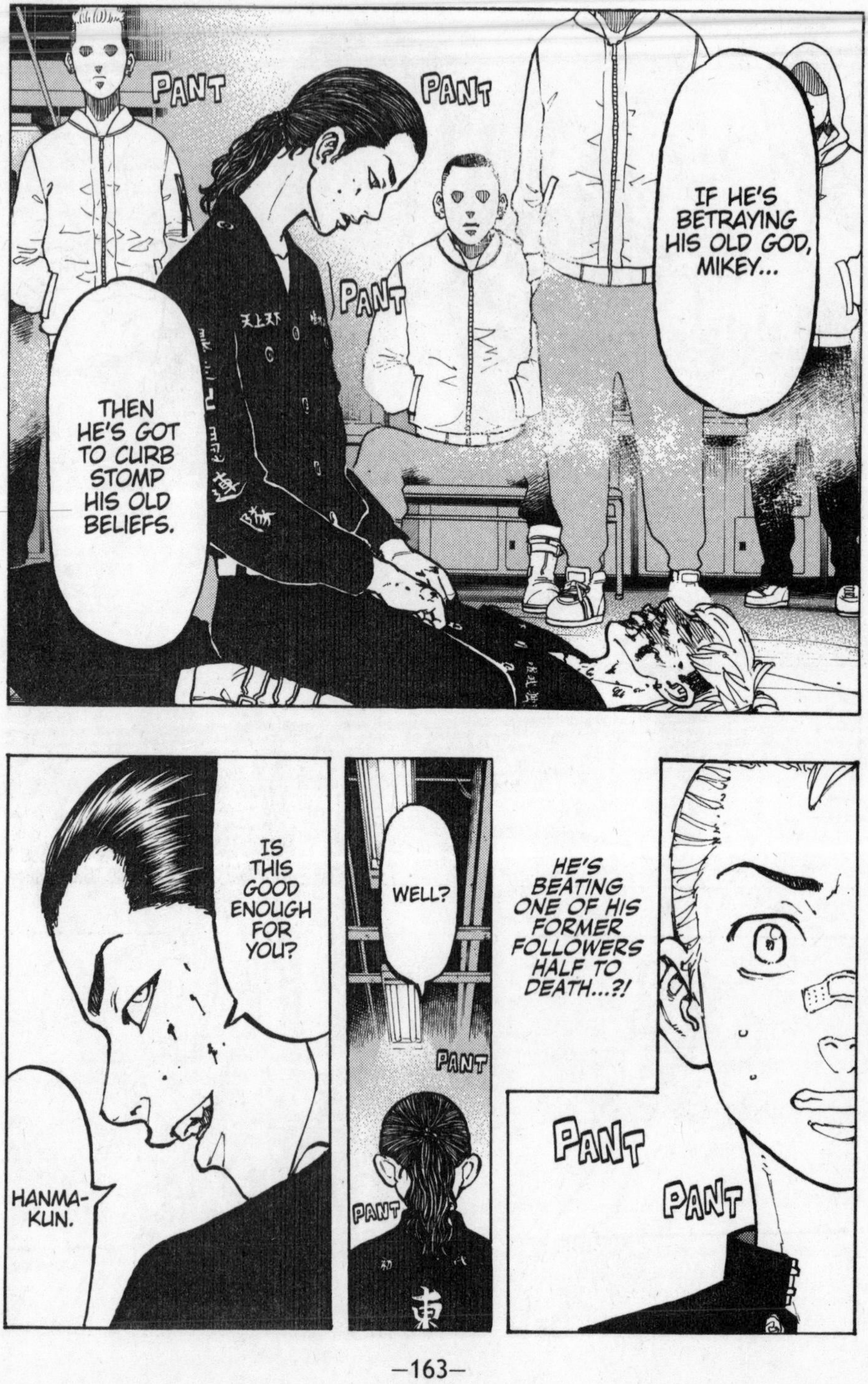
IF HE'S BETRAYING HIS OLD GOD, MIKEY...
PANT
PANT
PANT
THEN HE'S GOT TO CURB STOMP HIS OLD BELIEFS.
HE'S BEATING ONE OF HIS FORMER FOLLOWERS HALF TO DEATH...?!
PANT
PANT
WELL?
PANT
PANT
IS THIS GOOD ENOUGH FOR YOU?
HANMA-KUN.

FOR MY INITIATION INTO VALHALLA.

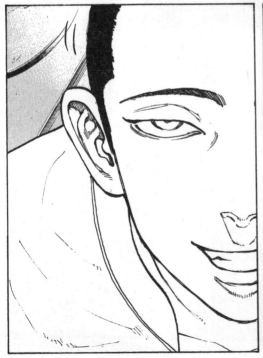

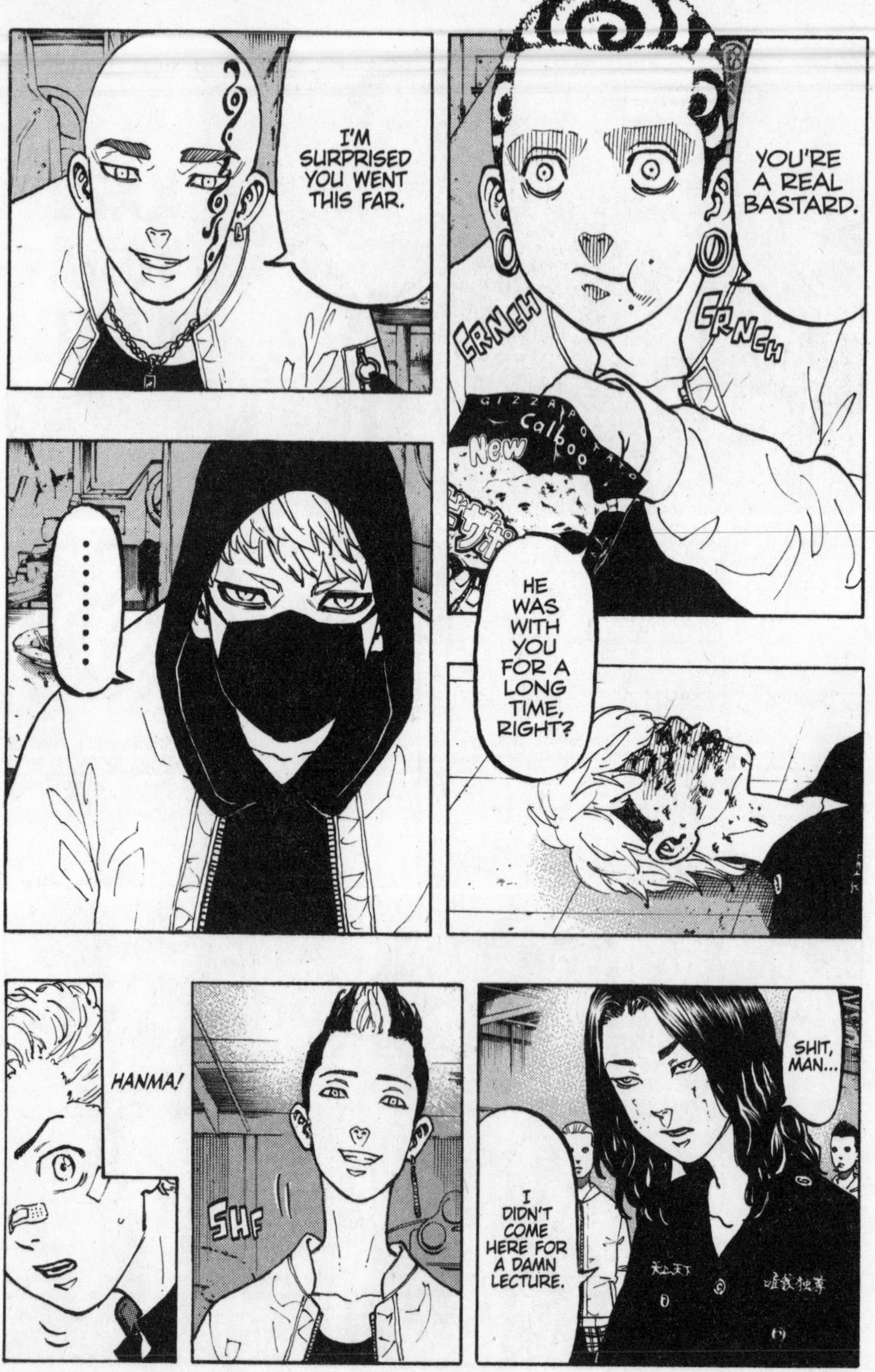
YOU'RE A REAL BASTARD.
CRNCH
CRNCH
I'M SURPRISED YOU WENT THIS FAR.
HE WAS WITH YOU FOR A LONG TIME, RIGHT?
......
SHIT, MAN...
I DIDN'T COME HERE FOR A DAMN LECTURE.
SHF
HANMA!

KAZU-
TORA-
AAA!!

YOU
READY?

YEAH?

HUH?

BA
DUM

YUP.

HERE
HE IS
...

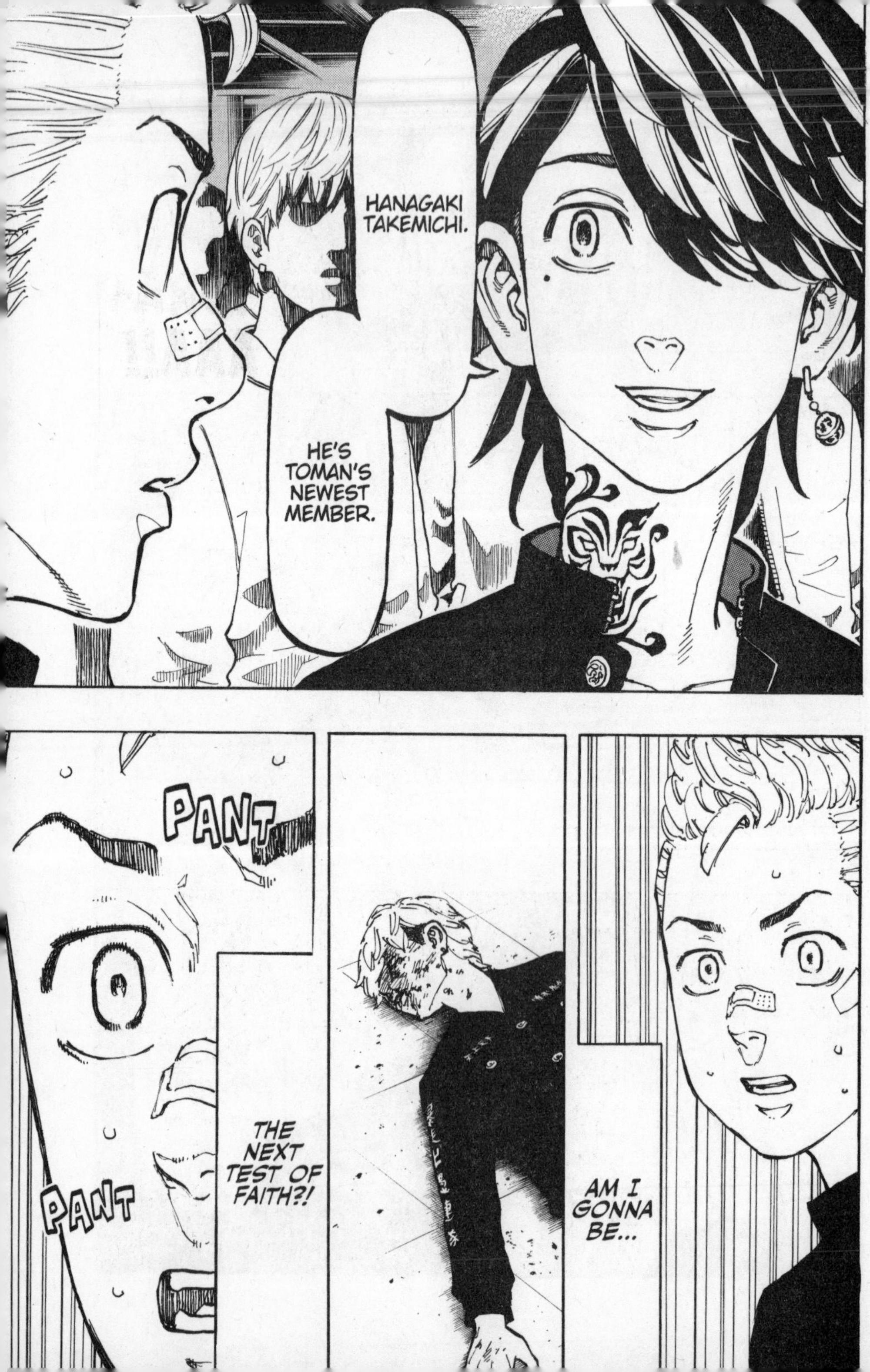

HANAGAKI TAKEMICHI.
HE'S TOMAN'S NEWEST MEMBER.
AM I GONNA BE...
THE NEXT TEST OF FAITH?!
PANT
PANT

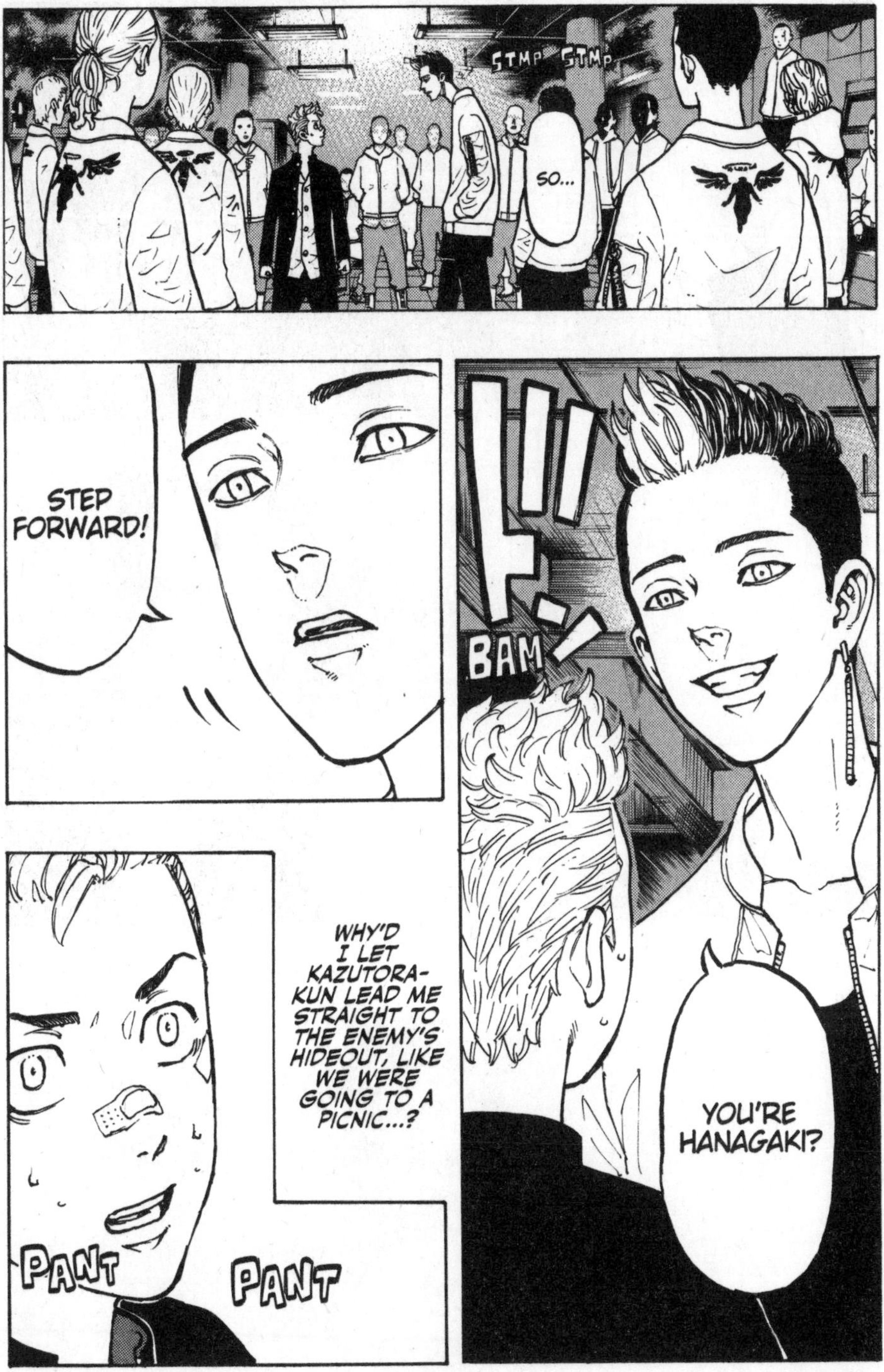
STMP STMP
SO...
BAM
YOU'RE HANAGAKI?
STEP FORWARD!
WHY'D I LET KAZUTORA-KUN LEAD ME STRAIGHT TO THE ENEMY'S HIDEOUT, LIKE WE WERE GOING TO A PICNIC...?
PANT
PANT

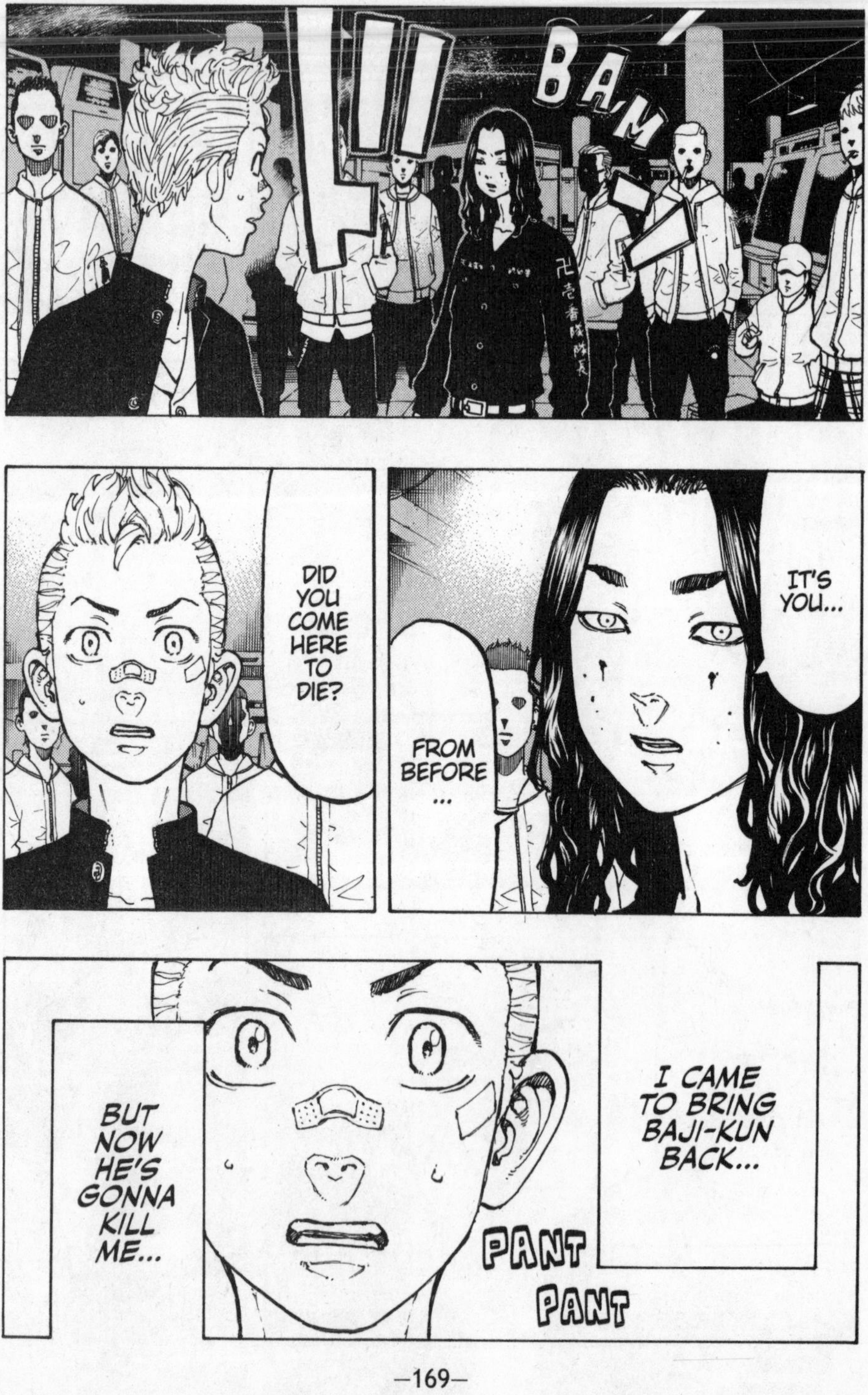
BAM
!!
IT'S YOU...
FROM BEFORE ...
DID YOU COME HERE TO DIE?
I CAME TO BRING BAJI-KUN BACK...
PANT PANT
BUT NOW HE'S GONNA KILL ME...

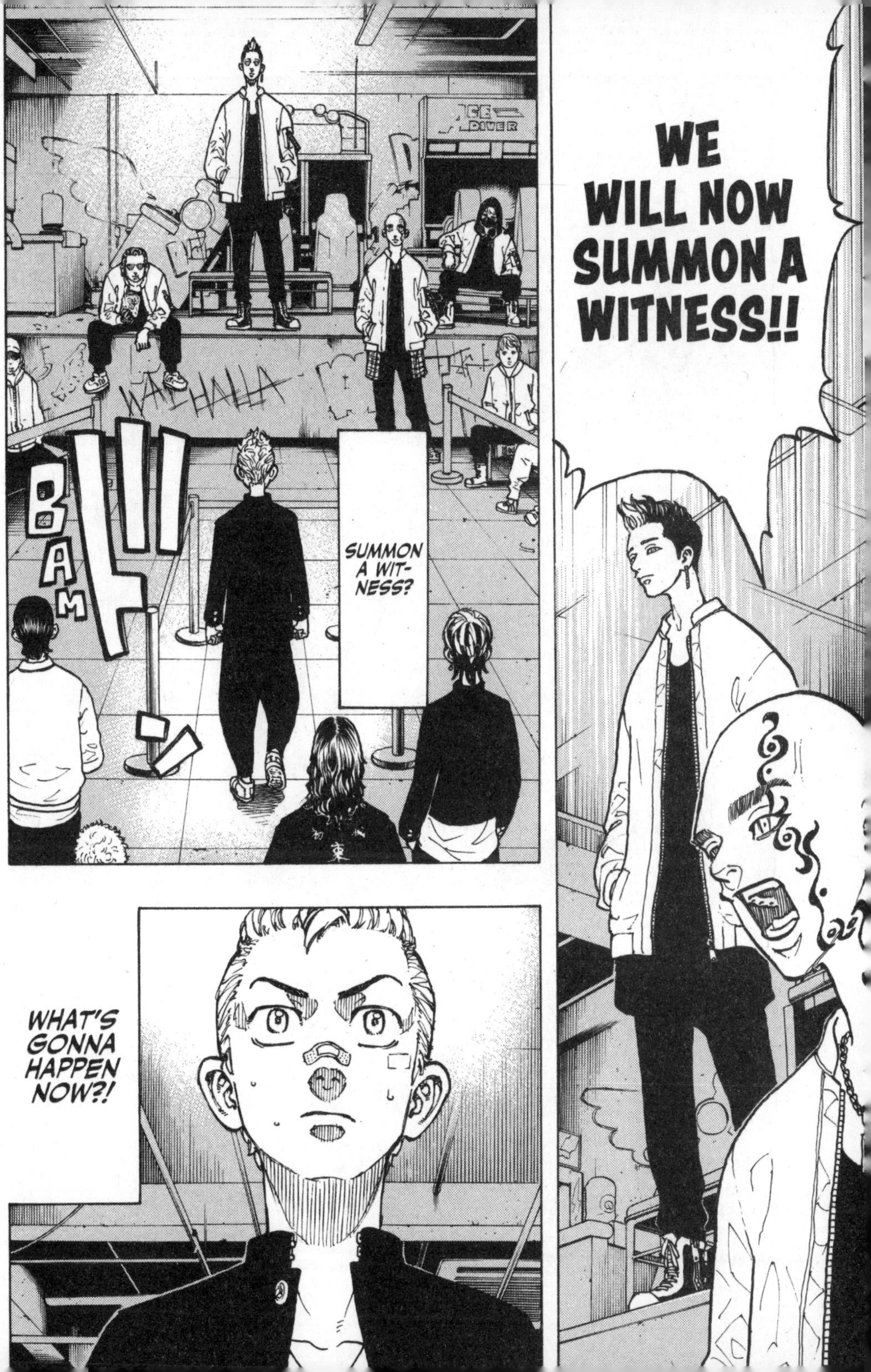
WE WILL NOW SUMMON A WITNESS!!
BAM
SUMMON A WIT- NESS?
WHAT'S GONNA HAPPEN NOW?!

CHAPTER 42: ONCE UPON A TIME

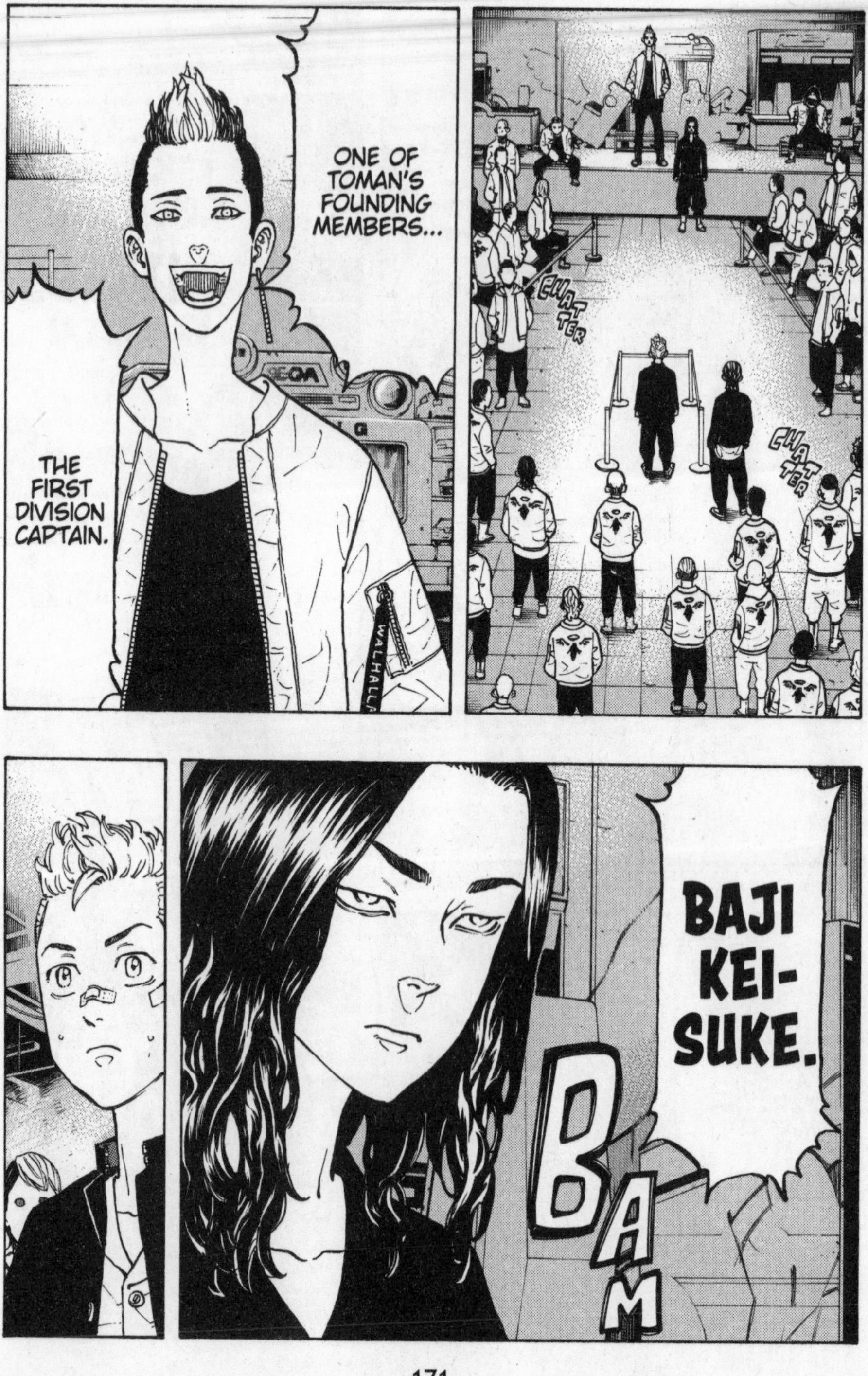

CHATTER
CHATTER
ONE OF TOMAN'S FOUNDING MEMBERS...
THE FIRST DIVISION CAPTAIN.
BAJI KEI-SUKE.
BAM
WALHALLA

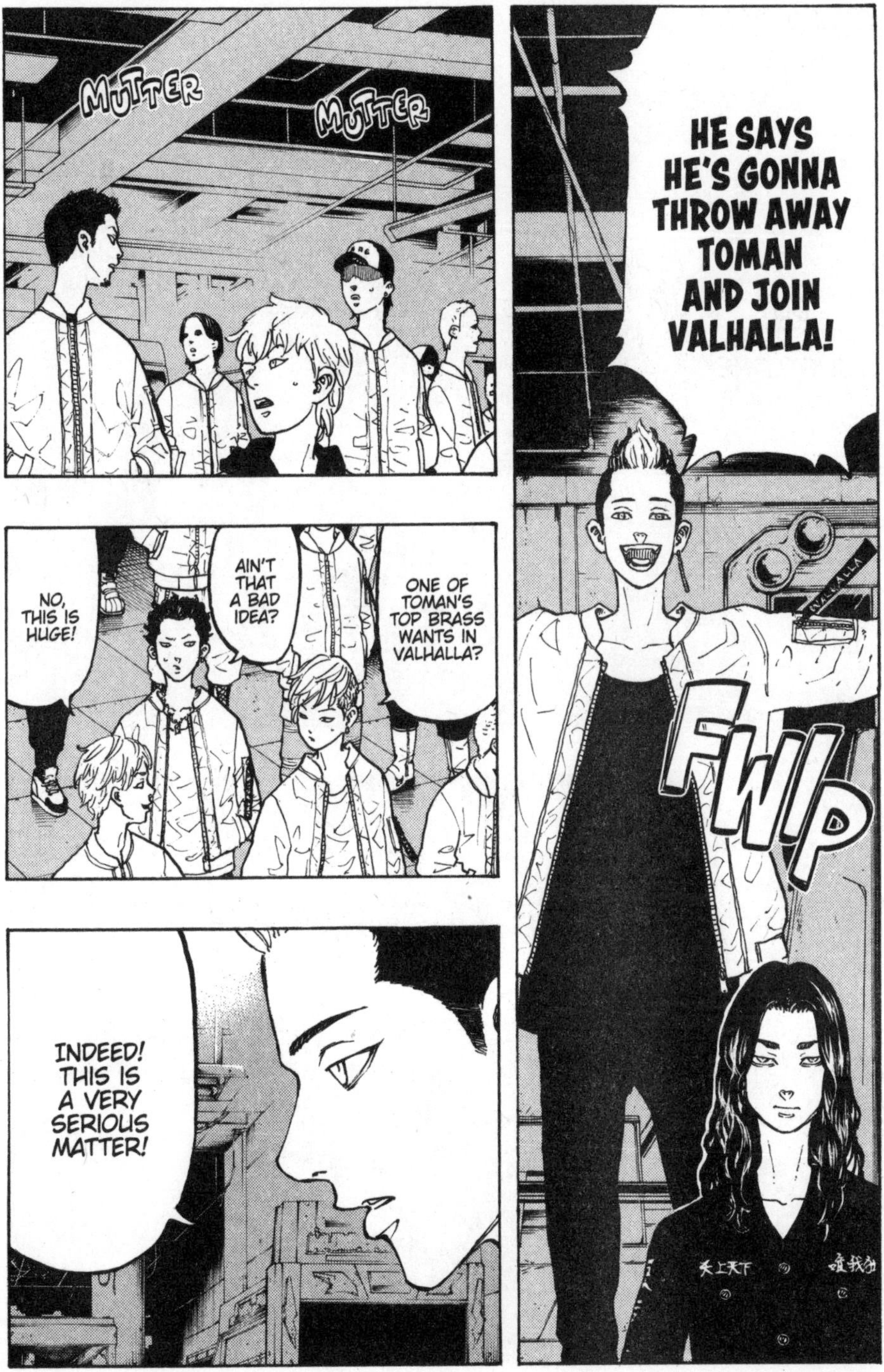
HE SAYS HE'S GONNA THROW AWAY TOMAN AND JOIN VALHALLA!
FWIP
MUTTER
MUTTER
ONE OF TOMAN'S TOP BRASS WANTS IN VALHALLA?
AIN'T THAT A BAD IDEA?
NO, THIS IS HUGE!
INDEED! THIS IS A VERY SERIOUS MATTER!

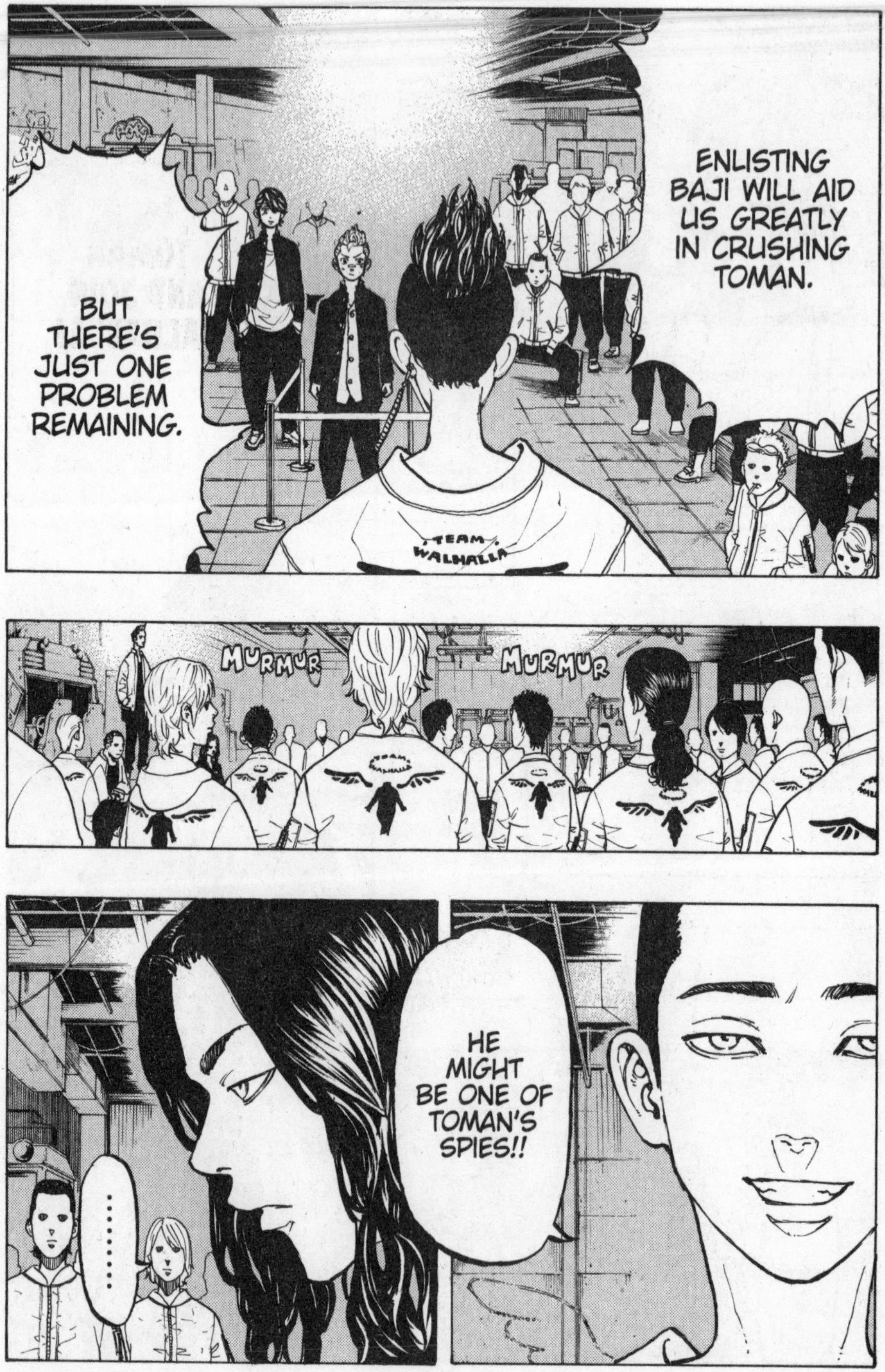
ENLISTING BAJI WILL AID US GREATLY IN CRUSHING TOMAN.
TEAM WALHALLA
BUT THERE'S JUST ONE PROBLEM REMAINING.
MURMUR
MURMUR
HE MIGHT BE ONE OF TOMAN'S SPIES!!
......

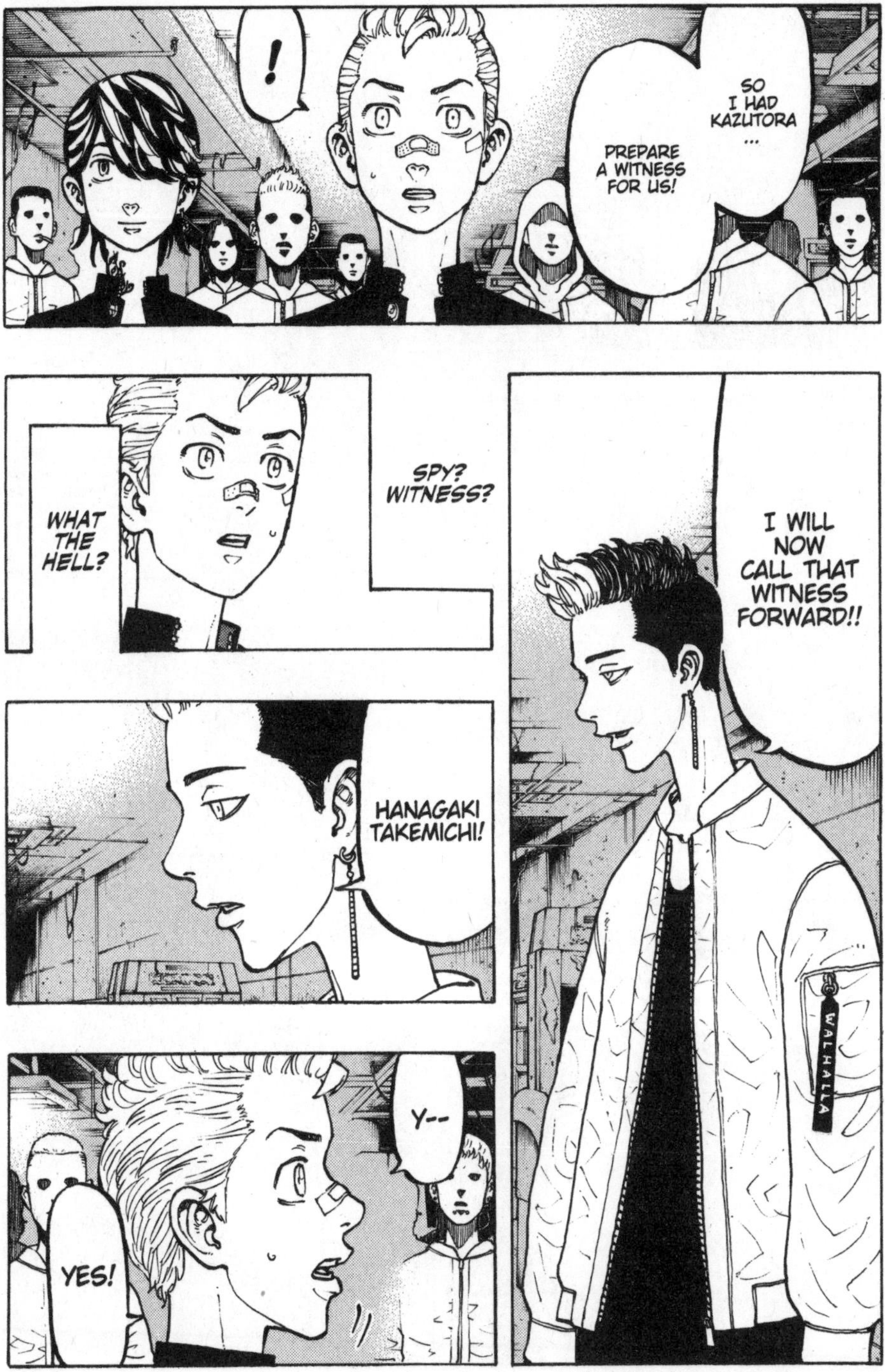
SO I HAD KAZUTORA ...
PREPARE A WITNESS FOR US!
!
I WILL NOW CALL THAT WITNESS FORWARD!!
WALHALLA
SPY? WITNESS?
WHAT THE HELL?
HANAGAKI TAKEMICHI!
Y--
YES!

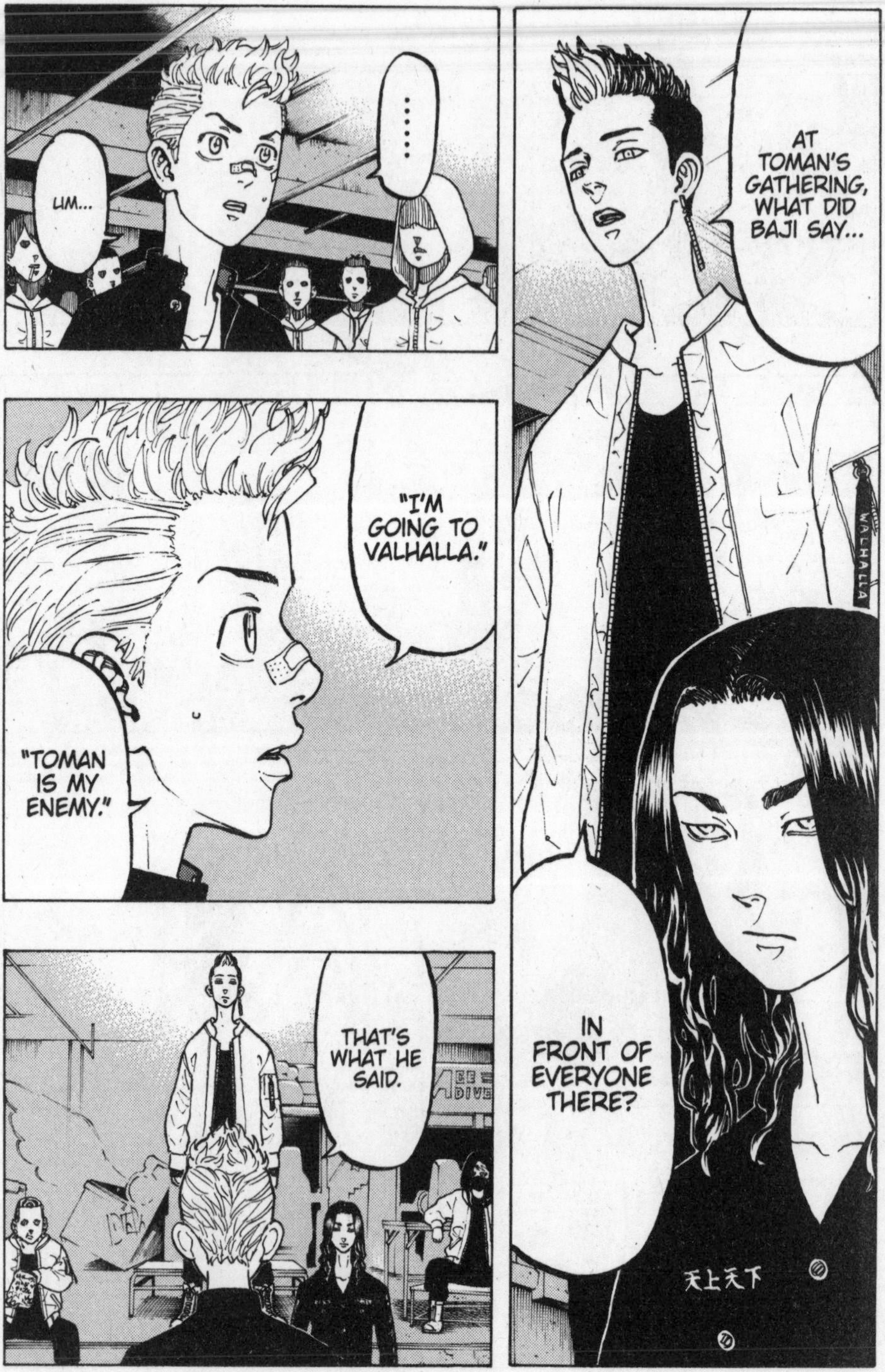
AT TOMAN'S GATHERING, WHAT DID BAJI SAY...
VALHALLA
IN FRONT OF EVERYONE THERE?
天上天下
......
UM...
"I'M GOING TO VALHALLA."
"TOMAN IS MY ENEMY."
THAT'S WHAT HE SAID.

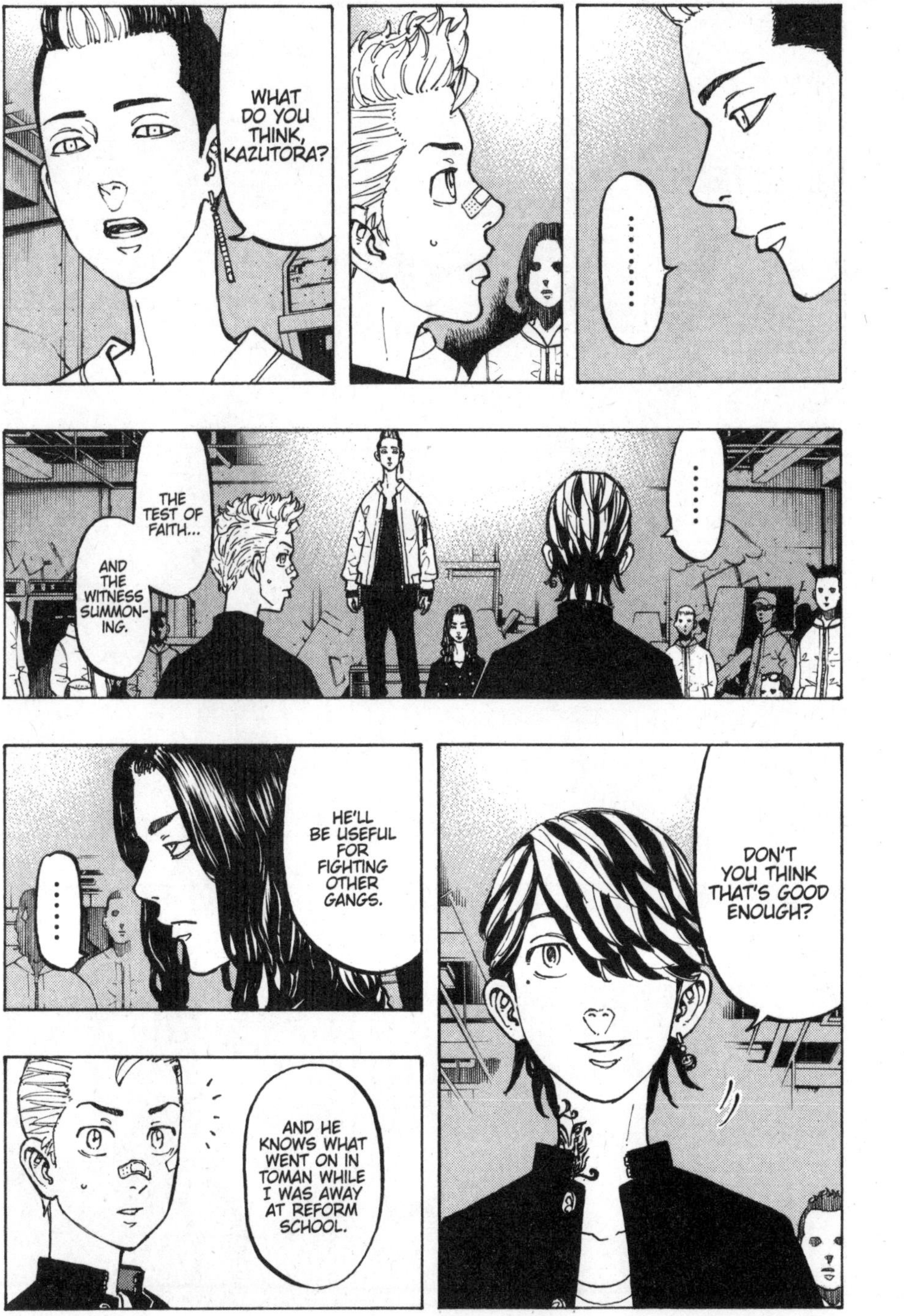

......
WHAT DO YOU THINK, KAZUTORA?
......
THE TEST OF FAITH...
AND THE WITNESS SUMMONING.
DON'T YOU THINK THAT'S GOOD ENOUGH?
HE'LL BE USEFUL FOR FIGHTING OTHER GANGS.
......
AND HE KNOWS WHAT WENT ON IN TOMAN WHILE I WAS AWAY AT REFORM SCHOOL.

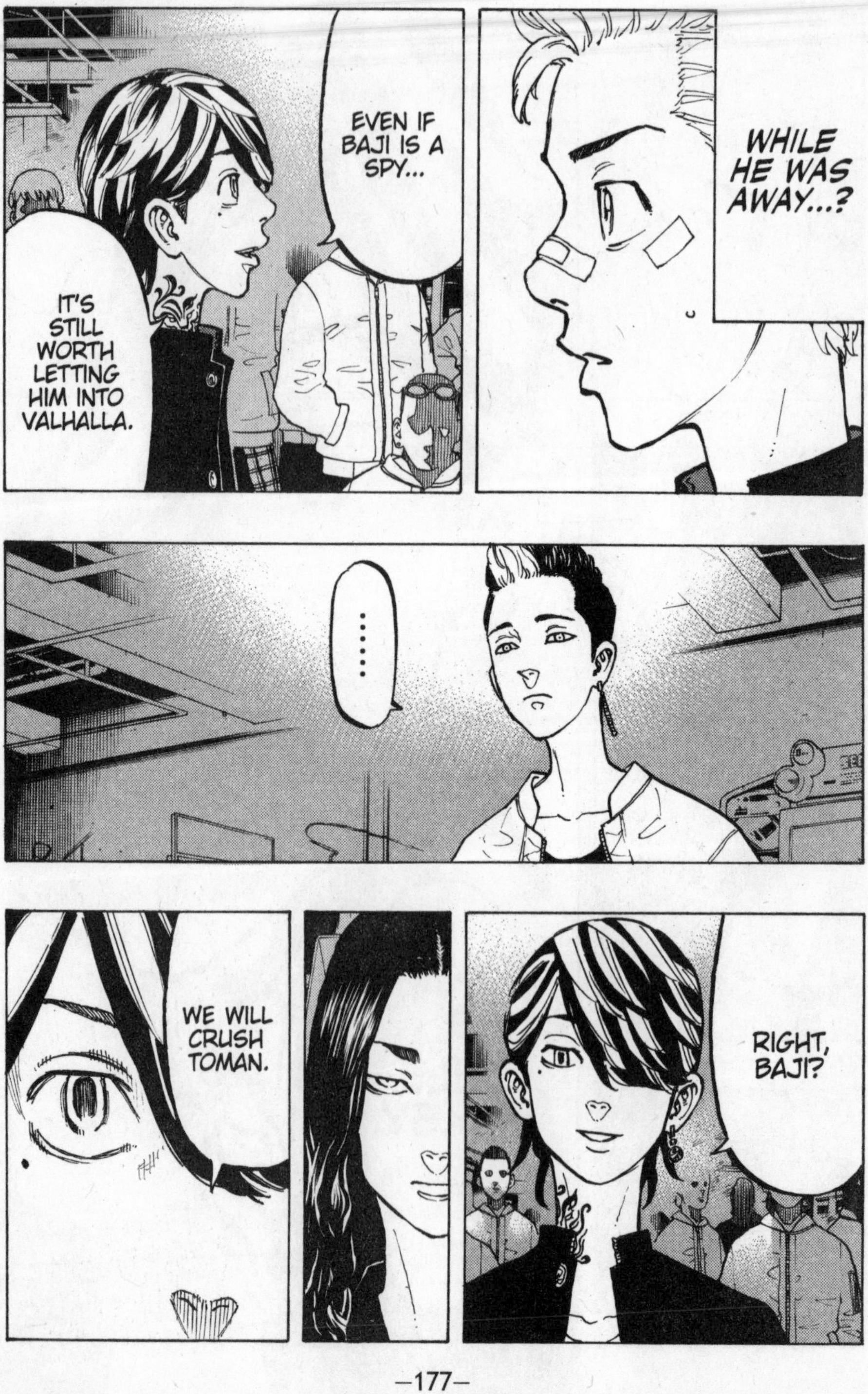
WHILE HE WAS AWAY...?
EVEN IF BAJI IS A SPY...
IT'S STILL WORTH LETTING HIM INTO VALHALLA.
......
RIGHT, BAJI?
WE WILL CRUSH TOMAN.

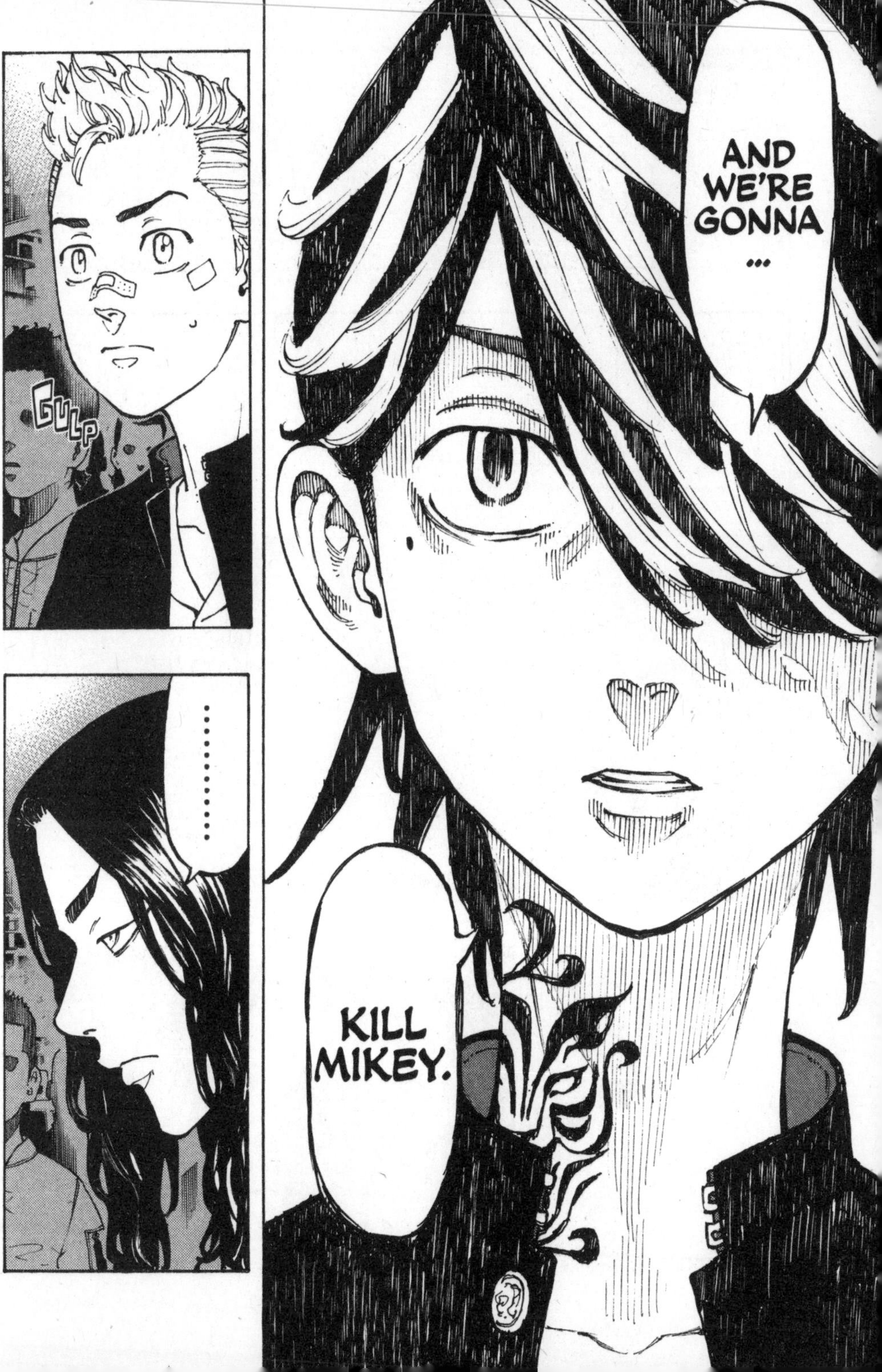
AND WE'RE GONNA ...
KILL MIKEY.
GULP
....

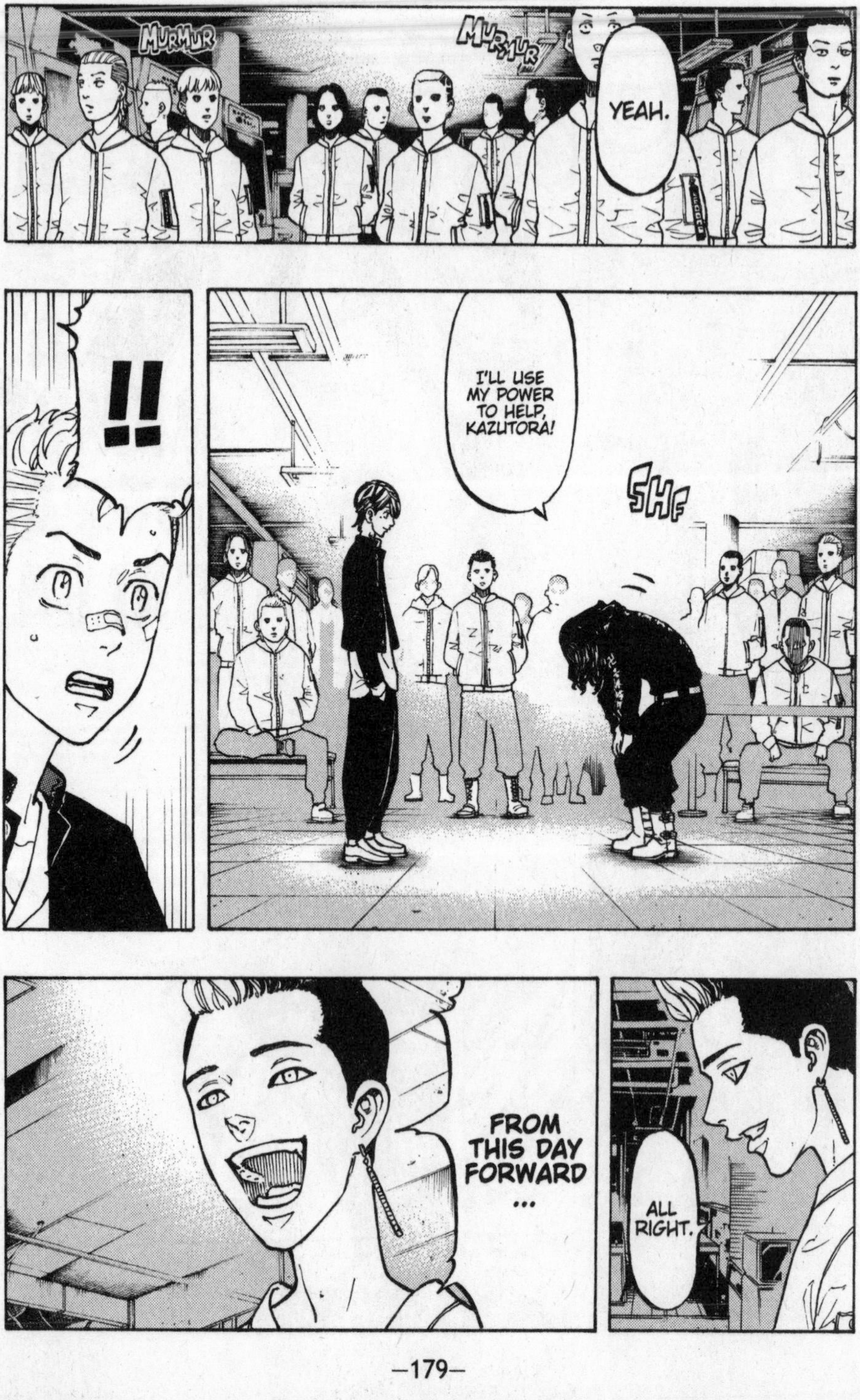
YEAH.
MURMUR
MURMUR
I'LL USE MY POWER TO HELP, KAZUTORA!
SHF
!!
ALL RIGHT.
FROM THIS DAY FORWARD ...

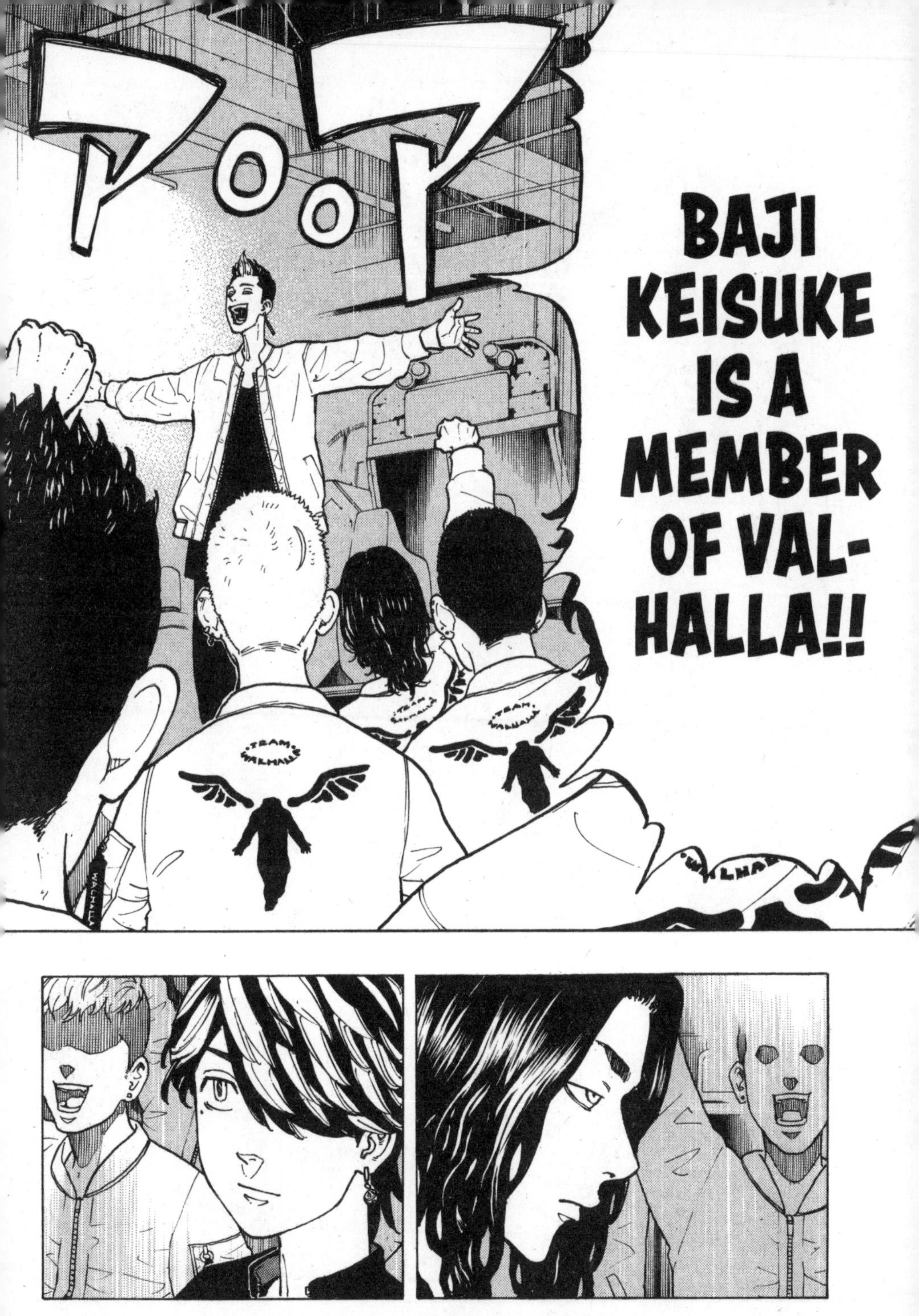
BAJI KEISUKE IS A MEMBER OF VAL- HALLA!!

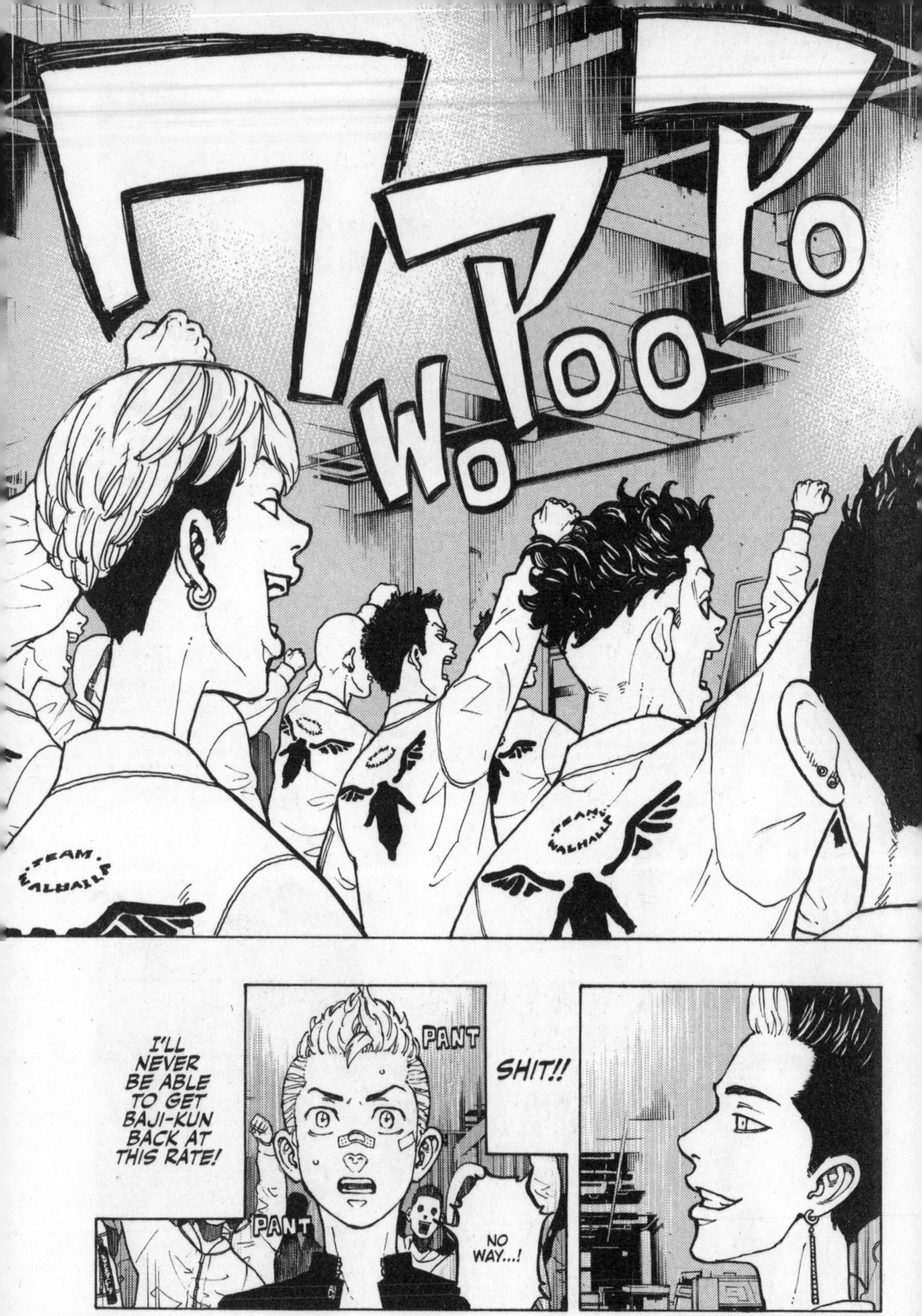
WOOOO
SHIT!!
PANT
I'LL NEVER BE ABLE TO GET BAJI-KUN BACK AT THIS RATE!
NO WAY...!
PANT

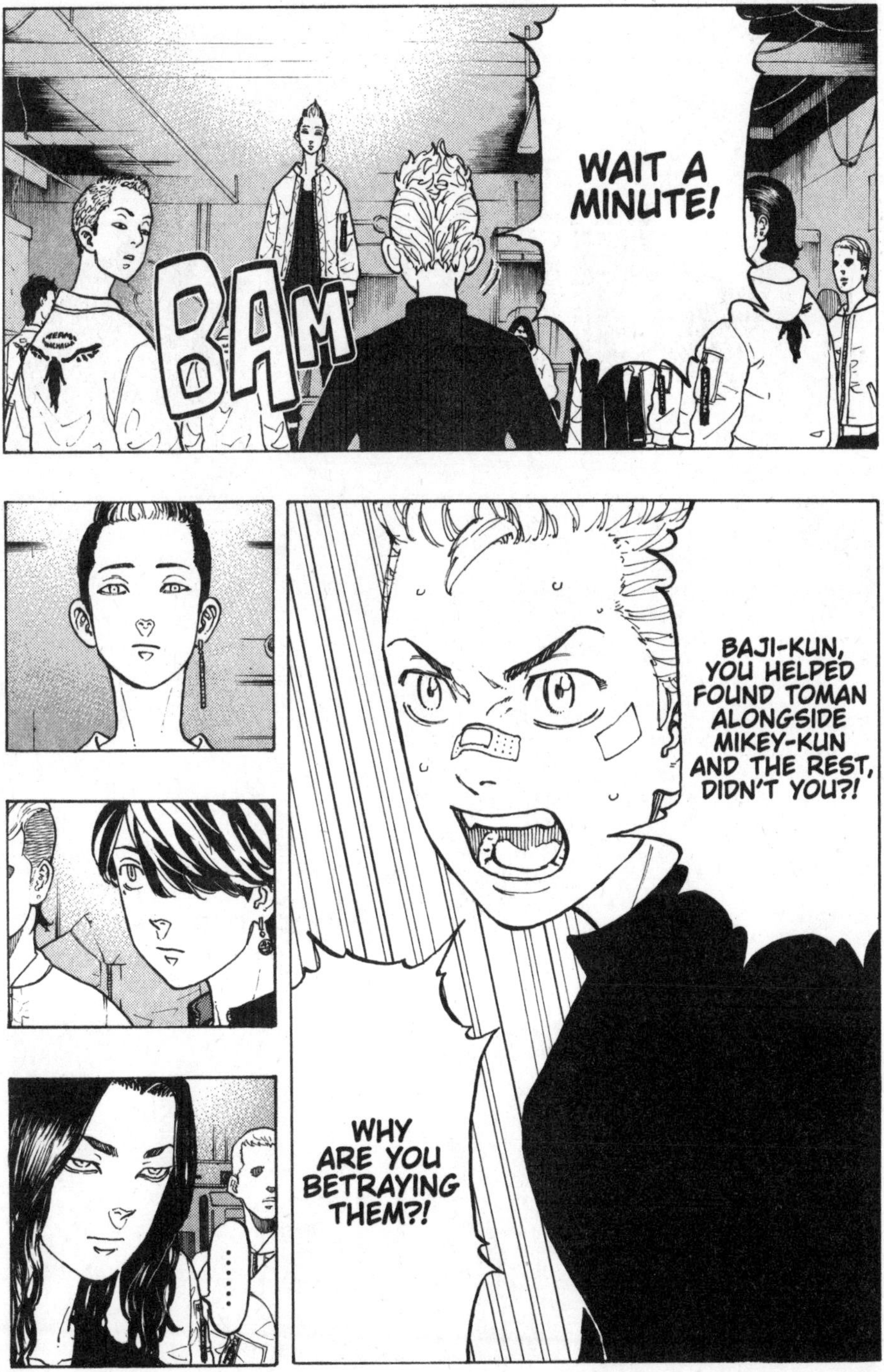
WAIT A MINUTE!
BAM
BAJI-KUN, YOU HELPED FOUND TOMAN ALONGSIDE MIKEY-KUN AND THE REST, DIDN'T YOU?!
WHY ARE YOU BETRAYING THEM?!
......

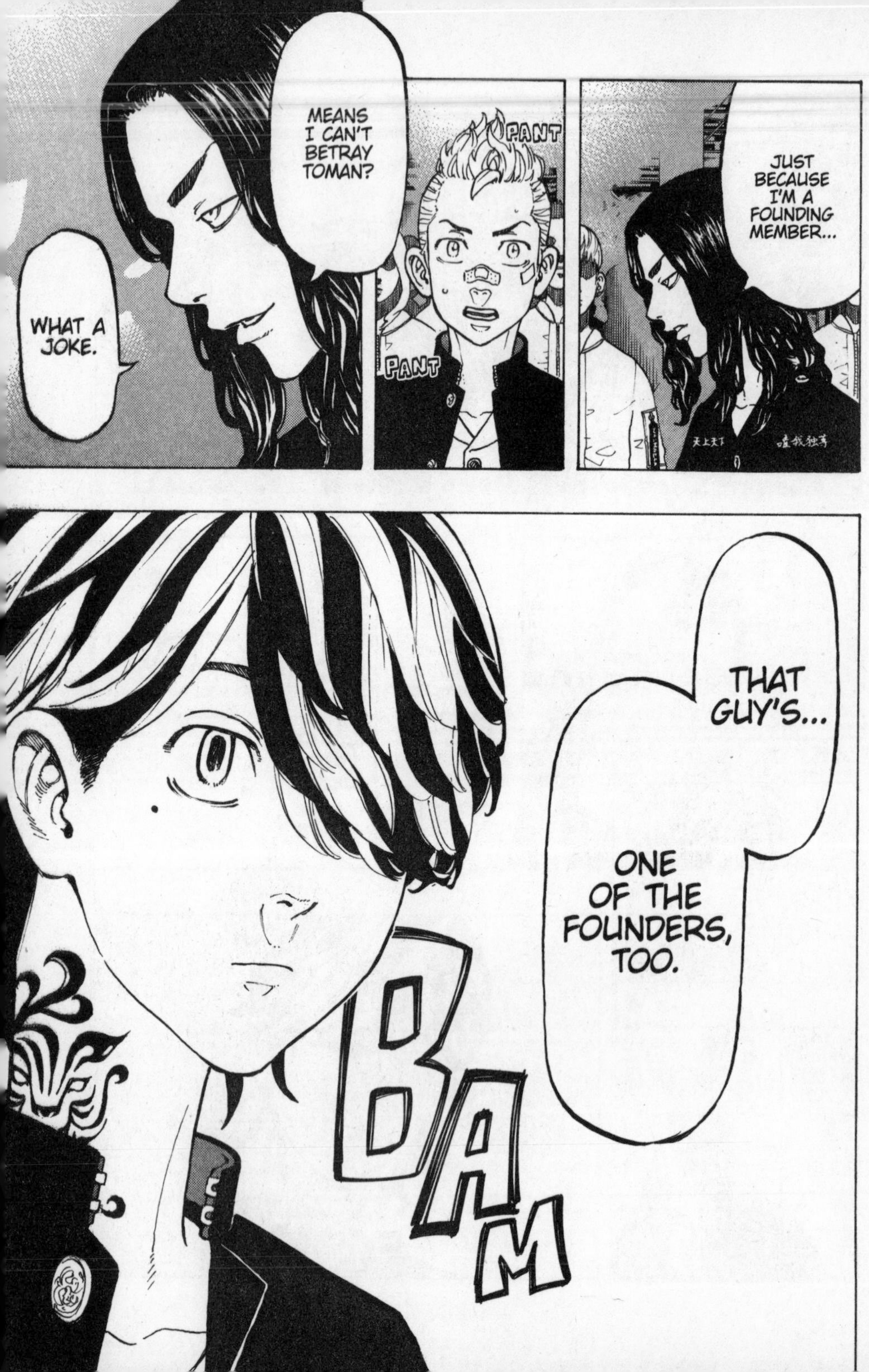
JUST BECAUSE I'M A FOUNDING MEMBER...
天上天下
唯我独尊
PANT
PANT
MEANS I CAN'T BETRAY TOMAN?
WHAT A JOKE.
THAT GUY'S...
ONE OF THE FOUNDERS, TOO.
BAM

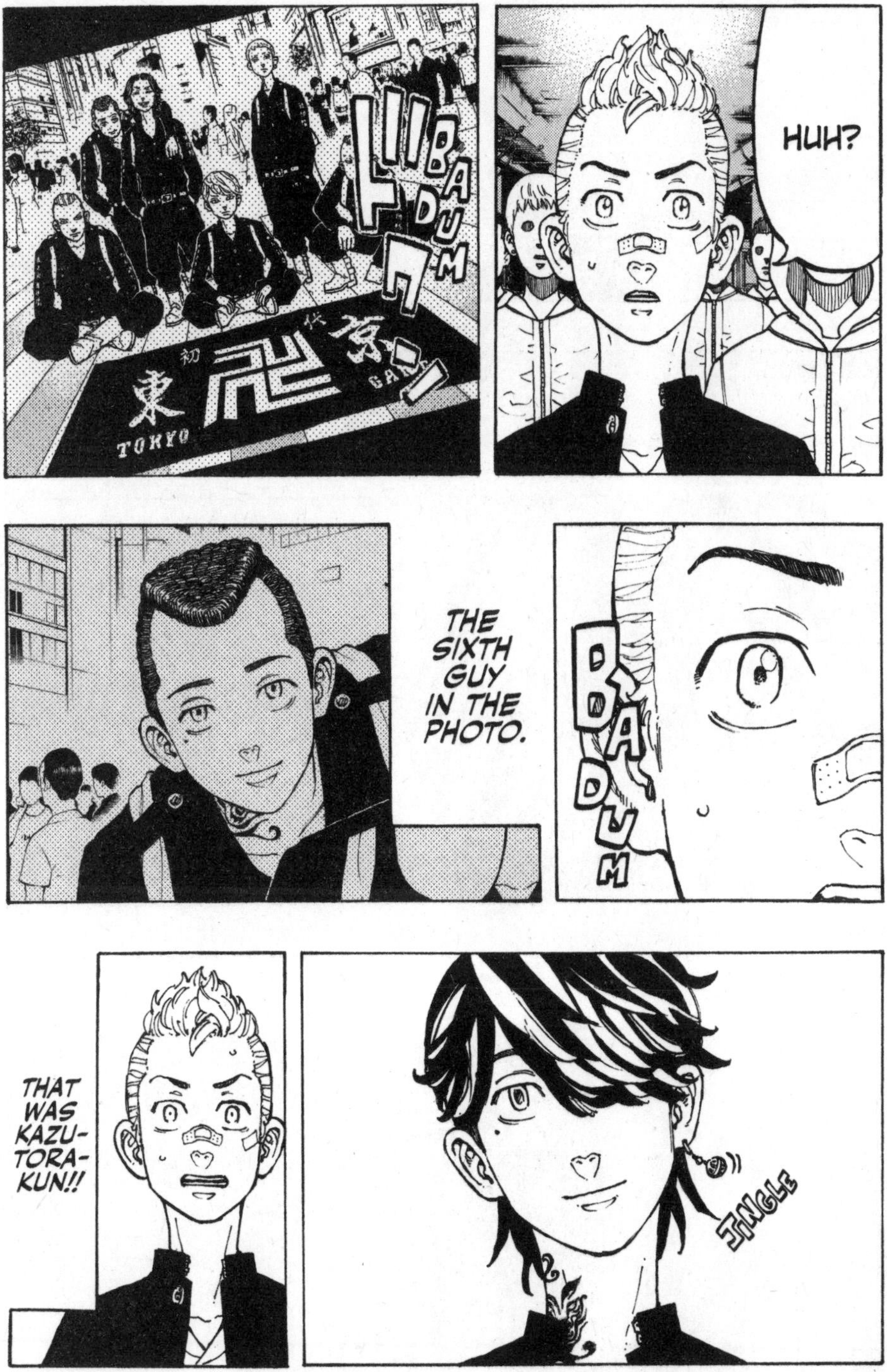
HUH?
BADUM
TOKYO
BADUM
THE SIXTH GUY IN THE PHOTO.
JINGLE
THAT WAS KAZUTORA-KUN!!

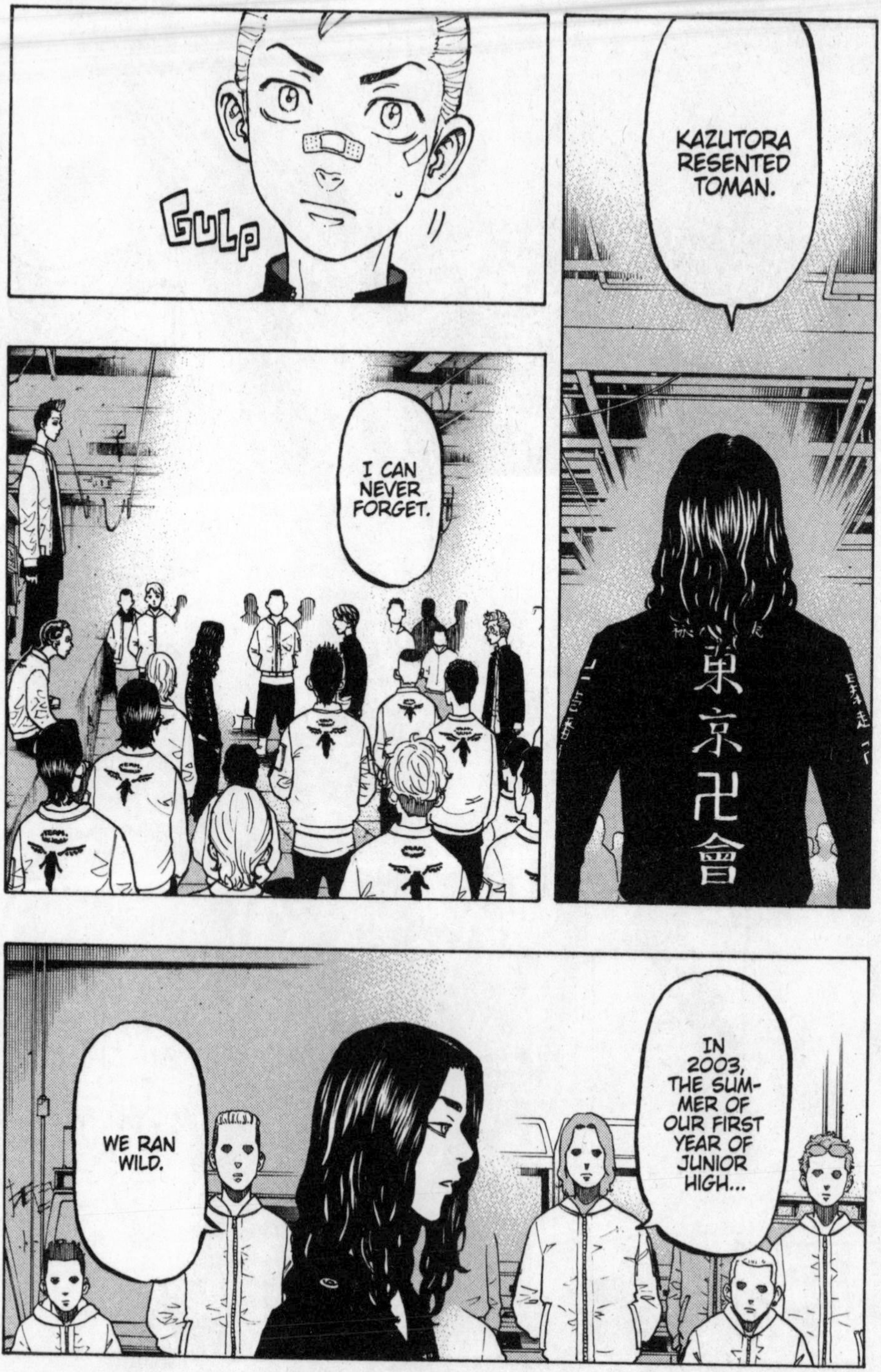
KAZUTORA RESENTED TOMAN.
東京卍會
GULP
I CAN NEVER FORGET.
IN 2003, THE SUMMER OF OUR FIRST YEAR OF JUNIOR HIGH...
WE RAN WILD.

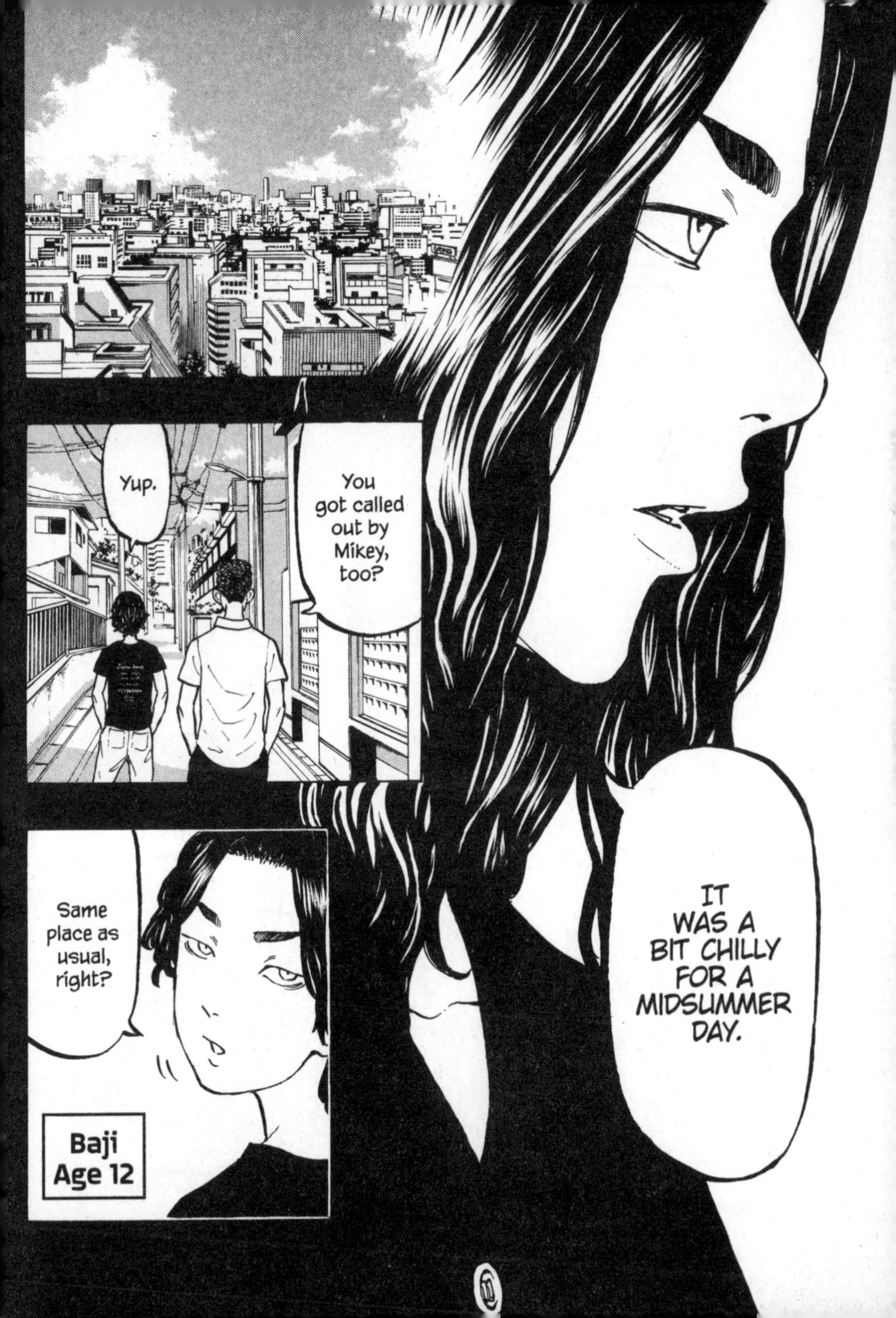
IT WAS A BIT CHILLY FOR A MIDSUMMER DAY.
You got called out by Mikey, too?
Yup.
Same place as usual, right?
Baji Age 12

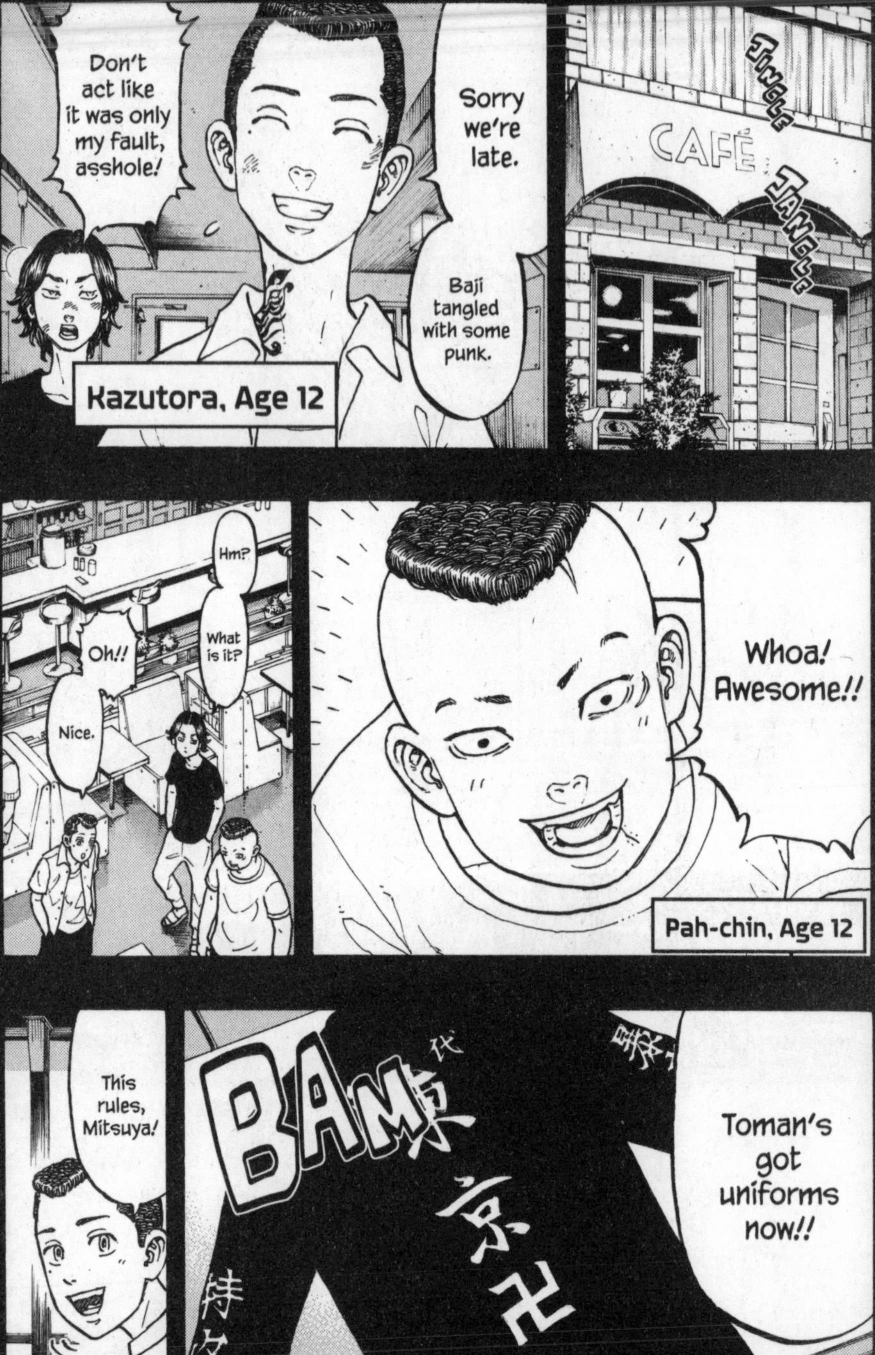
JINGLE
JANGLE
CAFÉ
Sorry we're late.
Baji tangled with some punk.
Don't act like it was only my fault, asshole!
Kazutora, Age 12
Whoa! Awesome!!
Pah-chin, Age 12
Hm?
What is it?
Oh!!
Nice.
Toman's got uniforms now!!
BAM
This rules, Mitsuya!

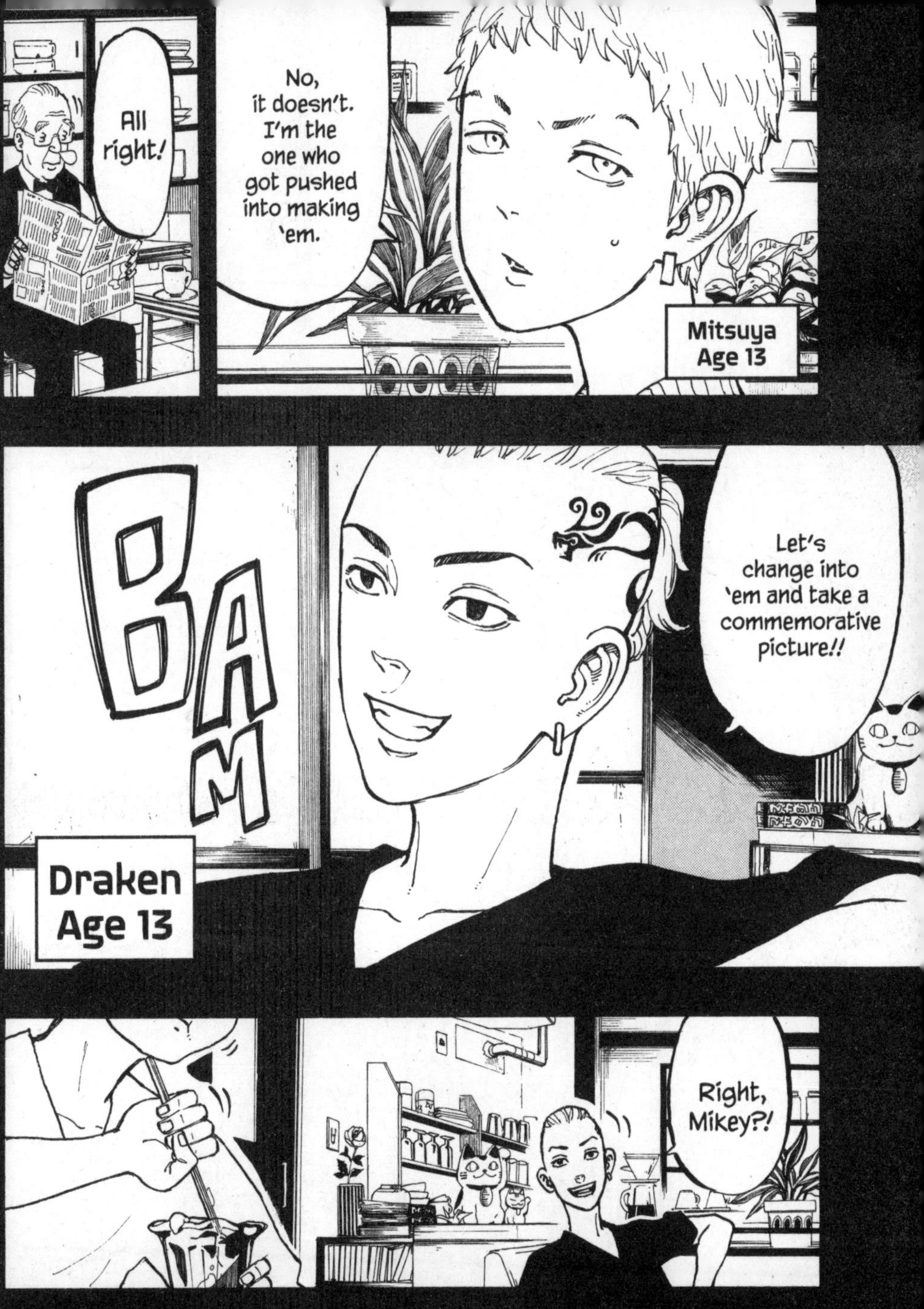
No, it doesn't. I'm the one who got pushed into making 'em.
Mitsuya Age 13
All right!
Let's change into 'em and take a commemorative picture!!
BAM
Draken Age 13
Right, Mikey?!

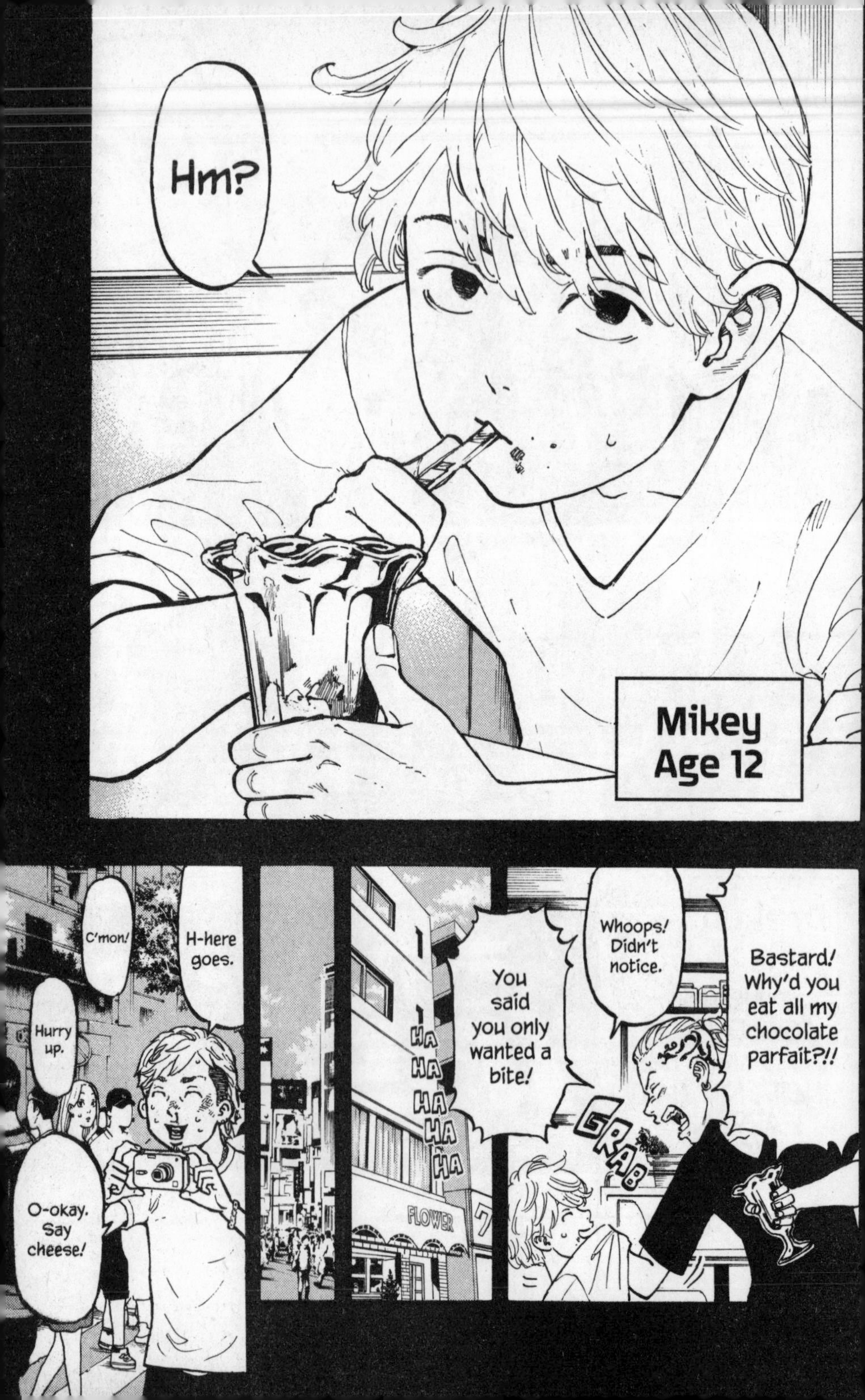
Hm?
Mikey Age 12
Bastard! Why'd you eat all my chocolate parfait?!!
Whoops! Didn't notice.
GRAB
You said you only wanted a bite!
HA HA HA HA HA
FLOWER
H-here goes.
C'mon!
Hurry up.
O-okay. Say cheese!

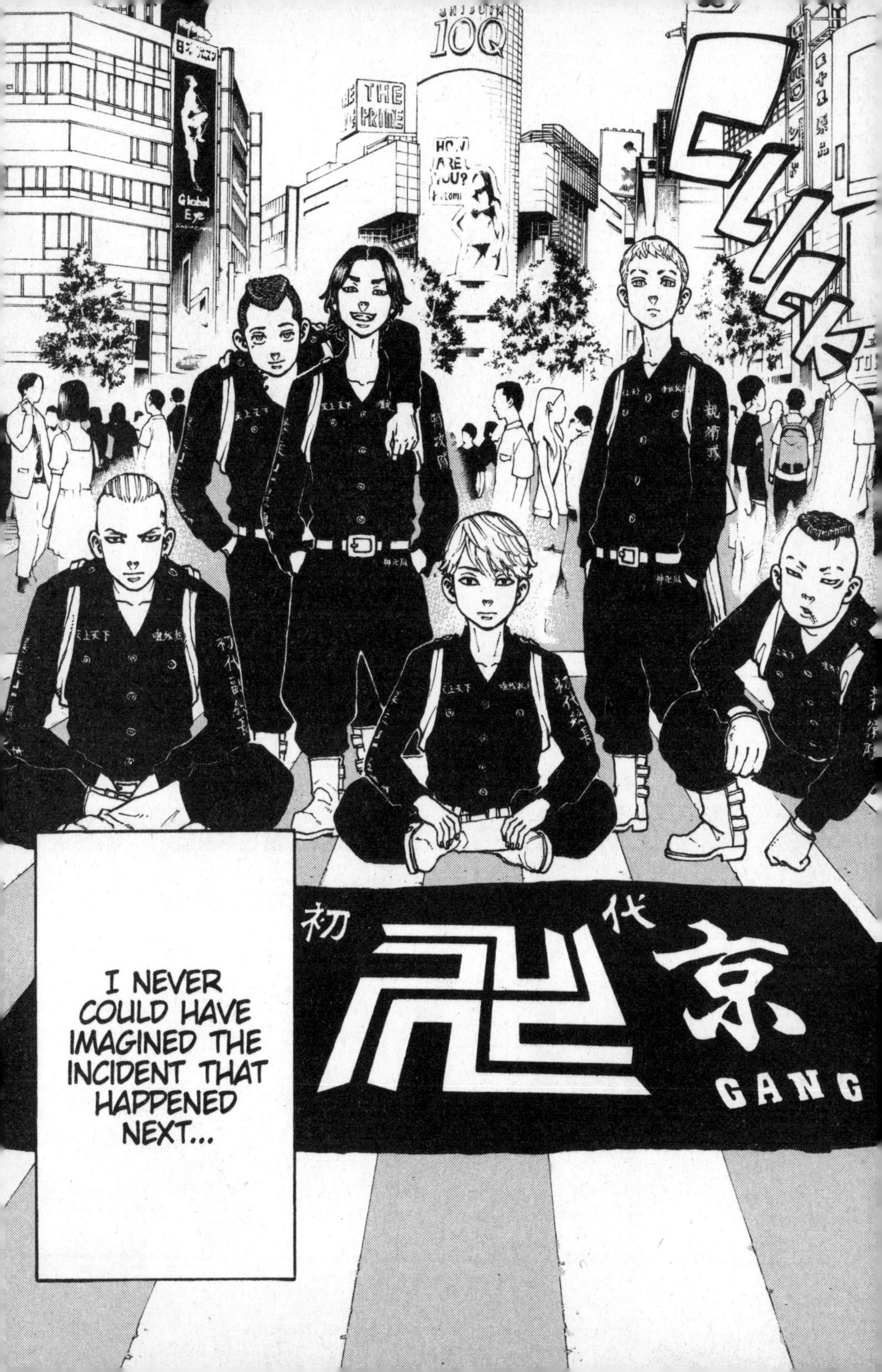

CLICK
10Q
THE PRIME
HOW ARE YOU?
Global Eye
初代
卍京
GANG
I NEVER COULD HAVE IMAGINED THE INCIDENT THAT HAPPENED NEXT...

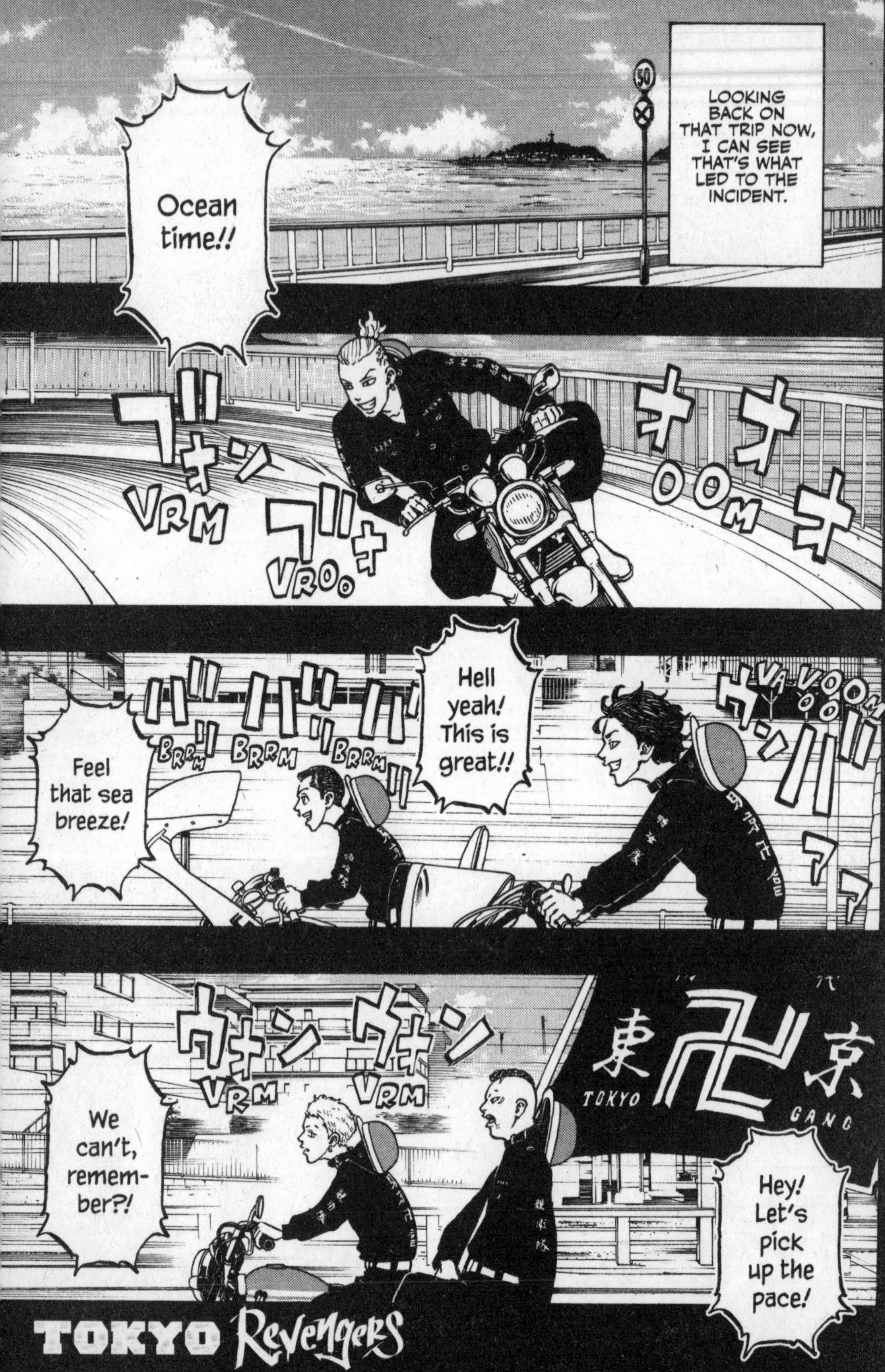
LOOKING BACK ON THAT TRIP NOW, I CAN SEE THAT'S WHAT LED TO THE INCIDENT.
Ocean time!!
OOM
VRM
VROo
VA VOOM
Hell yeah! This is great!!
BRRM BRRM BRRM
Feel that sea breeze!
TOKYO GANG
Hey! Let's pick up the pace!
VRM VRM
We can't, remember?!
TOKYO Revengers

CHAPTER 43: IN THOSE DAYS

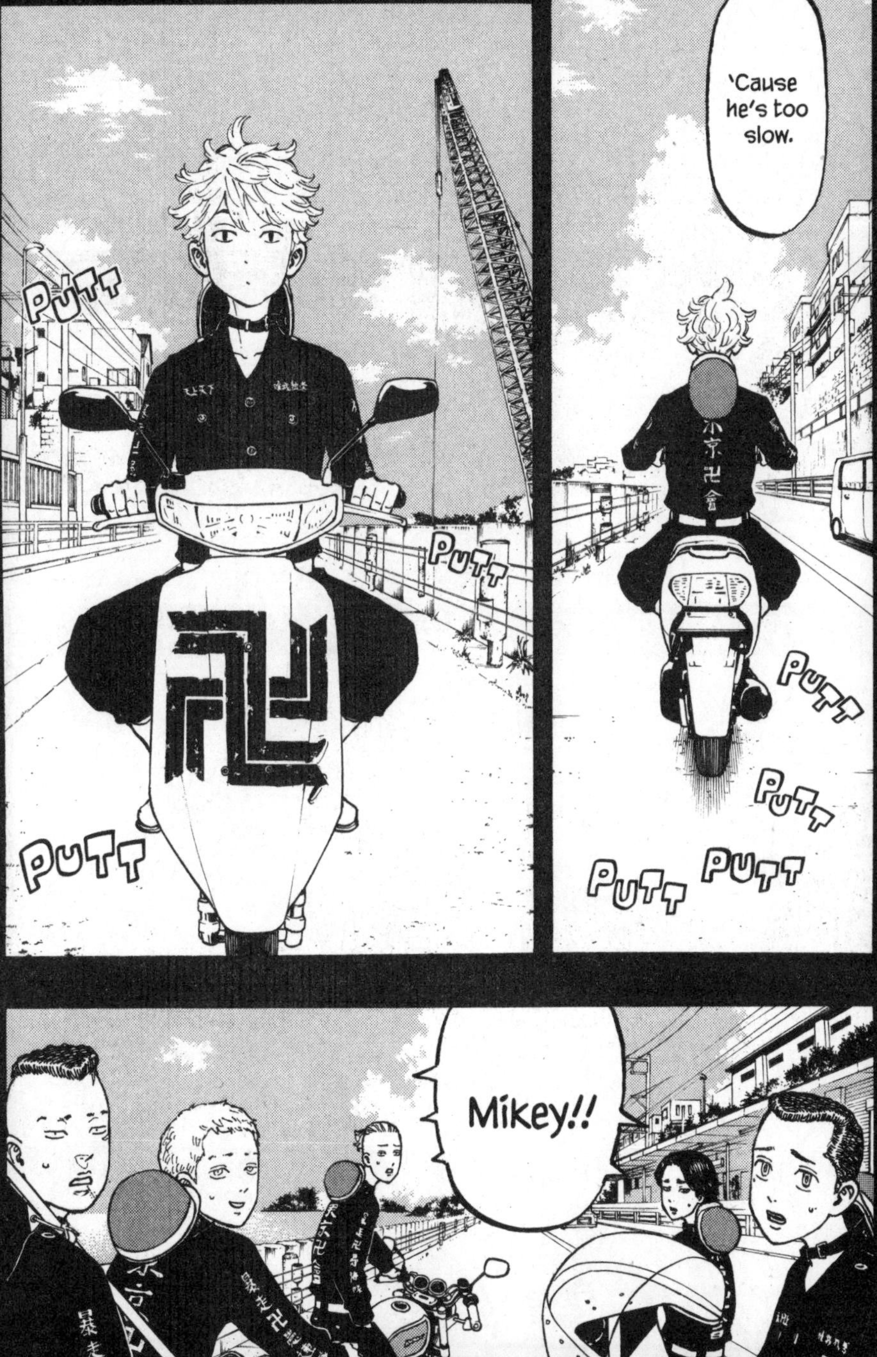

'Cause he's too slow.
PUTT
PUTT
PUTT
PUTT
PUTT
PUTT
PUTT
Mikey!!

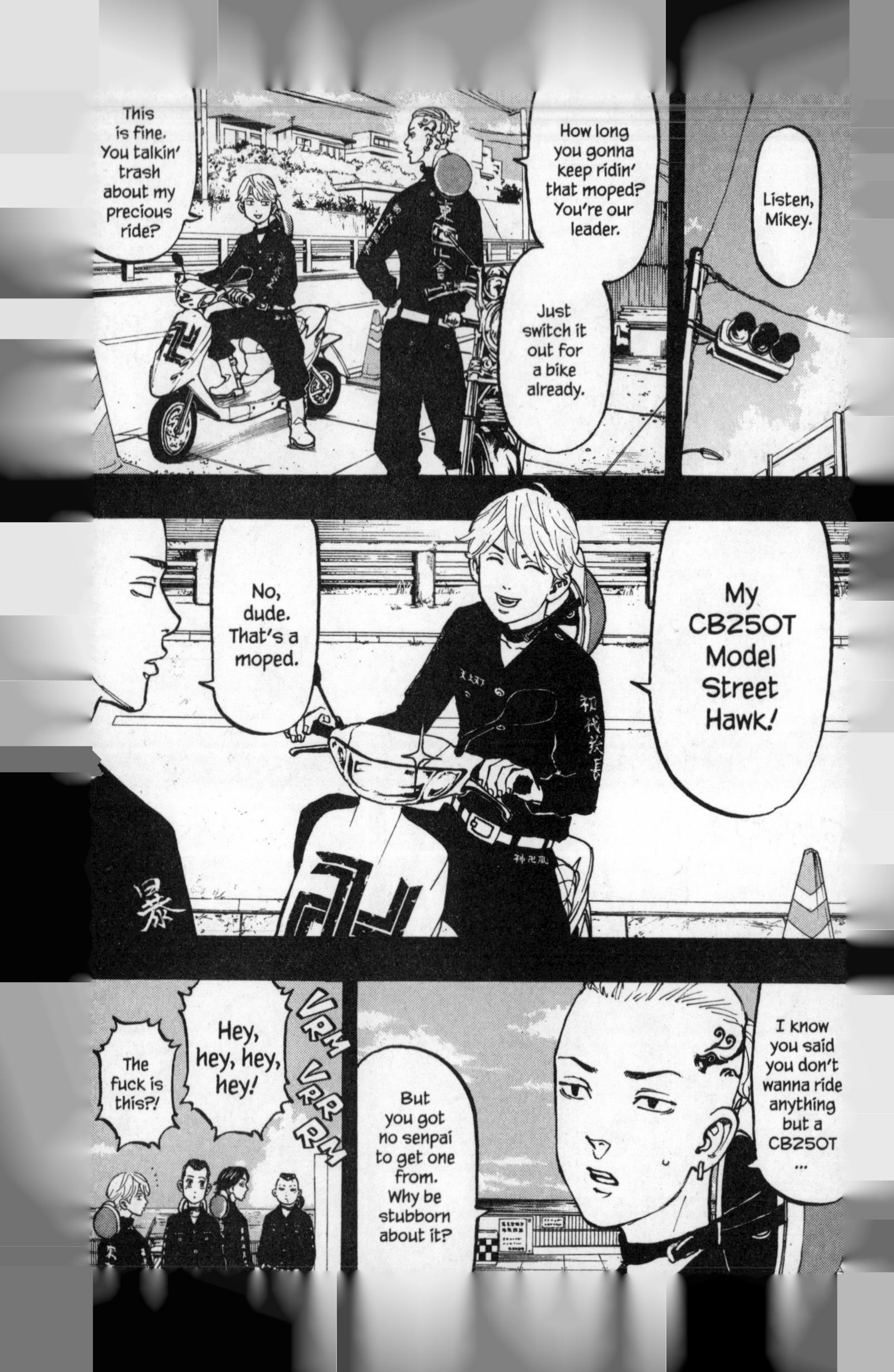

Listen, Mikey.
How long you gonna keep ridin' that moped? You're our leader.
Just switch it out for a bike already.
This is fine. You talkin' trash about my precious ride?
My CB250T Model Street Hawk!
No, dude. That's a moped.
I know you said you don't wanna ride anything but a CB250T ...
But you got no senpai to get one from. Why be stubborn about it?
VRM VRR RM
Hey, hey, hey, hey!
The fuck is this?!

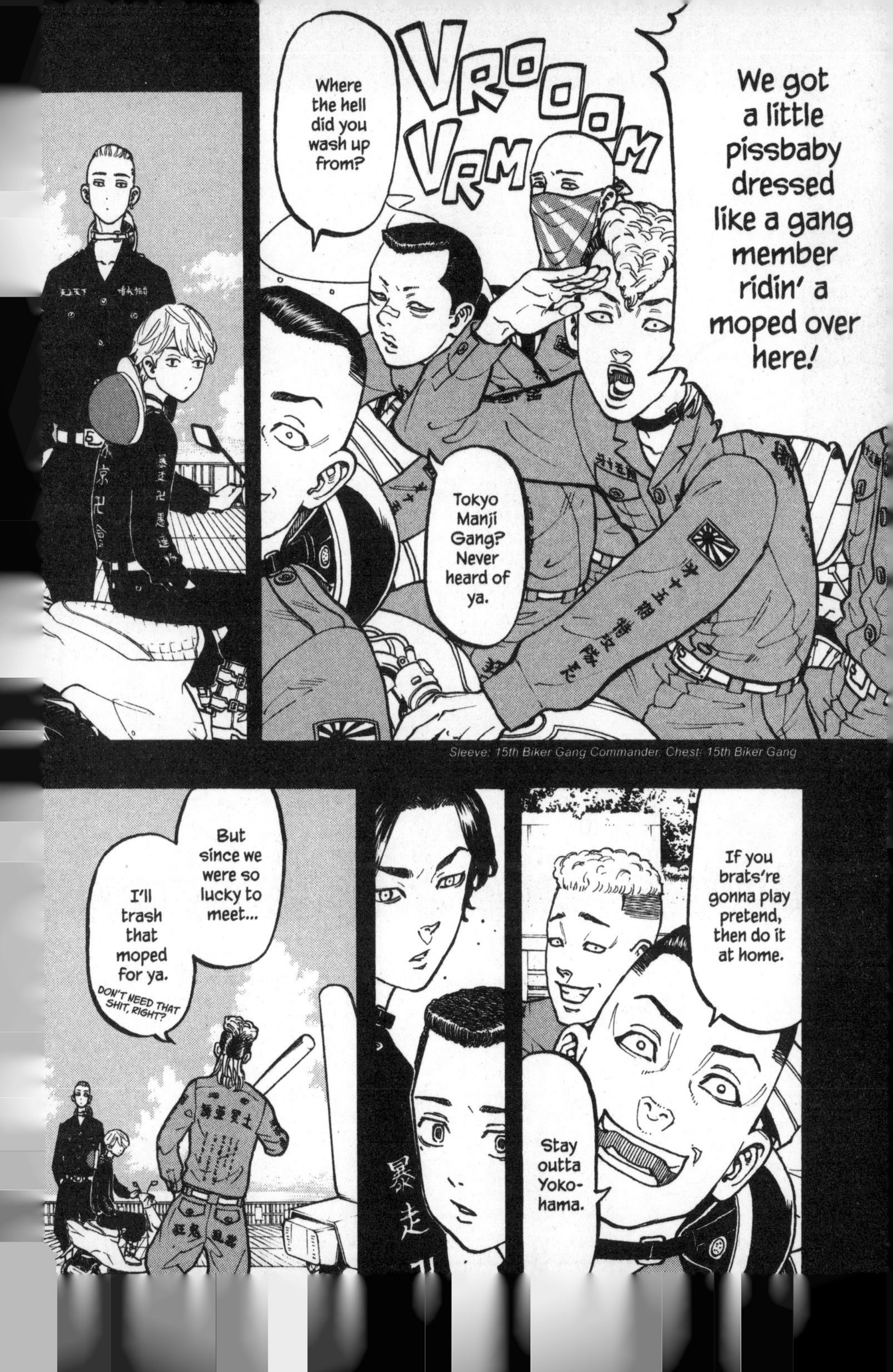
We got a little pissbaby dressed like a gang member ridin' a moped over here!
VROOOOM
VRM
Where the hell did you wash up from?
Tokyo Manji Gang? Never heard of ya.
If you brats're gonna play pretend, then do it at home.
Stay outta Yoko-hama.
But since we were so lucky to meet...
I'll trash that moped for ya.
DON'T NEED THAT SHIT, RIGHT?
Sleeve: 15th Biker Gang Commander. Chest: 15th Biker Gang

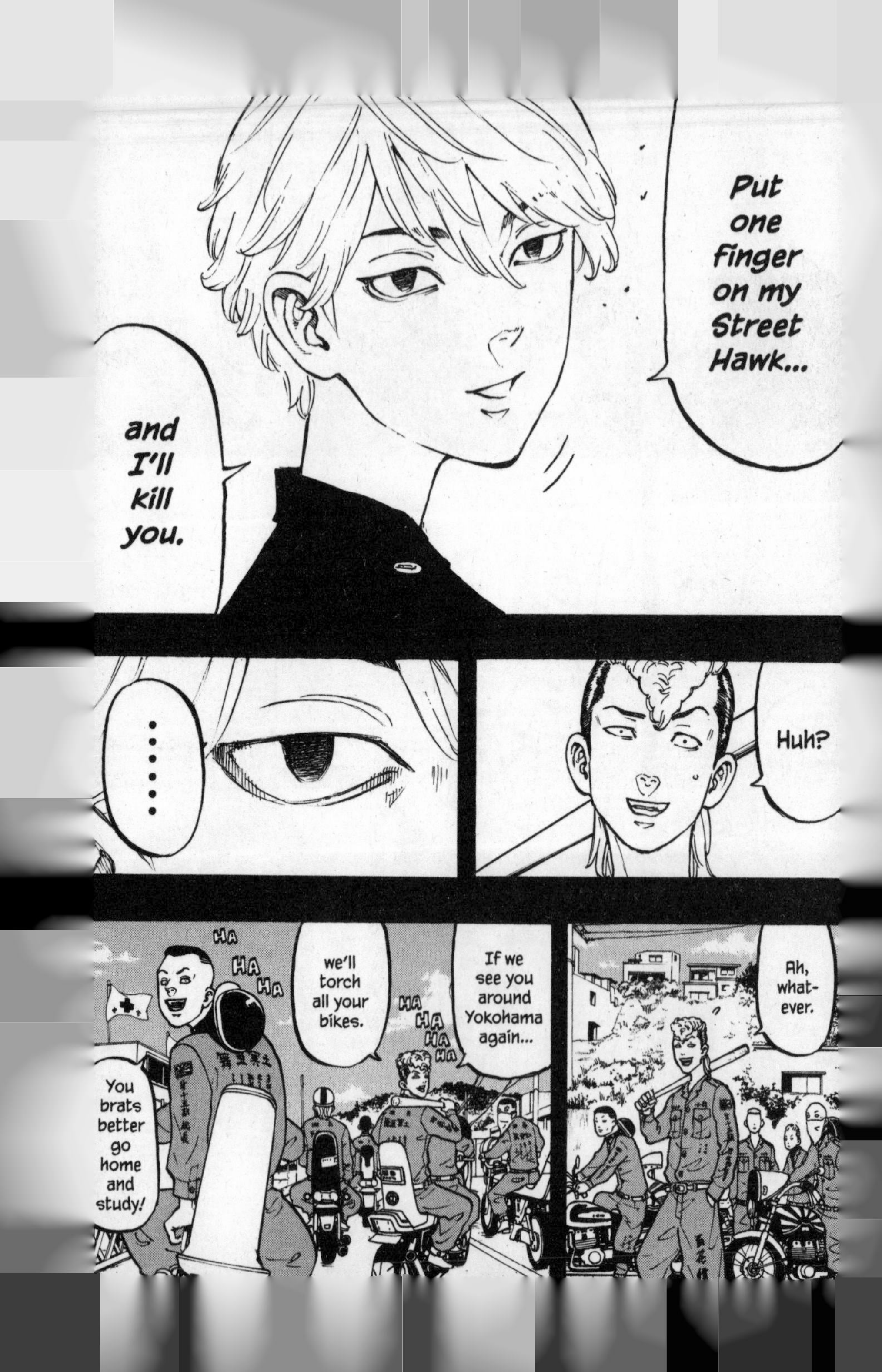
Put one finger on my Street Hawk...
and I'll kill you.
Huh?
......
Ah, whatever.
If we see you around Yokohama again...
HA HA HA HA
we'll torch all your bikes.
HA HA HA
You brats better go home and study!

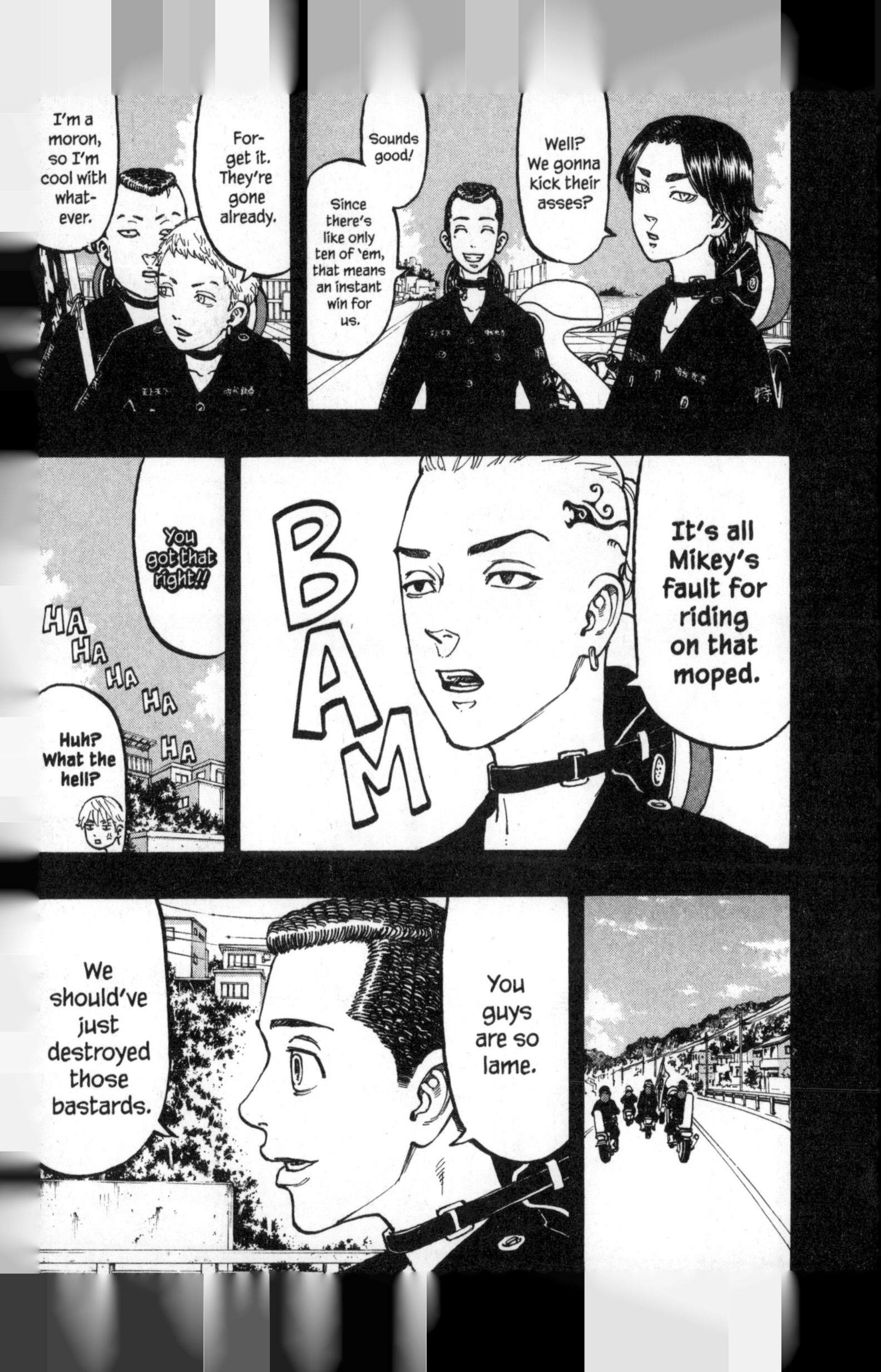
Well? We gonna kick their asses?
Sounds good!
Since there's like only ten of 'em, that means an instant win for us.
For-get it. They're gone already.
I'm a moron, so I'm cool with what-ever.
It's all Mikey's fault for riding on that moped.
BAM
You got that right!!
HA HA HA HA HA
Huh? What the hell?
You guys are so lame.
We should've just destroyed those bastards.

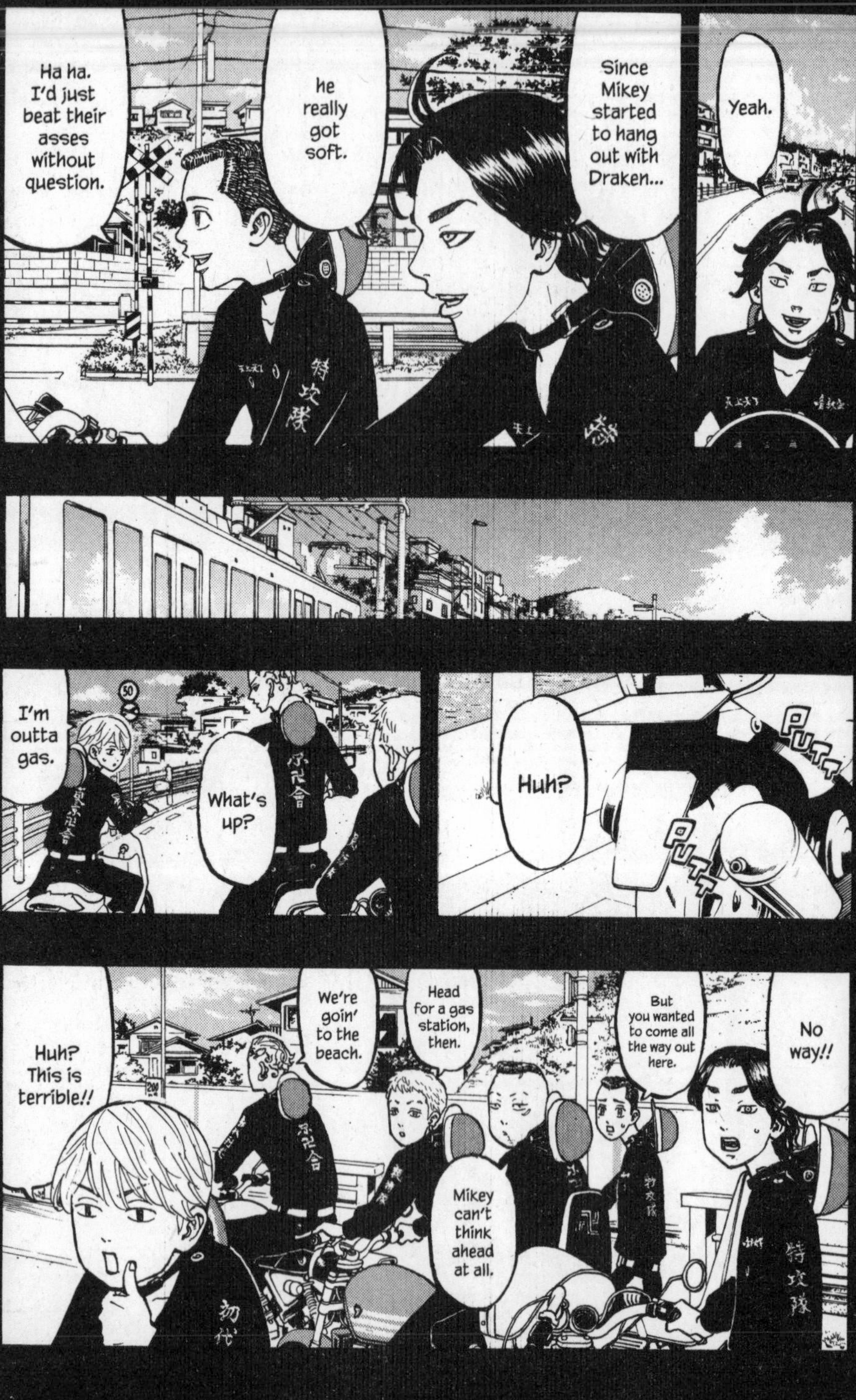
Yeah.
Since Mikey started to hang out with Draken...
he really got soft.
Ha ha. I'd just beat their asses without question.
PUTT
Huh?
PUTT
What's up?
I'm outta gas.
No way!!
But you wanted to come all the way out here.
Head for a gas station, then.
We're goin' to the beach.
Mikey can't think ahead at all.
Huh? This is terrible!!

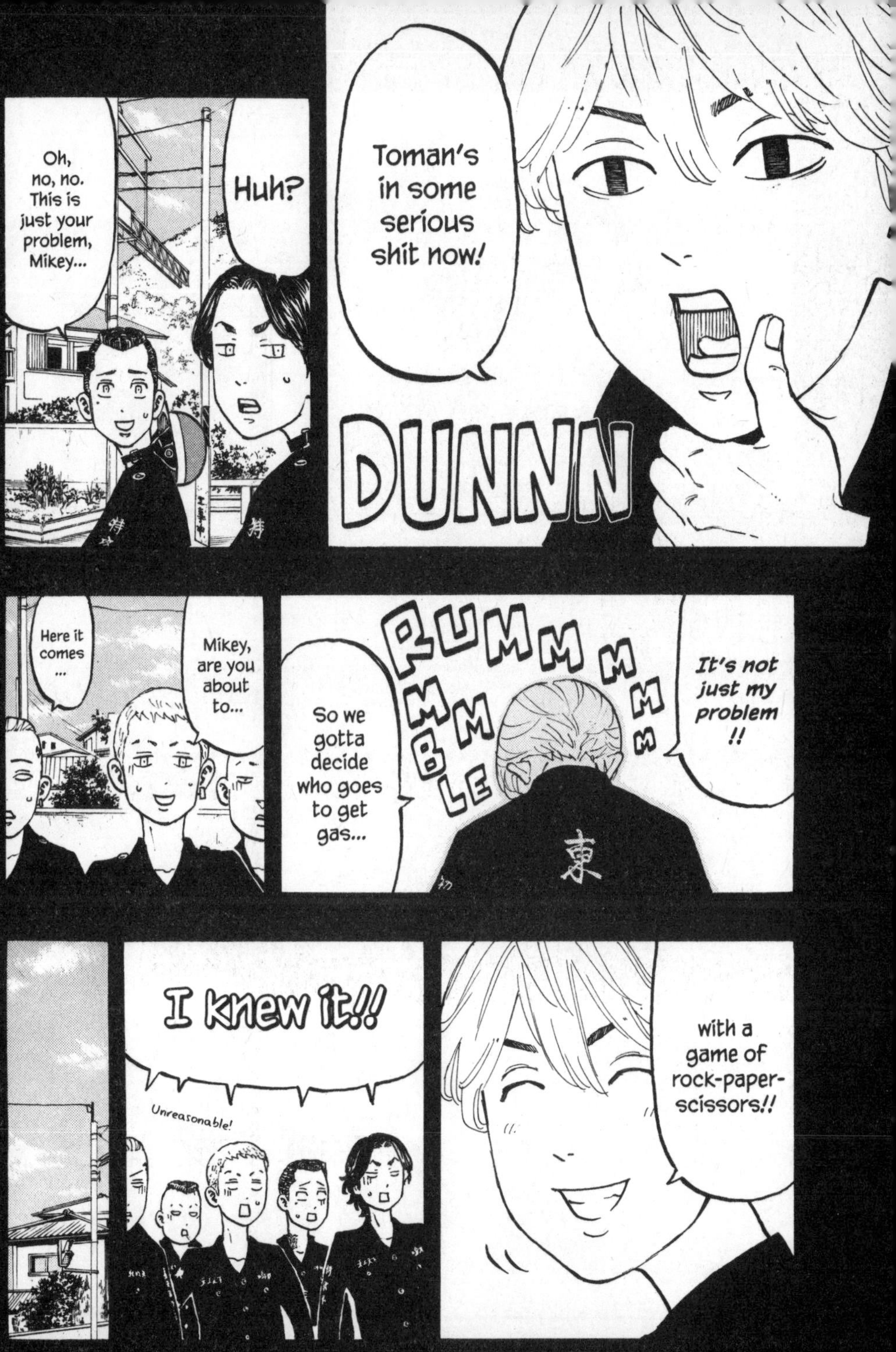
Toman's in some serious shit now!
DUNNN
Huh?
Oh, no, no. This is just your problem, Mikey...
It's not just my problem!!
RUMMMMMMMMMBLE
So we gotta decide who goes to get gas...
Mikey, are you about to...
Here it comes...
with a game of rock-paper-scissors!!
I knew it!!
Unreasonable!

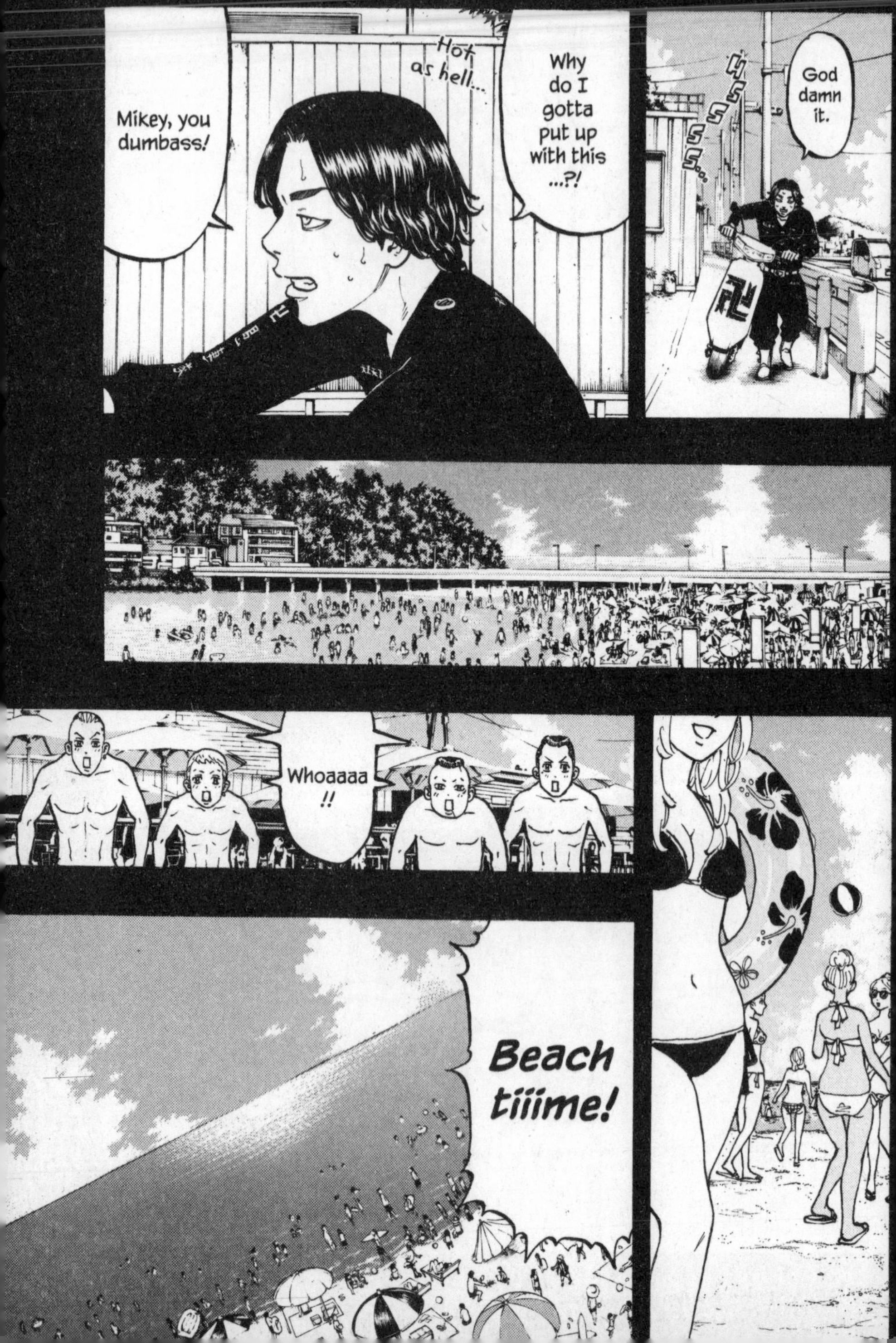
HSSSS...
God damn it.
Why do I gotta put up with this ...?!
Hot as hell...
Mikey, you dumbass!
Whoaaaa !!
Beach tiiime!

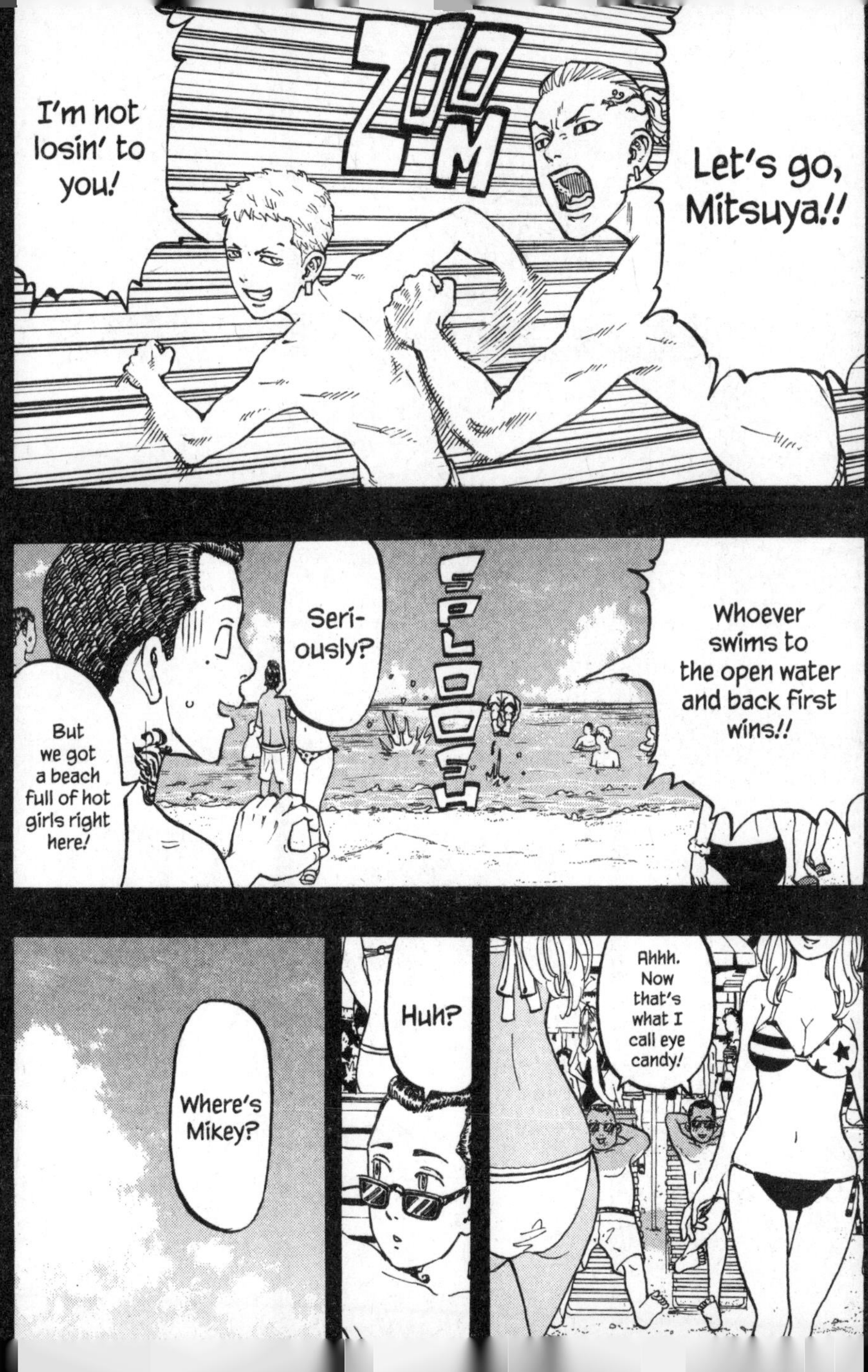
Let's go, Mitsuya!!
ZOOM
I'm not losin' to you!
Whoever swims to the open water and back first wins!!
SPLOOSH
Seri-ously?
But we got a beach full of hot girls right here!
Ahhh. Now that's what I call eye candy!
Huh?
Where's Mikey?

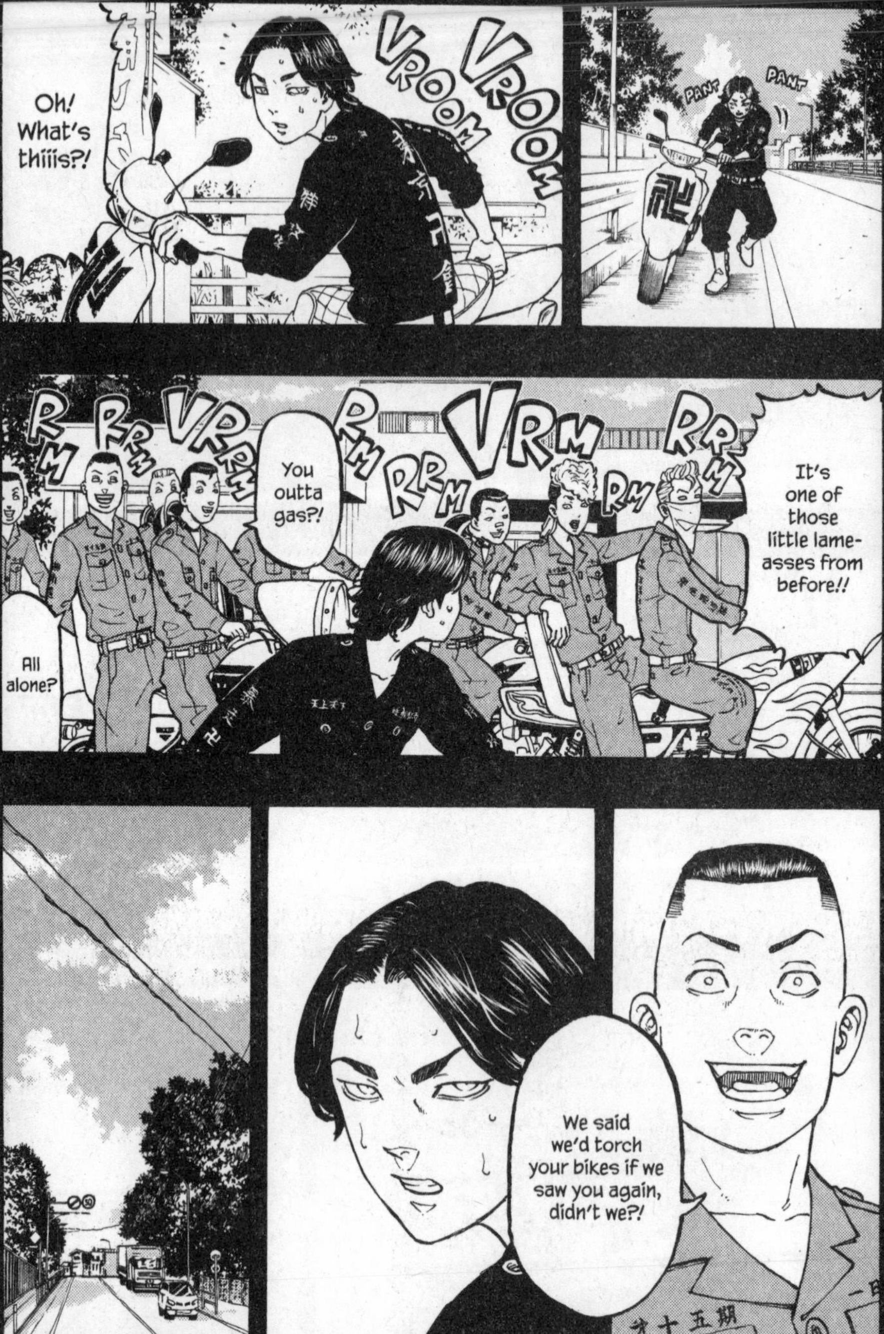
PANT PANT
VROOM VROOM
Oh! What's thiiis?!
It's one of those little lame-asses from before!!
RRRM
RM
VRM
RRRM
RRRM
You outta gas?!
VRRRM
RRRM
RRM
All alone?
We said we'd torch your bikes if we saw you again, didn't we?!

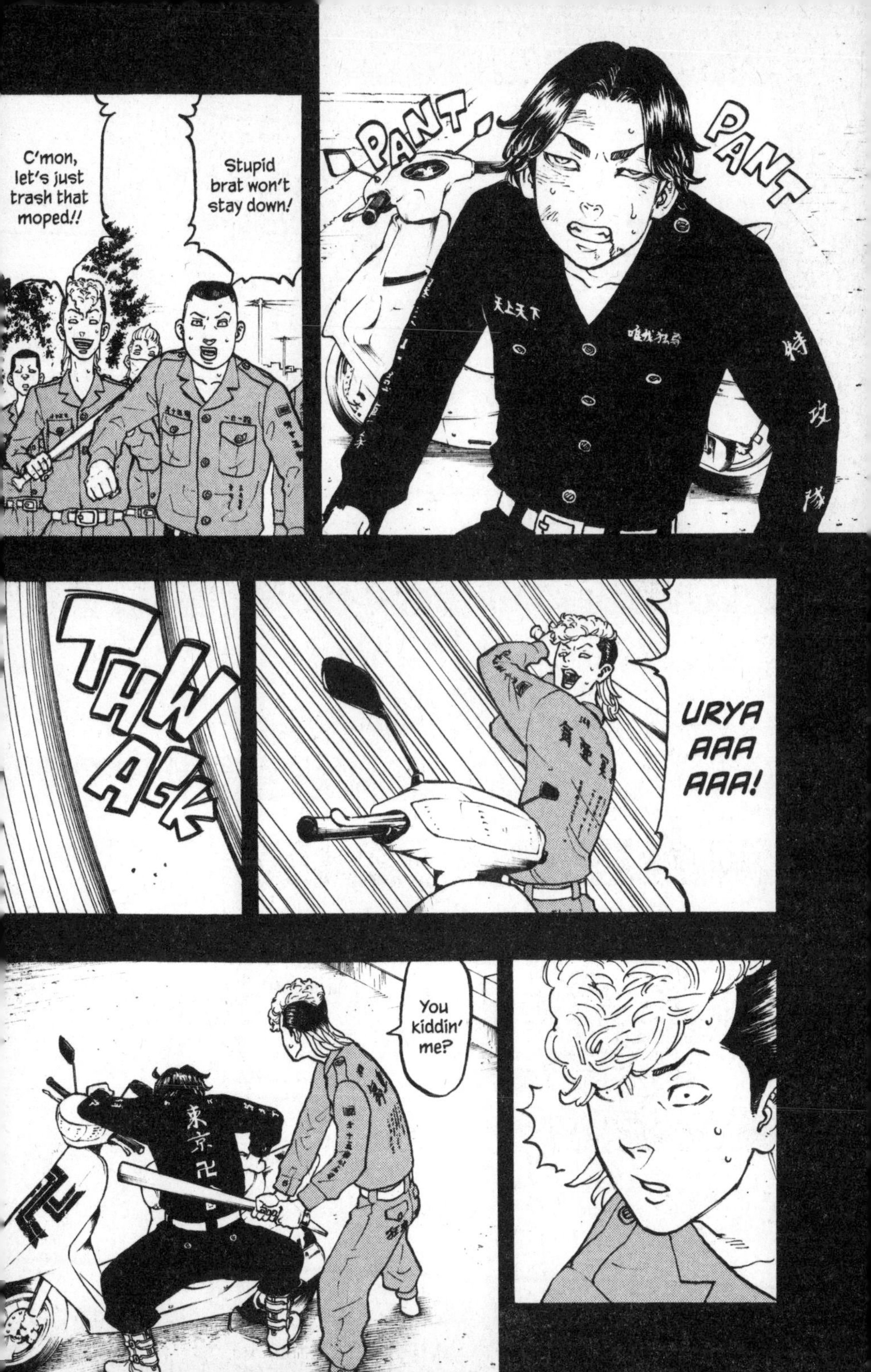
PANT PANT
Stupid brat won't stay down!
C'mon, let's just trash that moped!!
URYA AAA AAA!
THWACK
You kiddin' me?

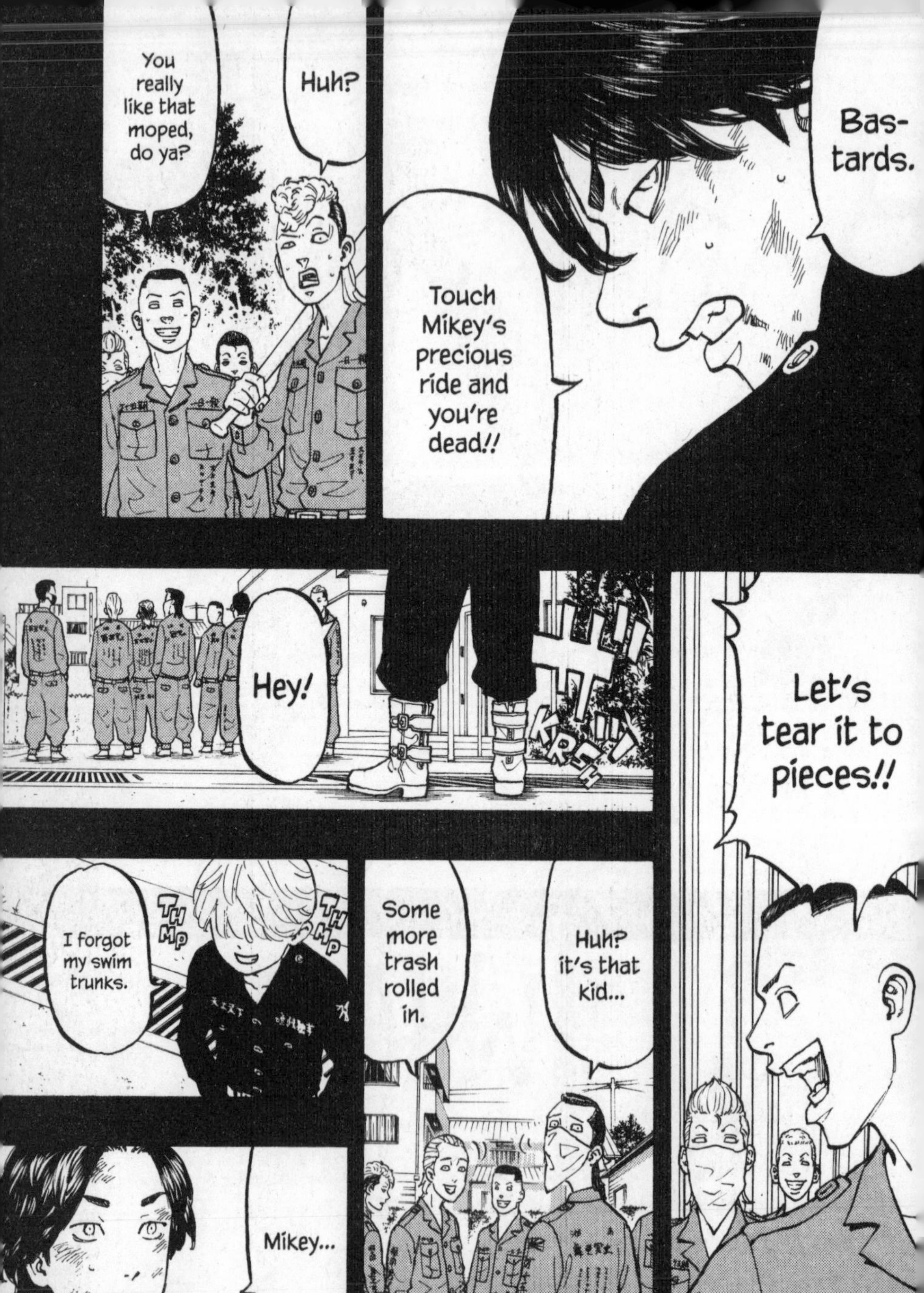
Bas-
tards.
Touch Mikey's precious ride and you're dead!!
Huh?
You really like that moped, do ya?
Let's tear it to pieces!!
KRSH
Hey!
Huh? it's that kid...
Some more trash rolled in.
THMP
THMP
I forgot my swim trunks.
Mikey...

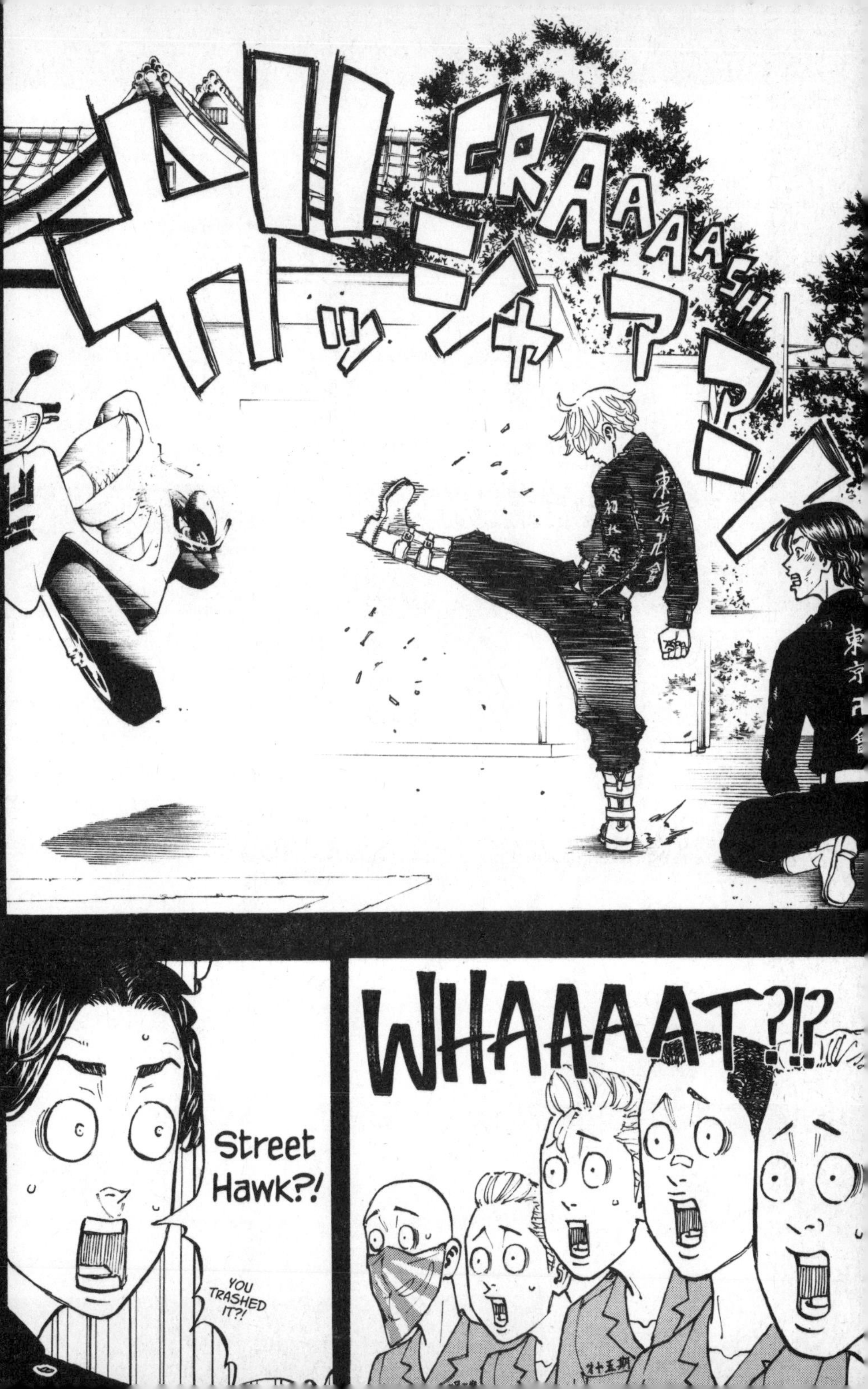
CRAAAASH
WHAAAAT?!?
Street Hawk?!
YOU TRASHED IT?!

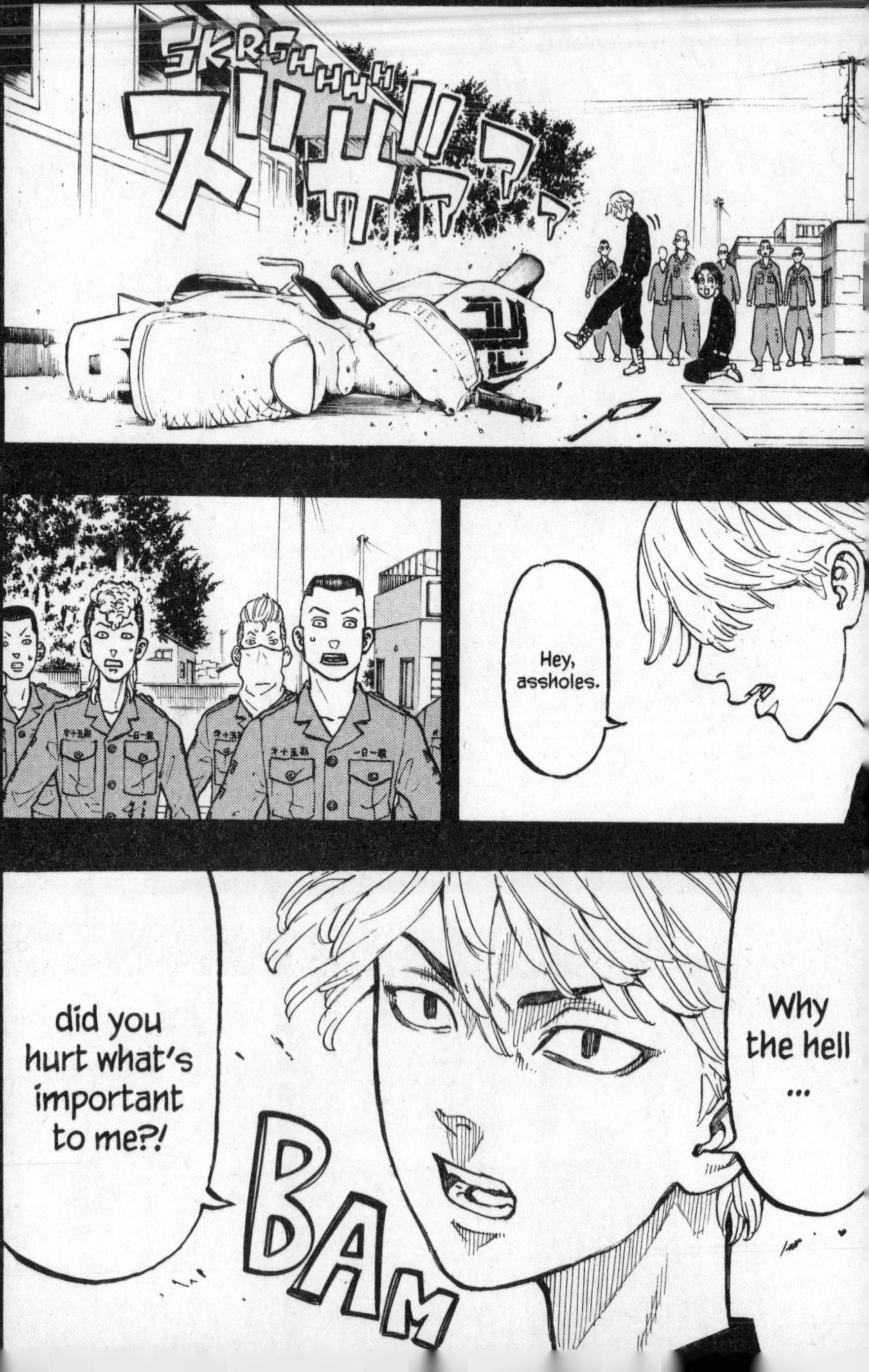
SKRSHHHH
Hey, assholes.
Why the hell ...
BAM
did you hurt what's important to me?!

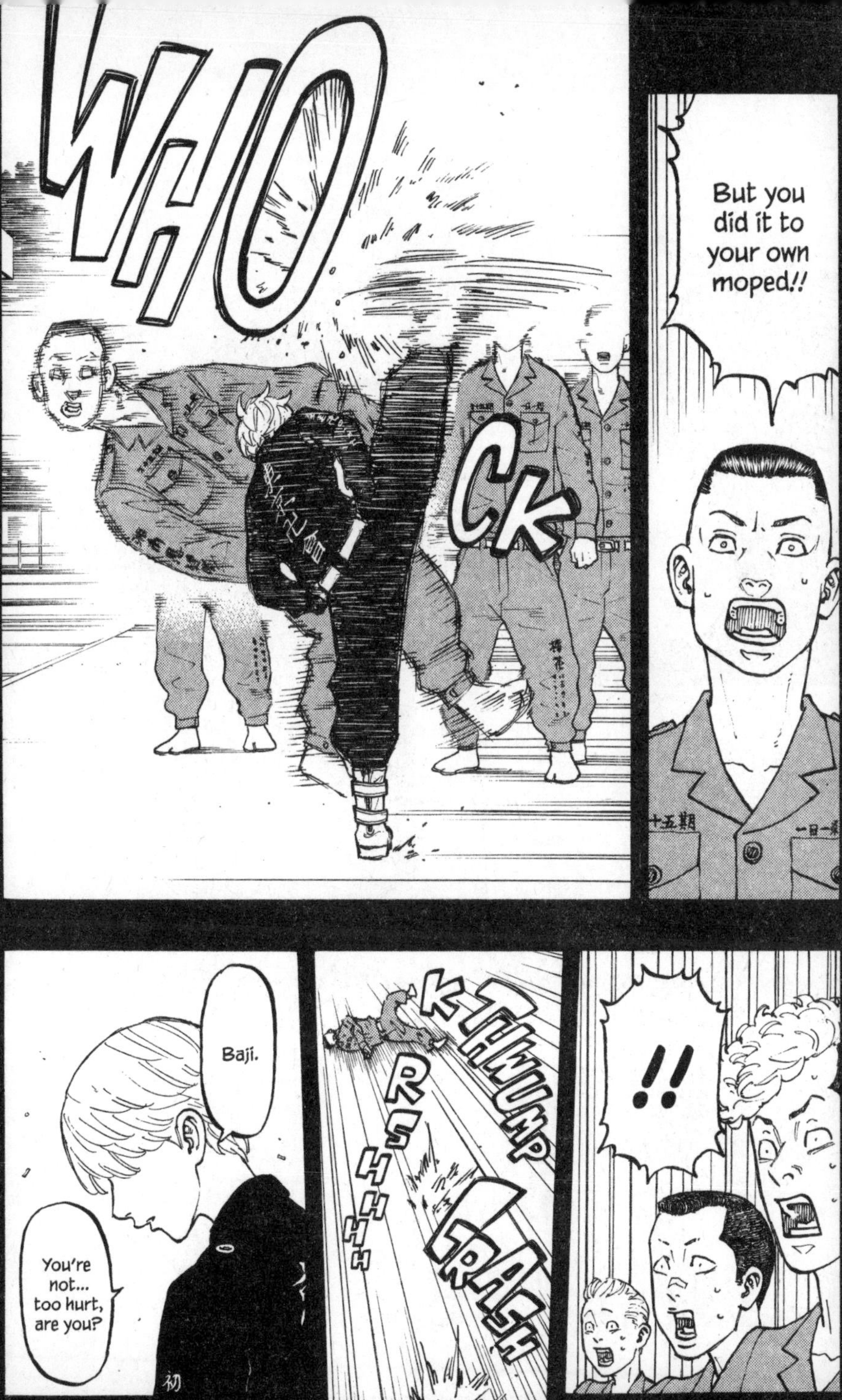

But you did it to your own moped!!
WHO
CK
!!
KTHWUMP
CRASH
RSHHHHHH
Baji.
You're not... too hurt, are you?

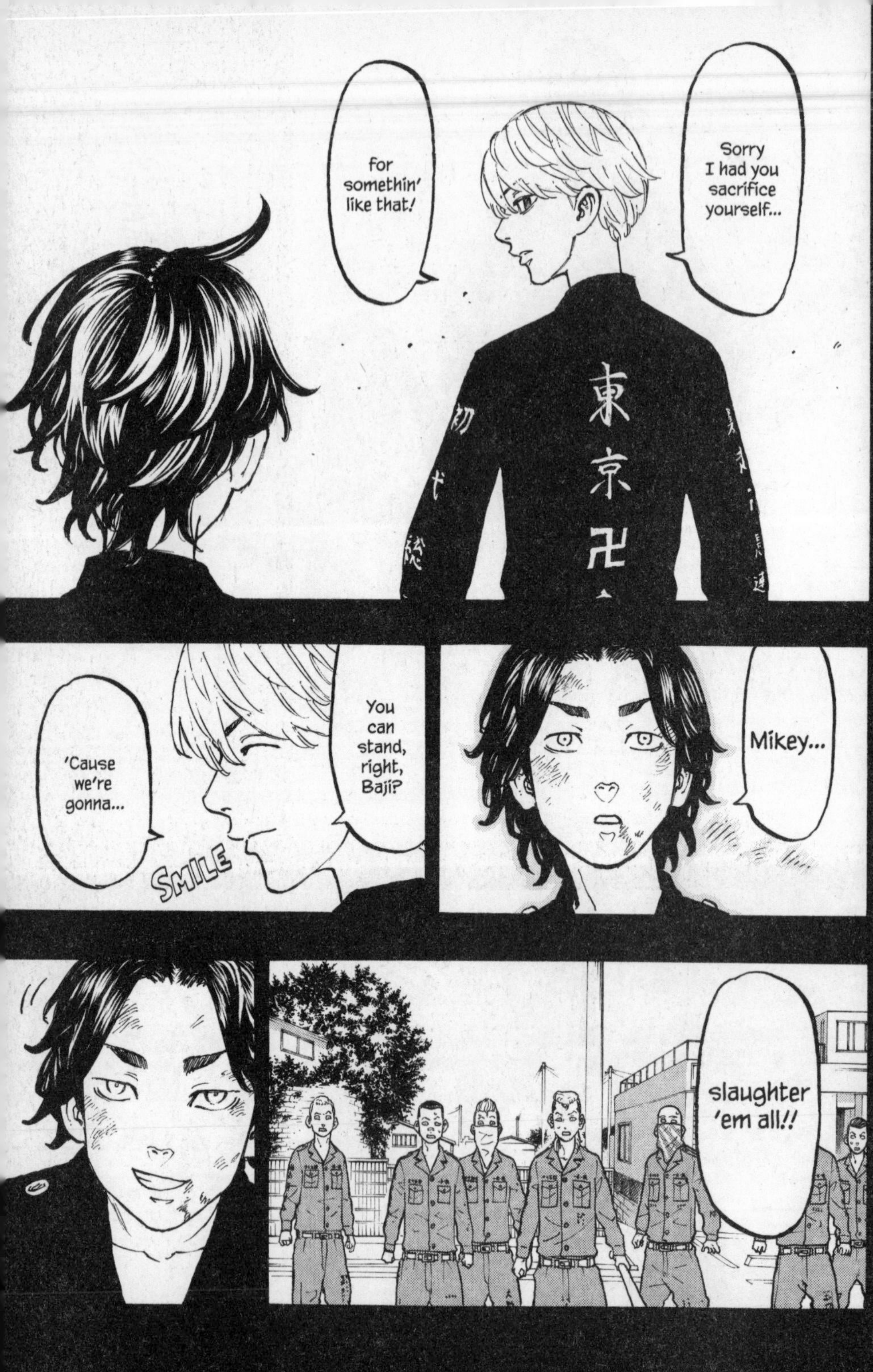

Sorry I had you sacrifice yourself...
for somethin' like that!
東京卍
Mikey...
You can stand, right, Baji?
'Cause we're gonna...
SMILE
slaughter 'em all!!

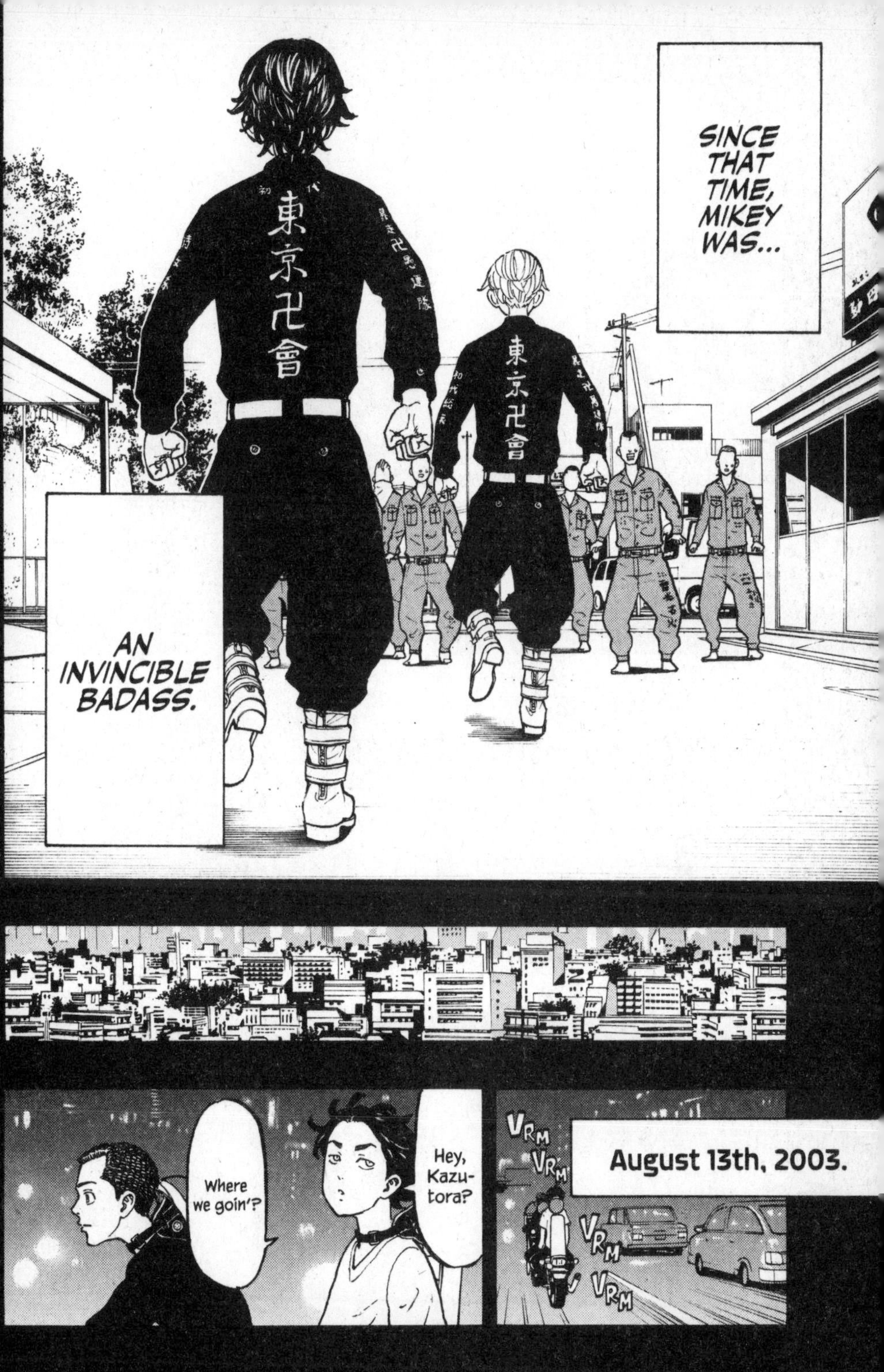
SINCE THAT TIME, MIKEY WAS...
東京卍會
東京卍會
AN INVINCIBLE BADASS.
VRM VRM
VRM VRM
August 13th, 2003.
Hey, Kazutora?
Where we goin'?

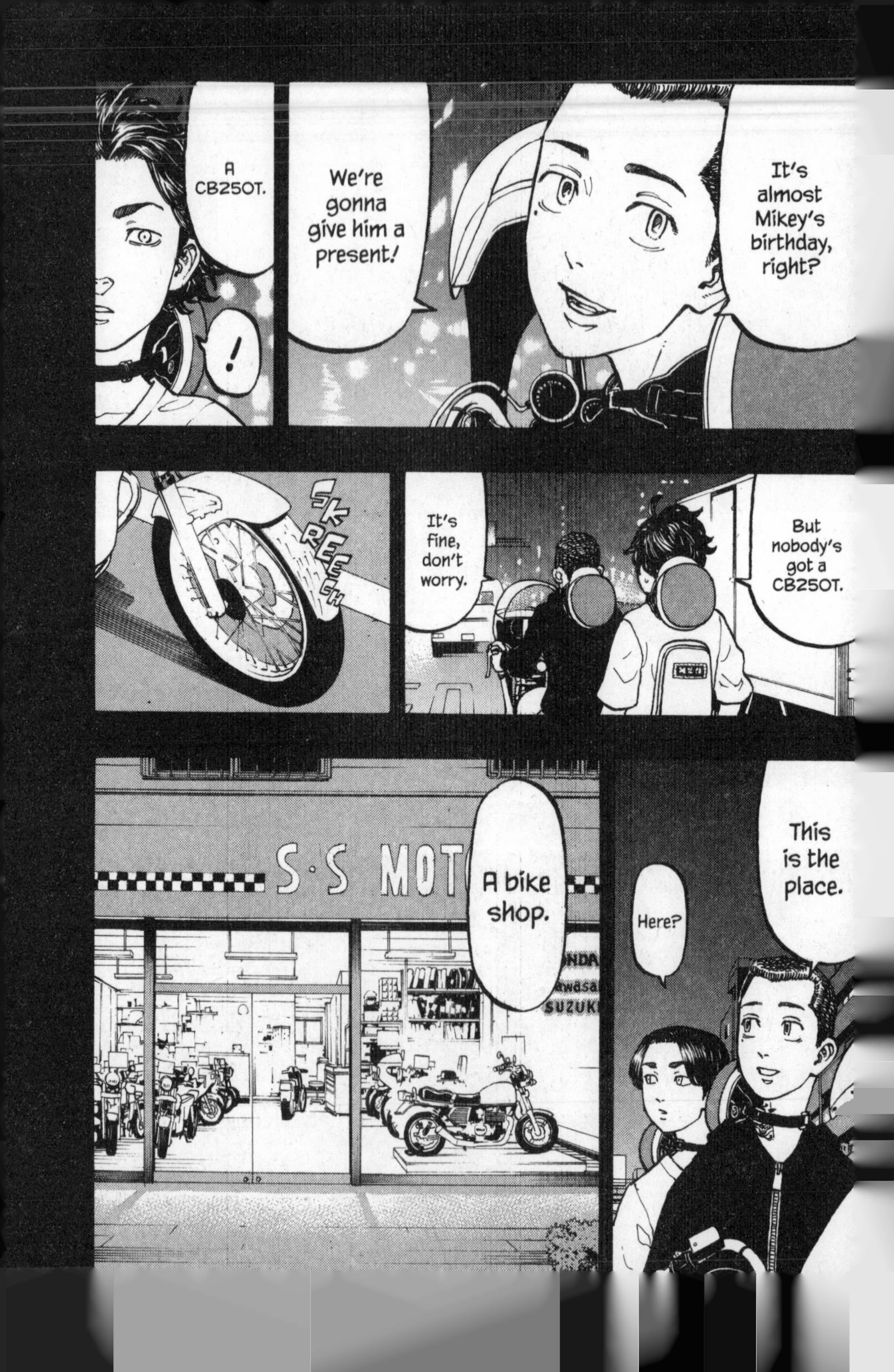

It's almost Mikey's birthday, right?
We're gonna give him a present!
A CB250T.
!
But nobody's got a CB250T.
It's fine, don't worry.
SKREECH
This is the place.
Here?
A bike shop.

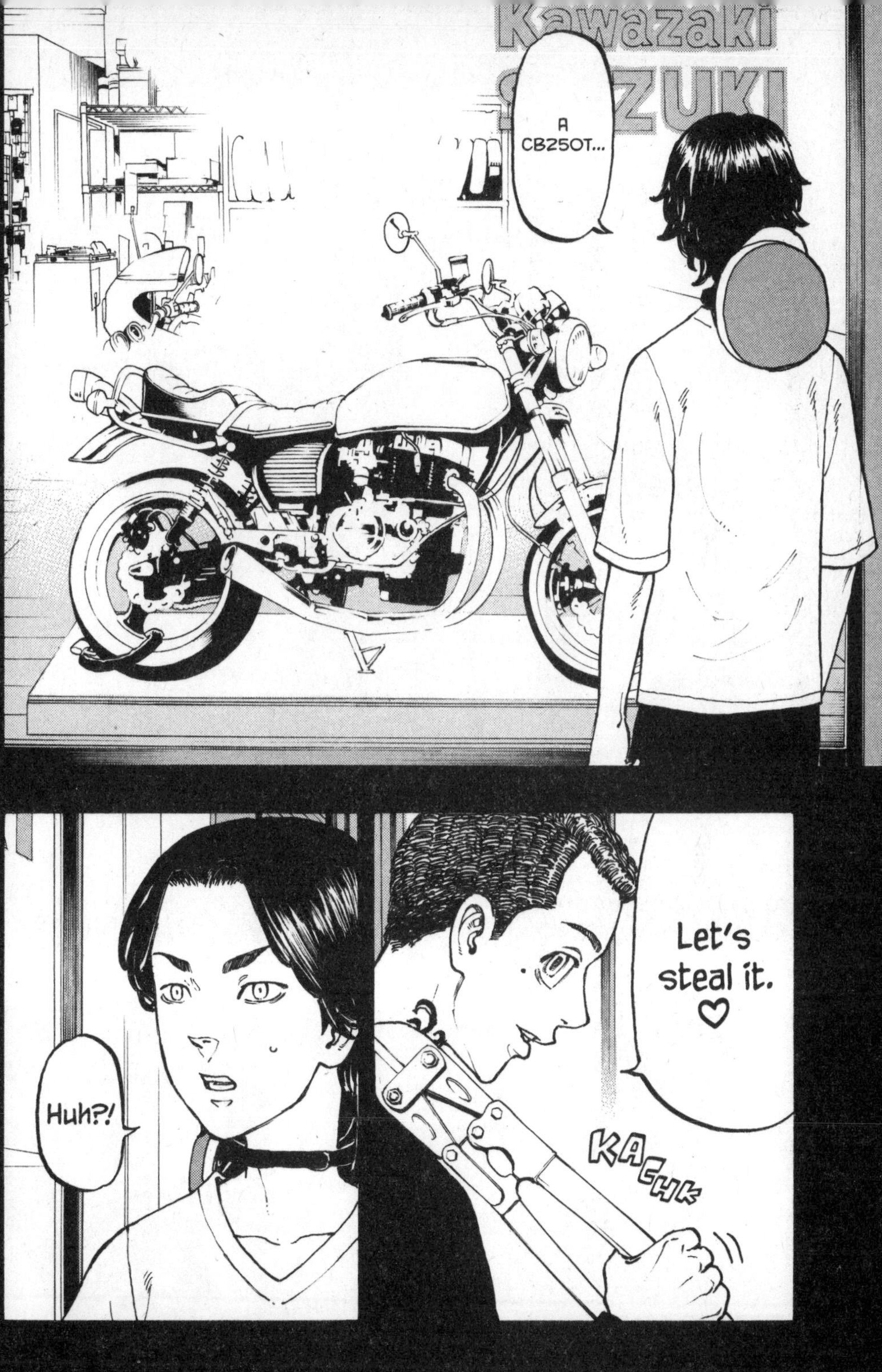
Kawazaki
ZUKI
A CB250T...
Let's steal it. ♡
KACHK
Huh?!

CHAPTER 44: SCREW UP

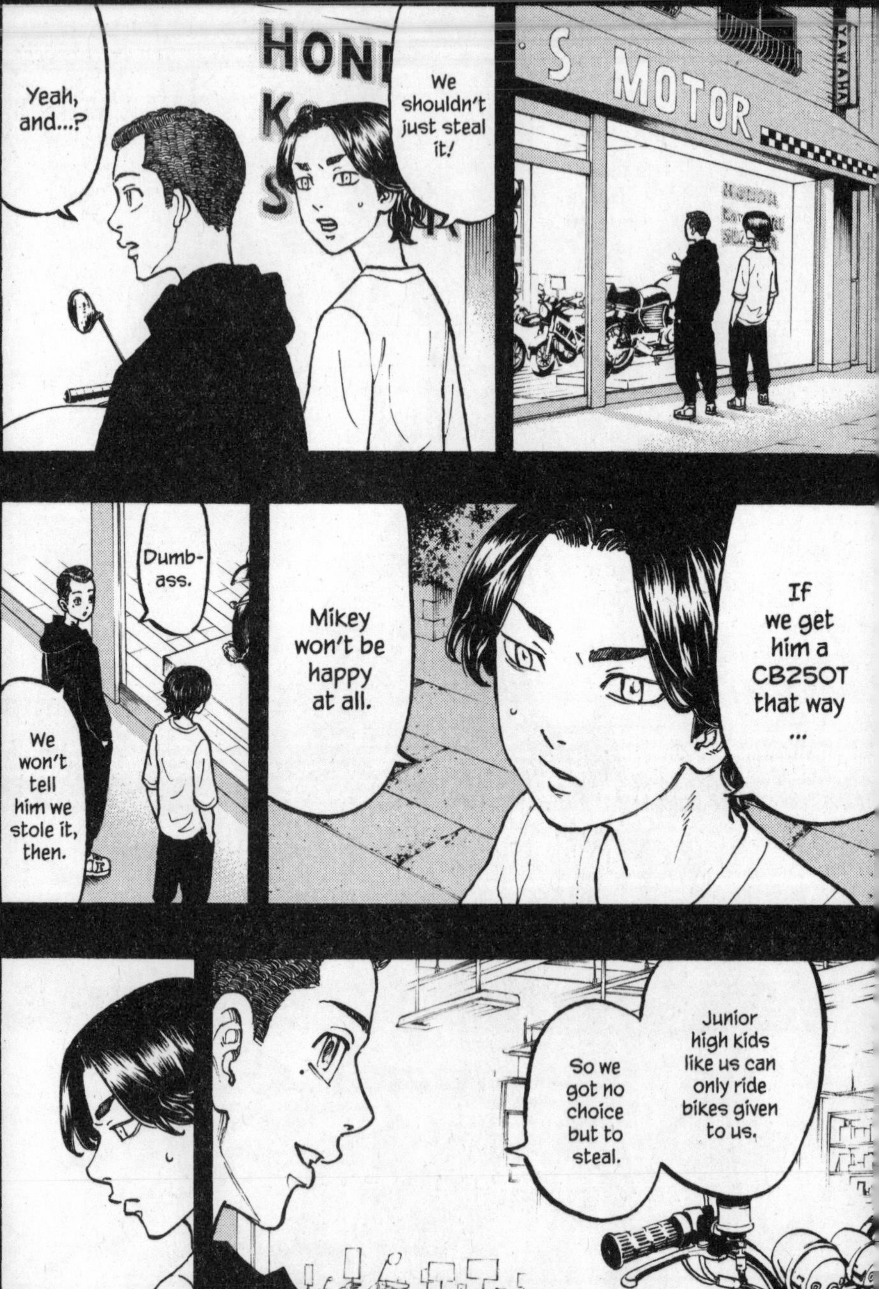

S MOTOR
YAMAHA
We shouldn't just steal it!
Yeah, and...?
If we get him a CB250T that way ...
Mikey won't be happy at all.
Dumb-ass.
We won't tell him we stole it, then.
Junior high kids like us can only ride bikes given to us.
So we got no choice but to steal.

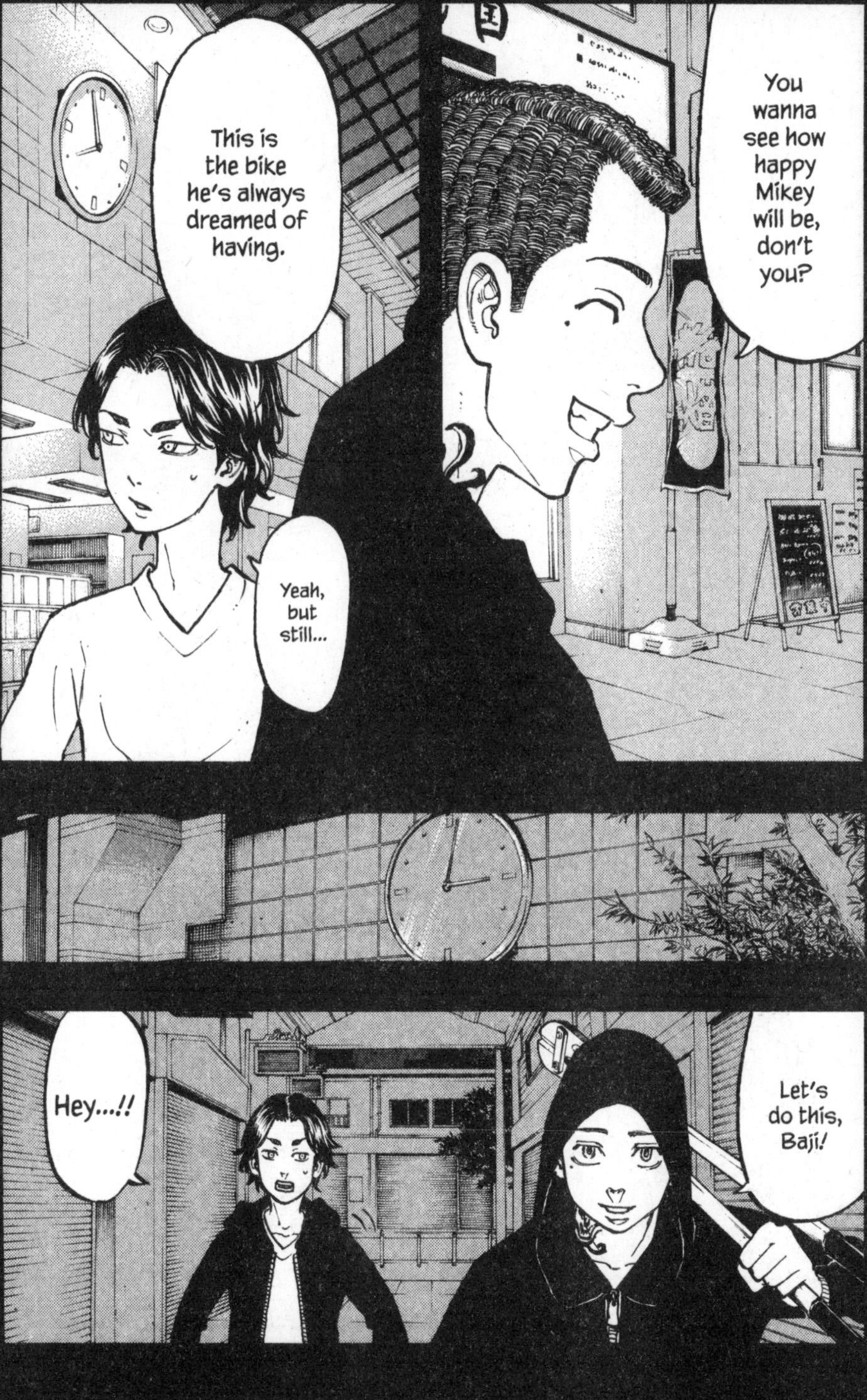
You wanna see how happy Mikey will be, don't you?
This is the bike he's always dreamed of having.
Yeah, but still...
Let's do this, Baji!
Hey...!!

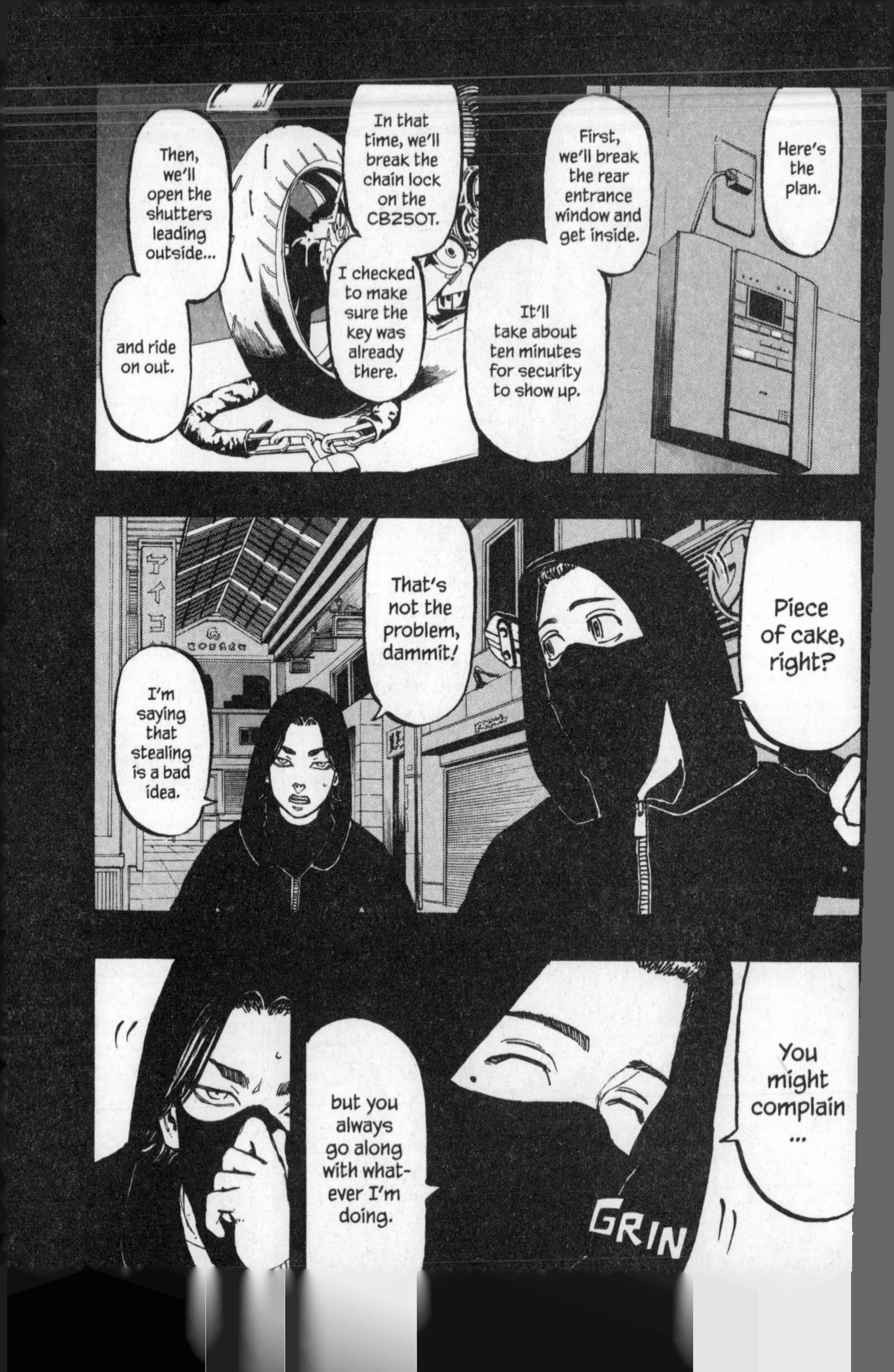
Here's the plan.
First, we'll break the rear entrance window and get inside.
It'll take about ten minutes for security to show up.
In that time, we'll break the chain lock on the CB250T.
I checked to make sure the key was already there.
Then, we'll open the shutters leading outside...
and ride on out.
Piece of cake, right?
That's not the problem, dammit!
I'm saying that stealing is a bad idea.
You might complain ...
GRIN
but you always go along with whatever I'm doing.

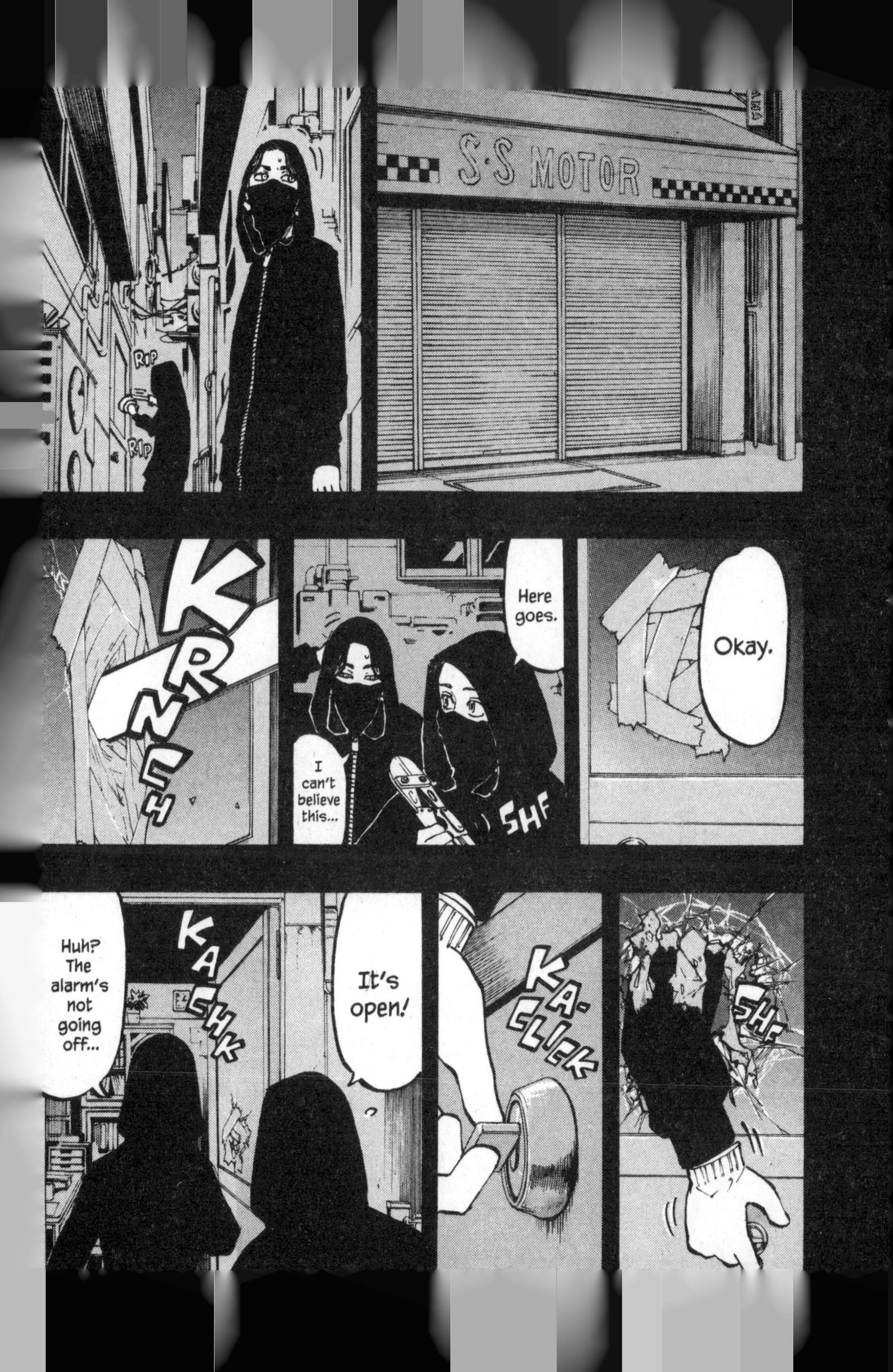
S·S MOTOR
RIP
RIP
Okay.
Here goes.
I can't believe this...
SHF
KRNCH
SHF
KA-CLICK
It's open!
KACHK
Huh? The alarm's not going off...

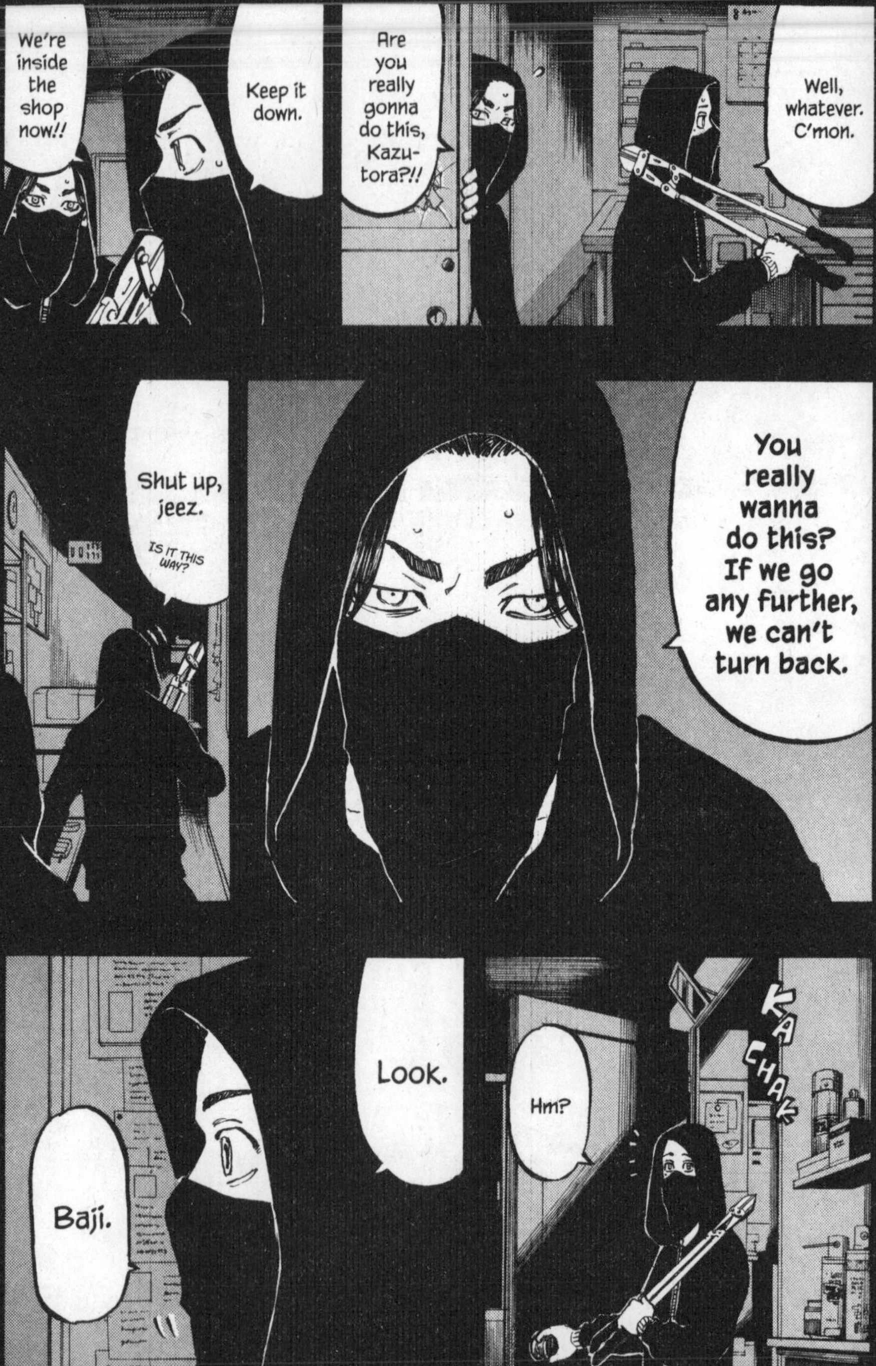
Well, whatever. C'mon.
Are you really gonna do this, Kazutora?!!
Keep it down.
We're inside the shop now!!
You really wanna do this? If we go any further, we can't turn back.
Shut up, jeez.
IS IT THIS WAY?
KACHAK
Hm?
Look.
Baji.

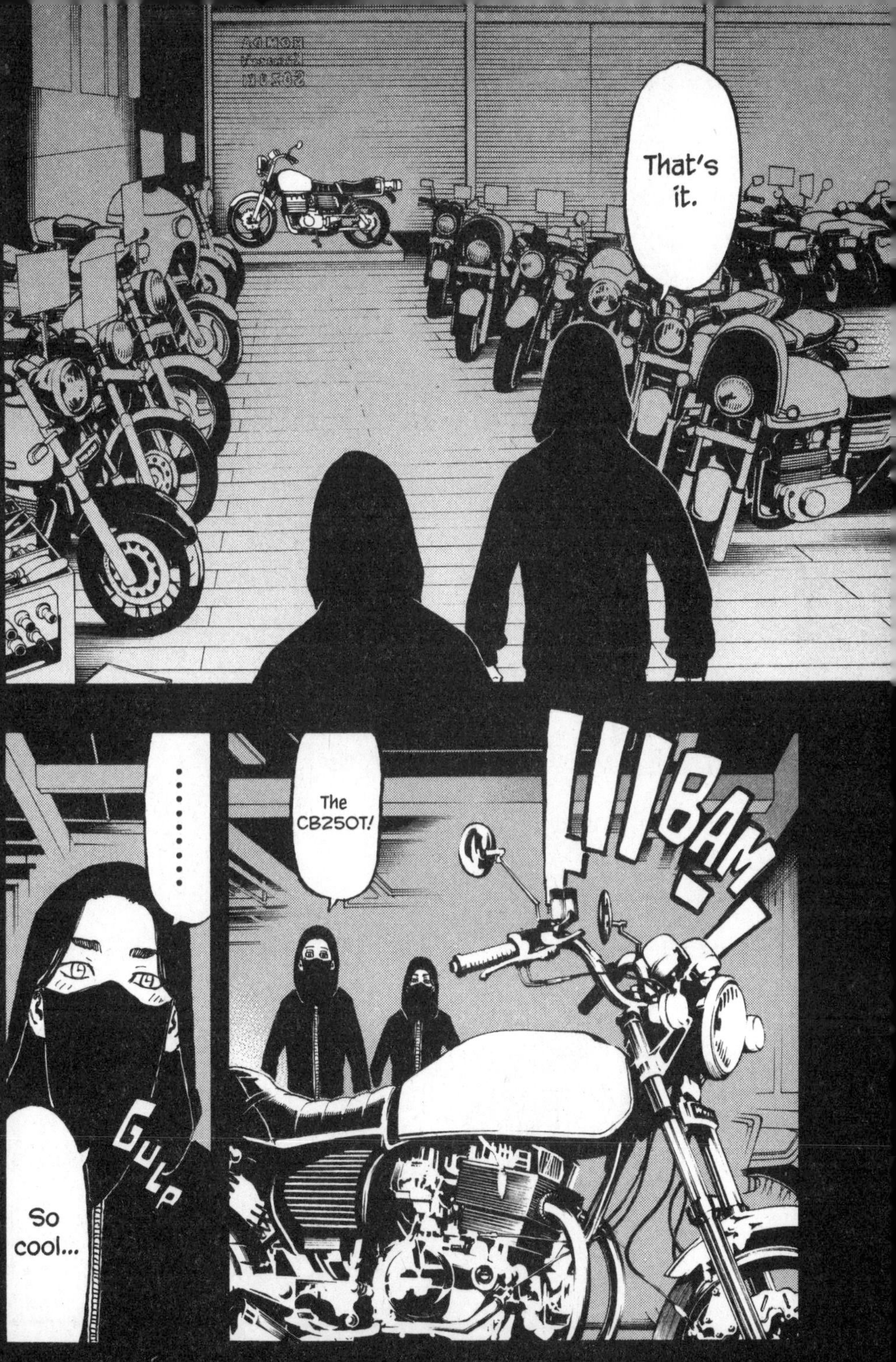
That's it.
The CB250T!
BAM
......
GULP
So cool...

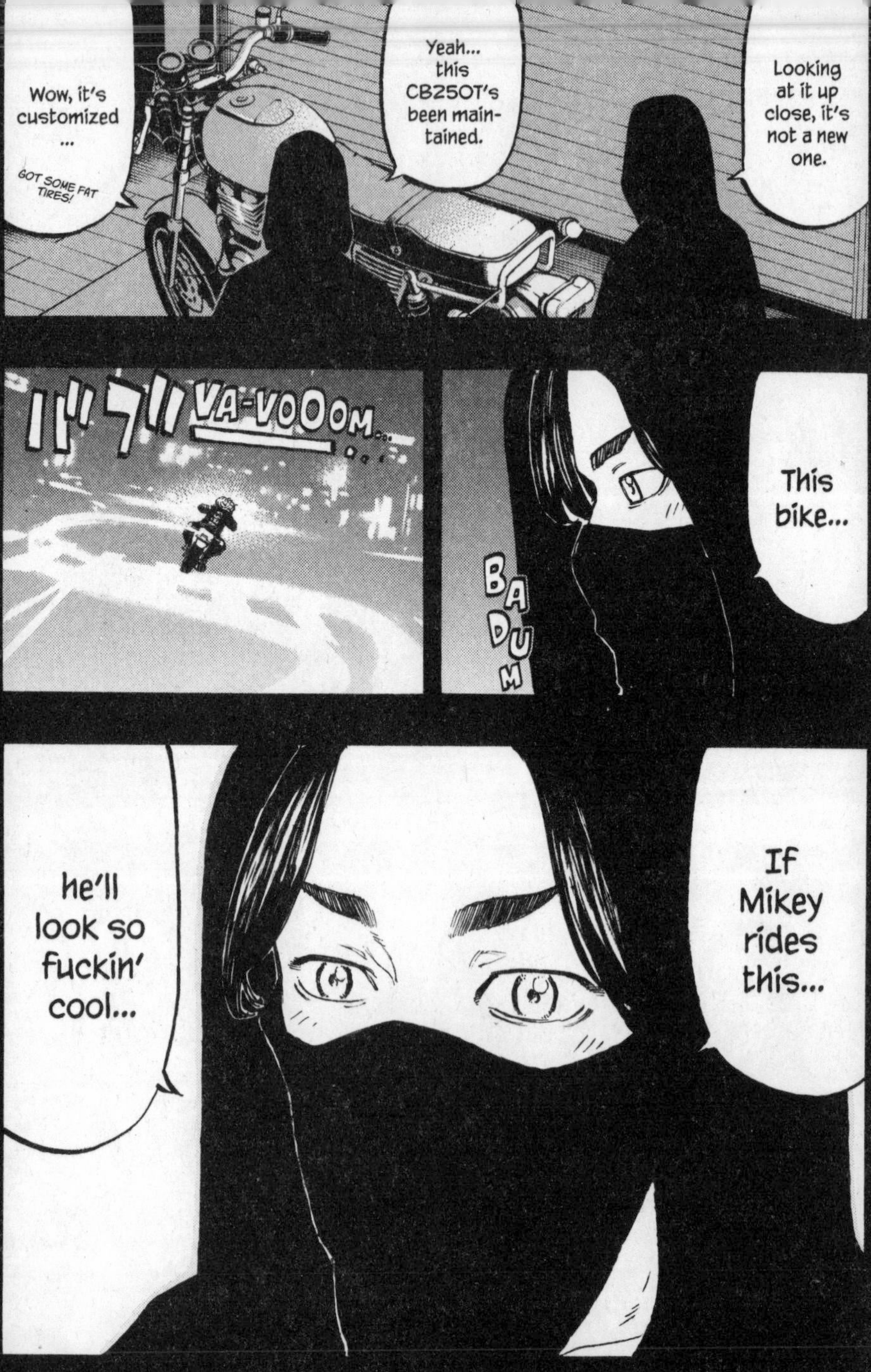
Looking at it up close, it's not a new one.
Yeah... this CB250T's been maintained.
Wow, it's customized ...
GOT SOME FAT TIRES!
This bike...
BADUM
VA-VOOOM...
If Mikey rides this...
he'll look so fuckin' cool...

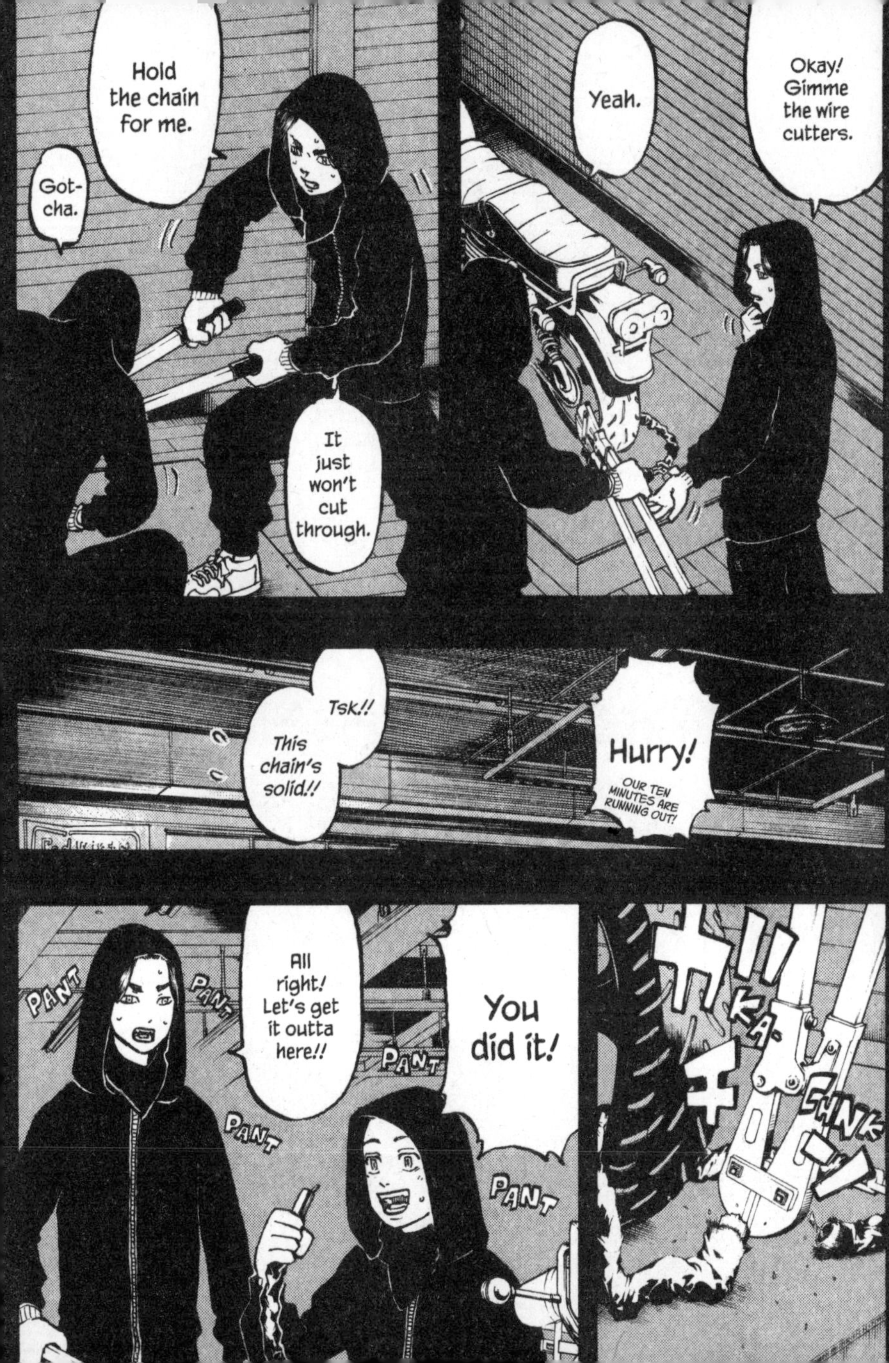
Okay! Gimme the wire cutters.
Yeah.
Hold the chain for me.
Got-cha.
It just won't cut through.
Hurry!
OUR TEN MINUTES ARE RUNNING OUT!
Tsk!! This chain's solid!!
KA-CHNK
You did it!
All right! Let's get it outta here!!
PANT
PANT
PANT
PANT
PANT

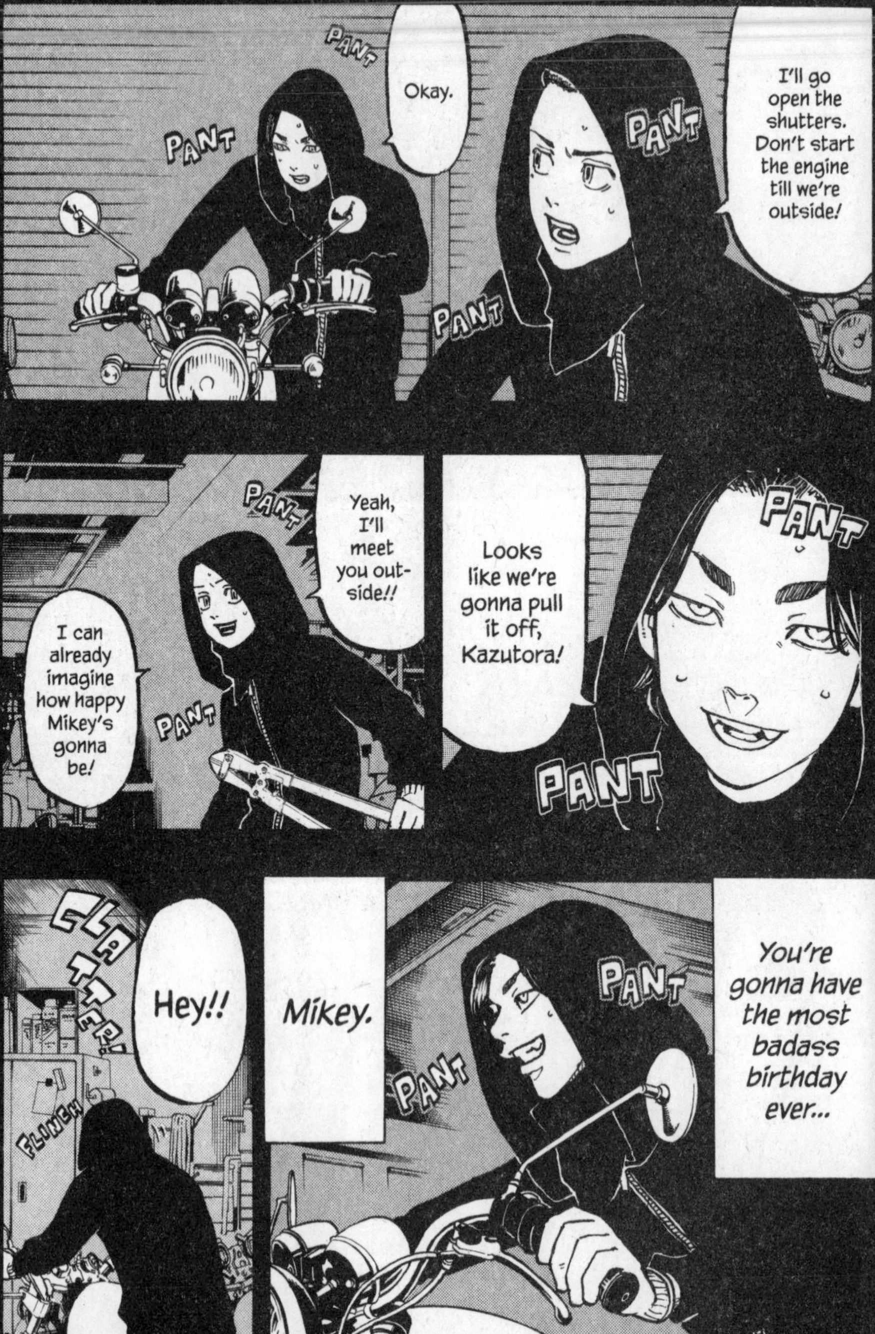
PANT
I'll go open the shutters. Don't start the engine till we're outside!
PANT
Okay.
PANT
PANT
PANT
Looks like we're gonna pull it off, Kazutora!
PANT
PANT
Yeah, I'll meet you out-side!!
I can already imagine how happy Mikey's gonna be!
PANT
You're gonna have the most badass birthday ever...
PANT
PANT
Mikey.
Hey!!
CLATTER!
FLINCH

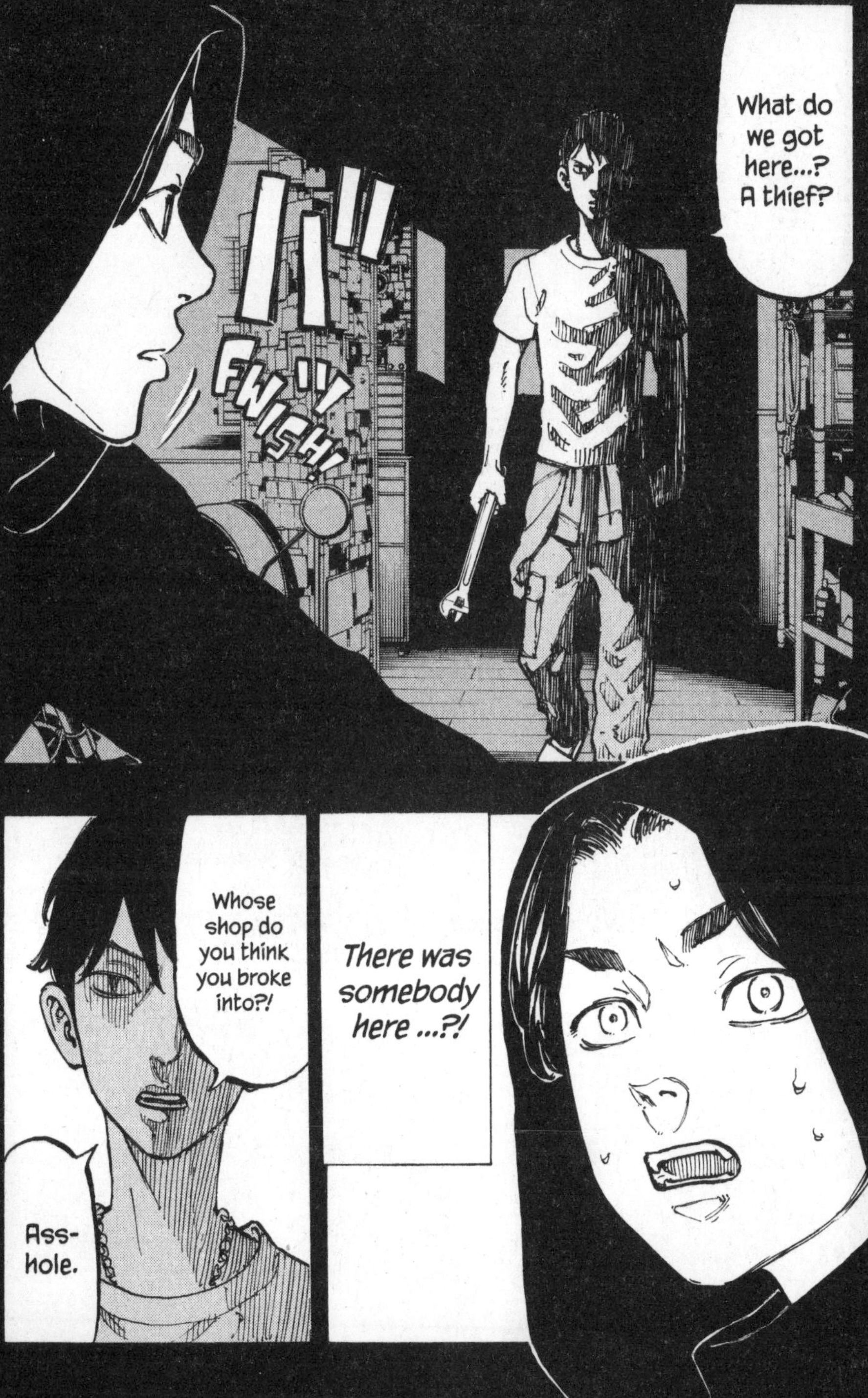What do we got here...? A thief?
FWISH!
There was somebody here ...?!
Whose shop do you think you broke into?!
Ass-hole.

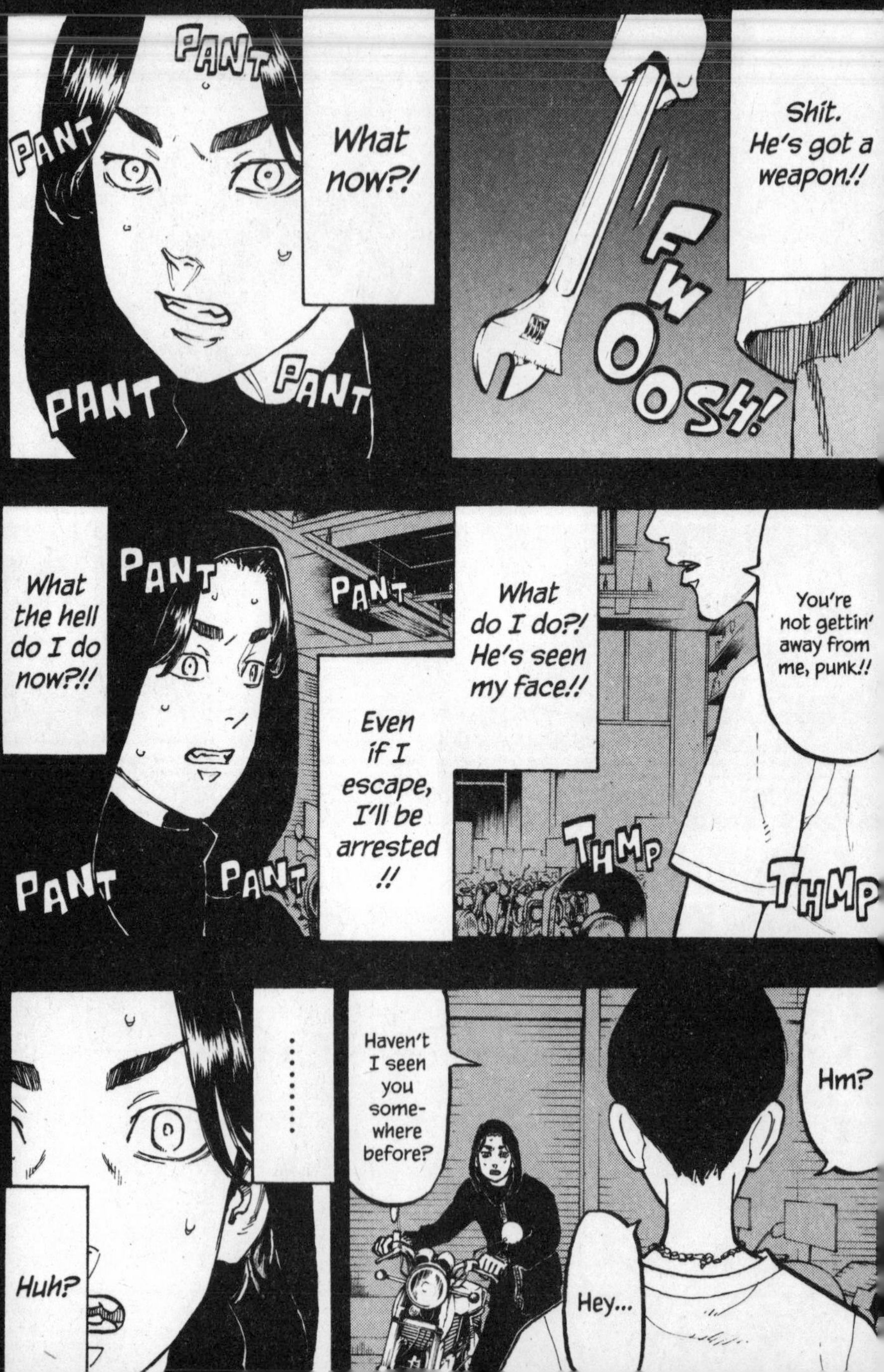

Shit. He's got a weapon!!
FWOOSH!
What now?!
PANT
PANT
PANT
PANT
You're not gettin' away from me, punk!!
THMP
THMP
What do I do?! He's seen my face!!
Even if I escape, I'll be arrested!!
PANT
PANT
What the hell do I do now?!!
PANT
PANT
Hm?
Haven't I seen you somewhere before?
Hey...
......
Huh?

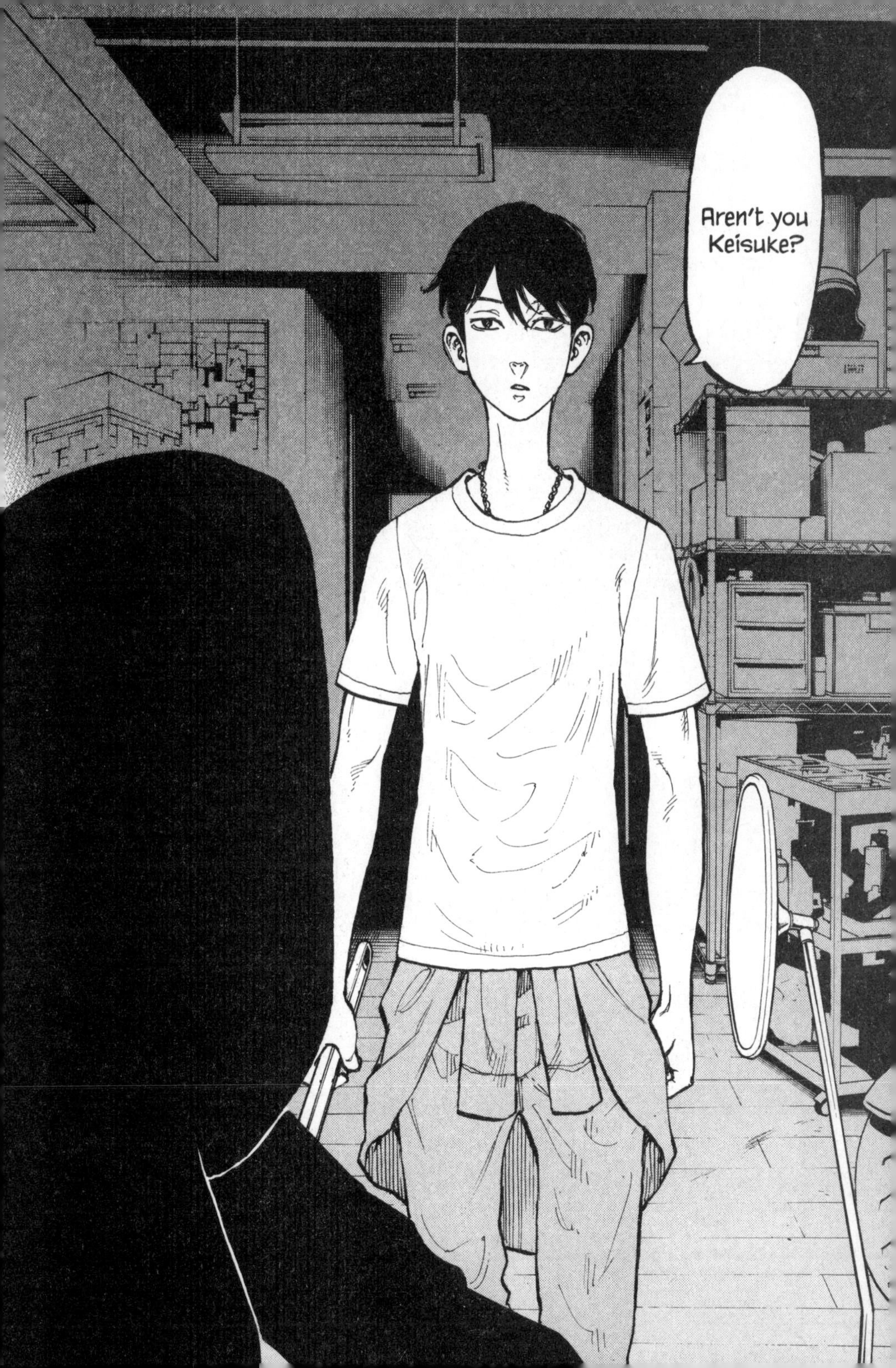
Aren't you Keisuke?

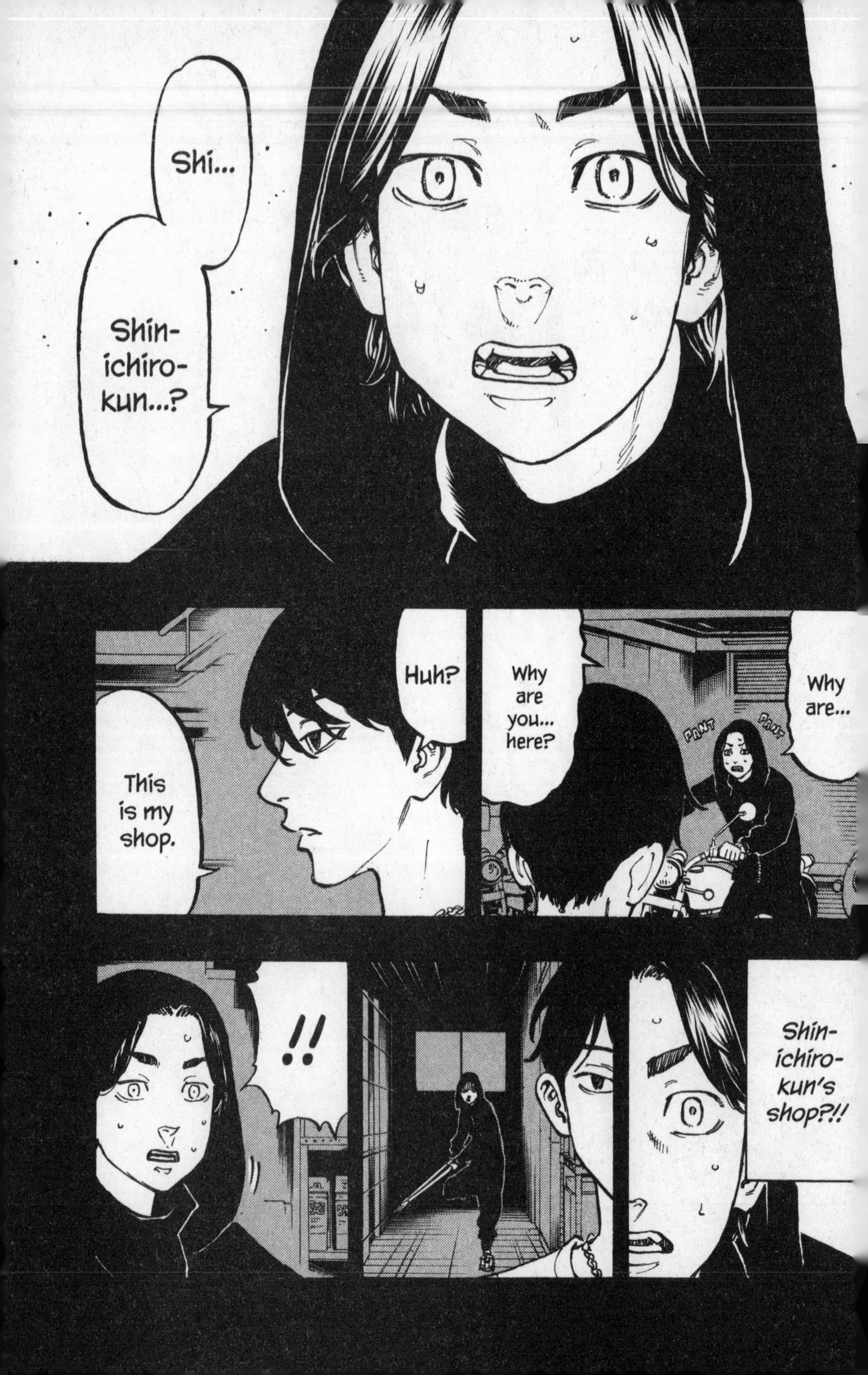
Shi...
Shin-ichiro-kun...?
Why are...
PANT
PANT
Why are you... here?
Huh?
This is my shop.
Shin-ichiro-kun's shop?!!
!!

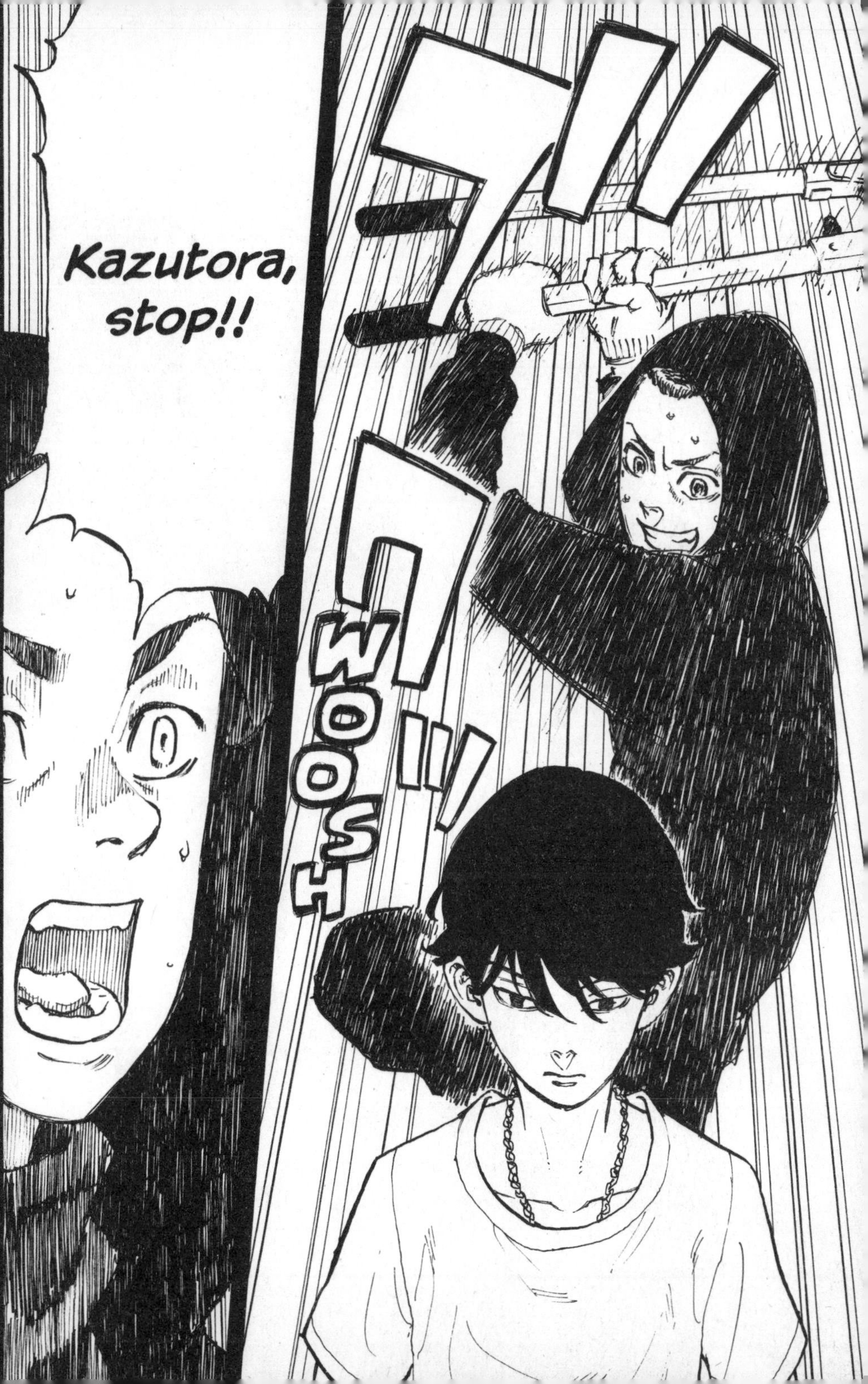
WOOSH
Kazutora, stop!!

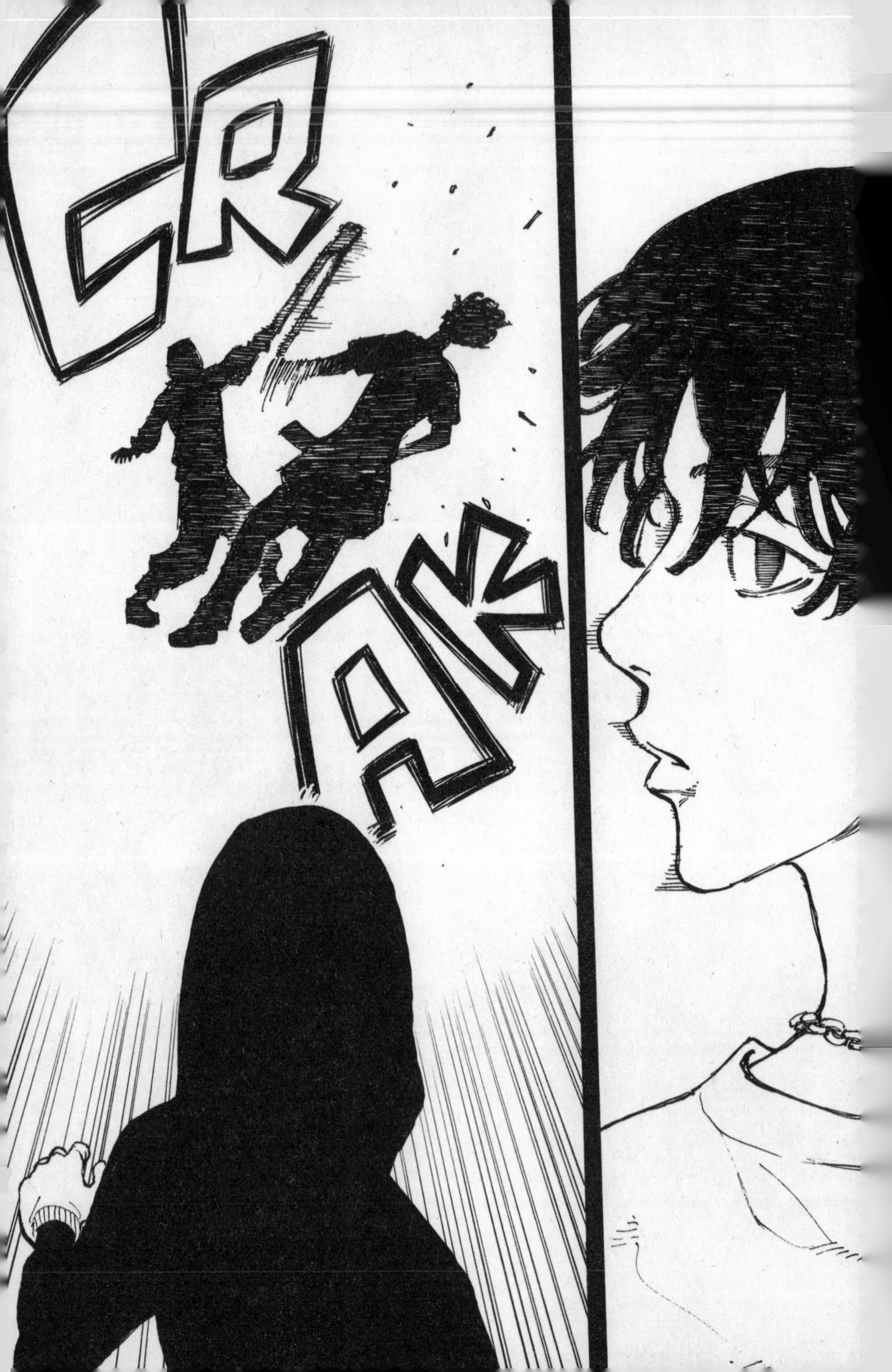
CRACK

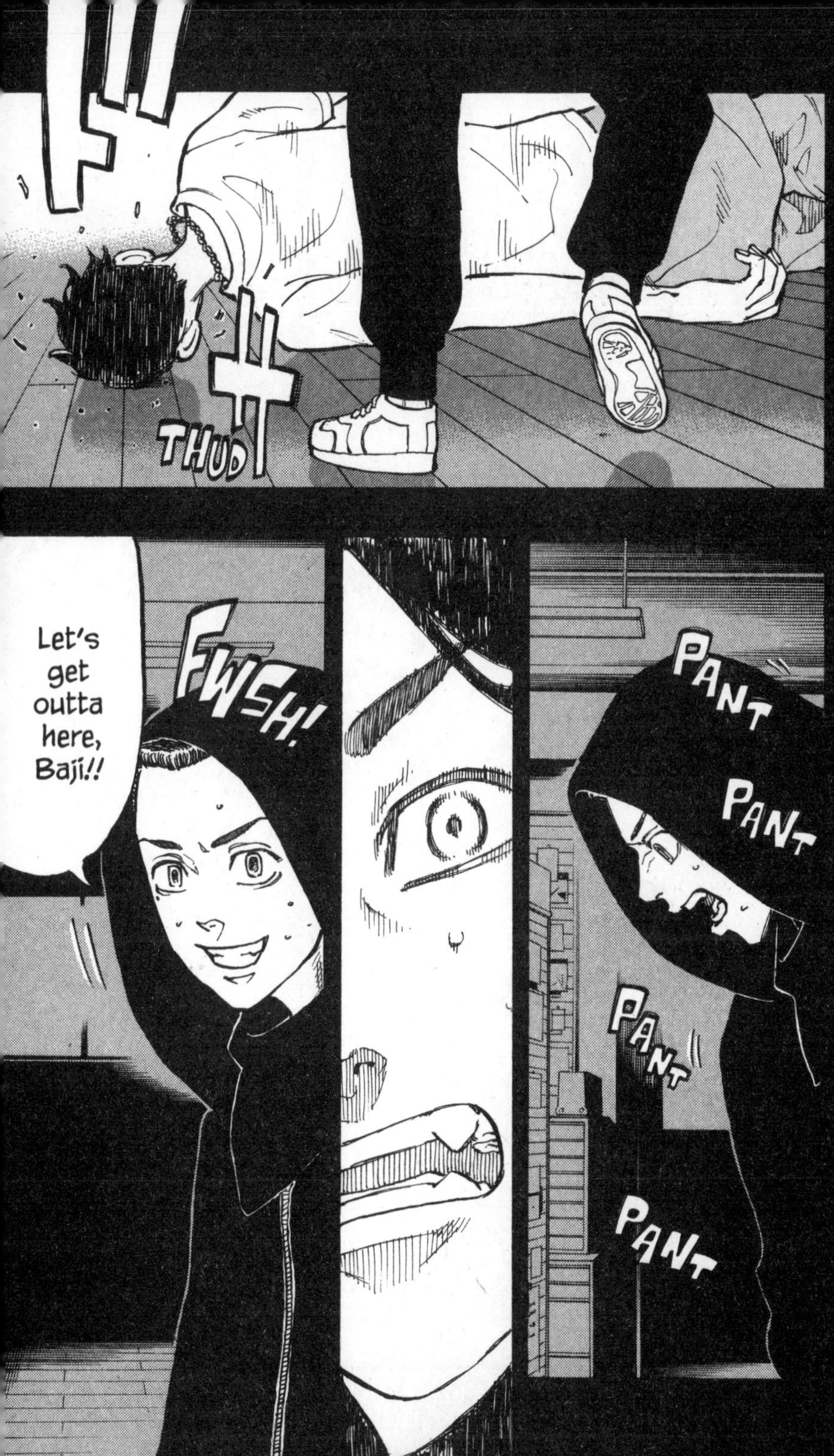
THUD
PANT
PANT
PANT
PANT
FWSH!
Let's get outta here, Baji!!

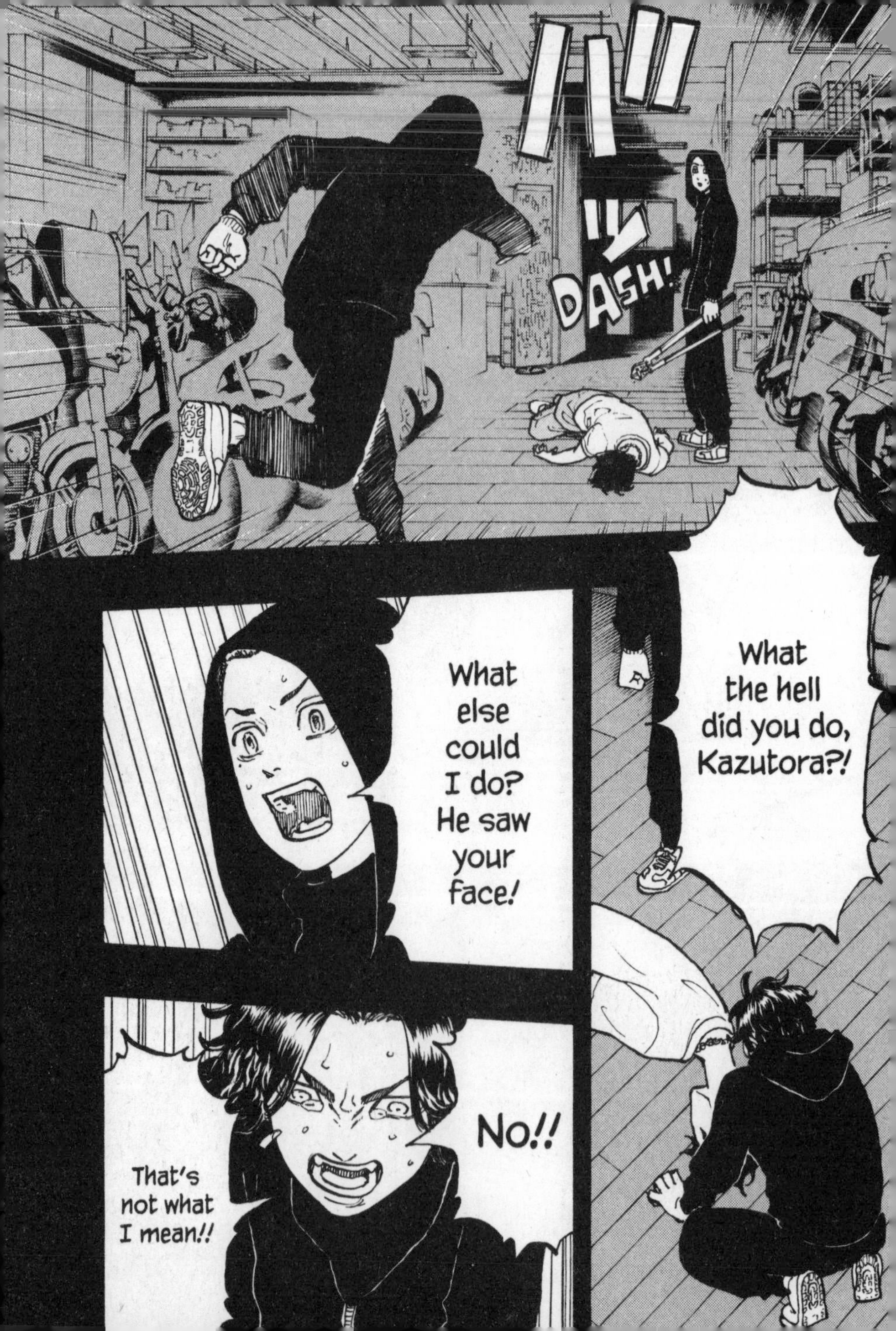
DASH!
What the hell did you do, Kazutora?!
What else could I do? He saw your face!
No!!
That's not what I mean!!

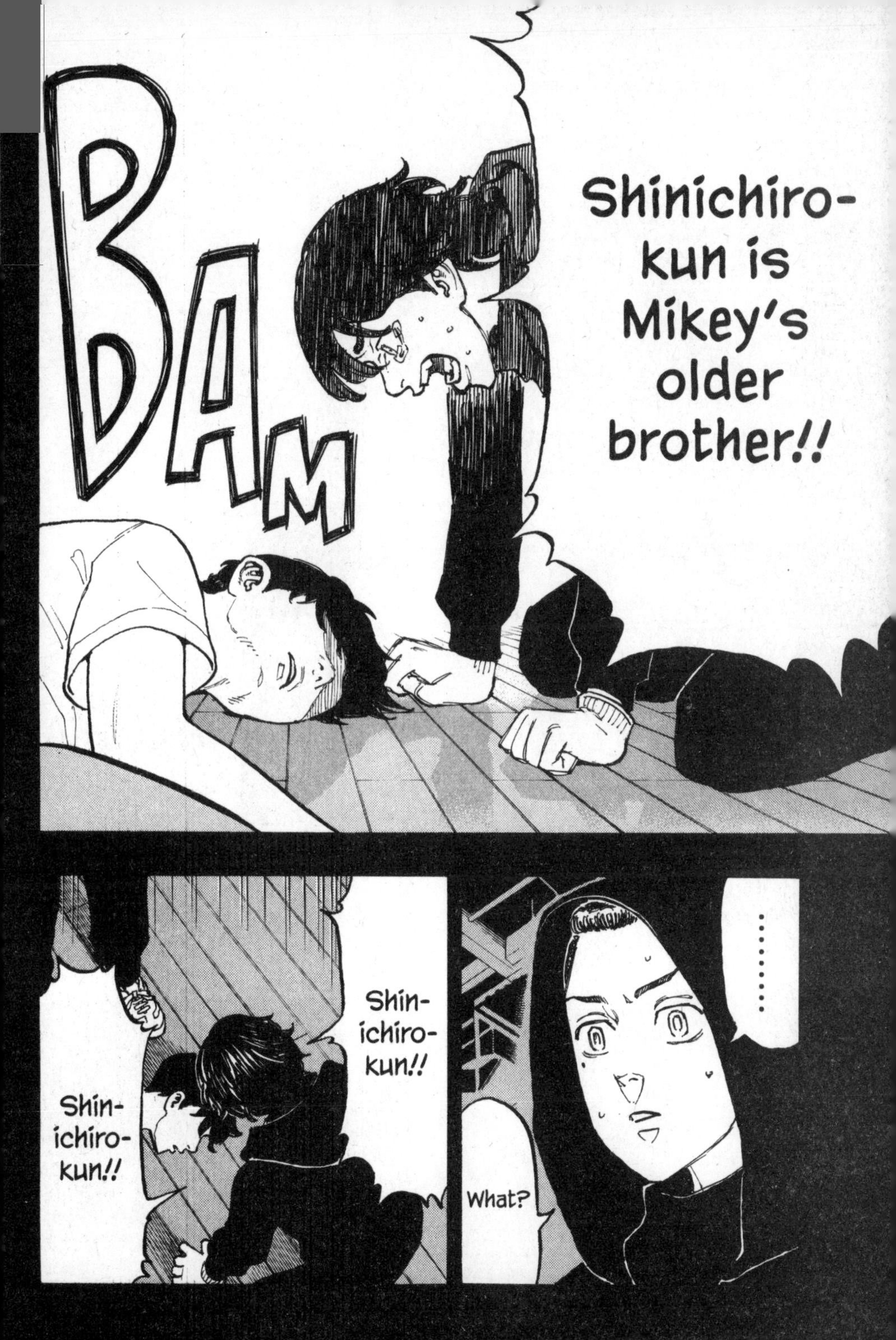
Shinichiro-kun is Mikey's older brother!!
BAM
......
What?
Shin-ichiro-kun!!
Shin-ichiro-kun!!

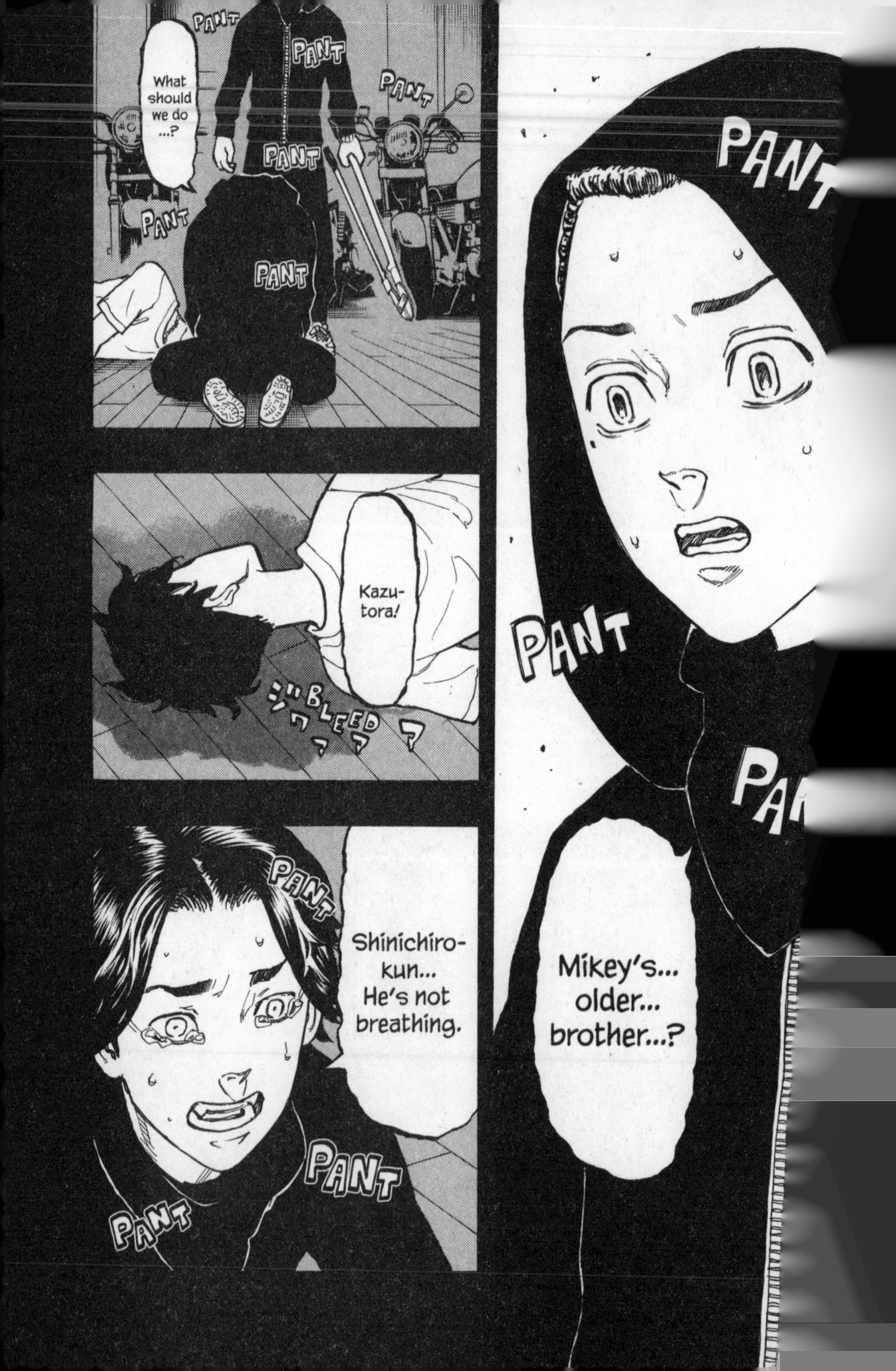

PANT
What should we do ...?
PANT
PANT
PANT
PANT
PANT
Kazu-tora!
BLEED
PANT
Shinichiro-kun... He's not breathing.
PANT
PANT
PANT
PANT
PANT
Mikey's... older... brother...?

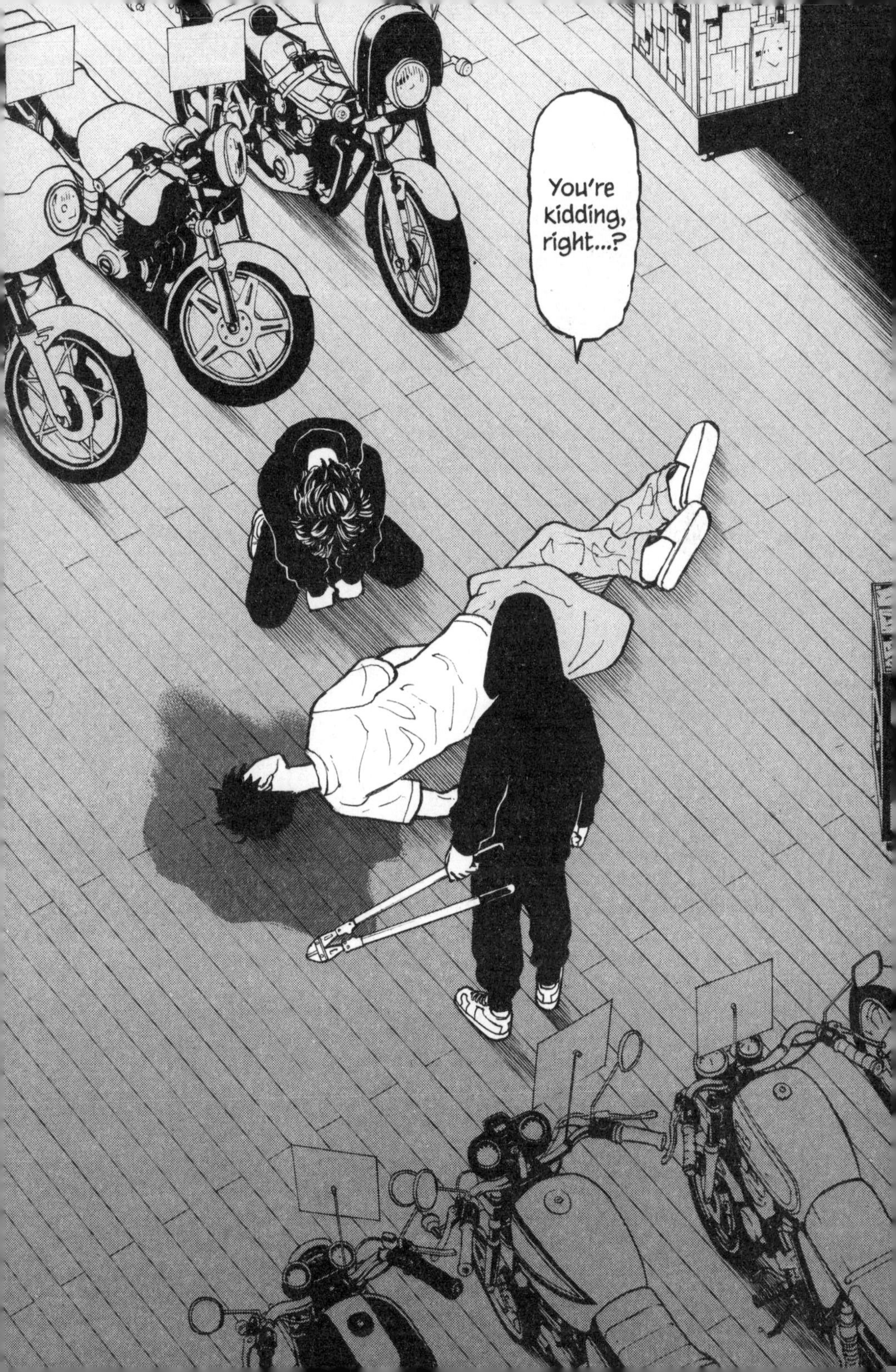
You're kidding, right...?

CHAPTER 45: TAKE OUT ON

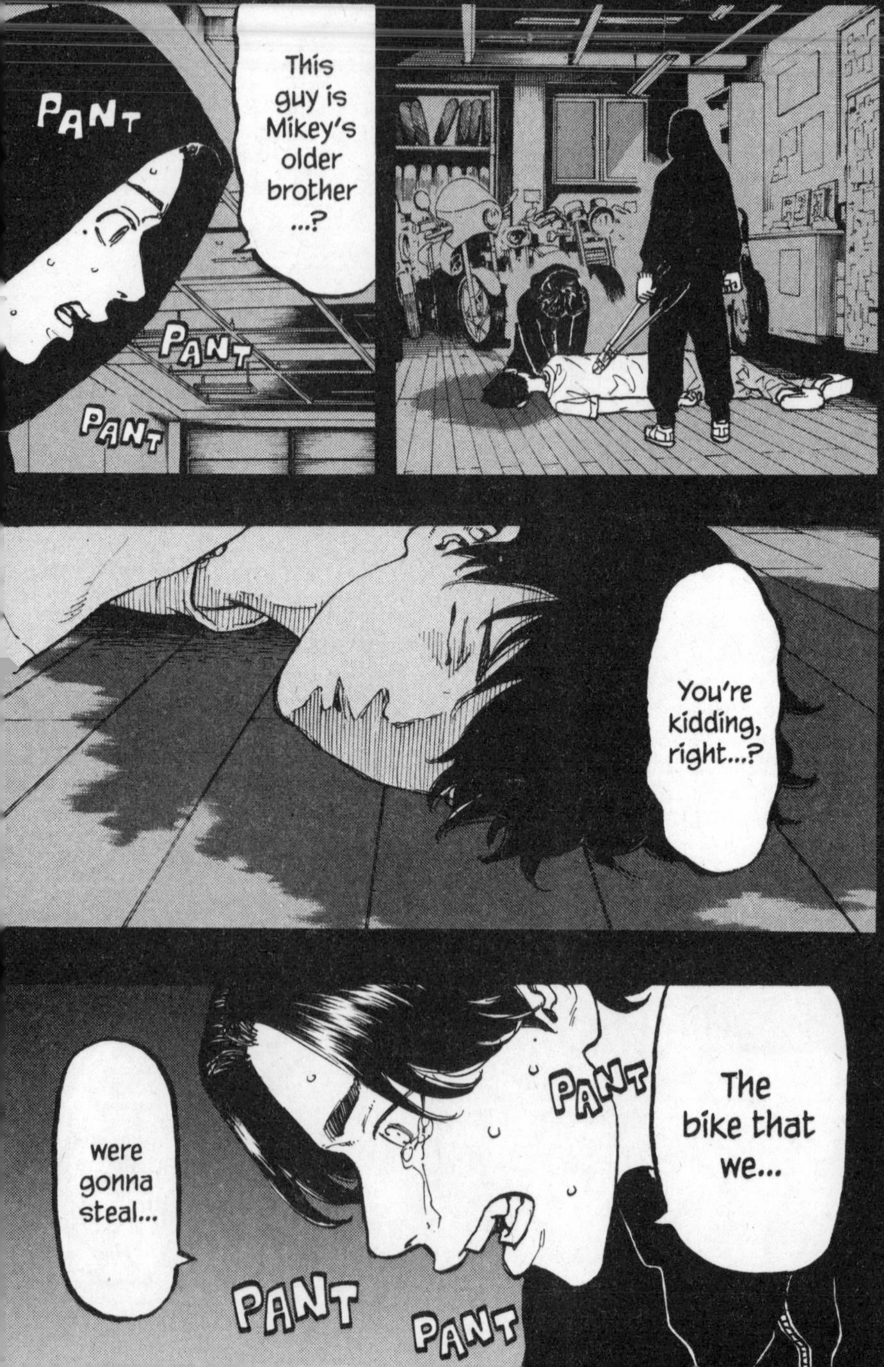
This guy is Mikey's older brother ...?
PANT
PANT
PANT
You're kidding, right...?
The bike that we...
PANT
were gonna steal...
PANT
PANT

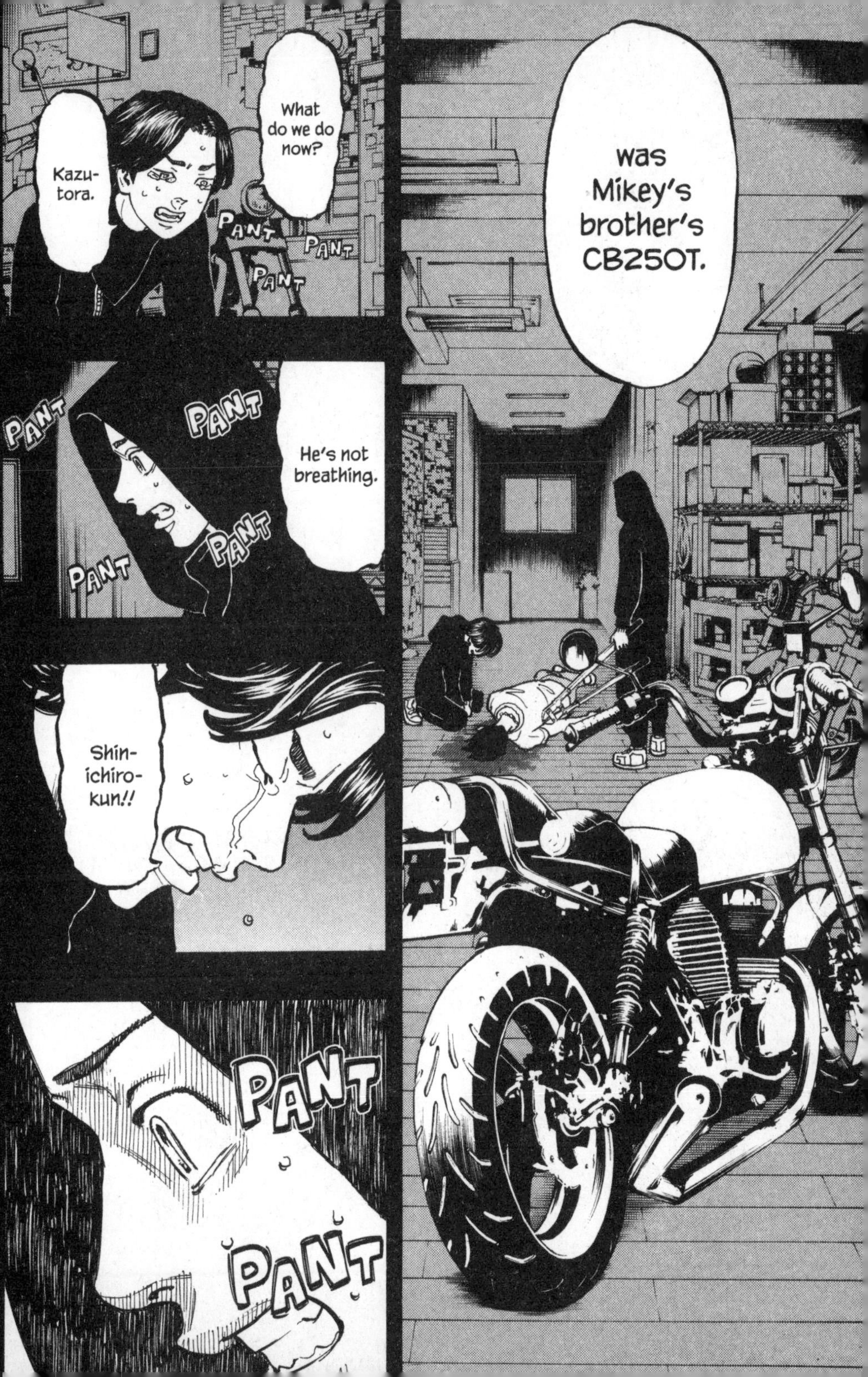
was Mikey's brother's CB250T.
What do we do now?
Kazu-tora.
PANT
PANT
PANT
PANT
He's not breathing.
PANT
PANT
PANT
Shin-ichiro-kun!!
PANT
PANT

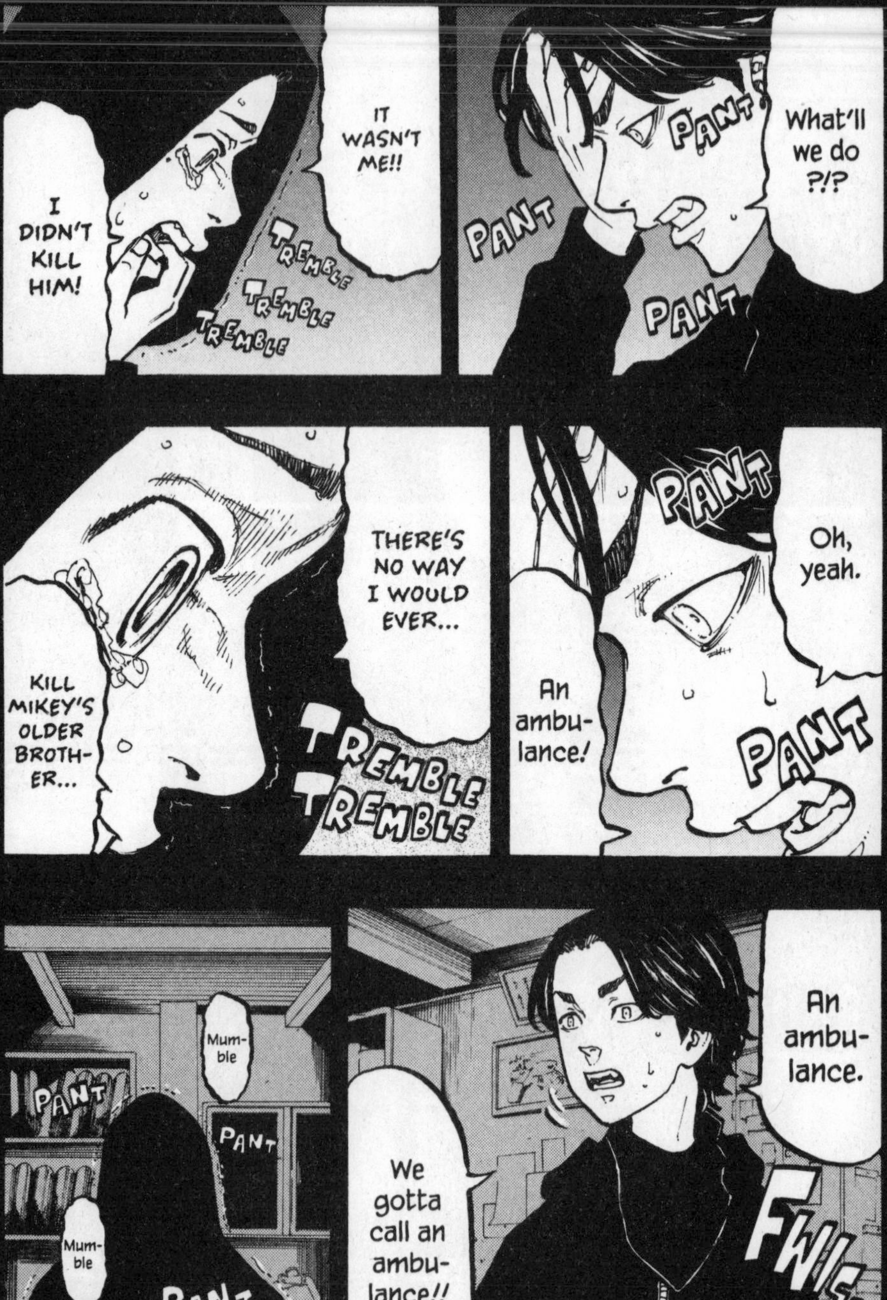
PANT
What'll we do ?!?
PANT
PANT
IT WASN'T ME!!
I DIDN'T KILL HIM!
TREMBLE
TREMBLE
TREMBLE
PANT
Oh, yeah.
An ambulance!
PANT
THERE'S NO WAY I WOULD EVER...
KILL MIKEY'S OLDER BROTHER...
TREMBLE
TREMBLE
An ambulance.
We gotta call an ambulance!!
FWISH!
Mumble
PANT
PANT
Mumble
PANT

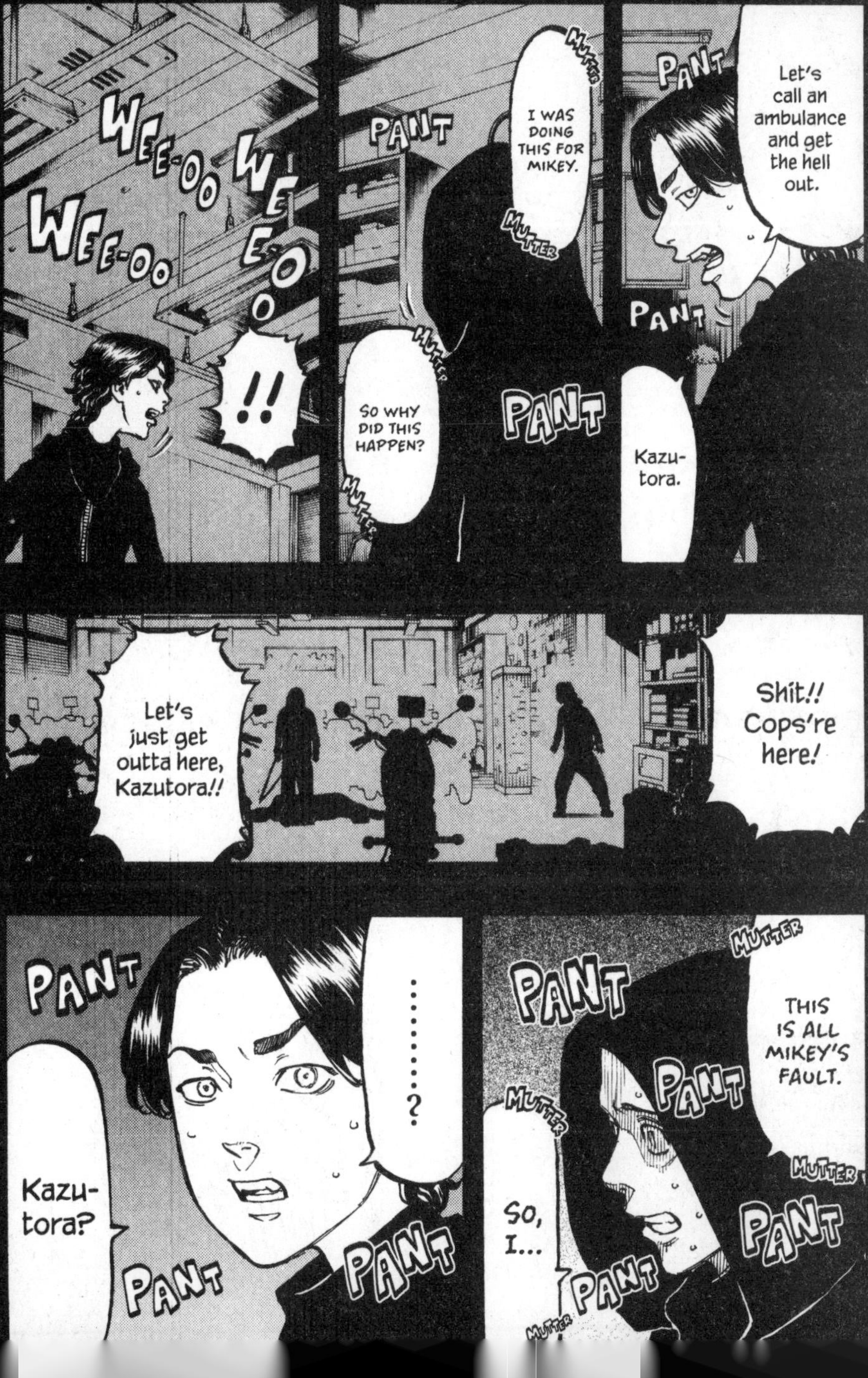
PANT
Let's call an ambulance and get the hell out.
PANT
Kazutora.
MUTTER
I WAS DOING THIS FOR MIKEY.
MUTTER
PANT
MUTTER
SO WHY DID THIS HAPPEN?
MUTTER
PANT
WEE-OO WEE-OO
WEE-OO
!!
Shit!! Cops're here!
Let's just get outta here, Kazutora!!
MUTTER
PANT
THIS IS ALL MIKEY'S FAULT.
PANT
MUTTER
MUTTER
PANT
So, I...
PANT
MUTTER
......?
PANT
Kazutora?
PANT
PANT

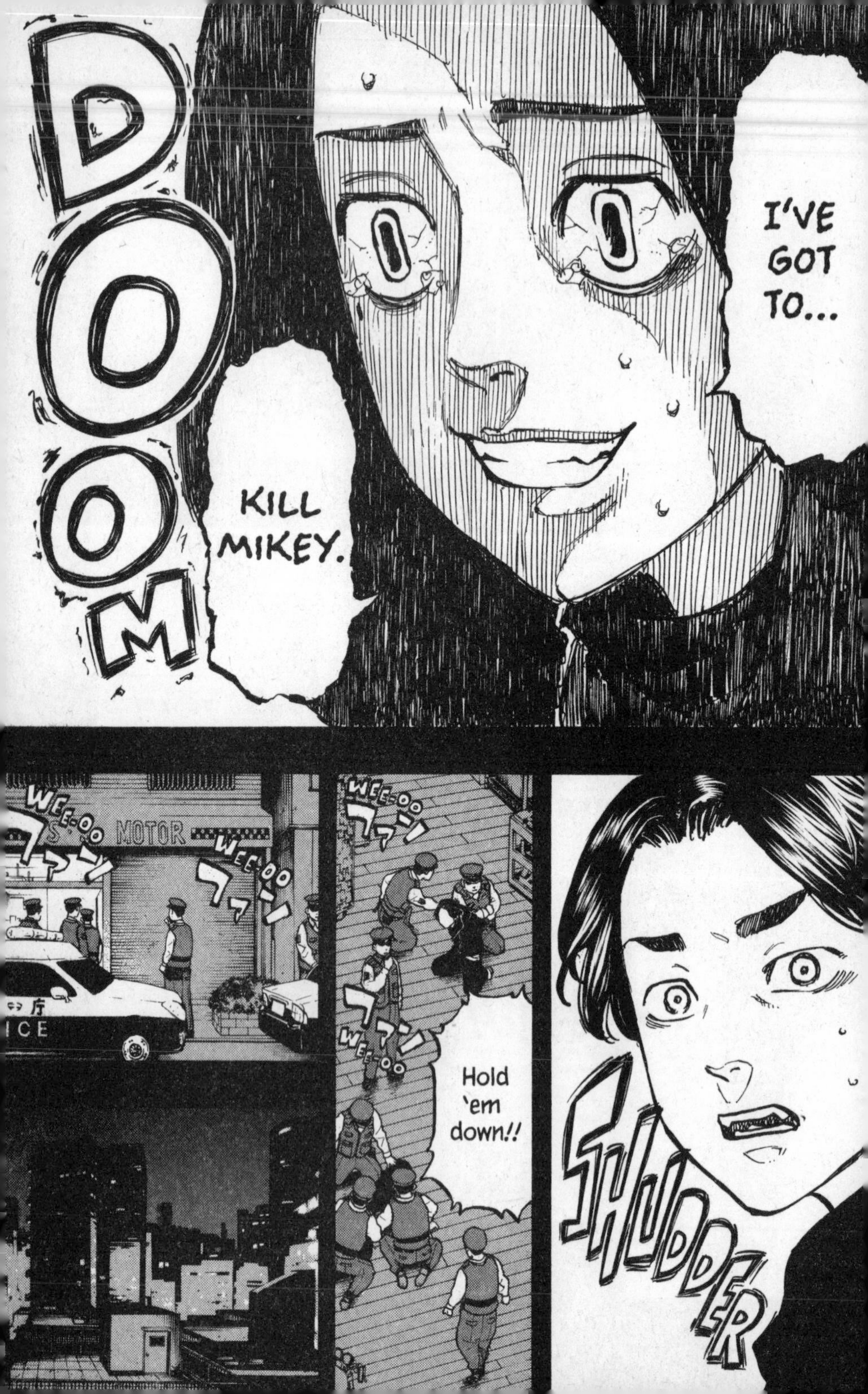
I'VE GOT TO...
KILL MIKEY.
DOOOM
SHUDDER
WEE-OO
WEE-OO
Hold 'em down!!
WEE-OO
MOTOR
WEE-OO
ICE

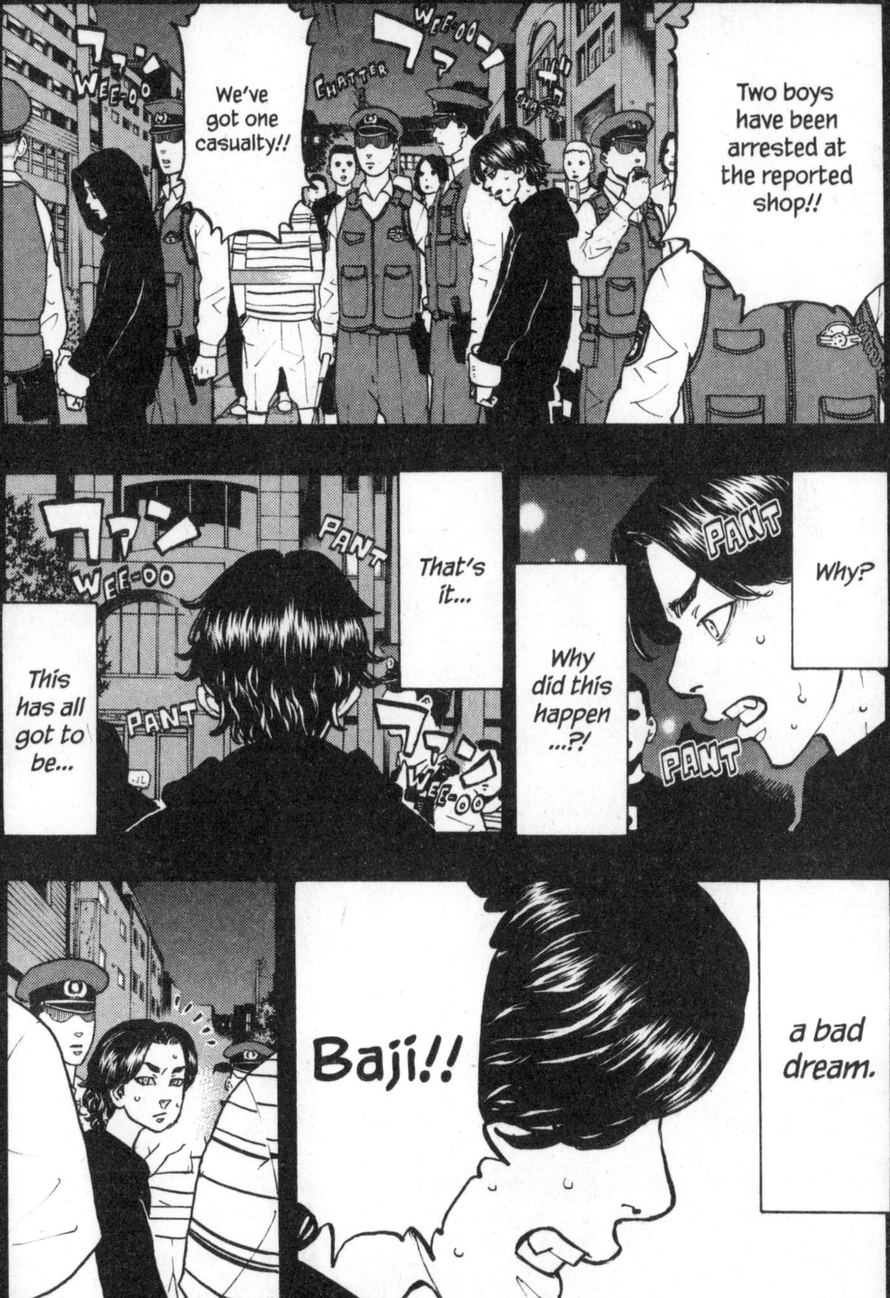
Two boys have been arrested at the reported shop!!
We've got one casualty!!
WEE-OO
CHATTER
WEE-OO
CHATTER
Why?
PANT
Why did this happen ...?!
PANT
That's it...
PANT
WEE-OO
This has all got to be...
PANT
WEE-OO
a bad dream.
Baji!!

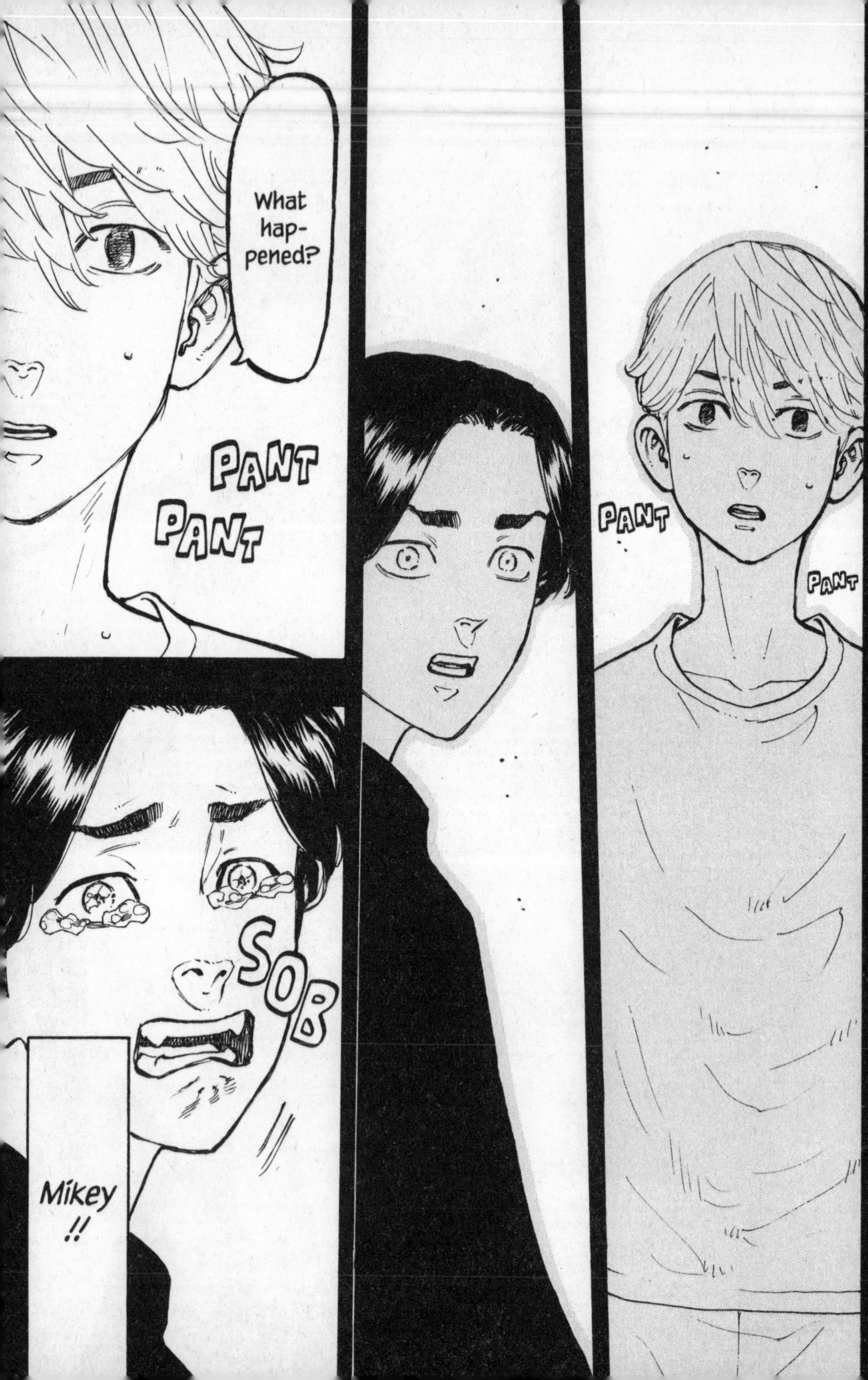
PANT
PANT
What hap-pened?
PANT
PANT
SOB
Mikey !!

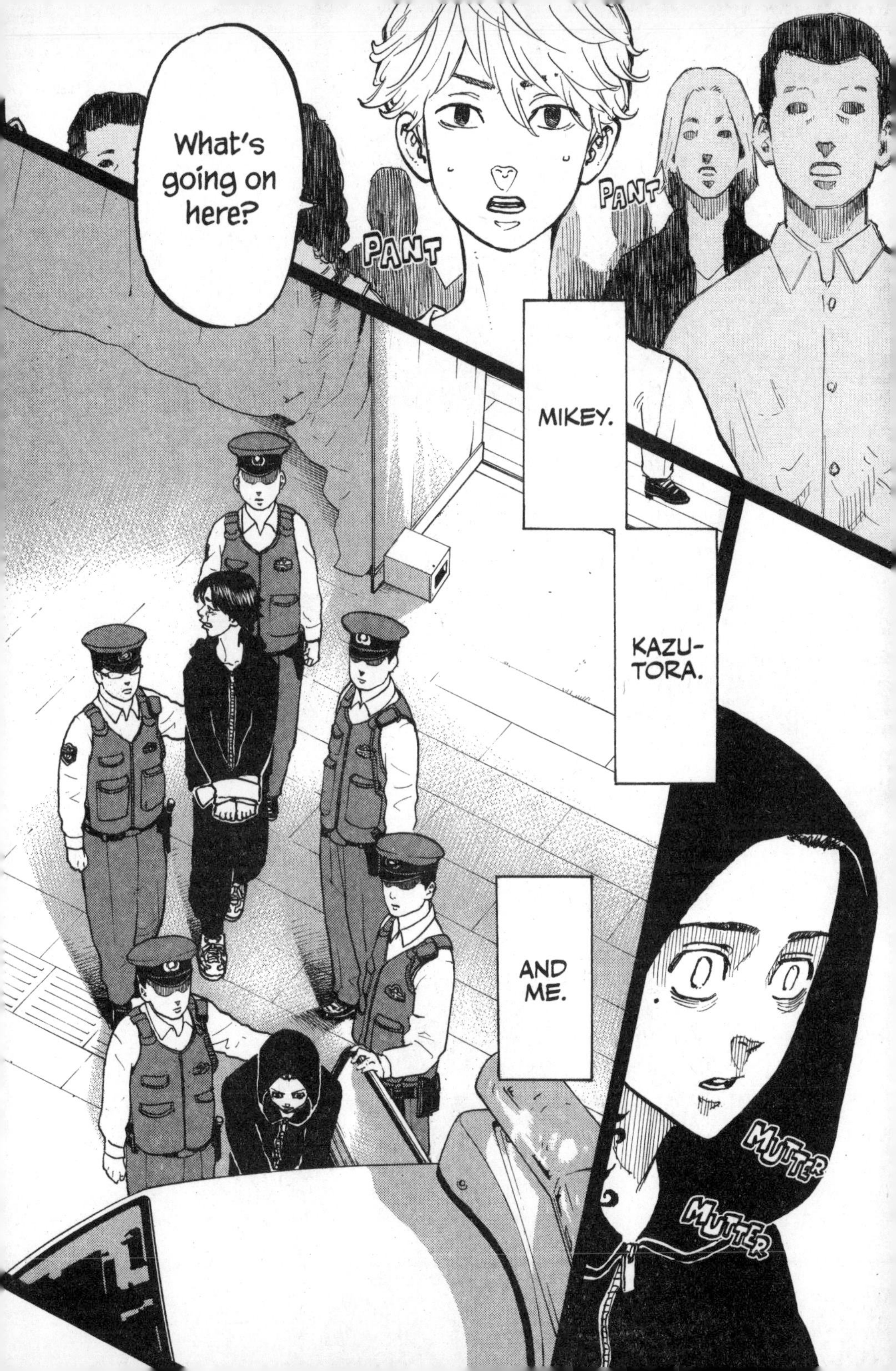

PANT
What's going on here?
PANT
MIKEY.
KAZU-TORA.
AND ME.
MUTTER
MUTTER

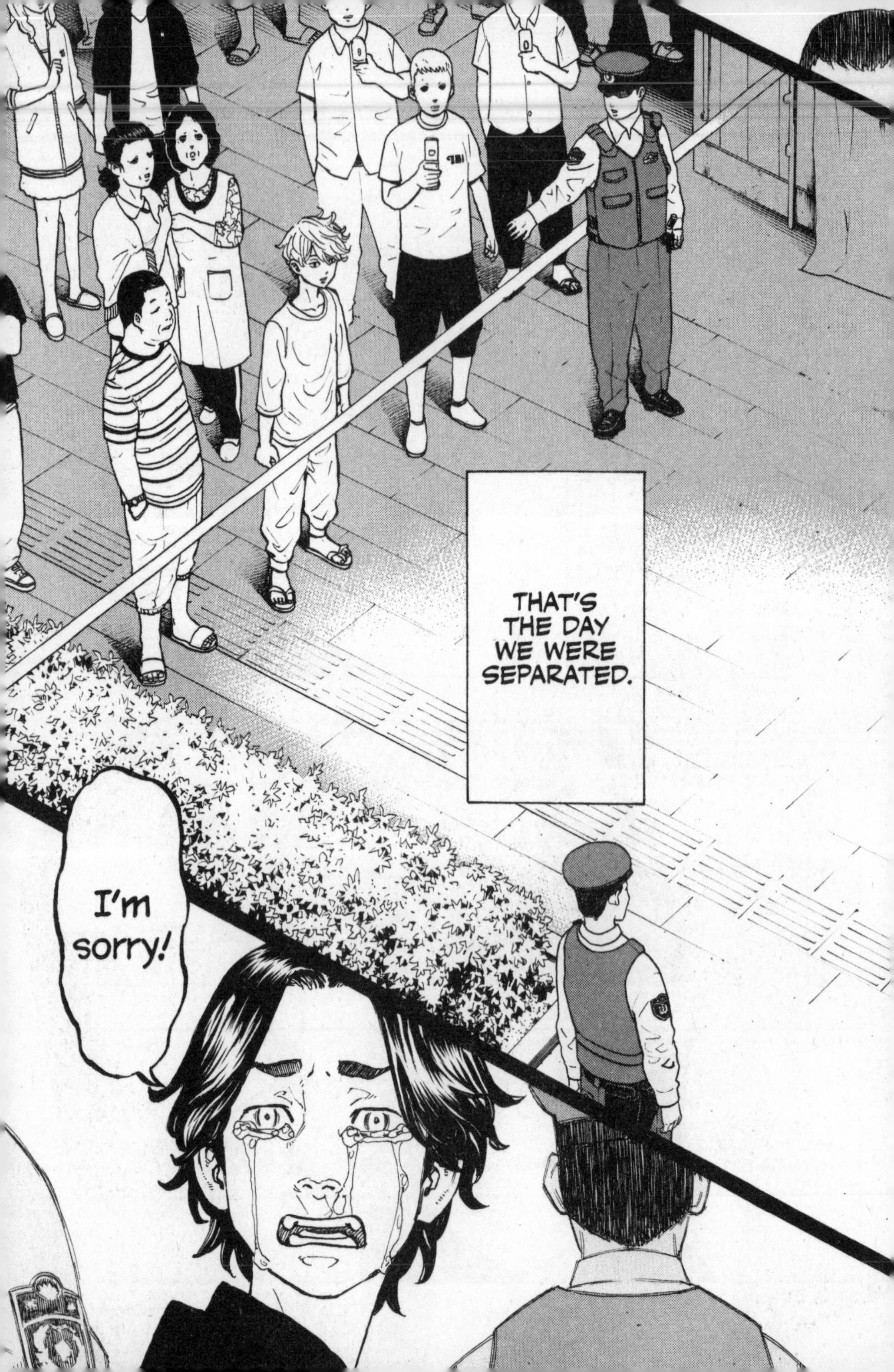
THAT'S THE DAY WE WERE SEPARATED.
I'm sorry!

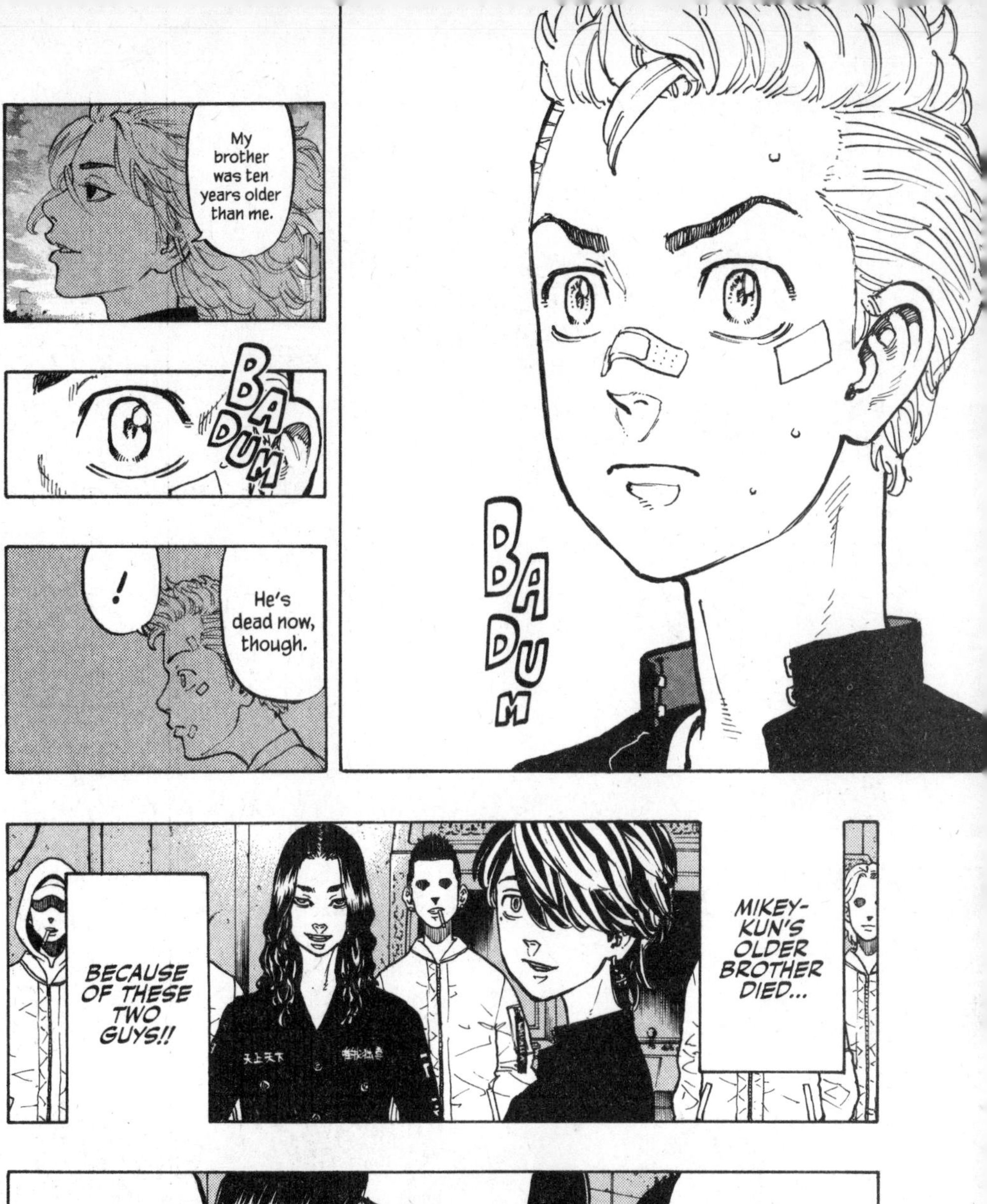
BADUM
My brother was ten years older than me.
BADUM
He's dead now, though.
!
MIKEY-KUN'S OLDER BROTHER DIED...
BECAUSE OF THESE TWO GUYS!!
KAZUTORA STOOD UP FOR ME, SO I DIDN'T END UP IN JUVIE.
I'VE BEEN WAITING FOR HIM TO GET RELEASED.

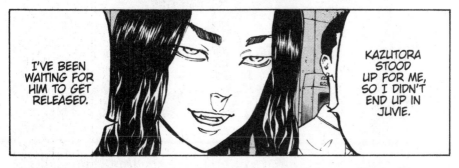

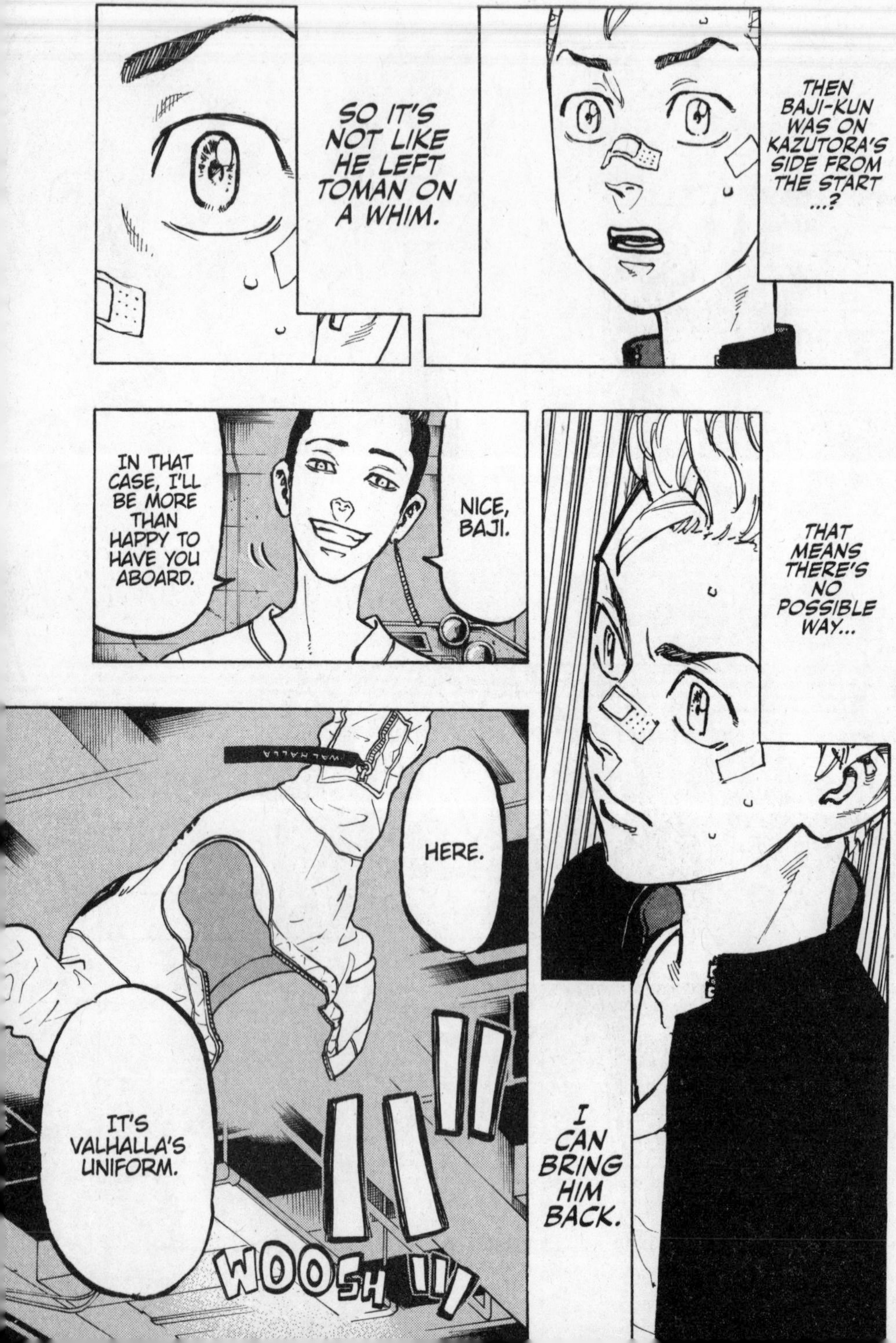
THEN BAJI-KUN WAS ON KAZUTORA'S SIDE FROM THE START ...?
SO IT'S NOT LIKE HE LEFT TOMAN ON A WHIM.
THAT MEANS THERE'S NO POSSIBLE WAY...
I CAN BRING HIM BACK.
NICE, BAJI.
IN THAT CASE, I'LL BE MORE THAN HAPPY TO HAVE YOU ABOARD.
HERE.
IT'S VALHALLA'S UNIFORM.
WOOSH

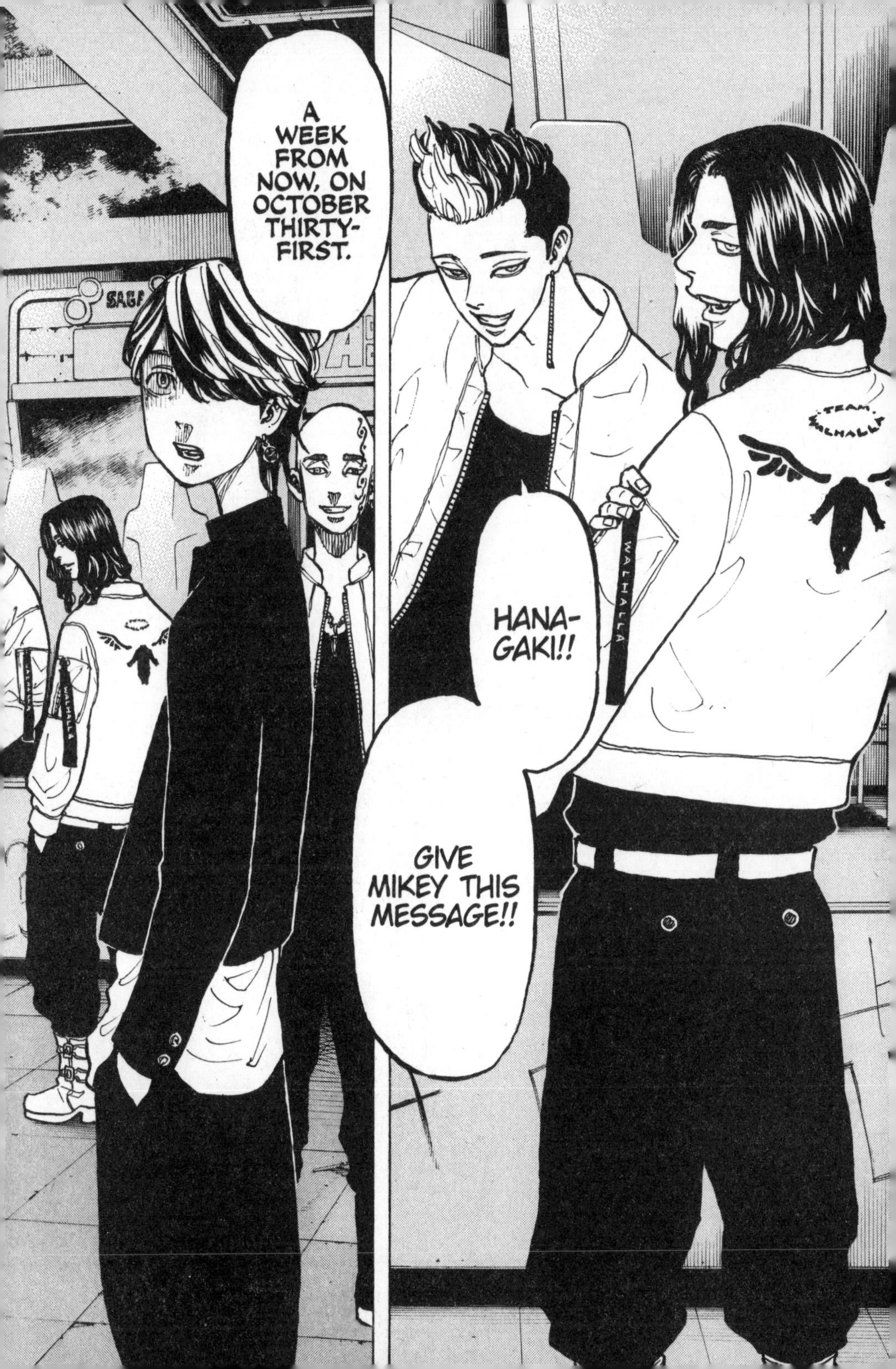
HANA-GAKI!!
GIVE MIKEY THIS MESSAGE!!
A WEEK FROM NOW, ON OCTOBER THIRTY-FIRST.

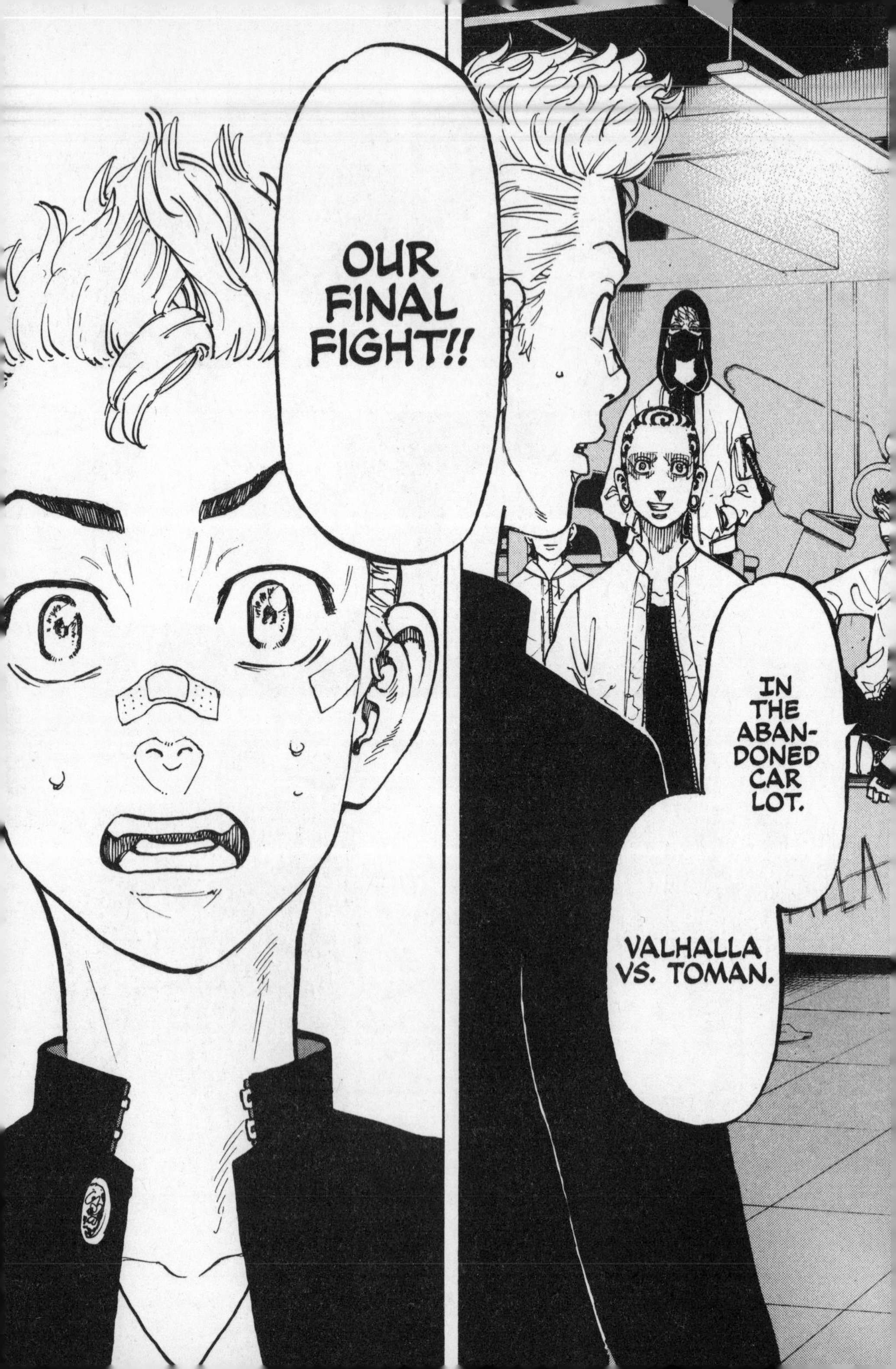
IN THE ABANDONED CAR LOT.
VALHALLA VS. TOMAN.
OUR FINAL FIGHT!!

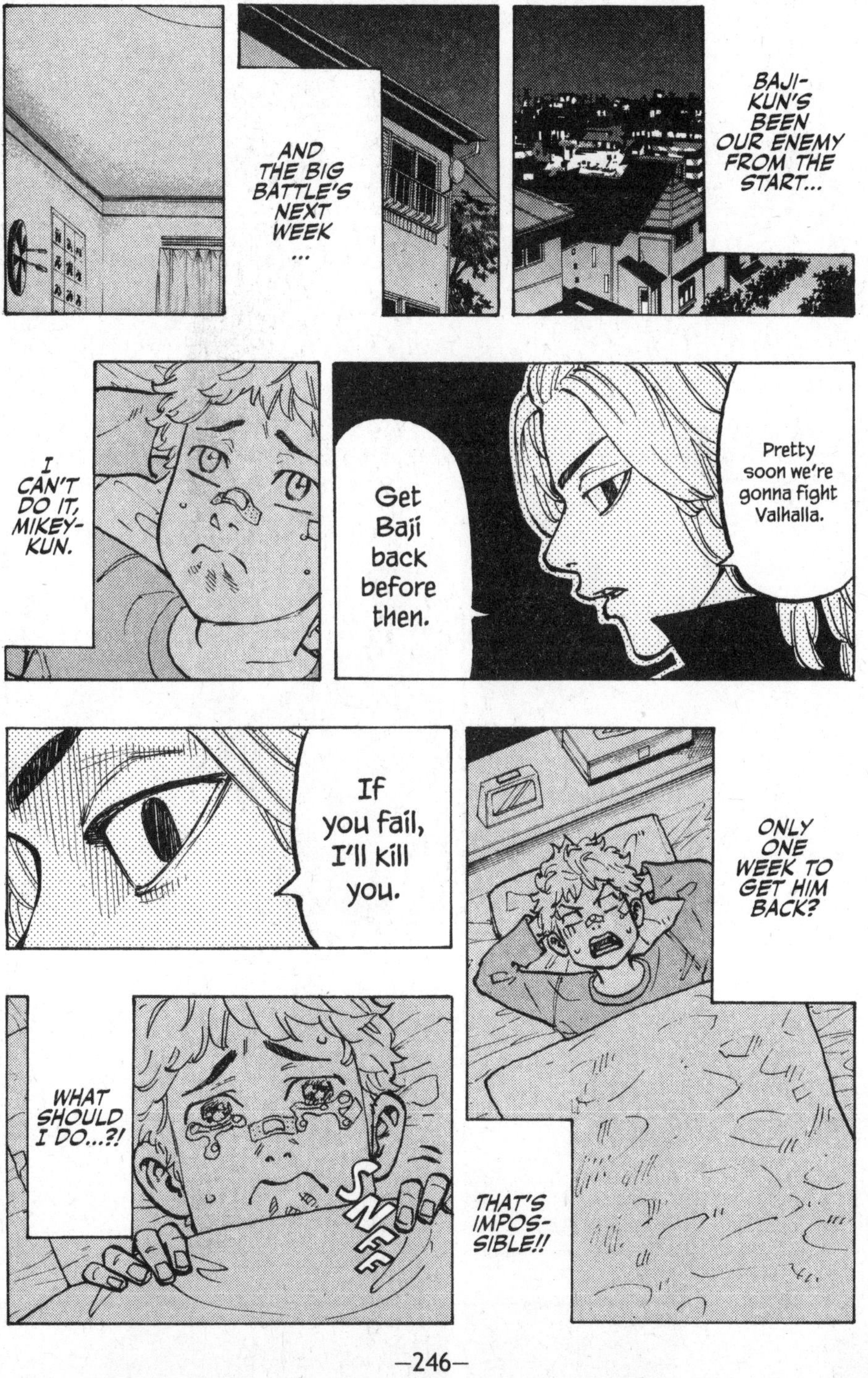
BAJI-KUN'S BEEN OUR ENEMY FROM THE START...
AND THE BIG BATTLE'S NEXT WEEK...
Pretty soon we're gonna fight Valhalla.
Get Baji back before then.
I CAN'T DO IT, MIKEY-KUN.
ONLY ONE WEEK TO GET HIM BACK?
THAT'S IMPOSSIBLE!!
If you fail, I'll kill you.
WHAT SHOULD I DO...?!
SNFF

SIGH ...

DIDN'T SLEEP A WINK...

EVEN THOUGH I'M ACTUALLY TWENTY-SIX.

THE NEXT DAY.

HOW DO I EXPLAIN THIS TO MIKEY-KUN?

HUH?

CREAK

C'MERE!

CREAK

HEY!

POP A SQUAT.
CREAK
WHAT... WHO'S THAT SCARY DUDE ...?
HE'S TOTALLY UP TO NO GOOD! AND HE'S BEAT TO HELL, TOO.
YESTER-DAY WAS A TOTAL DISASTER FOR US BOTH, HUH?
JUST IGNORE HIM.
CREAK
HUH...?
PAUSE
YESTER-DAY?

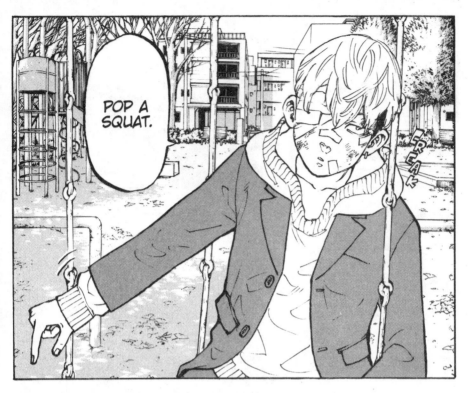

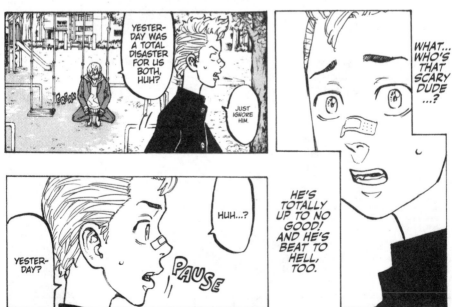

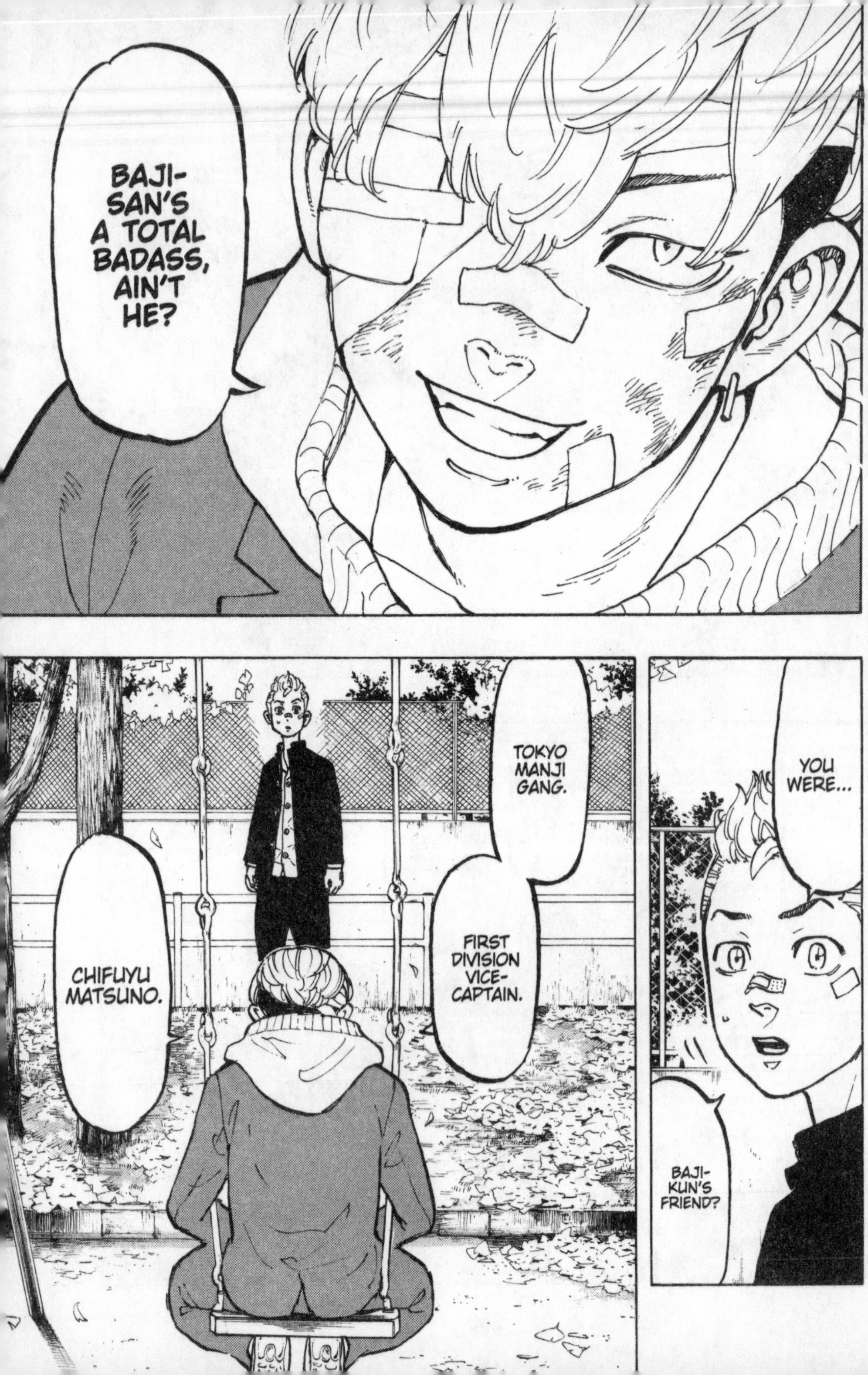
BAJI-SAN'S A TOTAL BADASS, AIN'T HE?
YOU WERE...
BAJI-KUN'S FRIEND?
TOKYO MANJI GANG.
FIRST DIVISION VICE-CAPTAIN.
CHIFUYU MATSUNO.

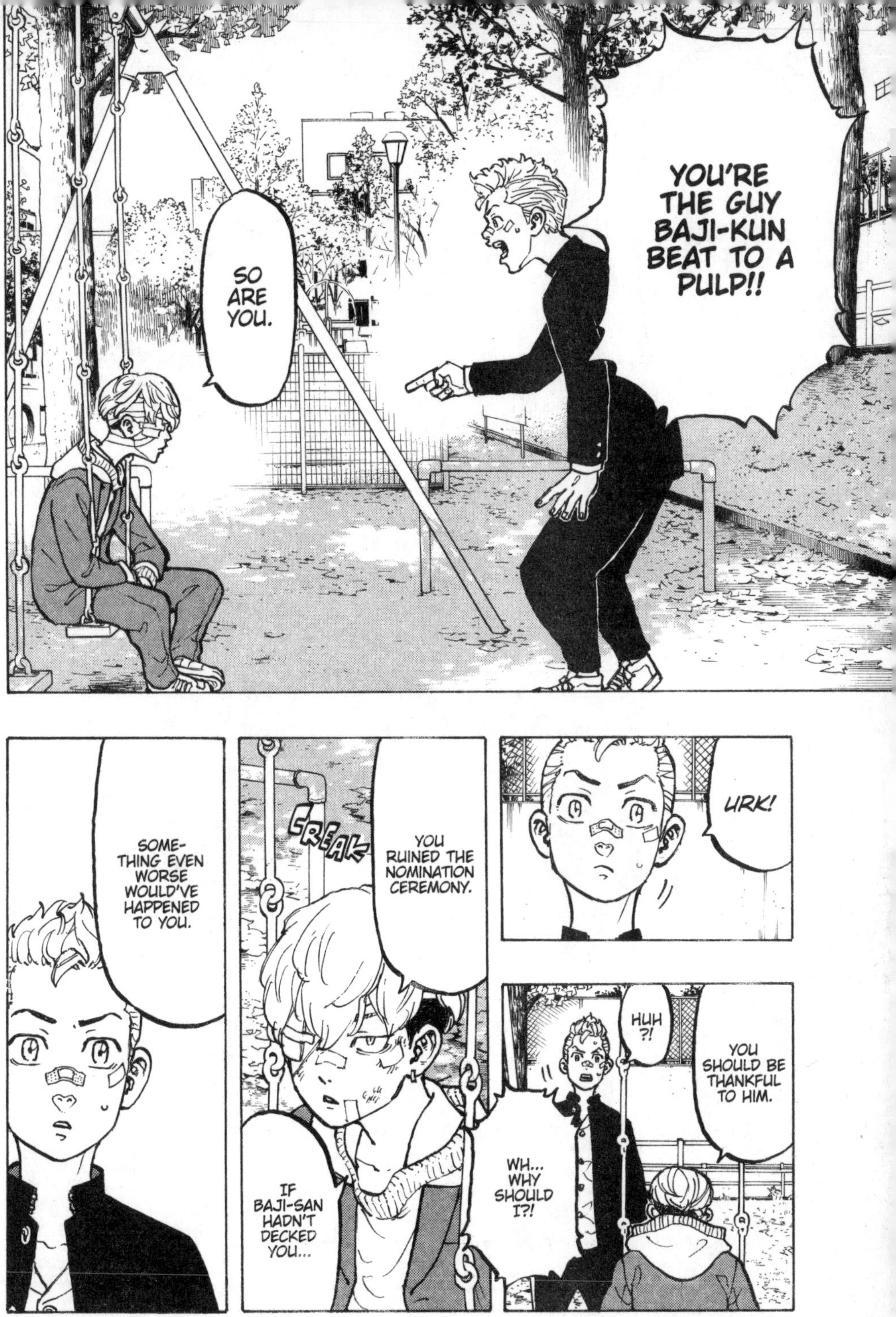
YOU'RE THE GUY BAJI-KUN BEAT TO A PULP!!
SO ARE YOU.
URK!
YOU SHOULD BE THANKFUL TO HIM.
HUH ?!
WH... WHY SHOULD I?!
CREAK
YOU RUINED THE NOMINATION CEREMONY.
IF BAJI-SAN HADN'T DECKED YOU...
SOME-THING EVEN WORSE WOULD'VE HAPPENED TO YOU.

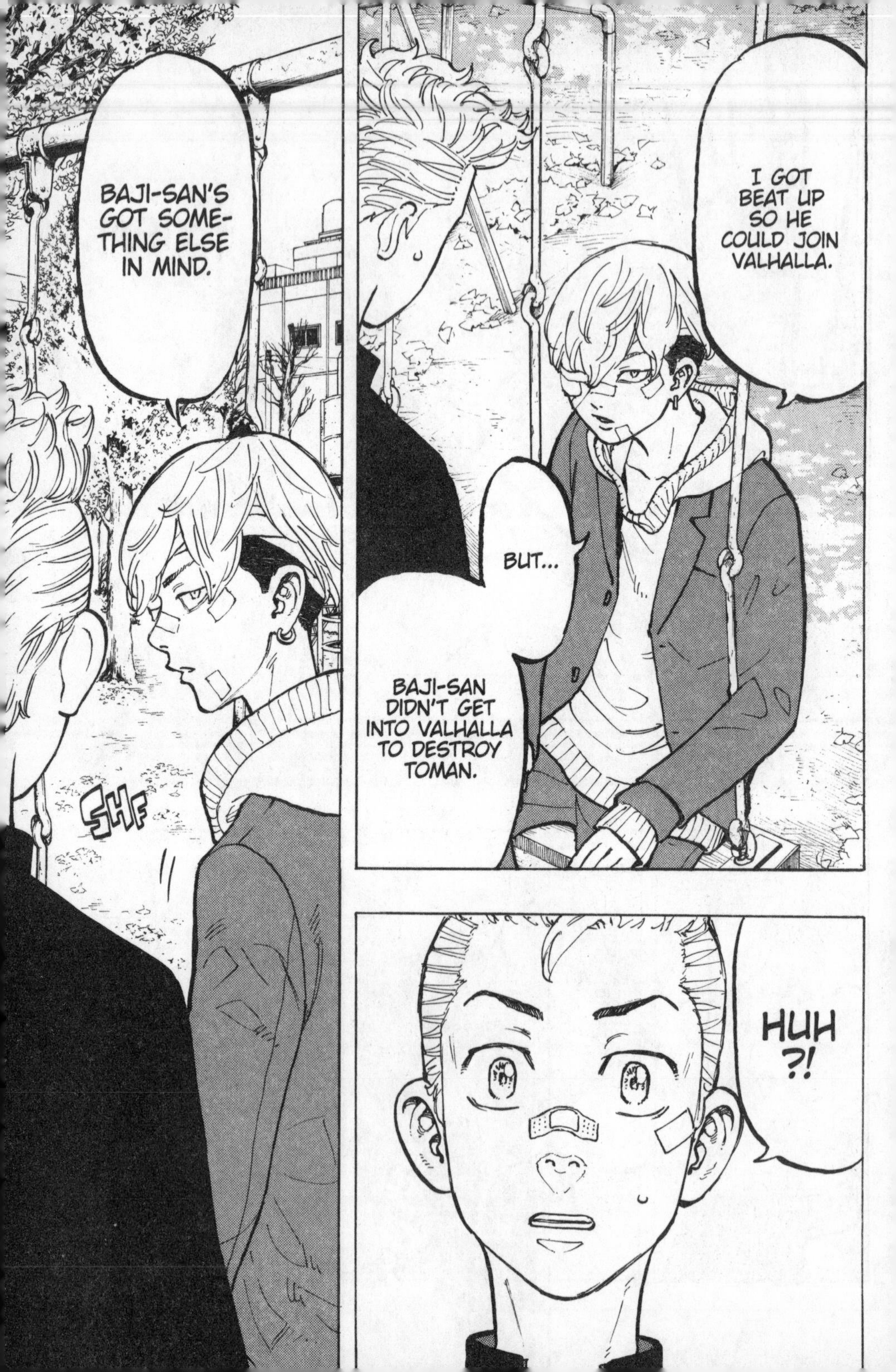
I GOT BEAT UP SO HE COULD JOIN VALHALLA.
BUT...
BAJI-SAN DIDN'T GET INTO VALHALLA TO DESTROY TOMAN.
HUH ?!
BAJI-SAN'S GOT SOME-THING ELSE IN MIND.
SHF

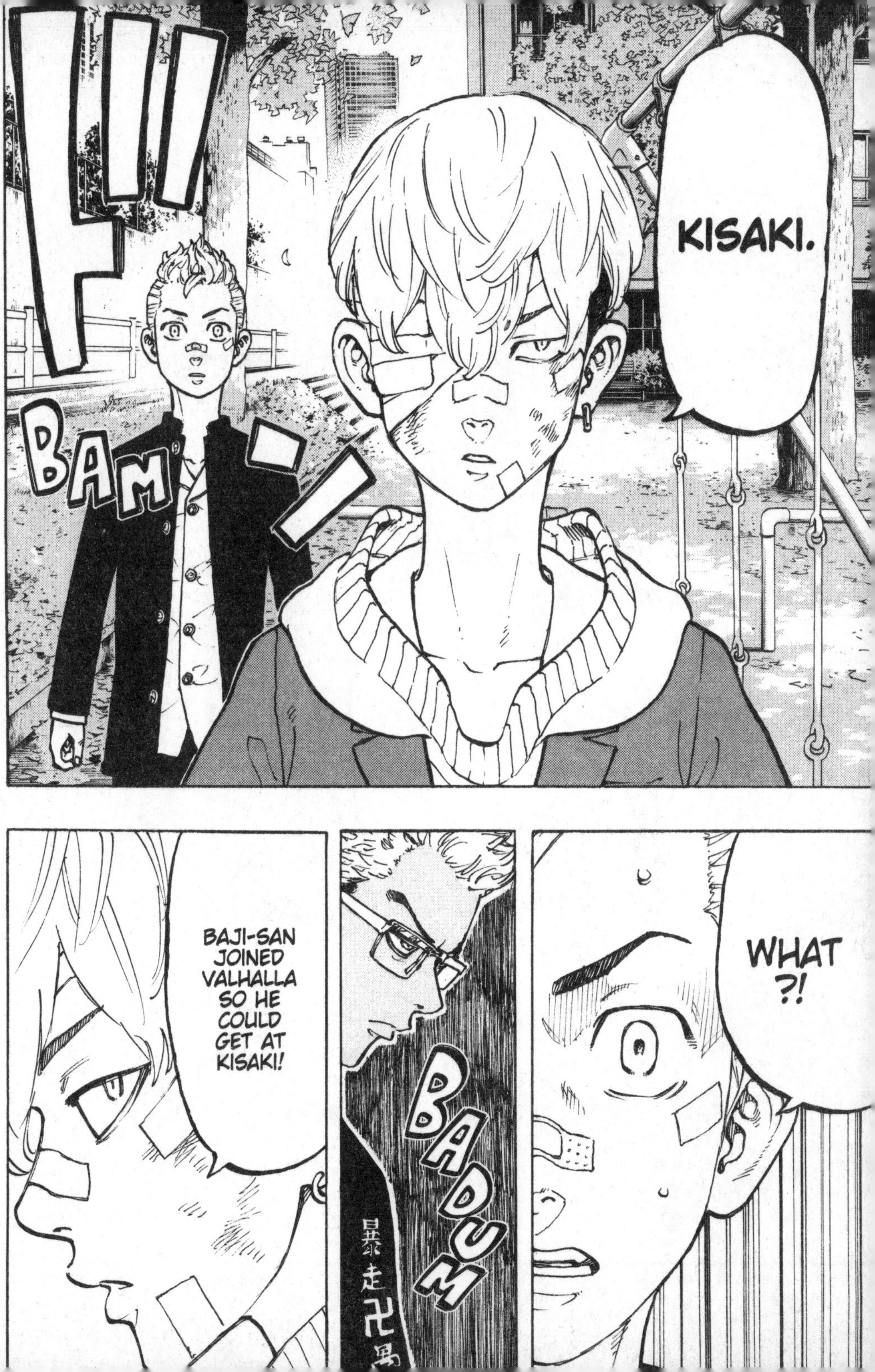
KISAKI.
!!!
BAM
WHAT ?!
BADUM
BAJI-SAN JOINED VALHALLA SO HE COULD GET AT KISAKI!

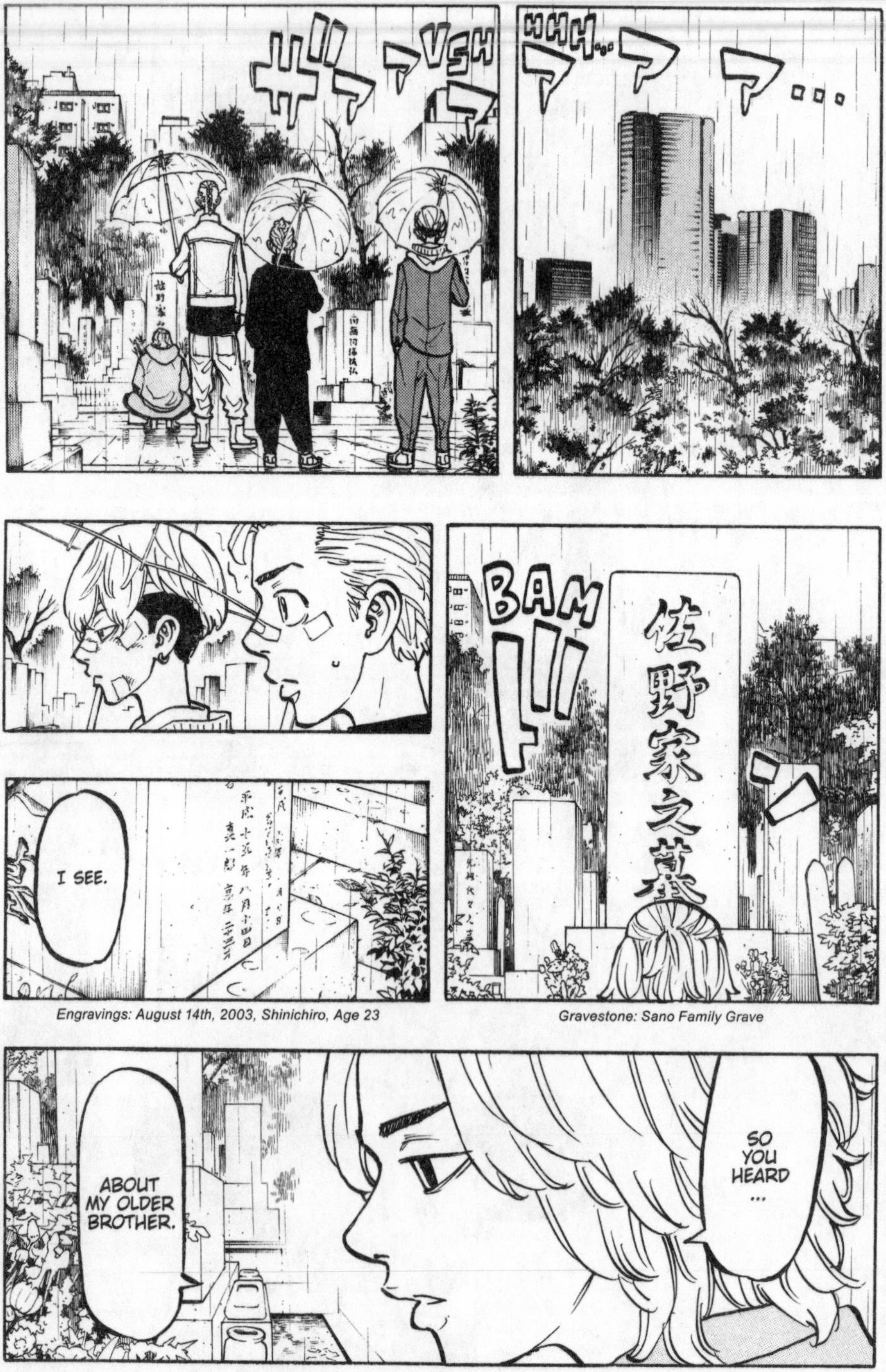
ザァァ VSH
HHH... ァ ァ ァ...
BAM
佐野家之墓
I SEE.
Gravestone: Sano Family Grave
Engravings: August 14th, 2003, Shinichiro, Age 23
SO YOU HEARD ...
ABOUT MY OLDER BROTHER.

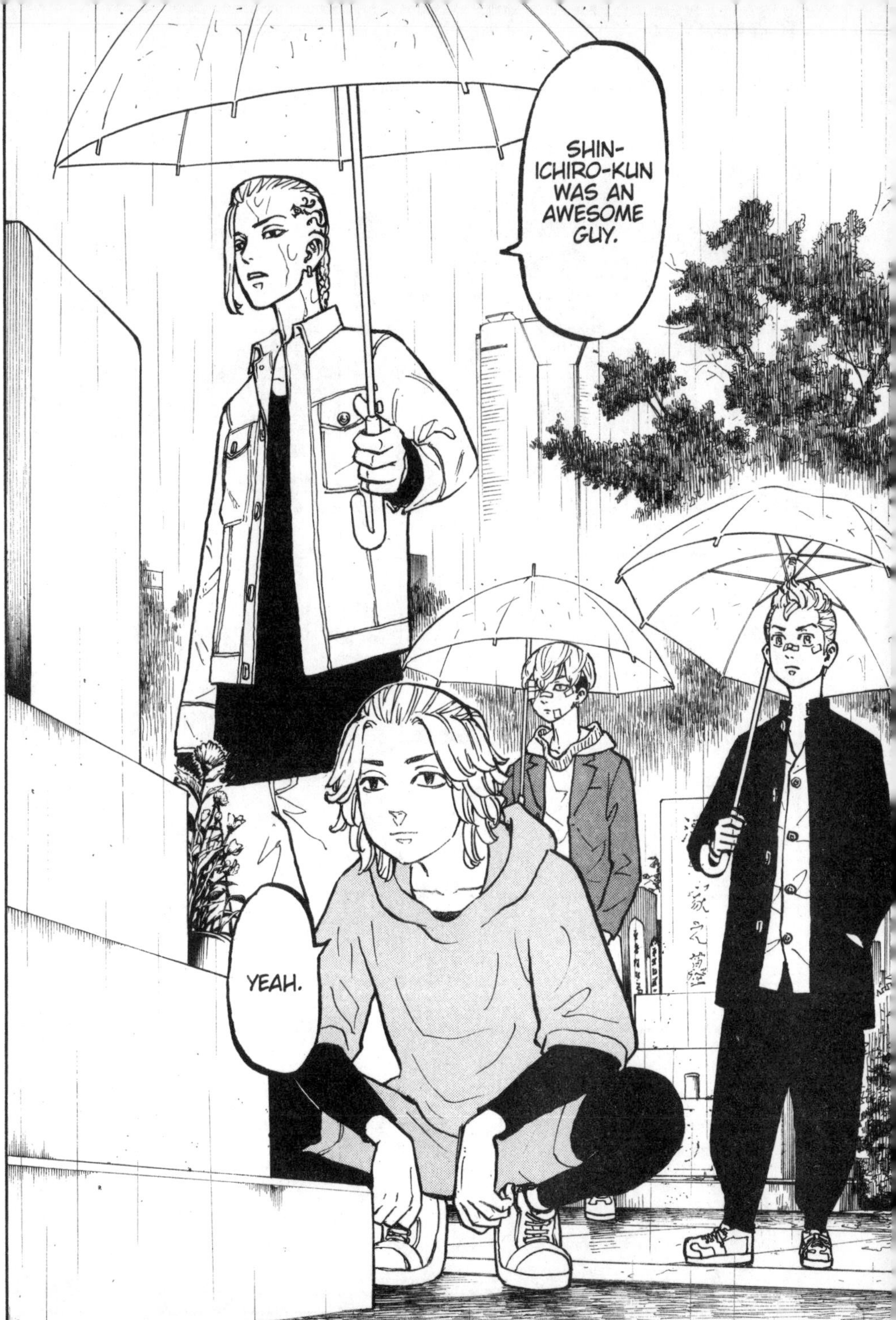
SHIN-ICHIRO-KUN WAS AN AWESOME GUY.
YEAH.

CHAPTER 46: MADE UP MY MIND

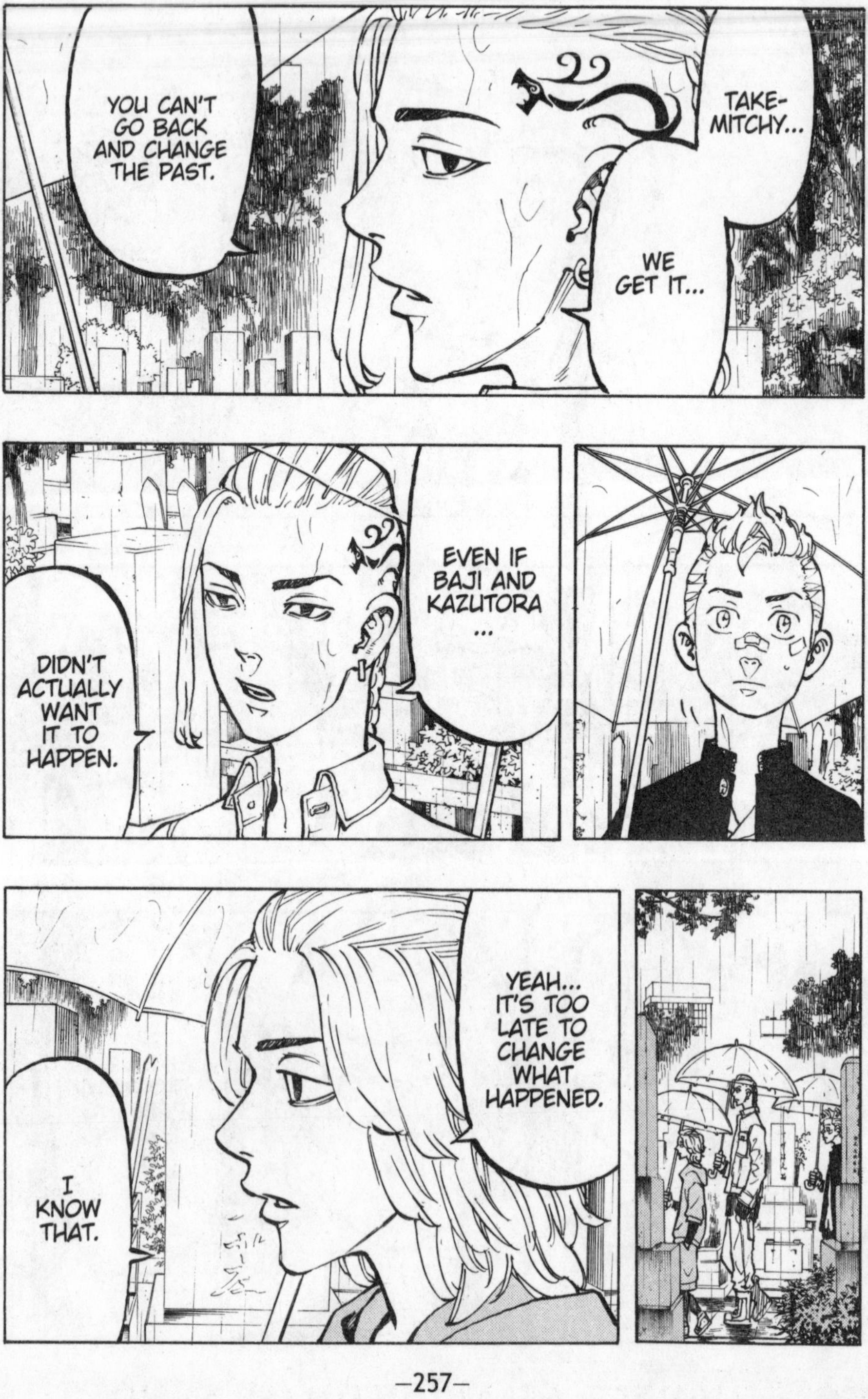
TAKE-MITCHY...
WE GET IT...
YOU CAN'T GO BACK AND CHANGE THE PAST.
EVEN IF BAJI AND KAZUTORA ...
DIDN'T ACTUALLY WANT IT TO HAPPEN.
YEAH... IT'S TOO LATE TO CHANGE WHAT HAPPENED.
I KNOW THAT.

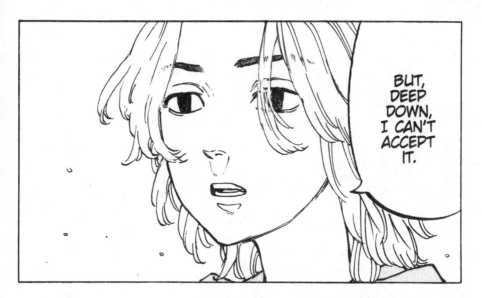

BUT, DEEP DOWN, I CAN'T ACCEPT IT.
THE CB250T THAT BAJI AND KAZUTORA WERE TRYING TO STEAL...
WAS THE ONE MY BROTHER RODE.
WHAT ?!!
THEY WANTED TO GIVE ME...
THAT BIKE AS A BIRTHDAY PRESENT, I KNOW IT.
BUT NOW THE CB250T IS A MEMENTO OF MY BROTHER.

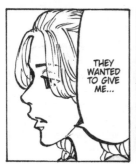

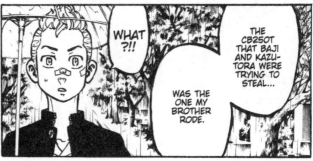

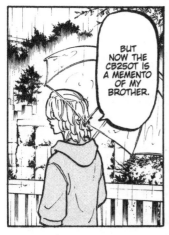

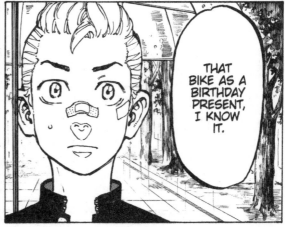

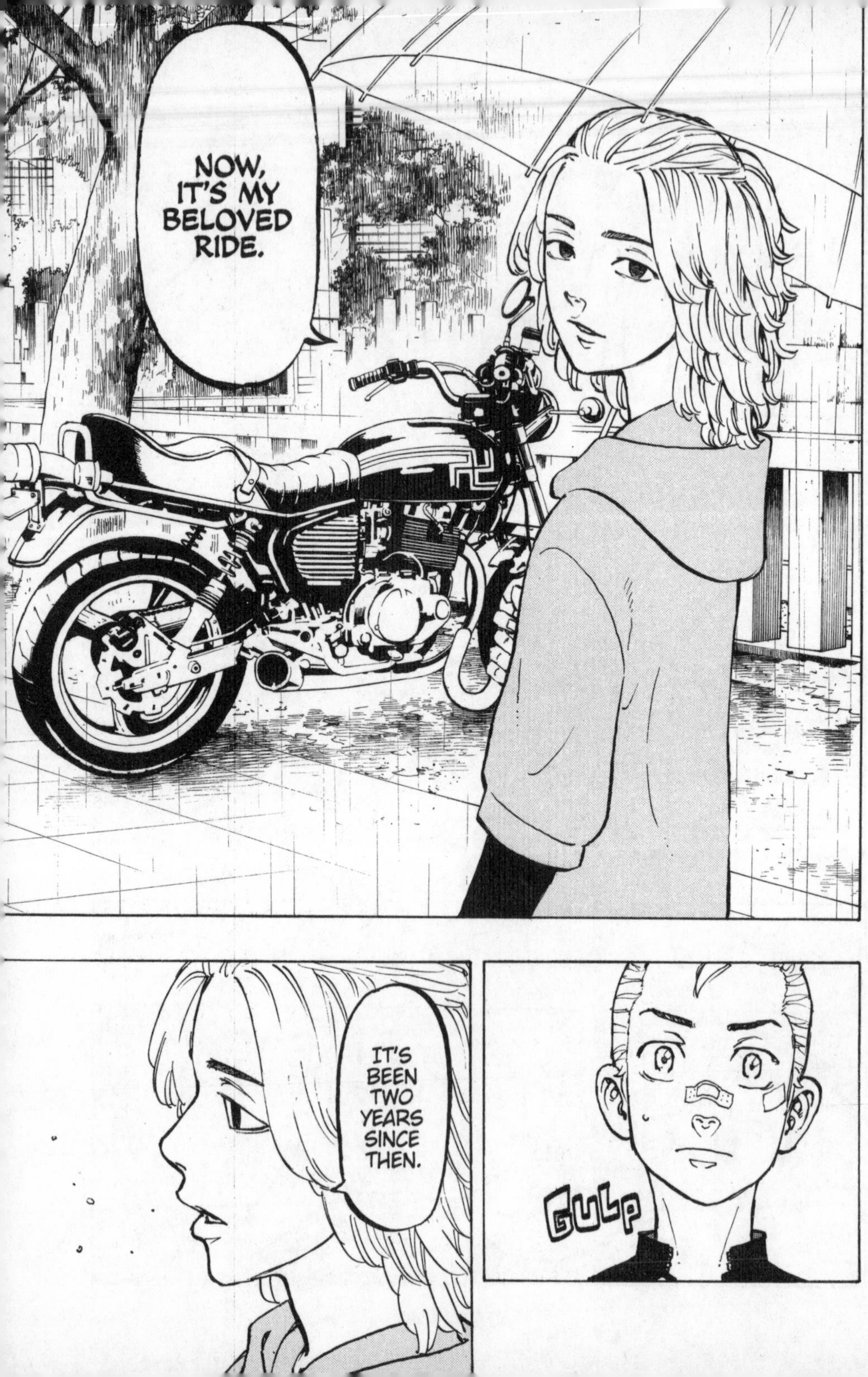
NOW, IT'S MY BELOVED RIDE.
GULP
IT'S BEEN TWO YEARS SINCE THEN.

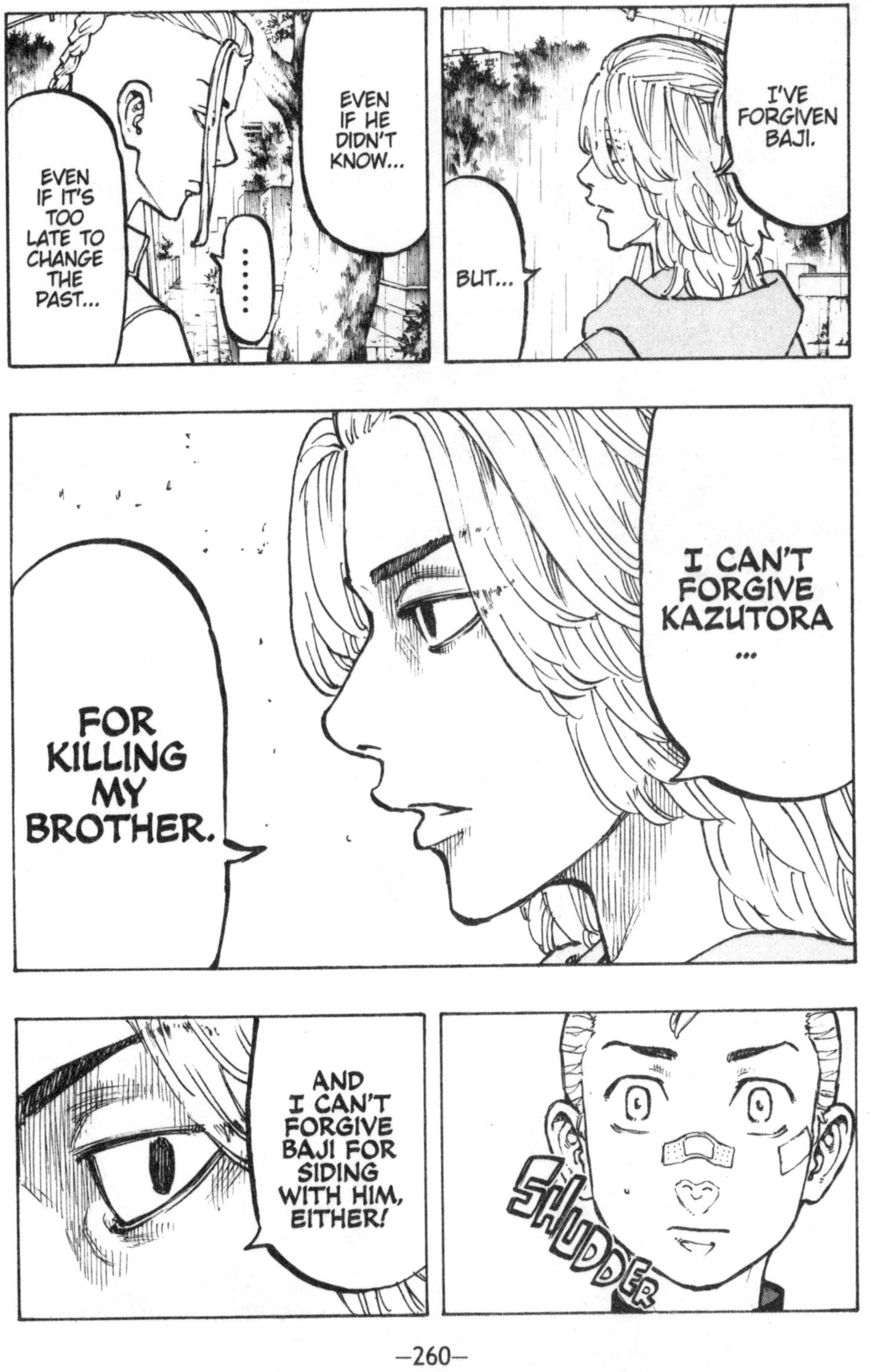
I'VE FORGIVEN BAJI.
BUT...
EVEN IF HE DIDN'T KNOW...
......
EVEN IF IT'S TOO LATE TO CHANGE THE PAST...
I CAN'T FORGIVE KAZUTORA ...
FOR KILLING MY BROTHER.
SHUDDER
AND I CAN'T FORGIVE BAJI FOR SIDING WITH HIM, EITHER!

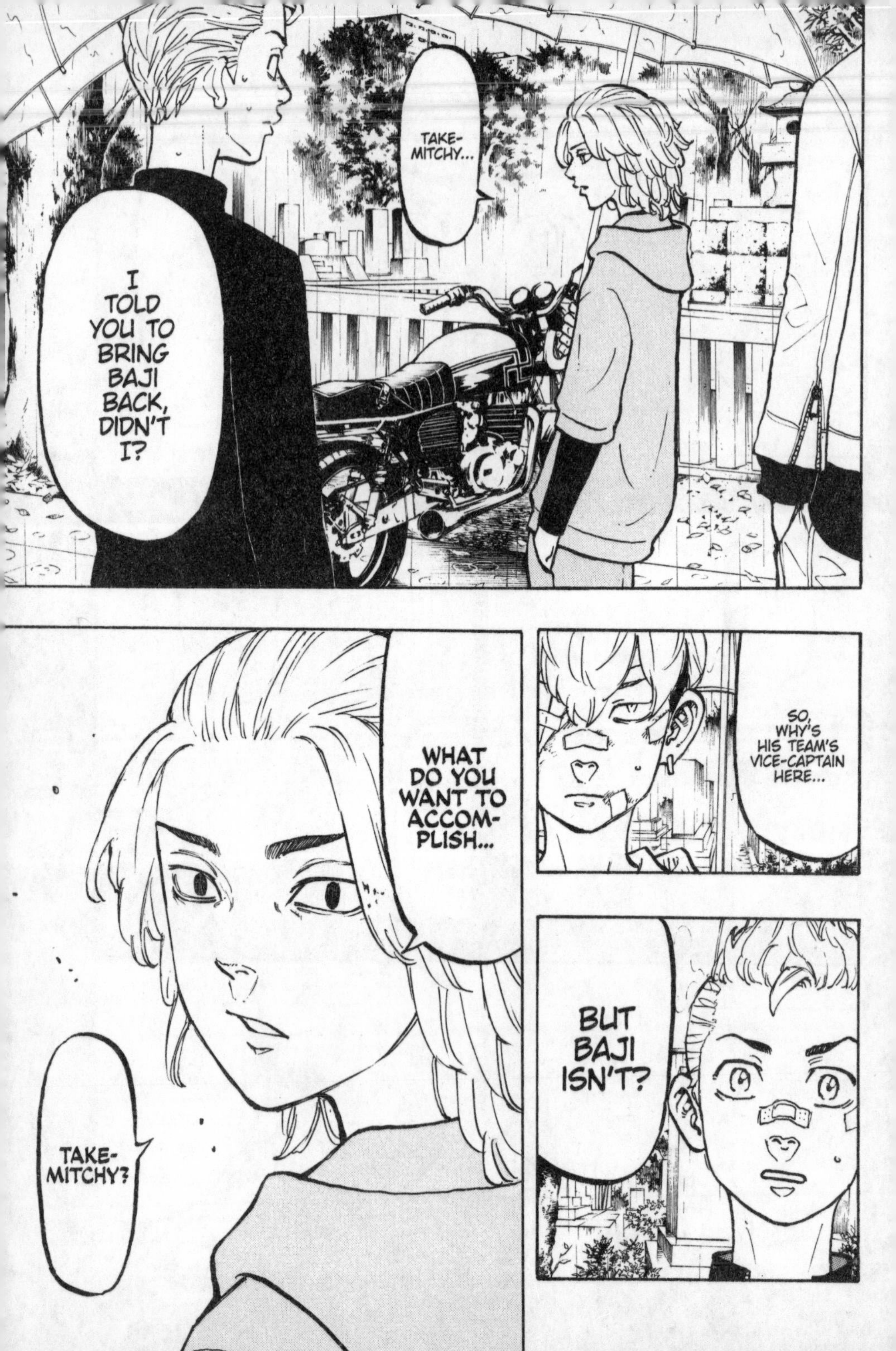
TAKE-MITCHY...
I TOLD YOU TO BRING BAJI BACK, DIDN'T I?
SO, WHY'S HIS TEAM'S VICE-CAPTAIN HERE...
BUT BAJI ISN'T?
WHAT DO YOU WANT TO ACCOMPLISH...
TAKE-MITCHY?

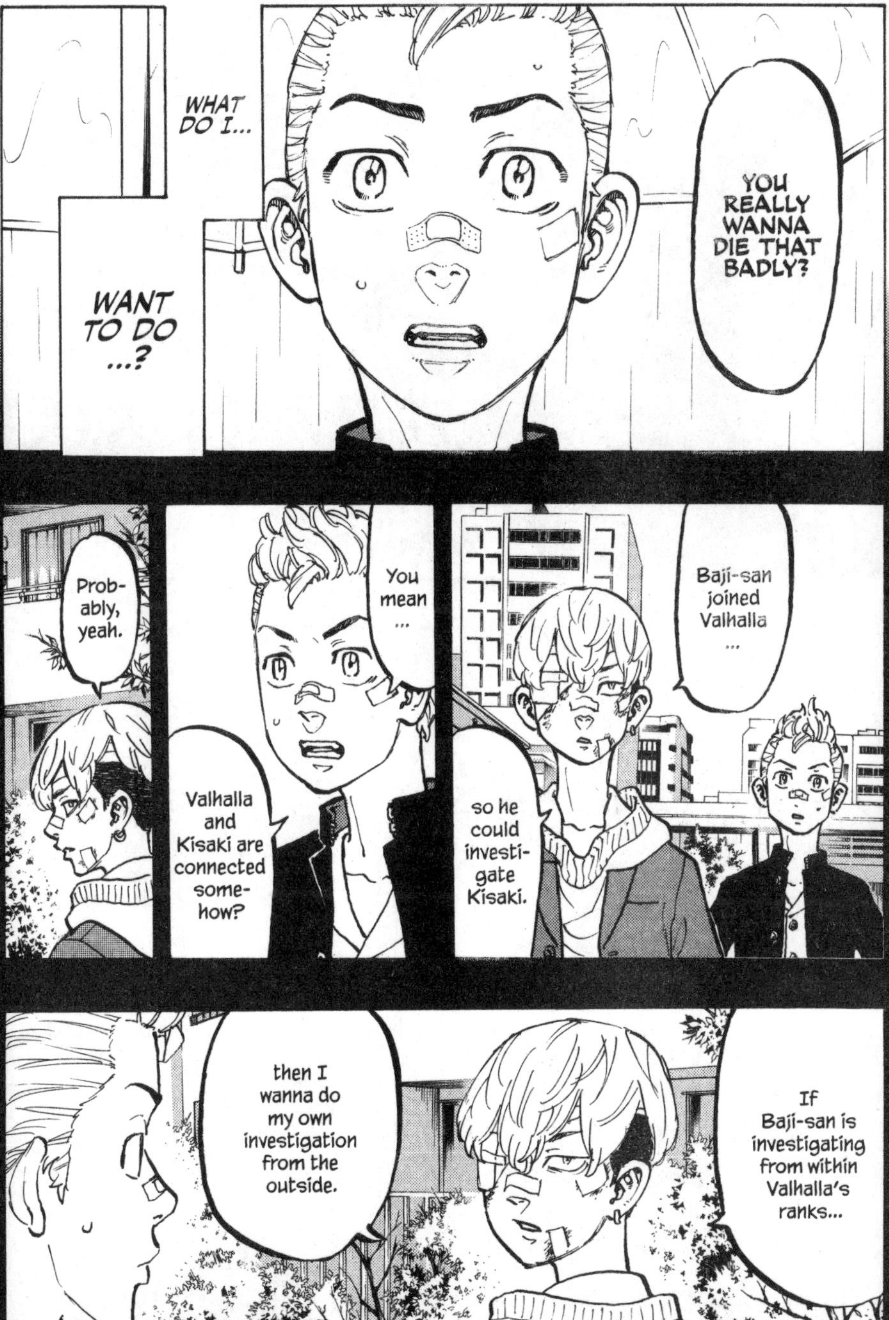

YOU REALLY WANNA DIE THAT BADLY?
WHAT DO I...
WANT TO DO ...?
Baji-san joined Valhalla ...
so he could investigate Kisaki.
You mean ...
Valhalla and Kisaki are connected somehow?
Probably, yeah.
If Baji-san is investigating from within Valhalla's ranks...
then I wanna do my own investigation from the outside.

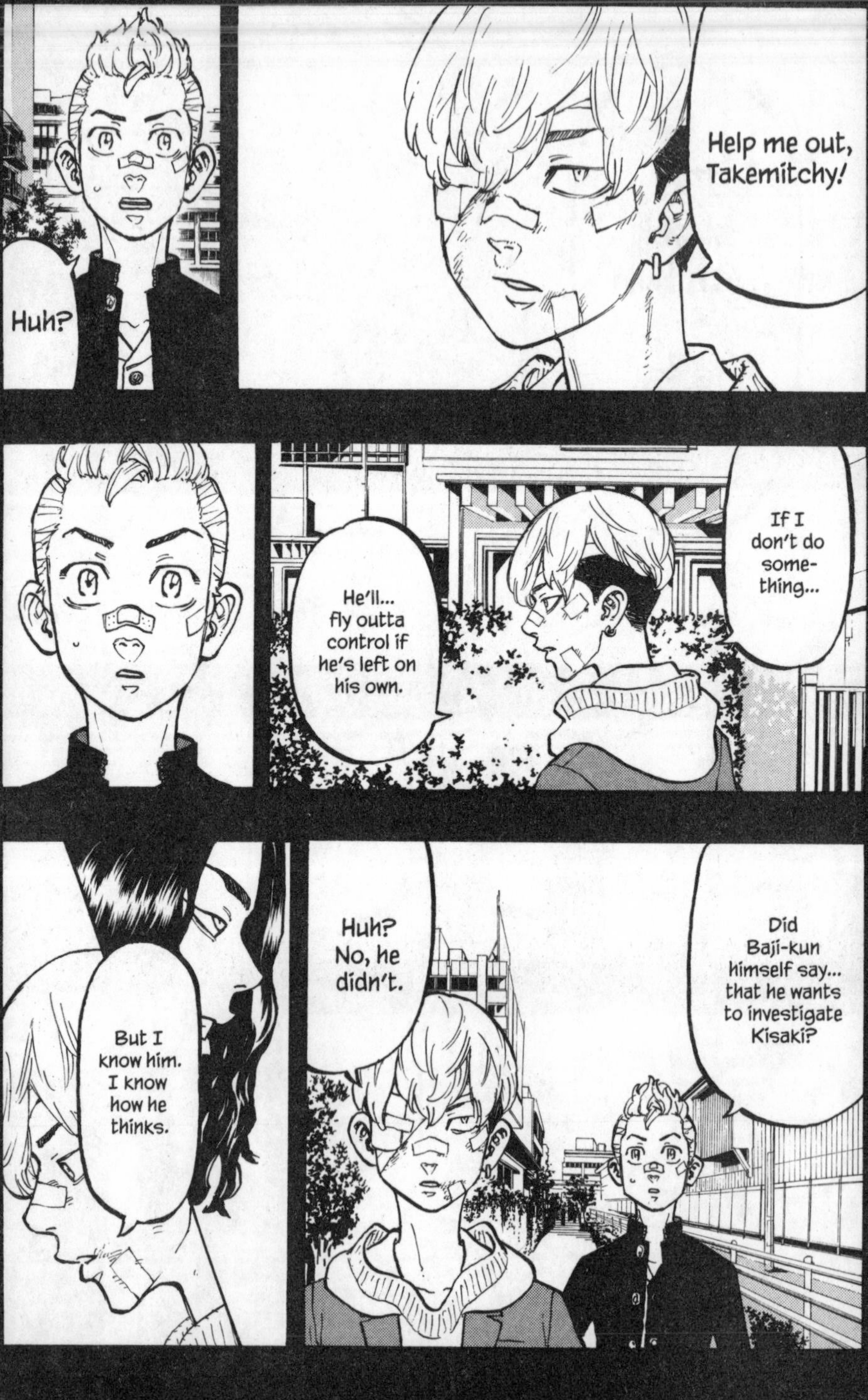
Help me out, Takemitchy!
Huh?
If I don't do some-thing...
He'll... fly outta control if he's left on his own.
Did Baji-kun himself say... that he wants to investigate Kisaki?
Huh? No, he didn't.
But I know him. I know how he thinks.

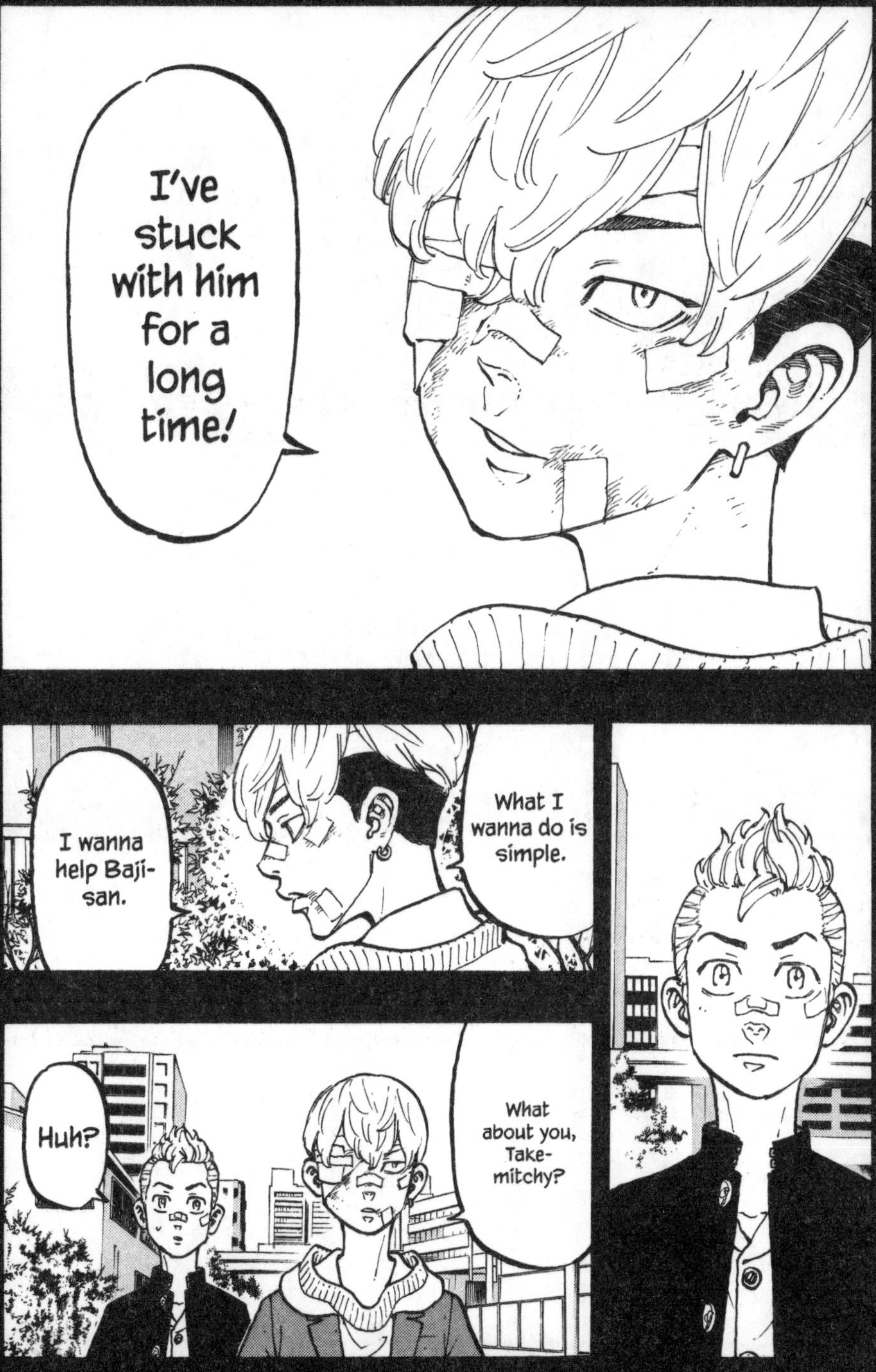
I've stuck with him for a long time!
What I wanna do is simple.
I wanna help Baji-san.
What about you, Take-mitchy?
Huh?

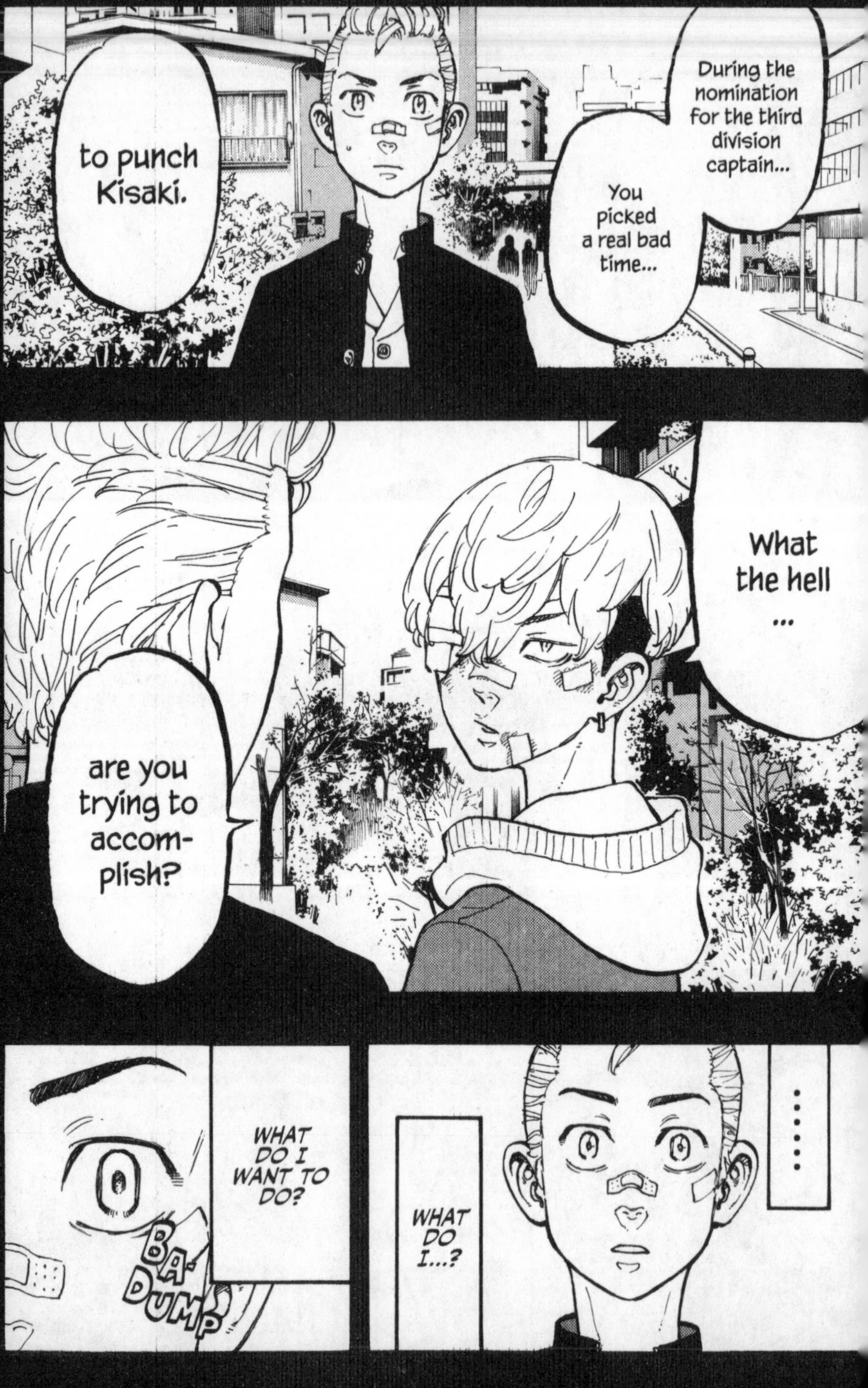
During the nomination for the third division captain...
You picked a real bad time...
to punch Kisaki.
What the hell ...
are you trying to accomplish?
......
WHAT DO I...?
WHAT DO I WANT TO DO?
BA-DUMP

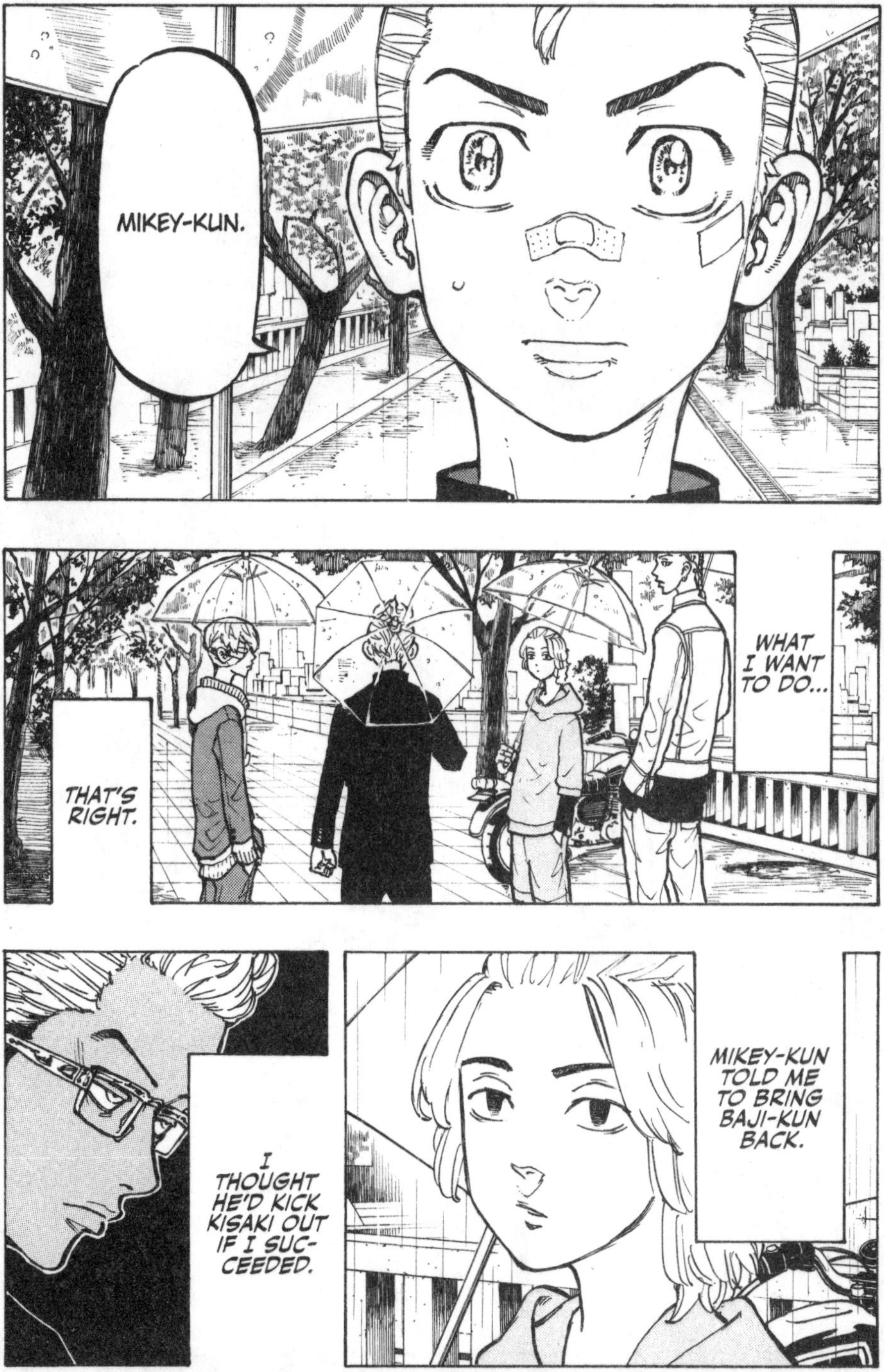
MIKEY-KUN.
WHAT I WANT TO DO...
THAT'S RIGHT.
MIKEY-KUN TOLD ME TO BRING BAJI-KUN BACK.
I THOUGHT HE'D KICK KISAKI OUT IF I SUC-CEEDED.

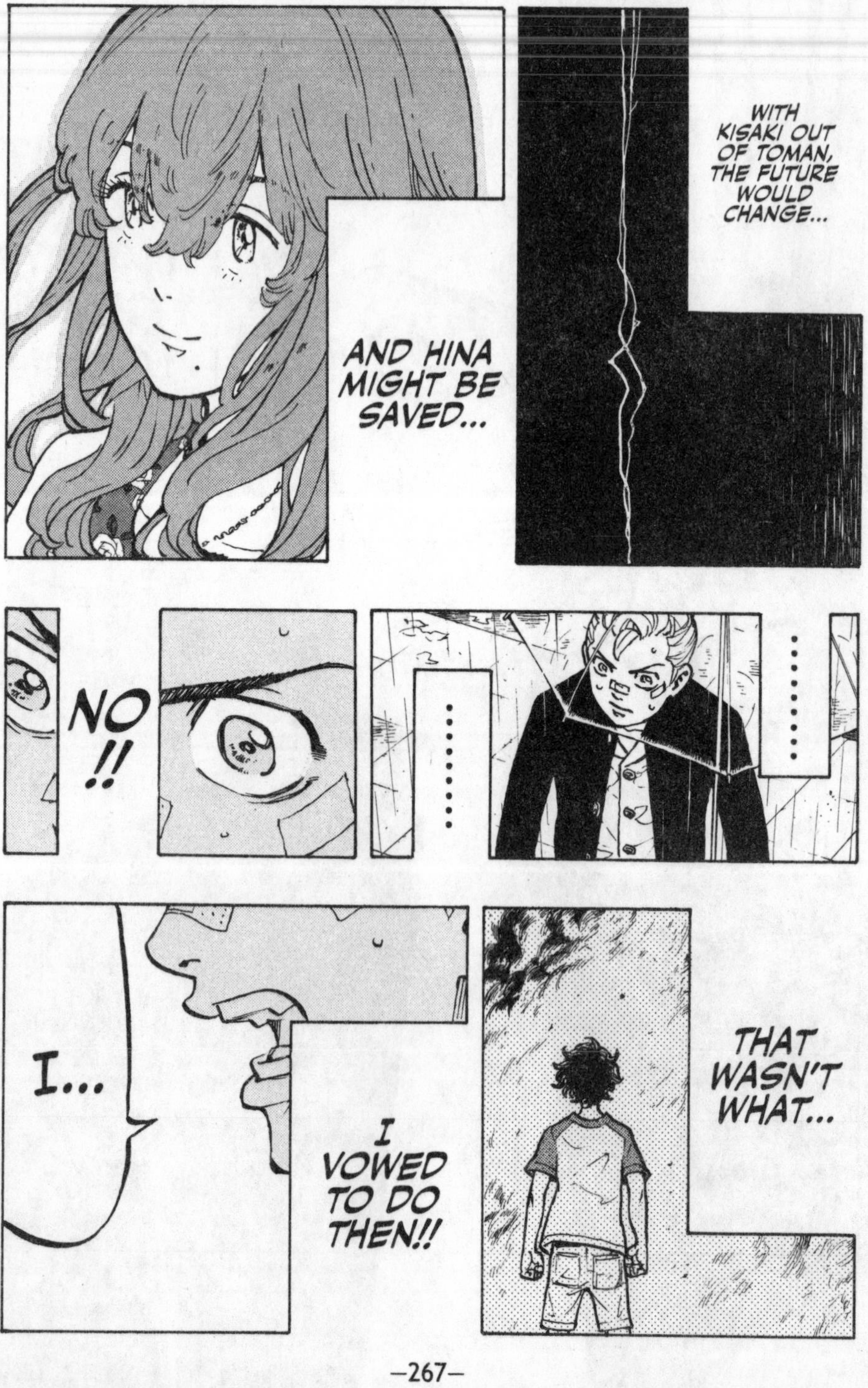

WITH KISAKI OUT OF TOMAN, THE FUTURE WOULD CHANGE...
AND HINA MIGHT BE SAVED...
......
......
NO !!
THAT WASN'T WHAT...
I...
I VOWED TO DO THEN!!

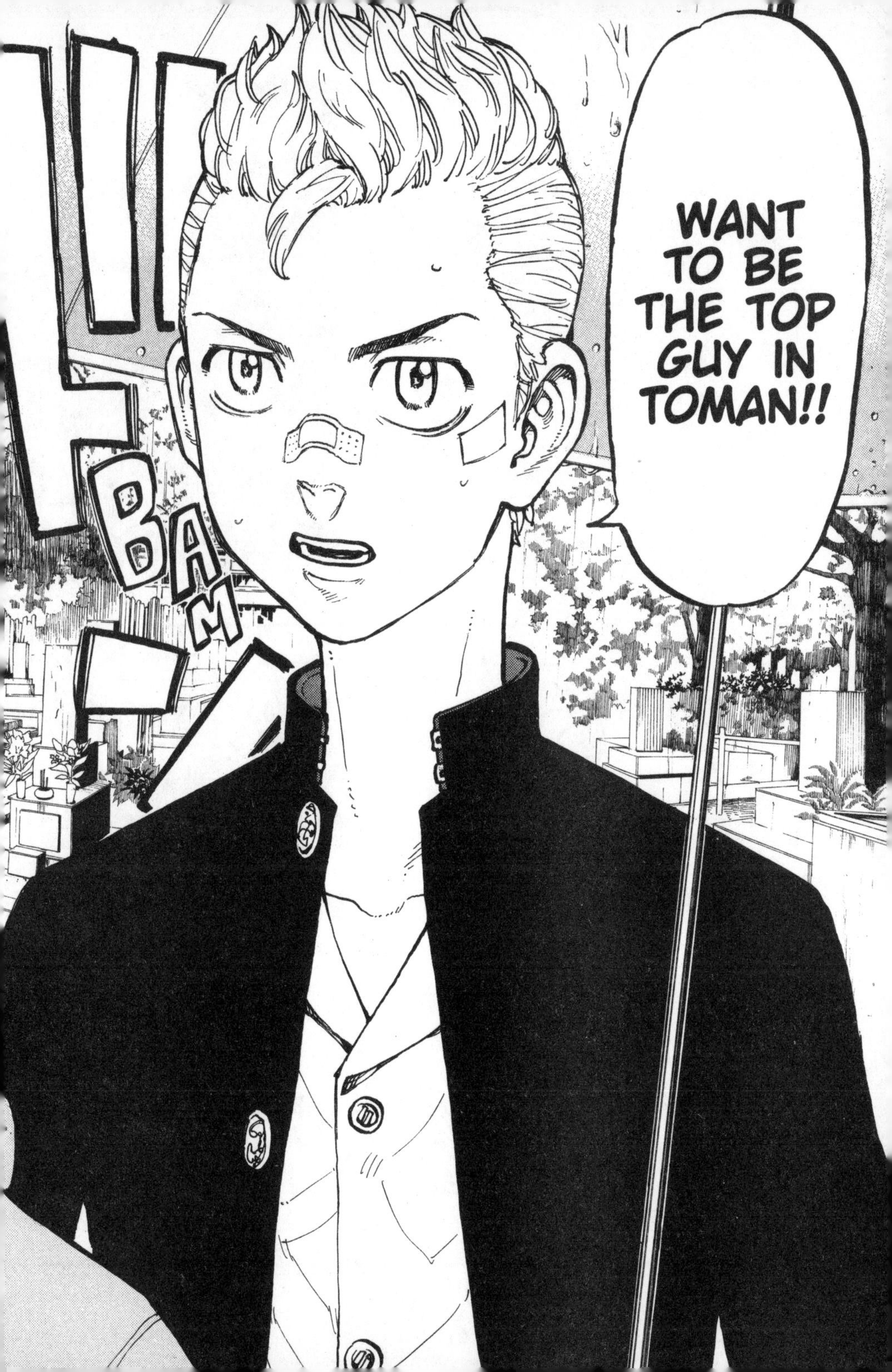
WANT TO BE THE TOP GUY IN TOMAN!!
BAM

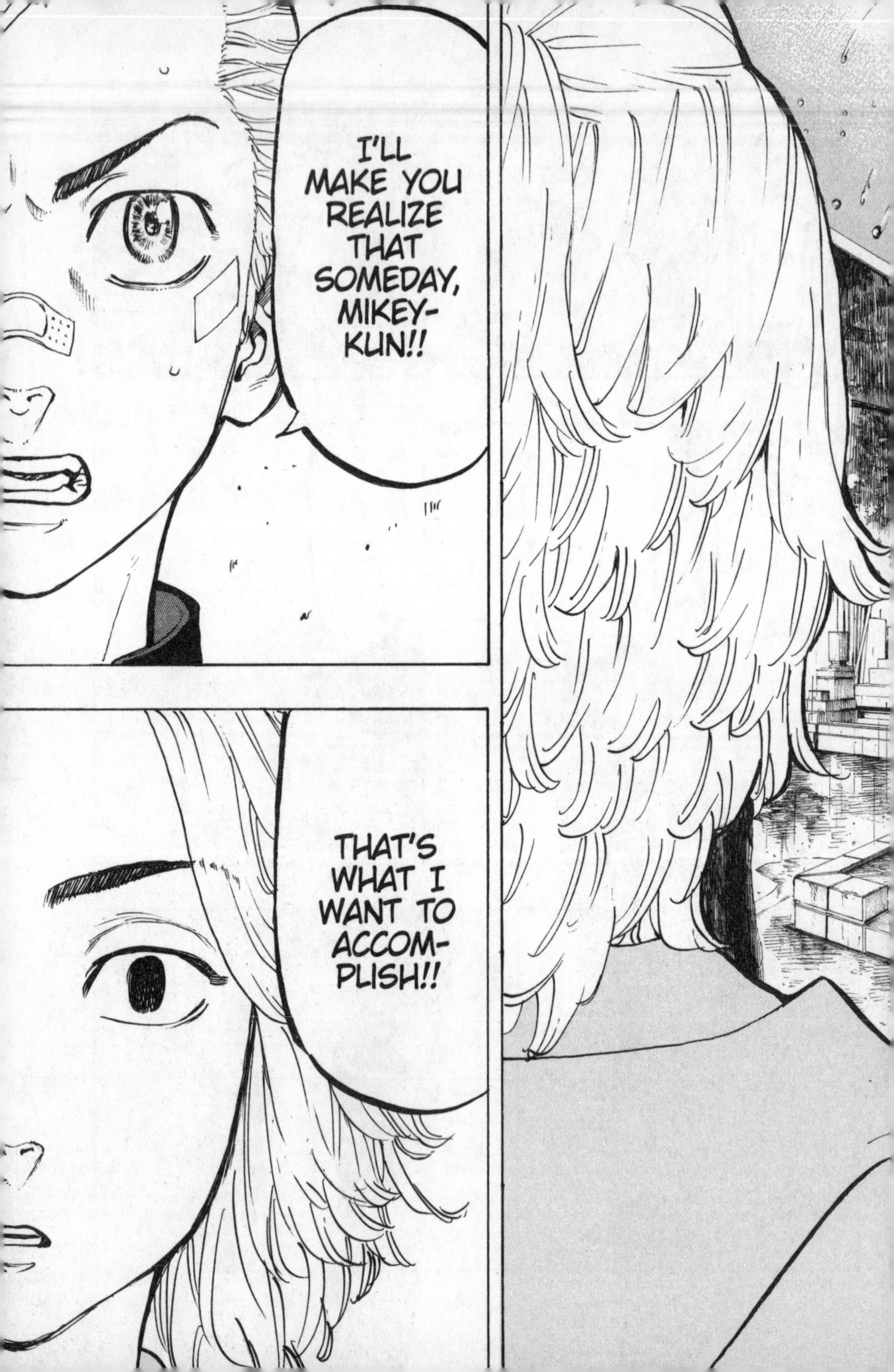
I'LL MAKE YOU REALIZE THAT SOMEDAY, MIKEY-KUN!!
THAT'S WHAT I WANT TO ACCOMPLISH!!

HA HA.

YEAH.

SMILE

THAT GUY... WHAT AN IDIOT.

BETTER CHECK YOURSELF, DUDE.

YOU WENT WAY BEYOND FAILING TO READ THE MOOD, THERE.

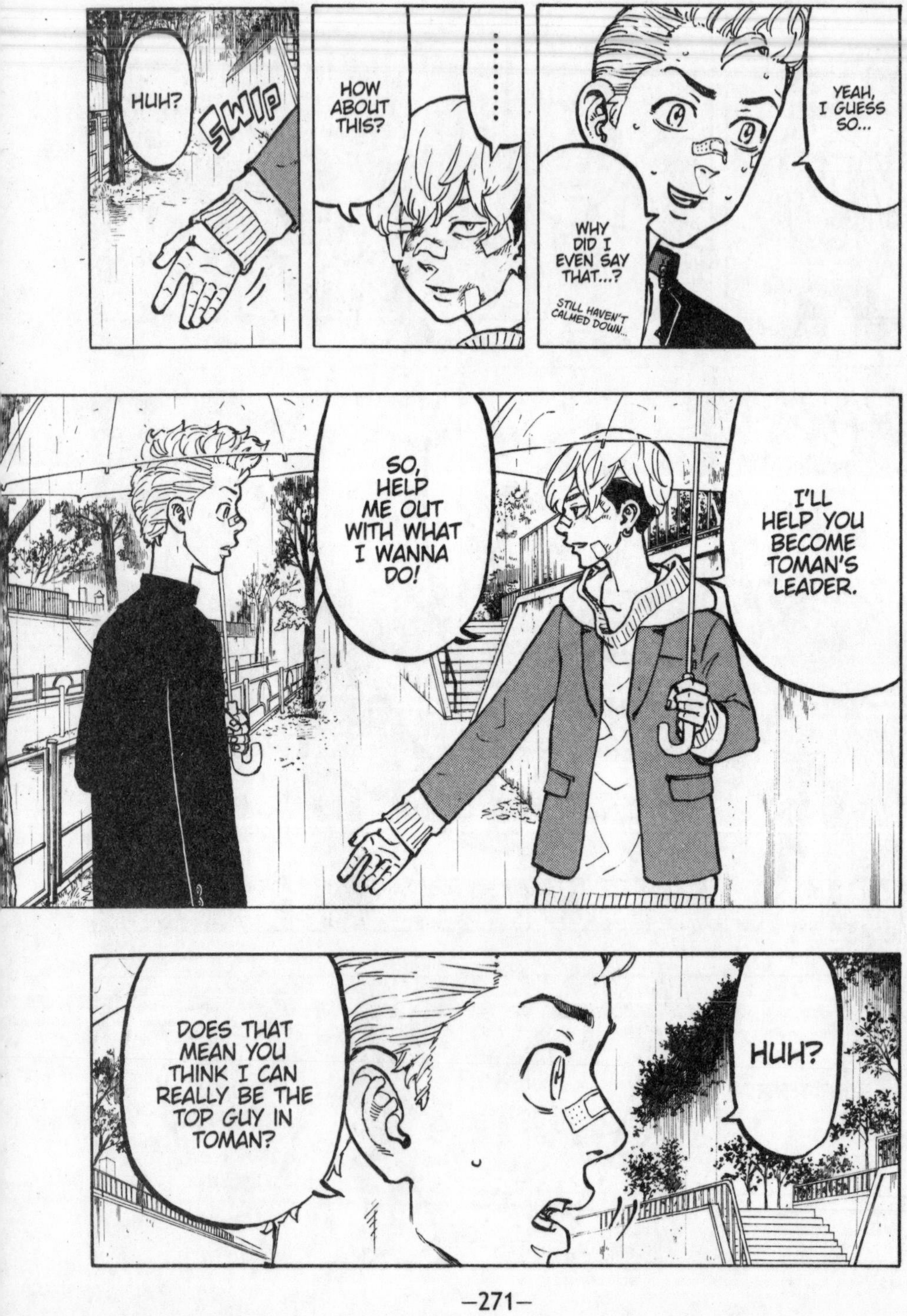
YEAH, I GUESS SO...
WHY DID I EVEN SAY THAT...?
STILL HAVEN'T CALMED DOWN...
......
HOW ABOUT THIS?
SWIP
HUH?
I'LL HELP YOU BECOME TOMAN'S LEADER.
SO, HELP ME OUT WITH WHAT I WANNA DO!
HUH?
DOES THAT MEAN YOU THINK I CAN REALLY BE THE TOP GUY IN TOMAN?

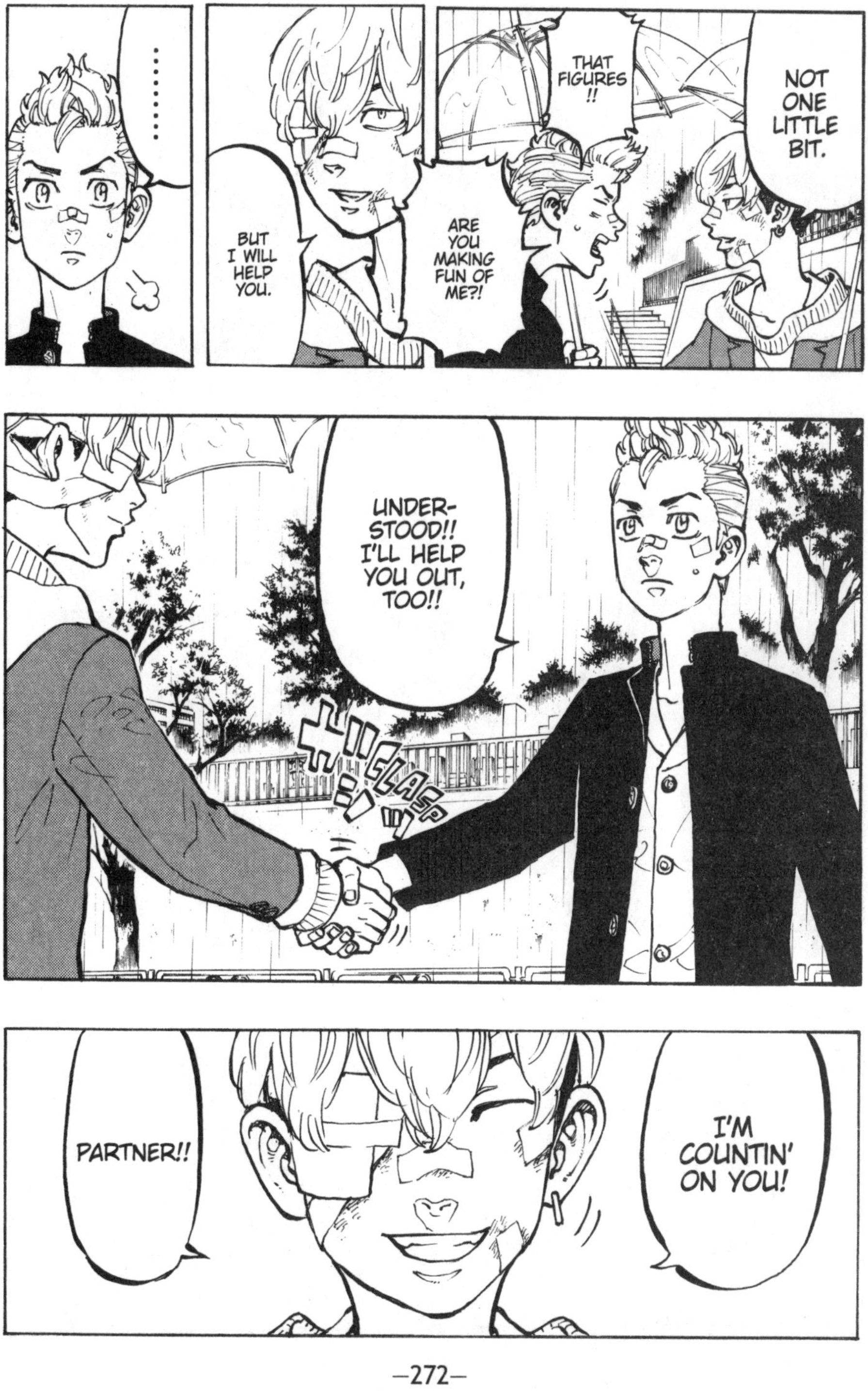

NOT ONE LITTLE BIT.
THAT FIGURES!!
ARE YOU MAKING FUN OF ME?!
BUT I WILL HELP YOU.
......
UNDER-STOOD!! I'LL HELP YOU OUT, TOO!!
CLASP
I'M COUNTIN' ON YOU!
PARTNER!!

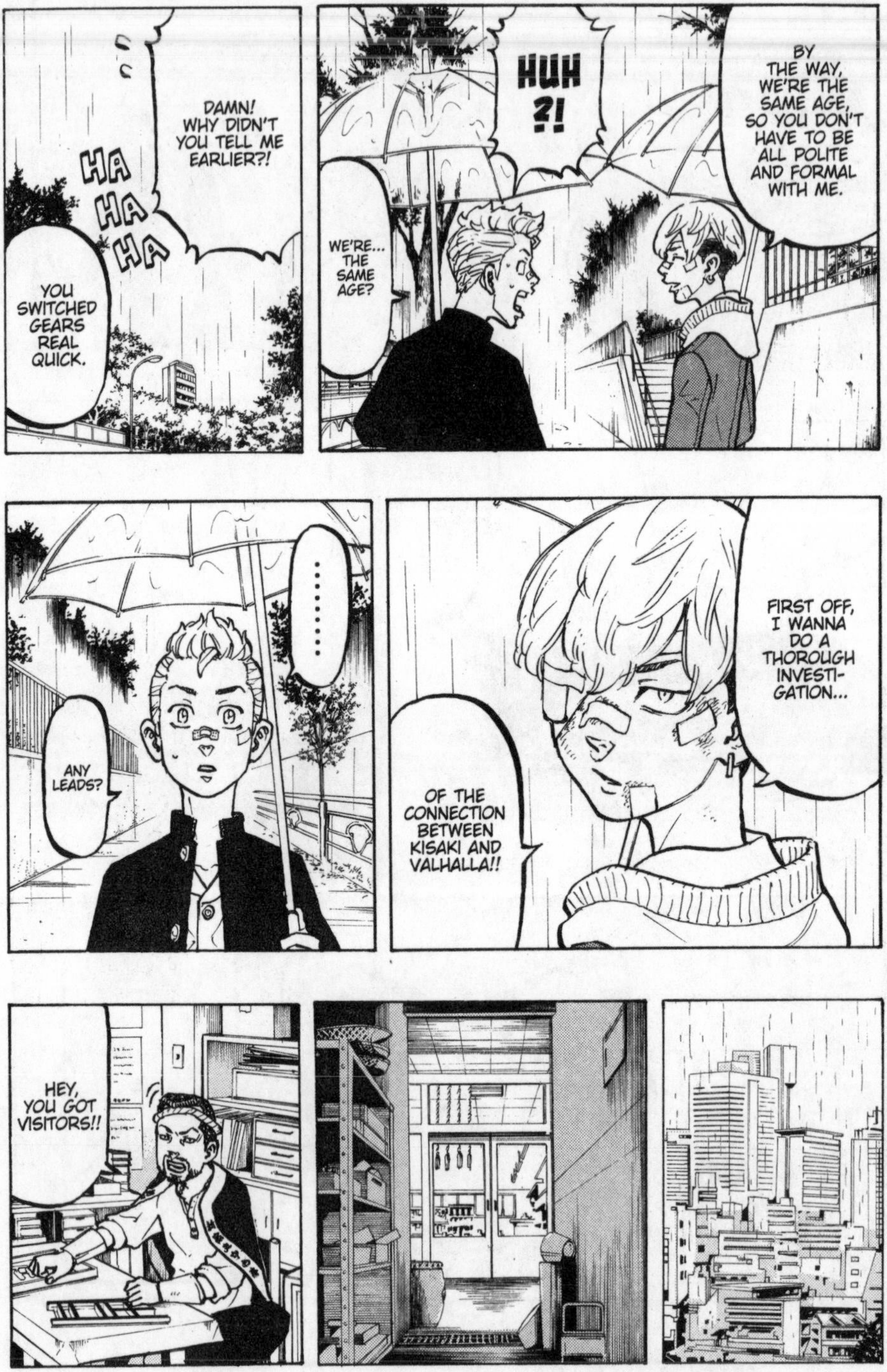
BY THE WAY, WE'RE THE SAME AGE, SO YOU DON'T HAVE TO BE ALL POLITE AND FORMAL WITH ME.
HUH ?!
WE'RE... THE SAME AGE?
DAMN! WHY DIDN'T YOU TELL ME EARLIER?!
HA HA HA
YOU SWITCHED GEARS REAL QUICK.
FIRST OFF, I WANNA DO A THOROUGH INVESTIGATION...
OF THE CONNECTION BETWEEN KISAKI AND VALHALLA!!
......
ANY LEADS?
HEY, YOU GOT VISITORS!!

HM?

WHO THE HELL'RE YOU GUYS?

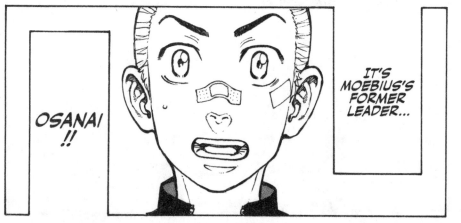

OSANAI!!

IT'S MOEBIUS'S FORMER LEADER...

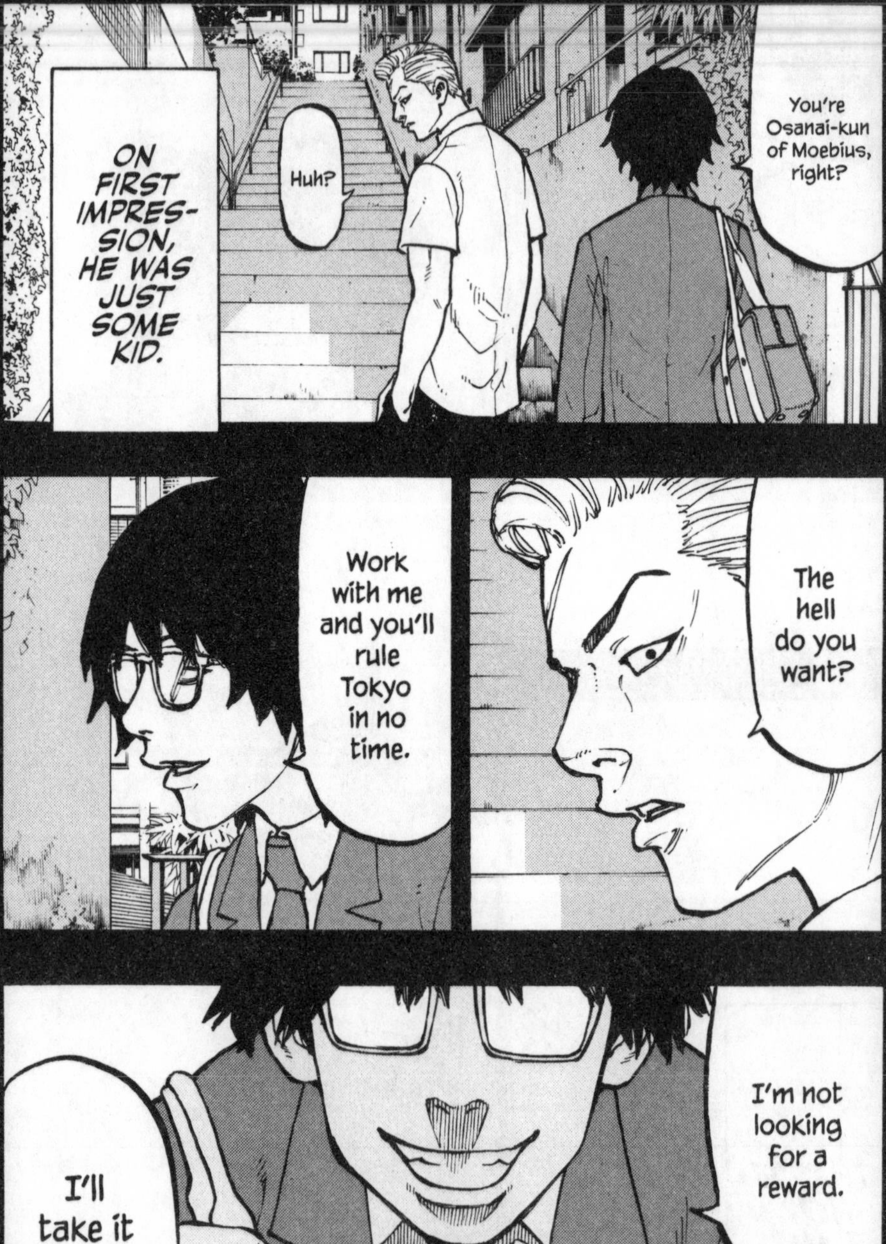
You're Osanai-kun of Moebius, right?
Huh?
ON FIRST IMPRES-SION, HE WAS JUST SOME KID.
The hell do you want?
Work with me and you'll rule Tokyo in no time.
I'm not looking for a reward.
I'll take it myself.

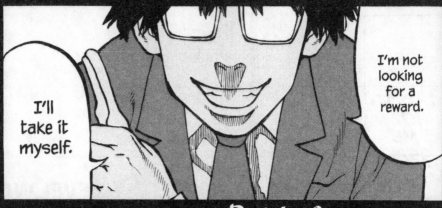

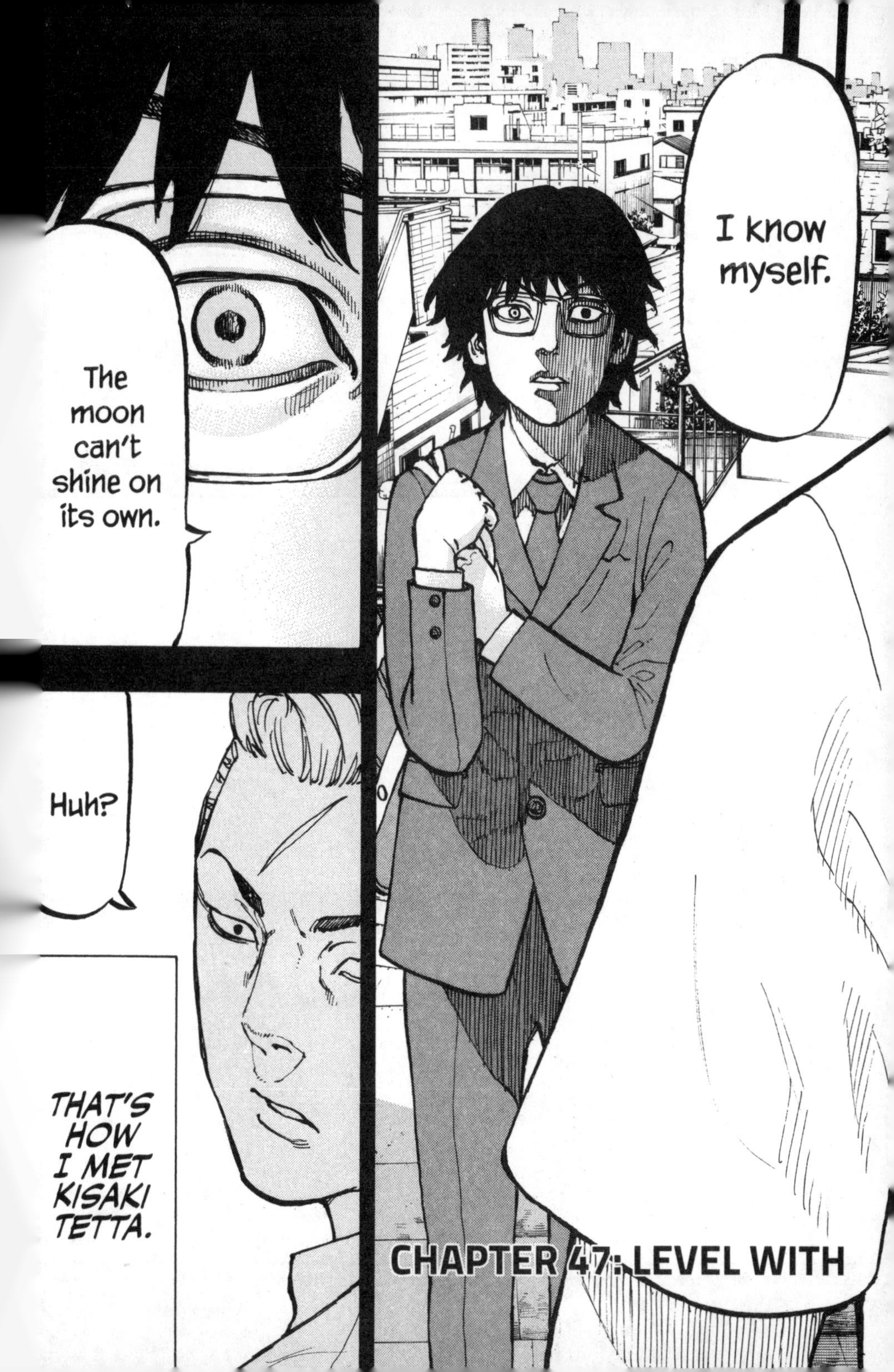
I know myself.
CHAPTER 47: LEVEL WITH
The moon can't shine on its own.
Huh?
THAT'S HOW I MET KISAKI TETTA.

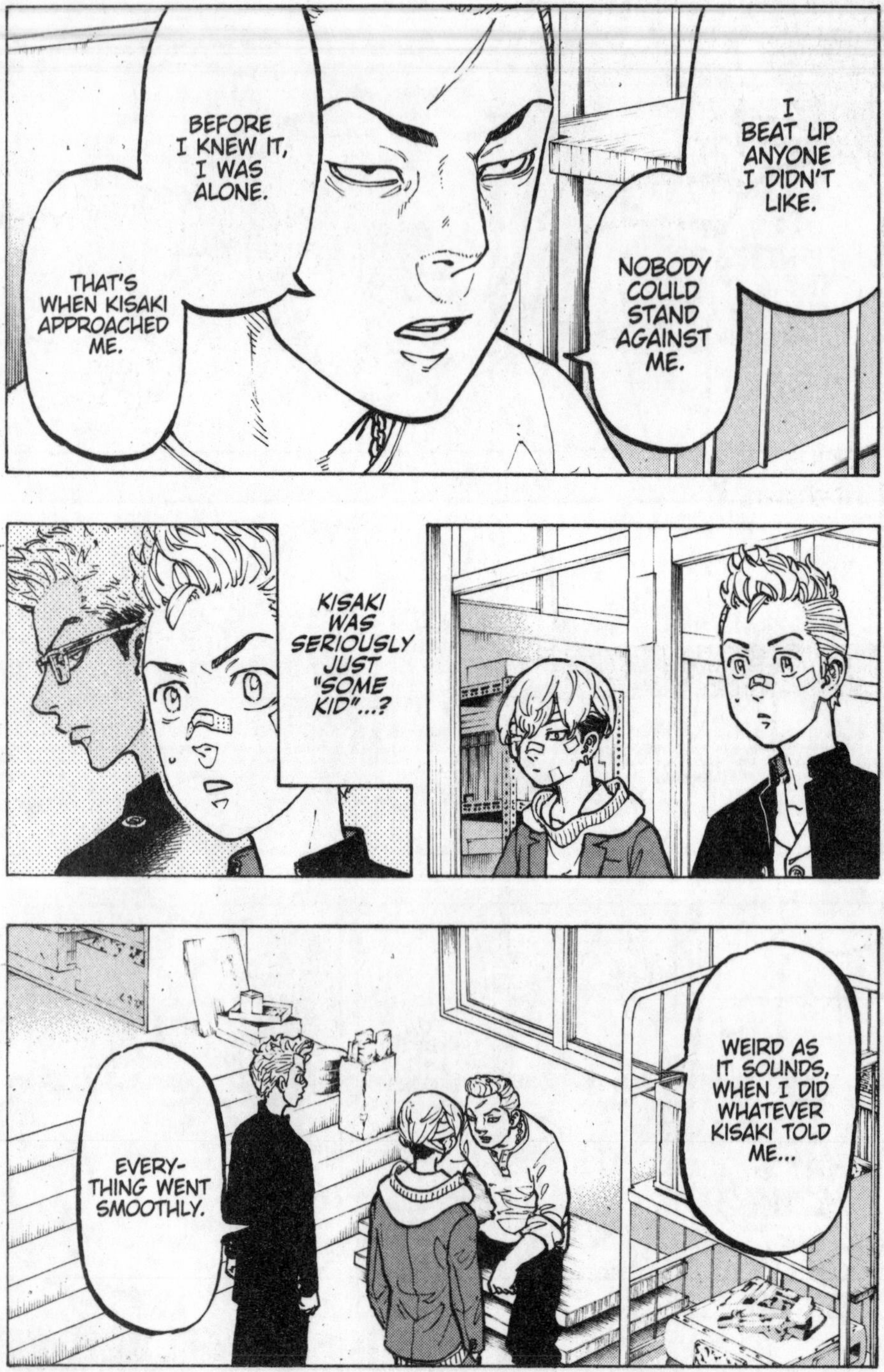
I BEAT UP ANYONE I DIDN'T LIKE.
NOBODY COULD STAND AGAINST ME.
BEFORE I KNEW IT, I WAS ALONE.
THAT'S WHEN KISAKI APPROACHED ME.
KISAKI WAS SERIOUSLY JUST "SOME KID"...?
WEIRD AS IT SOUNDS, WHEN I DID WHATEVER KISAKI TOLD ME...
EVERY-THING WENT SMOOTHLY.

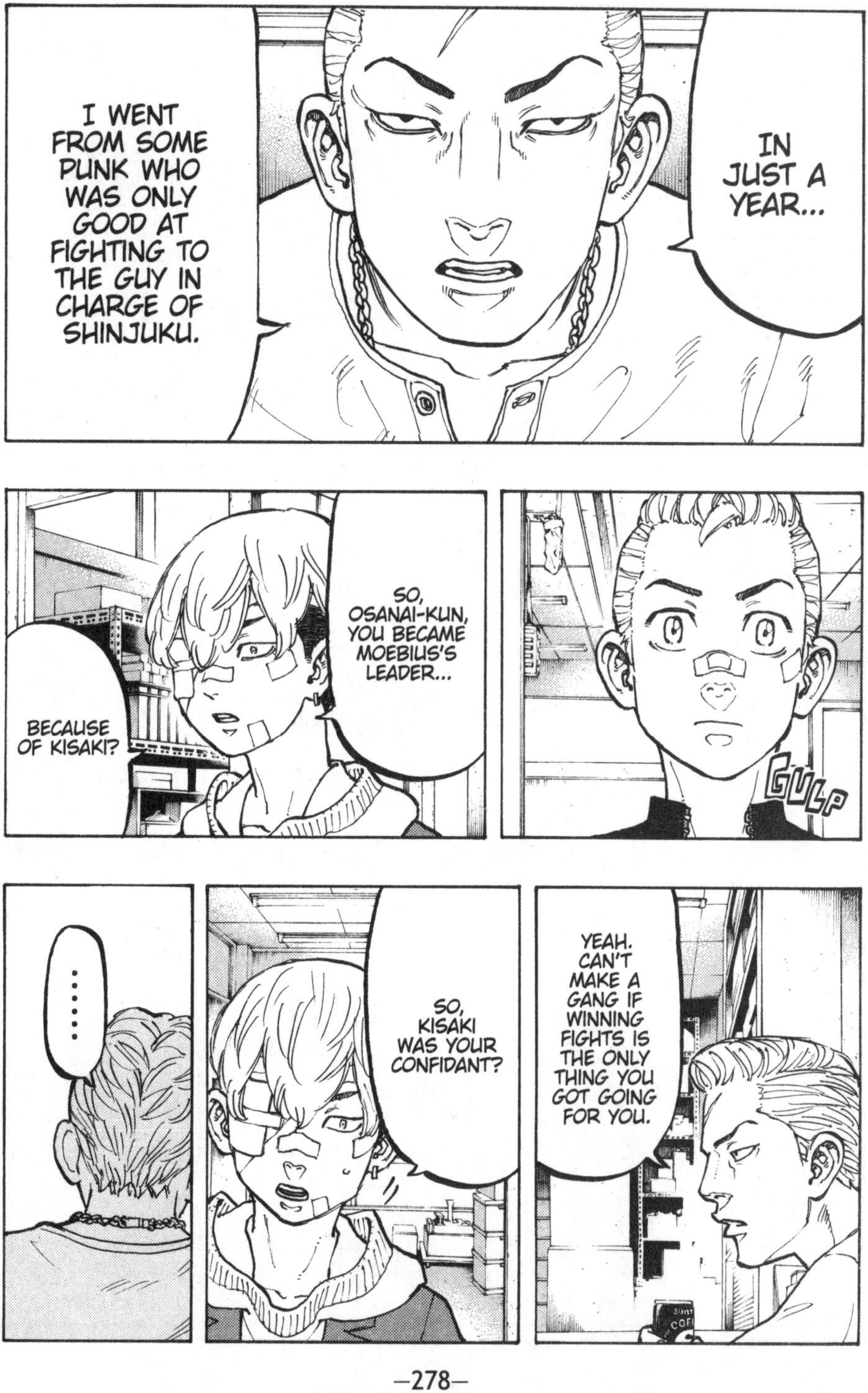
IN JUST A YEAR...
I WENT FROM SOME PUNK WHO WAS ONLY GOOD AT FIGHTING TO THE GUY IN CHARGE OF SHINJUKU.
GULP
SO, OSANAI-KUN, YOU BECAME MOEBIUS'S LEADER...
BECAUSE OF KISAKI?
YEAH. CAN'T MAKE A GANG IF WINNING FIGHTS IS THE ONLY THING YOU GOT GOING FOR YOU.
SO, KISAKI WAS YOUR CONFIDANT?
......

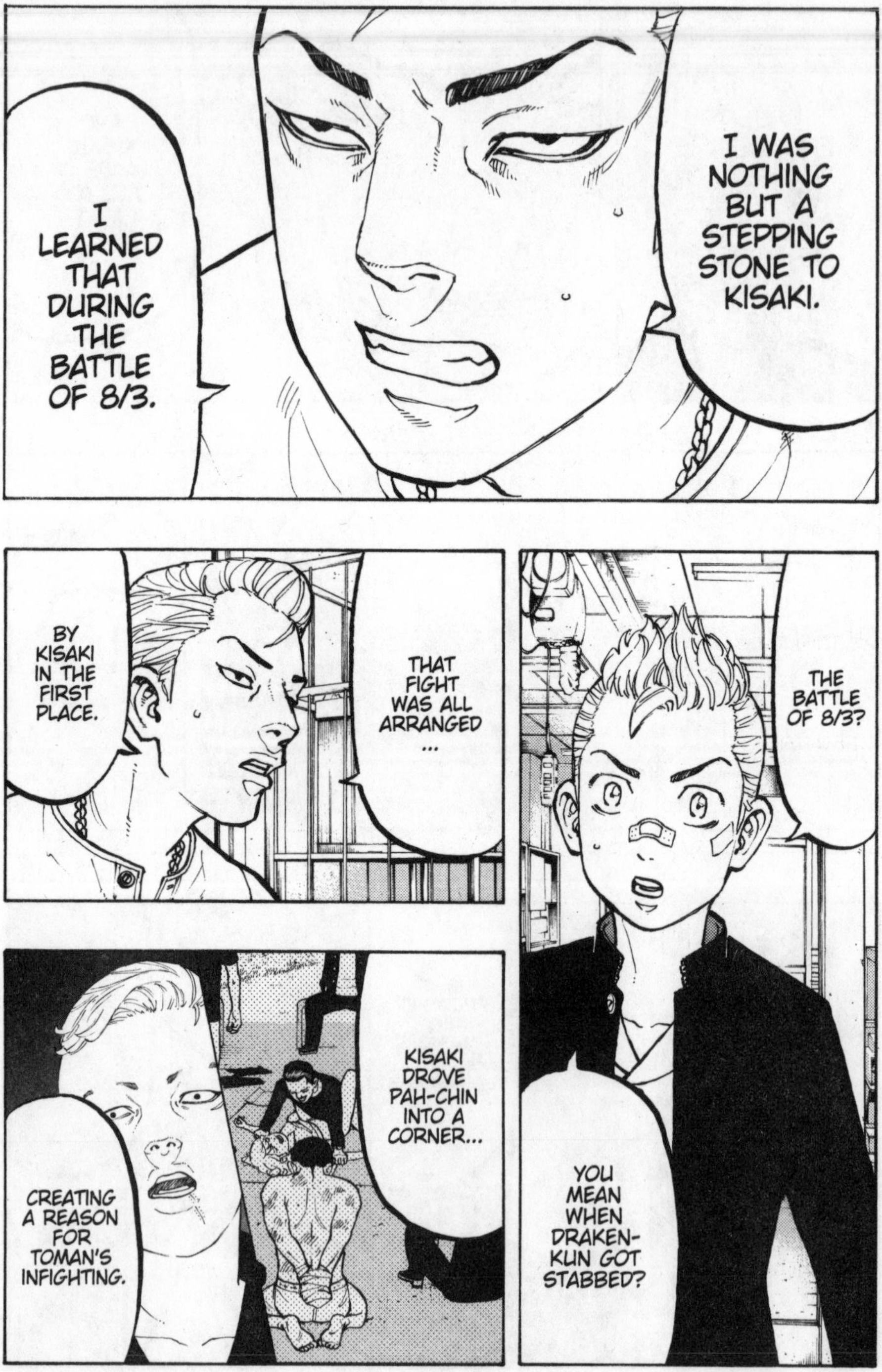
I WAS NOTHING BUT A STEPPING STONE TO KISAKI.
I LEARNED THAT DURING THE BATTLE OF 8/3.
THE BATTLE OF 8/3?
YOU MEAN WHEN DRAKEN-KUN GOT STABBED?
THAT FIGHT WAS ALL ARRANGED ...
BY KISAKI IN THE FIRST PLACE.
KISAKI DROVE PAH-CHIN INTO A CORNER...
CREATING A REASON FOR TOMAN'S INFIGHTING.

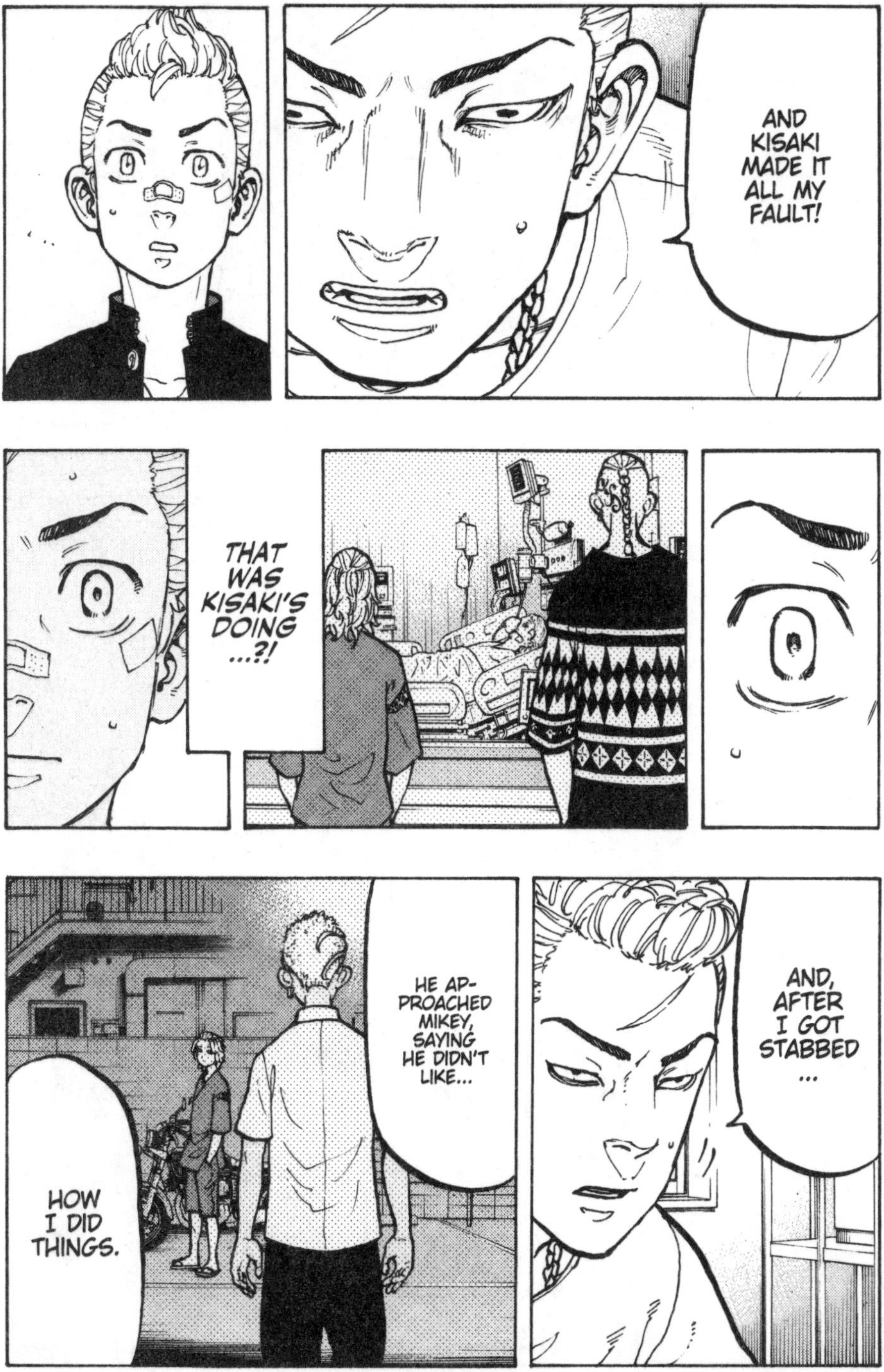
AND KISAKI MADE IT ALL MY FAULT!
. . .
THAT WAS KISAKI'S DOING ...?!
AND, AFTER I GOT STABBED ...
HE AP- PROACHED MIKEY, SAYING HE DIDN'T LIKE...
HOW I DID THINGS.

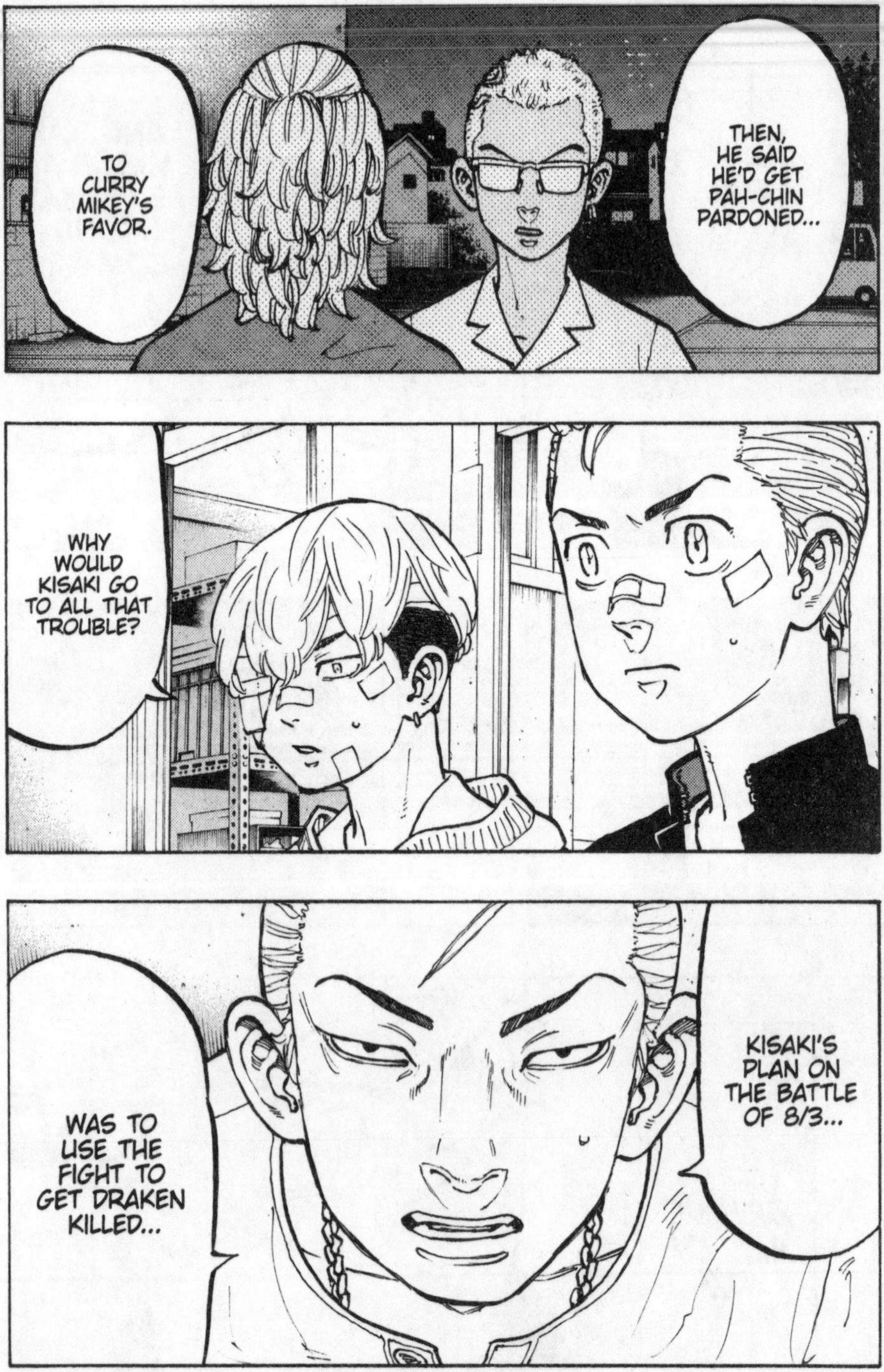
THEN, HE SAID HE'D GET PAH-CHIN PARDONED...
TO CURRY MIKEY'S FAVOR.
WHY WOULD KISAKI GO TO ALL THAT TROUBLE?
KISAKI'S PLAN ON THE BATTLE OF 8/3...
WAS TO USE THE FIGHT TO GET DRAKEN KILLED...

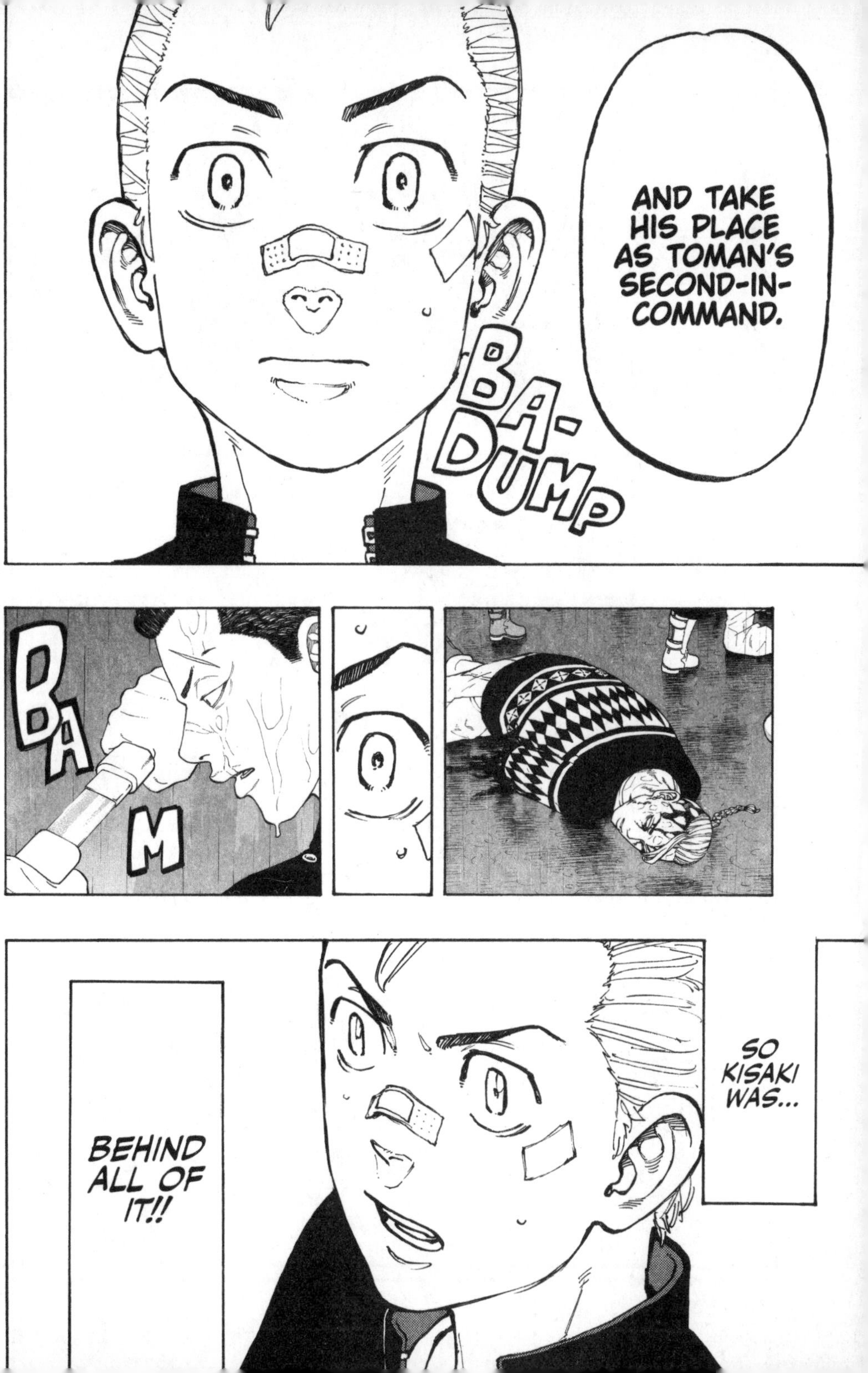
AND TAKE HIS PLACE AS TOMAN'S SECOND-IN-COMMAND.
BA-DUMP
BAM
SO KISAKI WAS...
BEHIND ALL OF IT!!

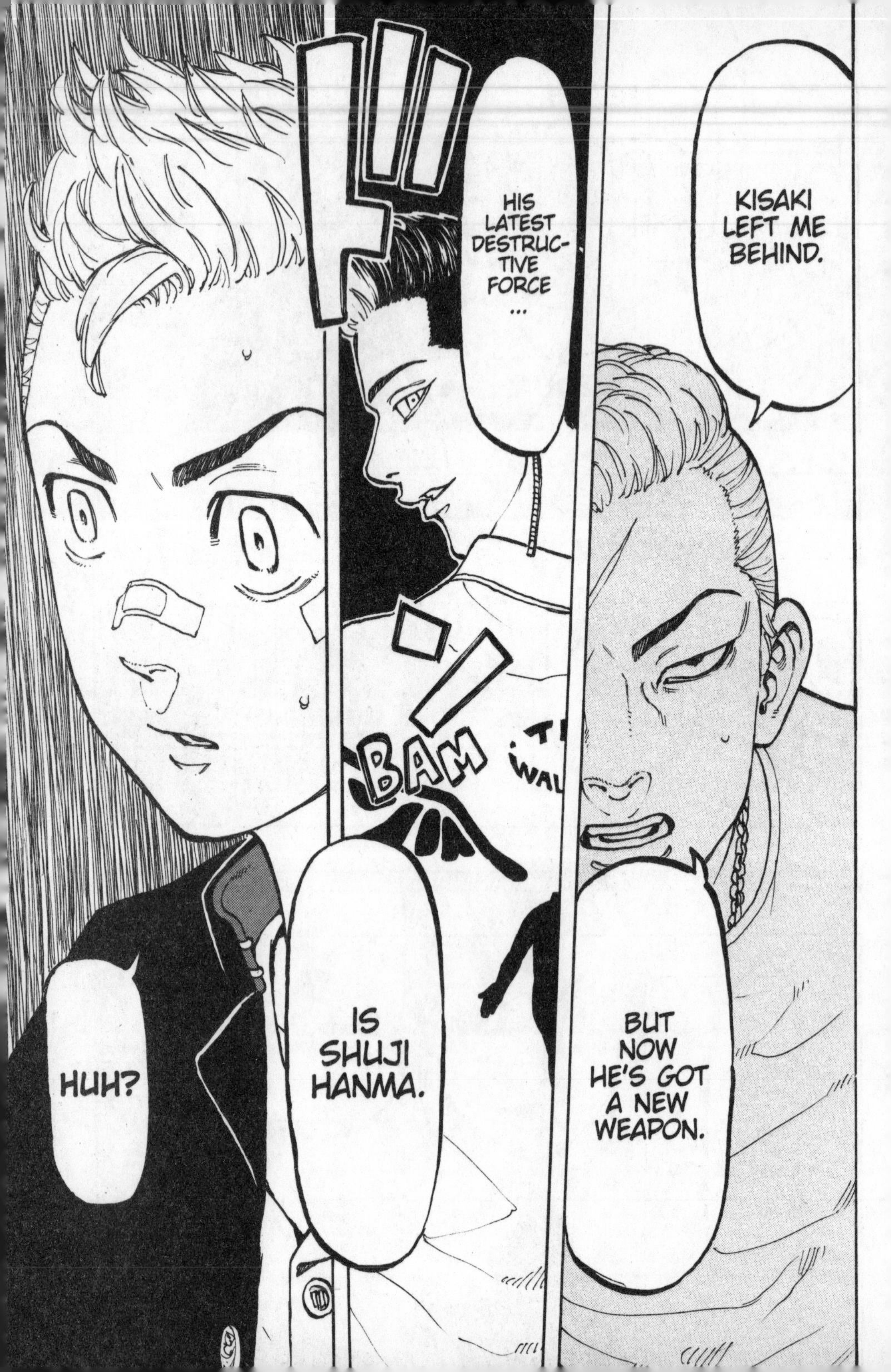
KISAKI LEFT ME BEHIND.
BUT NOW HE'S GOT A NEW WEAPON.
HIS LATEST DESTRUC-TIVE FORCE ...
BAM
IS SHUJI HANMA.
HUH?

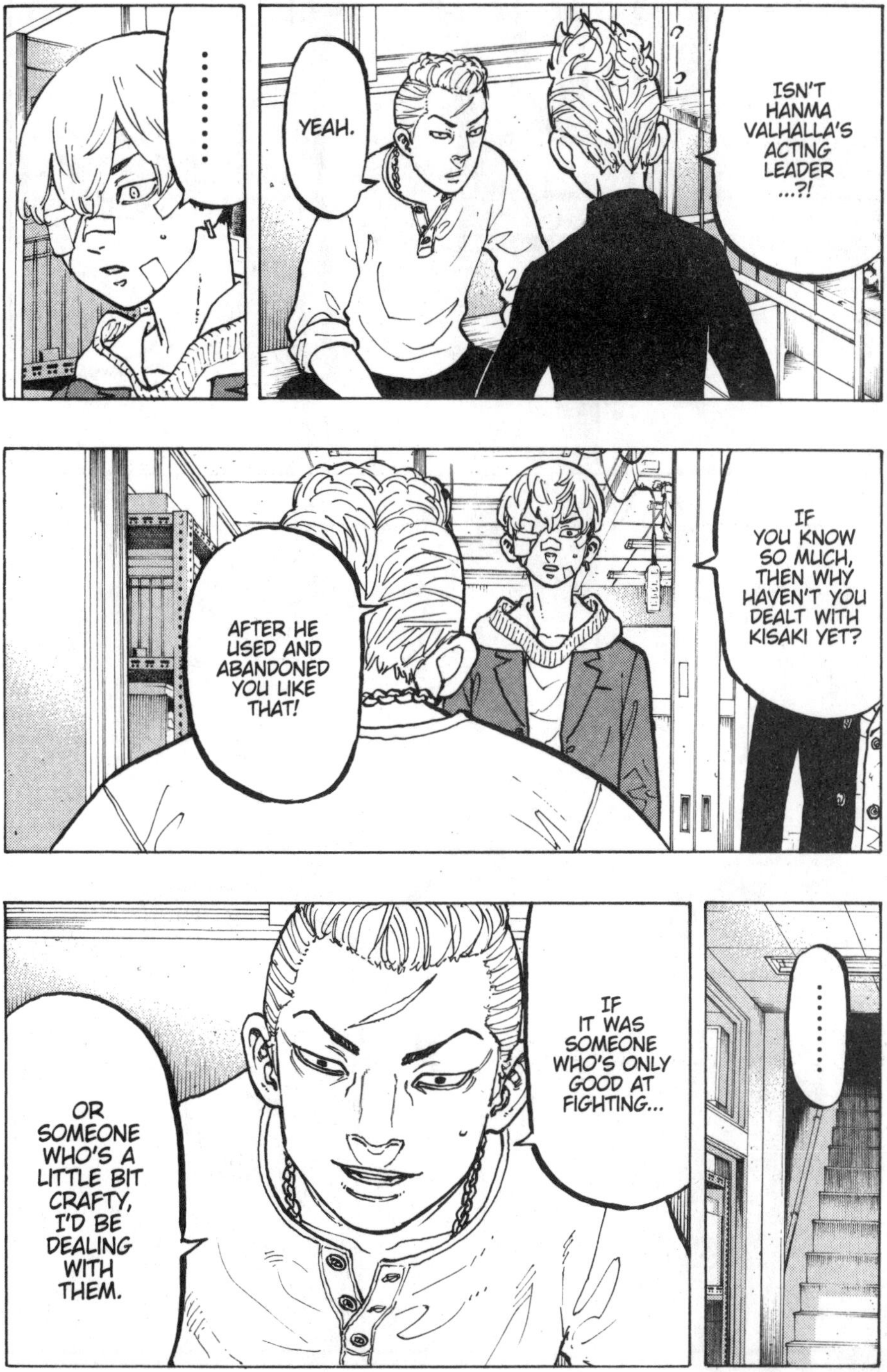
ISN'T HANMA VALHALLA'S ACTING LEADER ...?!
YEAH.
......
IF YOU KNOW SO MUCH, THEN WHY HAVEN'T YOU DEALT WITH KISAKI YET?
AFTER HE USED AND ABANDONED YOU LIKE THAT!
......
IF IT WAS SOMEONE WHO'S ONLY GOOD AT FIGHTING...
OR SOMEONE WHO'S A LITTLE BIT CRAFTY, I'D BE DEALING WITH THEM.

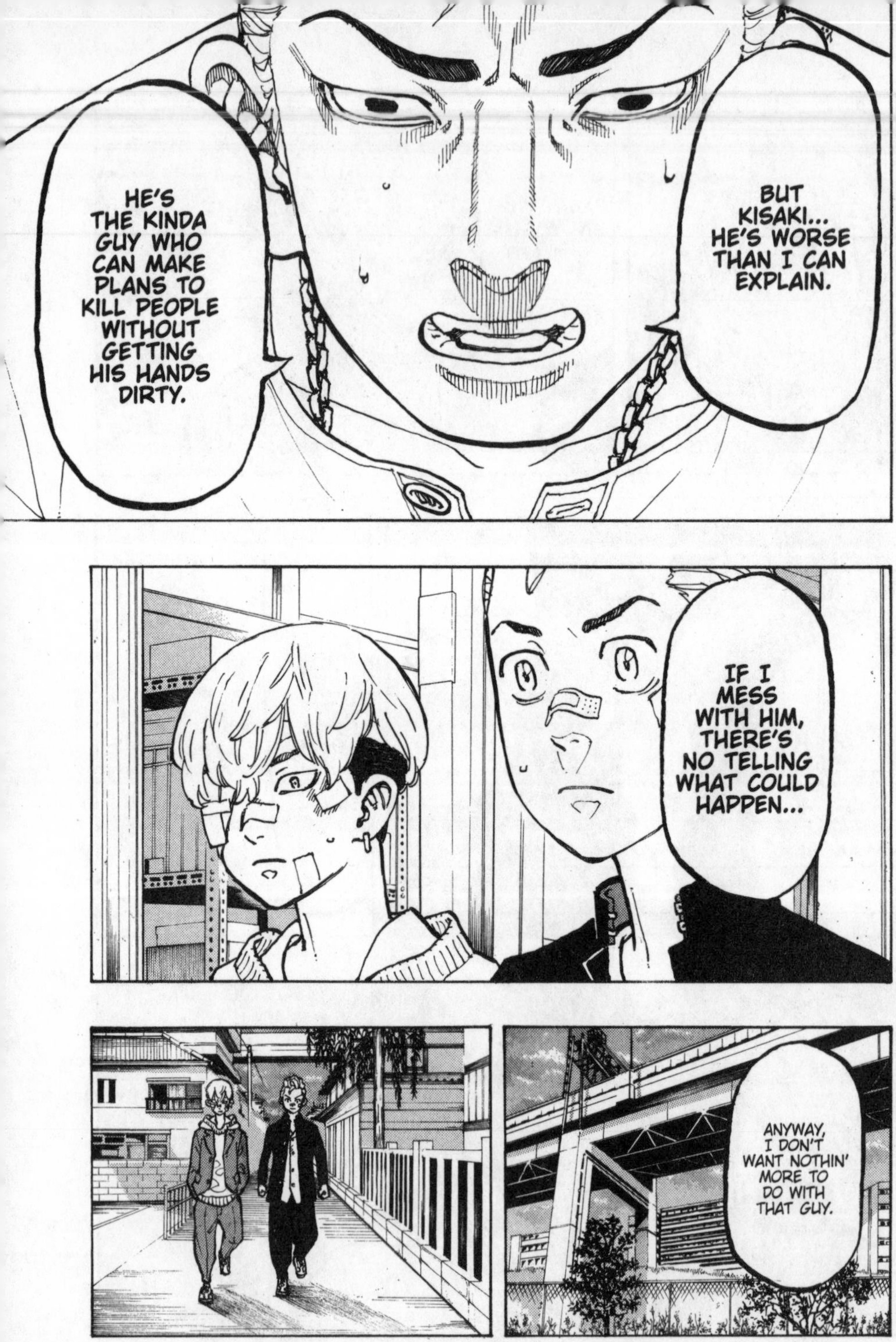
BUT KISAKI... HE'S WORSE THAN I CAN EXPLAIN.
HE'S THE KINDA GUY WHO CAN MAKE PLANS TO KILL PEOPLE WITHOUT GETTING HIS HANDS DIRTY.
IF I MESS WITH HIM, THERE'S NO TELLING WHAT COULD HAPPEN...
ANYWAY, I DON'T WANT NOTHIN' MORE TO DO WITH THAT GUY.

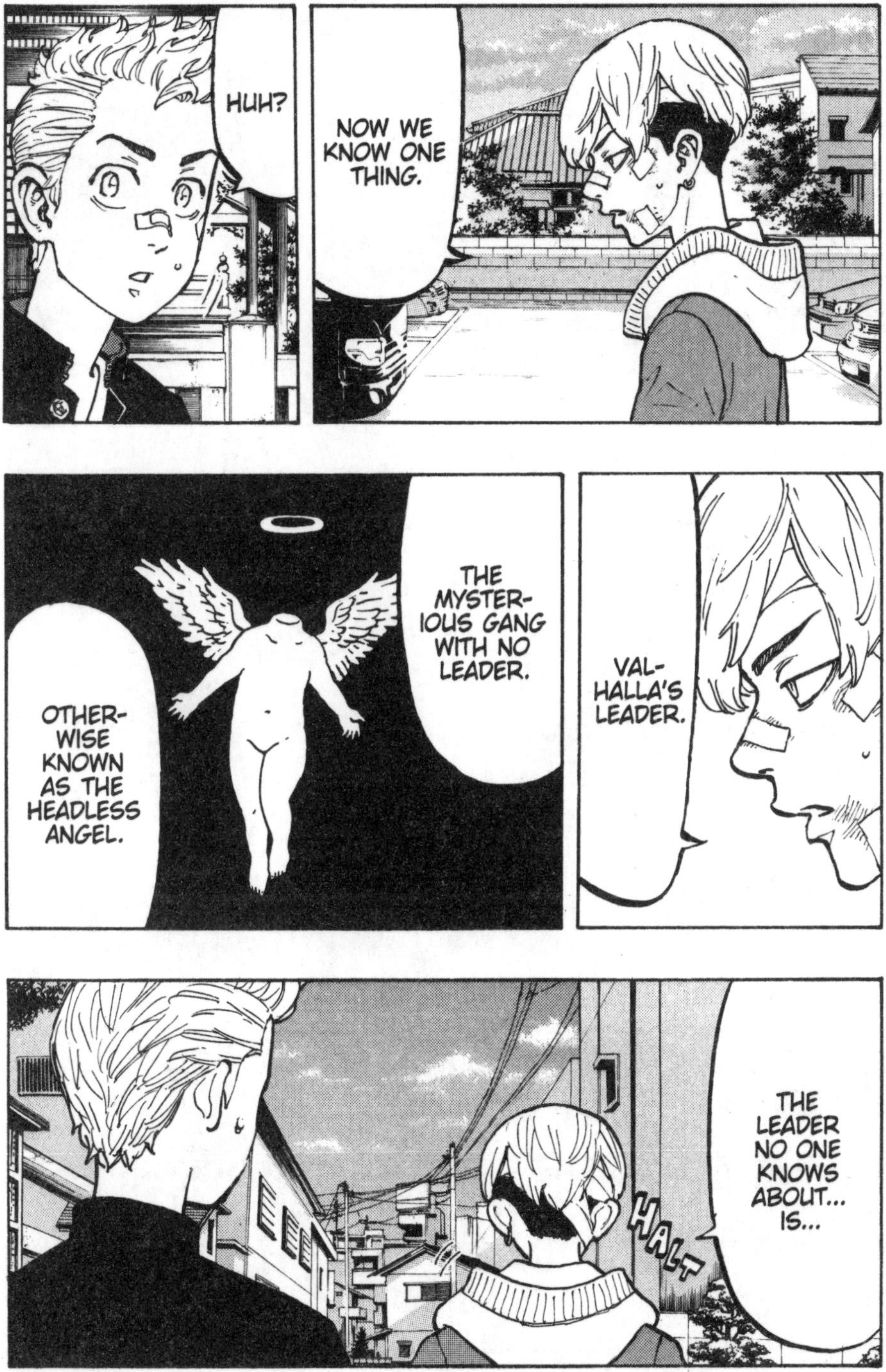

NOW WE KNOW ONE THING.
HUH?
VAL-HALLA'S LEADER.
THE MYSTER-IOUS GANG WITH NO LEADER.
OTHER-WISE KNOWN AS THE HEADLESS ANGEL.
THE LEADER NO ONE KNOWS ABOUT... IS...
HALT

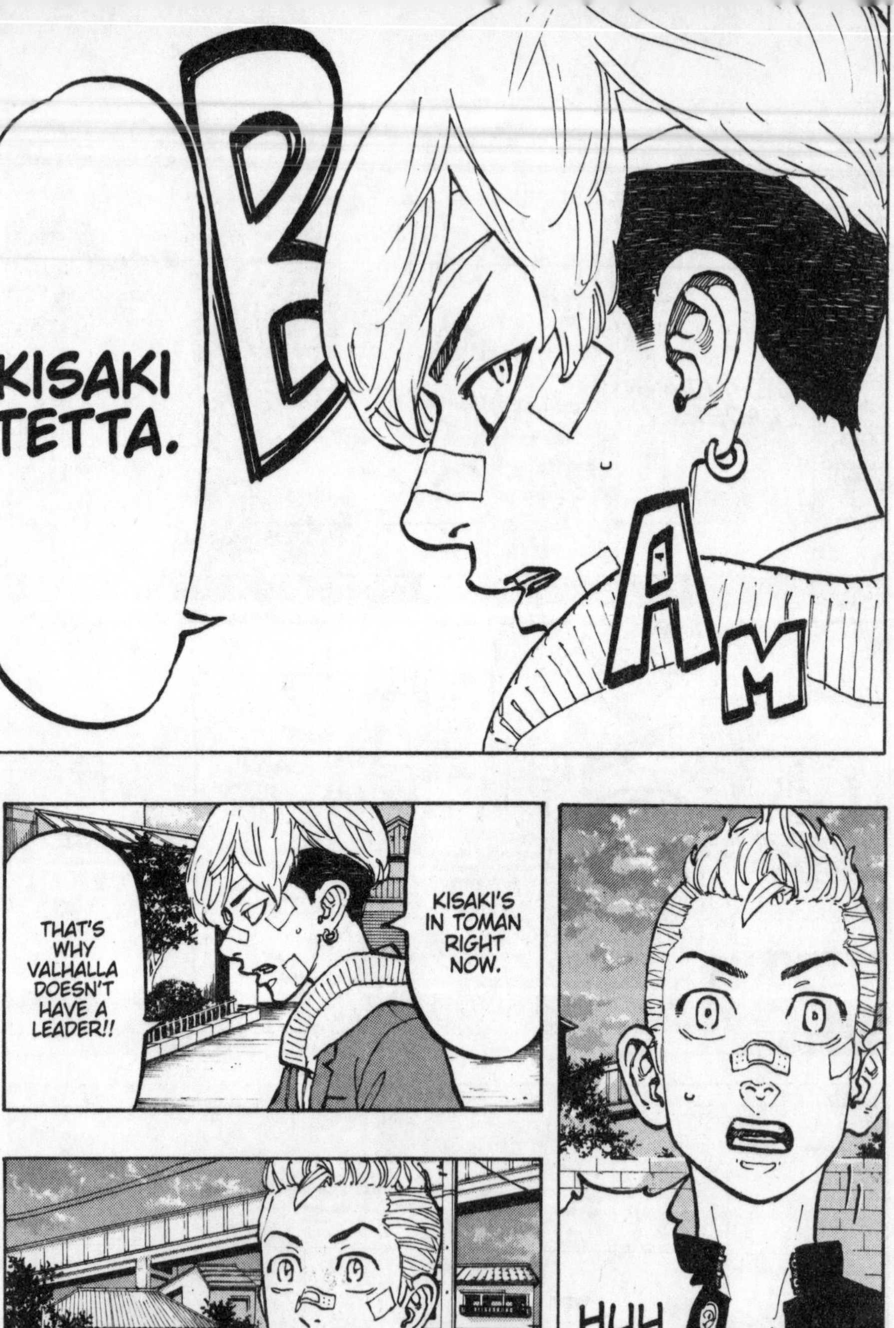
KISAKI TETTA.
HUH ?!
KISAKI'S IN TOMAN RIGHT NOW.
THAT'S WHY VALHALLA DOESN'T HAVE A LEADER!!

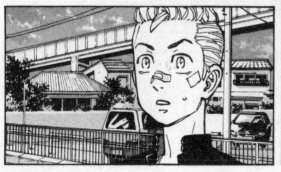

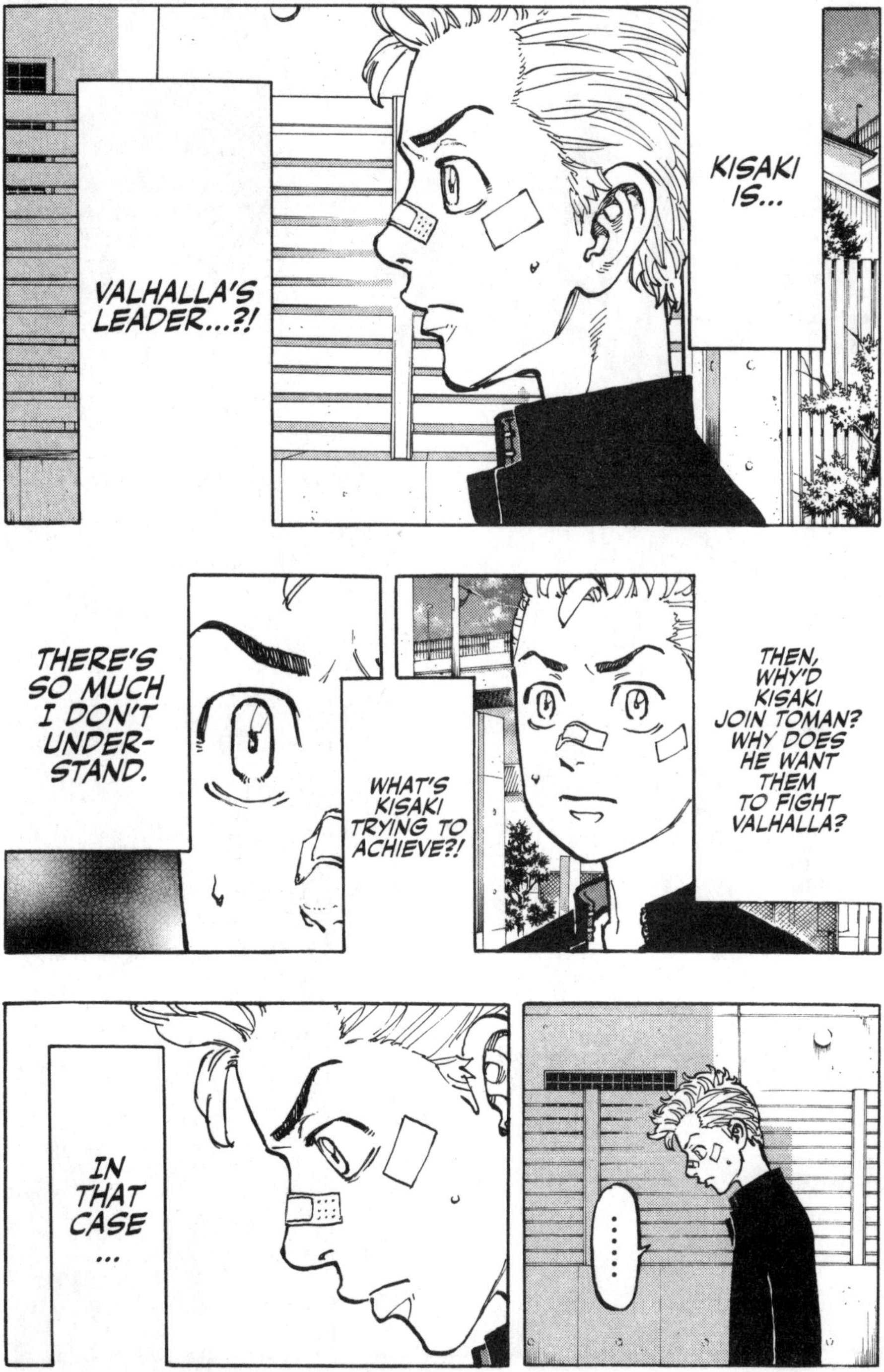
KISAKI IS...
VALHALLA'S LEADER...?!
THEN, WHY'D KISAKI JOIN TOMAN? WHY DOES HE WANT THEM TO FIGHT VALHALLA?
WHAT'S KISAKI TRYING TO ACHIEVE?!
THERE'S SO MUCH I DON'T UNDER-STAND.
......
IN THAT CASE ...

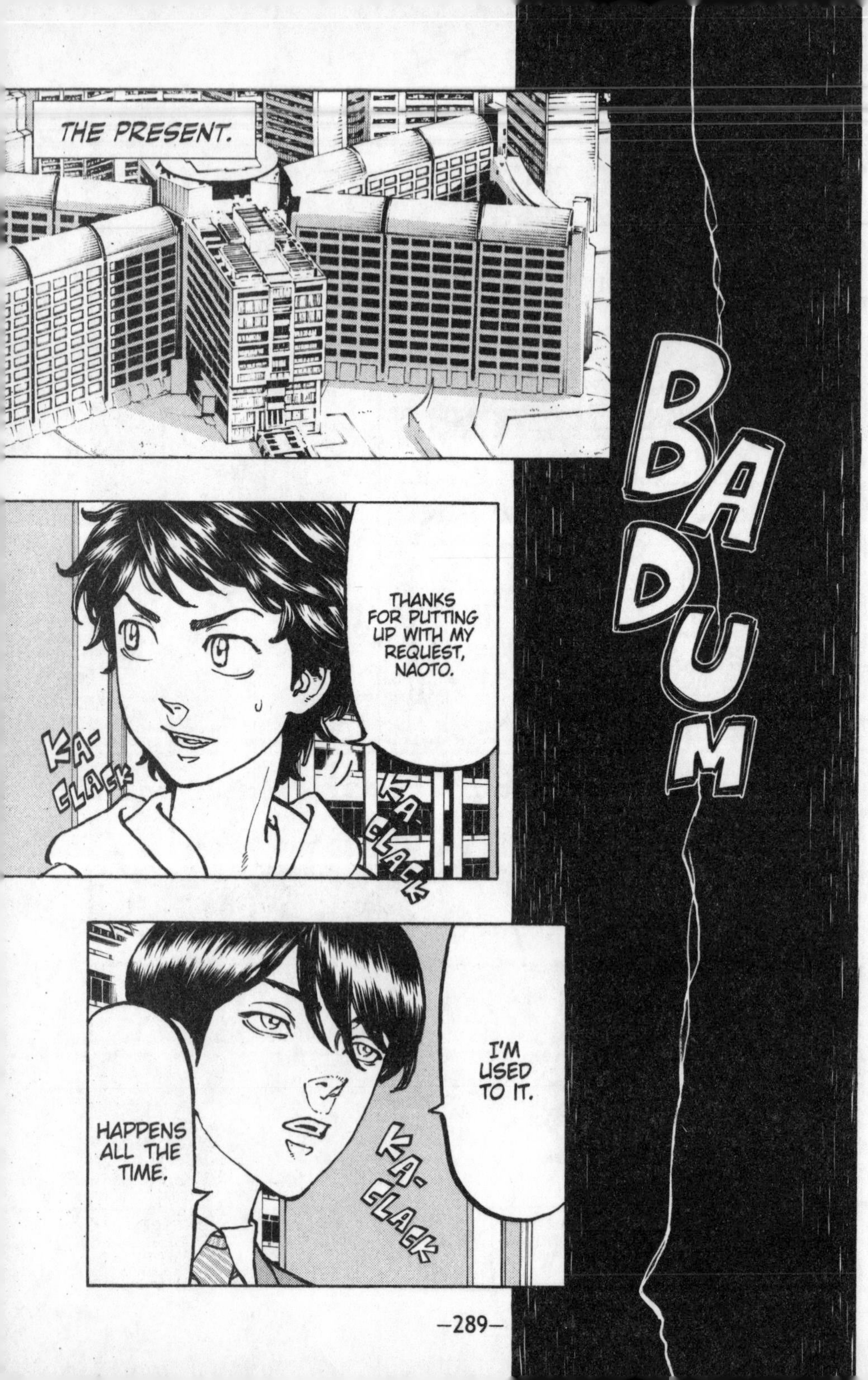
BADUM
THE PRESENT.
THANKS FOR PUTTING UP WITH MY REQUEST, NAOTO.
KA-CLACK
KA-CLACK
I'M USED TO IT.
HAPPENS ALL THE TIME.
KA-CLACK

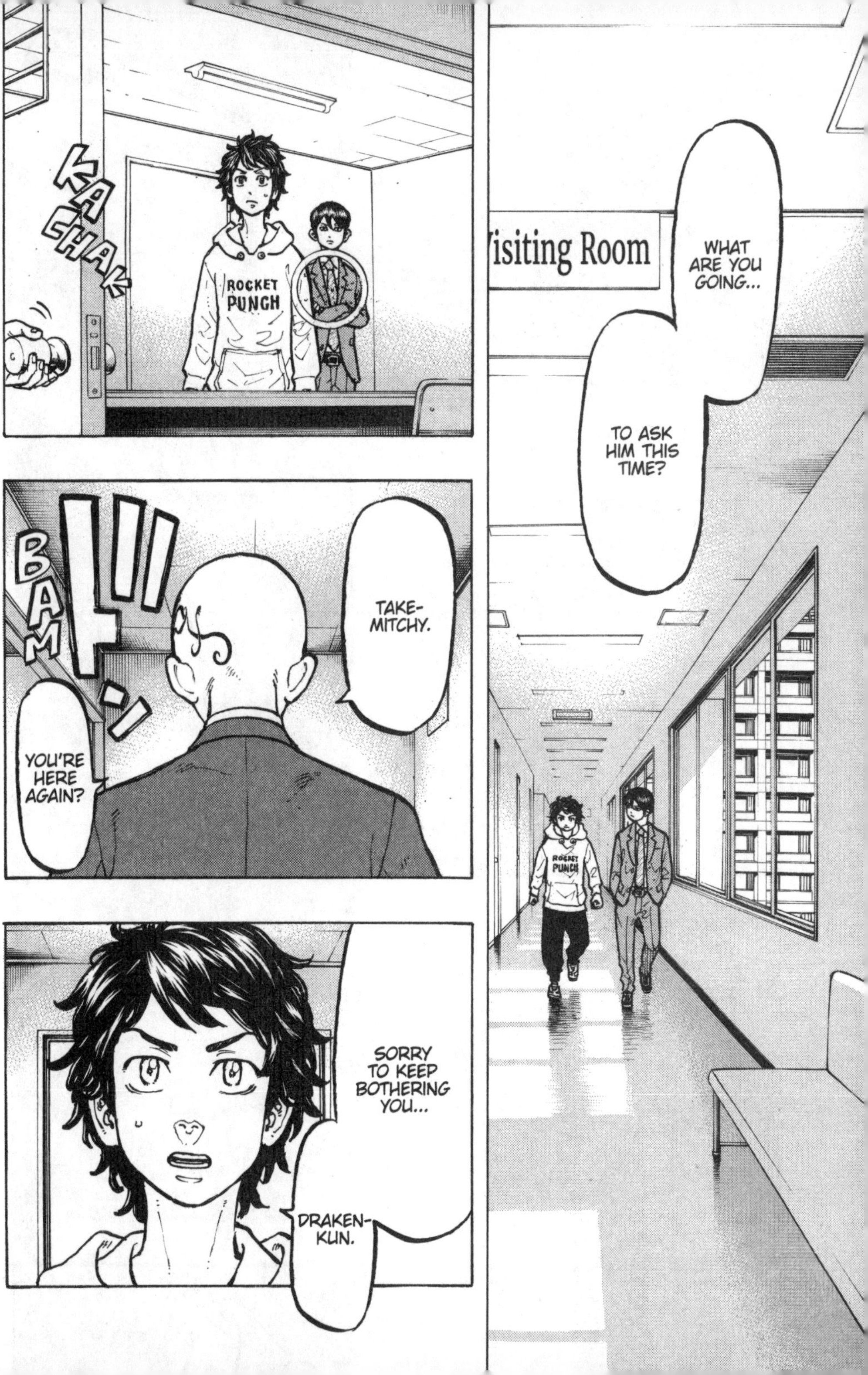

Visiting Room
WHAT ARE YOU GOING...
TO ASK HIM THIS TIME?
KACHAK
ROCKET PUNCH
TAKE-MITCHY.
BAM
YOU'RE HERE AGAIN?
SORRY TO KEEP BOTHERING YOU...
DRAKEN-KUN.

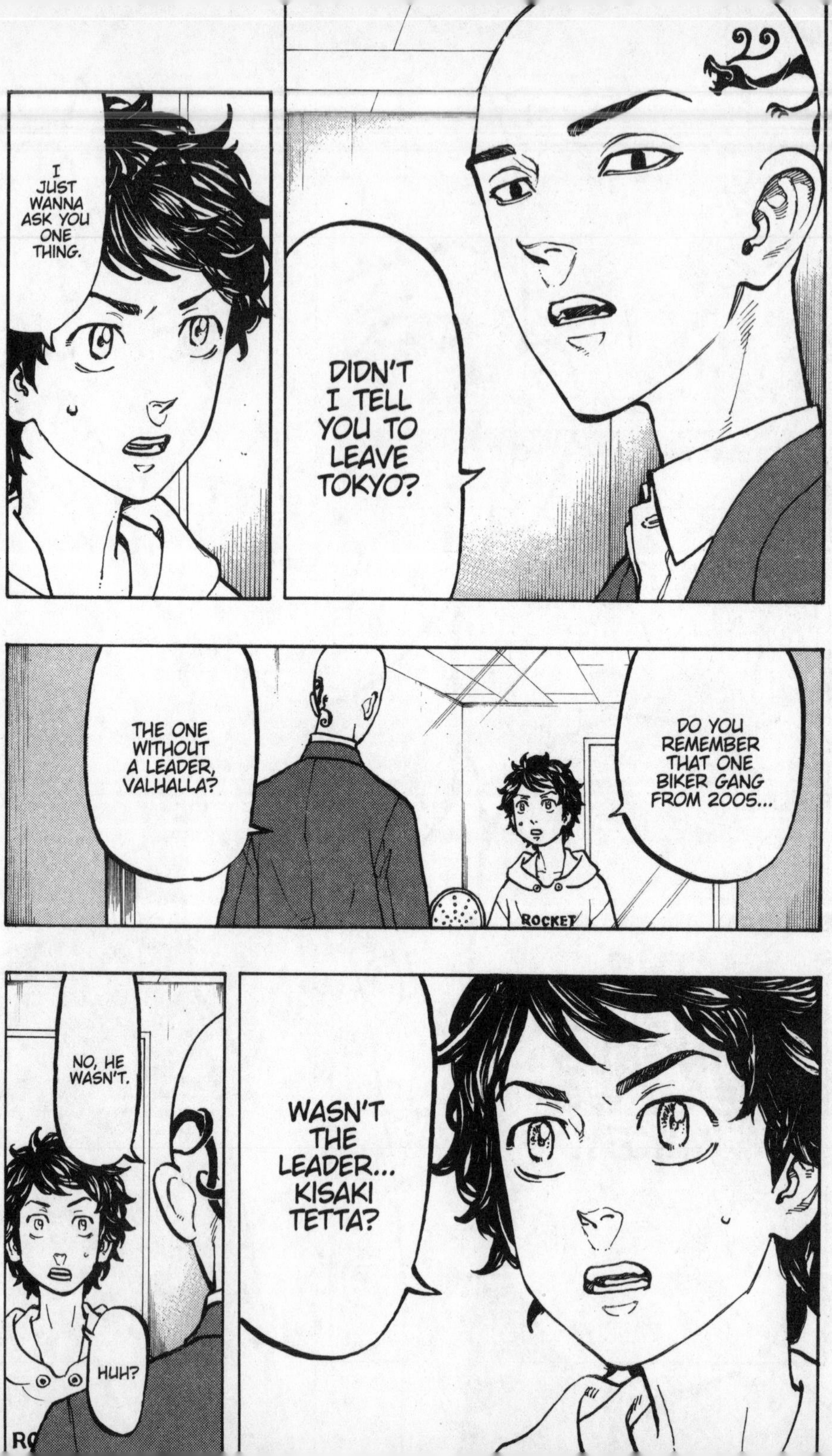
DIDN'T I TELL YOU TO LEAVE TOKYO?
I JUST WANNA ASK YOU ONE THING.
DO YOU REMEMBER THAT ONE BIKER GANG FROM 2005...
THE ONE WITHOUT A LEADER, VALHALLA?
ROCKET
WASN'T THE LEADER... KISAKI TETTA?
NO, HE WASN'T.
HUH?

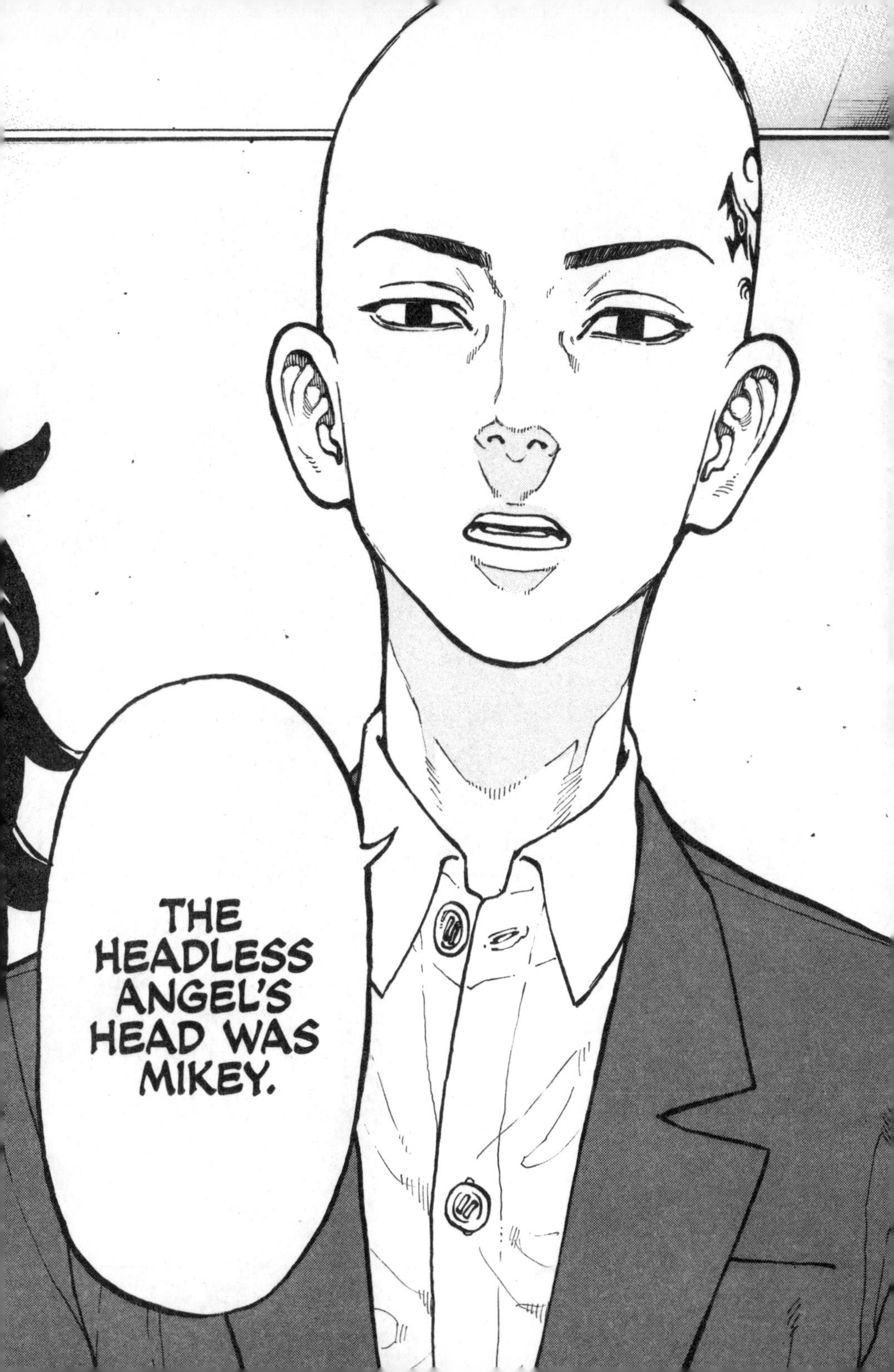
THE HEADLESS ANGEL'S HEAD WAS MIKEY.

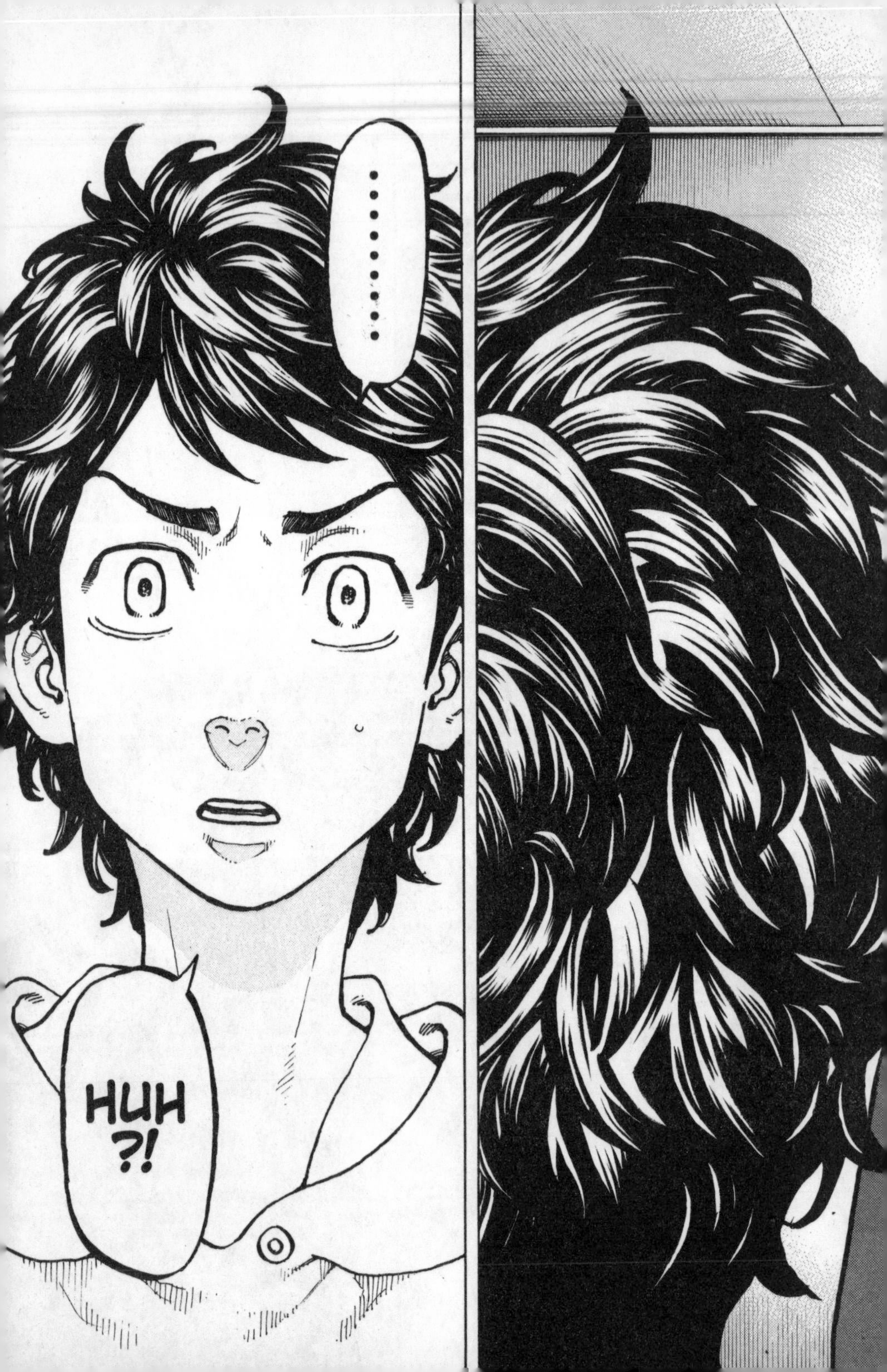
……
HUH ?!

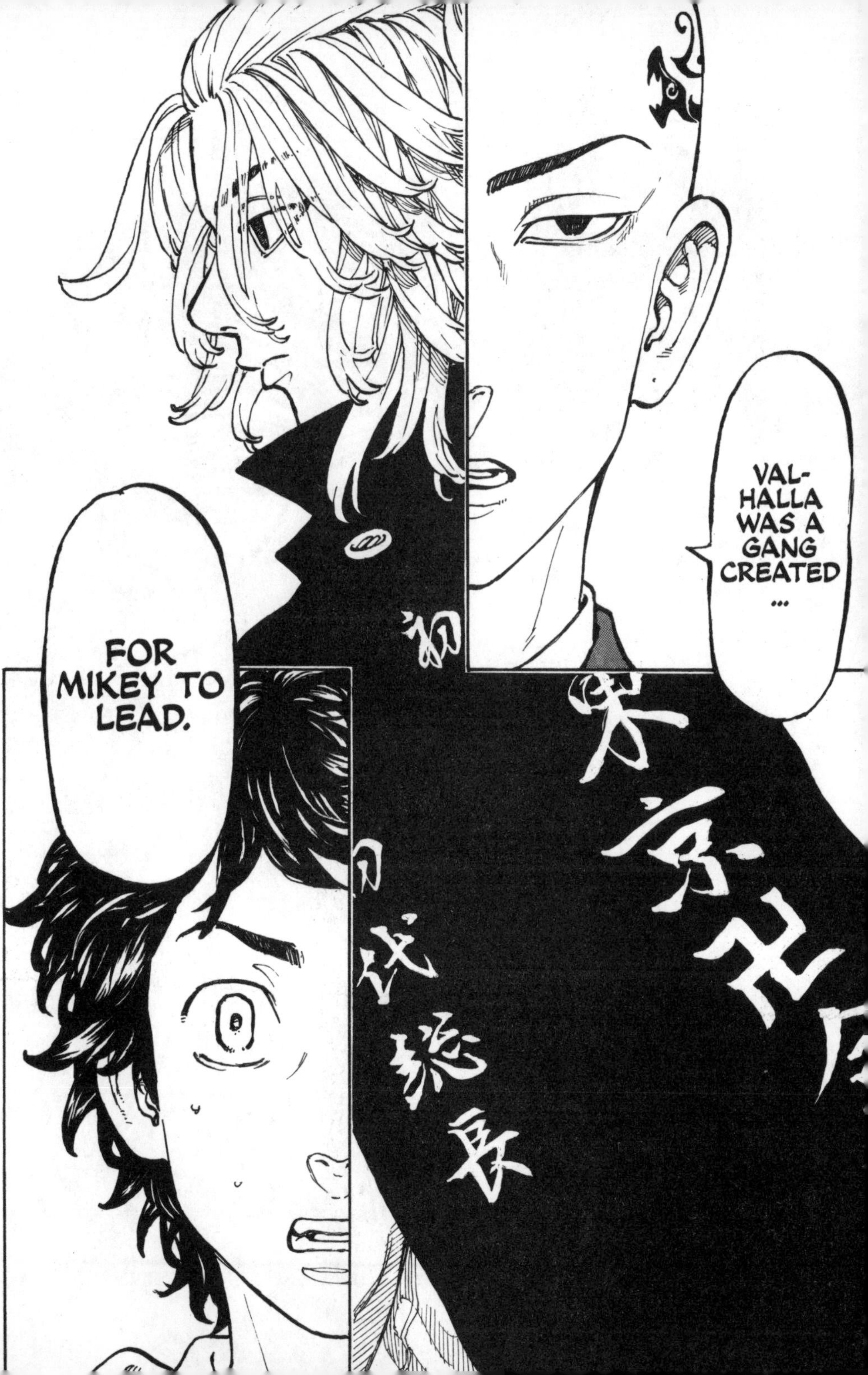
VAL-HALLA WAS A GANG CREATED ...
FOR MIKEY TO LEAD.

TOKYO Revengers

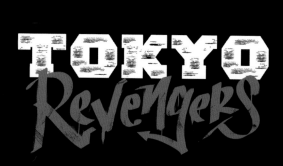

CHAPTER 48: NO WAY

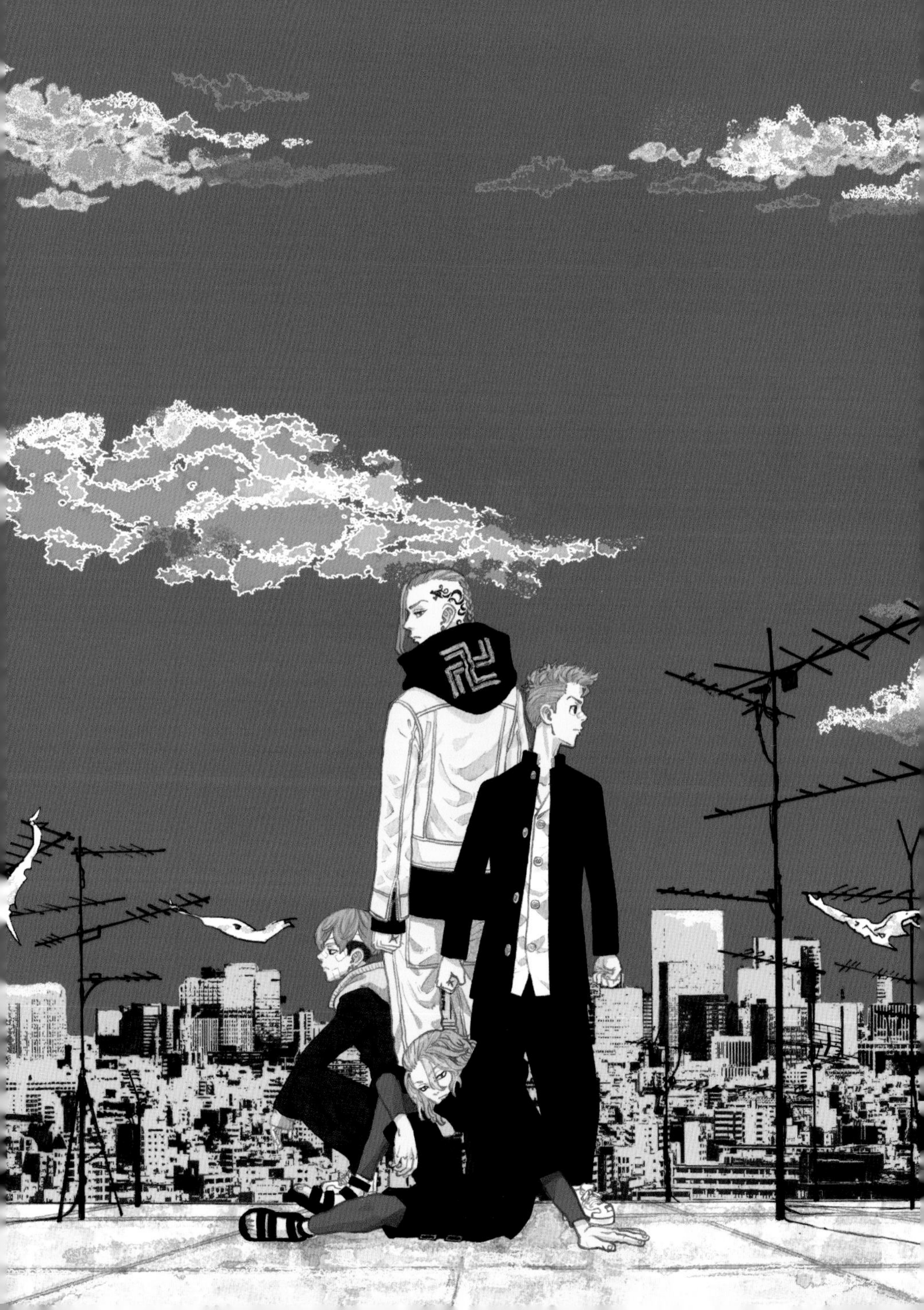

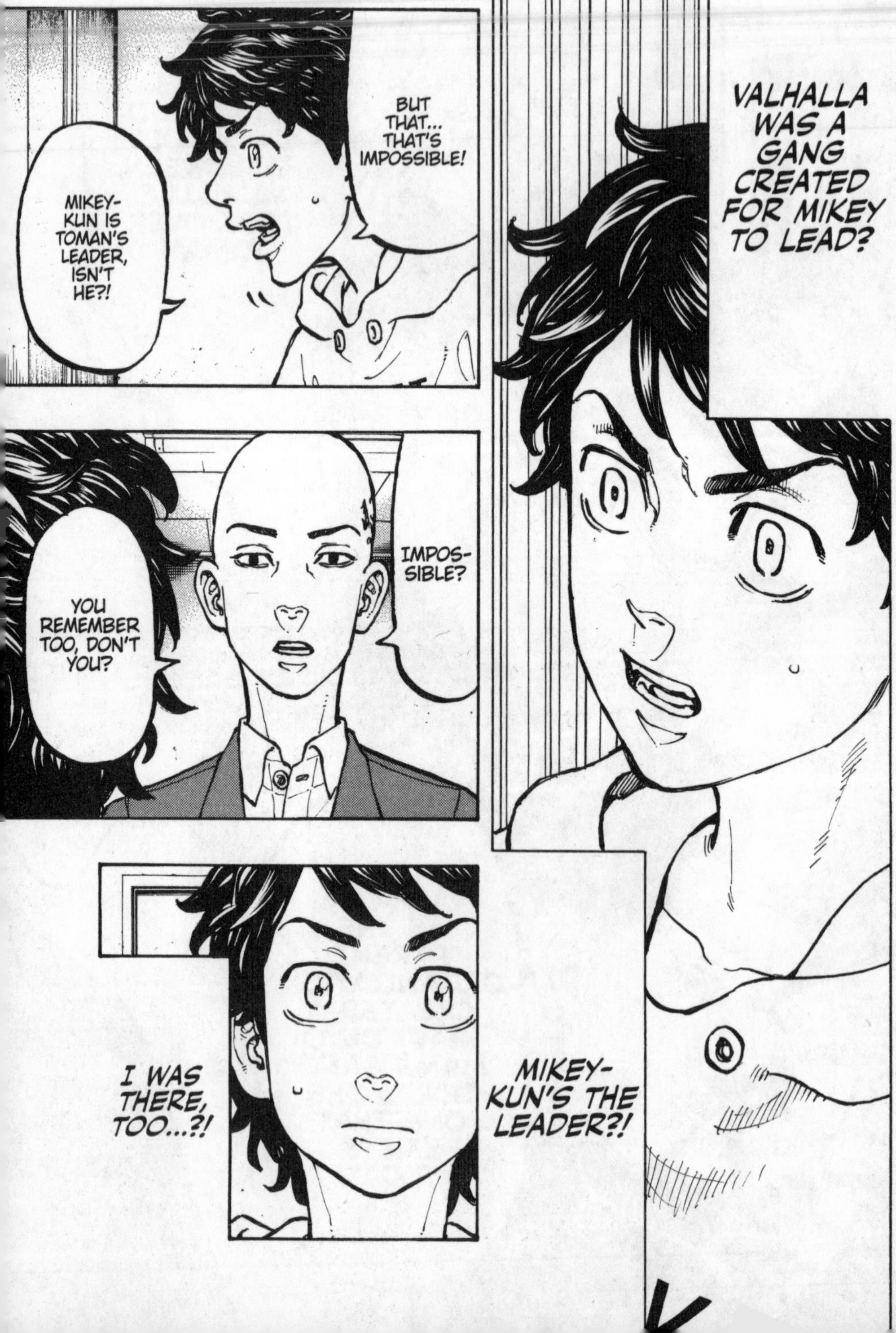
VALHALLA WAS A GANG CREATED FOR MIKEY TO LEAD?
BUT THAT... THAT'S IMPOSSIBLE!
MIKEY-KUN IS TOMAN'S LEADER, ISN'T HE?!
IMPOSSIBLE?
YOU REMEMBER TOO, DON'T YOU?
MIKEY-KUN'S THE LEADER?!
I WAS THERE, TOO...?!

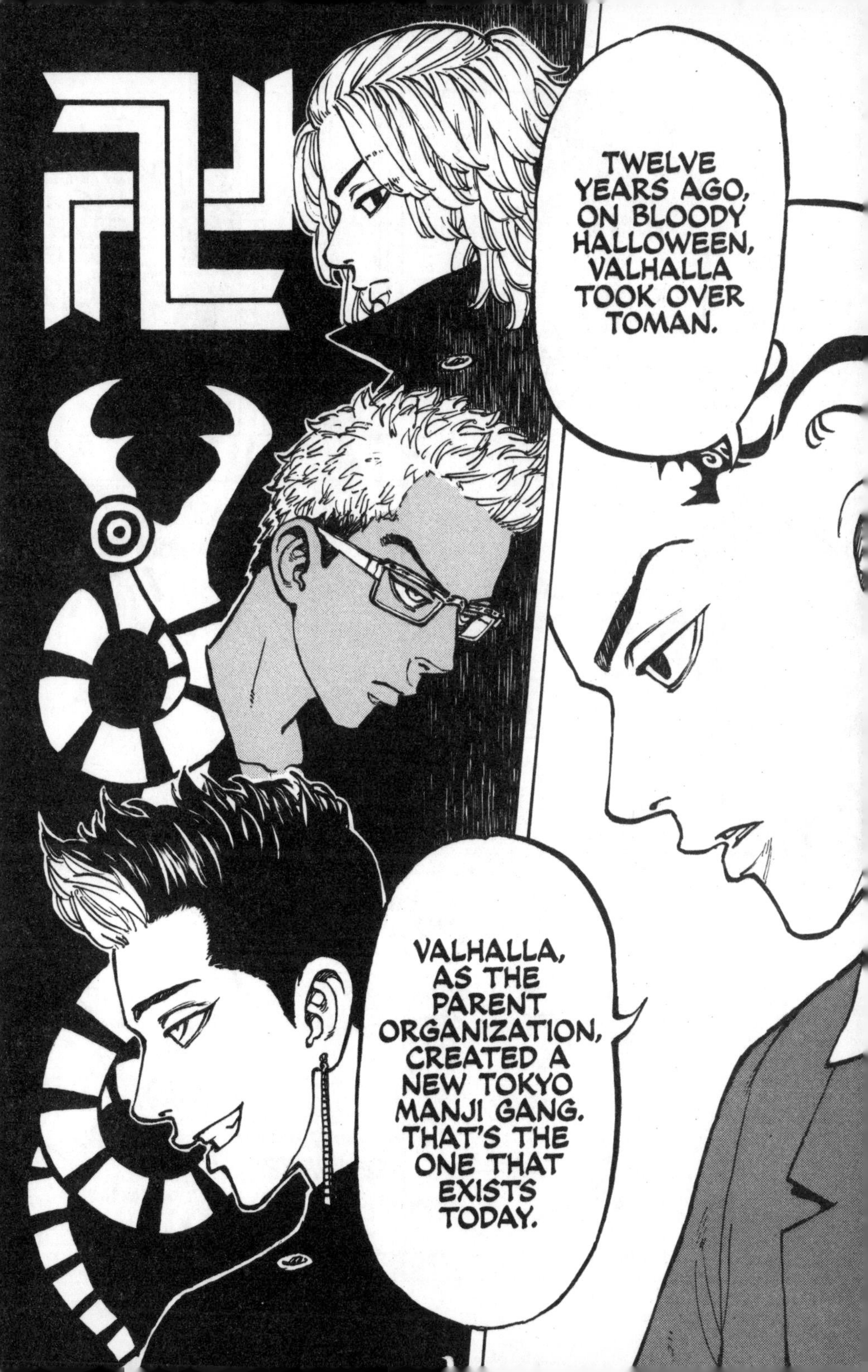
TWELVE YEARS AGO, ON BLOODY HALLOWEEN, VALHALLA TOOK OVER TOMAN.
VALHALLA, AS THE PARENT ORGANIZATION, CREATED A NEW TOKYO MANJI GANG. THAT'S THE ONE THAT EXISTS TODAY.

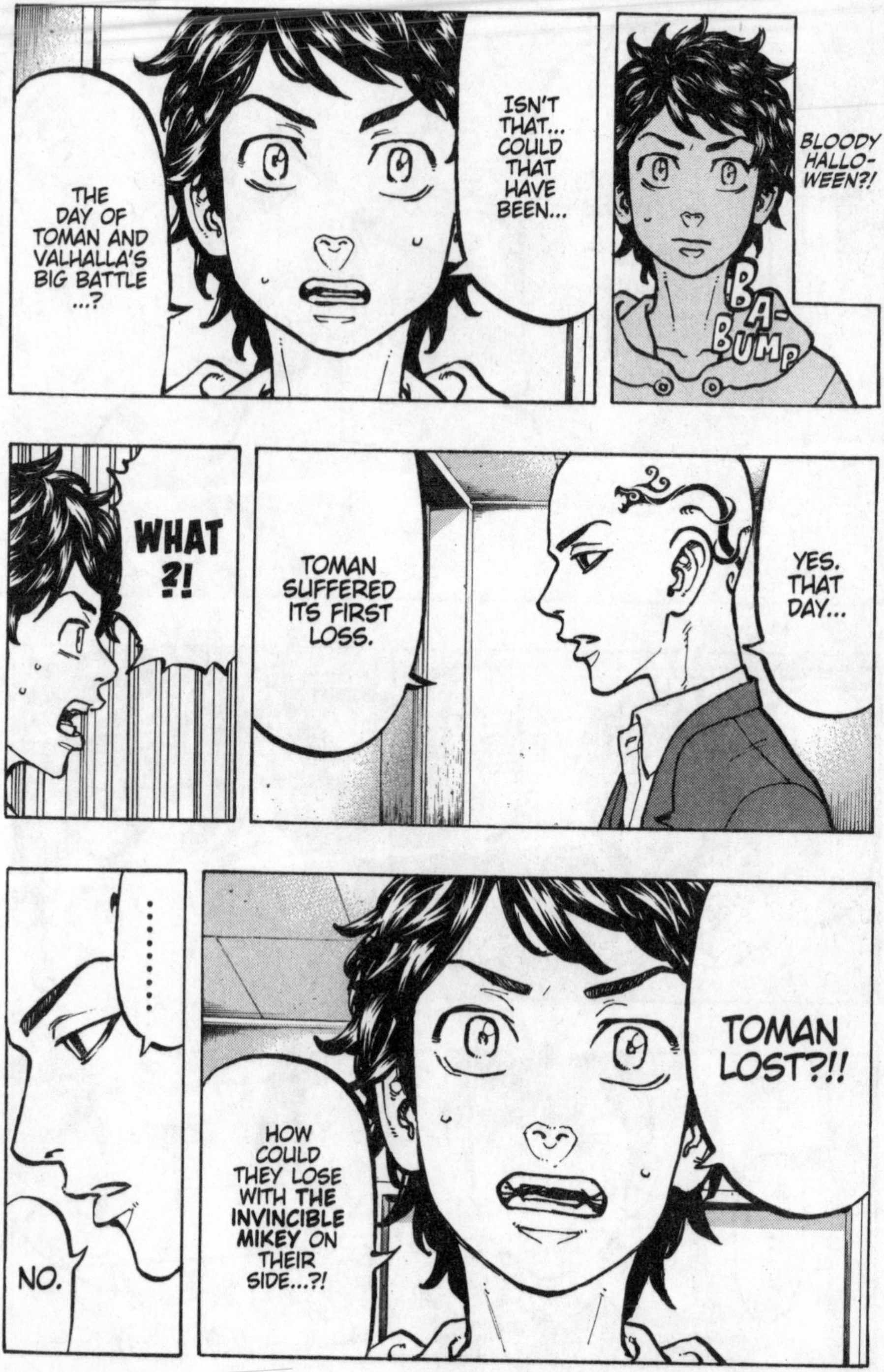
BLOODY HALLO-WEEN?!
BA-BUMP
ISN'T THAT... COULD THAT HAVE BEEN...
THE DAY OF TOMAN AND VALHALLA'S BIG BATTLE ...?
YES. THAT DAY...
TOMAN SUFFERED ITS FIRST LOSS.
WHAT ?!
TOMAN LOST?!!
HOW COULD THEY LOSE WITH THE INVINCIBLE MIKEY ON THEIR SIDE...?!
......
NO.

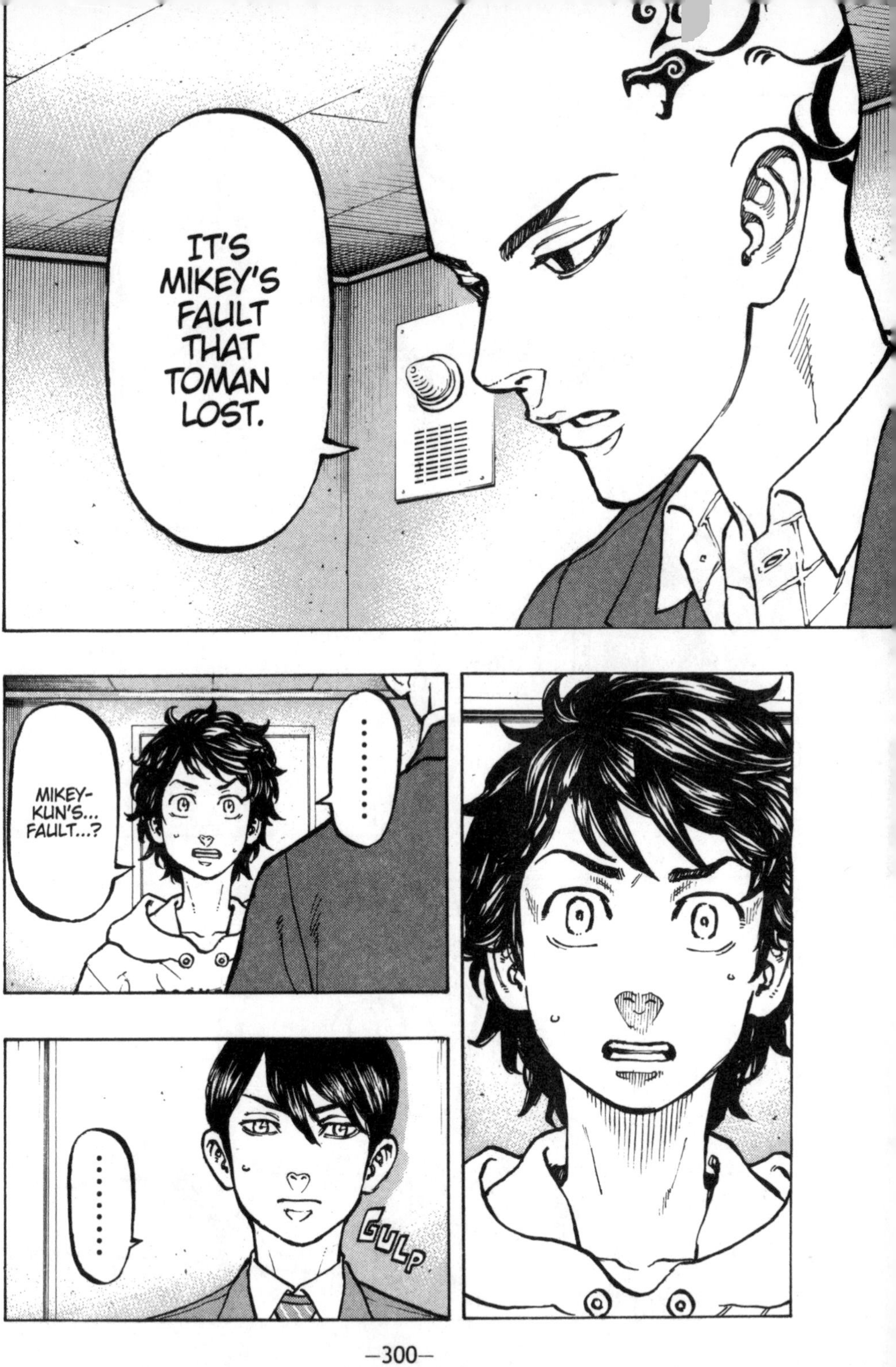
IT'S MIKEY'S FAULT THAT TOMAN LOST.
....
MIKEY-KUN'S... FAULT...?
....
GULP

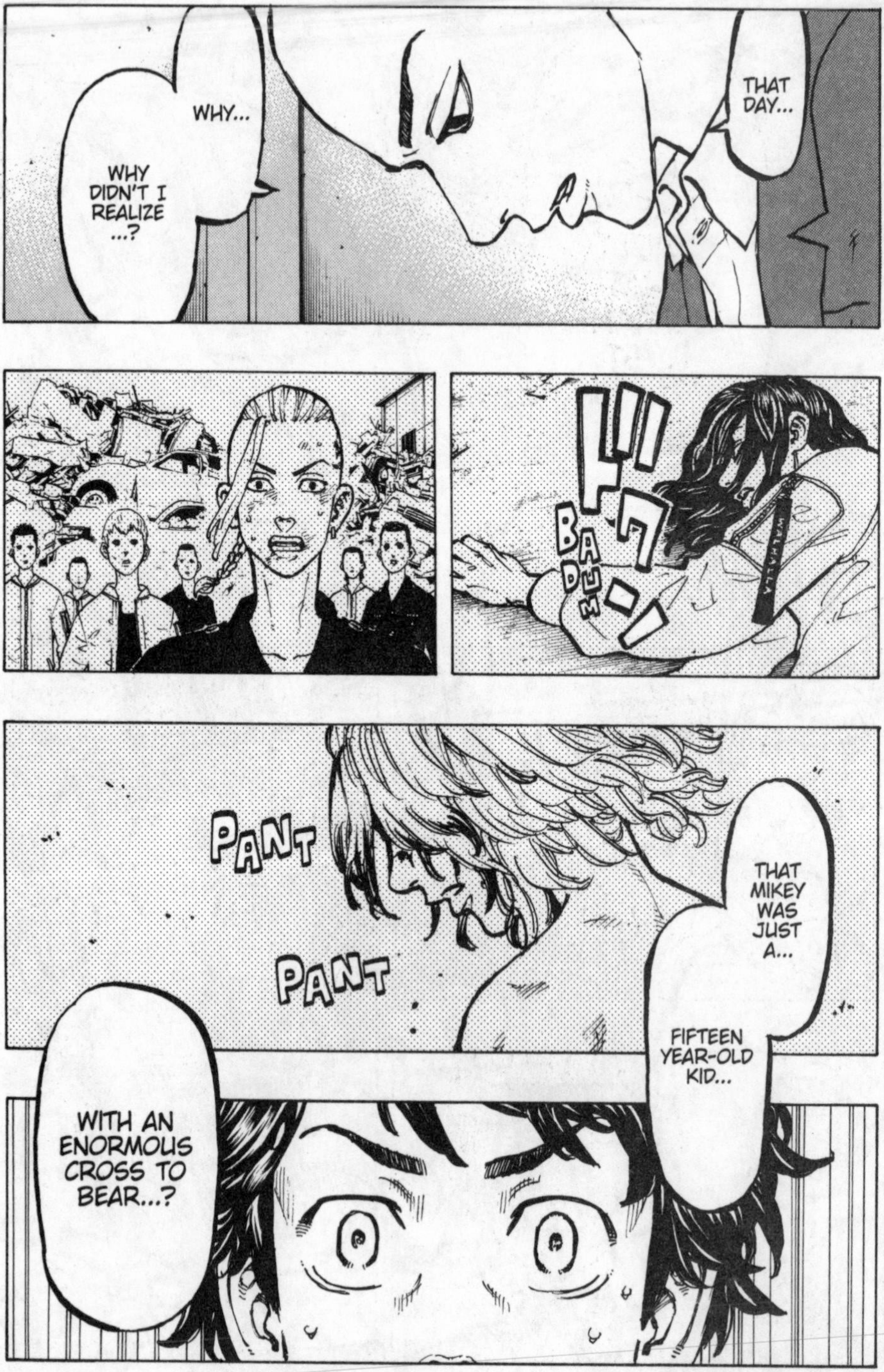
THAT DAY...
WHY...
WHY DIDN'T I REALIZE ...?
ドクンー!
BADUM
PANT
PANT
THAT MIKEY WAS JUST A...
FIFTEEN YEAR-OLD KID...
WITH AN ENORMOUS CROSS TO BEAR...?

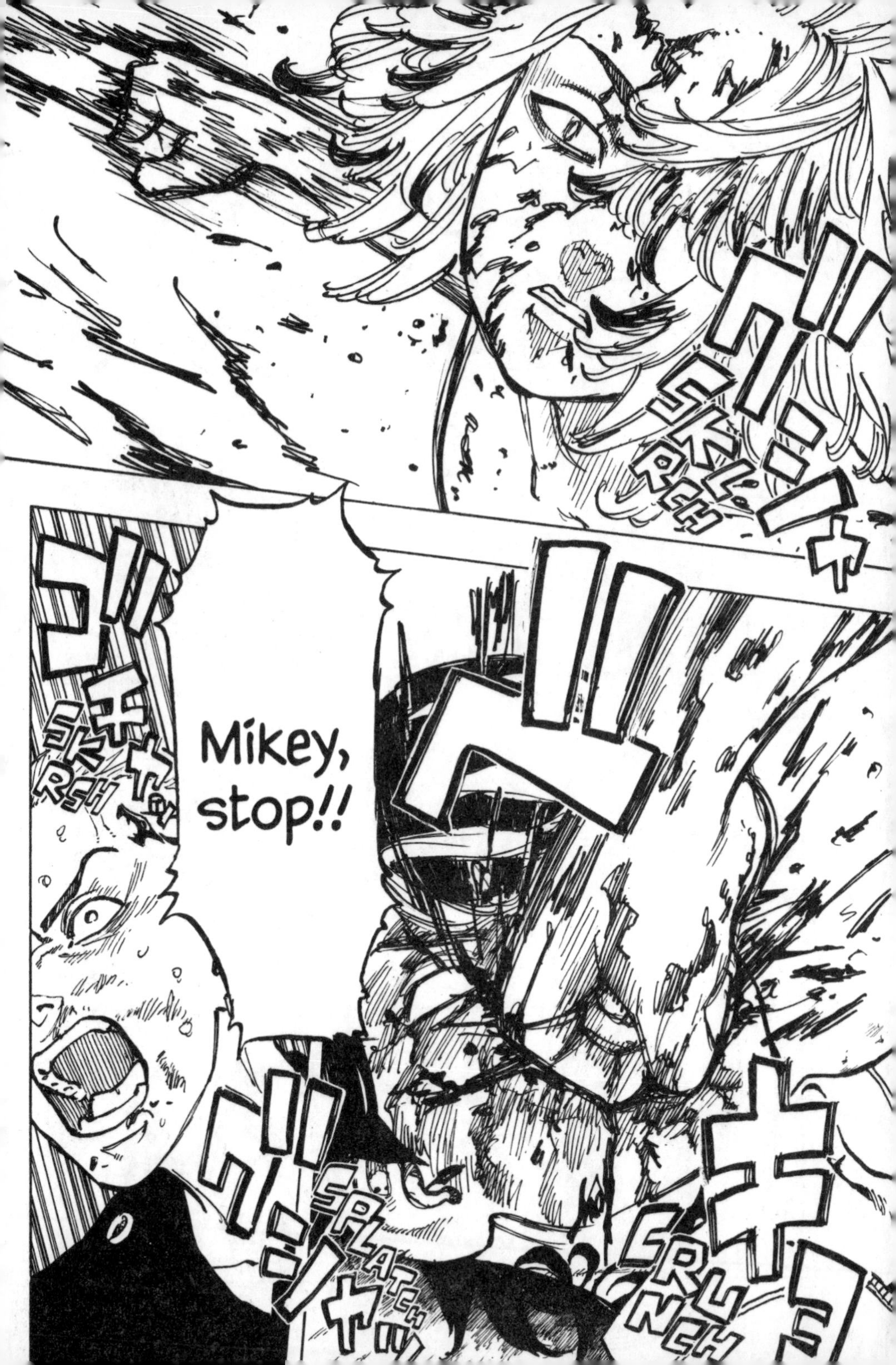
SKRCH
Mikey, stop!!
SKRSH
CRUNCH
SPLATCH

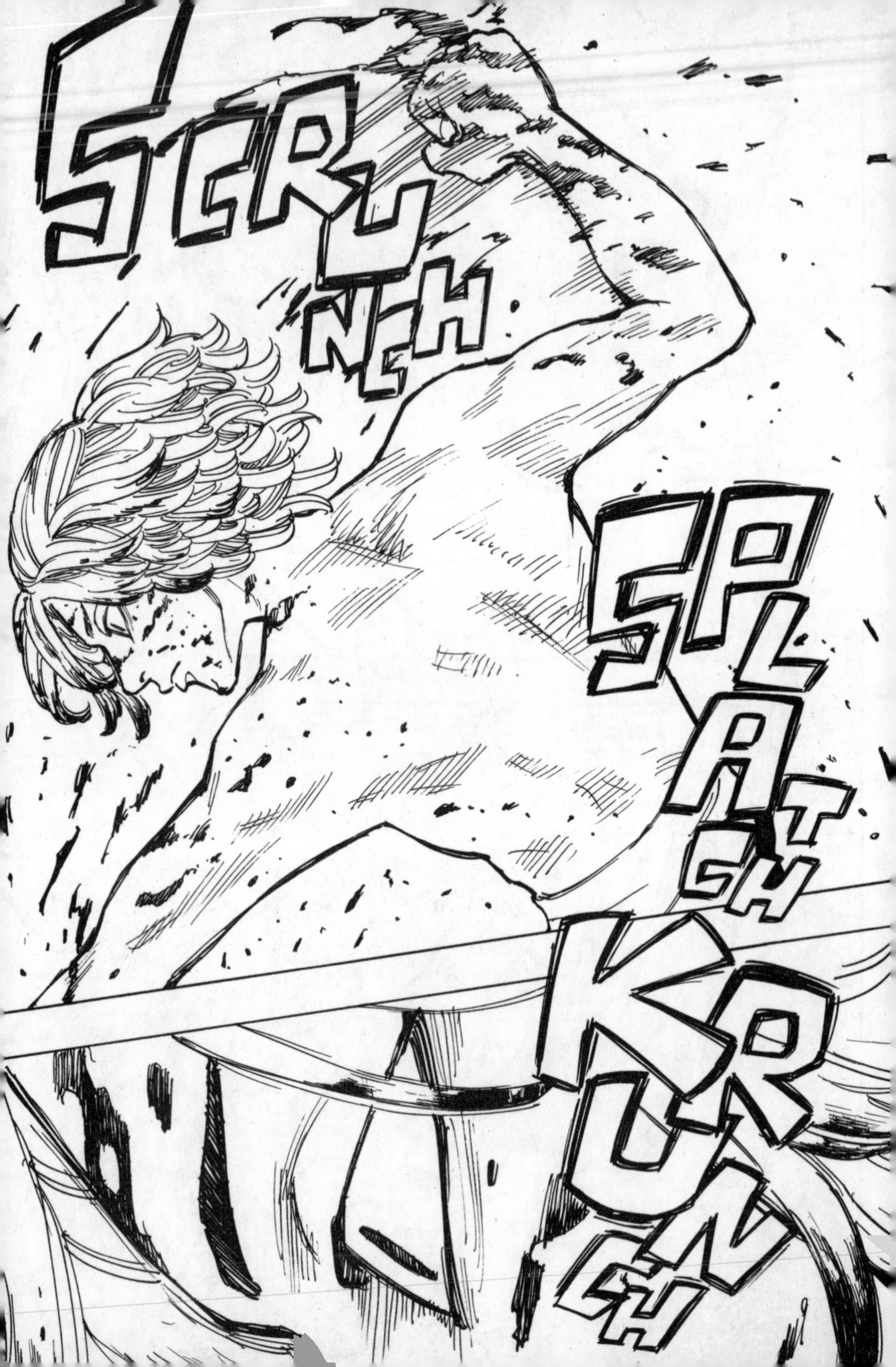
SCRUNCH
SPLATCH
KRUNCH

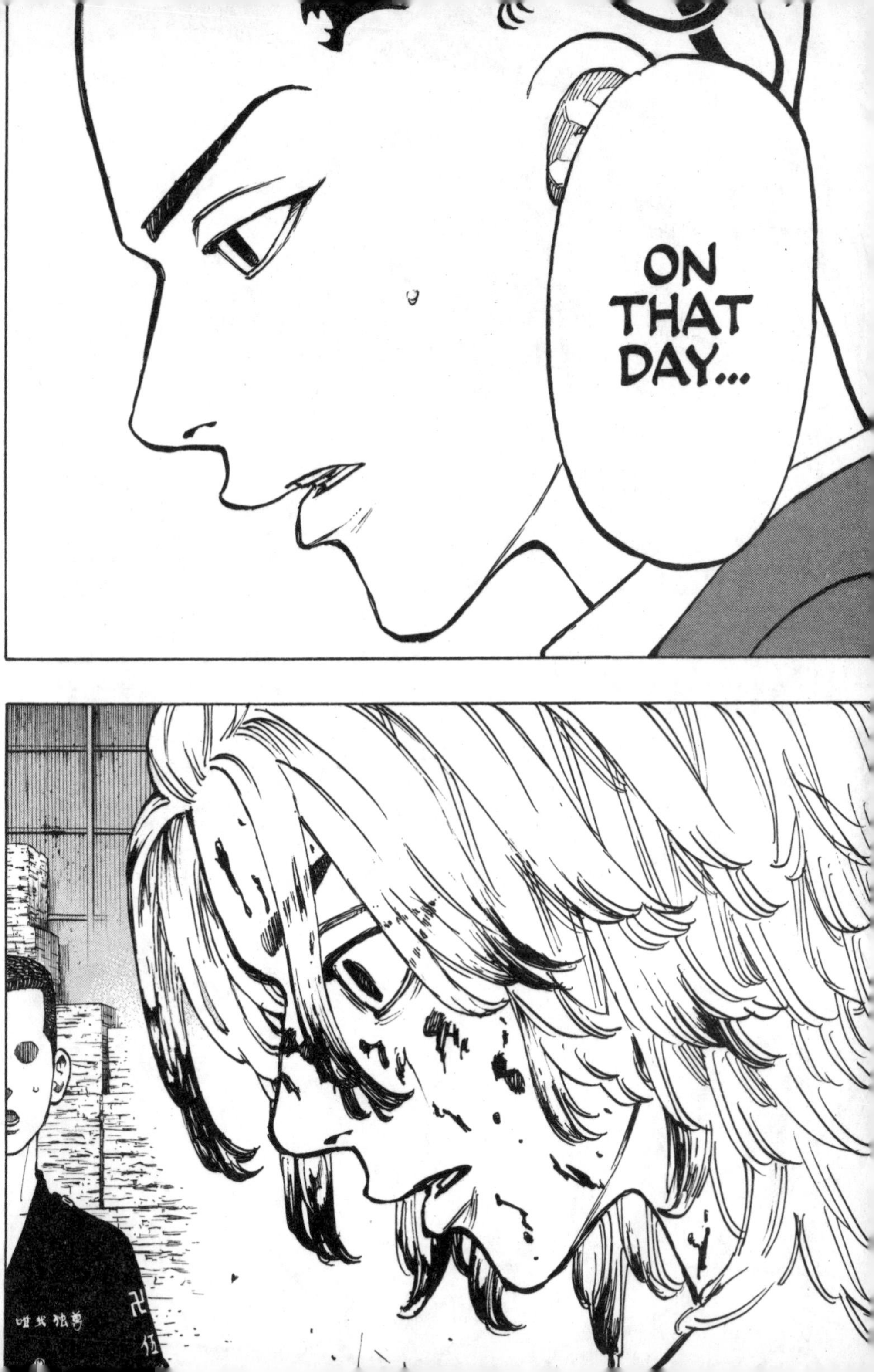
ON THAT DAY...

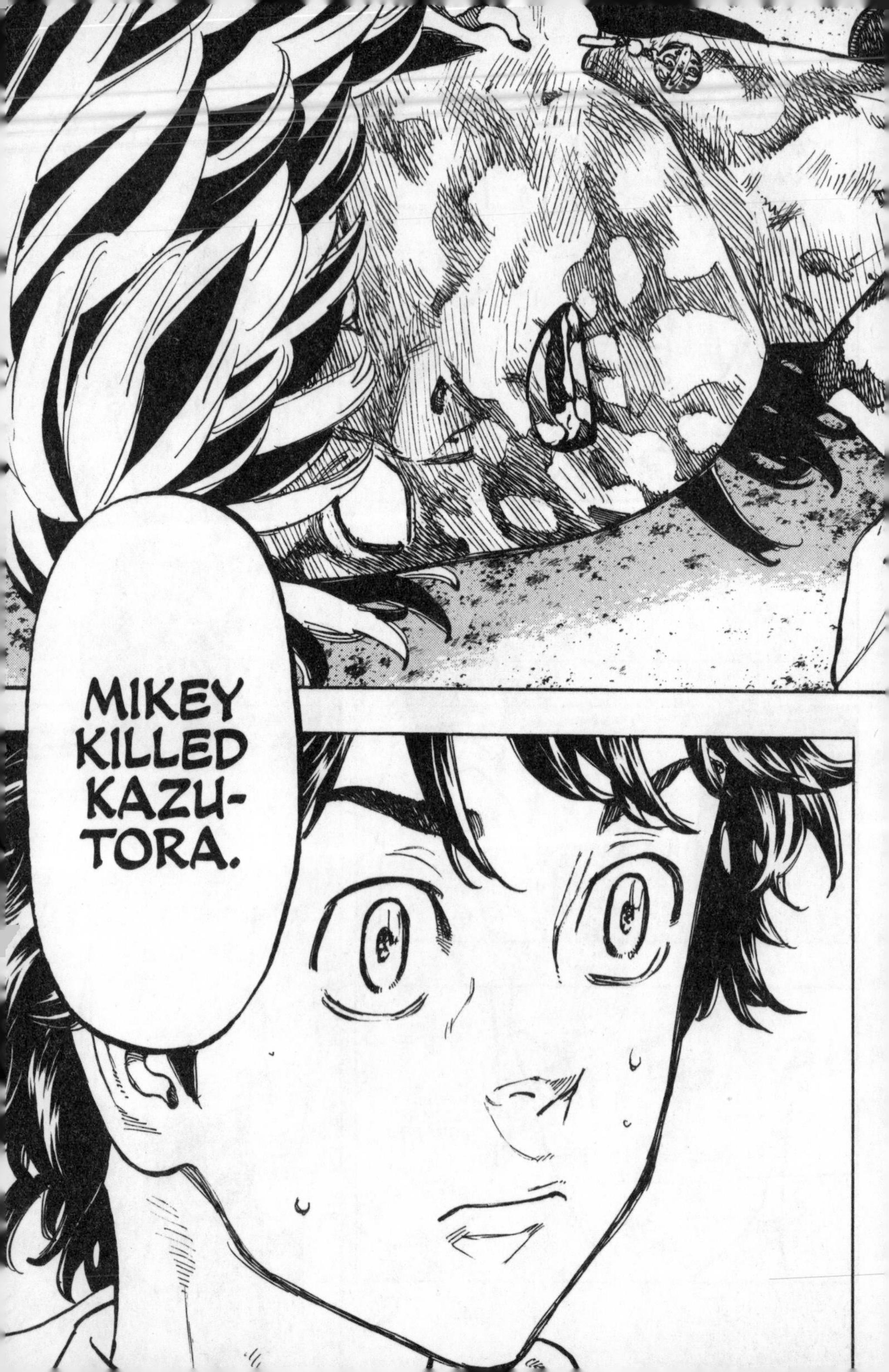
MIKEY KILLED KAZU-TORA.

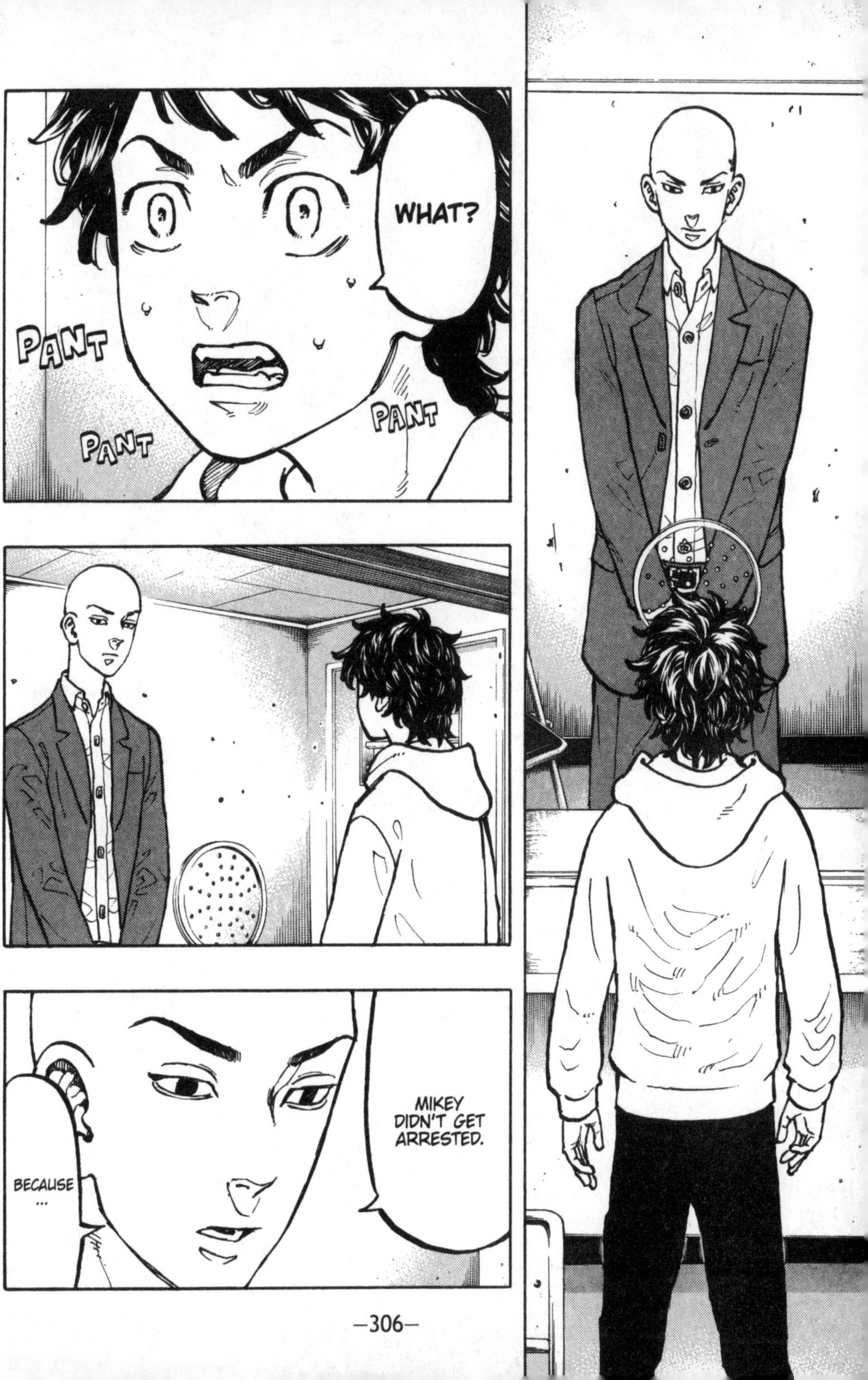
WHAT?
PANT
PANT
PANT
MIKEY DIDN'T GET ARRESTED.
BECAUSE ...

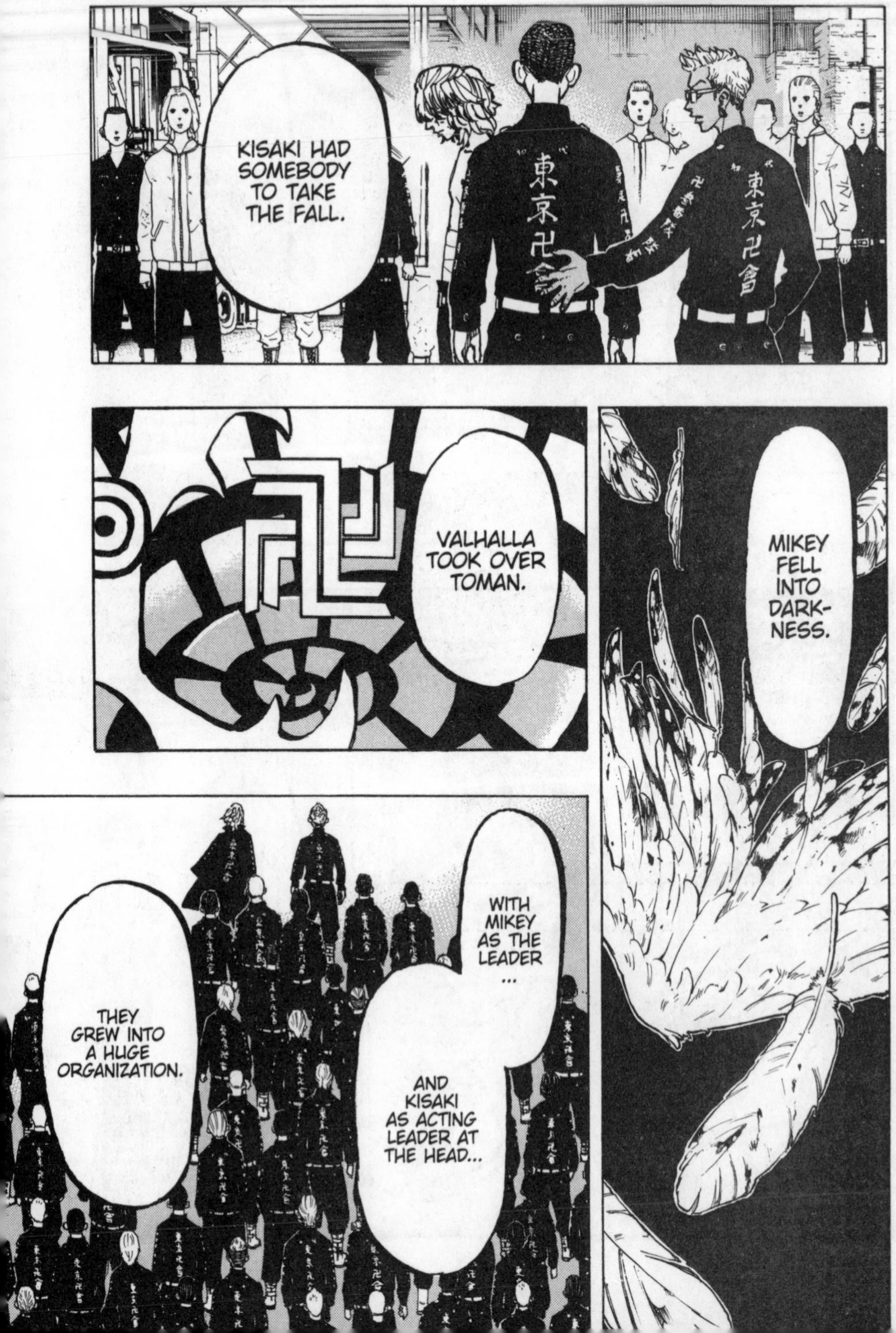
KISAKI HAD SOMEBODY TO TAKE THE FALL.
MIKEY FELL INTO DARK-NESS.
VALHALLA TOOK OVER TOMAN.
WITH MIKEY AS THE LEADER ...
AND KISAKI AS ACTING LEADER AT THE HEAD...
THEY GREW INTO A HUGE ORGANIZATION.

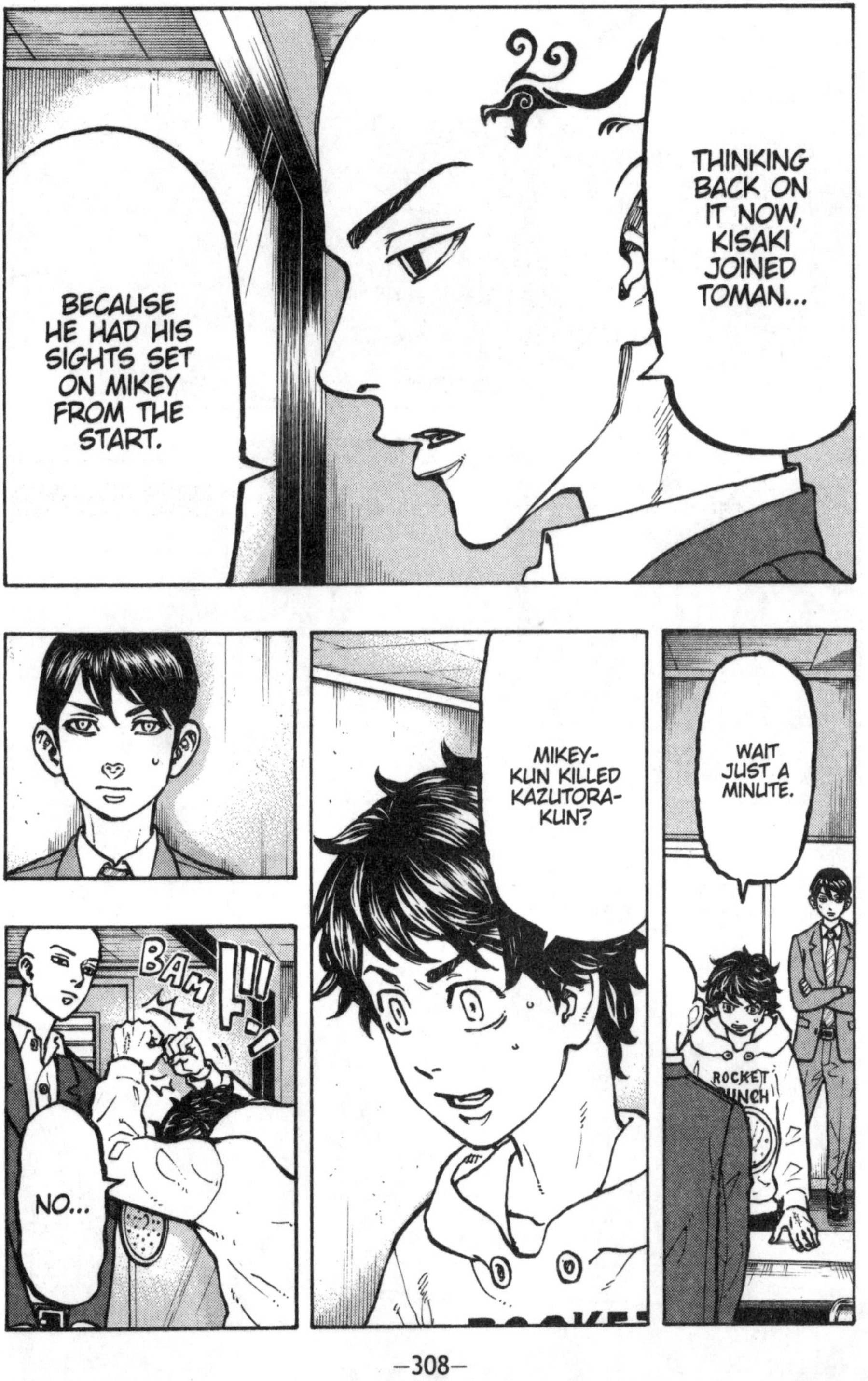
THINKING BACK ON IT NOW, KISAKI JOINED TOMAN...
BECAUSE HE HAD HIS SIGHTS SET ON MIKEY FROM THE START.
WAIT JUST A MINUTE.
MIKEY-KUN KILLED KAZUTORA-KUN?
BAM!!!
NO...

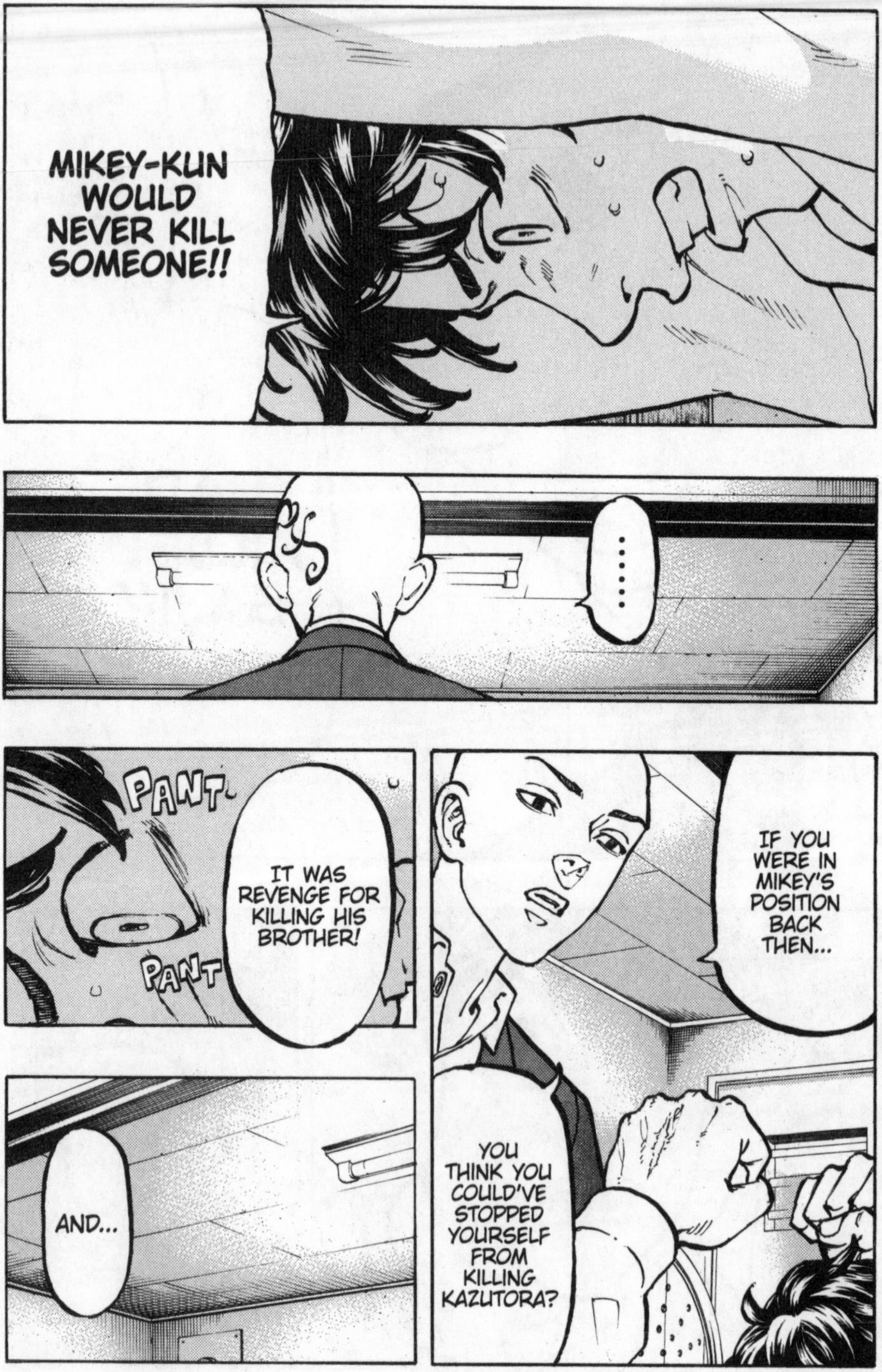
MIKEY-KUN WOULD NEVER KILL SOMEONE!!
......
IF YOU WERE IN MIKEY'S POSITION BACK THEN...
YOU THINK YOU COULD'VE STOPPED YOURSELF FROM KILLING KAZUTORA?
PANT
IT WAS REVENGE FOR KILLING HIS BROTHER!
PANT
AND...

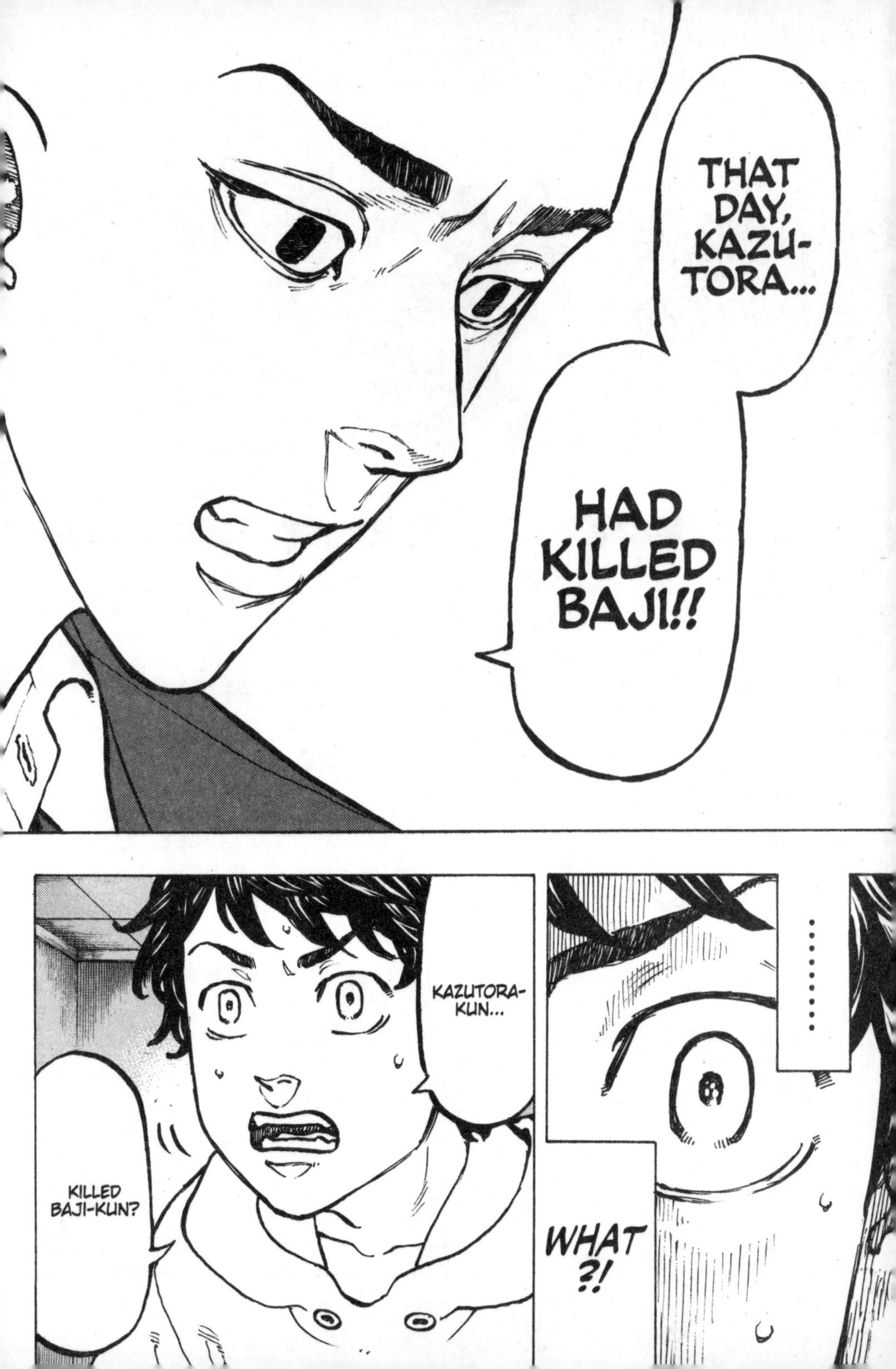
THAT DAY, KAZUTORA...
HAD KILLED BAJI!!
......
WHAT?!
KAZUTORA-KUN...
KILLED BAJI-KUN?

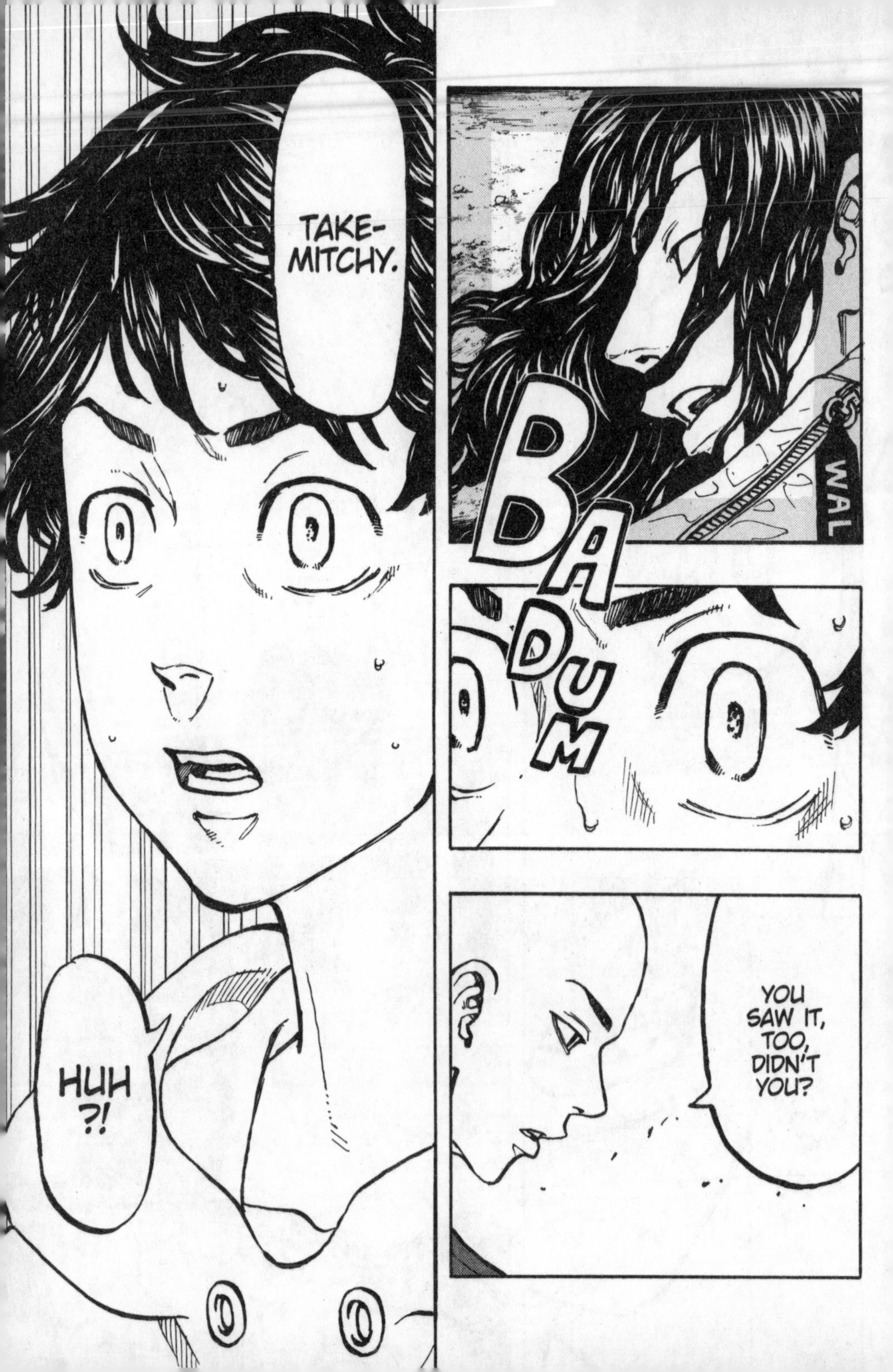
WAL
BADADUM
YOU SAW IT, TOO, DIDN'T YOU?
TAKE-MITCHY.
HUH ?!

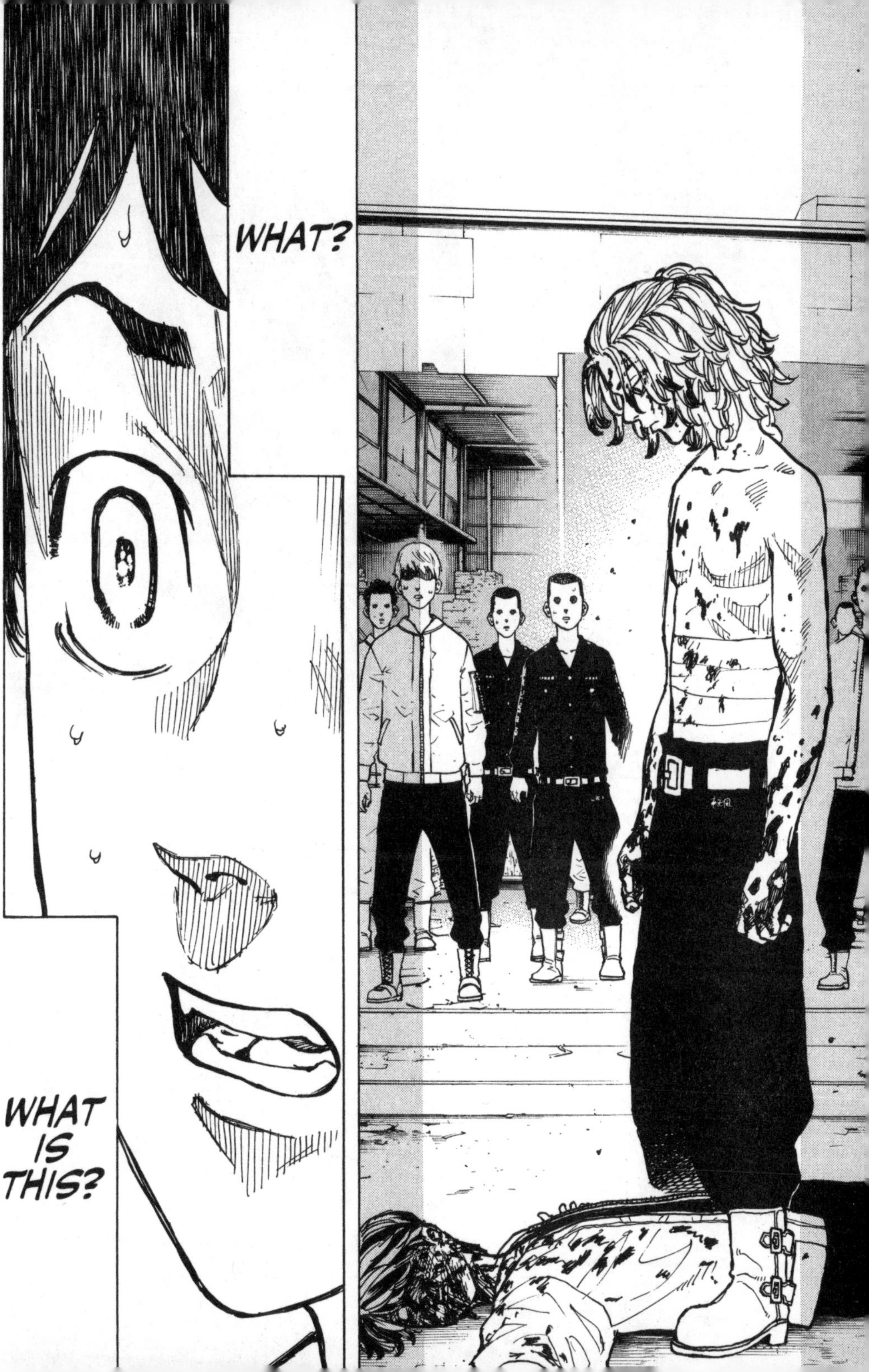
WHAT?
WHAT IS THIS?

MIKEY-KUN WOULD NEVER, EVER KILL ANYONE.

I KNOW THAT...

I BELIEVE THAT, BUT...

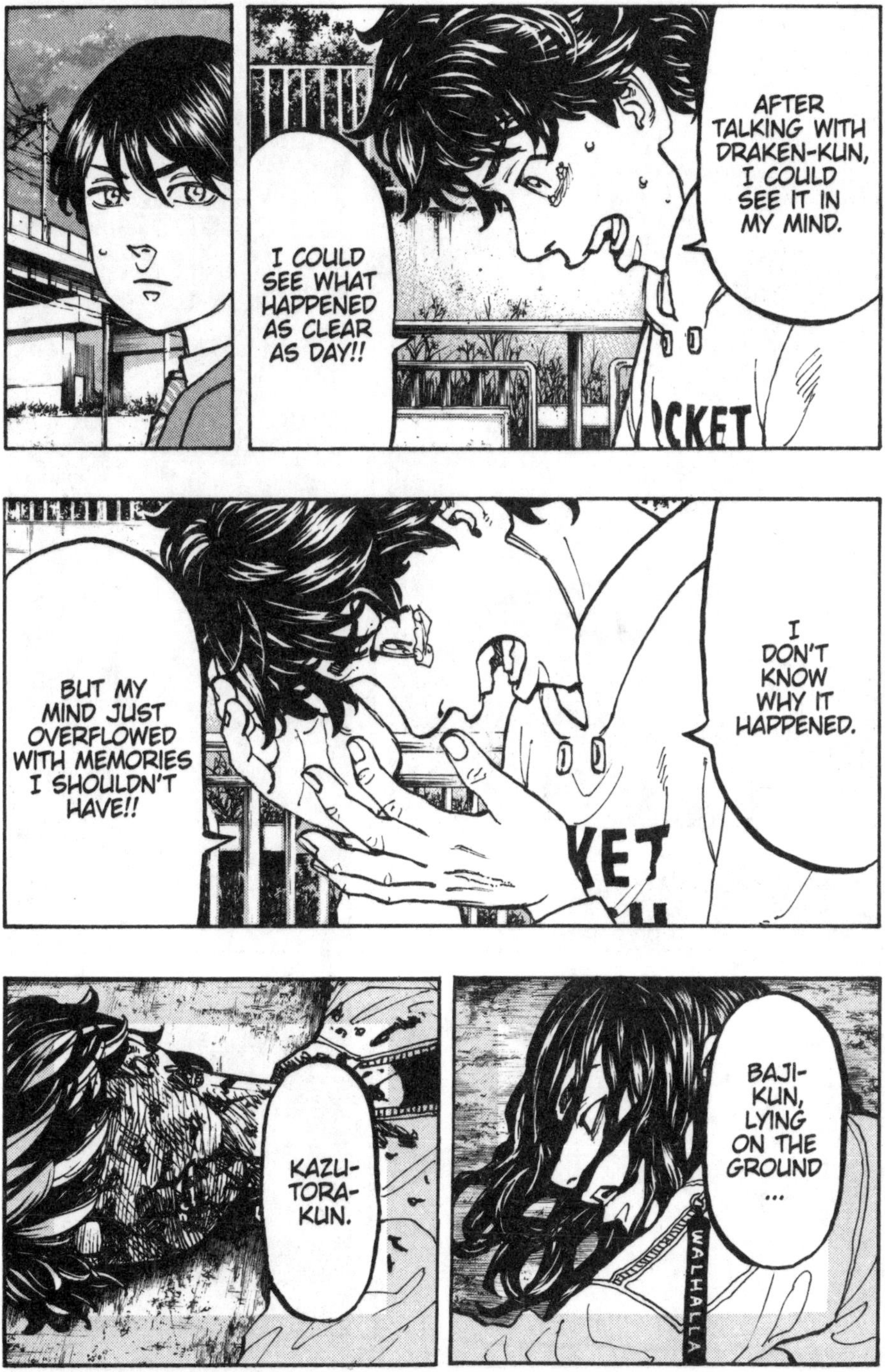
AFTER TALKING WITH DRAKEN-KUN, I COULD SEE IT IN MY MIND.
I COULD SEE WHAT HAPPENED AS CLEAR AS DAY!!
I DON'T KNOW WHY IT HAPPENED.
BUT MY MIND JUST OVERFLOWED WITH MEMORIES I SHOULDN'T HAVE!!
BAJI-KUN, LYING ON THE GROUND ...
WALHALLA
KAZUTORA-KUN.

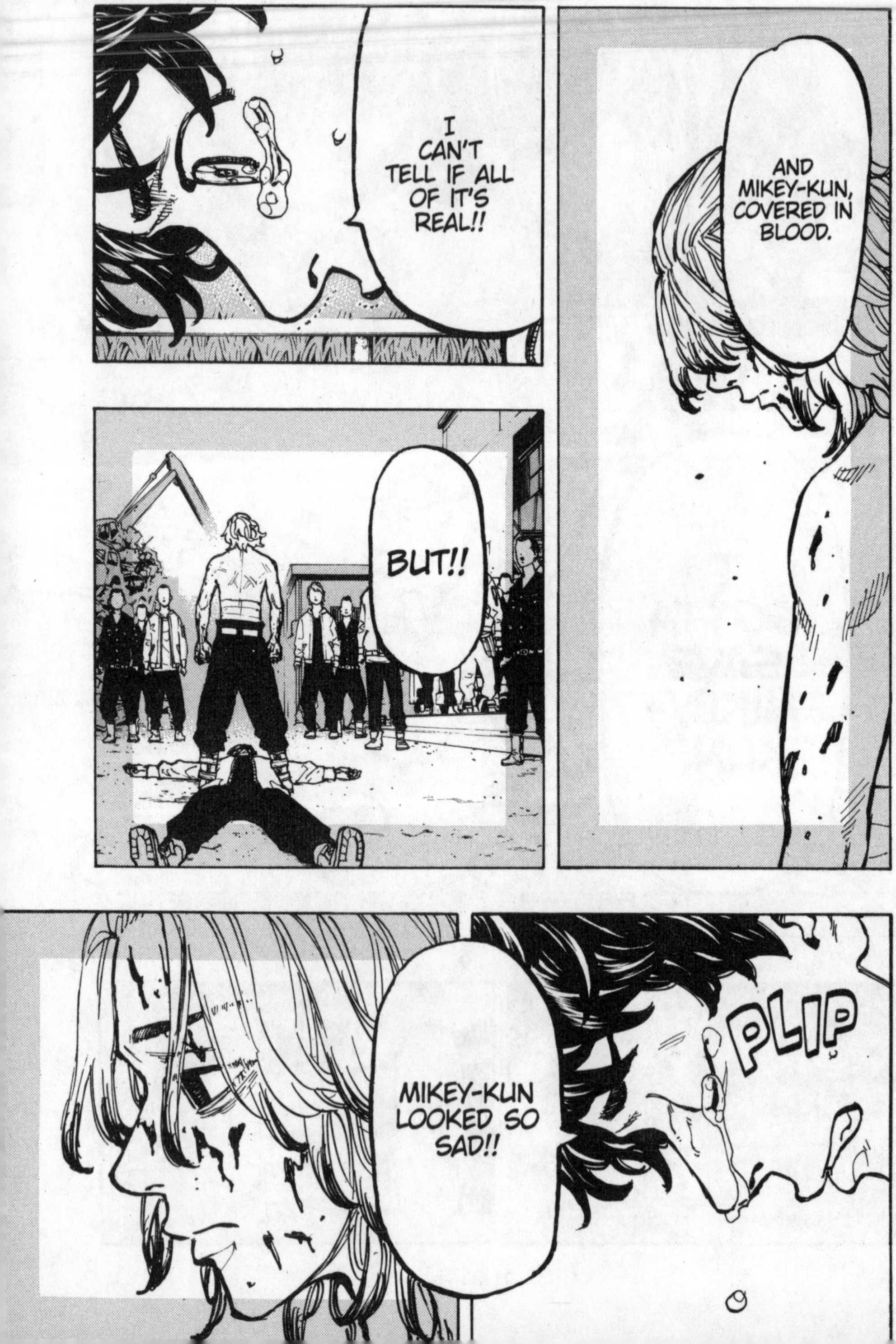
AND MIKEY-KUN, COVERED IN BLOOD.
I CAN'T TELL IF ALL OF IT'S REAL!!
BUT!!
PLIP
MIKEY-KUN LOOKED SO SAD!!

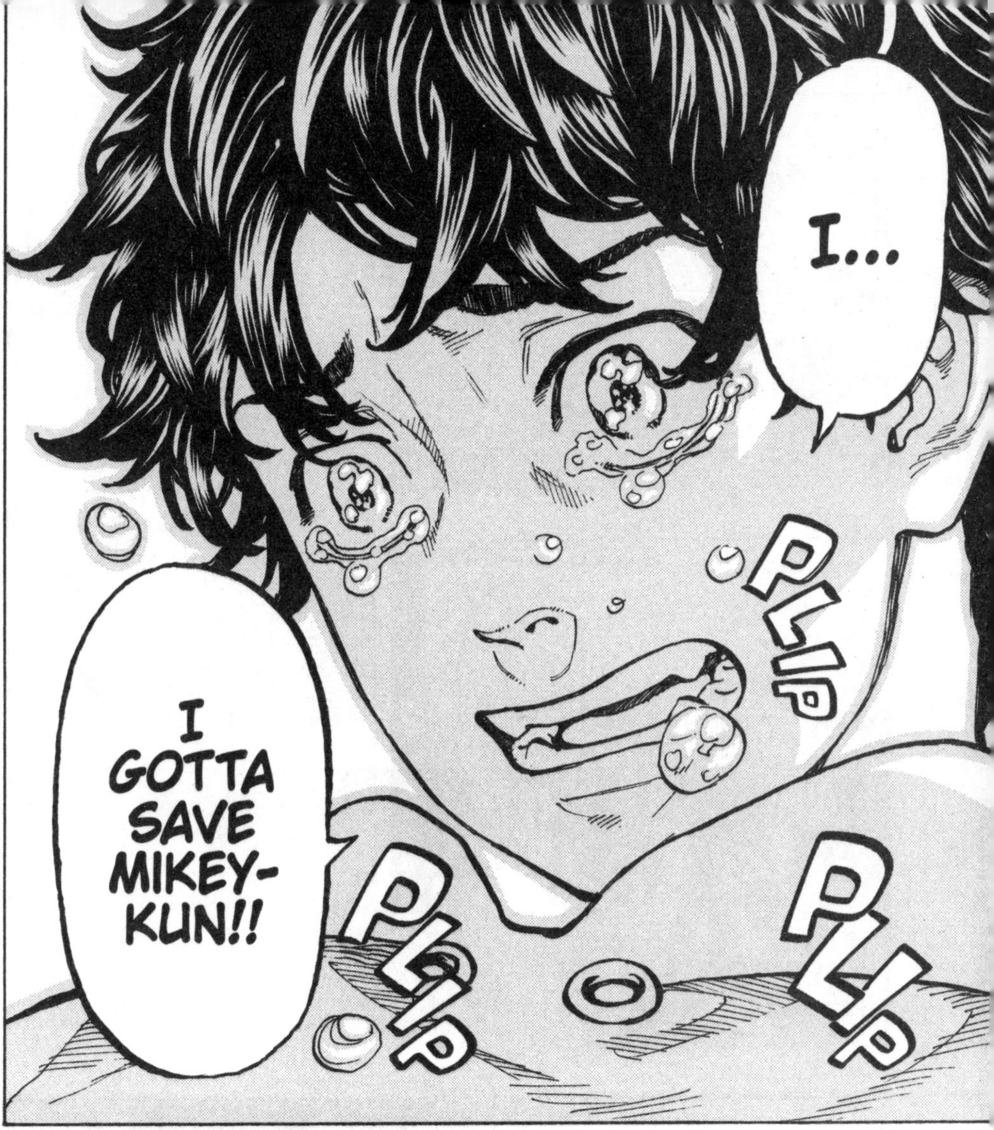
I...
PLIP
I GOTTA SAVE MIKEY-KUN!!
PLIP
PLIP
PLIP

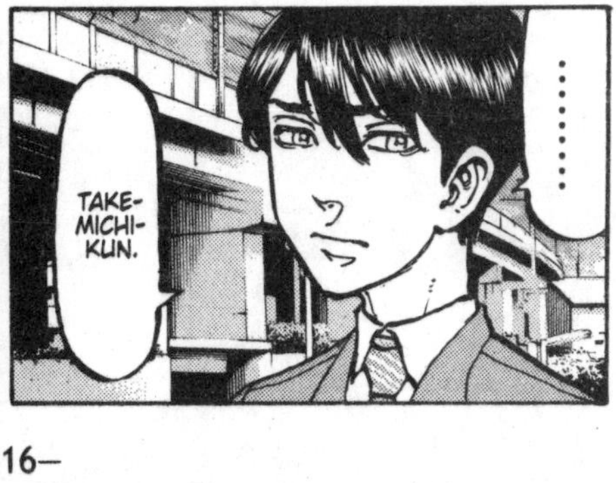
....
TAKE-MICHI-KUN.

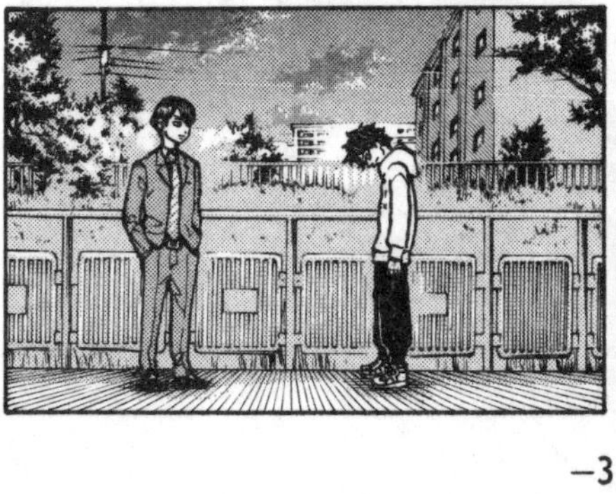

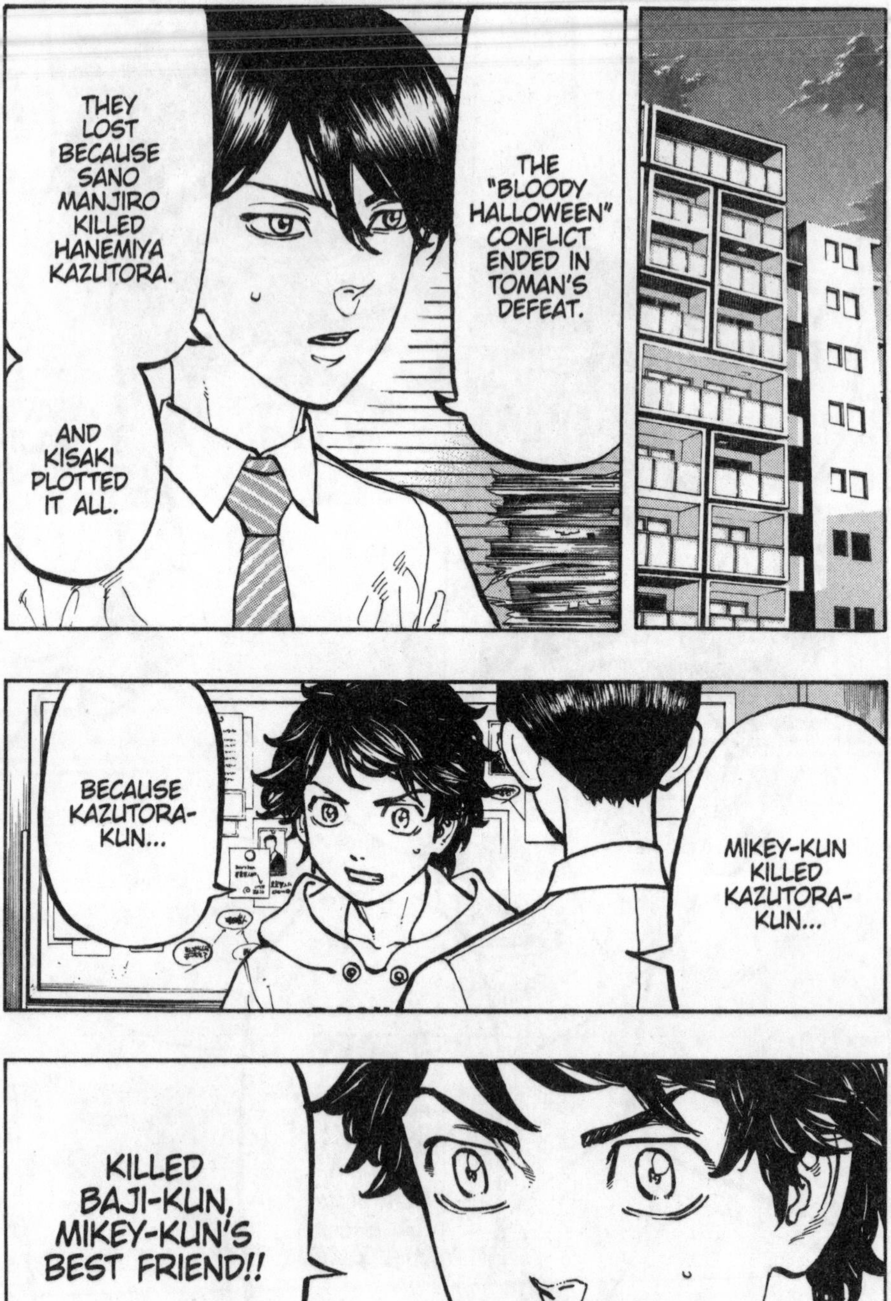
THE "BLOODY HALLOWEEN" CONFLICT ENDED IN TOMAN'S DEFEAT.
THEY LOST BECAUSE SANO MANJIRO KILLED HANEMIYA KAZUTORA.
AND KISAKI PLOTTED IT ALL.
MIKEY-KUN KILLED KAZUTORA-KUN...
BECAUSE KAZUTORA-KUN...
KILLED BAJI-KUN, MIKEY-KUN'S BEST FRIEND!!

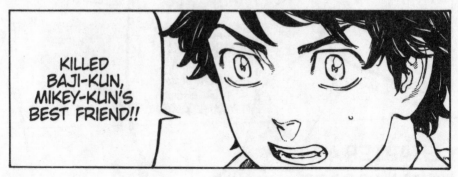

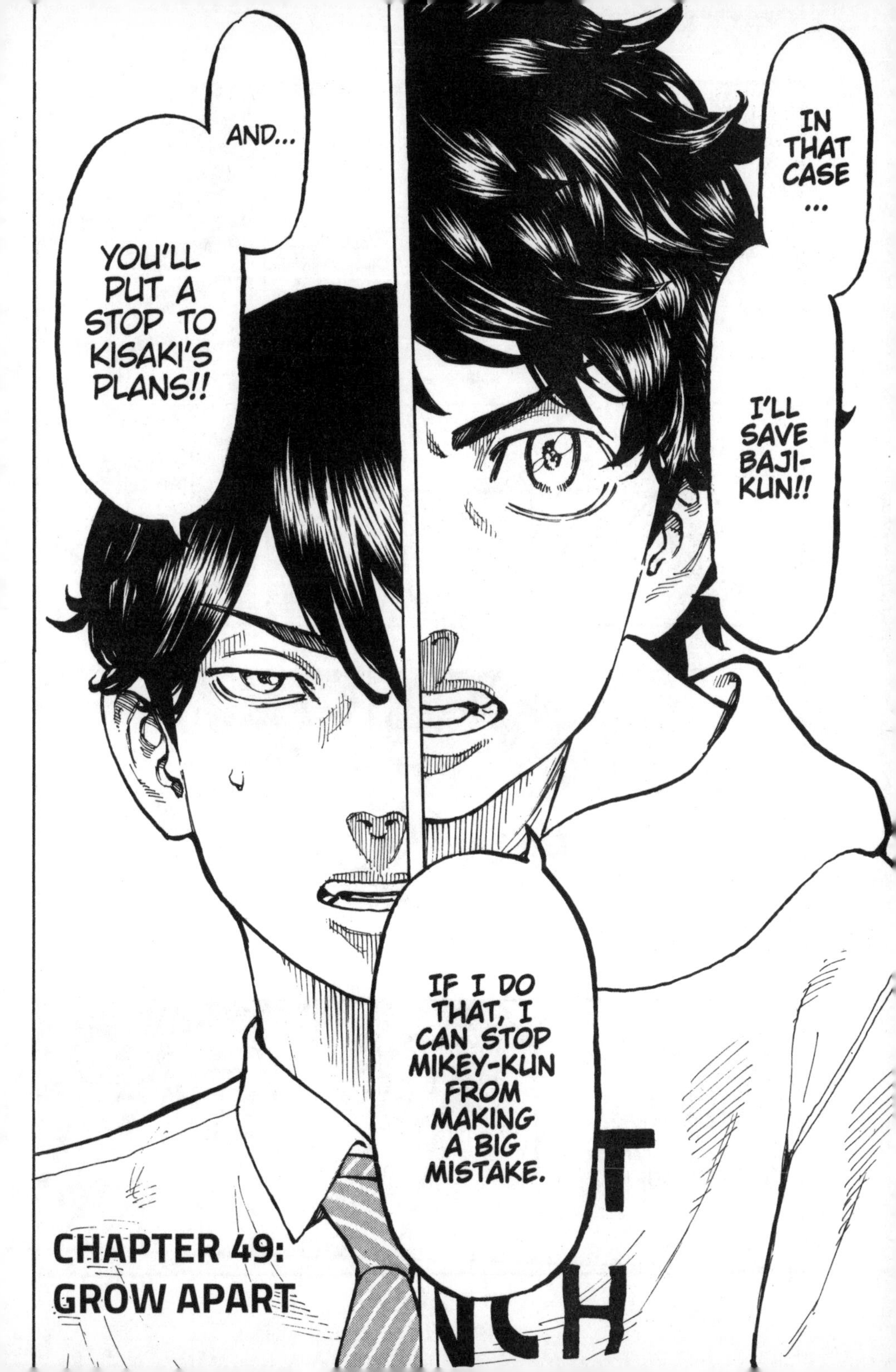
IN THAT CASE ...
I'LL SAVE BAJI-KUN!!
IF I DO THAT, I CAN STOP MIKEY-KUN FROM MAKING A BIG MISTAKE.
AND...
YOU'LL PUT A STOP TO KISAKI'S PLANS!!

CHAPTER 49: GROW APART

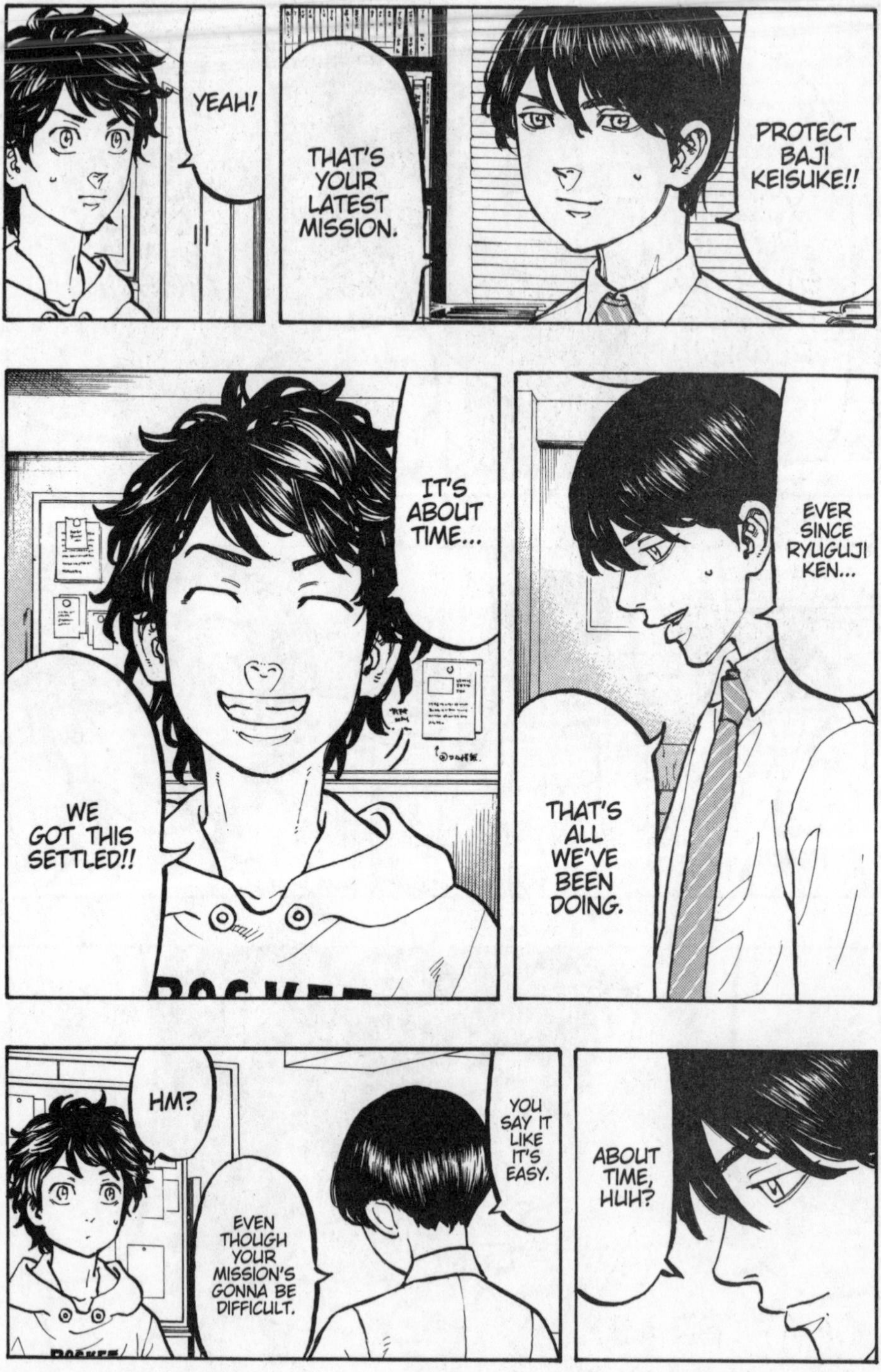
PROTECT BAJI KEISUKE!!
THAT'S YOUR LATEST MISSION.
YEAH!
EVER SINCE RYUGUJI KEN...
THAT'S ALL WE'VE BEEN DOING.
IT'S ABOUT TIME...
WE GOT THIS SETTLED!!
ABOUT TIME, HUH?
YOU SAY IT LIKE IT'S EASY.
HM?
EVEN THOUGH YOUR MISSION'S GONNA BE DIFFICULT.

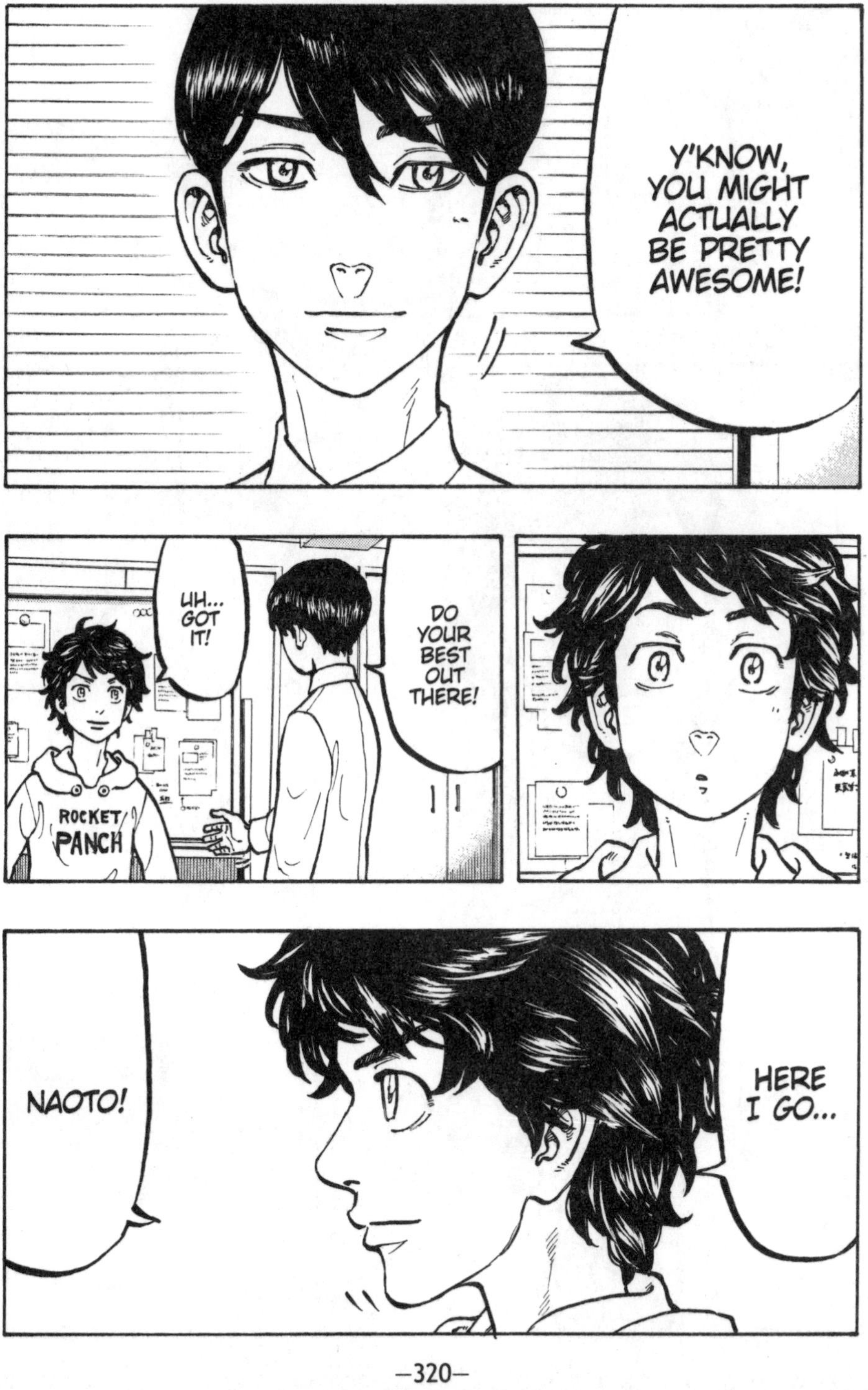
Y'KNOW, YOU MIGHT ACTUALLY BE PRETTY AWESOME!
DO YOUR BEST OUT THERE!
UH... GOT IT!
ROCKET PANCH
HERE I GO...
NAOTO!

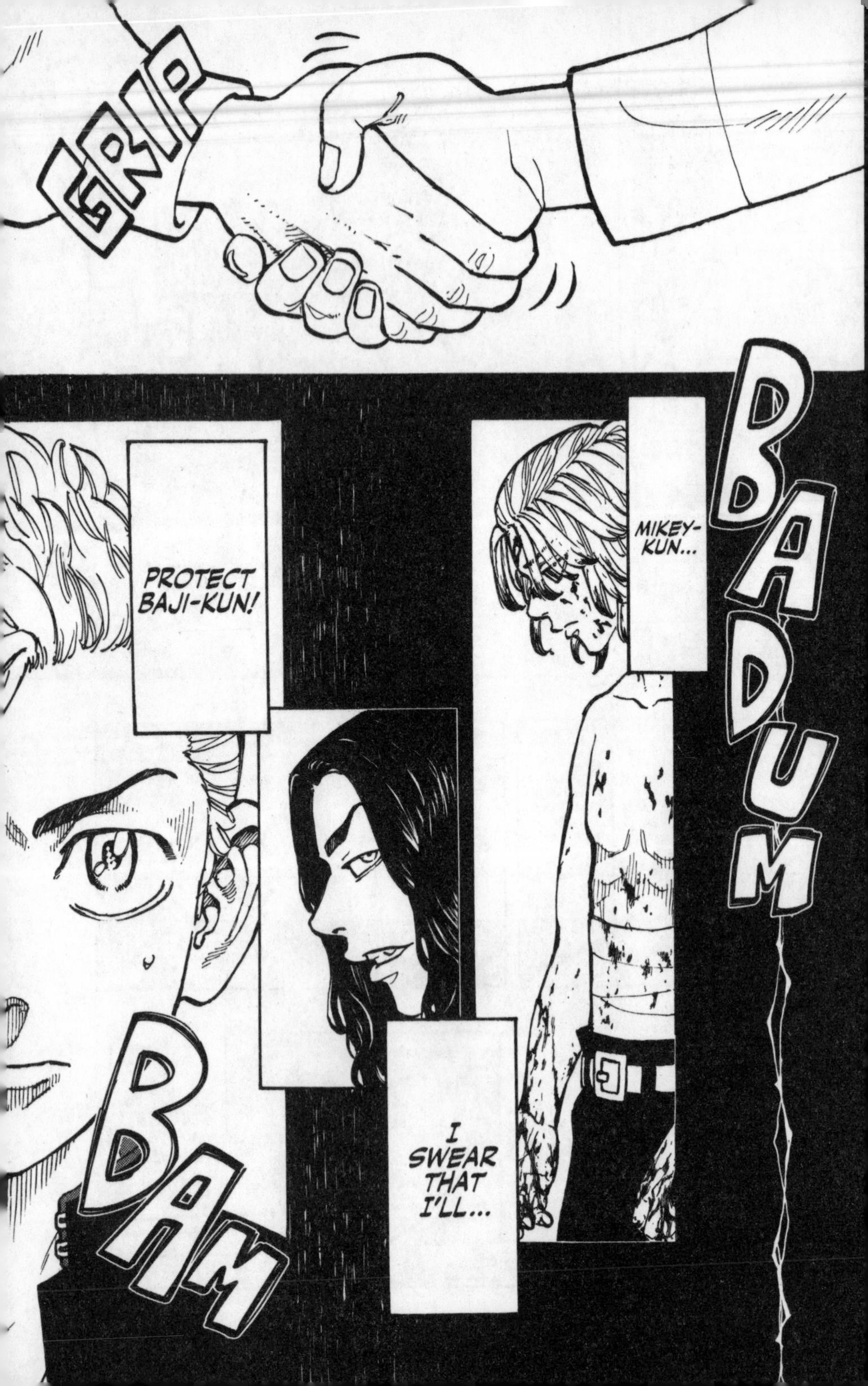
GRIP
BADUM
MIKEY-KUN...
I SWEAR THAT I'LL...
PROTECT BAJI-KUN!
BAM

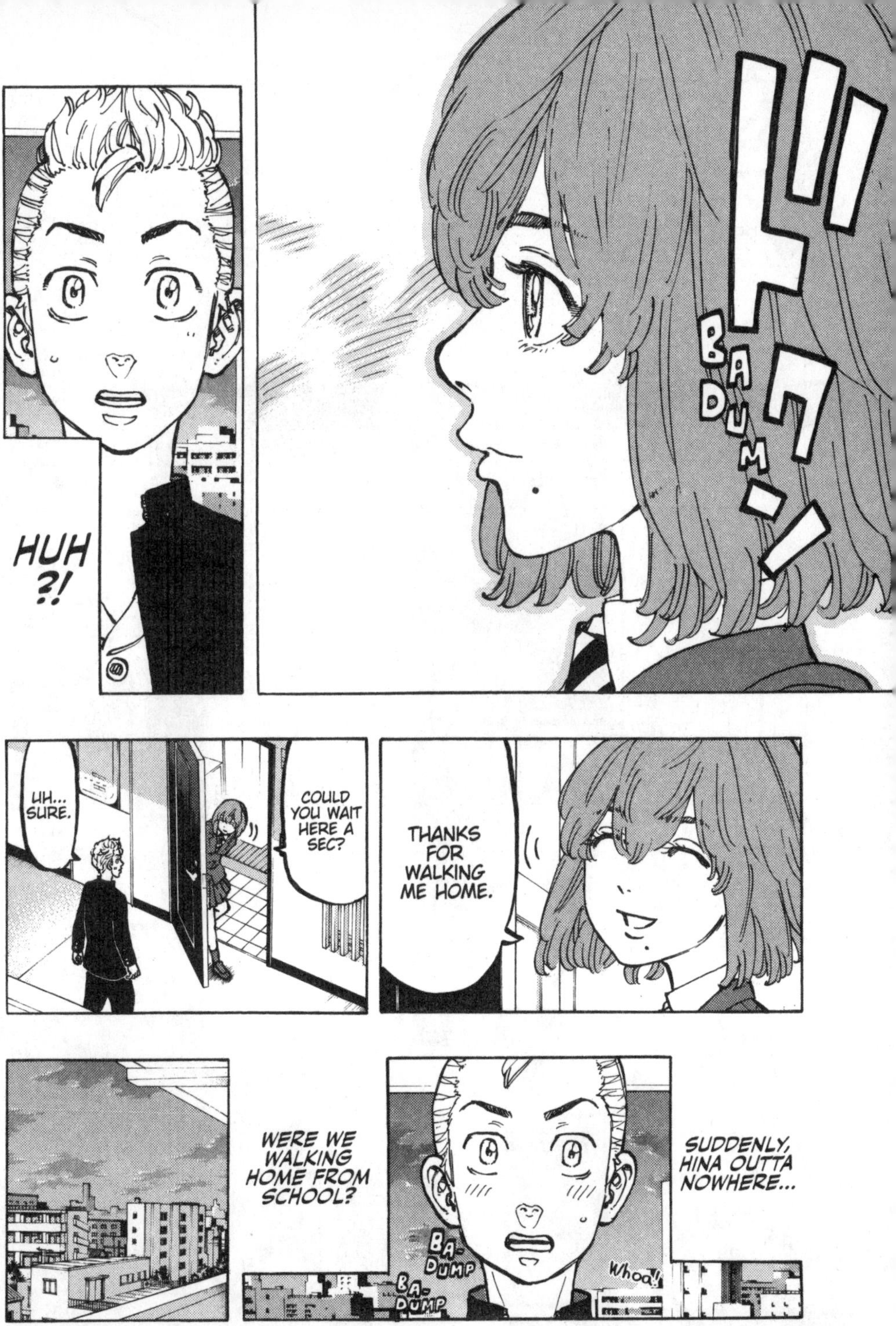
BADUM!
HUH ?!
THANKS FOR WALKING ME HOME.
COULD YOU WAIT HERE A SEC?
UH... SURE.
SUDDENLY, HINA OUTTA NOWHERE...
Whoa!!
BA-DUMP
BA-DUMP
WERE WE WALKING HOME FROM SCHOOL?

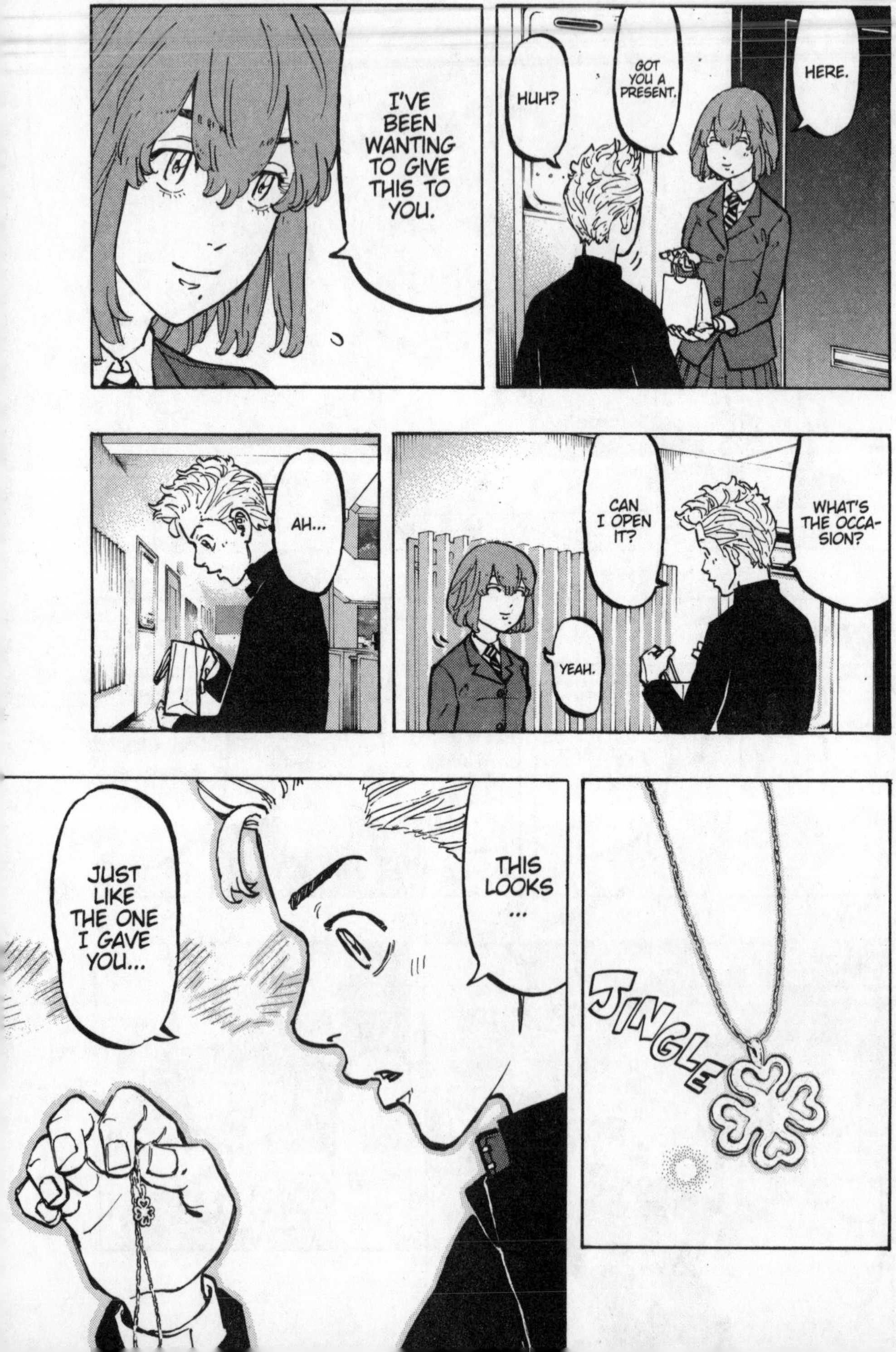
HERE.
GOT YOU A PRESENT.
HUH?
I'VE BEEN WANTING TO GIVE THIS TO YOU.
WHAT'S THE OCCA-SION?
CAN I OPEN IT?
YEAH.
AH...
JINGLE
THIS LOOKS ...
JUST LIKE THE ONE I GAVE YOU...

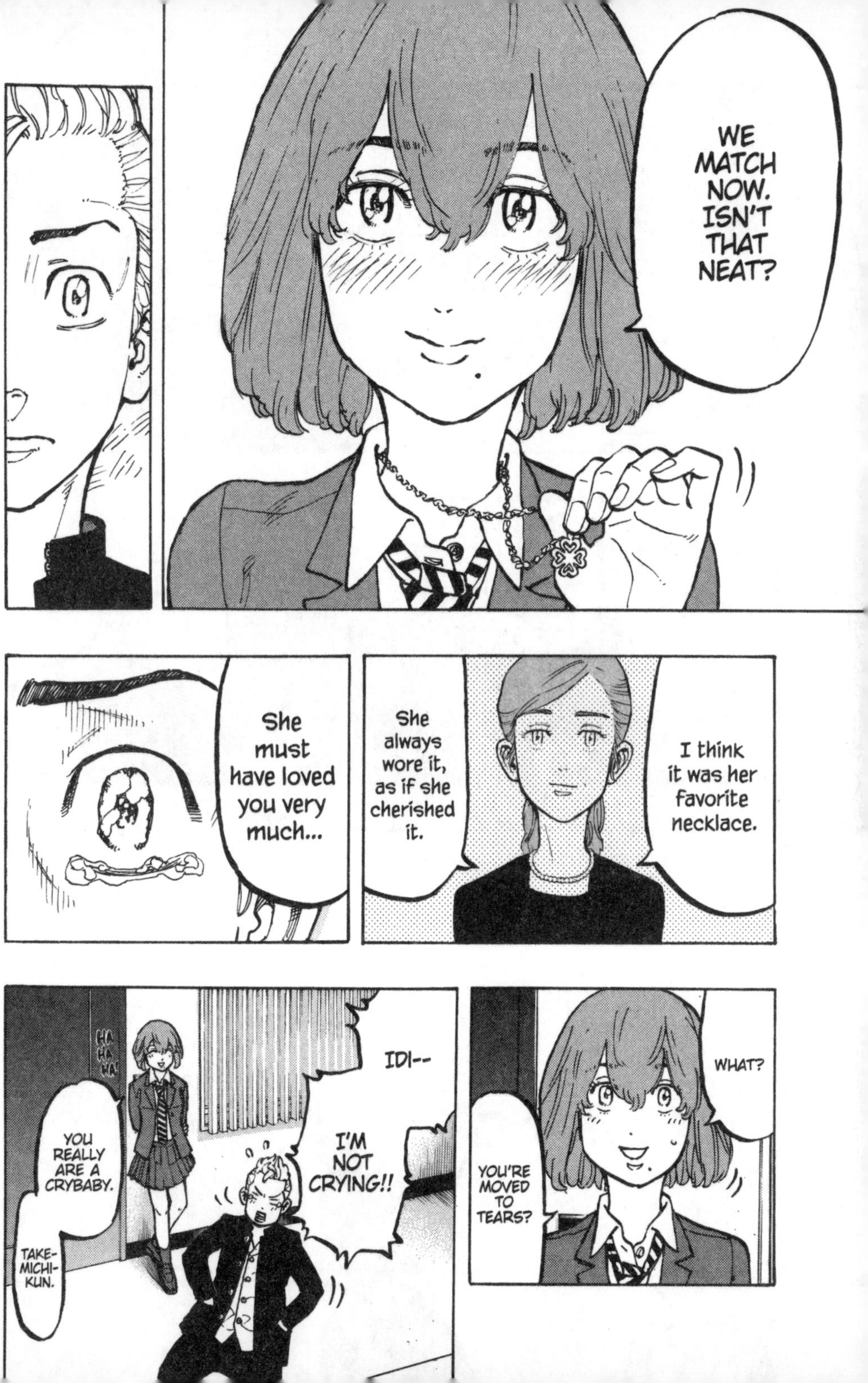
WE MATCH NOW. ISN'T THAT NEAT?
I think it was her favorite necklace.
She always wore it, as if she cherished it.
She must have loved you very much...
WHAT?
YOU'RE MOVED TO TEARS?
IDI--
I'M NOT CRYING!!
HA HA HA!
YOU REALLY ARE A CRYBABY.
TAKE-MICHI-KUN.

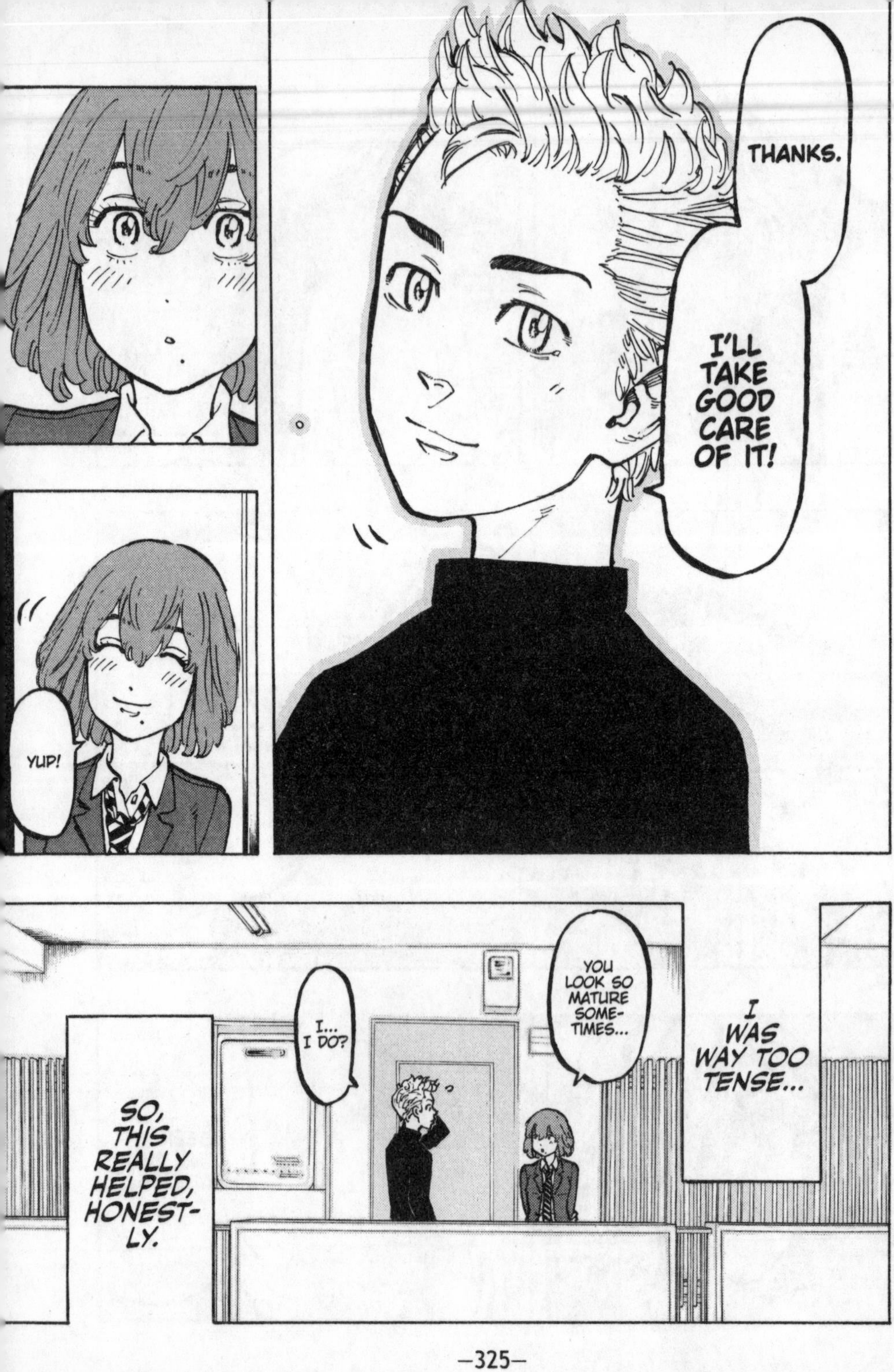
THANKS.
I'LL TAKE GOOD CARE OF IT!
YUP!
I WAS WAY TOO TENSE...
YOU LOOK SO MATURE SOME-TIMES...
I... I DO?
SO, THIS REALLY HELPED, HONEST-LY.

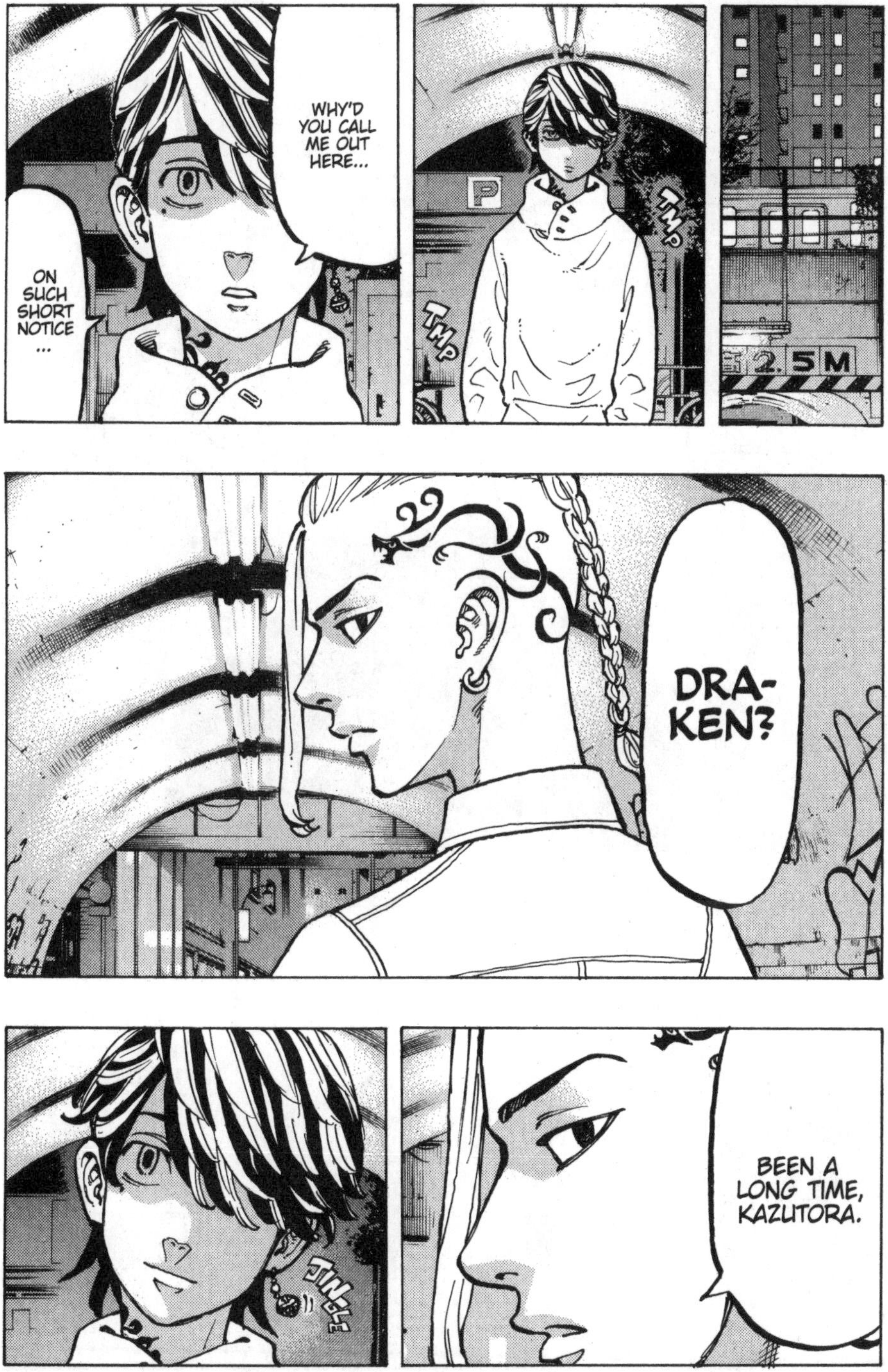
2.5M
TMP
TMP
WHY'D YOU CALL ME OUT HERE...
ON SUCH SHORT NOTICE ...
DRA-KEN?
BEEN A LONG TIME, KAZUTORA.
JINGLE

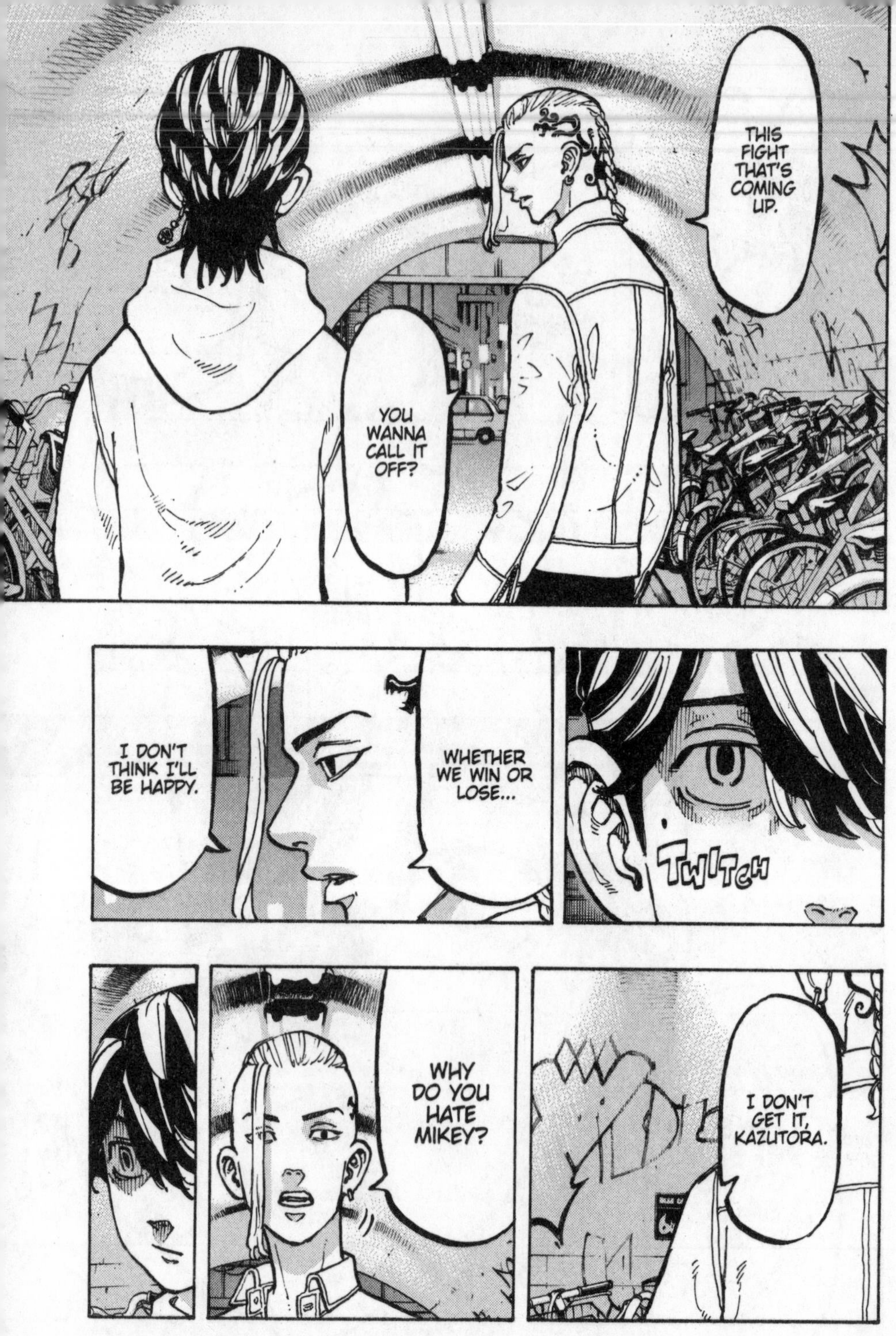

THIS FIGHT THAT'S COMING UP.
YOU WANNA CALL IT OFF?
TWITCH
WHETHER WE WIN OR LOSE...
I DON'T THINK I'LL BE HAPPY.
I DON'T GET IT, KAZUTORA.
WHY DO YOU HATE MIKEY?

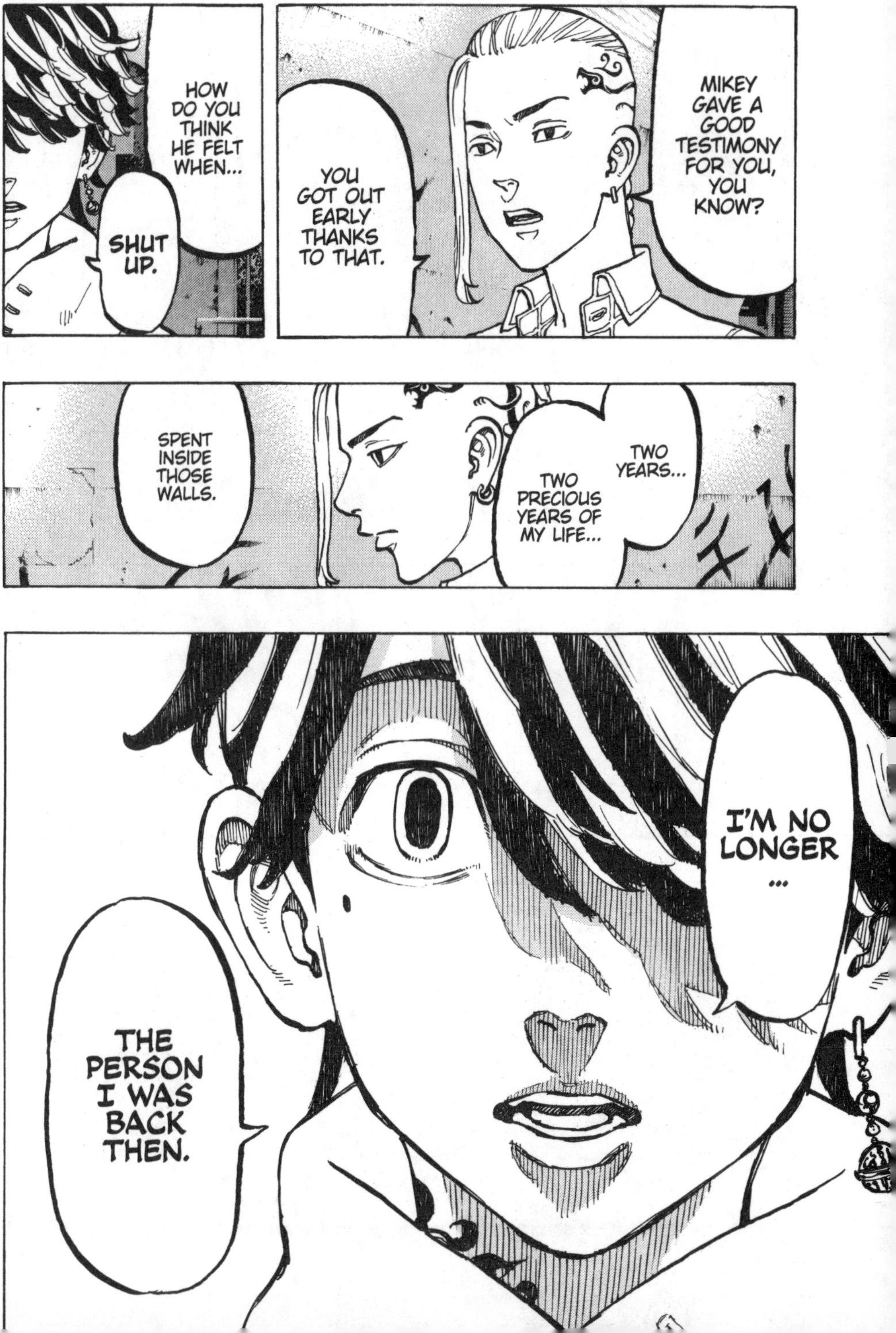
MIKEY GAVE A GOOD TESTIMONY FOR YOU, YOU KNOW?
YOU GOT OUT EARLY THANKS TO THAT.
HOW DO YOU THINK HE FELT WHEN...
SHUT UP.
TWO YEARS...
TWO PRECIOUS YEARS OF MY LIFE...
SPENT INSIDE THOSE WALLS.
I'M NO LONGER ...
THE PERSON I WAS BACK THEN.

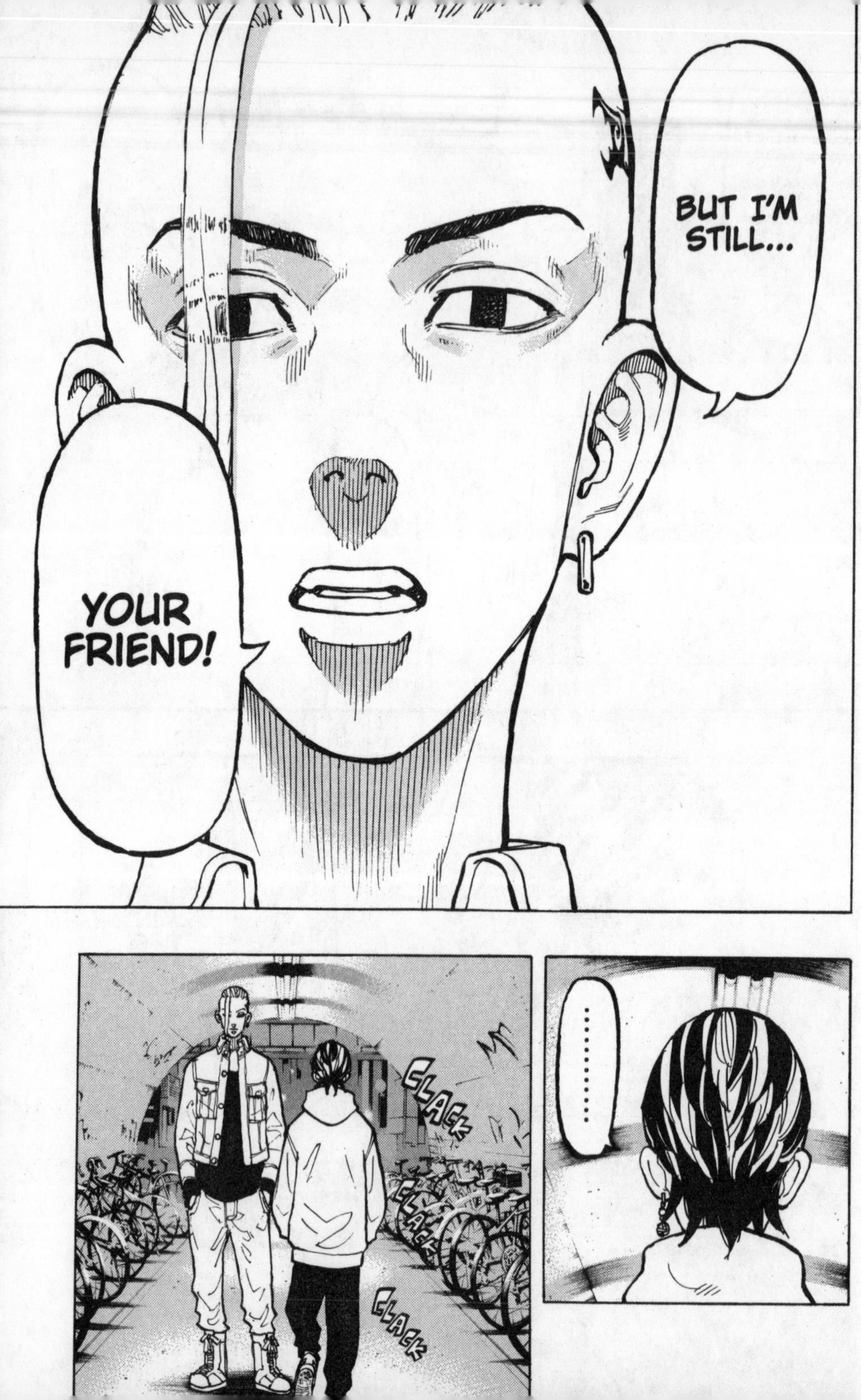
BUT I'M STILL...
YOUR FRIEND!
......
CLACK
CLACK
CLACK

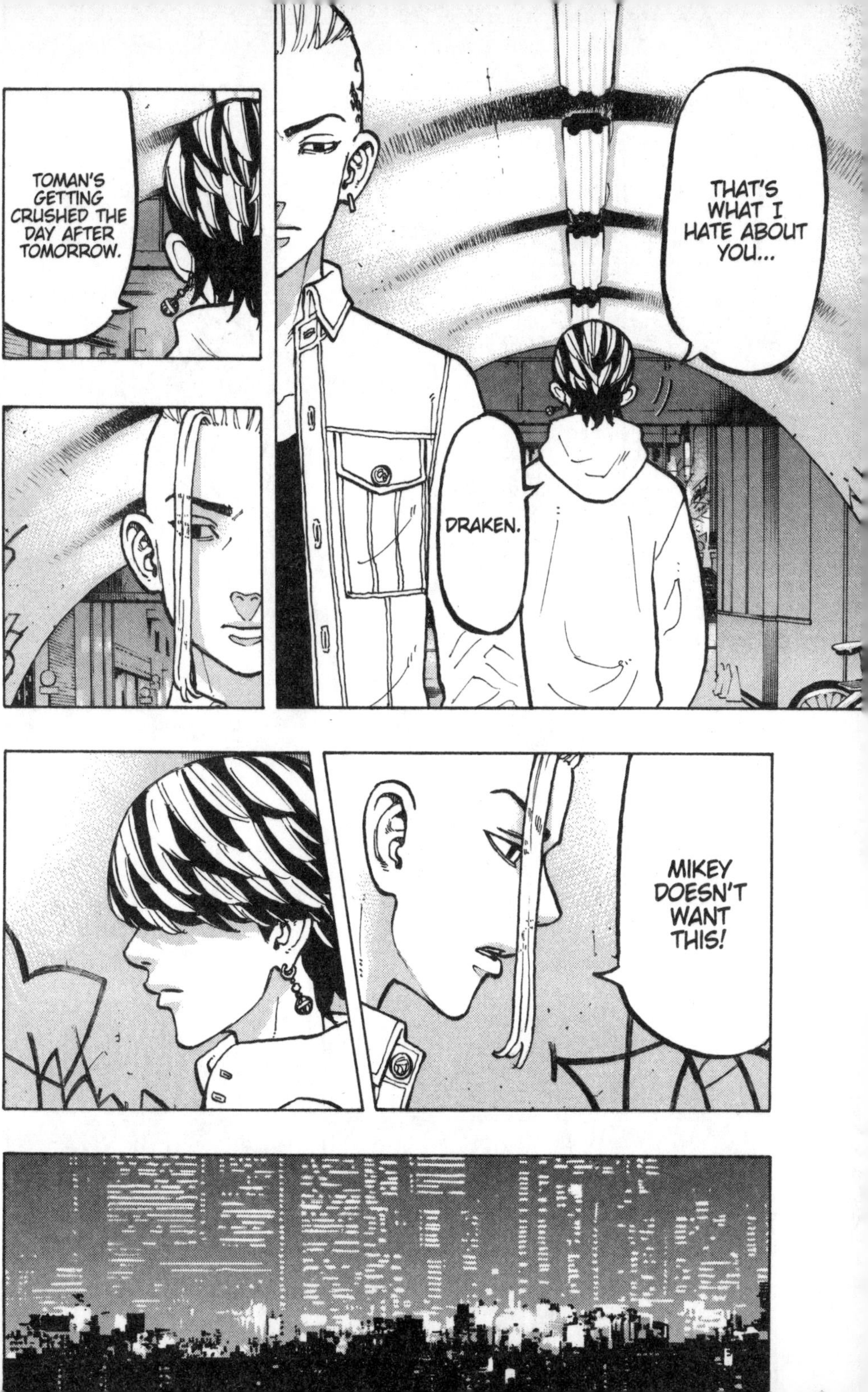
THAT'S WHAT I HATE ABOUT YOU...
DRAKEN.
TOMAN'S GETTING CRUSHED THE DAY AFTER TOMORROW.
MIKEY DOESN'T WANT THIS!

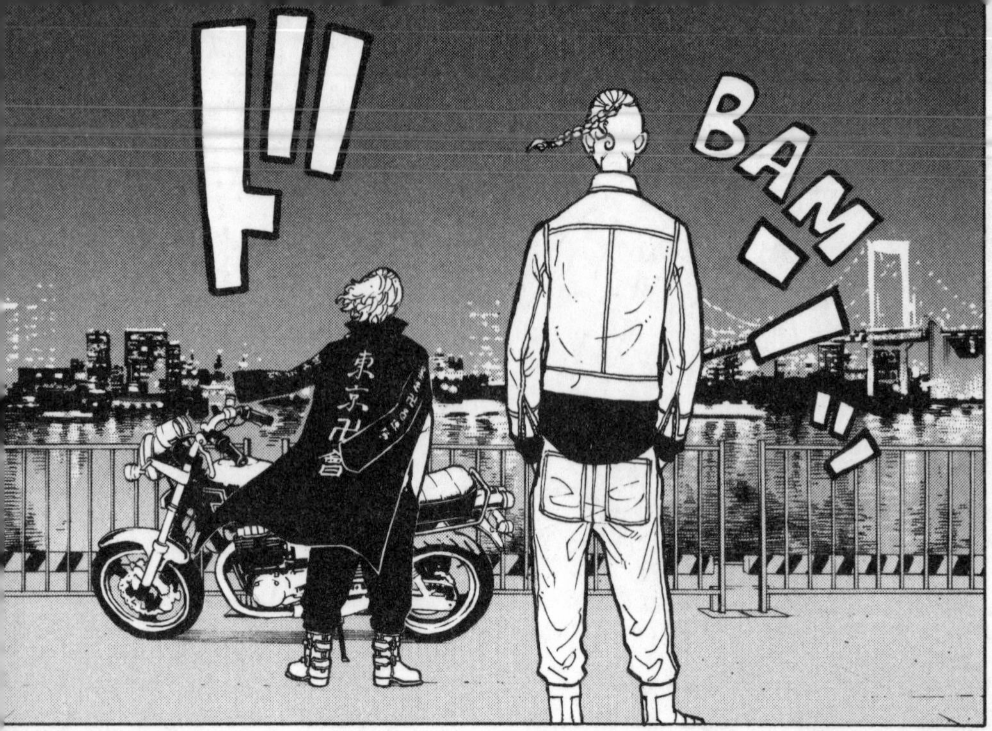
BAM
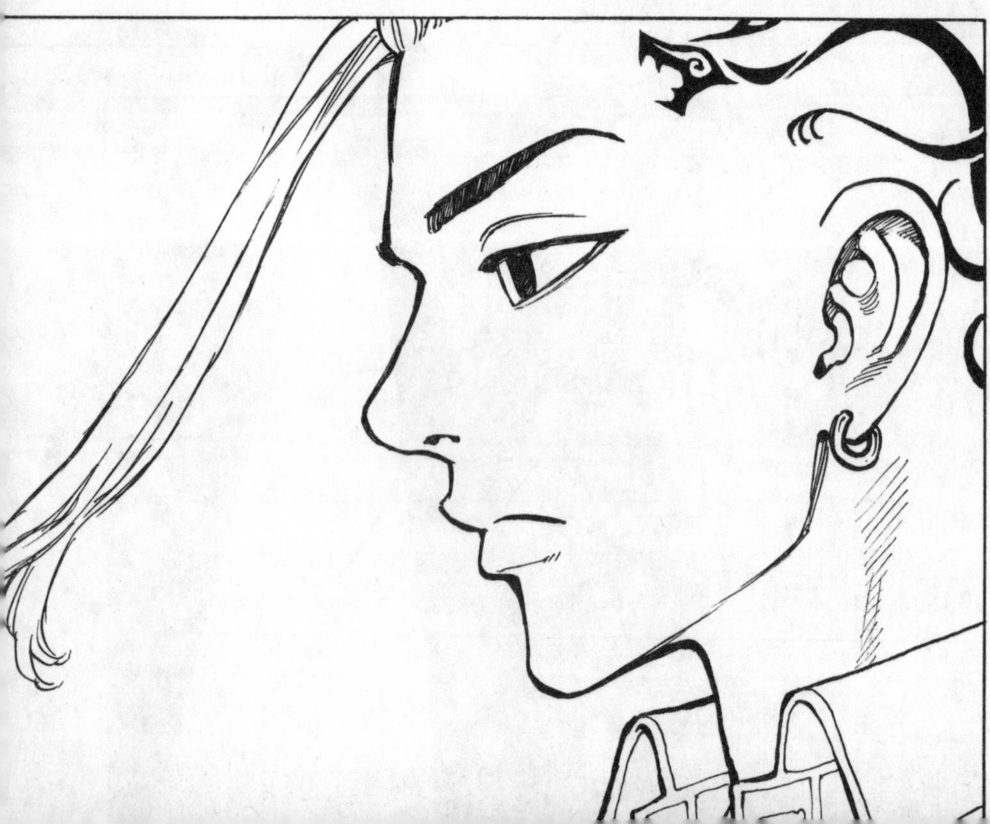

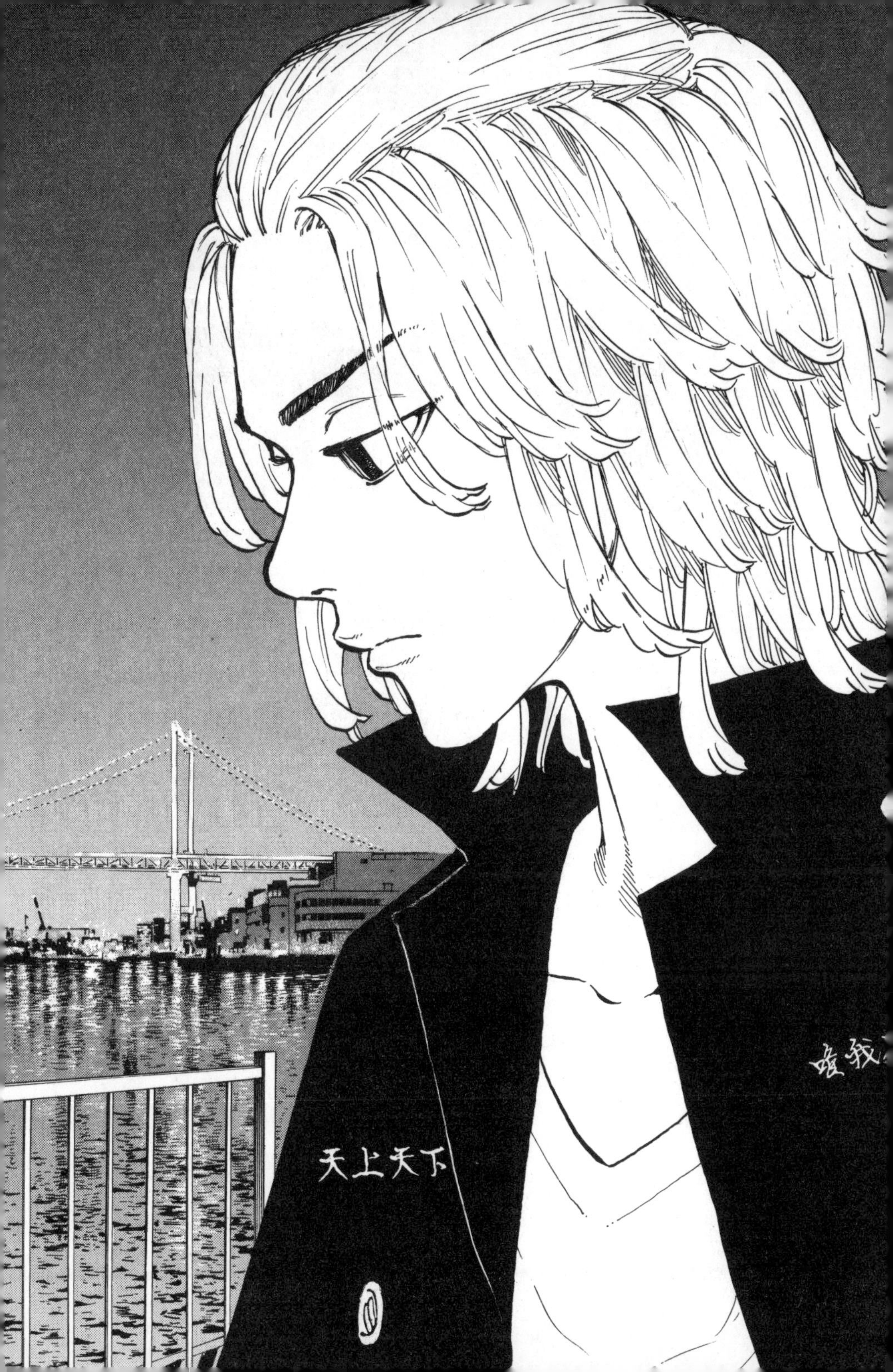
天上天下
唯我

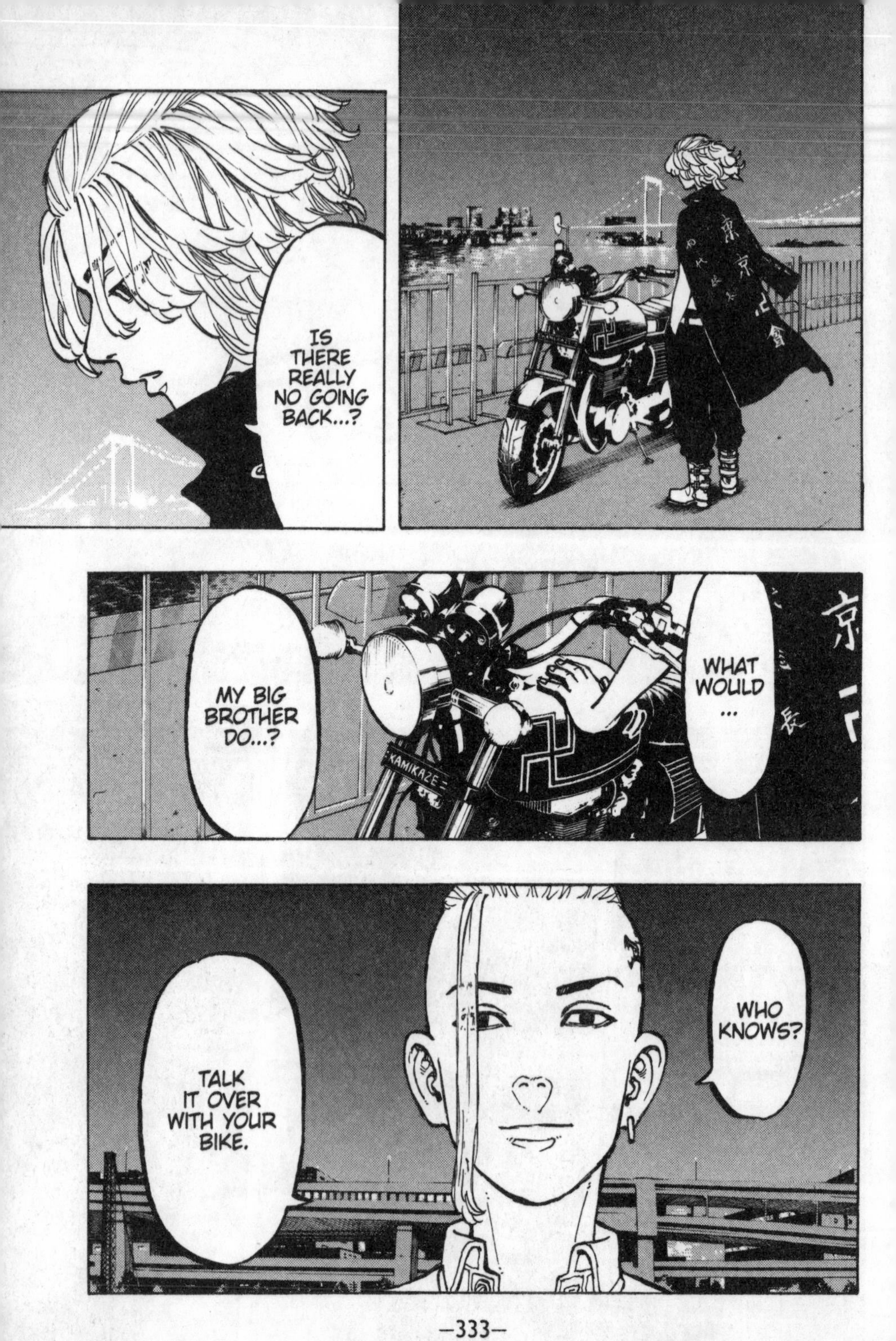
IS THERE REALLY NO GOING BACK...?
WHAT WOULD ...
MY BIG BROTHER DO...?
KAMIKAZE
WHO KNOWS?
TALK IT OVER WITH YOUR BIKE.

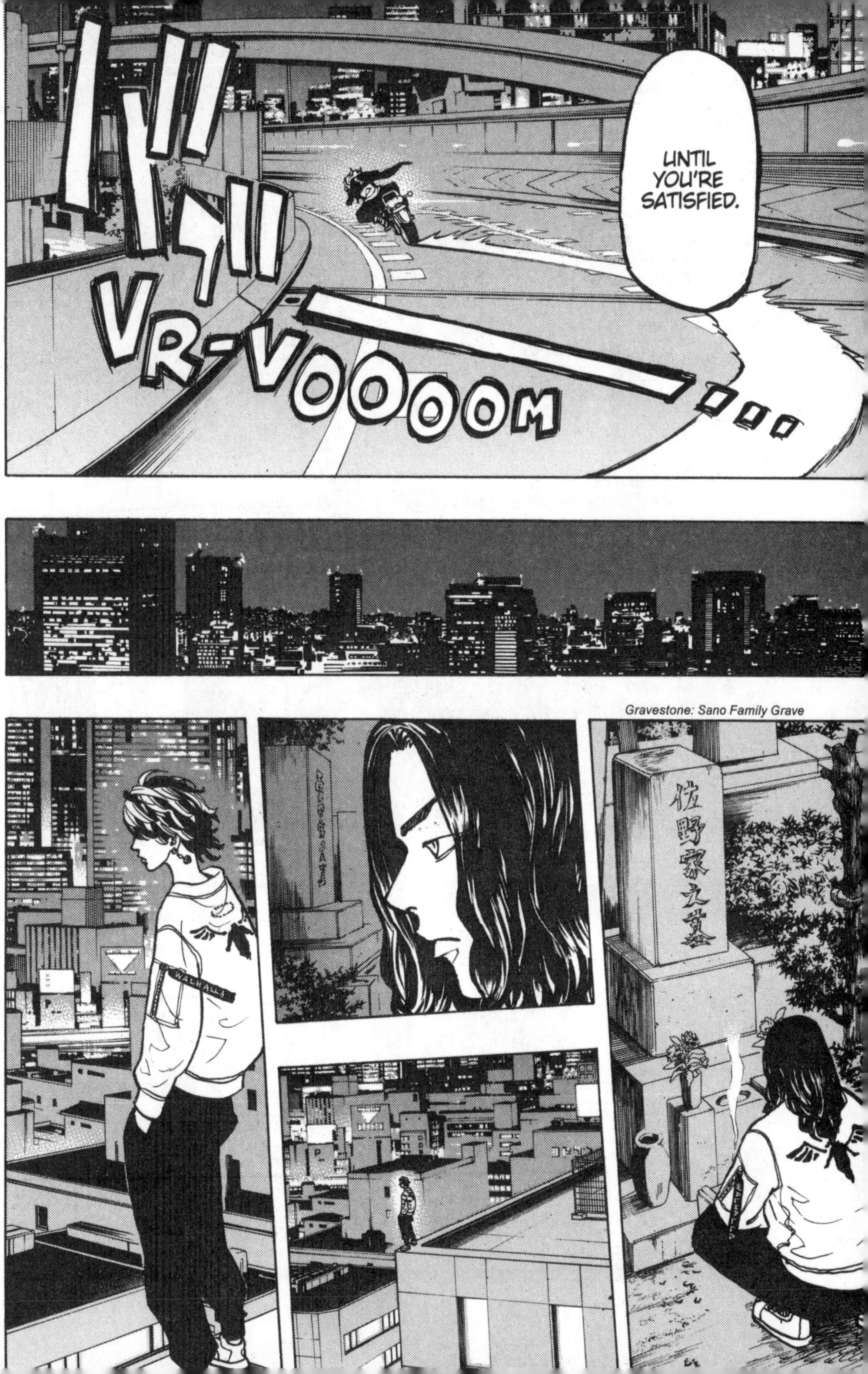

UNTIL YOU'RE SATISFIED.
VR-VOOOOM...
Gravestone: Sano Family Grave
佐野家之墓
WALHALLA

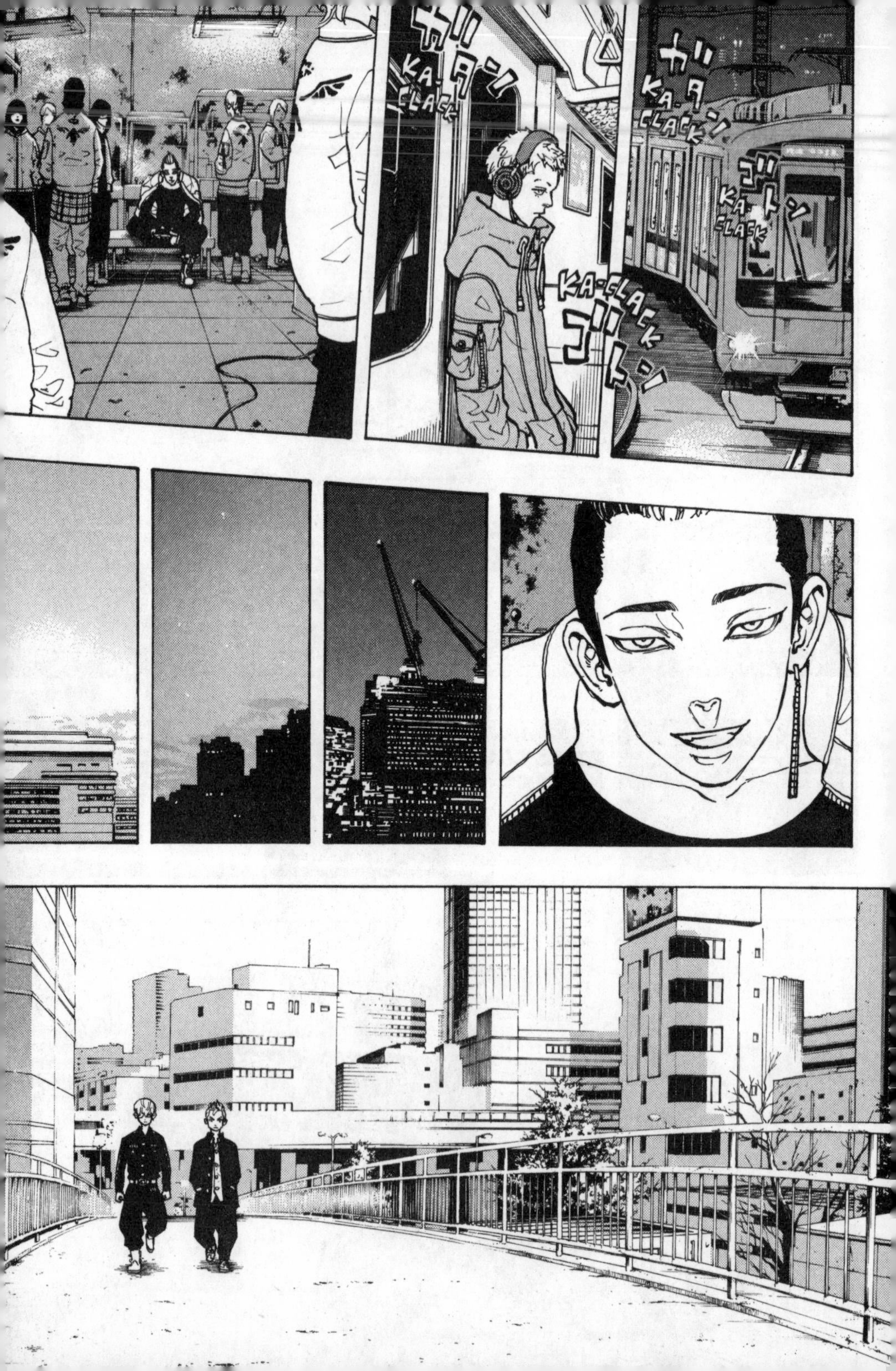

ガタ-ン!
KA-CLACK!
ゴトン
KA-CLACK
KA-CLACK
ゴトン!
ガタ-ン
KA-CLACK

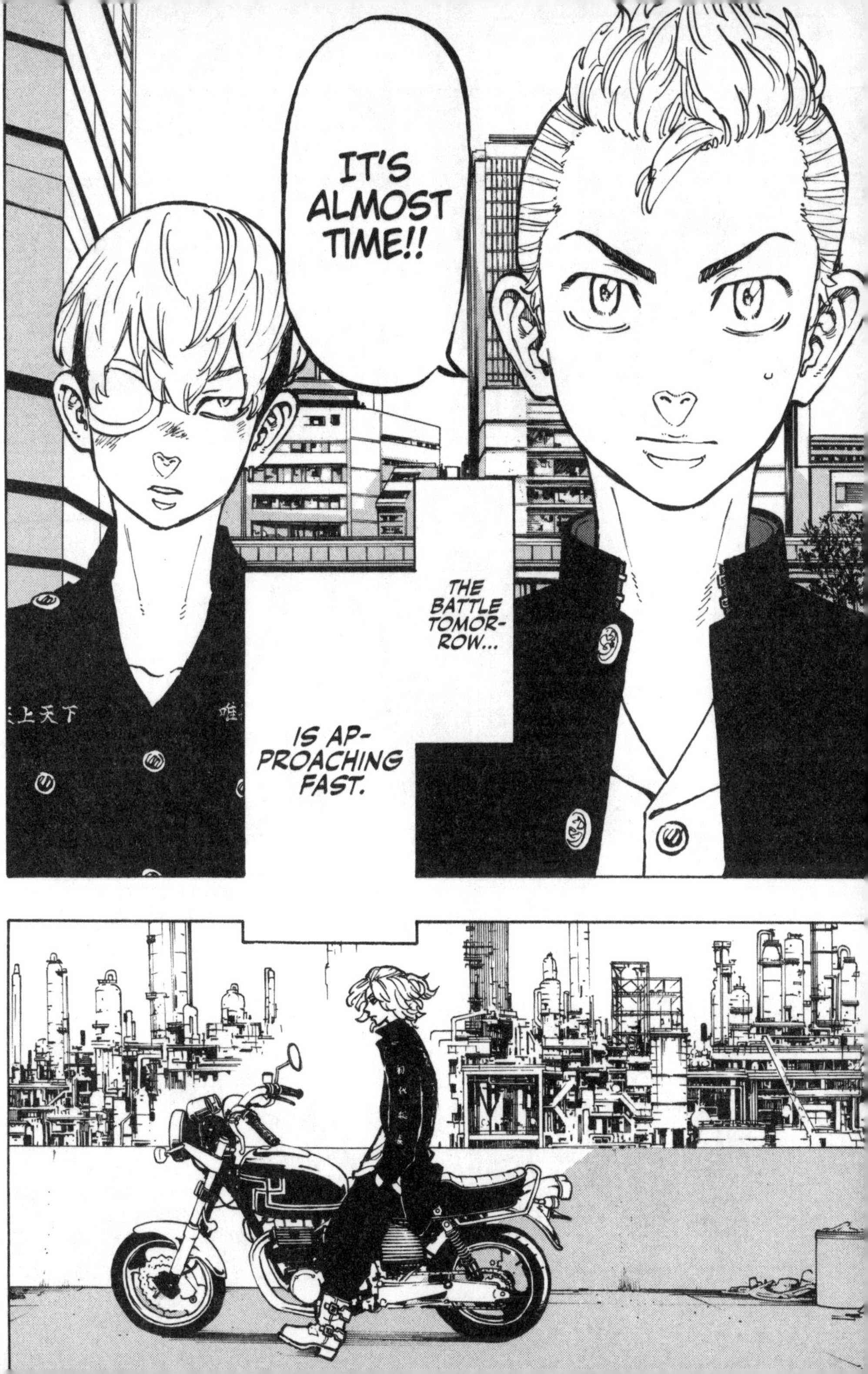
IT'S ALMOST TIME!!
THE BATTLE TOMORROW...
IS APPROACHING FAST.

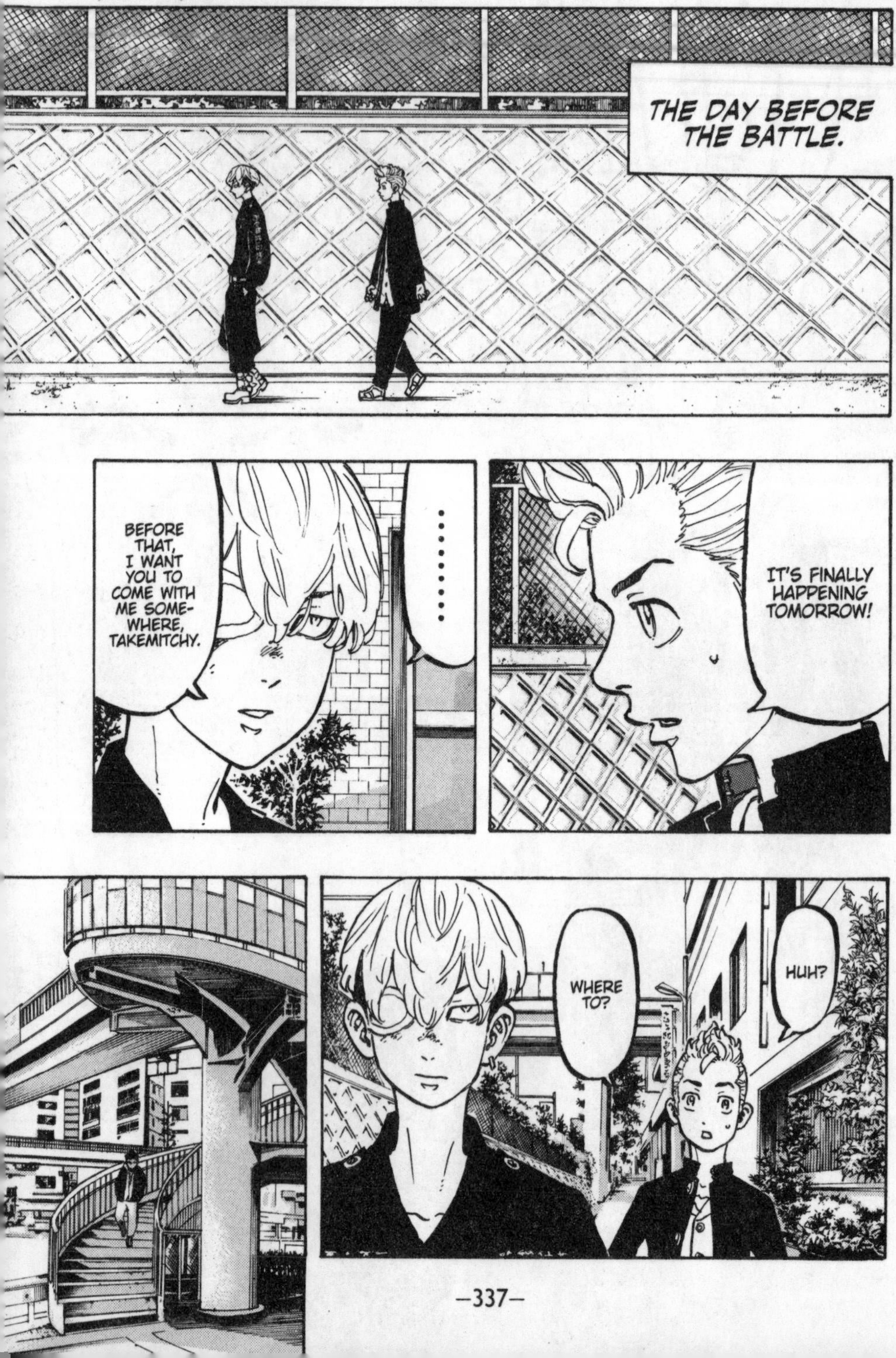
THE DAY BEFORE THE BATTLE.
IT'S FINALLY HAPPENING TOMORROW!
....
BEFORE THAT, I WANT YOU TO COME WITH ME SOME-WHERE, TAKEMITCHY.
HUH?
WHERE TO?

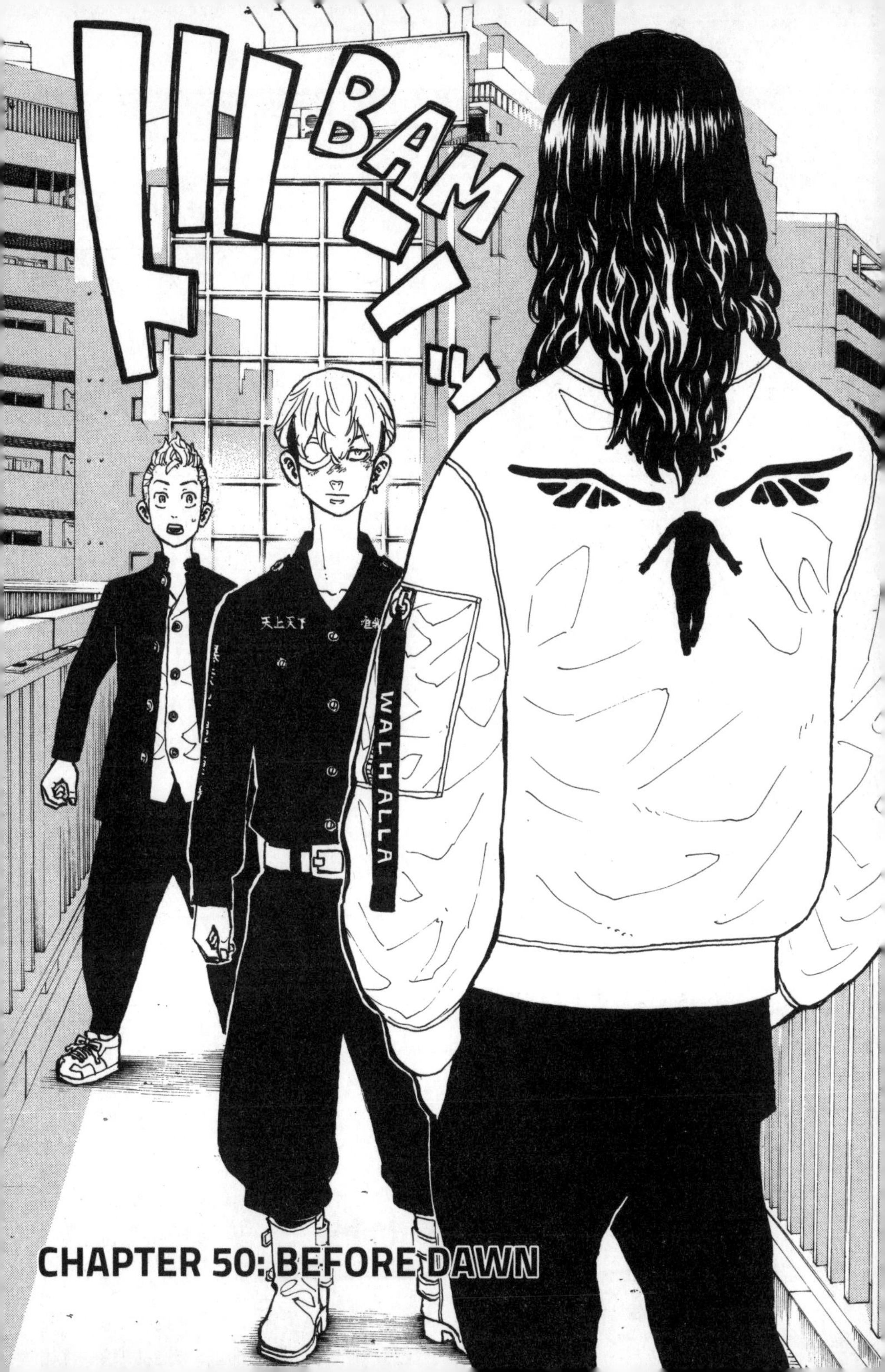
BAM
天上天下
WALHALLA

CHAPTER 50: BEFORE DAWN

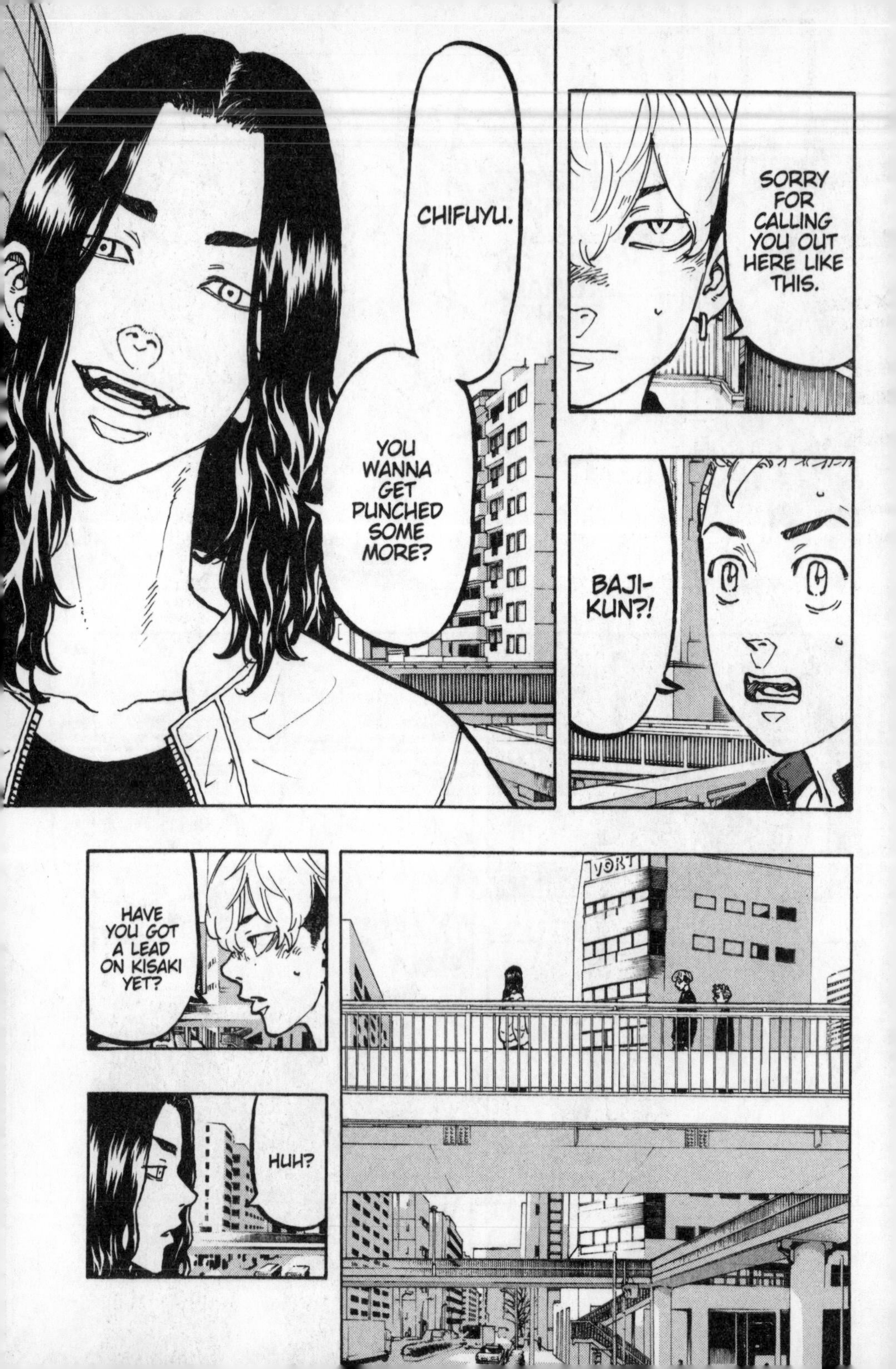
SORRY FOR CALLING YOU OUT HERE LIKE THIS.
BAJI-KUN?!
CHIFUYU.
YOU WANNA GET PUNCHED SOME MORE?
HAVE YOU GOT A LEAD ON KISAKI YET?
HUH?

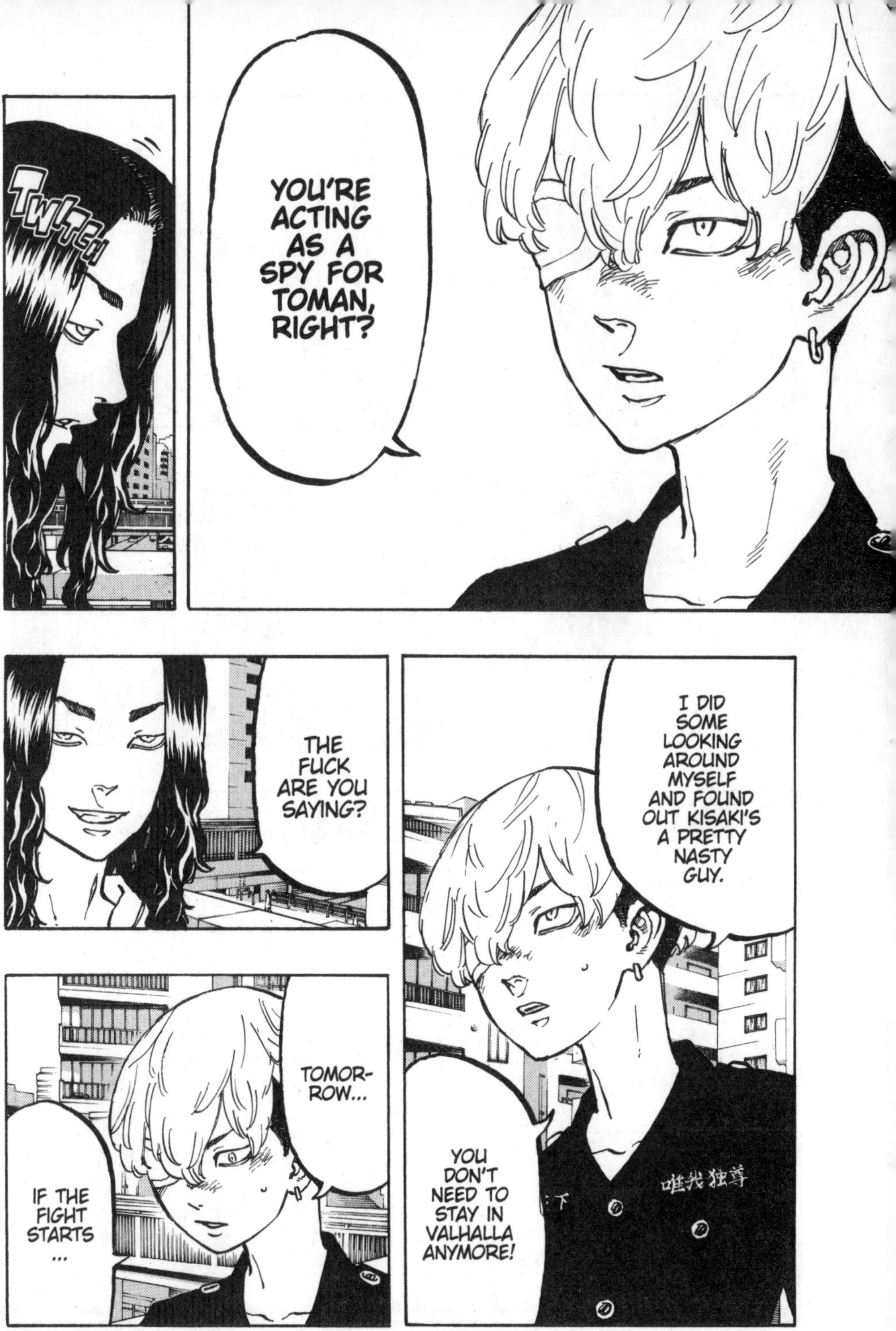
YOU'RE ACTING AS A SPY FOR TOMAN, RIGHT?
TWITCH
I DID SOME LOOKING AROUND MYSELF AND FOUND OUT KISAKI'S A PRETTY NASTY GUY.
YOU DON'T NEED TO STAY IN VALHALLA ANYMORE!
唯我独尊
THE FUCK ARE YOU SAYING?
TOMOR-ROW...
IF THE FIGHT STARTS ...

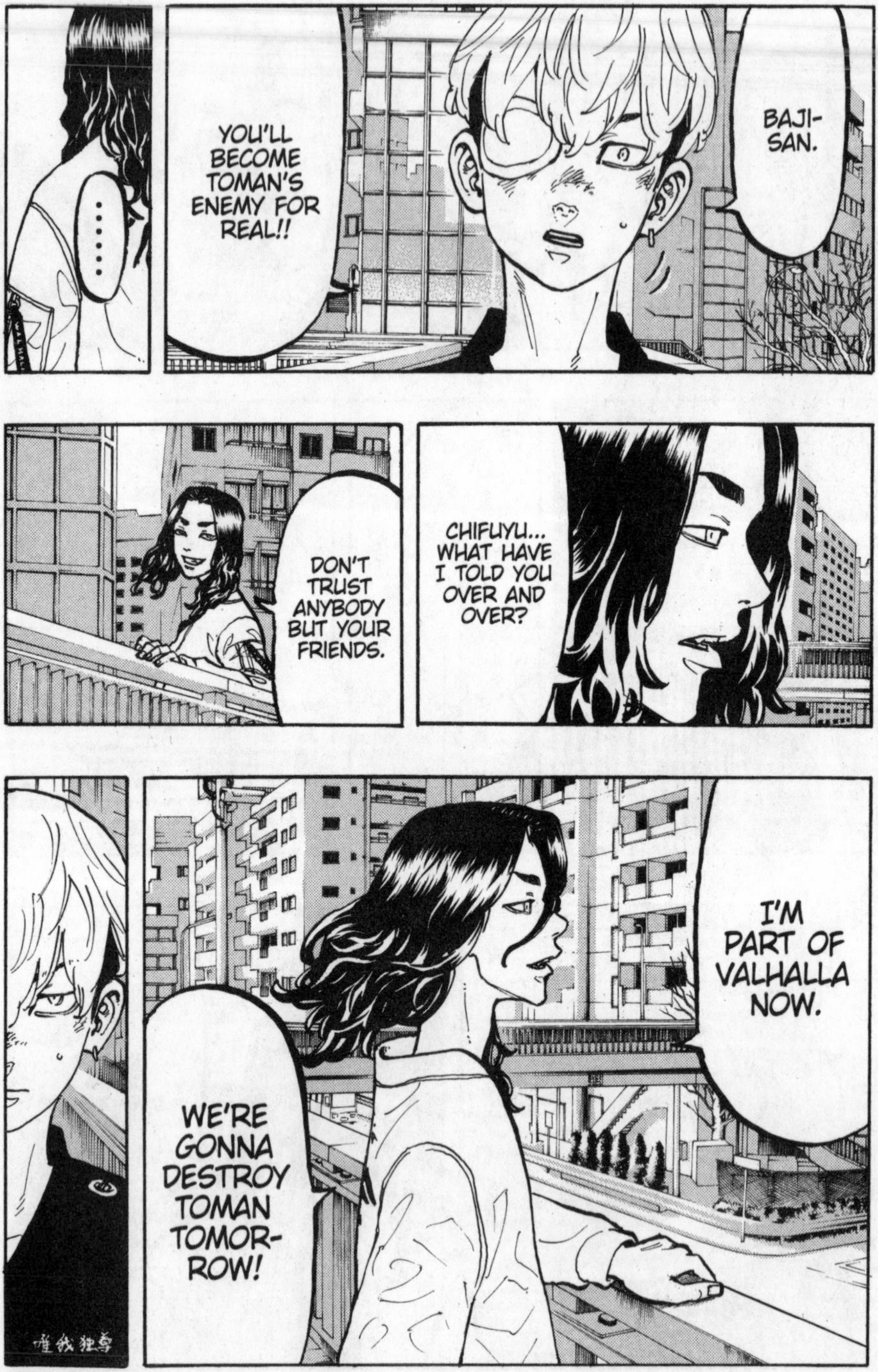
BAJI-SAN.
YOU'LL BECOME TOMAN'S ENEMY FOR REAL!!
......
CHIFUYU... WHAT HAVE I TOLD YOU OVER AND OVER?
DON'T TRUST ANYBODY BUT YOUR FRIENDS.
I'M PART OF VALHALLA NOW.
WE'RE GONNA DESTROY TOMAN TOMOR-ROW!
唯我独尊

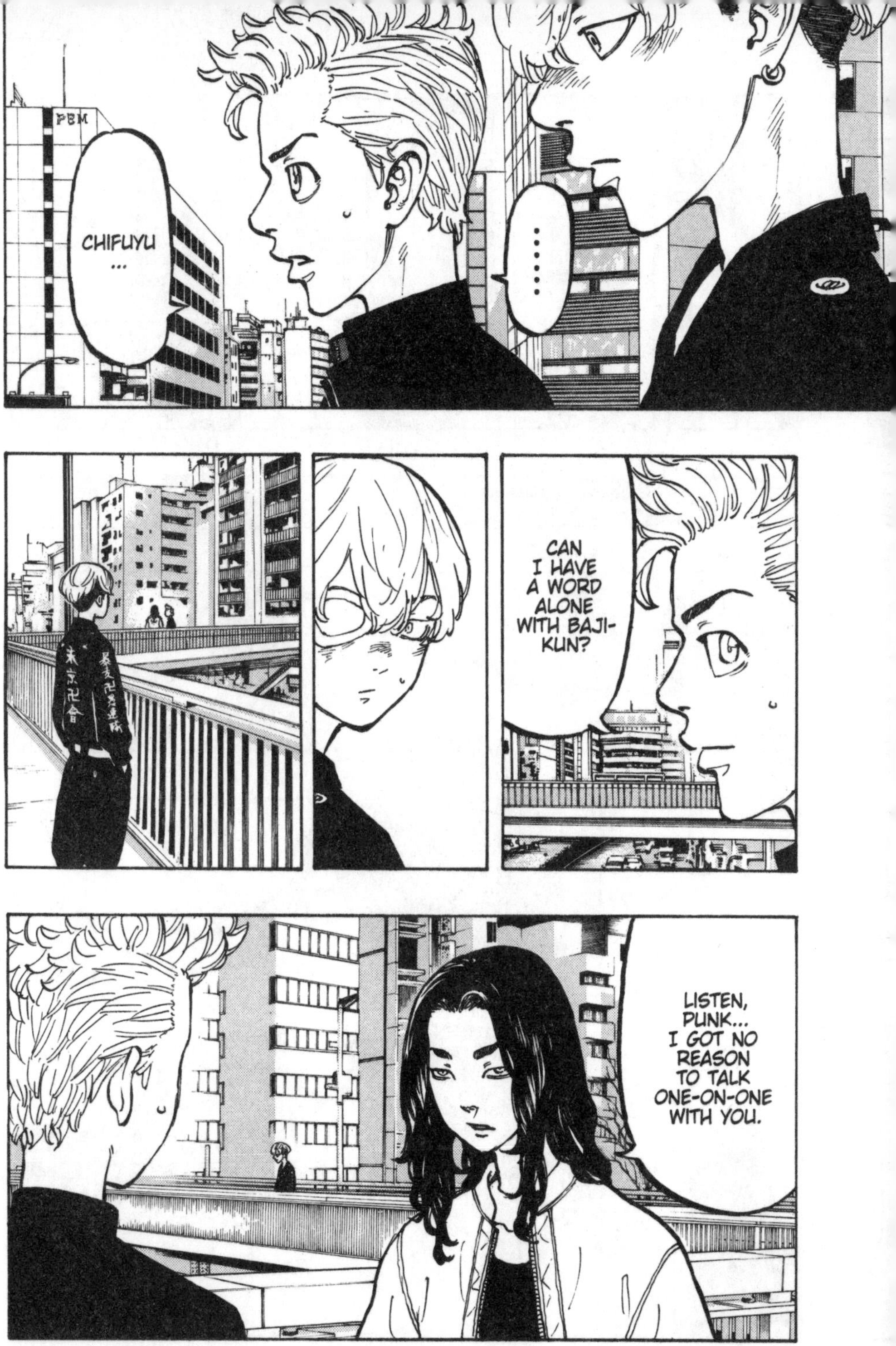
CHIFUYU ...
......
CAN I HAVE A WORD ALONE WITH BAJI-KUN?
LISTEN, PUNK... I GOT NO REASON TO TALK ONE-ON-ONE WITH YOU.

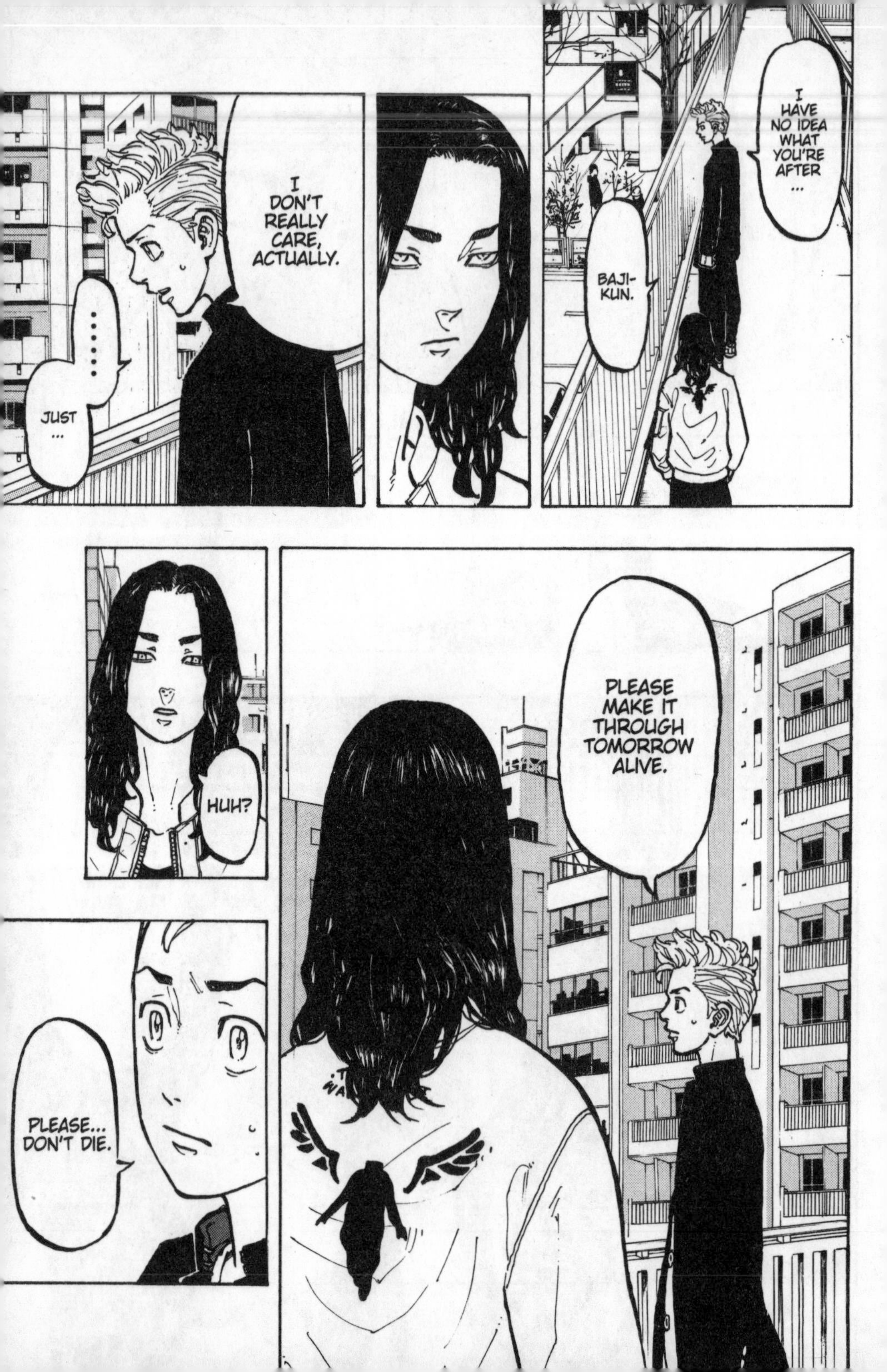
I HAVE NO IDEA WHAT YOU'RE AFTER ...
BAJI-KUN.
I DON'T REALLY CARE, ACTUALLY.
......
JUST ...
PLEASE MAKE IT THROUGH TOMORROW ALIVE.
HUH?
PLEASE... DON'T DIE.

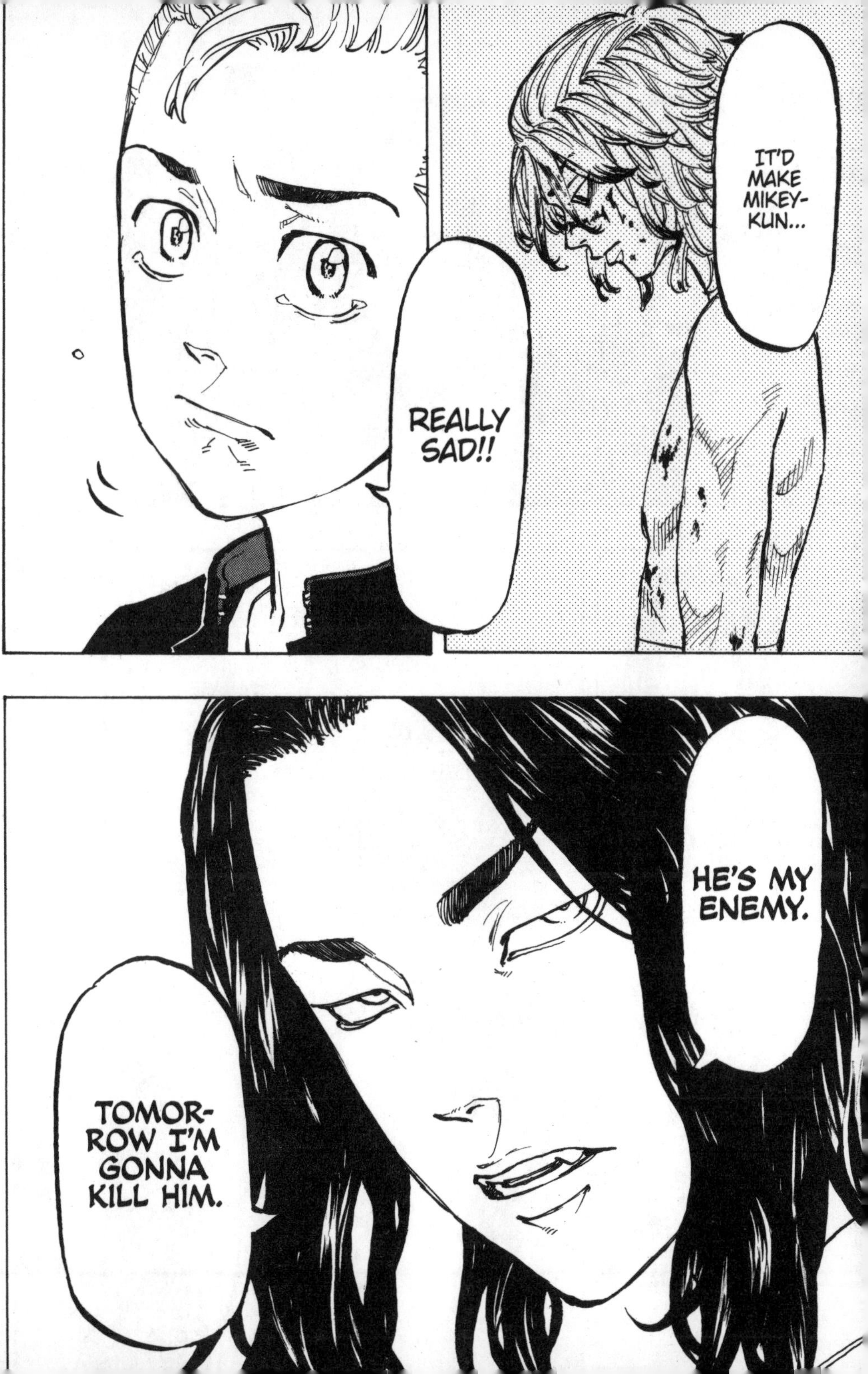
IT'D MAKE MIKEY-KUN...
REALLY SAD!!
HE'S MY ENEMY.
TOMOR-ROW I'M GONNA KILL HIM.

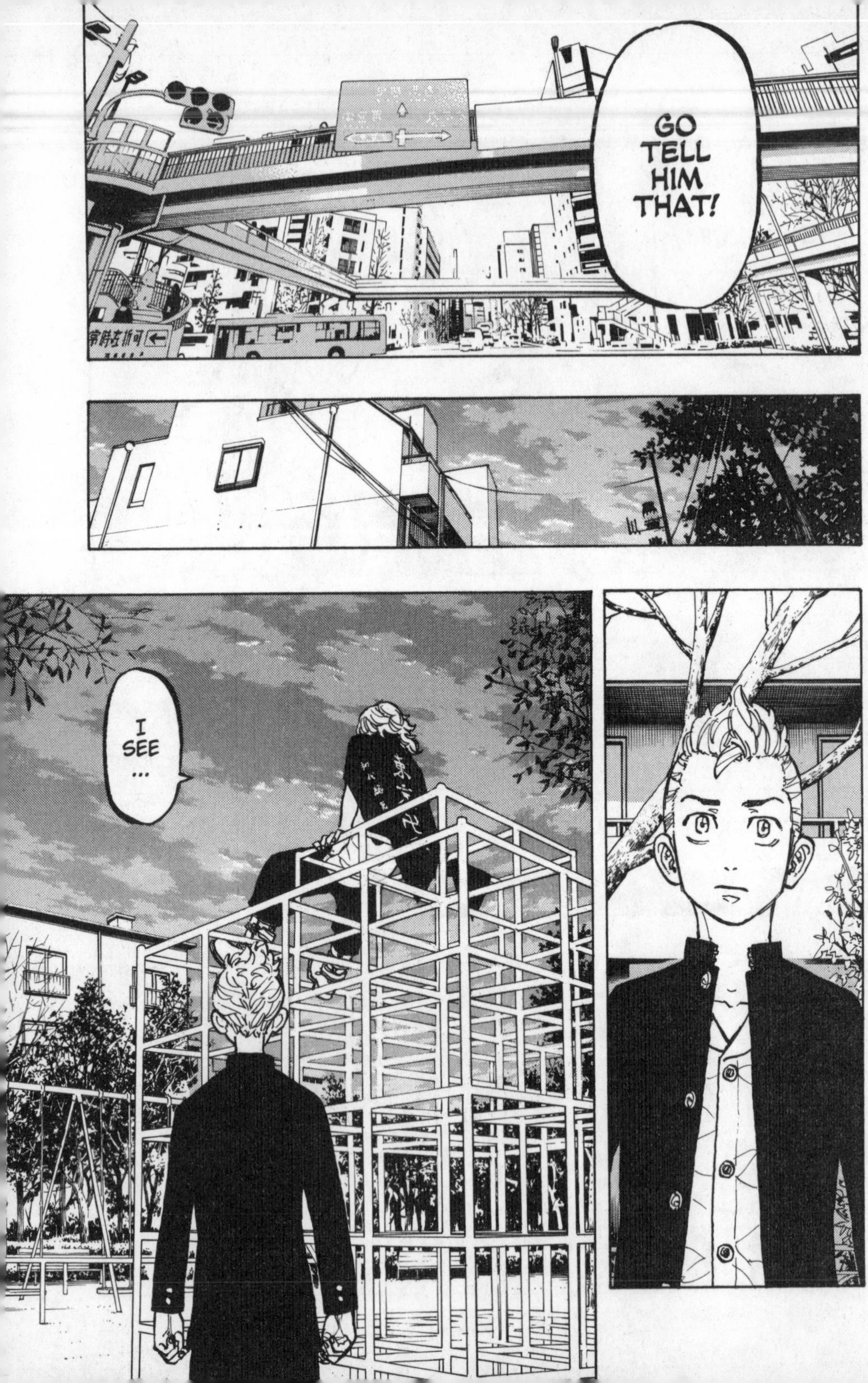
GO TELL HIM THAT!
I SEE ...

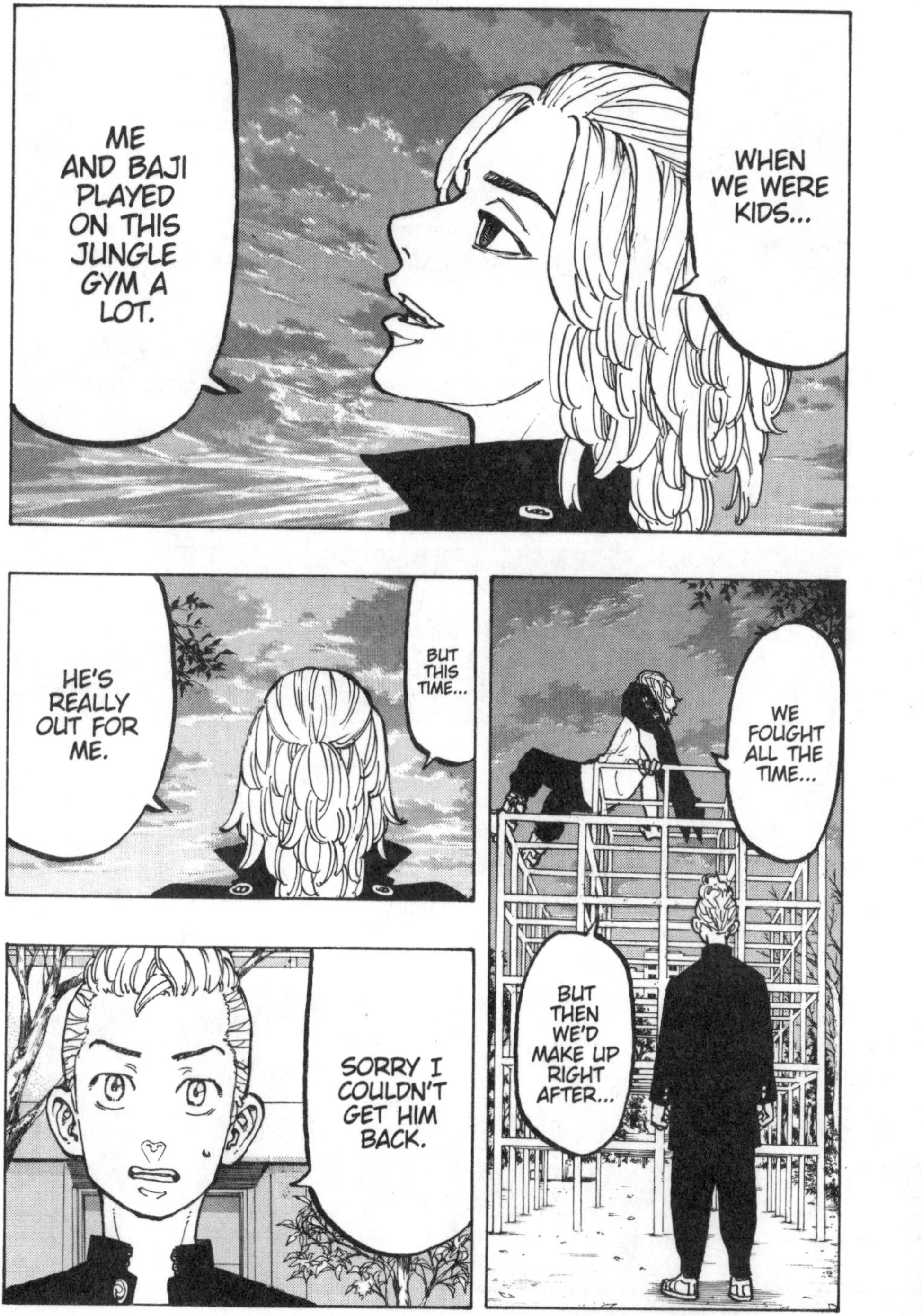
WHEN WE WERE KIDS...
ME AND BAJI PLAYED ON THIS JUNGLE GYM A LOT.
WE FOUGHT ALL THE TIME...
BUT THEN WE'D MAKE UP RIGHT AFTER...
BUT THIS TIME...
HE'S REALLY OUT FOR ME.
SORRY I COULDN'T GET HIM BACK.

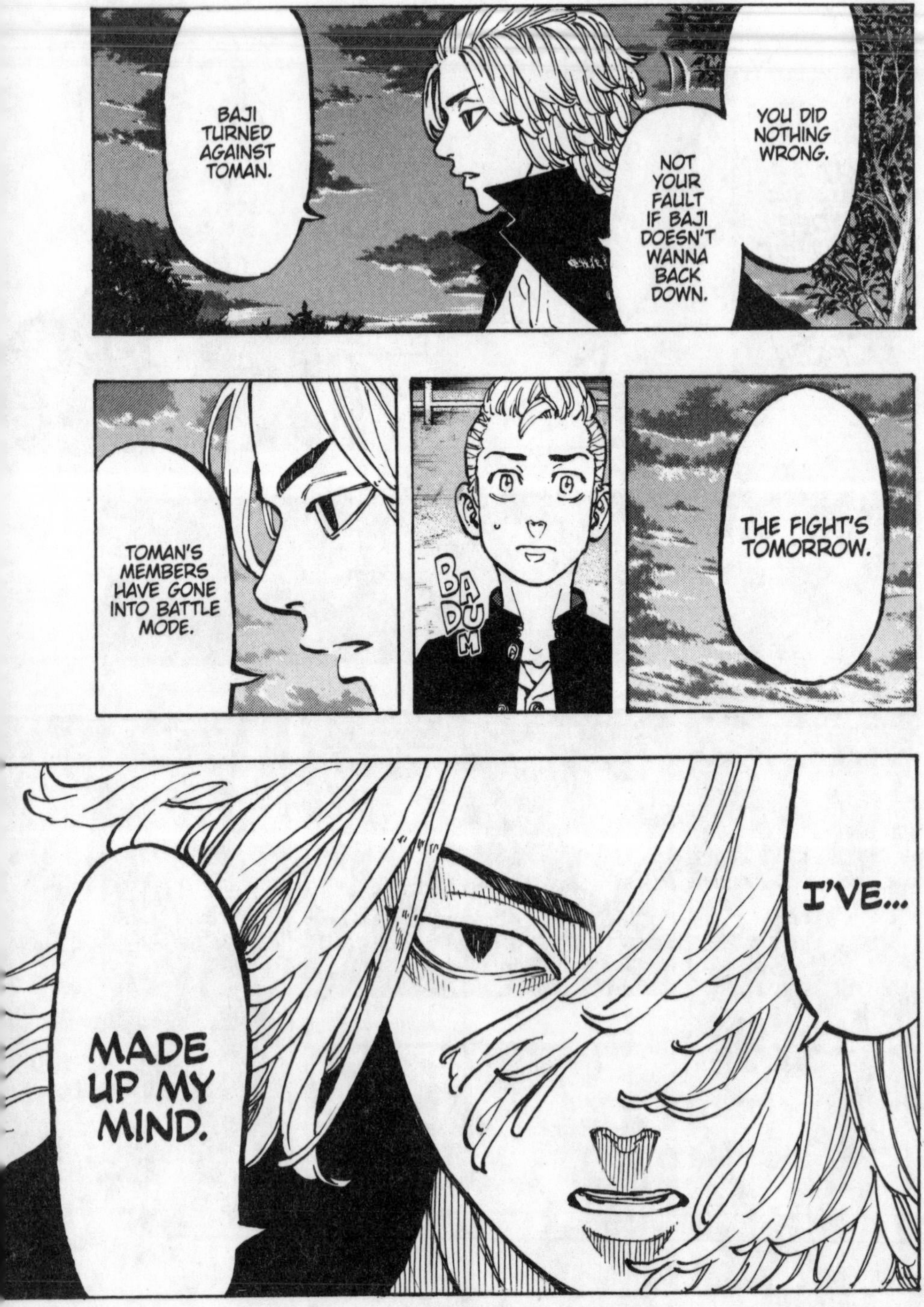
YOU DID NOTHING WRONG.
NOT YOUR FAULT IF BAJI DOESN'T WANNA BACK DOWN.
BAJI TURNED AGAINST TOMAN.
THE FIGHT'S TOMORROW.
BA DUM
TOMAN'S MEMBERS HAVE GONE INTO BATTLE MODE.
I'VE...
MADE UP MY MIND.

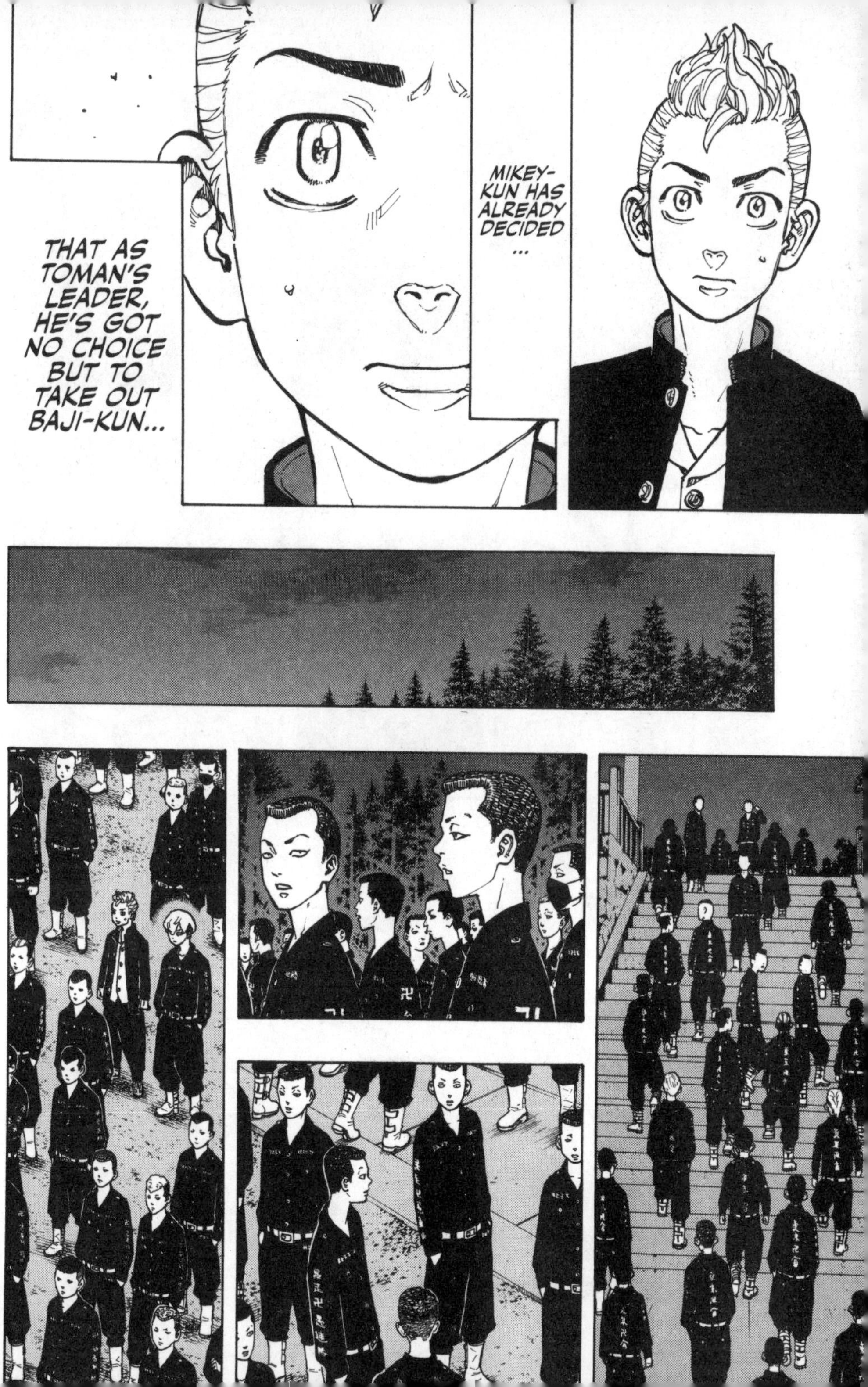
MIKEY-KUN HAS ALREADY DECIDED ...
THAT AS TOMAN'S LEADER, HE'S GOT NO CHOICE BUT TO TAKE OUT BAJI-KUN...

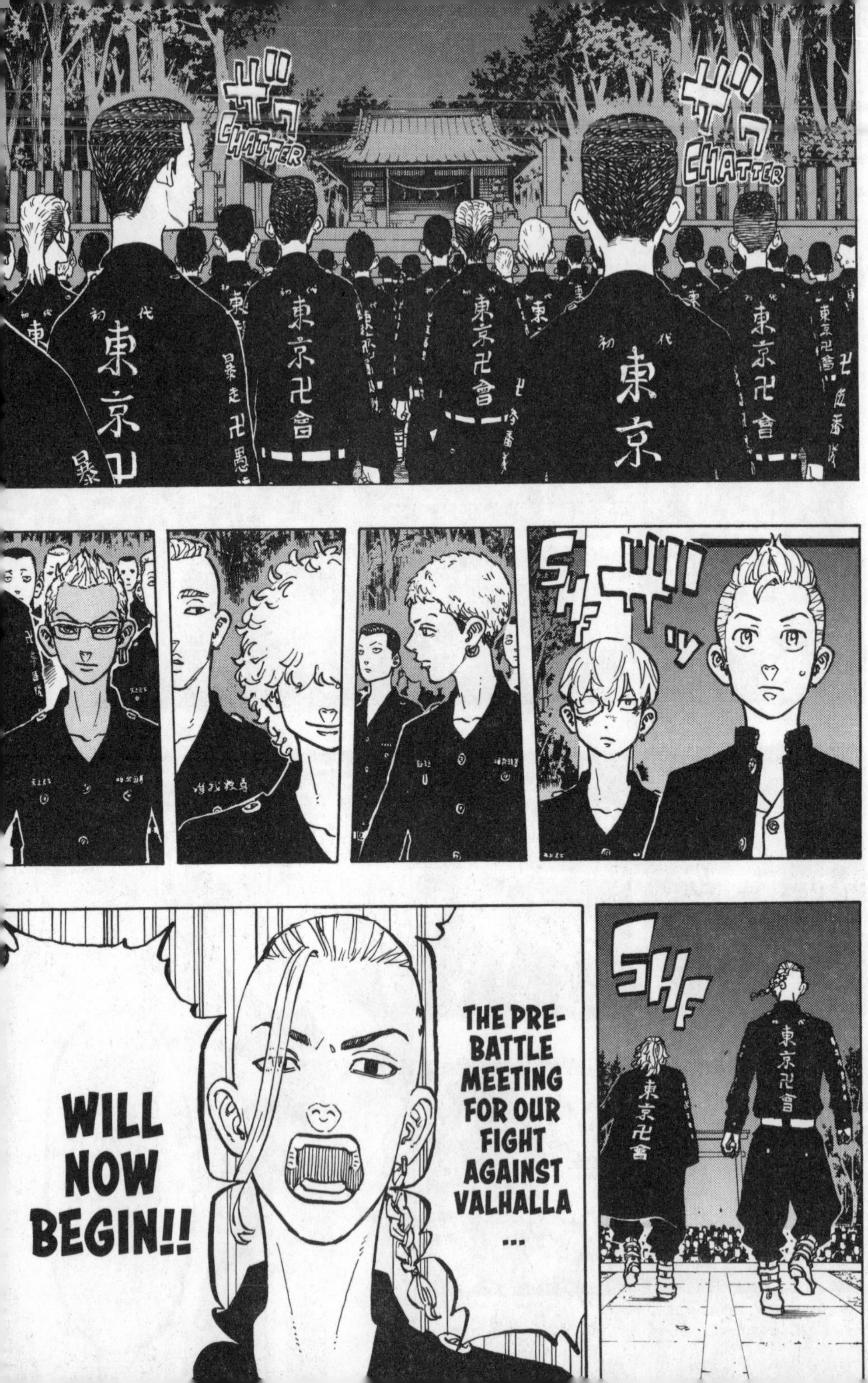

ザワ
CHATTER
ザワ
CHATTER
ザッ
SHF
SHF
THE PRE-BATTLE MEETING FOR OUR FIGHT AGAINST VALHALLA ...
WILL NOW BEGIN!!

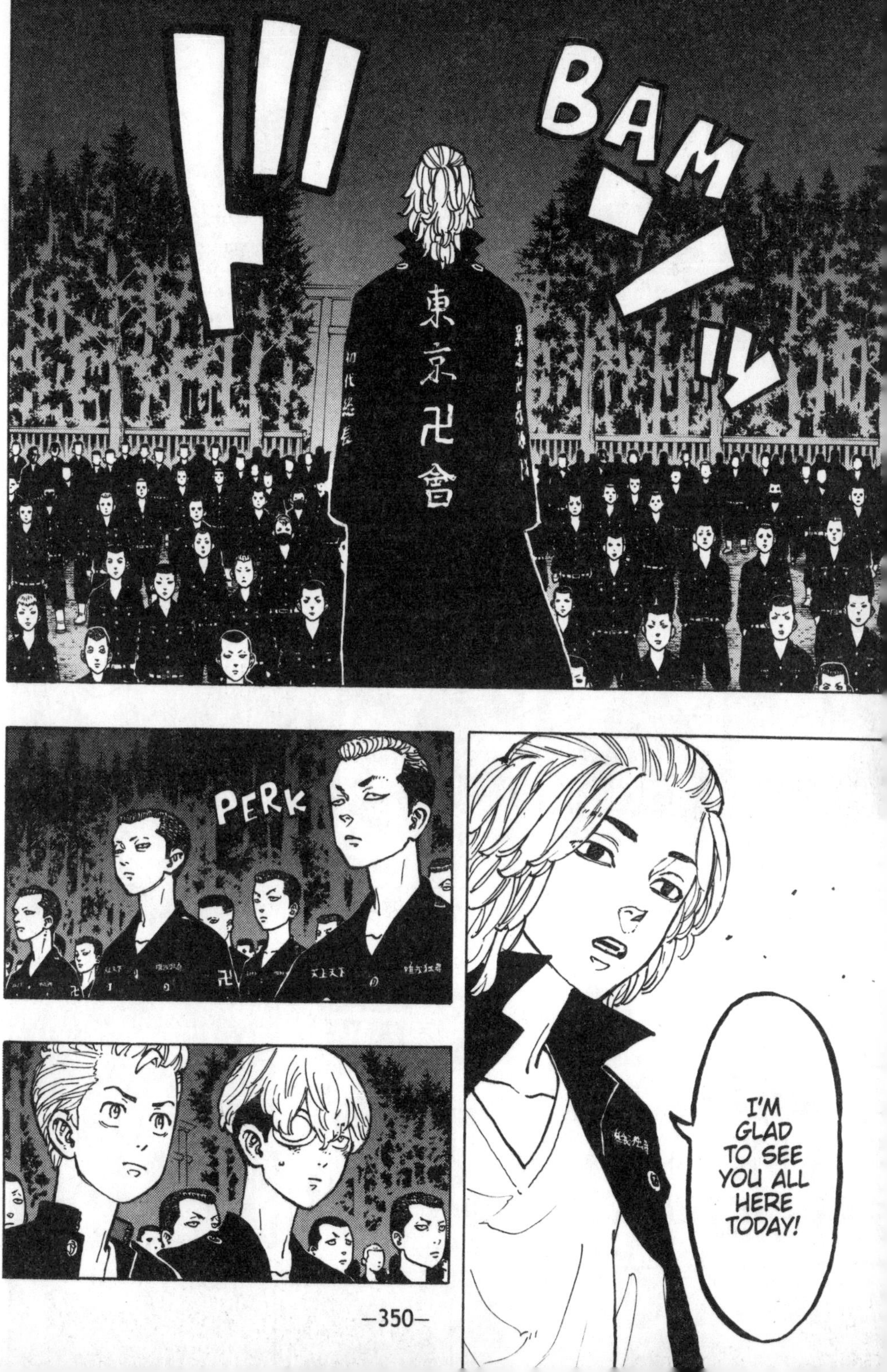

BAM
東京卍會
I'M GLAD TO SEE YOU ALL HERE TODAY!
PERK

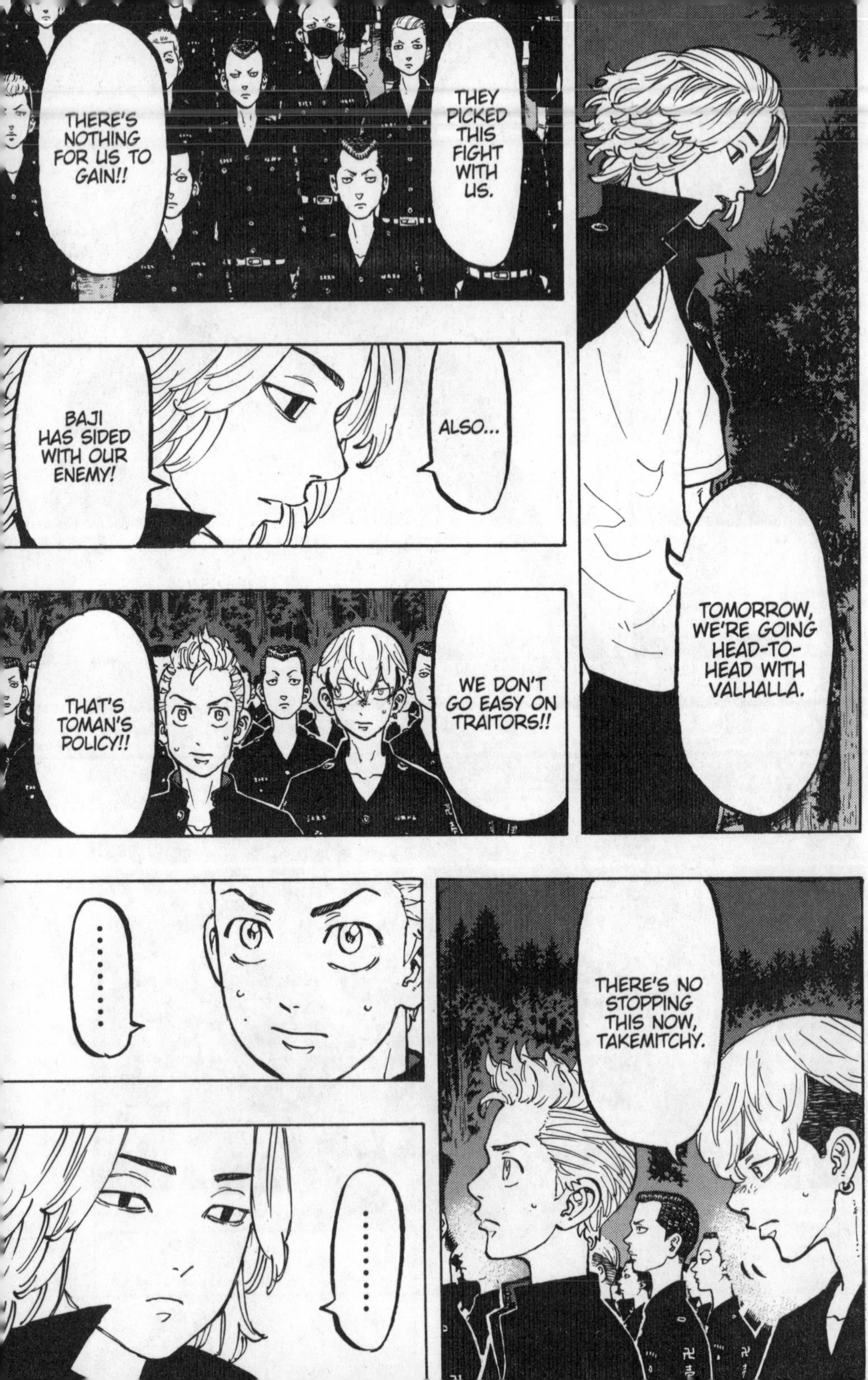
TOMORROW, WE'RE GOING HEAD-TO-HEAD WITH VALHALLA.
THEY PICKED THIS FIGHT WITH US.
THERE'S NOTHING FOR US TO GAIN!!
ALSO...
BAJI HAS SIDED WITH OUR ENEMY!
WE DON'T GO EASY ON TRAITORS!!
THAT'S TOMAN'S POLICY!!
THERE'S NO STOPPING THIS NOW, TAKEMITCHY.
......
......

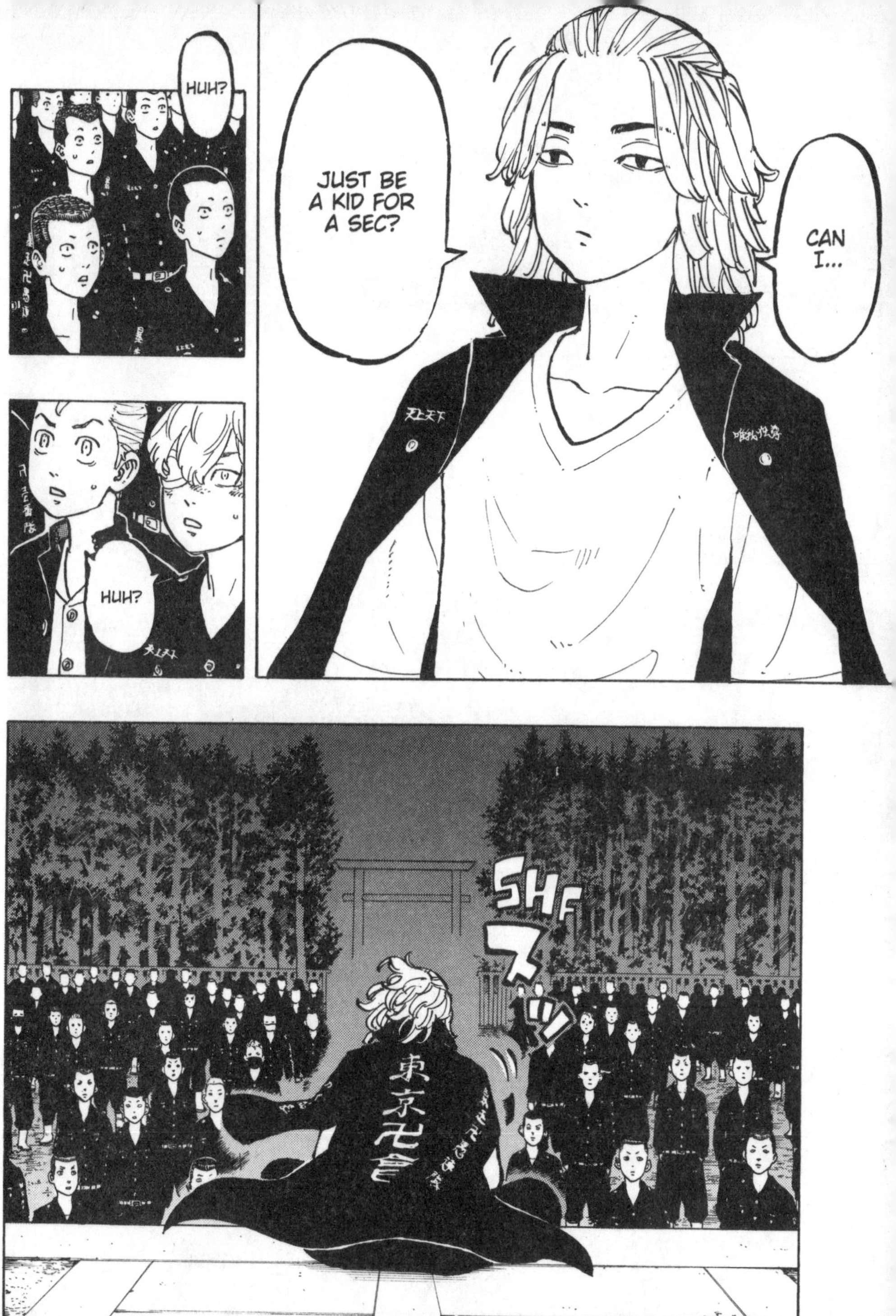
CAN I...
JUST BE A KID FOR A SEC?
HUH?
HUH?
SHF

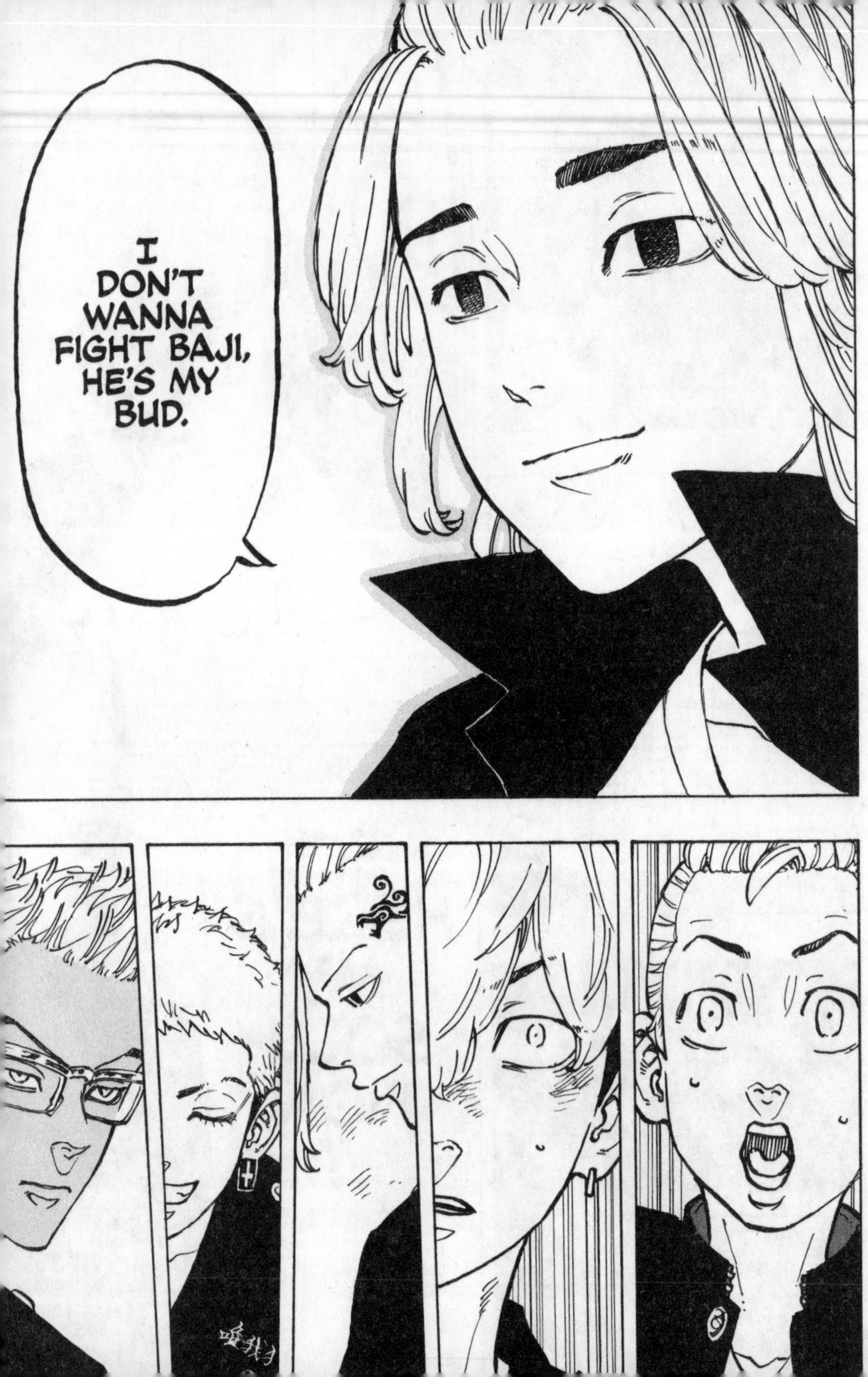
I DON'T WANNA FIGHT BAJI, HE'S MY BUD.

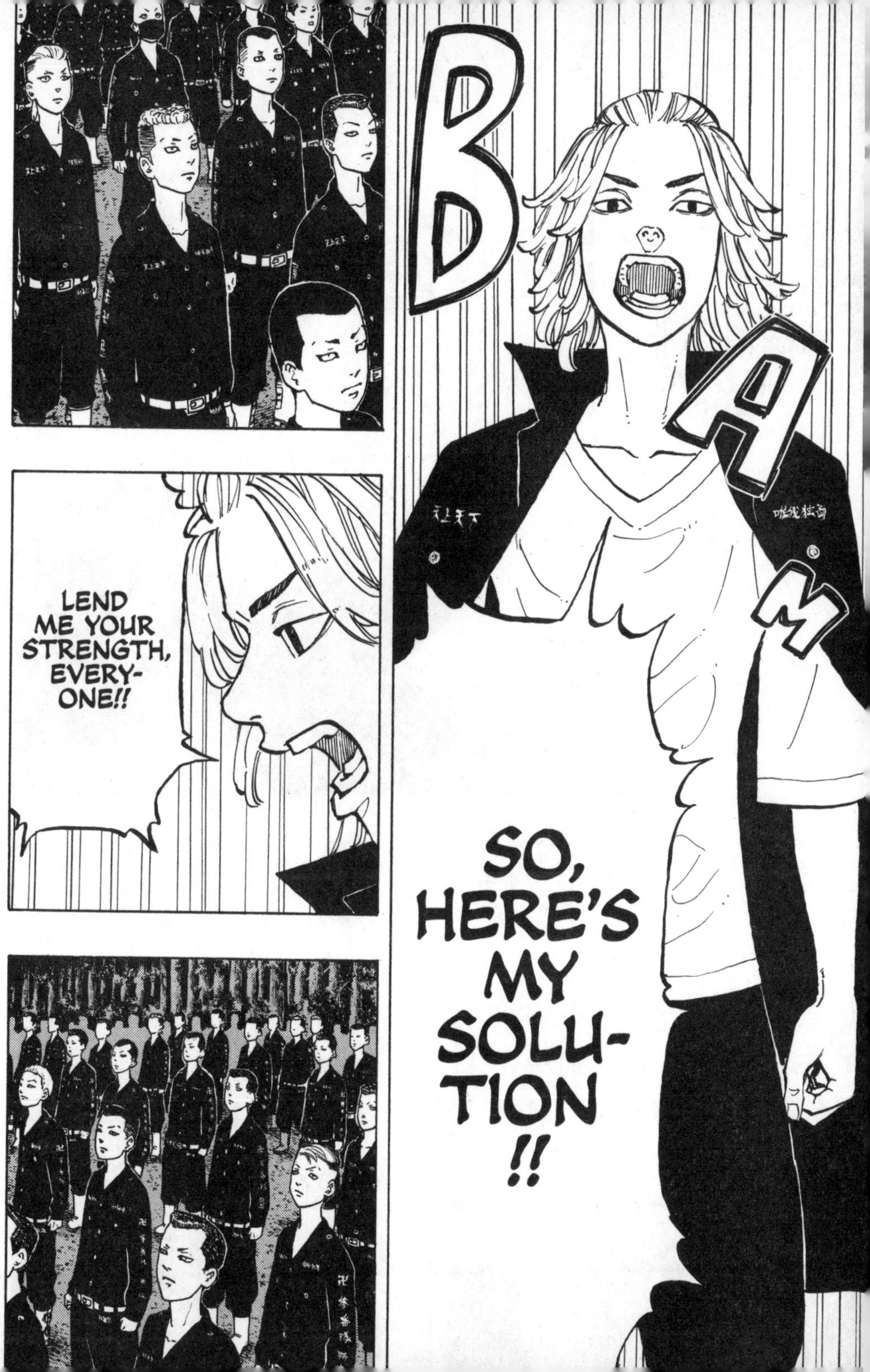
BAM
SO, HERE'S MY SOLUTION!!
LEND ME YOUR STRENGTH, EVERY-ONE!!

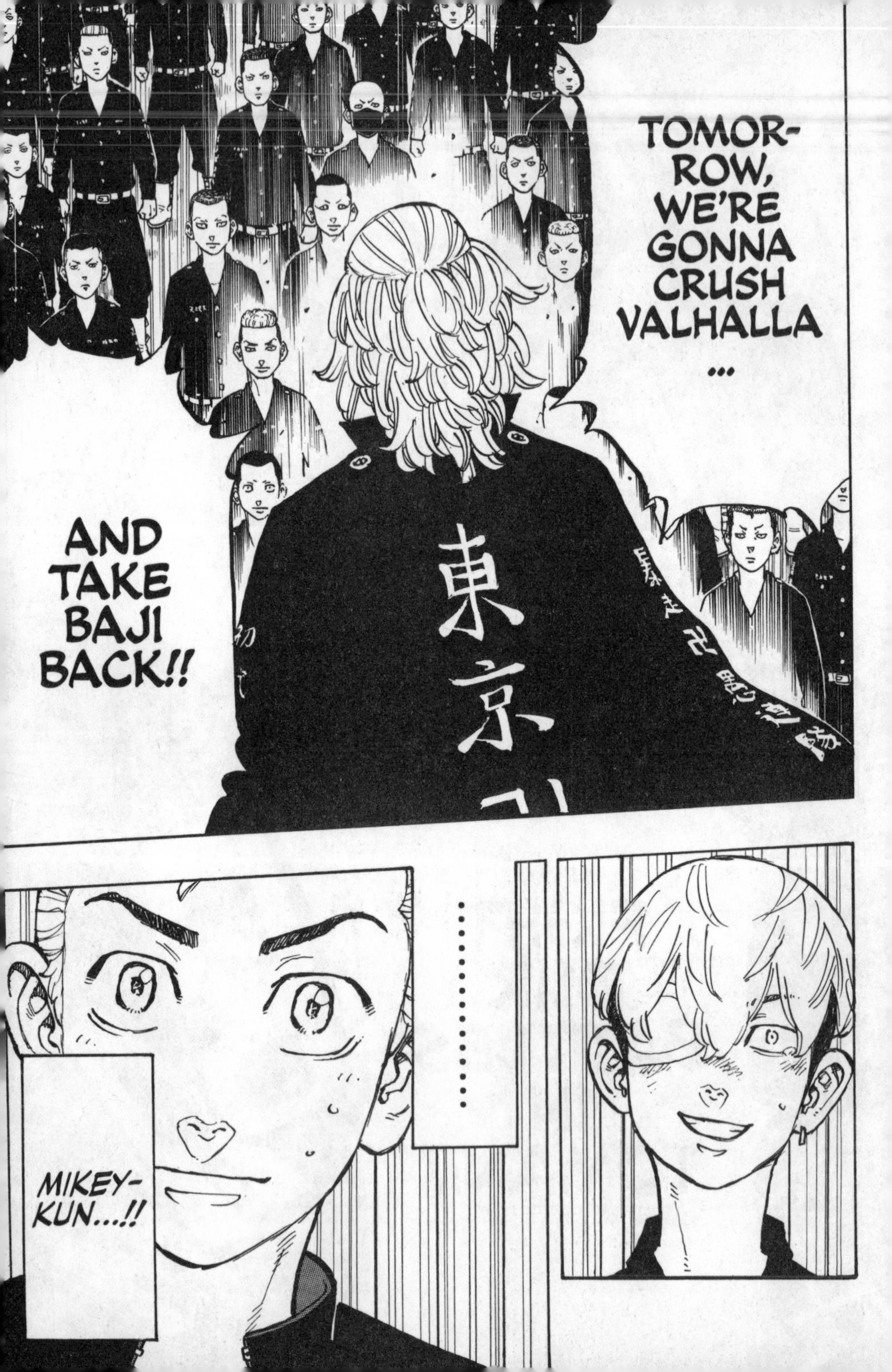
TOMOR-ROW, WE'RE GONNA CRUSH VALHALLA ...
AND TAKE BAJI BACK!!
....
MIKEY-KUN...!!

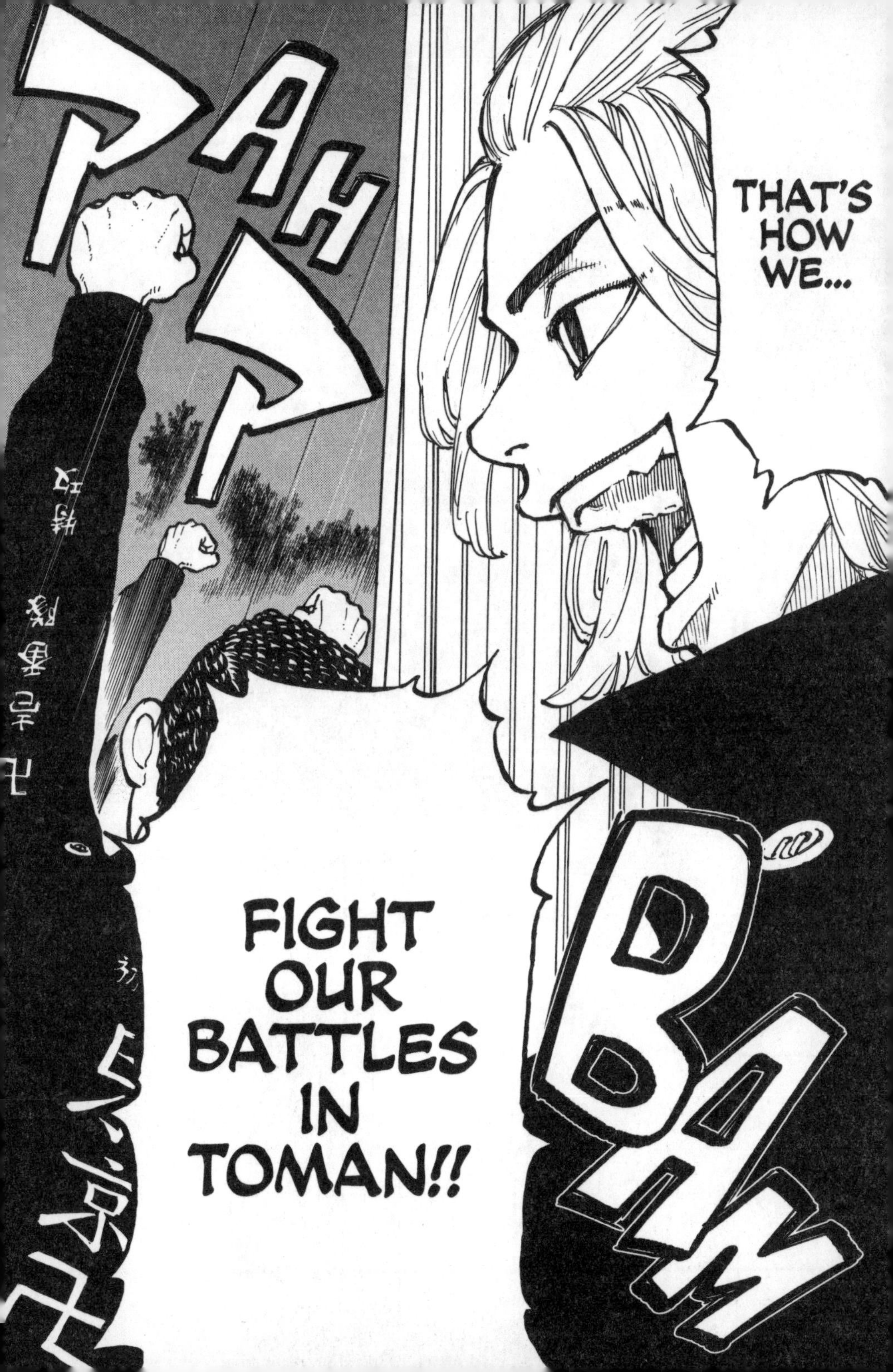
THAT'S HOW WE...
PAH
BAM
FIGHT OUR BATTLES IN TOMAN!!

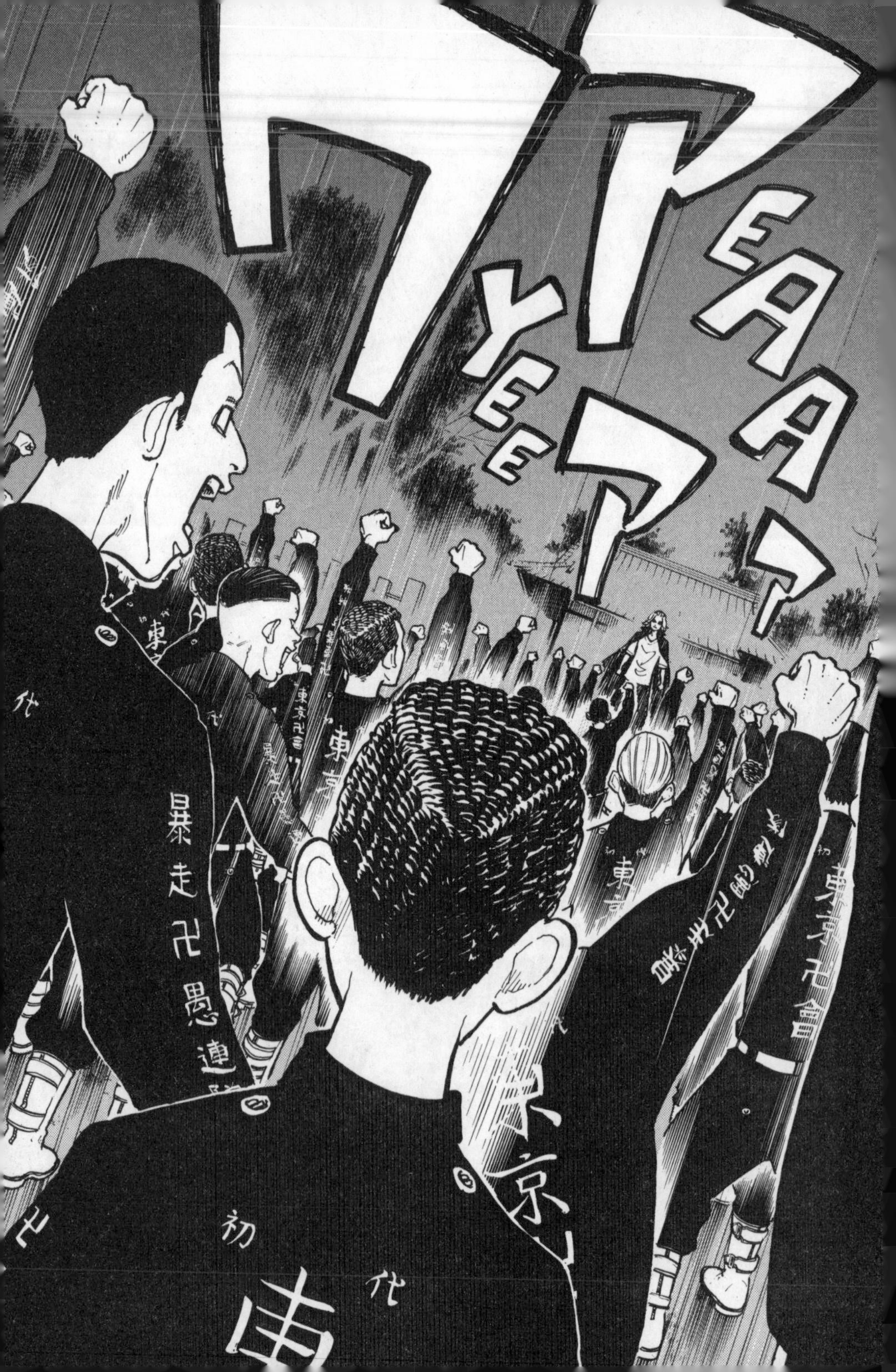
YEEEEAA

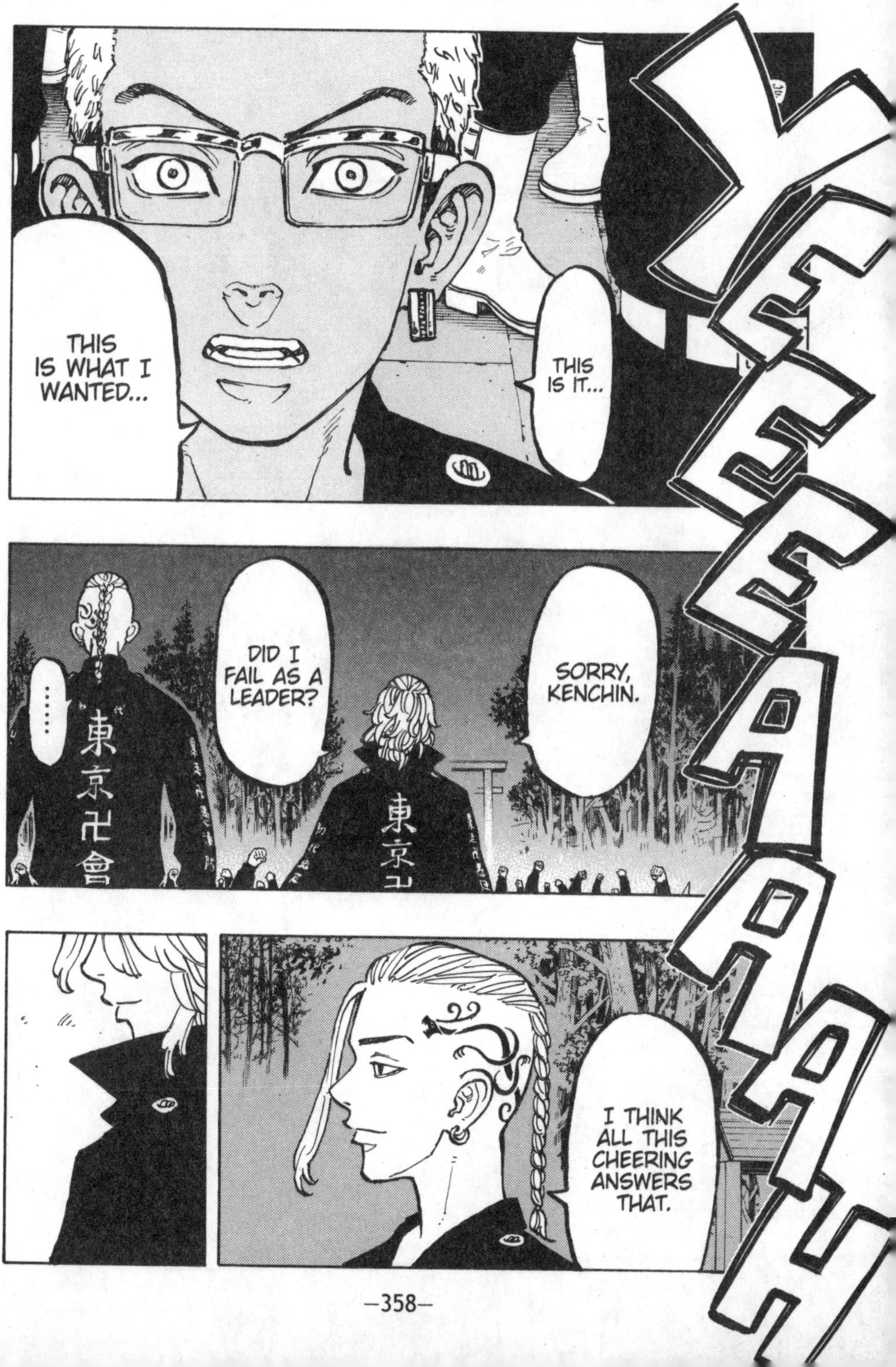
THIS IS IT...
THIS IS WHAT I WANTED...
SORRY, KENCHIN.
DID I FAIL AS A LEADER?
......
I THINK ALL THIS CHEERING ANSWERS THAT.

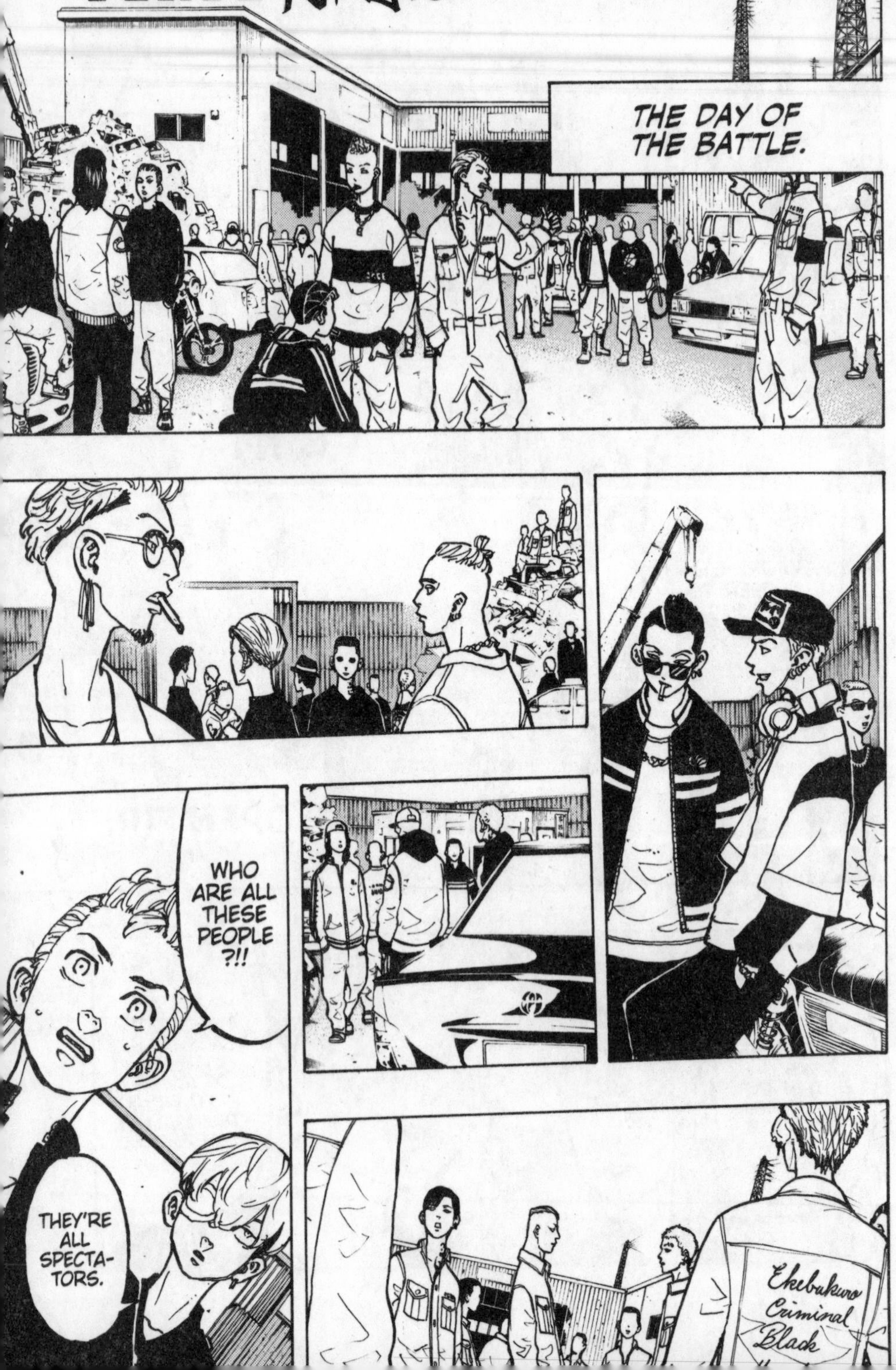
THE DAY OF THE BATTLE.
WHO ARE ALL THESE PEOPLE ?!!
THEY'RE ALL SPECTATORS.
Ekebukuro Criminal Black

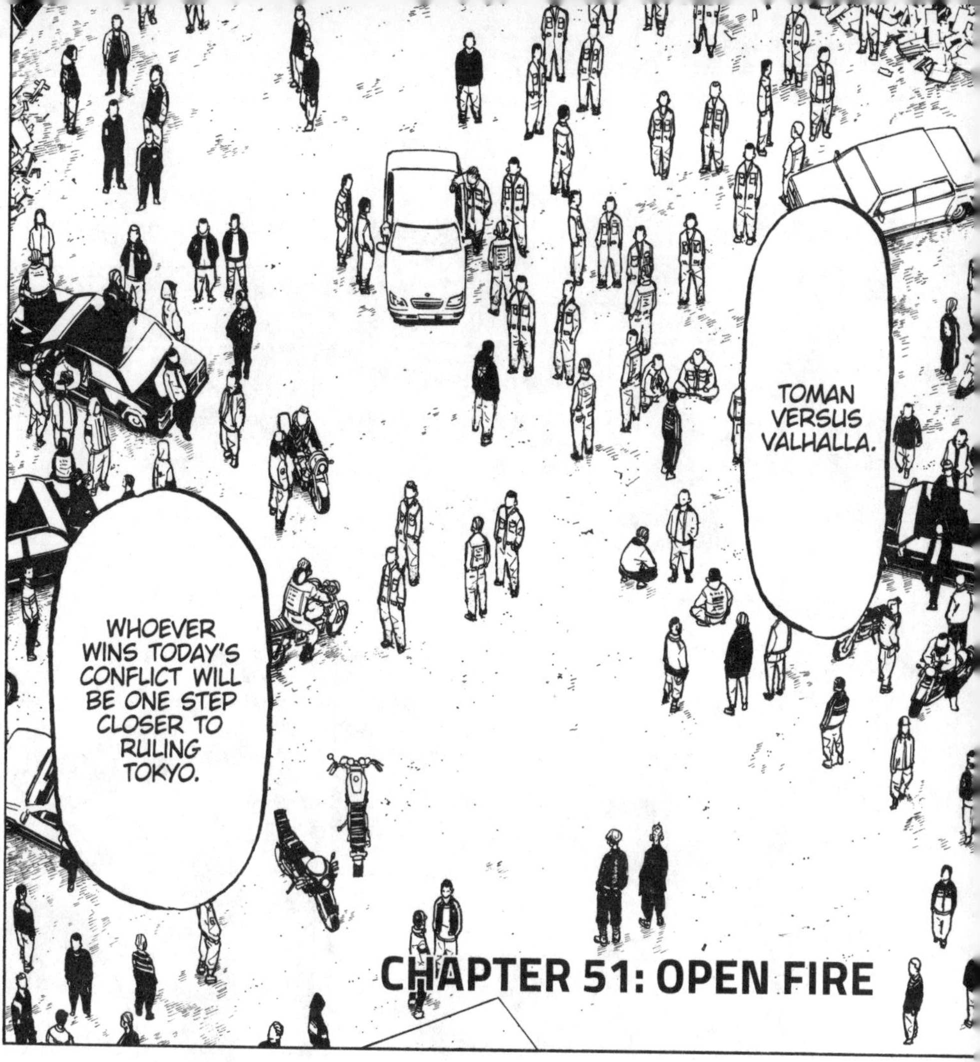
TOMAN VERSUS VALHALLA.
WHOEVER WINS TODAY'S CONFLICT WILL BE ONE STEP CLOSER TO RULING TOKYO.
CHAPTER 51: OPEN FIRE

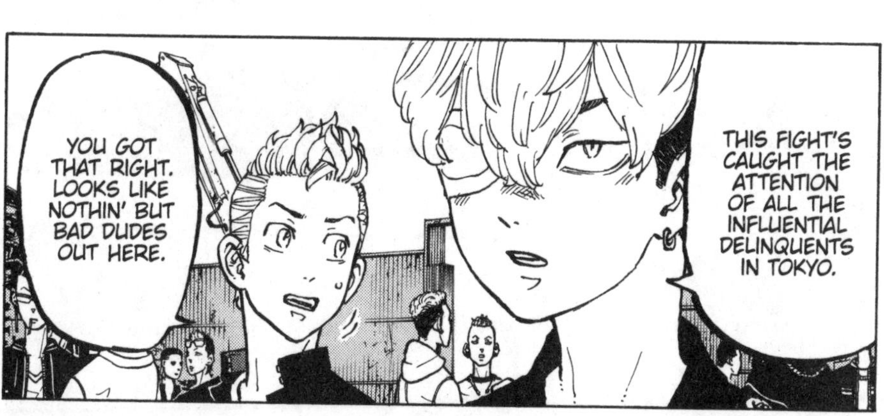
THIS FIGHT'S CAUGHT THE ATTENTION OF ALL THE INFLUENTIAL DELINQUENTS IN TOKYO.
YOU GOT THAT RIGHT. LOOKS LIKE NOTHIN' BUT BAD DUDES OUT HERE.

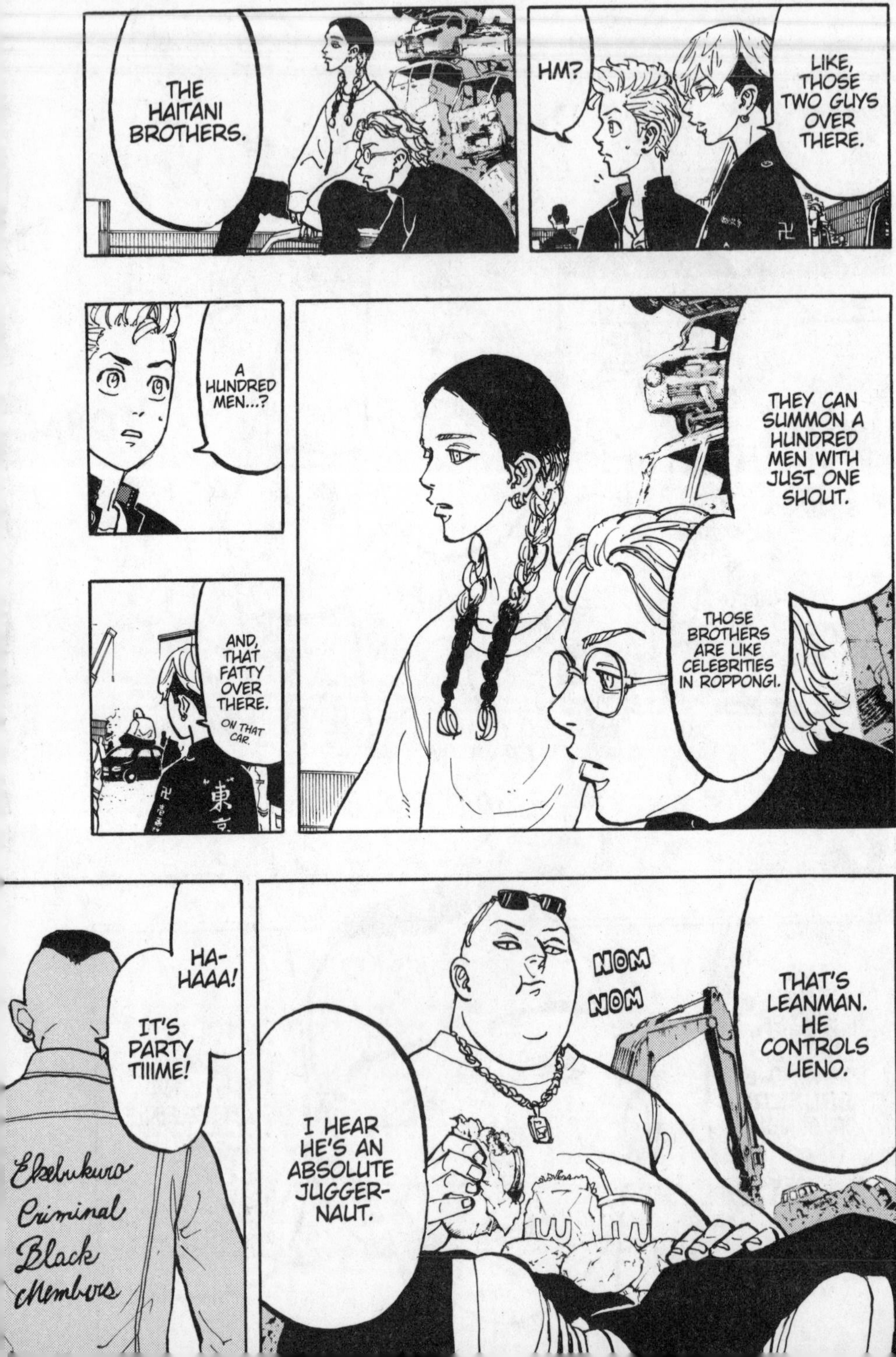

LIKE, THOSE TWO GUYS OVER THERE.
HM?
THE HAITANI BROTHERS.
THEY CAN SUMMON A HUNDRED MEN WITH JUST ONE SHOUT.
THOSE BROTHERS ARE LIKE CELEBRITIES IN ROPPONGI.
A HUNDRED MEN...?
AND, THAT FATTY OVER THERE.
ON THAT CAR.
THAT'S LEANMAN. HE CONTROLS UENO.
NOM NOM
I HEAR HE'S AN ABSOLUTE JUGGERNAUT.
HA-HAAA!
IT'S PARTY TIIIME!
Ikebukuro Criminal Black Members

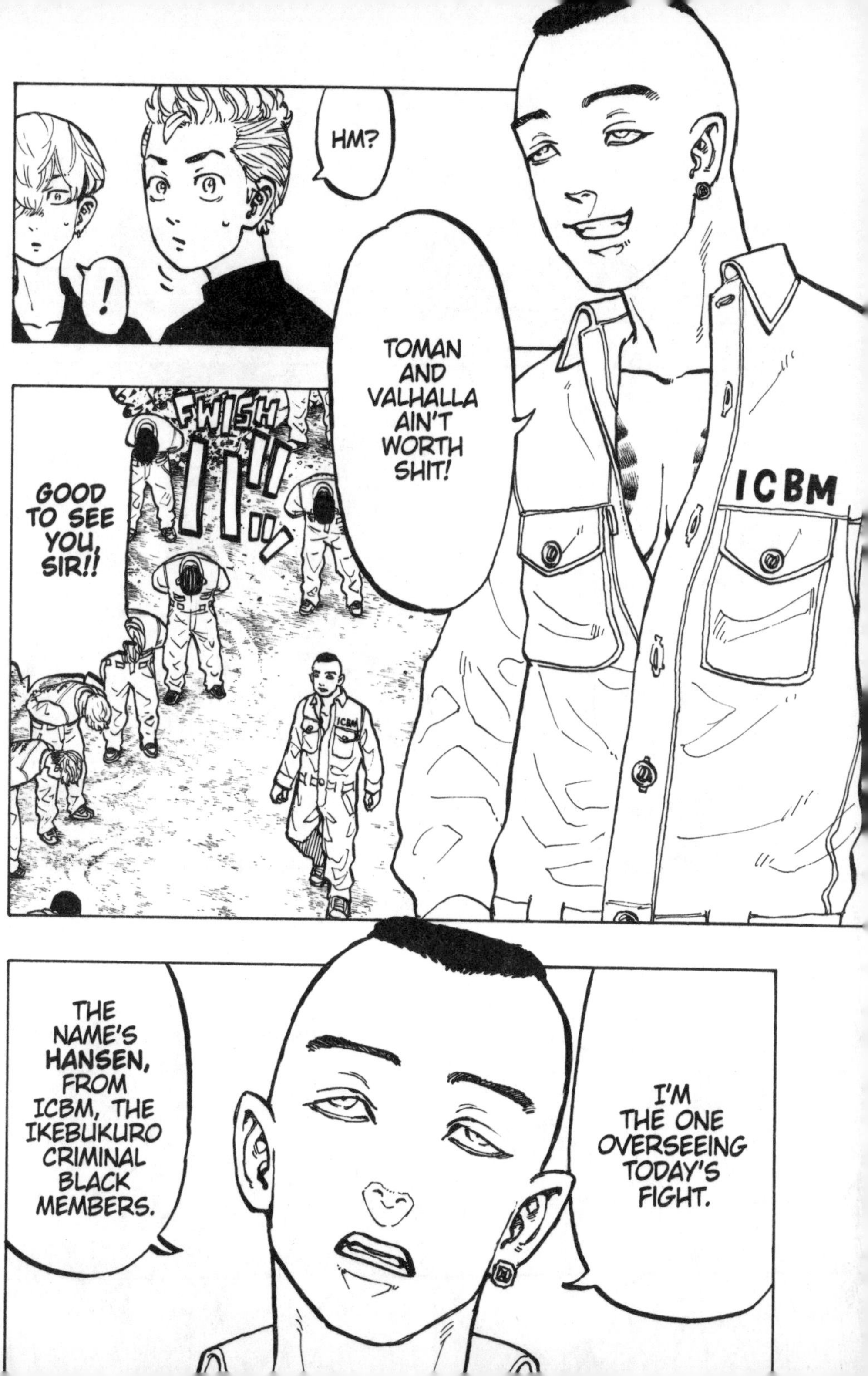
TOMAN AND VALHALLA AIN'T WORTH SHIT!
ICBM
HM?
!
FWISH
GOOD TO SEE YOU, SIR!!
THE NAME'S HANSEN, FROM ICBM, THE IKEBUKURO CRIMINAL BLACK MEMBERS.
I'M THE ONE OVERSEEING TODAY'S FIGHT.

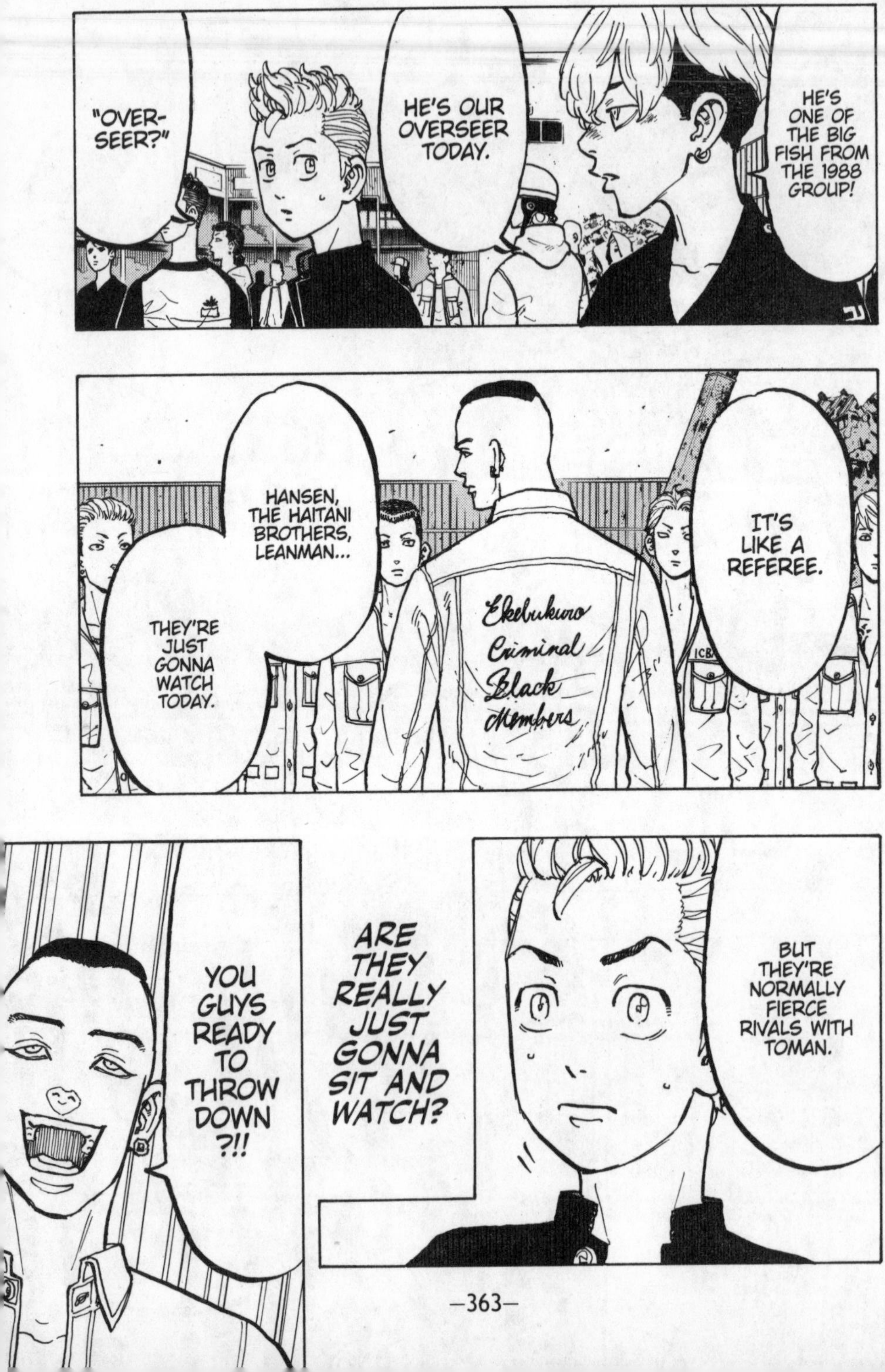
HE'S ONE OF THE BIG FISH FROM THE 1988 GROUP!
HE'S OUR OVERSEER TODAY.
"OVER-SEER?"
IT'S LIKE A REFEREE.
HANSEN, THE HAITANI BROTHERS, LEANMAN...
Ekebukuro Criminal Black Members
THEY'RE JUST GONNA WATCH TODAY.
BUT THEY'RE NORMALLY FIERCE RIVALS WITH TOMAN.
ARE THEY REALLY JUST GONNA SIT AND WATCH?
YOU GUYS READY TO THROW DOWN?!!

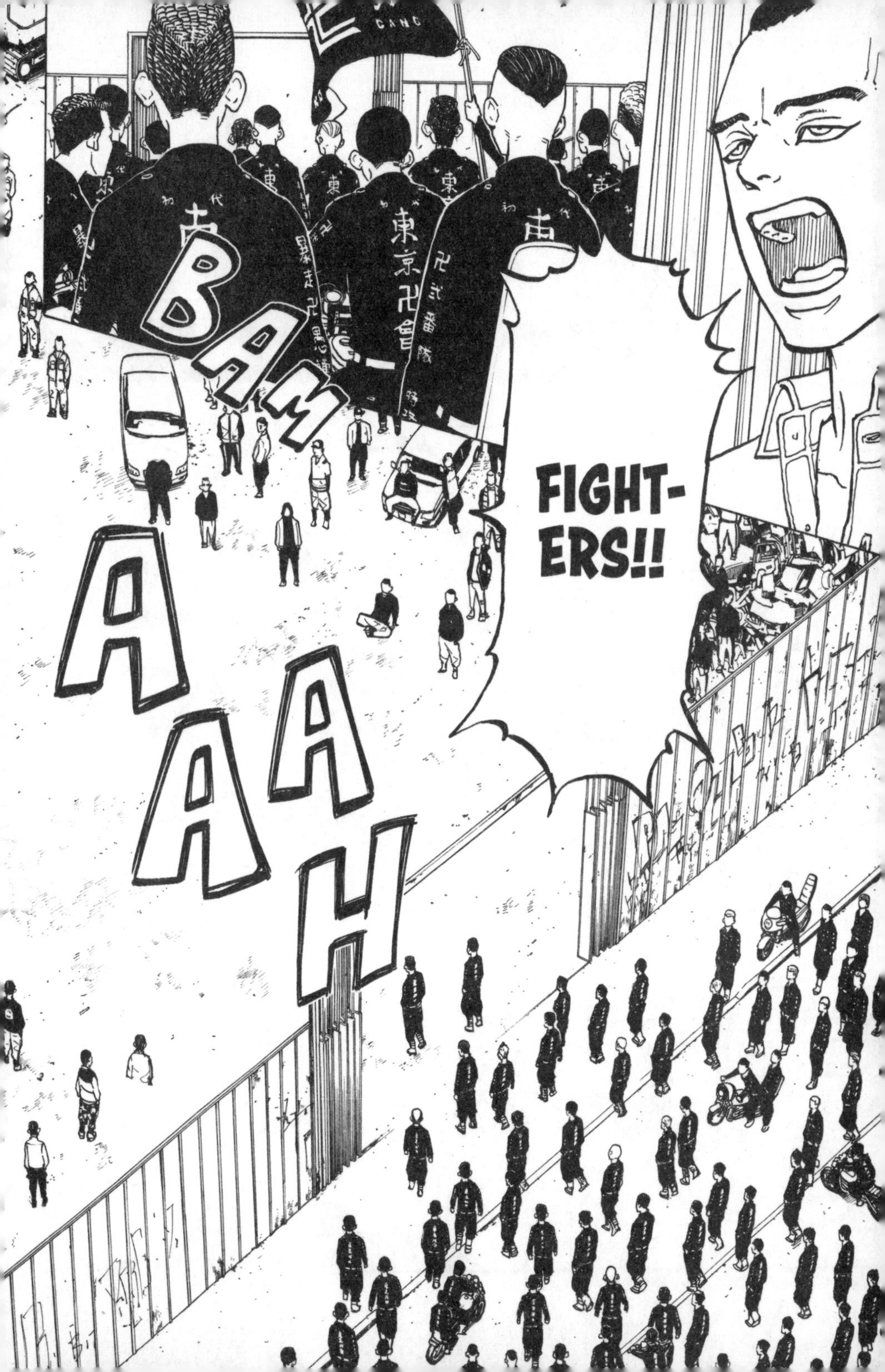
FIGHT-
ERS!!
BAM
AAAAH

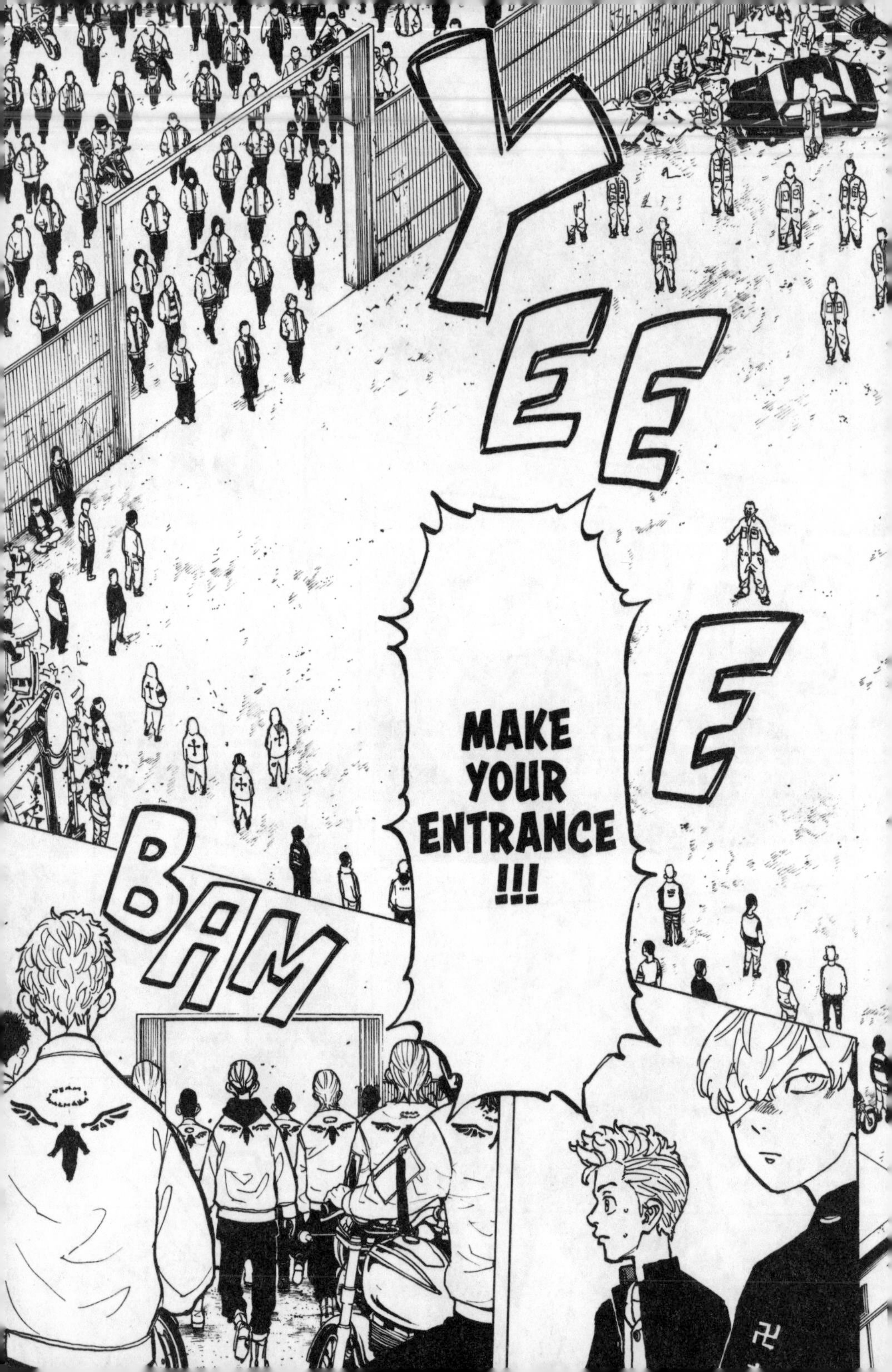
YEEE
MAKE YOUR ENTRANCE !!!
BAM

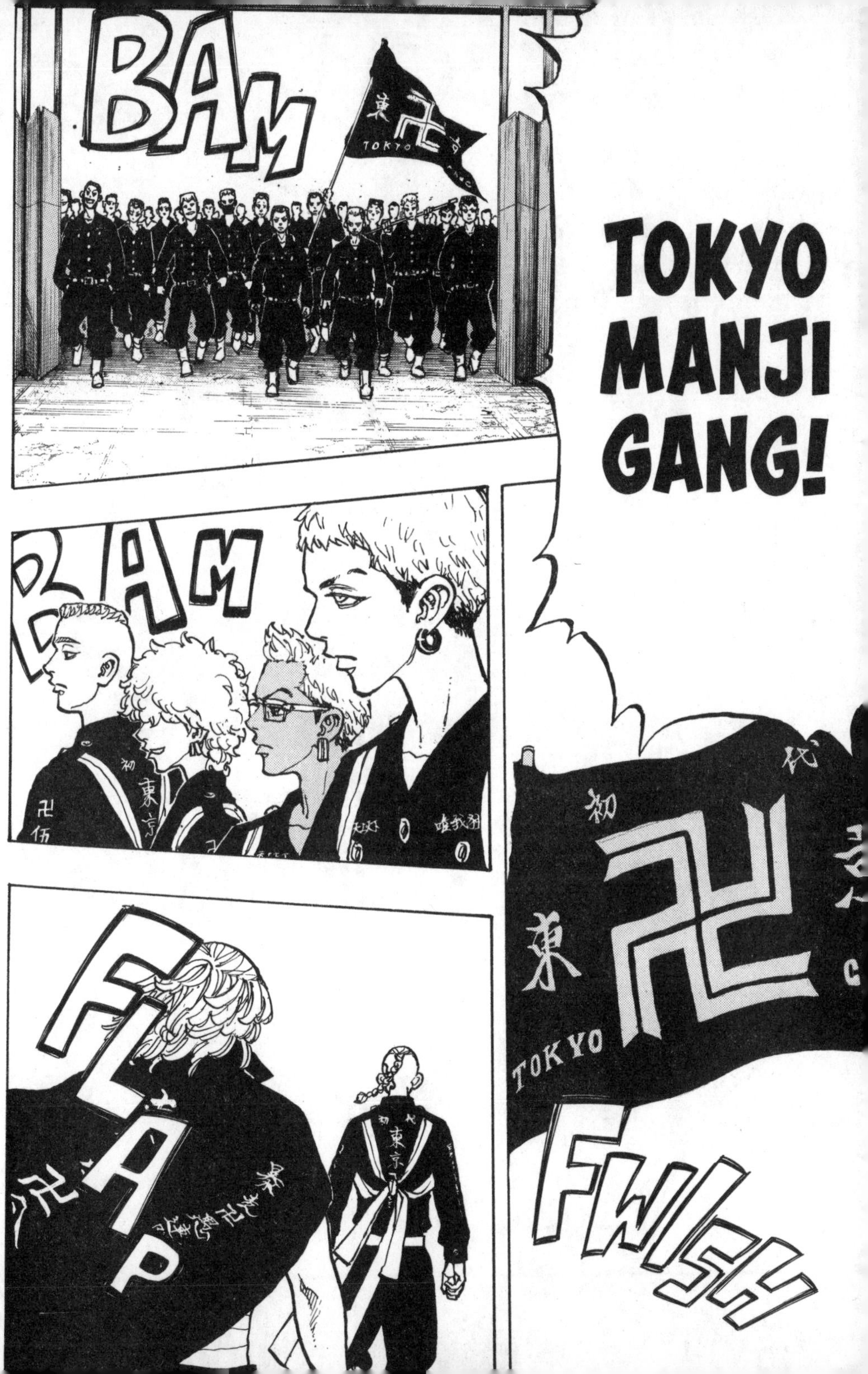
TOKYO MANJI GANG!
TOKYO
FWISH
BAM
TOKYO
BAM
FLAP

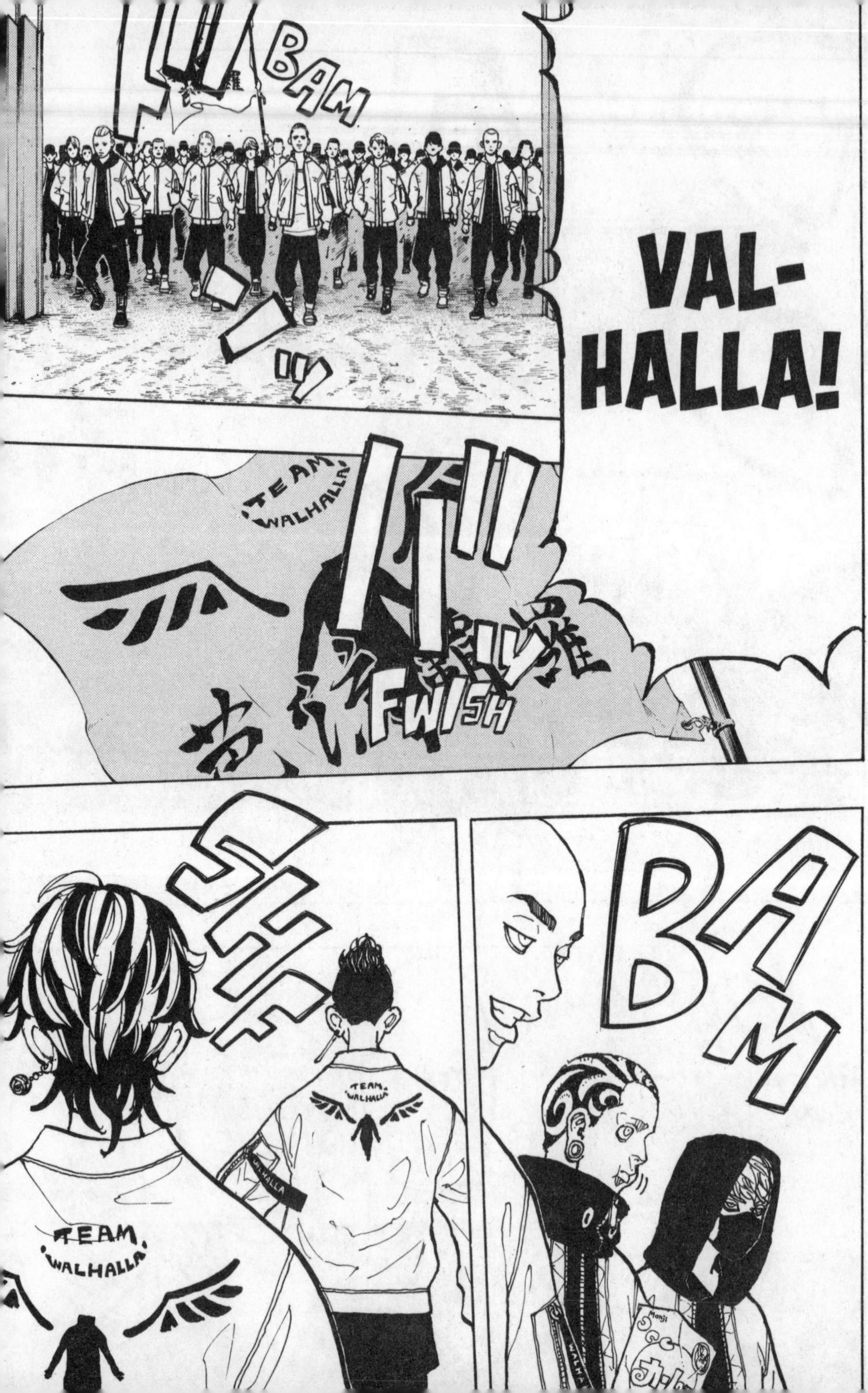
VAL-HALLA!
BAM
TEAM WALHALLA
FWISH
BAM
SHF
TEAM WALHALLA

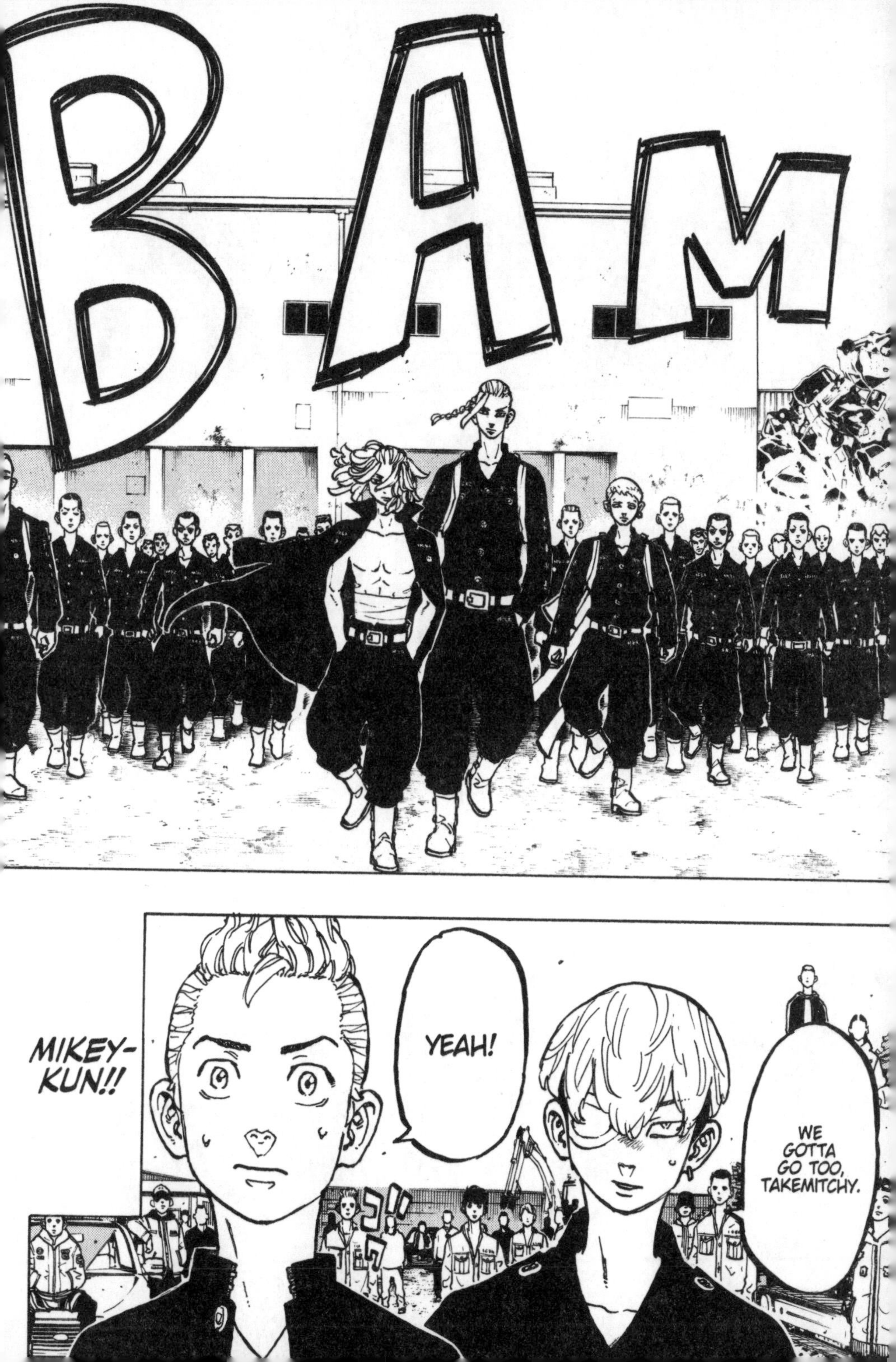
B.A.M
WE GOTTA GO TOO, TAKEMITCHY.
YEAH!
MIKEY-KUN!!

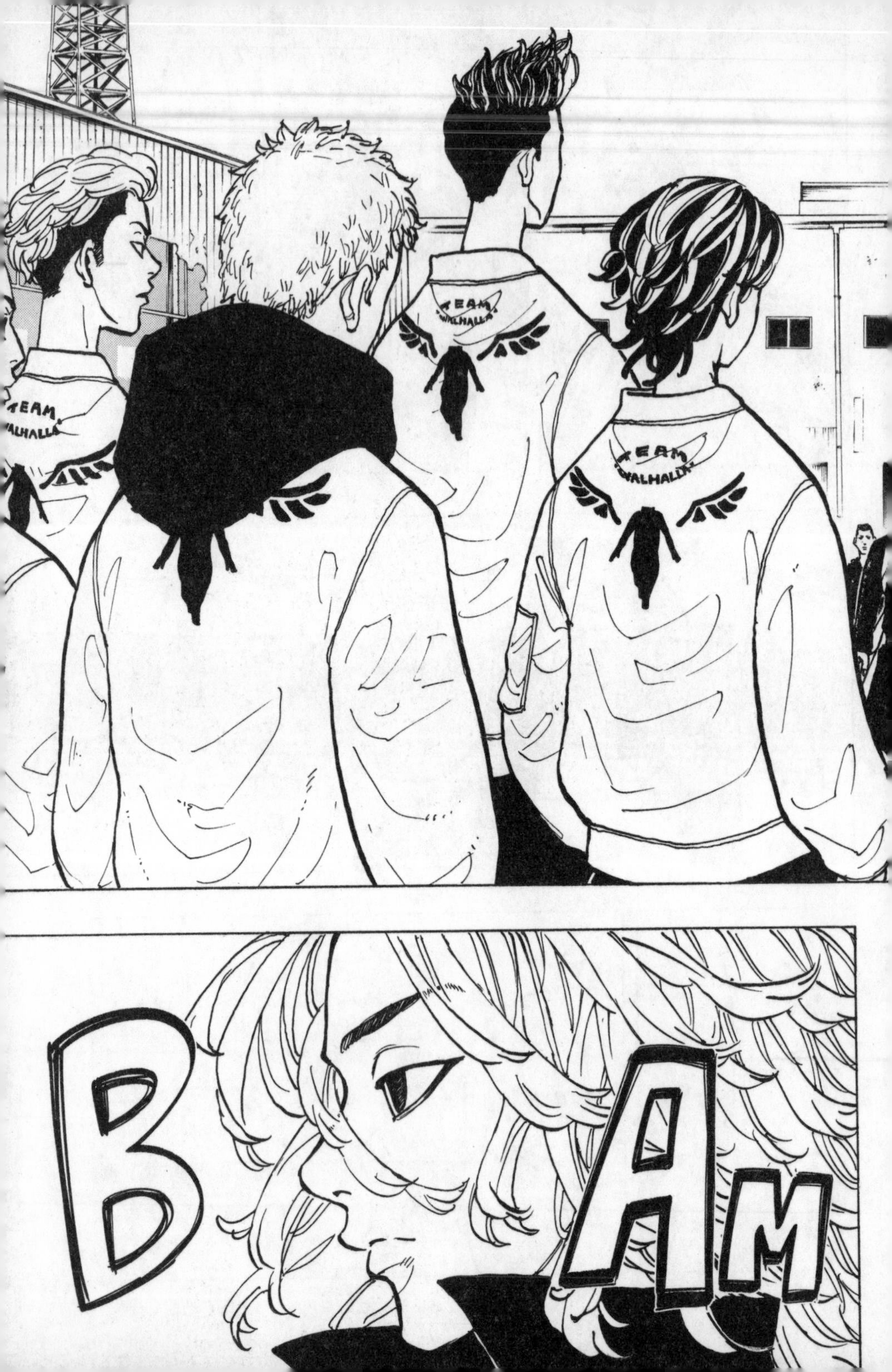
BAM

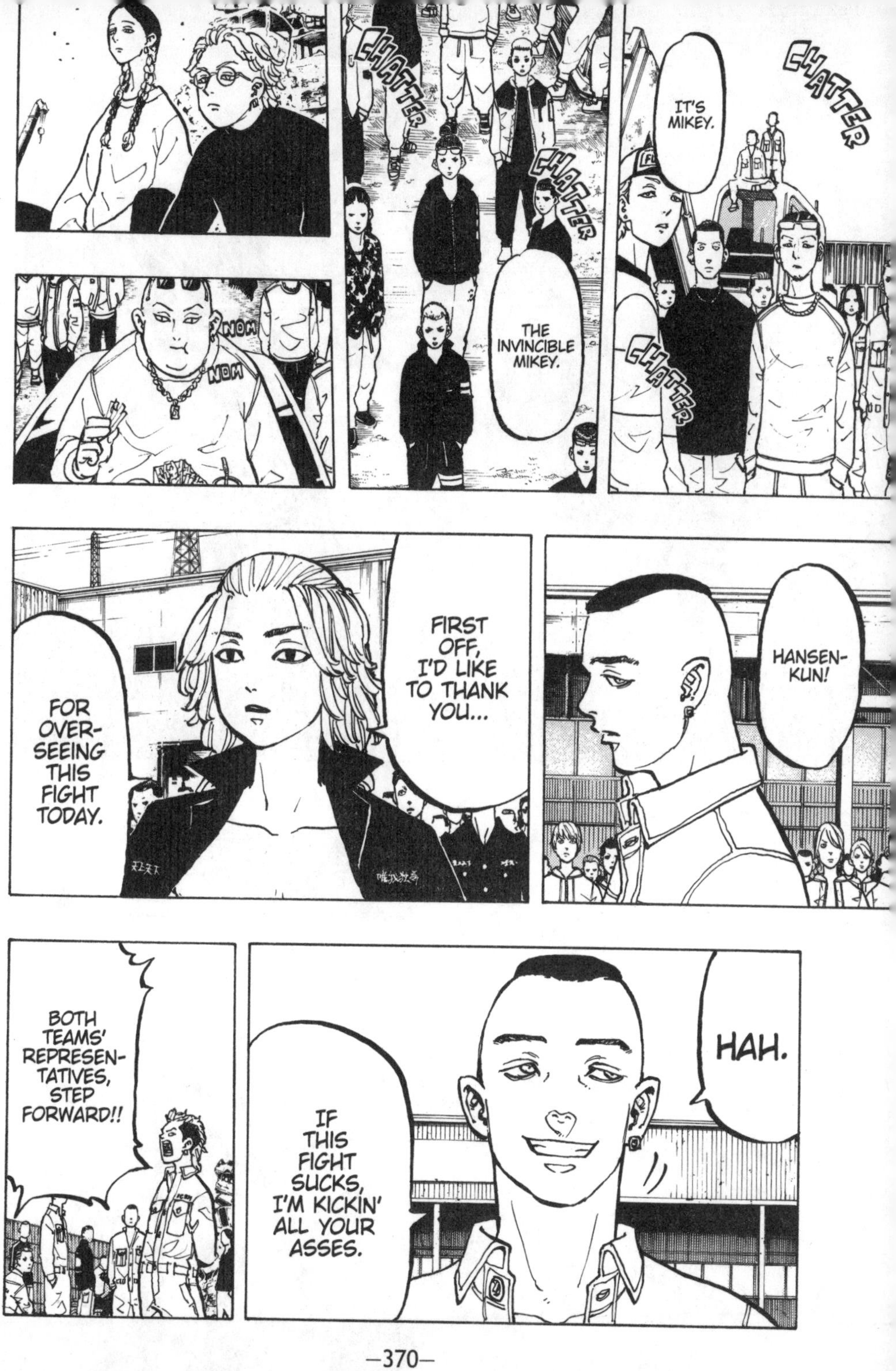
CHATTER
IT'S MIKEY.
CHATTER
CHATTER
CHATTER
THE INVINCIBLE MIKEY.
NOM
NOM
HANSEN-KUN!
FIRST OFF, I'D LIKE TO THANK YOU...
FOR OVERSEEING THIS FIGHT TODAY.
HAH.
IF THIS FIGHT SUCKS, I'M KICKIN' ALL YOUR ASSES.
BOTH TEAMS' REPRESENTATIVES, STEP FORWARD!!

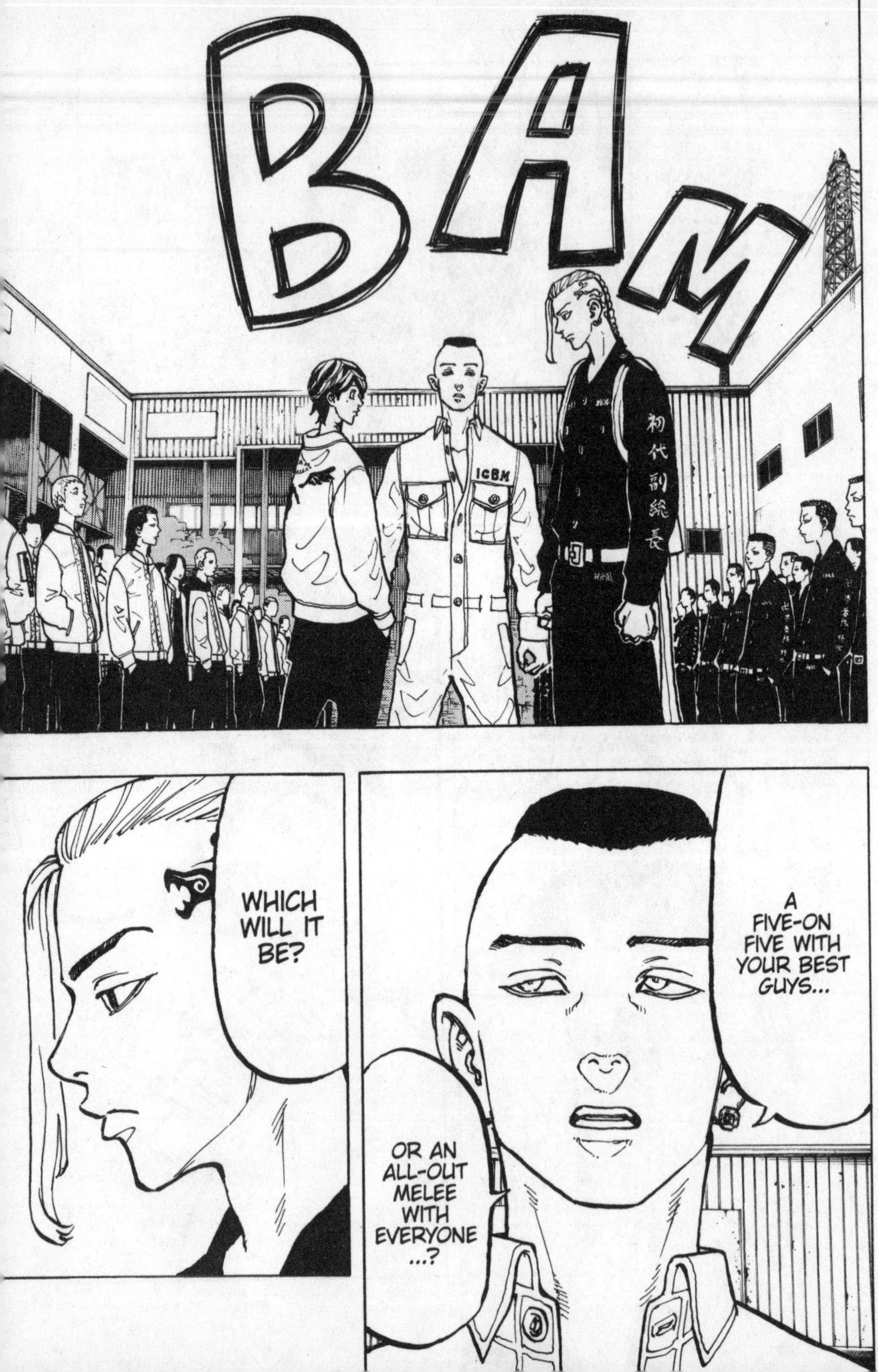
BAM
ICBM
初代副総長
A FIVE-ON FIVE WITH YOUR BEST GUYS...
OR AN ALL-OUT MELEE WITH EVERYONE ...?
WHICH WILL IT BE?

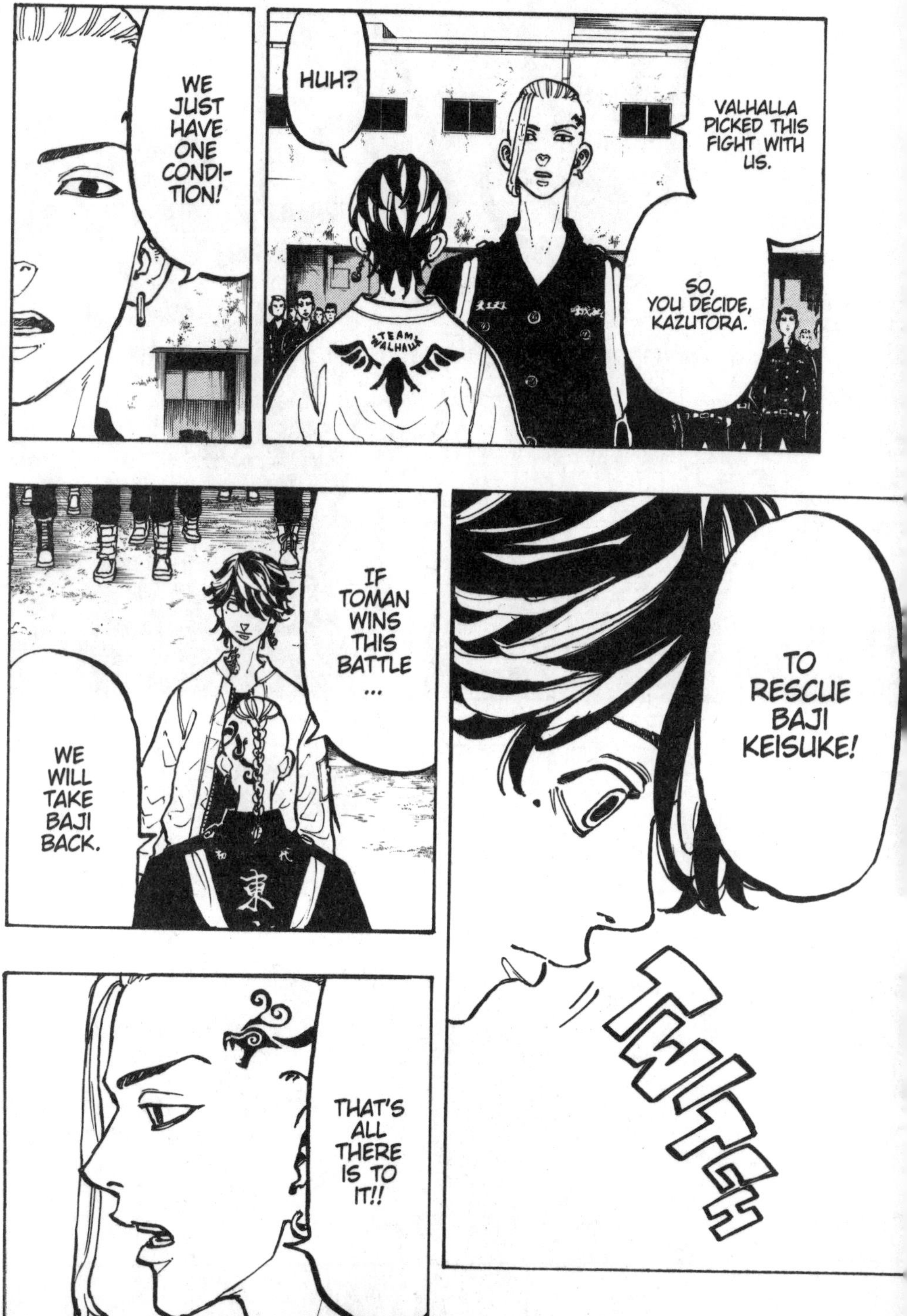
VALHALLA PICKED THIS FIGHT WITH US.
SO, YOU DECIDE, KAZUTORA.
HUH?
WE JUST HAVE ONE CONDITION!
TO RESCUE BAJI KEISUKE!
TWITCH
IF TOMAN WINS THIS BATTLE ...
WE WILL TAKE BAJI BACK.
THAT'S ALL THERE IS TO IT!!

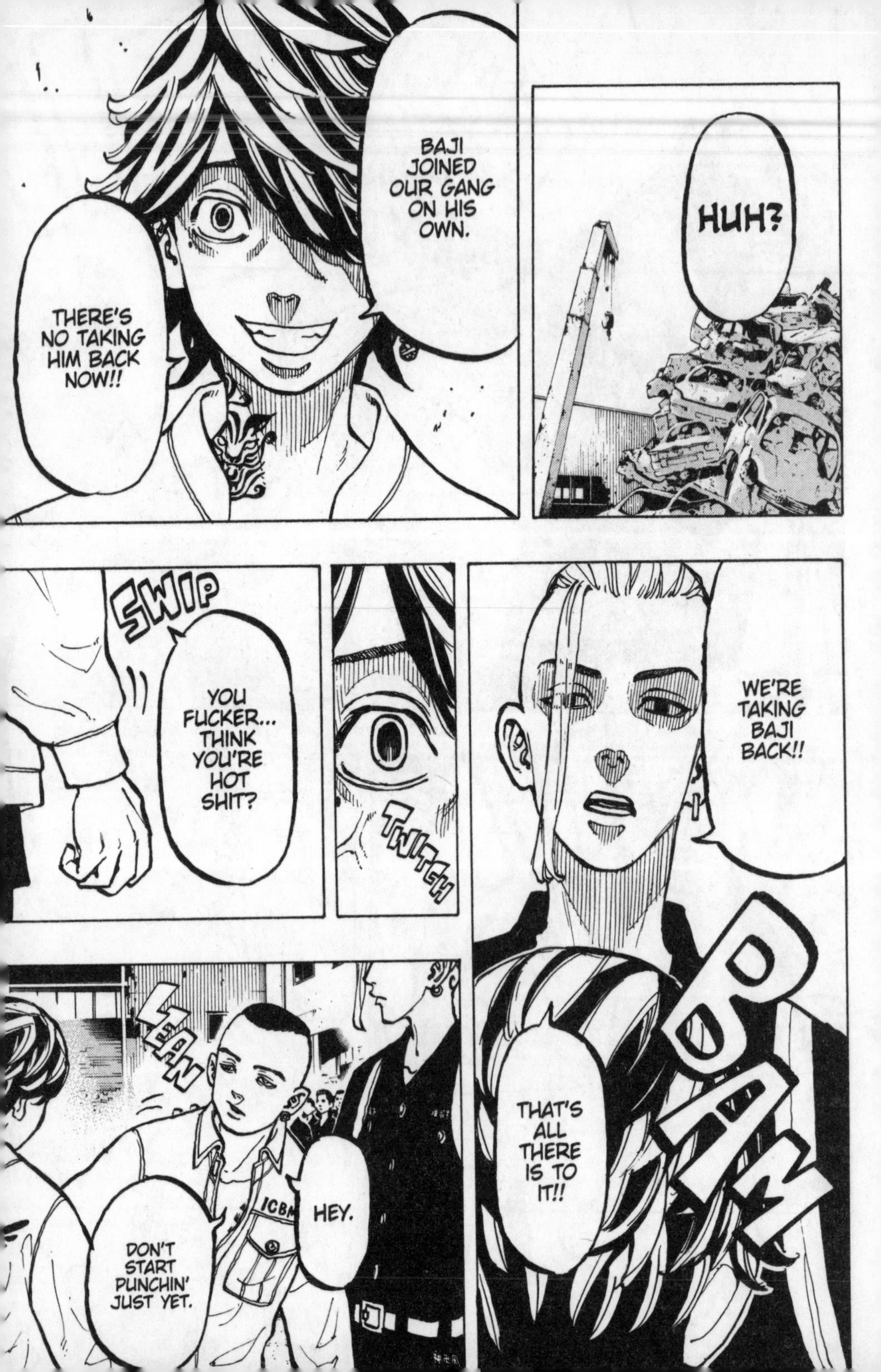
HUH?
BAJI JOINED OUR GANG ON HIS OWN.
THERE'S NO TAKING HIM BACK NOW!!
WE'RE TAKING BAJI BACK!!
BAM
THAT'S ALL THERE IS TO IT!!
TWITCH
SWIP
YOU FUCKER... THINK YOU'RE HOT SHIT?
LEAN
HEY.
DON'T START PUNCHIN' JUST YET.

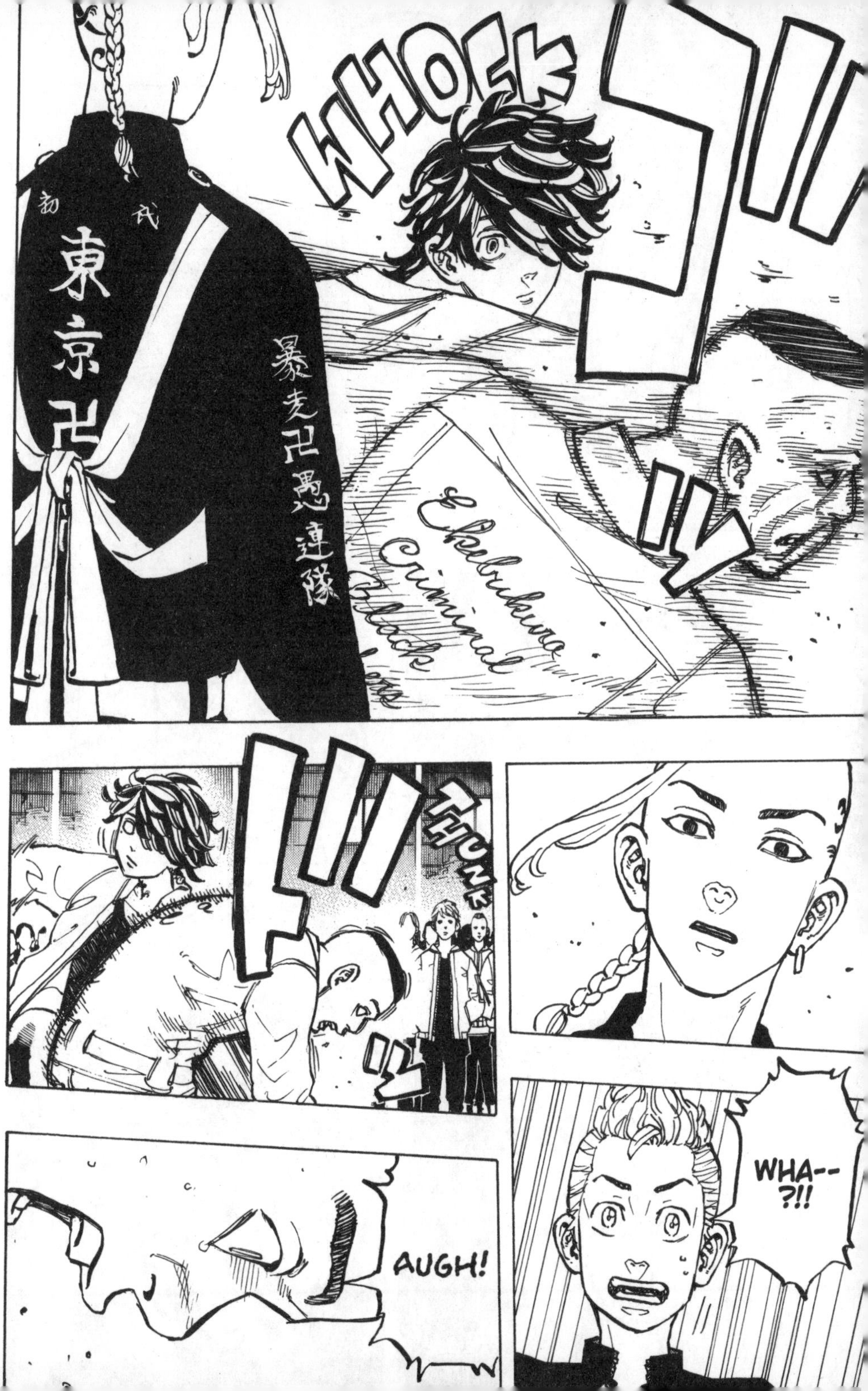
WHOCK
東京卍
暴走卍愚連隊
THUNK
WHA--?!!
AUGH!

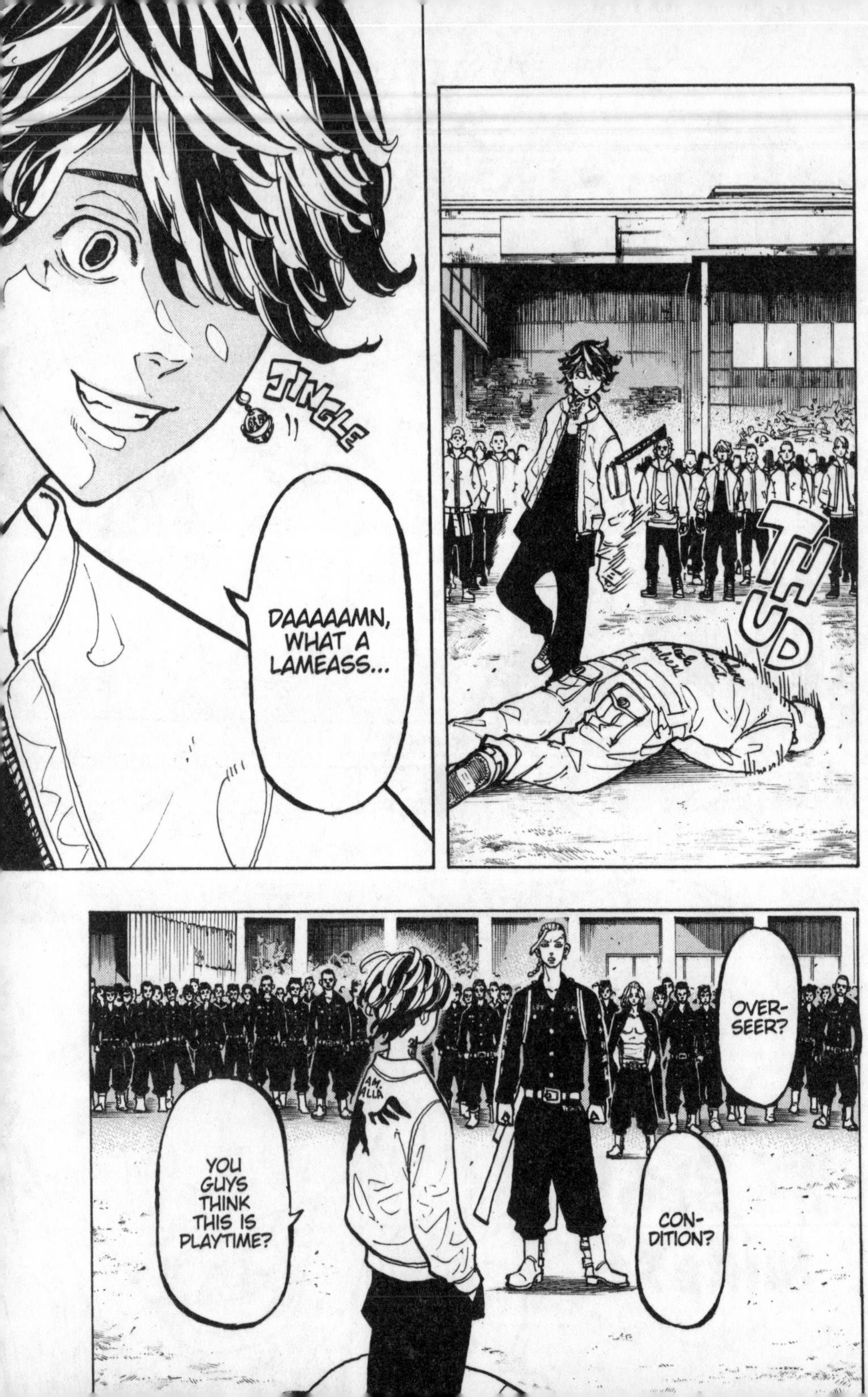
THUD
JINGLE
DAAAAAMN, WHAT A LAMEASS...
OVER-SEER?
CON-DITION?
YOU GUYS THINK THIS IS PLAYTIME?

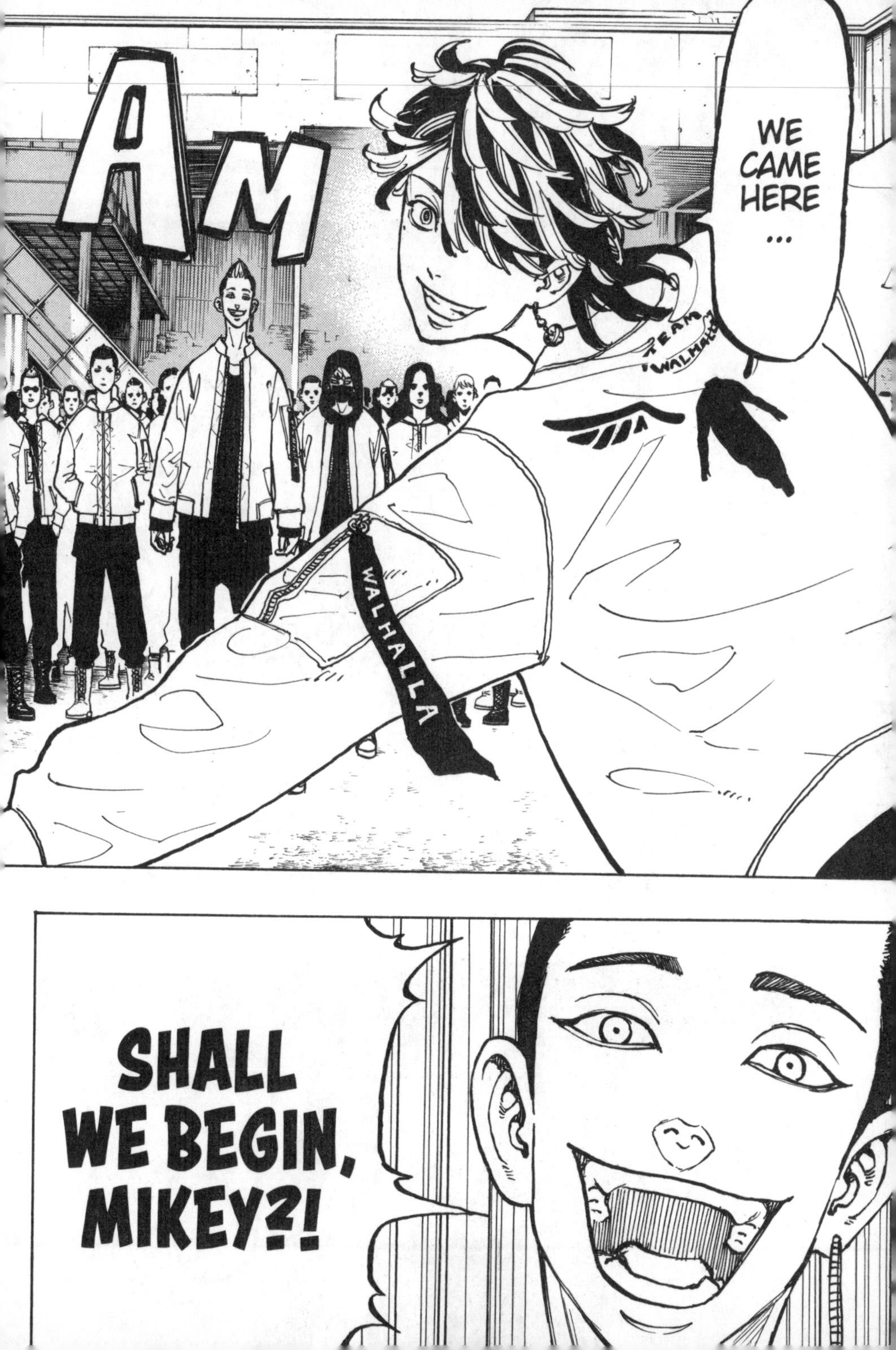
WE CAME HERE ...
AM
TEAM WALHALLA
WALHALLA
SHALL WE BEGIN, MIKEY?!

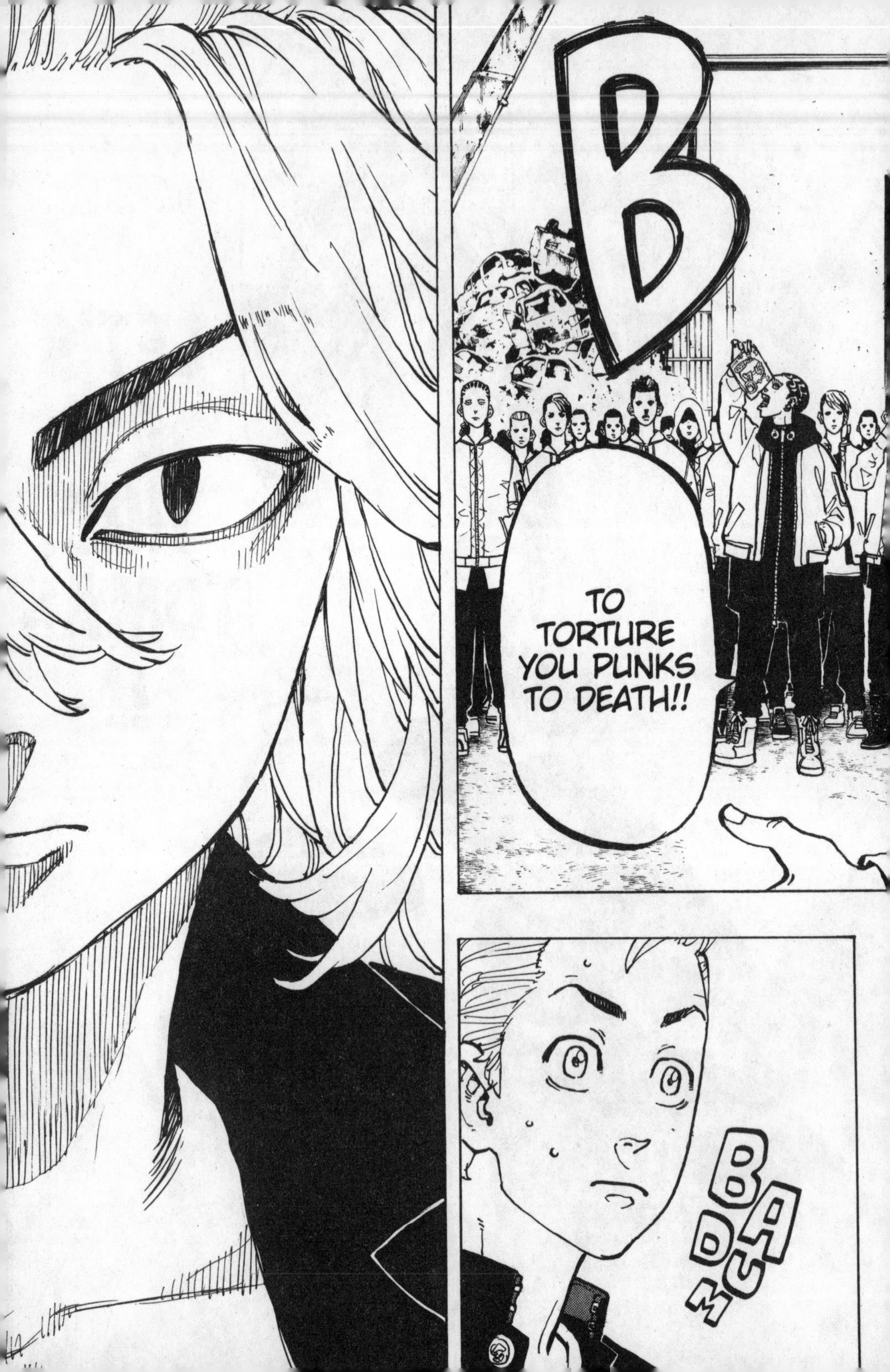
TO TORTURE YOU PUNKS TO DEATH!!
BADUM

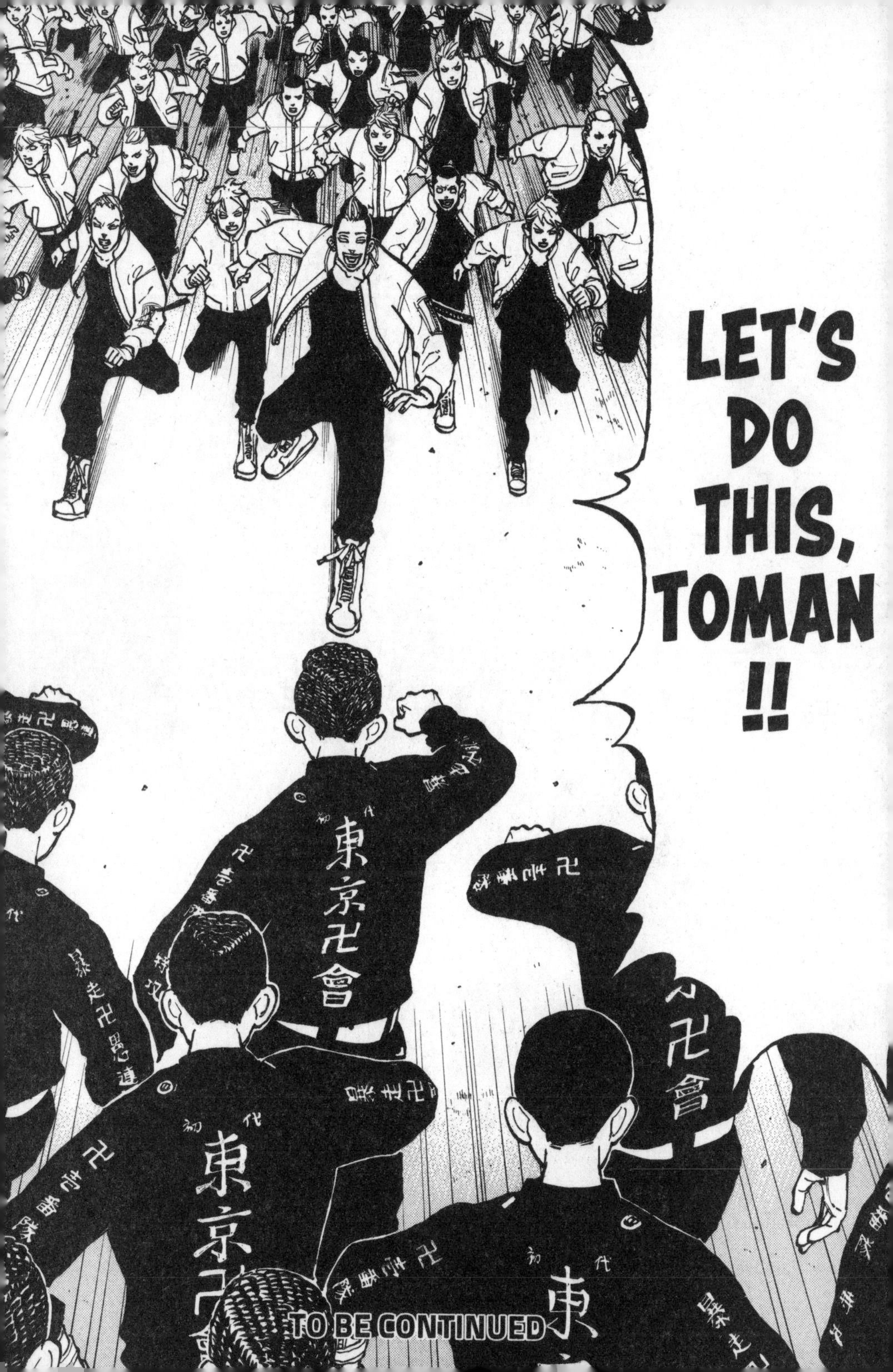
LET'S DO THIS, TOMAN!!
東京卍會
TO BE CONTINUED

TOKYO Revengers

SHIBUYA CROSSING

This photo of Toman's first generation was taken in the famous Shibuya Scramble Crossing in Tokyo. Behind them is the slightly obscured 109 department store (rendered as 10Q for this image, as it's fairly typical for well-known brand names to be slightly changed or spoofed by manga artists).

The Shibuya Scramble Crossing is notoriously crowded during the day. Violently forcing a stranger to take their picture under the eyes of hundreds of onlookers would be seen as a show of strength for these junior high school gang members.

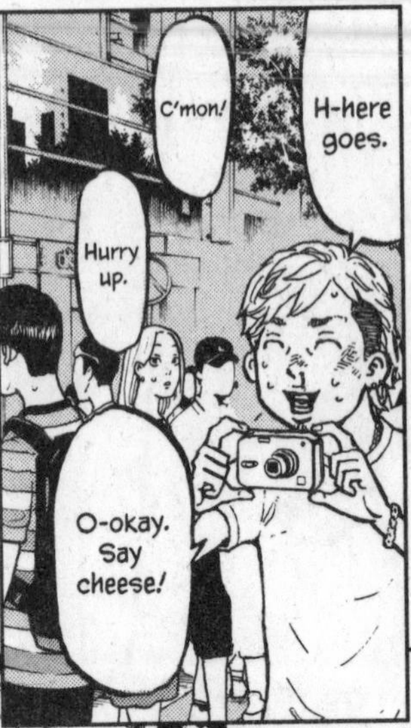
H-here goes.
C'mon!
Hurry up.
O-okay. Say cheese!

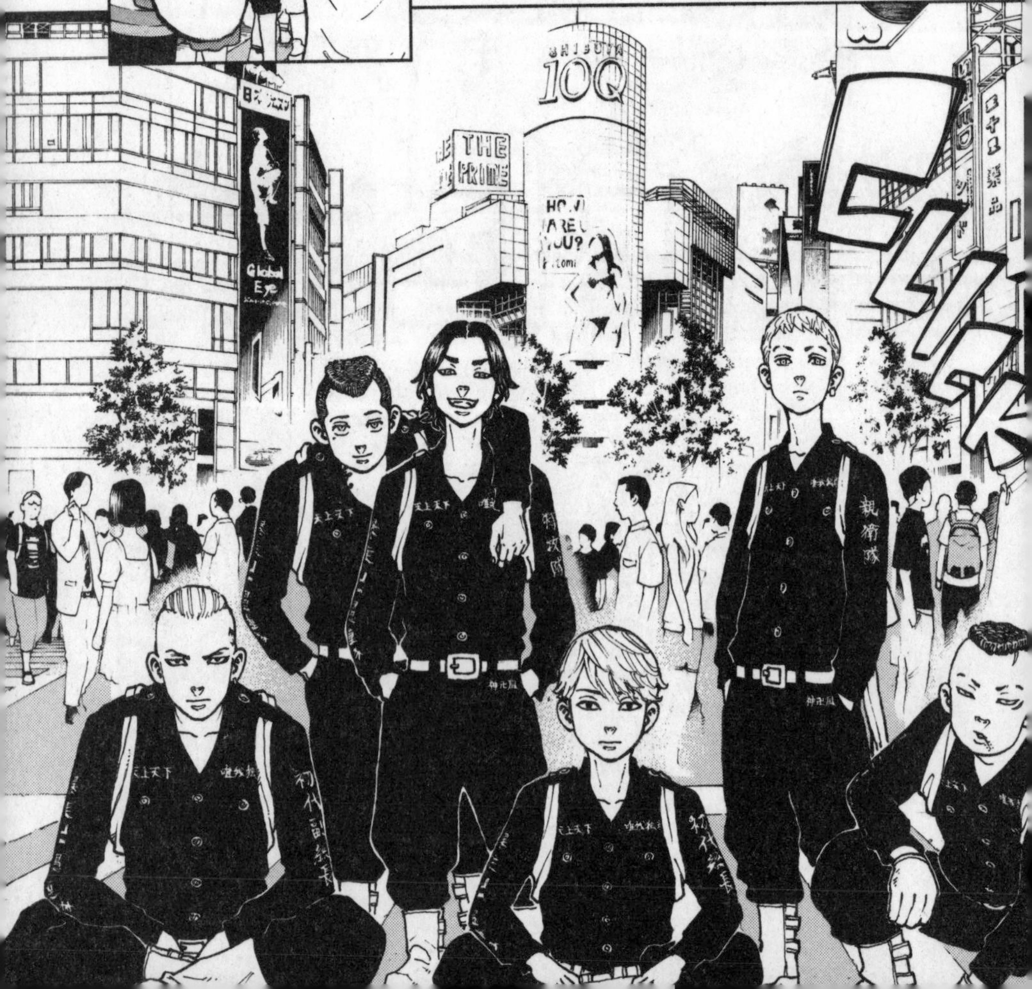
SHIBUYA
10Q
THE PRIME
Global Eye
CLICK

SHONAN MERMAIDS

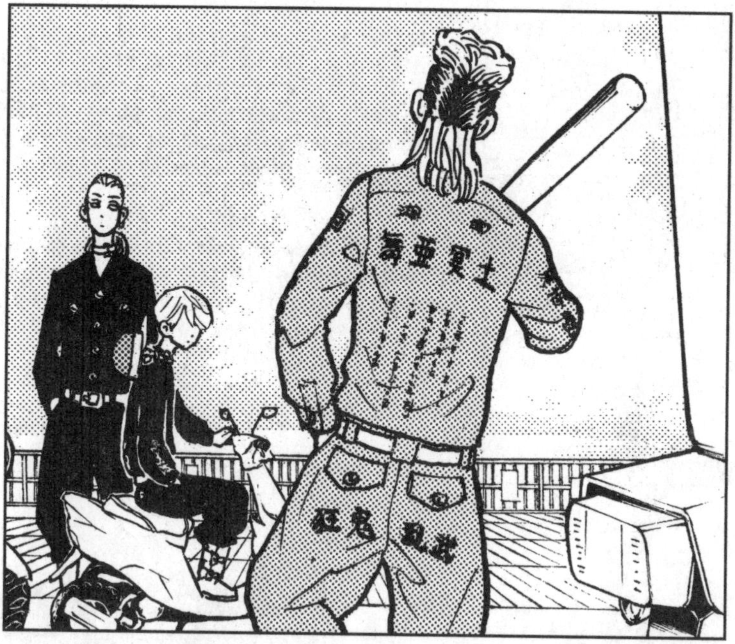

During Toman's first-generation beach trip in 2003, the gang ran into the Shonan Mermaids, a rival gang from the Shonan region, which is located along the coast of Sagami Bay in Kanagawa prefecture. Toman was traveling from Tokyo to the Yokohama area—which is along the Tokyo Bay, not Sagami Bay—but the Mermaids that Toman meets are from the 15th division of their gang, implying that the Mermaids are a large organization, with a huge territory. This is probably why they appear in Toman's path on their journey, despite being so far from their own home region.

The name Mermaid is written with the characters 舞 (dance), 亜 (Asia), and 冥土 (meido), a Japanese word for the Buddhist underworld. These characters aren't intended to be read literally, but were instead chosen to sound like "ma-a-meido," which is the Japanese pronunciation for mermaid.

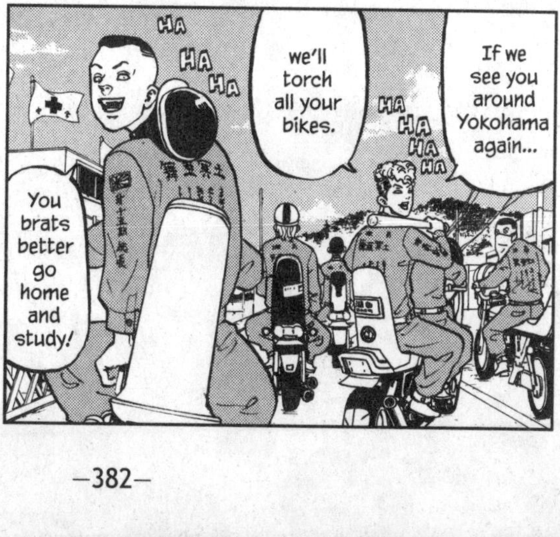
If we see you around Yokohama again...
HA HA HA HA
we'll torch all your bikes.
HA HA HA
You brats better go home and study!

TOKYO Revengers

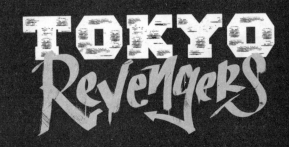

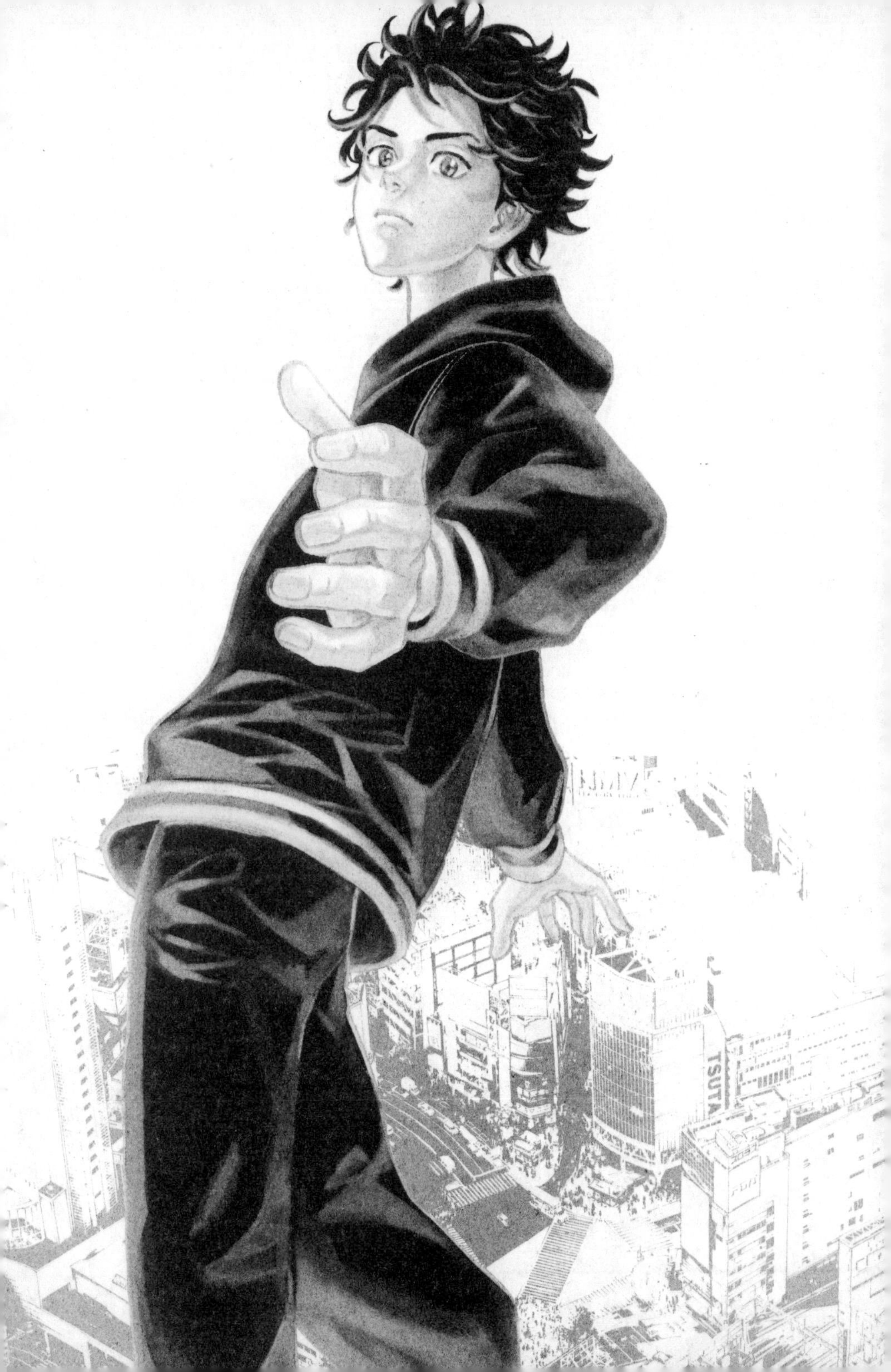
TSUTA

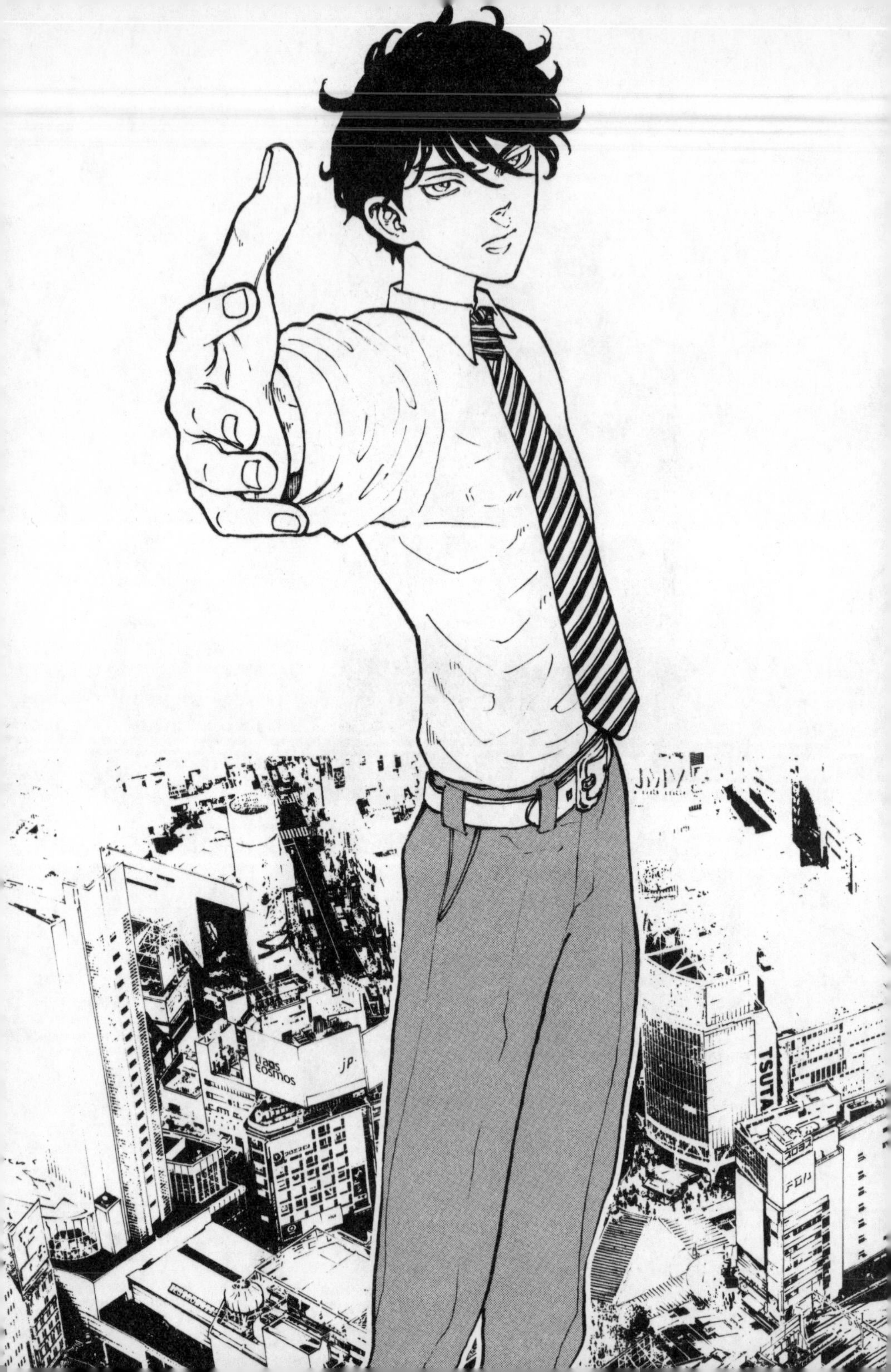
trans cosmos
.jp
TSUTA

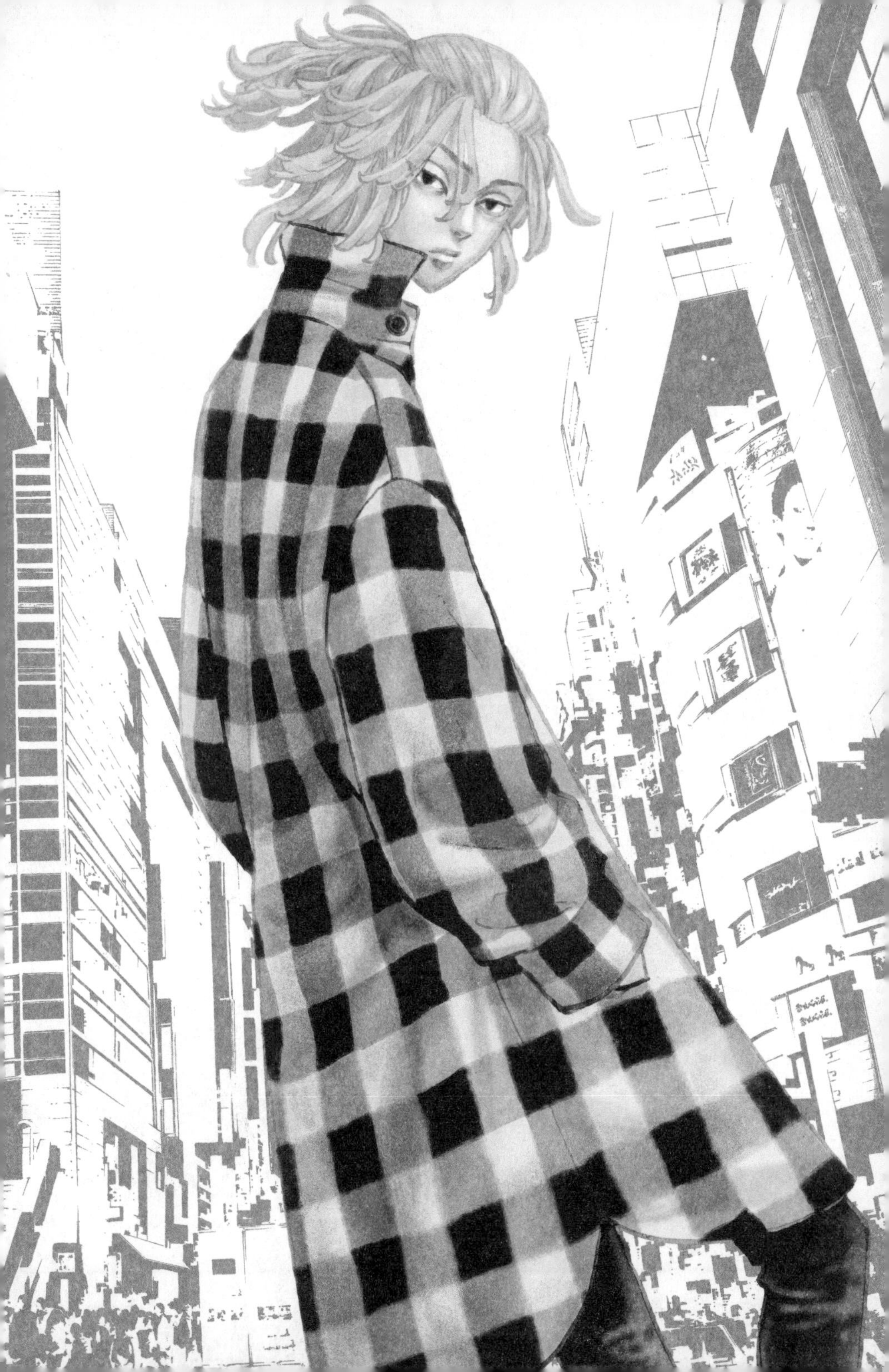

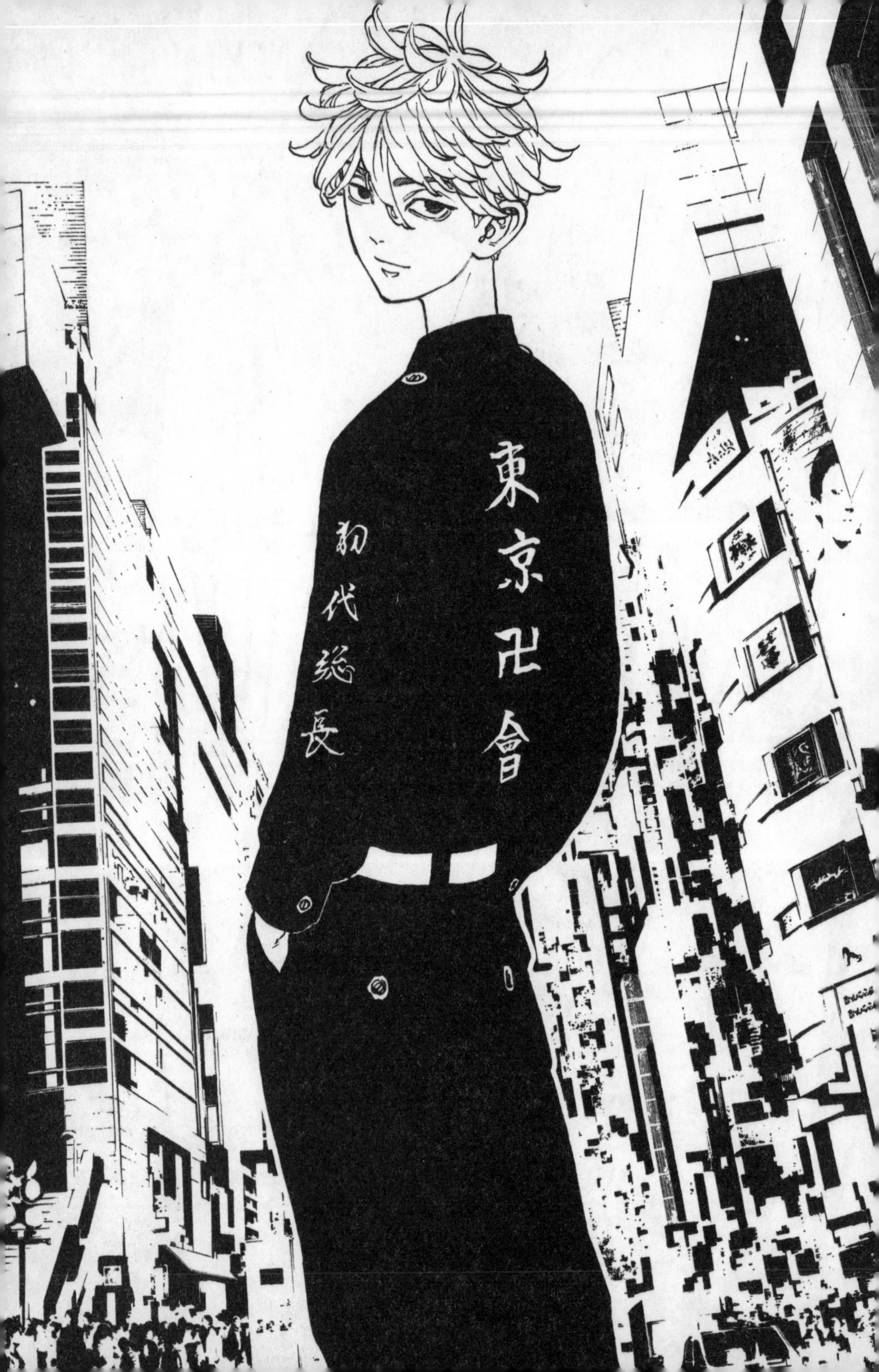
東京卍會
初代総長

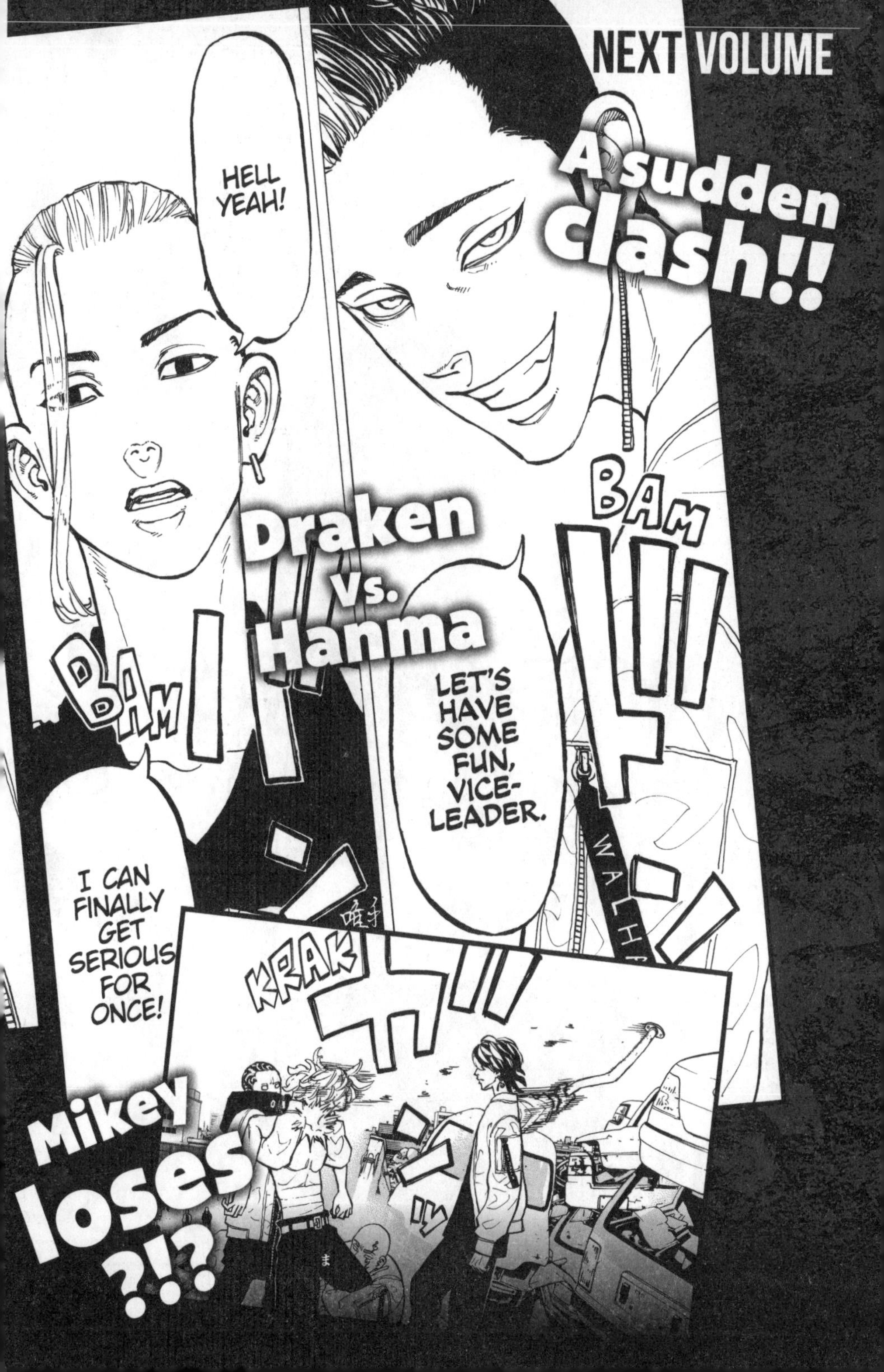
NEXT VOLUME
A sudden clash!!
BAM
LET'S HAVE SOME FUN, VICE-LEADER.
HELL YEAH!
Draken vs. Hanma
BAM
I CAN FINALLY GET SERIOUS FOR ONCE!
KRAK
Mikey loses?!?

TOKYO Revengers 7-8

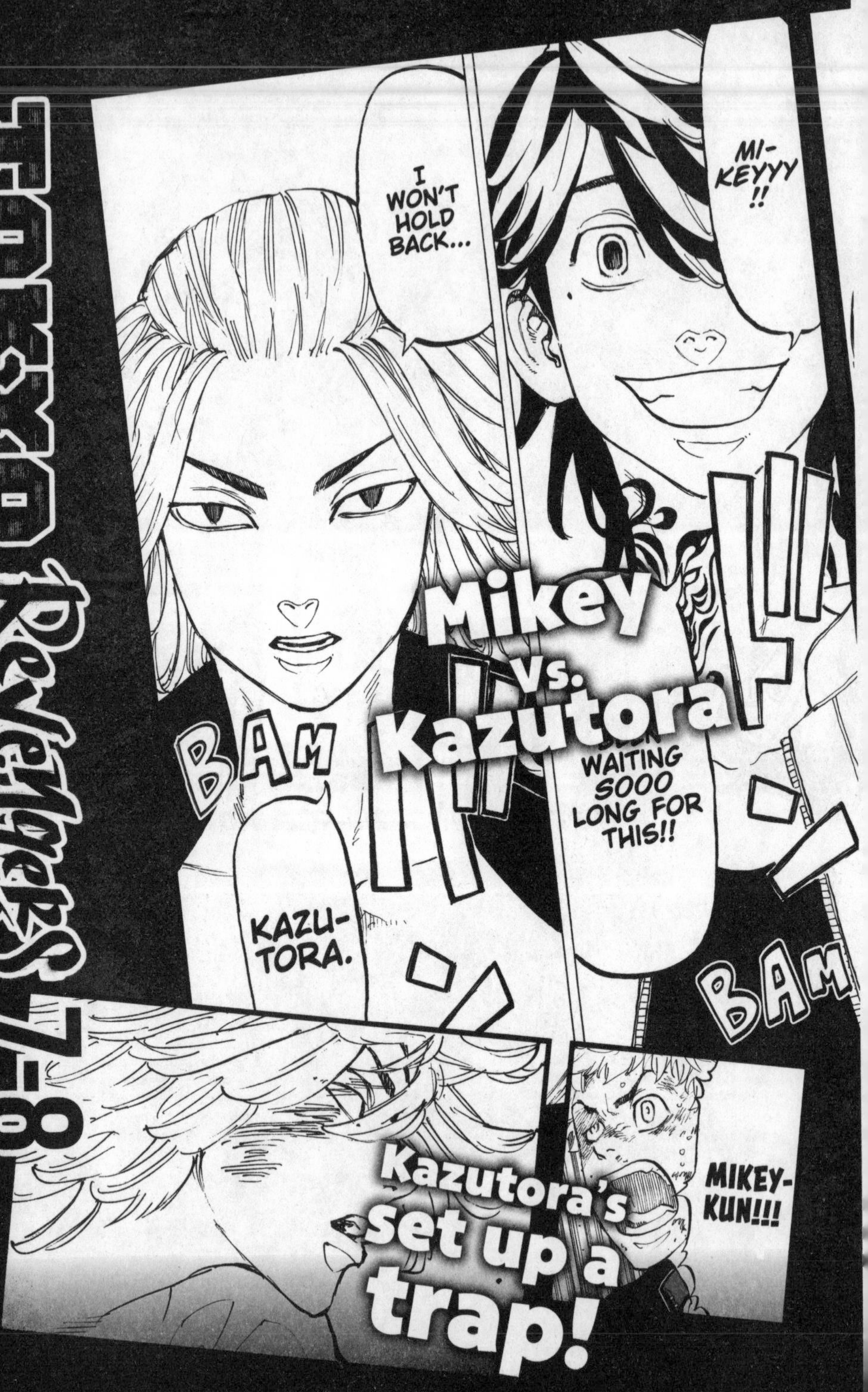

MI-KEYYY!!
WAITING SOOO LONG FOR THIS!!
BAM
I WON'T HOLD BACK...
KAZU-TORA.
BAM
Mikey vs. Kazutora
MIKEY-KUN!!!
Kazutora's set up a trap!

SEVEN SEAS ENTERTAINMENT PRESENTS

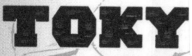

TOKY ES

story and art by KEN WAKUI

VOLUMES 5-6

TRANSLATION
Project Ceres

LETTERING
Robert Harkins

COVER AND LOGO DESIGN
H.Qi

PROOFREADER
Danielle King

EDITOR
Abby Lehrke

PRODUCTION DESIGNER
Christina McKenzie

PRODUCTION MANAGER
Lissa Pattillo

PREPRESS TECHNICIAN
Jules Valera

EDITOR-IN-CHIEF
Julie Davis

ASSOCIATE PUBLISHER
Adam Arnold

PUBLISHER
Jason DeAngelis

Tokyo Revengers Omnibus Vol. 3

First published in Japan in 2018 by Kodansha Ltd., Tokyo.
Publication rights for this English edition arranged through Kodansha Ltd., Tokyo.

Seven Seas press and purchase enquiries can be sent to Marketing Manager Lianne Sentar at press@gomanga.com. Information regarding the distribution and purchase of digital editions is available from Digital Manager CK Russell at digital@gomanga.com.

ISBN: 978-1-63858-622-7
Printed in Canada
First Printing: November 2022
10 9 8 7 6 5 4 3 2 1

READING DIRECTIONS

This book reads from *right to left*, Japanese style. If this is your first time reading manga, you start reading from the top right panel on each page and take it from there. If you get lost, just follow the numbered diagram here. It may seem backwards at first, but you'll get the hang of it! Have fun!!

1
2
3
4
5
6
7
8
9

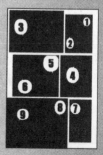

Follow us online: www.SevenSeasEntertainment.com